MW00565728

BUSINESS COMMUNICATION

BUSINESS COMMUNICATION

Second Edition

Deborah C. Andrews
University of Delaware

William D. Andrews
Westbrook College

Macmillan Publishing Company
New York
Maxwell Macmillan Canada
Toronto

The cover art and type, designed and produced by Thomas Slomka at Thomas William Design, was generated on a Macintosh II CI computer. The art was first designed in the traditional manner—on paper. Then through the use of a scanner, mouse, and keyboard, the design was recreated electronically using Adobe Illustrator 3.0 software. Once the final rendering was approved, reflective art was generated in the 4-Cast color printing system. The program data for the type were transferred to the Linotronic imagesetter at 1,200 lines of resolution. Both computer-generated images—art and type—were then brought together into a camera-ready mechanical, which was used to prepare the printing press and print the cover of this book.

Editor: Eben W. Ludlow
Development Editor: Nancy Perry
Production Supervisor: Andrew Roney
Production Manager: Valerie Sawyer
Text Designer: Eileen Burke
Cover Designer: Thomas William Design
Photo Researcher: Rachel Wolf/Diane Kraut
Illustrations: Waldman Graphics

This book was set in Meridien by Ruttle, Shaw & Wetherill, Inc., and printed and bound by Von Hoffmann Press, Inc.
The cover was printed by The Lehigh Press, Inc.

Copyright © 1992 by Macmillan Publishing Company,
a division of Macmillan, Inc.

Printed in the United States of America

All rights reserved. No part of this book may be reproduced or transmitted in any form or by any means, electronic or mechanical, including photocopying, recording, or any information storage and retrieval system, without permission in writing from the Publisher.

Earlier edition copyright © 1988 by Macmillan Publishing Company.

Macmillan Publishing Company
866 Third Avenue, New York, New York 10022

Macmillan Publishing Company is part of
The Maxwell Communication Group of Companies.

Maxwell Macmillan Canada, Inc.
1200 Eglinton Avenue East
Suite 200
Don Mills, Ontario M3C 3N1

Library of Congress Cataloging-in-Publication Data

Andrews, Deborah C.
Business communication/Deborah C. Andrews, William D. Andrews.
p. cm.
Includes index.
ISBN 0-02-303541-2
1. Business communication. 2. Business writing. I. Andrews, William D. (William David), 1945– II. Title.
HF5718.A743 1992
658.4'5—dc20 91-12905
CIP

Acknowledgments appear on pages 605–606, which constitute a continuation of the copyright page.

Printing: 1 2 3 4 5 6 7 Year: 2 3 4 5 6 7 8

This book is dedicated to the memory of
Joyce Andrews McKeller.

ABOUT THE AUTHORS

Deborah C. Andrews, Professor of English and Coordinator of the Business and Technical Writing Program at the University of Delaware, teaches undergraduate writing courses and conducts research on communication patterns in multinational organizations. Formerly, she taught business and technical writing at Drexel University, at Ohio State University (where she held a joint appointment in the departments of English and Metallurgical Engineering), and at Utah State University. A graduate of Middlebury College in Vermont, she completed advanced degrees at the University of Wyoming and the University of Pennsylvania. She has been a writing consultant for several organizations, including AT&T Technologies, the American Chemical Society, Dominion Textile, Inc., Duffield Associates, General Electric, Hercules, Inc., and the National Science Foundation. She has written many scholarly articles and also co-authored a textbook, *Technical Writing: Principles and Forms,* with Margaret Blickle.

William D. Andrews is President of Westbrook College in Portland, Maine. He was on the faculty at Ohio State University and then served as Dean of Academic Affairs at the Philadelphia College of Textiles and Science, where he also taught courses in management and in business communication. He has been a consultant to various government, business, and not-for-profit organizations, and he currently serves on the governing boards of a symphony orchestra, medical center, housing facility for the elderly, and several higher education associations. A graduate of the University of Pittsburgh, he earned a doctorate from the University of Pennsylvania and an M.B.A. in management from Penn's Wharton School. He has written many scholarly articles.

Together, William and Deborah Andrews have published a brief guide to writing for managers, *Write for Results,* as well as articles and papers. For a more personal look at their strategies for collaboration, see "*FYI:* Collaborating to Write This Textbook," on pp. 204–205.

PREFACE

This edition of *Business Communication*—like the first edition—provides the tools for succeeding in business through effective communication. By *succeeding* we mean you are

- Meeting the goals of the organization.
- Meeting the goals of the people you work with.
- Meeting your personal goals.

By *effective communication* we mean simply writing and reading, talking and listening that work. Strategies for making communication work fill the text. We explain both the *why* and the *how* for writing and speaking. That explanation derives from management theory as well as from research on the writing process, on listening and speaking, on document design, and on visual presentation of business information.

We don't give easy answers. Business—and communicating in business—is complex. There are few easy answers. But we do provide a simple structure for explaining the strategies necessary to succeed within that complexity.

WHAT'S NEW IN THE SECOND EDITION

Students and teachers told us the strategies presented in the first edition helped them to achieve successful communication. This edition preserves that proven approach. It also incorporates additional features and expanded discussions to make the approach even more vivid and engaging.

FYI: Commentaries from Corporate Executives, Leading Practitioners, and Researchers

A major feature new to this edition is the series of *FYI* boxes in which experts speak from their own experience about significant issues and events in business communication. Some of these commentaries focus on solving a specific corporate problem—for example, on how a food service organization might indicate the nutritional value of many foods across the multiple languages represented by Olympic athletes, or on how a health-care concern decides when faxes and phone calls are not enough and a face-to-face meeting with a joint venture partner in Japan is necessary. Other *FYIs* provide practical advice for students—on interviewing, on conducting research, and on using videos in presentations. Written specifically for this edition of *Business Communication,* the *FYIs* indicate both the diversity and the common ground in the way authorities communicate in organizations and speak about their communication strategies.

Expanded Models and Examples

Accompanying the FYIs and other discussions are new documents and visuals that bring the culture of corporations, government agencies, and not-for-profit organizations into the text. The selection represents organizations based in Canada, Hong Kong, Germany, Australia, and Japan as well as the United States. Sources include Baxter Healthcare, Hercules, Inc., Conoco Inc., Du Pont, McDonald's, Swissair, Dominion Textile, Hershey Foods, Hill and Knowlton Asia Ltd., ARASERVE, The Asia Foundation, Lufthansa, Informationszentrale der Elektrizitätswirtschaft EV, and the Travelers. Multiple examples from the same organization suggest the range of their communications.

To show students how other students compose documents and presentations, we've also enhanced the number and range of student writings. Contributors represent a wide variety of majors, including accounting, finance, marketing, management, retailing, fashion merchandising, information systems, sports and recreation, and natural resources.

i Enhanced Contextual Approach

The first edition was widely cited for the way it established the *context* of communication before instructing students in strategies and forms for writing and reading and for listening and speaking within that multifaceted environment. This edition enhances and expands on that contextual approach. Four elements of the context receive special attention: the international dimension, collaborative presentation, communications technology, and visuals and document design. You'll recognize that four-fold approach immediately as you skim the headings in the "What's Ahead" section at the beginning of each chapter. Here's a preview.

- **Expanded Coverage of the International and Multicultural Context.** Because international and multicultural issues set the context for business communication in the 21st century, the chapter on communicating in the global economy has been revised, expanded, and placed up front—as Chapter 3. This chapter sets the context for discussing the forms and strategies for such communication in the rest of the text. Chapters 20, 21, and 22 (based on Chapters 23, 24, and 25 in the first edition) have been greatly expanded with examples and strategies for listening and talking across cultures.

- **Expanded Coverage of Collaborative Communication.** In its discussion of group writing and speaking, the first edition charted territory not then commonly covered in such textbooks. This edition continues to explore strategies for group problem-solving and communication in writing and speaking. The chapter devoted to the topic (Chapter 11) has been expanded, as has the chapter on meetings (Chapter 21). Moreover, exercises grouped in a category called "for collaboration" are a consistent feature at the end of each chapter.

• **Expanded Coverage of Communications Technology.** The revised chapter on technology (Chapter 10) reflects changes in the workplace—and changes in student familiarity with computers. It surveys the impacts of electronic technology on the forms and conduct of organizational communication and on the meaning of business information. *The Wall Street Journal* reported recently that a Gallup poll of 500 offices found laser printers in 57 percent, fax machines in 78 percent, personal computers in 87 percent, and copiers in 94 percent of them. Moreover, the machines were dispersed throughout the company, not just in central locations.[1] Implications of such technology, summarized in Chapter 10, surface throughout *Business Communication.*

• **Expanded Coverage of Visuals and Document Design.** Visuals are an international language of business. Far beyond mere "visual aids," tables, figures, and videos are essential tools for organizational communication. Increases in the power and ease of use of personal computers and video recorders have been matched by decreases in price. This edition reflects these changes in the techniques for producing visuals. Chapter 6 on visuals includes even more examples, particularly of computer-generated visuals, and it covers the use of color and of photography. A full-color feature on photography in annual reports complements the chapter. Chapters 7 and 10 discuss some implications of desktop publishing systems for document design.

• **Expanded Discussion of Framing a Response—and Sounding Right.** A new chapter, "Communicating in Organizations: Frameworks" (Chapter 2), helps students characterize each communication situation before shaping their response—in a memo, letter, report, proposal, meeting, or interview. The chapter combines issues of both writing and oral presentation. It pulls together the elements of a communications response in a grid that defines the organizational functions, purposes, forms, and modes—from routine to customized. The grid underlies subsequent discussions of the writing process (in Part II) and the listening and speaking process (in Part V). It also underlies the chapter-by-chapter analysis of different forms.

This edition places even more emphasis on *voice,* the matter of how you sound, especially in customized documents. Being correct grammatically and using the right form for communication are critical, or course, but the issues of *voice* go beyond grammar and format, as the discussion makes clear. Moreover, the FYIs and the models provide students with the opportunity to hear how experts speak differently.

Other Changes in Pedagogy and Structure

Enhancements in the content of the text are matched by enhanced pedagogical tools. These changes also directed a few changes in the structure of *Business Communication.*

[1] Albert R. Karr, "Labor Letter," 2 April 1991, p. 1.

• **Chapter-opening headings and questions** are grouped under two logos. Under an **i,** like the symbol commonly found on European information signs, you'll find the headings that map the chapter to come. Under a **?,** the American-based symbol for traveler information, you'll find questions that help students to grasp the essential content of the chapter.

• **Chapter summaries.** The chapter-opening questions are answered in summary statements at the end of the chapter's discussion.

• **Expanded exercises** provide opportunities to apply concepts from the text. For each chapter, you'll find exercises in three categories. First, "For Discussion" items examine implications of the chapter topics. Second, exercises "For Writing" (or drawing, or speaking, as appropriate) give students practice in creating documents, graphics, or talks to match the forms and context addressed in the chapter. Finally, a set of exercises, "For Collaboration," highlights projects that engage a team.

• **Short cases.** Those teachers who enjoyed using the short cases in Chapter 2 of the first edition as ice-breakers in class will find that most have moved to the *Instructor's Resource Manual and Case Book,* which contains updated versions and new cases.

• A new **appendix on documentation** clarifies for students the sometimes complex issue of indicating sources in a report.

• **Procedures and specialized corporate documents** (including the annual report) have been combined in a special section in the back (Part VII). The chapters are thus unobtrusive if teachers choose not to cover these forms. Those teachers interested in discussing them will find that the specialized documents chapter in particular has been revised to emphasize how one *reads* and responds to corporate documents rather than how one writes them.

SUPPLEMENTS FOR TEACHERS AND STUDENTS

Several supplemental materials aid both teachers and students in using this text.

Instructor's Resource Manual and Case Book

This comprehensive paperback guides teachers in matching features of *Business Communication* to their personal approach to conducting the course. It shows options in syllabi and course sequence. It suggests solutions to exercises. It expands on each topic, chapter by chapter, giving teachers additional information and examples to bring into the classroom. A special feature new to this edition is the series of one page (or shorter) cases, some of which appeared in Chapter 2 of the first edition. The cases are ready for duplication as handouts to introduce concepts early in the course and where applicable throughout.

Specialized Instructor's Manual

Teachers interested in giving the class an international focus will find *Teaching Business Communication: The International Dimension* an additional aid in their pursuit. This specialized manual provides approaches, exercises, and cases that amplify the already abundant multicultural discussions in *Business Communication*. It was prepared by Linda Beamer of California State University, Los Angeles, who was formerly a cross-cultural business consultant in Toronto, Canada.

Study Guide

Written by Larry R. Andrews of Kent State University, this guide leads the student vigorously through the text. For each chapter of *Business Communication* it includes a chapter summary, learning objectives, short-answer quizzes, study or discussion questions, and extensive applications in the form of document revision exercises and a case-study writing problem. There are also reviews of spelling, grammar, mechanics, and usage, with extensive exercises.

Test Bank

Also prepared by Larry R. Andrews, the test bank offers 1500 items, both multiple choice and essay questions, keyed to specific sections of the text. The test bank is available in a printed version and as Microtest ® Test Preparation System software for both IBM and Macintosh computers.

Transparencies

Seventy two-color transparencies bring key items from text to screen as well as offer new supplementary examples. All are referenced in the instructor's resource manual.

ACKNOWLEDGMENTS

This book, like much of the writing the book discusses, was a collaborative effort. We'd especially like to thank all the *FYI* contributors, whose names are listed at the end of the main contents section. Their contributions often went well beyond their boxes in the text.

In addition, we'd like to thank the following people: James Edris, Director of Investor Relations, Hershey Foods Corporation; A. Ingrid Ratsep, Senior Project Manager, Duffield Associates; Sirio DeLuca, Director of Marketing, Dominion Industrial Fabrics Company; Becky Worley, R. John Brockmann, and John Jebb, University of Delaware; William R. Brown, Philadelphia College of Textiles and Science; and at Macmillan, all those named on the copyright page, especially Nancy Perry, Patricia Smythe, Andrew Roney, and Eben Ludlow.

As we rewrote the several drafts of this text, we profited from the comments of the following reviewers, whose insight and detailed suggestions we deeply appreciate:

William H. Baker, Department of Information Management, Brigham Young University
John D. Beard, Department of Marketing, Wayne State University
Pauline A. Buss, Department of English, William R. Harper College
Carol David, Department of English, Iowa State University
Caroll J. Dierks, Computer Information Systems Department, University of Northern Colorado
Roger W. Ellis, Department of Business Education and Office Administration, Bloomsburg University
Robert A. Gieselman, Department of Mechanical and Industrial Engineering, University of Illinois at Urbana-Champaign
Larry Honl, Department of Business Education and Administrative Management, University of Wisconsin-Eau Claire
Celest A. Martin, College Writing Program, University of Rhode Island
Carol M.H. Shehadeh, Department of Humanities, Florida Institute of Technology
Henrietta Nickels Shirk, Department of English, Northeastern University
Vincent C. Trofi, Department of Business Administration, Providence College
John L. Waltman, Department of Management, Eastern Michigan University
James Wyllie, Communications Arts Department, Southern Alberta Institute of Technology

D. C. Andrews owes a continuing special thanks to the Unidel Foundation, which supported her research in international business communication.

In the end, the major collaborators were our students. This book is theirs.

BRIEF CONTENTS

PART I: INTRODUCTION 1

1. The Challenges of Business Communication in the Global Economy 3
2. Communicating in Organizations: Frameworks 14
3. Communicating in Organizations: The Global and Multicultural Environment 32

PART II: WRITING IN CONTEXT 51

4. Macrocomposing: Organizing Yourself to Write 53
5. Microcomposing: Finding Your Voice 76
6. Composing with Visuals 96
   Special Feature: Communicating with Photographs in Corporate Annual Reports
7. Revising and Designing 128
8. Understanding Business Information 149
9. Accessing the Sources of Business Information 163
10. Communicating with Electronic Technology 179
11. Collaboration: Managing Group Communication 196

PART III: MEMOS AND LETTERS 217

12. Memos 219
13. Elements of Letter Writing 240
14. Managing Routine Letters 261
15. The Routine and Beyond: Negative Situations 276
16. Customized Letters to Persuade 298

PART IV: PROPOSALS AND REPORTS 321

17. Bids and Proposals 323
18. Elements of Business Reporting 344
19. Formal Reports 363

PART V: LISTENING AND TALKING 401

20. Elements of Oral Communication 403
21. Telephone Calls and Meetings 422
22. Business Presentations 447

PART VI: EMPLOYMENT COMMUNICATION 475

23. Resumes and Cover Letters 477
24. The Interview . . . and Beyond 508

PART VII: SPECIAL FORMS OF BUSINESS COMMUNICATION 527

25. Procedures and Instructions 529
26. Documents of the Corporation 554

HANDBOOK 574

APPENDIX: Documenting Sources of Information 595

INDEX 607

CONTENTS

PART I
INTRODUCTION
1

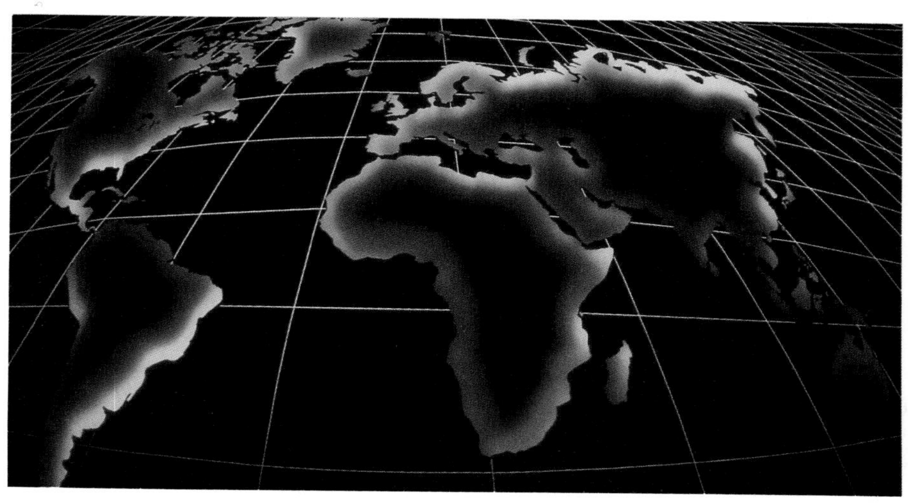

1

THE CHALLENGES OF BUSINESS COMMUNICATION IN THE GLOBAL ECONOMY
3

BUSINESS IN THE 21ST CENTURY 4
WORKING SMARTER THROUGH GOOD COMMUNICATION 8
FYI: Why Study Business Communication? 8
HOW SUCCESSFUL COMMUNICATION HELPS YOU 9
Achieve Job Success 9
Gain Personal Satisfaction 10
Meet Ethical and Social Obligations 10
THE CHALLENGE OF SUCCESSFUL BUSINESS COMMUNICATION 11
SUMMARY 12
EXERCISES 12

2

COMMUNICATING IN ORGANIZATIONS: FRAMEWORKS
14

DEFINING BUSINESS COMMUNICATION 16
A COMMUNICATION MODEL 16
Applying the Communication Model 17
THE NATURE OF BUSINESS ORGANIZATIONS 18
THE DIRECTION OF COMMUNICATION 18
ORGANIZATIONAL FUNCTIONS OF BUSINESS COMMUNICATION 20
Definition 20
Control 21
Maintenance 22
PURPOSES OF BUSINESS COMMUNICATION 22
Recording 22
Informing 23
Persuading 24
FORMS OF BUSINESS COMMUNICATION 24
Written Forms 24
Oral Forms 25
Nonverbal Forms 25
Electronic Forms 26
Convergence of Forms 26
MODES OF BUSINESS COMMUNICATION 26
Routine Communication 27
Customized Communication 27
Mixed Modes of Communication 28
SUMMARY 28
EXERCISES 29

3

COMMUNICATING IN ORGANIZATIONS: THE GLOBAL AND MULTICULTURAL ENVIRONMENT
32

THE GLOBAL ECONOMY 33
A Network of Investments and People 33
Global Decision Making 34
GEOGRAPHIC DISPERSION 34
Differences in Space and Time 34
Overcoming Geography with Technology 36

CULTURAL DIVERSITY 37
Definition of Culture 37
Multiculturalism in the United States and Canada 37
Language Differences 38
Similarities in Organizational Structure 38
Differences in Context 39
TALKING AND WRITING 40 • MAKING AND IMPLEMENTING DECISIONS 40 • RECRUITING 40 • TRUSTING 41 • MAINTAINING RELATIONSHIPS 41
BELIEVING IS SEEING 41
TALKING AND LISTENING ACROSS CULTURES 43
WRITING AND READING ACROSS CULTURES 43
FYI: A Dinner Invitation in Korea 44
FYI: Bilingual Publications 45
SUMMARY 46
EXERCISES 46

PART II
WRITING IN CONTEXT
51

4
MACROCOMPOSING: ORGANIZING YOURSELF TO WRITE
53

ORGANIZING THE MESSAGE: PRINCIPLES 55
Identify the Purpose 56
Imagine the Reader 56
Recognize Multiple Readers 57
Understand the Form 57
ORGANIZING THE MESSAGE: TOOLS AND TECHNIQUES 58
Control Statement 58
Direct and Indirect Order 59
Introduction-Middle-Ending 59
Routine Forms and Formats 59

Conventional Patterns 60
CAUSE AND EFFECT 60 • CLASSIFICATION AND ANALYSIS 60 • COMPARISON AND CONTRAST 61 • PARALLELISM 61 • NARRATIVE 61
ORGANIZING THE INFORMATION: NONLINEAR TECHNIQUES 62
Data-dumping 62
Picturing 65
Mapping Your Mind 66
FYI: Clustering 66
ORGANIZING THE DOCUMENT: OUTLINES 67
The Nonlinear Outline 68
ORGANIZING YOURSELF: MANAGING THE PROCESS 69
Make a Schedule 70
Make an Outline 70
Warm Up 70
Play to Your Strengths 71
Be Ready to Change 71
Keep Writing 71
SUMMARY 72
EXERCISES 72

5

MICROCOMPOSING: FINDING YOUR VOICE 76

THE ELEMENTS OF VOICE 78
WORDS 79
Concrete and Abstract Words 79
Denotation and Connotation 80
Content and Structure Words 80
VERBS 81 • VERBIAGE 82
Discriminatory Language 82
Levels of Usage 83
FYI: Acronyms 84
FORMAL AND INFORMAL LANGUAGE 84 • JARGON 84
Word Play 85
SENTENCES 85
Length 85
Parallelism 86
Branching 86
VOICES 87
The Corporate Voice 88
The Legal Voice 90
The Ethics of Voice 90
AN ENGAGING VOICE 91
SUMMARY 92
EXERCISES 92

6

COMPOSING WITH VISUALS
96

THINKING VISUALLY 97
COMMUNICATING VISUALLY 97
FYI: **Visualizing the Law 98**
Consolidating and Recording Information 100
Summarizing and Reinforcing a Message 100
Unifying the Document 103
Providing Dramatic Impact 103
Reducing Text 105
Crossing Language Barriers 106
SELECTING THE APPROPRIATE VISUAL FORM 106
FYI: **Olympic Colors 106**
Tables and Matrixes 108
Line Graphs 110
Organizational Charts and Flowcharts 112
Schedules 113
Bar Charts 113
Pie Charts 115
Pictorial Charts 116
Maps 118
Drawings 118
Photographs 119
FYI: **Communicating with Photographs 119**
TESTING THE VISUAL 119
Accuracy 120
Distortion 120
Documentation 120
THE VISUAL PAGE 120
Guidelines for Using Visuals 121
SUMMARY 123
EXERCISES 124
SPECIAL FEATURE: Communicating with Photographs in Corporate Annual Reports

7

REVISING AND DESIGNING
128

RESEEING 129
A REVISING ROUTINE 132
Guidelines for Revising 132
Revising with a Computer 133
MACROREVISING 133
Use Conventional Formats 134

State the Controlling Idea 134
Use Parallel Headings 134
Develop Strong Paragraphs 136
MARKING COMPONENTS 136 • PACING THE READING 138
Design the Text as a Visual 139
MICROREVISING 141
Focusing 141
Emphasizing 142
Proofreading 142
READABILITY 142
SUMMARY 143
FYI: Measuring Readability 144
EXERCISES 146

8

UNDERSTANDING BUSINESS INFORMATION
149

THE ROLE OF INFORMATION IN BUSINESS COMMUNICATION 150
TYPES OF BUSINESS INFORMATION 151
USING DIFFERENT TYPES OF INFORMATION 152
CHARACTERISTICS OF GOOD BUSINESS INFORMATION 154
Accuracy 155
Timeliness 155
Relevance 155
Reliability 155
Sensibleness 156
PATTERNS OF INFORMATION USE 156
Using Information to Record 157
Using Information to Inform 157
Using Information to Persuade 157
GUIDELINES FOR INTERPRETING INFORMATION 158
SUMMARY 160
EXERCISES 160

9

ACCESSING THE SOURCES OF BUSINESS INFORMATION
163

SEARCHING FOR INFORMATION 164
SOURCES OF BUSINESS INFORMATION 166
Personal Observation 166
Interview 167
GUIDELINES FOR THE INTERVIEW 167

Survey 169

GUIDELINES FOR DEVELOPING THE QUESTIONNAIRE 170 • GUIDELINES FOR SELECTING THE POPULATION 171

Literature 172

PRIMARY MATERIALS 172 • PRINT INDEXES 173 • ELECTRONIC INDEXES 175

FYI: **Find It Fast** 176

SUMMARY 176

EXERCISES 176

10

COMMUNICATING WITH ELECTRONIC TECHNOLOGY 179

THE ELECTRONIC MEDIA 181

PRODUCTION 181

Wordprocessing 181

Desktop Publishing 182

Electronic Paper 182

THE ELECTRONIC CONTEXT FOR COMMUNICATION 185

Hypertext 185

The Merging of Oral and Written Media 185

FACSIMILE TRANSMISSION 185

FYI: **Hypermedia** 186

ELECTRONIC MAIL 186

FYI: **Local Norms in E-Mail** 188

ELECTRONIC BULLETIN BOARDS AND CONFERENCES 188

The Electronic Workplace 189

THE PANCAKE ORGANIZATION 190 • DECENTRALIZATION 190

THE COSTS OF COMPUTING 191

Privacy 191

The 24-Hour Workday 192

Physiological Effects 192

Psychological Effects 193

SUMMARY 193

EXERCISES 194

11

COLLABORATION: MANAGING GROUP COMMUNICATION 196

COLLABORATION: THE ORGANIZATIONAL WAY 197

Forms of Collaborative Writing 198

Advantages of Collaborative Writing 199

WHO'S RESPONSIBLE? 200
HOW GROUPS FORM AND FUNCTION 201
Formation of Groups 202
Group Processes 202
GROUP WRITING 203
Guidelines for Group Writing 203
FYI: **Collaborating to Write This Textbook 204**
FYI: **Making Assignments 206**
GROUP ORAL PRESENTATIONS 209
Guidelines for Group Oral Presentations 209
REVIEWING AND EDITING THE WORK OF OTHERS 212
Guidelines for Editing the Work of Others 212
SUMMARY 213
EXERCISES 214

PART III

MEMOS AND LETTERS

217

12

MEMOS

219

DEFINING MEMOS 221
FYI: **The One-Page Memo 225**
THE FUNCTIONS OF MEMOS 225
Meeting Organizational Goals 225
USING A MEMO TO RECORD THE MINUTES OF A MEETING 226
Meeting Personal Goals 228
GUIDELINES FOR WRITING MEMOS 230
Identify the Context 231
Review Your Communication Options 231
Determine the Structure 231
Distribute the Information 232
Conform to Conventions 234
Edit and Revise 235
Evaluate Against All Goals 235
WHEN MEMOS GO AWAY 236
SUMMARY 237
EXERCISES 237

13

ELEMENTS OF LETTER WRITING
240

LETTERS AND PHONE CALLS 241
CONNECTING ETHICALLY WITH THE READER 243
Be Honest 243
Value the Reader's Time 243
Use the Reader's Code 244
Consider the Reader's Self-Interest 245
PLANNING LETTERS 245
Timing 245
Organizing: Routine and Customized Letters 245
Dictating 246
GUIDELINES FOR DICTATING 246
Writing Within the Law 247
THE LETTERLY VOICE 248
CONVENTIONS 249
Standard Elements 250
SENDER'S ADDRESS 250 • DATE 250 • INSIDE ADDRESS 250 • ATTENTION LINE 250 • SUBJECT LINE 250 • SALUTATION 250 • COMPLIMENTARY CLOSE 251 • SIGNATURE 251 • OTHER NOTATIONS 251 • SUBSEQUENT PAGES 252
Format 252
WRITING LETTERS INTERNATIONALLY 252
FYI: Communicating with a Japanese Partner 254
SUMMARY 254
EXERCISES 258

14

MANAGING ROUTINE LETTERS
261

PLANNING ROUTINE LETTERS 262
REQUESTING 264
Placing an Order 264
Inviting 264
Requesting Information 266
INFORMING 266
Confirming and Thanking 266
Responding to a Request for Information 268
Writing about a Policy or Procedure 268
Writing About an Account 271
Covering an Enclosure 273
SUMMARY 273
EXERCISES 273

15

THE ROUTINE AND BEYOND: NEGATIVE SITUATIONS
276

A ROUTINE APPROACH TO NEGATIVE SITUATIONS 277
Refusing an Invitation 278
Writing About Problems with an Order 278
Refusing a Claim 278
WRITING BEYOND THE ROUTINE 280
Have the Right Person Sign the Letter 280
Place the Explanation Strategically 280
Check the Sound of Your Voice 281
ANNOUNCING BAD NEWS 282
REFUSING REQUESTS 283
DEALING WITH PROBLEMS IN A PRODUCT OR SERVICE 287
Writing the Complaint 288
Responding to the Complaint 289
FYI: **Rudeness Never Works 292**
SUMMARY 292
EXERCISES 294

16

CUSTOMIZED LETTERS TO PERSUADE
298

ESTABLISHING COMMON GROUND 299
SELLING 300
Know What You Are Selling 300
Know the Reader You Are Selling It To 300
Show Why the Reader Needs What You Are Selling 300
Treat the Reader Ethically 301
PLANNING THE SALES LETTER: THE AIDA APPROACH 301
Attention 301
Interest 302
Desire 302
Action 302
WRITING THE SALES LETTER 303
WRITING A PERSUASIVE INVITATION 303
REQUESTING A RESPONSE TO A QUESTIONNAIRE 306
ASKING FOR A LETTER OF RECOMMENDATION 307
WRITING A LETTER OF RECOMMENDATION 309
WRITING LETTERS WITH COMPLEX INFORMATION 310
SUMMARY 316
EXERCISES 316

PART IV

PROPOSALS AND REPORTS

321

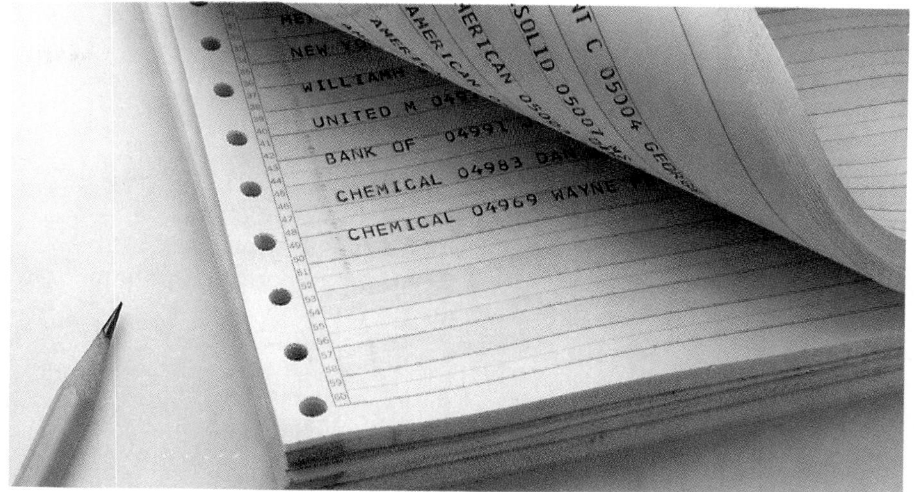

17

BIDS AND PROPOSALS

323

SOLVING BUSINESS PROBLEMS 324
REQUEST FOR BID 325
BIDS 326
Guidelines for Solicited Bids 326
INVESTIGATIONS: PROBLEMS OF FACT, MEANS, VALUE 328
Problem of Fact: Informative Report 328
Problem of Means: Interpretive Report 328
Problem of Value: Persuasive Report 329
REQUEST FOR PROPOSAL 329
PROPOSALS: A CASE STUDY 329
STRATEGIES FOR PROPOSALS 330
Clearly Identify the Problem 334
Describe a Reasonable Approach to Solving the Problem 334
Show That You Can Carry Out the Proposed Approach 335
Present One Clear Message 336
THE STRUCTURE OF PROPOSALS 336
FYI: Proposal Writing 336
Introduction 337
Problem Statement 338
Objectives 339
Solution 339
Justification 339
Budget 340
SUMMARY 340
EXERCISES 341

18

ELEMENTS OF BUSINESS REPORTING
344

MEASURES OF ACCOUNTABILITY 345
CONTEXT FOR REPORTING 346
GATHERING INFORMATION 348
FYI: Electronic Reporting on Spotted Owls 348
Fact Sheets 349
ROUTINE REPORTS 351
The Progress Report 353
The Trip Report 353
A Routine Site Evaluation 356
SUMMARY 360
EXERCISES 360

19

FORMAL REPORTS
363

DEALING WITH COMPLEXITY 364
FYI: Objectivity in North American and Chinese Reports 368
Introduction 368
Middle 371
Ending 374
SPECIAL FEATURES OF THE FORMAL REPORT 374
Front Matter 374
LETTER (OR MEMO) OF TRANSMITTAL 374 • COVER 376 • TITLE PAGE 376 • TABLE OF CONTENTS 377 • LIST OF FIGURES AND LIST OF TABLES 377 • EXECUTIVE SUMMARY AND ABSTRACT 377 • PREFACE 377 • FOREWORD 379
Back Matter 379
APPENDIX 379 • REFERENCES AND/OR BIBLIOGRAPHY 379 • INDEX 379
READABILITY 380
Text 380
Visuals 381
Design 381
A STUDENT REPORT: A MANAGEMENT INFORMATION SYSTEM FOR A RESTAURANT 383
SUMMARY 395
EXERCISES 395

PART V

LISTENING AND TALKING

401

20

ELEMENTS OF ORAL COMMUNICATION
403

CHOOSING BETWEEN WRITING AND COMMUNICATING ORALLY 405
Guidelines for Choosing Speaking over Writing 405
NONVERBAL ELEMENTS 407
Body Language 407
EYES AND FACIAL EXPRESSION 407 • APPEARANCE 407 • MOVEMENT 408 • TOUCH 408
Setting 408
STRATEGIES FOR EFFECTIVE LISTENING 409
Recognizing Barriers 409
Getting the Message 411
Getting the Intent 412
Listening to a Different Culture 412
FYI: **Meishis in Japanese Business** 413
Listening to the Other Gender 414
STRATEGIES FOR EFFECTIVE TALKING 415
Guidelines for Talking 415
ETHICS OF ORAL COMMUNICATION 416
Gaining Compliance 417
The Rogerian Strategies for Managing Conflicts 417
Taking No for an Answer 418
SUMMARY 419
EXERCISES 419

21

TELEPHONE CALLS AND MEETINGS
422

PHONE CALLS 423
Outgoing Calls 424
GUIDELINES FOR CALLING 425
Incoming Calls 426
Voice Mail 426
MEETINGS 428
The Risks in Meetings 428
The Rewards of Meetings 429
ROUTINE AND CUSTOMIZED MEETINGS 430
Regular Meetings 430
Task Forces 431
THE MEETING PROCESS 431
Group Dynamics 431
SOCIALIZATION 431 • CONFLICT 432 • CONSENSUS 432
Conducting a Meeting 432
PLANNING THE LOGISTICS 432 • SETTING THE AGENDA 433 • LEADING THE DISCUSSION 434
Attending a Meeting 435
Using Meetings to Solve Problems 435
GUIDELINES FOR SOLVING PROBLEMS IN MEETINGS 435
MEETING INTERNATIONALLY 436
Preparing 436
MEETING CUSTOMS AND LOGISTICS 437 • DOCUMENTS 437
Participating 437
FYI: Deciding to Meet Abroad 438
MEETING BY PHONE AND ELECTRONICALLY 439
Teleconferencing 439
Electronic Meetings 441
SUMMARY 444
EXERCISES 444

22

BUSINESS PRESENTATIONS
447

THE CONTEXT FOR PRESENTATIONS 448
DETERMINING THE CONTEXT FOR YOUR TALK 449
Analyze the Audience 449
CHARACTERIZE 450 • COUNT 450
Assess the Setting 450
TIMING 451 • ARRANGEMENTS 452

Identify the Purpose 452
ORGANIZING YOUR INFORMATION 453
Ho-Hum! 453
Why Bring That Up? 453
FYI: Corporate Speech Writing: Framing the Facts 454
For Instance? 455
So What? 456
PREPARING THE VISUALS 456
Overheads and Slides 458
Video 462
FYI: Seven Cs for Video Success 462
PRACTICING 463
PRESENTING 464
Keep Control 464
Talk with the Audience 467
Using Question-and-Answer Sessions Strategically 467
GUIDELINES FOR USING QUESTIONS STRATEGICALLY 468
Think Multiculturally 468
SUMMARY 470
EXERCISES 470

PART VI
EMPLOYMENT COMMUNICATION
475

23
RESUMES AND COVER LETTERS
477

SELF-INVENTORY 479
MARKET INVENTORY 479
Career-Planning Office or Agency 479
State and Federal Employment Offices 479
FYI: The Job Search 481

Newspapers 481
Professional Job Listings 482
Sources of Information about Companies 483
Word of Mouth 483
SOLICITING RECOMMENDATIONS 483
MANAGING THE RESUME—PART I: CONTENT 484
Heading 484
Objective 487
Education 487
Experience and Skills 487
Personal Information 490
References 491
MANAGING THE RESUME—PART II: DESIGN 491
WRITING THE COVER LETTER 492
Attention 494
Interest 494
Desire 495
Action 496
Letters That Work 497
SUMMARY 501
EXERCISES 501

24

THE INTERVIEW . . . AND BEYOND
508

GOALS FOR INTERVIEWS 509
CONDUCTING THE INTERVIEW 510
Setting the Stage 510
Asking Questions 510
Paying Attention 510
Taking Notes 512
Concluding Gracefully 512
THE EMPLOYMENT INTERVIEW 512
Preparing 513
Participating in a Face-to-Face Interview 513
FYI: **The Employment Interview as Role Play 516**
Participating in a Telephone Interview 516
AFTER THE INTERVIEW 518
Deciding 518
Accepting an Offer 519
Declining an Offer 520
Responding to a Rejection 520
PERFORMANCE REVIEWS 520
SUMMARY 521
EXERCISES 524

PART VII

SPECIAL FORMS OF BUSINESS COMMUNICATION

527

25

PROCEDURES AND INSTRUCTIONS
529

GETTING READY TO WRITE 531
Target the User 531
Set the Goals 532
Understand the Procedure 532
MATERIALS AND TOOLS 533 • TIME 533 • RANGE OF STEPS OR ACTIONS 533 • BEST SEQUENCE 533 • NECESSARY PRECAUTIONS 533 • FURTHER INFORMATION 533
WRITING THREE TYPES OF PROCEDURES 534
Step-by-Step Instructions 534
HOW TO DO SOMETHING 534 • HOW TO GET SOMEWHERE 536
Manuals 539
SOFTWARE MANUALS 539 • CROSS-CULTURAL CONCERNS 540
Codes of Practice and Behavior 541
DESIGNING THE PROCEDURE 543
TESTING THE PROCEDURE 545
Validating and Verifying 545
VALIDATION 545 • VERIFICATION 545
Revising to Simplify 545
YOUR VOICE AS AN INSTRUCTOR 547
SUMMARY 549
EXERCISES 550

26

DOCUMENTS OF THE CORPORATION
554

INTERNAL DOCUMENTS 555
Documents That Define 555
GOAL STATEMENT 556 • POLICY STATEMENT 556 • STRATEGIC PLAN 558
Documents That Control 558
Documents That Maintain 559
Employee Publications 560
EXTERNAL DOCUMENTS 560
FYI: **Redirecting and Redesigning the Hercules *Horizons* 560**
Customer-Relations Documents 562
SERVICE ANNOUNCEMENTS 562 • NEWSLETTERS 562
Reports for Investors 564
THE CONTEXT FOR ANNUAL REPORTS 564 • READING ANNUAL REPORTS 564
FYI: **The CEO's Letter to Shareholders 566**
OTHER REPORTING OCCASIONS 567
Press Releases 568
FYI: **A Glimpse at PR in the 21st Century 570**
SUMMARY 570
EXERCISES 571

HANDBOOK
574

ERROR MESSAGES 575
Faulty Agreement 575
Fragments 576
Lack of Parallelism 576
Misplaced Modifiers 577
Dangling Modifiers 578
Shifts in Point of View 579
Shifty or Missing Subjects 580
Mixed Metaphors 580
PUNCTUATION 580
The Comma 581
The Semicolon 582
The Colon 583
The Dash 584
Parentheses 584

Brackets 584
The Period 585
The Exclamation Point 585
Quotation Marks 585
The Apostrophe 586
The Hyphen 587
Underlining and Boldface 587
ABBREVIATION, CAPITALIZATION, AND NUMBER USE **588**
Abbreviation 588
Capitalization 589
Numbers 590
FREQUENTLY MISUSED WORDS AND PHRASES **590**

APPENDIX
DOCUMENTING SOURCES OF INFORMATION
595

WHEN TO DOCUMENT SOURCES **596**
WHEN TO REQUEST PERMISSION TO REPRINT MATERIAL **597**
DOCUMENTING WRITTEN COMMUNICATIONS **597**
Citing Published Material 601
Citing Unpublished Material 601
DOCUMENTING ORAL PRESENTATIONS **603**

INDEX
607

For Your Information: Special Commentaries

"Why Study Business Communication?" by Robert D. Gieselman 8
"A Dinner Invitation in Korea" by Lt. Petra M. Gallert 44
"Bilingual Publications" by Maurice Boucher 45
"Clustering" by Thomas F. Carney 66
"Acronyms" by Donna Lee Cheney 84
"Visualizing the Law" by Bertram Wolfson 98
"Olympic Colors" by John R. Farquharson 106
"Communicating with Photographs" by Philip Douglis 119
"Measuring Readability" by Janice C. Redish 144
"Find It Fast" by Marie Flatley 176
"Hypermedia" by Rebecca B. Worley 186
"Local Norms in E-Mail" by JoAnne Yates 188
"Collaborating to Write This Textbook" by William D. Andrews and Deborah C. Andrews 204
"Making Assignments" by Jone Rymer 206
"The One-Page Memo" by William Cheney 225
"Communicating with a Japanese Partner" by Ken Charhut 254
"Rudeness Never Works" by Jean Bohner 292
"Proposal Writing" by Brent Worley 336
"Electronic Reporting on Spotted Owls" by Henrietta Nickels Shirk 348
"Objectivity in North American and Chinese Reports" by Linda Beamer 368
"Meishis in Japanese Business" by Mohammed Ahmed 413
"Deciding to Meet Abroad" by Ken Charhut 438
"Corporate Speech Writing: Framing the Facts" by Ellen J. Roberts 454
"Seven Cs for Video Success" by Ed Ziegler 462
"The Job Search" by Beth Berret 481
"The Employment Interview as Role Play" by Robert J. Myers 516
"Redirecting and Redesigning the Hercules *Horizons*" by Ida G. Crist 560
"The CEO's Letter to Shareholders" by Crystal C. Bell 566
"A Glimpse at PR in the 21st Century" by Wilma K. Mathews 570

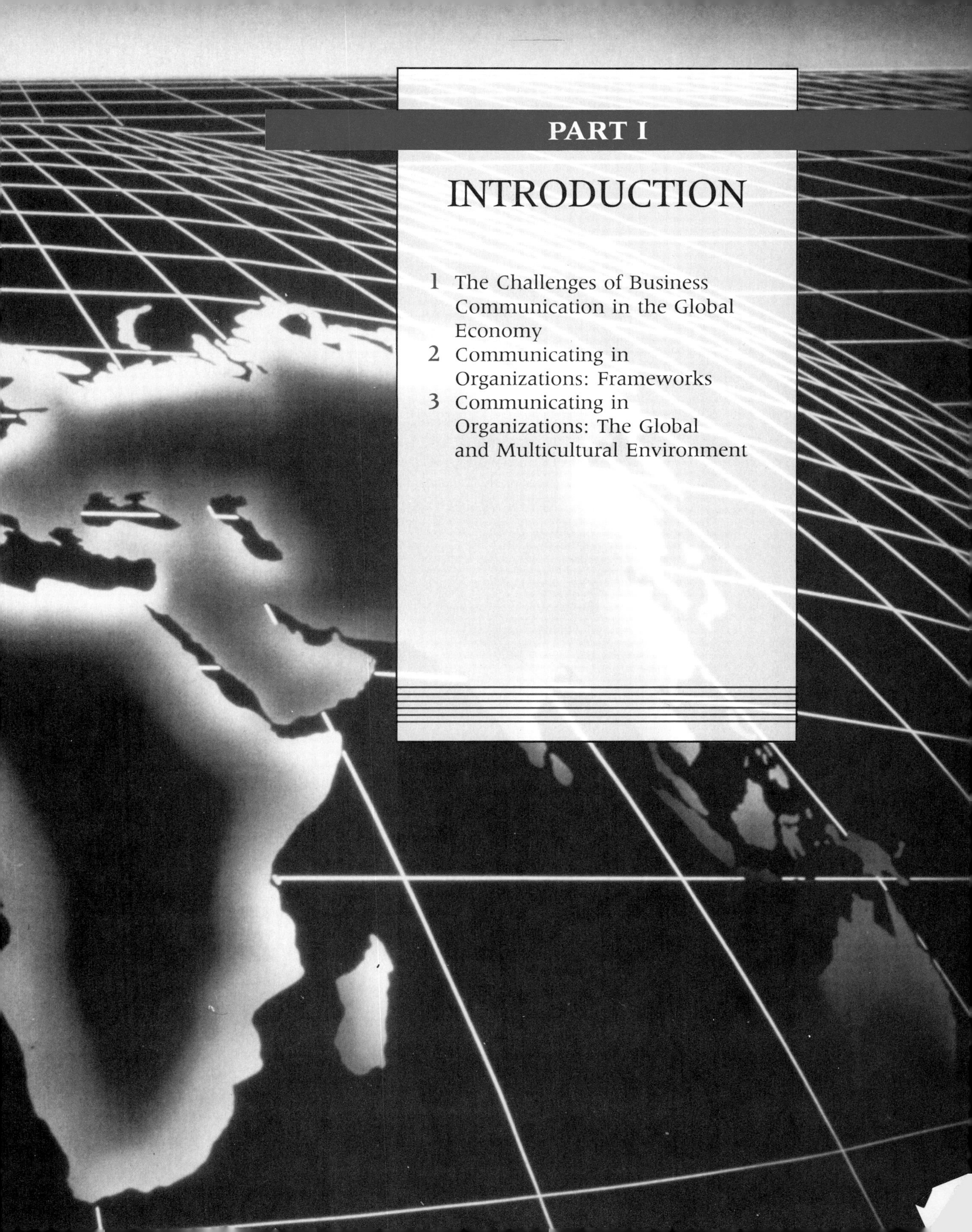

PART I

INTRODUCTION

1 The Challenges of Business Communication in the Global Economy
2 Communicating in Organizations: Frameworks
3 Communicating in Organizations: The Global and Multicultural Environment

INTRODUCTION TO PART I

"Business *Is* Communication."

Do you agree? You can answer the question because you already know a lot about both business and communication. In your daily life and in whatever work experience you have or may be having now, you have learned a lot about communication. After all, you speak, listen, read, and write evey day, on the job and off. You have also practiced business—certainly as a consumer, probably in a full- or part-time job. You see, hear, and read news about business every day on television and radio and in newspapers and magazines.

As a college student, you have probably already studied both business and communication. You may have had one or more courses, general or specialized, in aspects of business. You have probably studied writing, and perhaps speaking, in an English or communication course.

The first three chapters of this textbook are meant as a bridge from your prior study and practice of both business and communication to your formal study of business communication. They are meant to set the stage, building on what you already know and can do. They also introduce new information: concepts, issues, and themes that will enrich your study of business communication as you proceed through the course for which this book serves as text.

Chapter 1 briefly describes the changing nature of business practice and outlines the benefits you can enjoy from good communication skills. It will help you answer the question you probably have in mind as you begin your course: "Why should I study business communication?"

Chapter 2 offers a set of *frameworks* for viewing the study of business communication. It provides a simplified theoretical framework for understanding what communication is and how it works. It describes typical business functions and shows how communication serves each. Overviews of the forms and modes of business communication give you a preview of what kind of business communication you will use as you study and practice.

Chapter 3 rounds out the introduction by describing the global and multicultural economy in which all businesspeople practice and communicate. The *challenges* described in the first chapter and the *frameworks* presented in the second chapter must all be understood in the context of the evolving world of international and multicultural business.

You probably already know much about the ideas and issues that these three chapters present. Some points may also be new. All should be exciting to you as you embark on your formal study of business communication, bringing to bear what you have already learned to meet the challenges that lie ahead for businesspeople in the 21st century.

1 THE CHALLENGES OF BUSINESS COMMUNICATION IN THE GLOBAL ECONOMY

What's Ahead

BUSINESS IN THE 21ST CENTURY
WORKING SMARTER THROUGH GOOD COMMUNICATION
FYI: Why Study Business Communication?
HOW SUCCESSFUL COMMUNICATION HELPS YOU
Achieve Job Success
Gain Personal Satisfaction
Meet Ethical and Social Obligations
THE CHALLENGE OF SUCCESSFUL BUSINESS COMMUNICATION
SUMMARY
EXERCISES

Do You Know 

- What are some changes that will occur in business in the 21st century?
- What is the role of communication in business—now and in the next century?
- How can good communication help you personally?

- A salesperson driving on a California freeway uses her car phone to leave a message in her supervisor's electronic mailbox in Orlando, Florida.
- A hospital administrator in Chicago interviews a Spanish-speaking applicant for a job in the critical-care unit.
- A senior consultant in a public accounting firm in Munich prepares a financial analysis of investment prospects in Poland for a manufacturer of printing equipment in Buxton, Maine.
- A benefits manager in Atlanta writes a summary of a new health care program that must be included in the company's newsletter for employees in the United States, Mexico, and Japan.
- A recent college graduate, planning to open a restaurant near St. Louis, develops a financing plan to present to the local bank as part of a loan application.

The year is 2015, and you could be the salesperson, hospital administrator, consultant, benefits manager, or entrepreneur. You are a businessperson in the 21st century, and your job is to *communicate.* A college student today, in the 20th century, you will pursue your business career in the 21st century. Are you ready?

BUSINESS IN THE 21ST CENTURY

What will a business career in the 21st century be like? Many aspects of business life will resemble those of the 1990s. Businesses will manufacture goods and produce services. Customers will purchase the goods and services. Financial resources will be focused on producing what customers want in a manner that yields the highest return to owners and investors. People will be recruited, hired, developed, managed, rewarded, fired, and retired. New businesses will begin. Some will fail. Others will merge and recombine. Governments will issue and enforce regulations on safety, the environment, and ethical practice. Unions will organize workers and demand changes in employment practices. In short, business in the 21st century will in many ways be like business in the 20th century.

But there will be obvious changes. No crystal ball is accurate enough to show us all of them, but by looking at trends in the last few decades, we can predict some:

• People working in business will demand and get more responsibility. Rather than being treated as interchangeable parts in a large machine, workers will have more influence over what they do and will participate more in decisions about how their employers make decisions and organize work. Differences between "employers" and "employees" will decrease as all members of a firm or organization work together to achieve goals.

• Businesses will be organized in new structures, with more emphasis on teams and groups. "Tall" structures with well-defined hierarchies have characterized corporate organizations. People report to (that is, are responsible to) others above them, in a pyramid form with many employees at the bottom reporting upward to key executives and finally through these people to a chief executive officer at the top. This form of organization is already evolving toward a "flat" or "pancake" model with fewer layers of management between the "top" and the "bottom." Flatter organizations promote direct relationships among employees and emphasize teamwork and collaborative problem-solving at all levels. "Upward" and "downward" communication—from workers to supervisors and supervisors to workers—will remain important, but "sideways" communication *among* all employees will become more common and more important to achieving the success of businesses.

• Businesses and the people in them will be concerned about the world around them, especially about the natural environment. The need to protect the environment will affect business decisions about what products are made and how they are made and used. The goal of maximizing profit will be tempered by respect for the natural environment. Oil producers, chemical companies, and automobile manufacturers already work under tight restrictions. These restrictions will become even tighter. Great new business opportunities will emerge as firms recycle products and produce new ones that

Concern for the natural environment, as reflected in corporate and community recycling programs, will be a growing influence on business practice and communication.

B►

If your company has gotten this complicated,

In any complex organization, size can create obstacles. And many firms are using information technology to help get past them.

But instead of trying to run around obstacles, Andersen Consulting suggests that you eliminate them entirely.

Working from a total business perspective, we look for ways to simplify your company's fundamental processes. We help you remove barriers between departments. Between individuals. Between your company and its business goals.

© 1990 Andersen Consulting

Like complicated board games, business structures can create obstacles. Many organizations are being simplified to remove barriers, increase participation, and promote communication.

reduce pollution, degrade readily in nature, and require fewer nonrenewable resources in their manufacture and distribution.

• Markets for goods and services will be worldwide, not national. Firms will buy and sell globally and will organize and operate their businesses with less attention to their "home" countries. Increasingly, raw materials will be mined or extracted in one area of the world, shipped to another for finishing, and sold in yet another.

• Technology will play a larger role in how businesses operate. Rather than taking the place of people, technology—especially in the form of computers and related electronic processes—will ease some of the burdens of work and will enable workers to accomplish more in less time. The greater use of technology will further increase the need for a work force that is better educated and more flexible than in the past.

• Information will continue to grow dramatically as research produces new observations and interpretations. We not only will know more but also will have more ways to record, store, and transfer what we know. In other

you should fold.

Then, after a clearer path has been established, we apply the information technology that will speed you on your way.

Using this combination of business and technological skills, Andersen Consulting has helped simplify operations for leading companies in almost every industry.

We invite you to join the fold.

ANDERSEN CONSULTING
ARTHUR ANDERSEN & CO., S.C.

Where we go from here.

words, both information itself and our ability to *use* it will increase to the point where simply managing information will be a key business function.

• Distinctions between private and public forms of enterprise will blur as governments and businesses work in partnerships and increasingly affect each other's goals and practices. Private businesses will be subject to government regulation and will operate with more sensitivity to *public* needs as expressed by citizens through the political process.

• New forms of financing and organizing business will emerge, causing growth in both very large businesses and very small ones. There will be more giant corporations—and more "mom-and-pop" businesses. The individual entrepreneur who wants to open a restaurant, write a new software package for a microcomputer, or develop a more efficient lighting fixture will be supported and encouraged by traditional capital markets. At the same time, very large businesses will add to their products and services by adopting entrepreneurial methods that encourage individual effort and that bring small firms under their corporate umbrellas.

WORKING SMARTER THROUGH GOOD COMMUNICATION

What will these changes mean for you, the businessperson of the 21st century? At the very least, business life will be exciting. It always has been, but with continuing changes along the lines suggested, business is going to be even more challenging and satisfying in the next century.

You might be a member of a project team developing a computerized inventory-control system for a large agribusiness venture in the Middle East, working with colleagues from Japan, Brazil, and Saudi Arabia. You might be spending 18-hour days in your garage, refining a new detergent that degrades safely in the water system—and talking to local bankers about financing while you communicate with potential customers in Europe to locate your best market. Or you might be supervising a team of information specialists working to reduce the time it takes to process insurance claims at a hospital.

Whatever business you pursue in the 21st century, you will have to work hard and work "smart"—just as businesspeople in the 20th century do. *Communication* will be central to everything you do in business, in the next century as in this one. You will need to talk, listen, read, and write. You will need to identify and understand information, to arrange it so that others understand and can use it, and to transfer that information in a form that helps you and others know and reach goals—your own, as well as those of your business. In a simple sense, business *is* communication. It follows that good communication means good business—for you and for your company. In the 21st century, good communication will be even more important

WHY STUDY BUSINESS COMMUNICATION?

Robert D. Gieselman
Former Executive Director, Association for Business Communication;
Professor of Engineering Communication, University of Illinois at Urbana-Champaign

Nearly everyone talks about the importance of good communication. One has only to pick up a newspaper or magazine to find statements by executives in business, government, and the professions about how vital communication is in the workplace, how it is the lifeblood of organizations, and how it can affect your career advancement. Various studies of how executives spend their time at work reveal that about all they do is communicate: they spend nearly 100 percent of their workday reading, writing, talking, and listening.

We take all this for granted; no one disputes it. Indeed, knowledgeable people have been making similar statements at least since the time of Aristotle. Yet, there is a disquieting feeling that, despite all the emphasis on communication, we do not seem to make adequate progress toward improvement. Why?

Part of the problem may be in the very nature of communication. We engage in communication so constantly and intensely all of our lives that we simply take it for granted. It is such a normal part of our lives that we seldom think about it, certainly not consciously or critically. We speak, we write, and we assume that we have communicated. Often we have not. Truly, the great enemy of communication is the

to business and personal success than it has been in the 20th century. In "*FYI:* Why Study Business Communication?" one of the leading American authorities on the topic explains why communication skills are so important.

HOW SUCCESSFUL COMMUNICATION HELPS YOU

In the next chapter, you will look at the ways in which communication works in business. Right now, it's worth thinking about the value of communication to you, the businessperson. Successful communication helps you

- Achieve job success.
- Gain personal satisfaction.
- Meet ethical and social obligations.

Achieve Job Success

Job success depends on many factors, from your specialized skills and knowledge to simple luck. Over and over in surveys and personal statements, however, business leaders point to good communication skills as being among the two or three most important characteristics needed for success. Being able to write and speak clearly and effectively complements one's technical abilities and reflects one's understanding of people, the two dimensions of management most often cited as keys to organizational and individual success. The evidence is overwhelming that good communicators succeed in business.

illusion of it. Thus, part of the answer may be that we need to recognize the illusory nature of communication and redouble our efforts to monitor our communicative efforts, to solicit feedback, and to engage in careful follow-up.

Another path to success is to recognize that communication occurs between *people*. You cannot communicate well unless you focus on the human element, considering carefully what people want and need, what they already know, and what you expect them to do. You cannot ignore power relationships and other organizational dynamics.

A middle manager in a firm for which I served as a consultant once asked my advice about one of her subordinates. She said, "Bill seems to get whatever he wants around here. He doesn't just write memos; he talks to people first and tells them he'll get back to them in writing. Then, when they see his written requests, they remember that they've already discussed matters and they usually go along. He sets them up; that's why he's so successful. What should I do?" My answer was easy: "Promote him."

To be a successful communicator, emulate Bill: Focus on people, pre-communicate, communicate, and follow-up. Good luck.

The headquarters of the European Economic Community (Common Market) is the center of activities that reflect both globalization and cooperation affecting businesses in Europe and throughout the world.

Gain Personal Satisfaction

Personal satisfaction comes in part from job success, but it also extends well beyond promotions, raises, and pats on the back for work well done. Writing a clear report or delivering a powerful speech gives you a feeling of mastery that reinforces your self-confidence and sense of achievement and promotes personal satisfaction. Being able to summarize a complex legal situation in a single-page memo or to produce an imaginative visual that captures the connection between market share and volume growth provides an immediate pleasure and reward that go well beyond simple job success. It just feels good to do well.

Meet Ethical and Social Obligations

When you hear on the news about "scandals" in government and on Wall Street or about workers suing their former employers for unfair dismissal, you realize that businesspeople face ethical issues every day. Although it may not be easy to define or establish ethical and social obligations, all of us feel such obligations and try to meet them in our daily lives. Meeting them on the job will become even more important to individuals and businesses in the century ahead.

Successful communication provides a way of satisfying ethical and social obligations. Communication depends on *trust,* on the assumption of the honesty, integrity, and fair dealing that must accompany relations with other people. As business grows more global, establishing and retaining trust among people of differing values and business practices will provide new ethical challenges. Honest communication affirms membership in the human race. It says that you respect others and want them to respect you.

The Quakers have a saying with broad nonsectarian application, especially in business communication: "In all your dealings, leave other people at least as well off as you found them." If in everyday speech, office memos, corporate advertising campaigns, and the preparation of annual reports—to name just a few instances of business communication—you behave in a way that conforms with this advice, then you have communicated well.

THE CHALLENGE OF SUCCESSFUL BUSINESS COMMUNICATION

This textbook will help you understand and improve the communication skills that lie at the heart of business and that will help you to succeed on the job, to develop self-confidence, and to meet your obligations to others. But business has never been—and won't be in the 21st century—a matter of rules and regulations or cookbook recipes. Business works through people, who every minute of every business day listen, learn, think, apply principles, and try new approaches. As they do so, they grow and develop, reaching for goals, adjusting procedures, and looking for what works best. They succeed—and their business prospers—because they *communicate*. That's what this book is about. We hope that it will help you—as a student of business in the 20th century, and as a successful businessperson of the 21st century.

As businesses expand globally, familiar symbols take new forms, and messages must be communicated in different languages, as seen in this fast food restaurant in Quebec.

SUMMARY

- Although many aspects of business will not change from today to the next century, some trends apparent even now will increase greatly and change the nature of business life. As a businessperson in the 21st century, you will see

  - More emphasis on individual effort and responsibility in businesses.
  - Greater concern for the environment.
  - The challenge of global markets.
  - Advances in technology.
  - Continuing growth in information and its use.
  - New organizational structures that simplify reporting relationships.
  - Fewer distinctions between the public and private sectors.
  - New approaches to financing and organizing that will create more very large and very small business organizations.

- As many social, economic, and political forces change business practice in the years ahead, the ability to communicate quickly and effectively will play a larger role in business success, which will make good communication skills even more important for personal and professional growth.
- The ability to communicate well will help you, as a businessperson in the 21st century, to reach your career goals, to achieve personal satisfaction and gain self-confidence, and to meet your ethical obligations to others and to your society.

EXERCISES

For Discussion

1. What career do you plan to pursue? Do you think that that career will change as we enter the 21st century? How?
2. List the skills that you think are important for success in your chosen field. Where do communication skills rank in that list?
3. Which of these business positions do you think will exist in the year 2050? Why?

Secretary	Human resource manager
Accountant	Data-processing clerk
Market researcher	Salesperson
Environmental quality monitor	Manager of information

4. Select one of the business positions listed in Exercise 3 that you think will still exist in the year 2050 and speculate about how the job may change from what it is today—in the educational qualifications required, in advancement possibilities, in the level of responsibility, and in job content. Why will these changes occur? How important will communication skills be in the position?
5. If businesses become more environmentally aware, how will the need to communicate—both within a business and outside it—be affected? Will there need to be more or less communication? What will need to be communicated? To whom?

For Writing

6. If you hold a job (full time or part time) while attending college, keep a log for one day that shows
   a. the amount of time you spend in communicating—with fellow workers, customers, suppliers, government agencies, and the general public.
   b. the form each communication takes: oral, written, or electronic.

   Write a one-page essay describing how much of your job is devoted to communication.
7. Discuss with a member of your family how much time he or she spends in communication each day on the job. Write a brief report summarizing your discussion. Are you surprised by the amount of time the person spends in communication on the job? Is it more or less time than you expected?
8. Select one of the business trends outlined in this chapter (for example, environmental concerns or new forms of organization). Read the business section of your local newspaper for several days to look for examples of the trend you selected. Using examples you found in the newspaper, write a brief essay on the trend.

For Collaboration

9. Form a team of three or four students from your class to analyze this business situation:

   Sandra Myers and Randy Becker are applying for the position of management trainee at the Global Department Stores. Myers has a degree in psychology. Becker has a degree in fashion merchandising. The head of the training program wants to hire Becker because of his specialized education, but the head of the human resource department favors Myers because she thinks the study of psychology is good preparation for dealing well with fellow workers and customers. The two heads agree that they want to hire the applicant with "the best communication skills."

   Your analysis of this situation should consider the following questions:
   a. Why are communication skills considered so important for the job?
   b. How might courses in fashion merchandising have helped Becker develop good communication skills?
   c. How might Myers's study of psychology have helped her develop good communication skills?

   Now suggest a way to help identify the applicant with the best communication skills. (For example, an interview, a role-playing situation, or a paper test of writing skills.) Discuss why you selected this test and how it will identify good communication skills.

   As a team, report to your class on the results of your analysis and describe and defend the method you developed for identifying good communication skills. As a class, vote on which team's method is best and discuss why.

2 COMMUNICATING IN ORGANIZATIONS

Frameworks

What's Ahead

DEFINING BUSINESS COMMUNICATION
A COMMUNICATION MODEL
Applying the Communication Model
THE NATURE OF BUSINESS ORGANIZATIONS
THE DIRECTION OF COMMUNICATION
ORGANIZATIONAL FUNCTIONS OF BUSINESS COMMUNICATION
Definition
Control
Maintenance
PURPOSES OF BUSINESS COMMUNICATION
Recording
Informing
Persuading
FORMS OF BUSINESS COMMUNICATION
Written Forms
Oral Forms
Nonverbal Forms
Electronic Forms
Convergence of Forms
MODES OF BUSINESS COMMUNICATION
Routine Communication
Customized Communication
Mixed Modes of Communication
SUMMARY
EXERCISES

Do You Know 

- What is business communication?
- What happens when we communicate?
- What is a business organization?
- What functions does communication serve in business?
- What purposes does communication serve in business?
- What different forms can business communication take?
- What modes of communication are typical in business?

- The president and the chairman of the board of Valero Energy Corporation give a presentation to stock analysts in Los Angeles about their company's prospects and then answer questions about projected demand for natural gas and its impact on future earnings.
- A college freshman working at South Freeport Marine asks the dockmaster for a 50-cent-an-hour raise in recognition that she has worked for the marina for three years.
- The executive director of the United Way in Medford, Oregon, writes a memo to the heads of all participating community agencies to solicit suggestions on new ways to recognize the contributions of senior citizens to the annual fundraising campaign.
- A consultant for McKinsey and Company meets with the owner of a small biotechnology firm in Iowa to review plans for exporting its product, a pregnancy-testing kit, to the People's Republic of China.

All these situations are examples of business communication. When we write, speak, read, and listen to achieve business goals, we practice business communication. This chapter will help you explore essential theoretical and conceptual issues, which serve as background to the study of business communication. You need a good grasp of these ideas and concepts to develop effective business communication skills.

In this chapter, you will explore a number of *frameworks* that set the context for understanding and practicing purposeful communication on the job. First, you'll study a *model* for communication: a simplified description of how communication occurs at the most general level. Then, you'll look at the three primary *functions* that communication serves within business organizations. Within any of those functions, you'll see that communication can serve three *purposes*. You'll also briefly examine the *forms* that business communication can take. Finally, you'll see two *modes* that communication can follow.

The purposes, forms, functions, and modes of business communication are the frameworks within which this book presents descriptions and advice on how to be an effective business communicator in the 21st century.

DEFINING BUSINESS COMMUNICATION

Two definitions will help you understand business communication:

> A *business* is an organization, that is, a collection of persons, structures, and processes that function together to achieve one or more goals.
>
> *Communication* is the transfer of information to achieve a goal, which can be either understanding or action.

Putting these together, we can say that

> Business communication is the transfer of information to help an organization achieve its goals.

Of course, not all speaking, writing, reading, and listening on the job fits this definition. The person who shouts with joy when the computer program she is working on produces the right result is "speaking on the job," but her shout does not fall within our meaning because it is not goal-oriented, that is, is not aimed at achieving an outcome. We are concerned with *instrumental* communication: writing, speaking, reading, and listening to achieve a goal. (Nonverbal communication—that is, gestures, looks, and other ways of using body language to express feelings—can be instrumental, too; generally, however, it is expressive rather than instrumental.) While focusing here on the instrumental, you need to remain aware of the other forms of communication and of their presence in business situations. But business communication as we use the term in this book is always instrumental, that is, always aimed at a goal.

A COMMUNICATION MODEL

Figure 2–1 is a simple model of communication that will help you understand how instrumental communication works on the job. The key elements in this model are the *sender* (S) and the *receiver* (R). But instrumental communication starts with the *goal,* the result that the sender desires to achieve *through the receiver.* That goal can be *understanding* or *action.* In other words, the sender may wish the receiver to comprehend something (understanding) or to do something (action). To achieve the goal, the sender encodes a *message* in a *medium.* The medium is the form that the message takes—written, oral, nonverbal, or electronic. Once he or she receives the message, the receiver returns another message to the sender, again encoded in some form. This feedback message allows the sender to see whether the original goal has been accomplished.

This model captures the simplest of communication acts, but communication is rarely as easy and direct as the model implies. Human communication is not a static transfer of one bit of information to one receiver with one intention. It is a dynamic activity, a set of interconnected loops with messages moving back and forth in various media between one or more senders and receivers. That's what makes communication challenging—and fun.

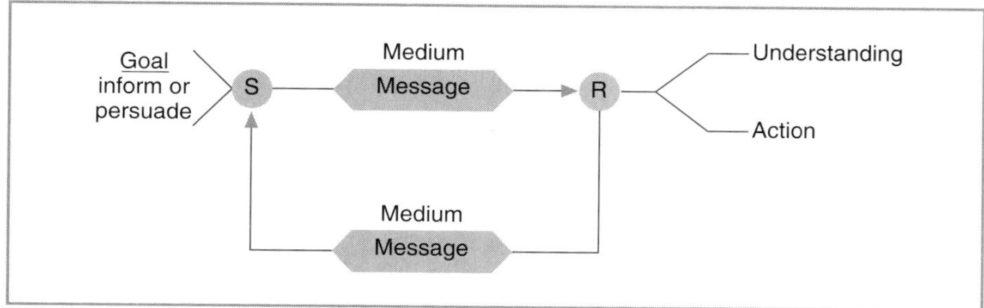

FIGURE 2–1.
A simplified model of communication.

Applying the Communication Model

We can illustrate the complexity of communication by applying our simple model to a common situation. Suppose you are sitting in a draft in your classroom because the professor opened the window. Your *goal* is to get the professor to close the window; that is the *action* you want him to take. You raise your hand and ask the professor to close the window. The medium of your message is both nonverbal (getting attention by raising your hand) and oral (the request itself). The professor sees your hand and hears your words; in other words, he receives the message. He may act or not. If he closes the window, your communication has achieved its goal. The loop is closed: You got what you wanted.

It's possible to imagine other ways in which this communication situation might unfold. You might pass a note to the professor (same message, different medium). You might write a complaint to the dean of students (same message, different medium, different receiver, and longer time frame for expected response). You might squirm, glance angrily at the open window, pull your coat over your shoulders, don gloves, stamp your feet, that is, use body language to convey your point (same message, nonverbal medium).

It is also possible, of course, for you to decide not to communicate at all but to get up and close the window yourself. You take action directly rather than attempting to transfer information to another to cause him to take the action. You could also communicate, but not instrumentally: You could simply scream, "It's freezing in here"—not to achieve a specific outcome but simply to vent your anger.

If, however, you choose not to take direct action nor to use words to express anger noninstrumentally, then you might select from many options in messages and media. Each varies with and depends on your desired goal. The *receiver* likewise has many options in action or understanding and in feedback.

Thus, a seemingly simple, commonplace situation is really quite complex. Presenting it in a visual model, as in Figure 2–1, is somewhat deceptively simple, but such a model is useful as long as you remember the range of possibilities available in messages, media, receivers, and feedback. All of these choices are related to the intended *goal:* what you want. Purpose is therefore central to instrumental communication.

Now look back to the four examples at the beginning of this chapter that show people communicating on the job. Who is the sender? Who is the receiver? What is the goal? What media are used for sending? What feedback can occur? If you can answer these questions, you are well on your way to understanding the complex and exciting nature of business communication.

THE NATURE OF BUSINESS ORGANIZATIONS

Purposefulness, or goal orientation, is also the key characteristic of the organization. We'll repeat the definition of an organization given above: a collection of persons, structures, and processes that function together to achieve one or more goals.

The persons are those employed in the organization. The structures are the formal units or building blocks that comprise the organization. For example, an organization might consist of three divisions: manufacturing, sales, and administration. Each of these might in turn have divisions or subgroups. These are related to one another through *reporting lines:* The head of each subgroup reports to the head of a division, who reports to the head of the whole organization. Structures are linked by processes, which are the actions that occur as the organization does its work (for example, manufacturing or marketing). We can put these elements together to form a simple picture of an organization: people working together in defined units to accomplish goals.

THE DIRECTION OF COMMUNICATION

As you saw in Chapter 1, the ways in which businesses are organized are changing. In many businesses, the traditional "tall" structure, or pyramid, is giving way to the "flat" structure, or pancake (see Figure 2–2). Although people still "report to" (that is, are responsible to) supervisors, who in turn report to other supervisors, the layers of management are reduced, and teamwork rather than reporting relationship is valued. Communication is directly affected by the nature of the organization.

In all organizations, tall or flat, there must be *vertical* communication, both *upward,* toward higher levels of authority, and *downward,* toward those with lower levels of authority. For example, information about how a business is performing—sales data, market share, production schedules, and cash flow—is reported upward, from those close to the operations to those who make executive and policy decisions. In turn, those executive and policy decisions are reported downward, to those who implement them.

There is also always *horizontal* communication in organizations: across reporting lines, among people at the same or similar levels of authority. As organizations become flatter, sideways or horizontal communication assumes even greater importance. Increasing emphasis on teams requires constant communication among team members. (See Chapter 11 on collaborative comunication for specific advice on working in teams.) If you have played on a sports team, you are familiar with the advice coaches often give to

FIGURE 2–2.
Implications of two forms of organizational charts for communication. A "tall" organization (top) emphasizes upward and downward communication. In a "flat" structure (bottom), teamwork and sideways communication are most valued.

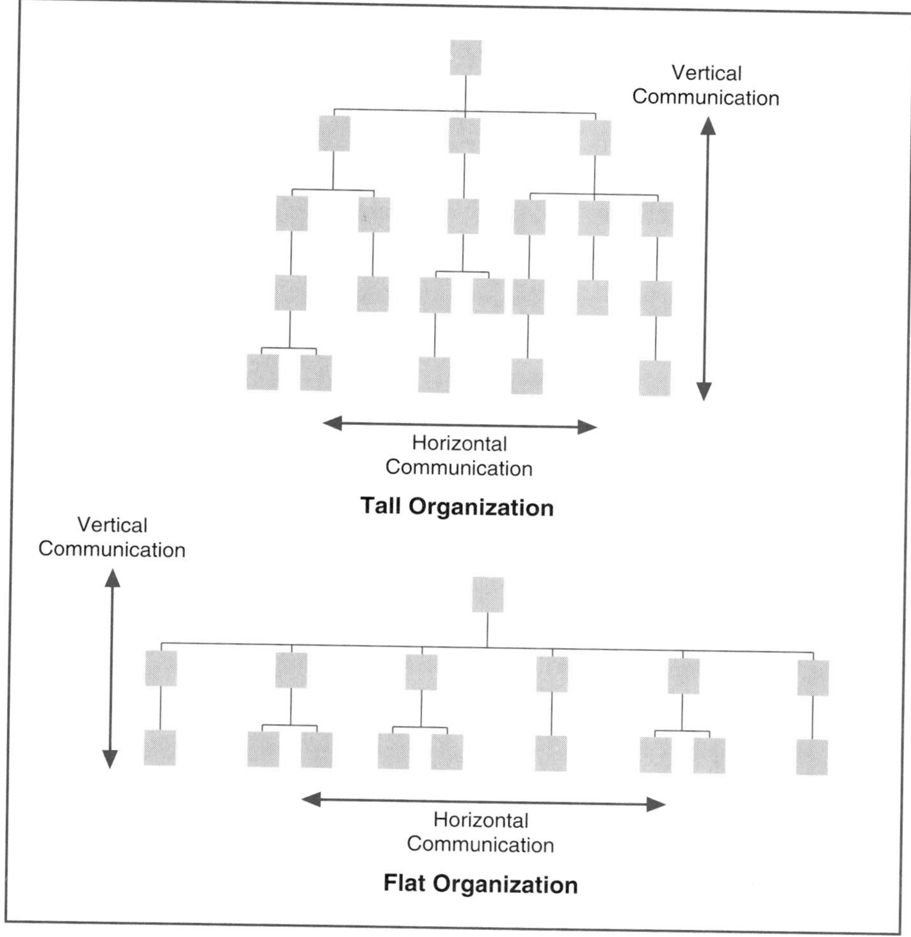

players: "*Talk* to each other." That's just another way of saying, "Communicate horizontally."

Regardless of the shape of the organization—flat, tall, or somewhere in between—you should recognize the wide range of organizations in modern society. The military is an example of a particularly tall organization, with soldiers at the bottom of the pyramid and the commander-in-chief sitting alone at the top. Small entrepreneurial firms of a dozen or so people, who may be both "workers" and "owners," reflect the flat structure. There are as many structures as there are firms. And both horizontal and vertical communication are required in all.

In this book our discussion of business communication is applicable to all organizations. We use the term *business* and the term *organization* interchangeably, for convenience. "Business communication" goes on in Fortune 500 companies, small software firms, churches, colleges, government agencies, sports teams, fraternities, and so on.

The common feature of these organizations is that they are goal-oriented. The goals obviously vary, from saving souls (in the case of a church) to increasing return to investors (in the case of a business enterprise). Because business is goal-oriented, it should be obvious that in business communication, goals are of the utmost importance.

ORGANIZATIONAL FUNCTIONS OF BUSINESS COMMUNICATION

Within an organization, communication serves three broad functions: *definition, control,* and *maintenance.* An organization has to define itself and articulate its mission or goals. It has to say what it's all about and what it tries to achieve. This is *definition,* the highest level of organizational communication. An organization also has to *do* what it defines as its mission or goal, and the activities aimed at achieving goals have to be planned and monitored. This is *control.* While it seeks its goals within its mission, an organization also has to maintain itself, that is, it has to keep going as an organization. This is *maintenance.*

Definition

To survive and prosper, a company has to know its business. It has to say clearly and precisely what it does and why—to its employees, management, customers, stockholders, and many publics. This is *definition.*

A company that prospered by selling metal safes to banks found that when the explosive growth in branch banking ended, the firm's sales fell rapidly, and its very existence as a business was threatened. Recognizing that it was not in the "safe business" but in the "bank support business," the company shifted to the production of electronic teller machines, a growing market. The company's survival depended on a sharp definition of its business, and this definition required communication.

The process of definition began on an informal level, with officers of the firm talking among themselves about markets, products, and opportunities for growth in a new banking environment. The discussion spread outward to the sales force, whose members were asked to talk to their customers about what products banks would need in the future as their business changed. These discussions led to memos and proposals, formal written documents that the officers and the board of directors debated and finally approved. Then the newly sharpened definition of the company had to be communicated widely, first throughout the organization itself, to all employees on whom success depended, and then to the customers, the financial institutions, the news media, and the various publics with which the firm dealt. Brochures and newsletters were created, executives gave speeches to employees and stock analysts, and new marketing materials were developed to support the sales force in explaining the company's orientation. Throughout this process, words and pictures and numbers had to be put together to create the right definition of what the company was and what business it was in.

Definition saved the company. And communication—at first oral and informal, later written and formal, internal and external—supported the critical definition function.

Annual shareholder meetings offer important opportunities for businesses to *define* themselves, to project a corporate image, and to announce key corporate goals.

Control

Once an organization has defined itself and communicated that definition both inside and outside, the work of meeting the goal begins. For the former safe manufacturer, new business operations began. Electronic teller machines were designed, built, sold, distributed, and maintained. Communication again played a key role. Designs were proposed. Manufacturing processes were developed to build the machines. Advertising literature was developed showing specifications and prices. Orders were booked and processed. Machines were shipped and installed. Invoices were sent, payments recorded, bills and wages paid. At each point in these activities, people wrote, spoke, and listened to other people inside and outside the organization to produce results.

Communication provides the means of keeping track of all this purposeful activity so that the right work is done by the right people at the right time. This management function is called *control,* and successful communication is central to control. Facilitating the ongoing activities of the firm to help it achieve its goals is the second function of communication in organizations.

As a college student, you encounter this aspect of organizational communication frequently. When you register for a course, you write a number on a form that is processed by the registrar to produce a bill, put your name on a class roster, and generate a grade card that the instructor completes at the end of the term. That card, in turn, leads to an entry on your transcript, and when all the right entries have been made (and the bills paid), the college tells you and your employer that you have graduated. The college's business, graduating educated persons, is accomplished in part through this communication flow supporting the control function.

Maintenance

In addition to defining its business and carrying out that business, all organizations have to *maintain* themselves. They hire people and pay them; they open the doors in the morning and close them at night; they buy typewriters and microcomputers and paper; they clean the washrooms and polish the floors. Some of these activities are routine and unexciting, and they often seem distant from such others as production and sales that are at the heart of the firm's business. But these maintenance functions are crucial to helping the organization achieve its goals.

Communication supports the maintenance function. To hire a new person, you have to write a job description, place an ad, review applications, interview prospective employees, start a personnel file, and make sure that the new employee has a desk and that a check for him or her will be produced at the end of the pay period. These activities require constant and interrelated communication—oral and written, internal and external. The purpose of this communication is to maintain the organization so that it can do its work and meet its goals.

PURPOSES OF BUSINESS COMMUNICATION

All on-the-job communication serves one of three purposes: to *record,* to *inform,* or to *persuade.* Sometimes these overlap; for example, you might *record* information in a document whose overriding purpose is to *persuade.* The goal of communication as shown in the model in Figure 2–1 on page 17 is one of these three purposes. If you are writing to induce understanding, you *record* or *inform.* If your goal is to induce action, you communicate to *persuade.*

Recording

Businesses need to *record* a great deal: personnel information, sales data, the status of inventory, and so forth. When you communicate primarily to record, your focus is on the information itself and the need to make it accurate and accessible. Although other people read or listen to what is recorded, their special needs and interests are less important than simply getting the information right and getting it into a form that makes their access to it easy.

Many of the standard forms and reports produced in organizations are aimed at the recording purpose. You log in the number of items sold each day and the total price. You fill out an application for insurance or some other benefit. You list all the customers who entered the shop and the time they spent. You summarize the days of accrued vacation time available to each employee. You *record*—accurately, and in a form that makes the information accessible to potential users.

Informing

When you communicate to *inform,* you become more aware of the needs of your audience. *Who* is being informed? *Why?* Information is vital, but now you also think a bit more about the audience and potential use. Communicating to inform places extra burdens on you to know your audience and its interests in the material.

Sometimes you inform in response to a specific request. At other times, you inform on your own initiative. A log of items sold each day in a shop is a record. But if you notice a pattern in the sales—for example, 75 percent of the sales are for items under $10—you might decide to *inform* your supervisor of this trend, either because she asks you or because you think the fact is significant and you take the initiative to tell her. Your communication might be a simple oral statement: "Joan, I noticed that 75 percent of our sales are for under $10." Or you might write a brief memo summarizing the point and including daily figures as support.

When you move from recording to informing, you become aware of the receiver of the communication and begin to tailor its presentation to that person's needs and interests. If a request for information is specific, you take special care to respond with attention not just to the raw information but also to who requested it and why.

Communicating both within and outside their organizations, people of different interests and backgrounds work jointly to reach common business goals while still meeting personal objectives.

Persuading

The most challenging purpose of communication is *persuading*. When you write or speak to persuade, you often use data that have been recorded, but your focus shifts to the recipient because your purpose is to convince that person of something. If you noticed the sales pattern described above—75 percent of the items sold are priced under $10—you might try to convince your supervisor that more profits could be made if higher priced items were sold. You might write a memo to her recording the relevant data as the basis for trying to persuade her to do something to change the pattern.

Consideration of the audience and its needs becomes primary when you communicate to persuade. Whom are you writing or speaking to? What interest does she have in the topic? What does she already know about it? How much more information will she need to know before accepting your argument? What is the best way to structure that argument to make it persuasive? In communication designed to persuade, the accuracy and accessibility of the information remain important, but packaging that information for the specific audience requires special consideration.

FORMS OF BUSINESS COMMUNICATION

Whether you communicate to record, inform, or persuade, you have a choice of forms in which to express yourself. The form you select is the *medium* of communication, as seen in the model in Figure 2–1 on page 17. Although more than one form is often used, you need to distinguish among four basic types: written, oral, nonverbal, and electronic.

Written Forms

Written forms of business communication include memos, letters, reports, and such documents as newsletters, sales brochures, and annual reports. In most circumstances, the choice of communicating in writing is made for you. For example, you are asked by your supervisor to write a memo summarizing your attendance at a conference, or you receive a letter of complaint from a dissatisfied customer who requests that you respond. You can see, however, that a choice among forms is still present in these examples. When you are told to write a memo, you should obviously do so, but you might also decide to summarize the memo orally when you hand it to your supervisor. The angry customer needs a written response to his letter, but you might also phone him to signify that you take the complaint seriously and value his business.

Overwhelmed by paper, many businesses encourage nonwritten communication, and much is said about the "paperless office" of the future, when electronic means of communication will substitute for written forms (see Chapter 10). Avoiding a blizzard of paper makes good sense, and electronic communication *may* reduce paperwork, but written forms of communication are still common. They serve vital needs: to document carefully for legal purposes, to avoid ambiguity, to make sure that memories of conversations don't produce variant results, and to promote brevity and clarity.

"Putting it in writing" has many advantages that often outweigh the disadvantage of the paper blizzard.

Oral Forms

In sheer volume, oral communication is the most common form of business communication (see Chapter 20). In phone calls, sales presentations, and formal and informal meetings, millions and millions of words are used to carry on business. Oral communication is direct and instantaneous and produces immediate feedback. It takes time to write a memo, send it, and receive comments. Hours of work can be reduced to a few minutes of conversation, and the results of the conversation can be judged on the spot.

But oral communication has disadvantages. What someone tells you orally may not be as clear or focused as what he or she writes. You may misinterpret what was said, or others hearing it may reach different conclusions. Also, there is no legal record, unless of course the conversation is taped. And emotions, which can be carefully controlled in writing, may show in a conversation, thereby diverting attention from the issue at hand.

The pros and cons of oral communication need to be weighed carefully if you have the choice of speaking or of using another form. Sometimes you have no choice. If you are asked to present a five-minute summary to the president of your idea for improving profits, you can't very well ask to send a letter instead. But when you have the choice of speaking or using another form, make sure that the advantages of the oral form outweigh its disadvantages for the purpose and audience at hand.

Nonverbal Forms

In a conversation, much of the meaning is carried in a form other than words. We call this *nonverbal communication.* You raise an eyebrow, stare out the window while someone is speaking, shrug your shoulders, use hand gestures, or shift your weight from one foot to another. Body language, as this is often called, is important. You communicate interest (or lack of it), emotion, involvement, and attitude through gestures and body positions.

Nonverbal communication rarely substitutes for oral communication; rather, it complements it. Appropriate body language reinforces what is said in words. Pointing to a chart as you speak focuses the audience's attention. Frowning as you present negative information signals to the audience that this is not good news. Using certain hand gestures indicates enthusiasm about the topic.

Nonverbal communication, however, can detract from oral communication. Looking bored as you review statistics tells your audience that it, too, should find this topic dull. Shrugging your shoulders in response to a question suggests either ignorance or lack of concern on your part. Pointing to someone as you respond to his question may reflect a combative attitude.

In cultures foreign to your own, nonverbal communication takes on added significance. Many of the gestures and body positions that are natural in your own culture may have a special—even negative—meaning in another culture. Exercise care in such cases. Like written language, body language varies. Know the languages, verbal and nonverbal, of your audience, and use both accordingly.

Properly used, nonverbal communication is a powerful means of carrying messages, especially if it complements spoken communication. (See Chapter 20 for more advice on effective nonverbal communication.)

Electronic Forms

Electronic media of communication are increasingly common in business. (See Chapter 10 for a detailed discussion of the special features of various electronic media.) Sending electronic mail may substitute for writing a memo on paper and forwarding it through interoffice mail. A teleconference may replace face-to-face meetings.

The choice of electronic media must meet the general test of selection: Do the advantages outweigh the disadvantages? Speed is an obvious advantage. An equally obvious disadvantage is that with electronic communication, you may lose the "paper trail" that is so important in business, often for legal reasons. (There are, of course, ways to preserve files in electronic communication.) If the advantage of speed outweighs the disadvantage of losing the trail, then electronic communication is appropriate.

Convergence of Forms

You write a letter and send it via facsimile transmission (fax) to your branch office in Mexico City. Written communication or electronic communication? You make a formal presentation on business strategy to the board of directors and hand out a ten-page summary of key facts and recommendations. Oral? Written? Nonverbal? You tape that presentation and send it out to field offices. Electronic?

Forms are converging. Oral, written, nonverbal, and electronic forms of communication are coming to overlap, meld, merge, and intertwine. This is a good tendency, one you should both understand and exploit as a business communicator. The variety of forms available to you and your ability to use them together—simultaneously or in sequence—enhance your ability to communicate clearly and efficiently to varied audiences for varied purposes. The richness of possibilities in forms aids you in dealing with the complexities of business communication in an increasingly global marketplace.

MODES OF BUSINESS COMMUNICATION

Regardless of its function, purpose, or form, all business communication can be divided into routine and customized modes. Actually, these are better thought of as opposite poles on a continuum. At one end of the continuum is the routine mode; at the other is the customized mode. Many examples of business communication lie somewhere in between, not strictly routine or strictly customized but combining features of both.

Routine Communication

Routine communication is communication that is expected. The quarterly report on sales is produced and distributed quarterly, on a predictable date. Monthly progress reports are issued monthly. The employee newsletter reaches your desk on Friday afternoon, or Monday morning, or whenever. The annual report appears after the close of the fiscal year.

The predictability of routine communication goes beyond the fixed or known time of its production and distribution. A communication is routine if it is created according to fixed norms, patterns, or forms. A fill-in-the-blank memo or report, for example, is routine. The pacing of the information is controlled by the form. Even if the format is not of the fill-in variety, a memo or report can be routine if it is prepared according to an established pattern.

Letters in response to customer complaints (see Chapter 15) are good examples of routine communication. The writer follows a fixed form. For example:

Paragraph 1: Thank customer for letter, and note date of letter and nature of complaint.

Paragraph 2: Assure customer of our interest in hearing from him or her and our desire to respond positively.

Paragraph 3: Respond to specific issue raised in letter; admit problem and offer solution, or ask for more information.

Paragraph 4: Close by repeating thanks, expressing hope that solution is appropriate, and reiterating desire to maintain good relations.

You have probably received such a letter if you ever wrote to complain about a product or service. Sometimes you feel that the letter is "boilerplate"—an automatic response that fails to deal with the specifics of your complaint. If the routine is well handled, however, the letter does its work convincingly, meeting your needs. But the process by which it was produced is still *routine.*

Many business situations call for routine communication: at a fixed time, or following a format that does not vary greatly from situation to situation. In the routine mode, the individual recipient of the message is not as important as the message itself and the medium in which it is carried. The writer or speaker often works on automatic pilot.

Customized Communication

At the other end of our continuum is the customized communication. It is produced in response to a unique circumstance rather than a predictable one, and it is not governed by fixed formats or norms. The needs and interests of the recipient are especially important in shaping the communication. Nothing is automatic. The writer or speaker has to follow general conventions but shapes and controls the communication according to the very specific features of the circumstance.

For example, the president of the firm that is your largest customer calls to complain about the quality of service. No boilerplate response will do. A specially crafted letter, probably from your own president, is required. The letter not only has to be customized but has to *appear* customized—tailored to the individual and the unique circumstances.

Mixed Modes of Communication

No communication problem is unique, and every communication problem is different. Contradictory? Not really. Every situation, of course, has its own features, special twists and turns, and flavor. However, almost all can be examined for common patterns and characteristics.

The customized letter apologizing for poor service to the president of your largest customer is obviously not considered routine. But the response is likely to follow closely the general outline of the routine letter cranked out on demand. That's because the routine itself is set in response to generic features that are probably present even in the special circumstance. You'll find, therefore, that you can combine qualities of the routine and the customized in most business communication situations.

As a business communicator, you face both routine and special situations and must respond in both routine and specialized ways. You can't assume that every communication is routine—but you also can't assume that each is unique and therefore calls for a customized response. Be aware of the poles of the continuum, but also be aware that most cases fall somewhere in between.

SUMMARY

- Business communication is the transfer of information to help an organization achieve its goals. It is instrumental, or purposeful, aimed at an outcome.
- A simple model of communication includes a **sender** and a **receiver.** The sender has a **goal,** the desired outcome, which can be either understanding or an action on the part of the receiver. The **message** is the content sent from sender to receiver, and it is encoded in a **medium.** The receiver returns a **feedback** message to the sender to indicate how the message was received. Although this model appears static, communication is really dynamic, with messages and feedback moving back and forth rapidly and continuously.
- Business organizations are purposeful. They are always oriented toward the achievement of a goal or goals. This is true whether the organization is a production business like an auto manufacturer, a service business like a bank, or a nonprofit business like a school or church.
- In an organization, communication serves three functions: definition, control, and maintenance. **Definition** is the creation of the organization's mission and goals. **Control** is the monitoring of its purposeful activities. **Maintenance** includes all the functions necessary for the organization to maintain itself so that it can achieve its goals.
- Communication serves three general purposes: to record, to inform, and to persuade. **Recording** is oriented to the information itself and requires

you to stress accuracy and accessibility. **Informing** puts greater stress on the intended recipient of the message, causing you to tailor the recorded information to that person. **Persuading** requires great attention to the recipient of the message because you want that person to accept your argument.

- Business communication can take one of four forms: written, oral, nonverbal, or electronic, each with its special features, advantages, and disadvantages. In current business practice, the distinction among the forms is disappearing as the forms themselves converge: Electronic mail, for example, is both written and electronic.

- Business communication can be said to be either routine or customized. **Routine** communication occurs on a predictable schedule and according to fixed patterns and formats. **Customized** communication responds to special circumstances and does not follow fixed patterns or formats. In practice, most business communication combines features of both the routine and the customized.

EXERCISES

For Discussion

1. Collect examples of people communicating on the job. List specific illustrations of writing, speaking, or listening that are aimed at achieving a business goal.
2. List five business organizations that you have had some involvement with during the past week. (Don't forget the college you are enrolled in.) Apply the definition of a business given in this chapter to each of these organizations, and identify as best you can the persons, structures, and processes that together make up the organization. Based on the activities of these organizations, can you determine their goals? What are they in business to achieve? To maximize profit? To improve the life of the community? To increase the understanding of an issue?
3. Collect examples of written business communication, for example, an advertisement, a memo, or an employee newsletter. Use our definition of business communication to explain what is going on in each example and why.
4. Using the examples you collected for Exercise 3, apply the communication model to each. Identify sender, receiver, goal, message, medium, and feedback.
5. After you have gone to a store to make a purchase, write down the oral exchange between you and the clerk. Apply the communication model to this example of business communication, identifying sender, receiver, goal, message, medium, and feedback. Show this application visually, using the model in Figure 2–1 or altering it to better illustrate the flow of communication back and forth between you and the clerk.
6. Ask an employee of a business organization for a one-sentence *definition* of the firm. What is it in business for? Organizations that have a simple mission statement that all employees can easily grasp and communicate to others are generally considered likely to achieve success. Is the definition in this case clear and simple?

7. When you apply for a job, you engage in a variety of communications. Identify each of these, noting whether it is oral or written, what its goal is, and who are the sender and the receiver (examples: advertisement of an opening, your letter or phone inquiry, resume, interview, notice of appointment or wage, orientation packet for new employees). The hiring of employees is a maintenance function within a business. Discuss how each of the communications involved in your job search contributed to the maintenance of the business.

8. Fill in each of the boxes of the following chart with examples of business communication that you are familiar with. Across the top are the three *purposes;* down the side are the four *forms.* (For example, a letter in which you apply for a job would fall within "Written" communication to "Persuade.")

	Record	Inform	Persuade
Written			
Oral			
Nonverbal			
Electronic			

9. For the same communications as in Exercise 8, fill in this chart. This time the elements are the *organizational functions* and the *purposes.*

	Record	Inform	Persuade
Definition			
Control			
Maintenance			

For Writing

10. Many business situations call for communication, but often the participants are unclear about what to say or write to whom and why. Here is a typical example:

John Riley supervised the assembly room of a television-manufacturing plant. He oversaw the mounting of the sets in cabinets and the installation of the fittings: knobs, handles, and labels. He noticed that out of every dozen or so sets that came into his facility, one had screw holes on the bottom that were misaligned enough so that someone had to jiggle the set to match it up with the cabinet holes for final mounting. This process took extra time and thus reduced the productivity of Riley's group. He also feared that the rough handling of the sets required for the alignment would cause damage and would result in rejection by the quality control department, to which the sets were shipped when they left his assembly room.

Riley decided to call the engineering design department, which had final authority over the design of the sets. A junior engineer to whom he spoke told him to write a memo about the problem to the senior design engineer. Riley did so, but two months later, he had had no response. He discussed the problem at lunch with a fellow supervisor in the chassis room, from which the sets came into the assembly room. This person was surprised that Riley had even bothered to contact engineering design at all. He said that Riley should just have mentioned the problem directly to him, and he would have followed up on it right in the chassis room. Engineering design, he said, never liked to deal with production people. Even if they got involved, it would take months of study before they would agree to a design change, whereas he, as supervisor of the chassis room, could modify procedures on his own to correct the problem.

Write a one-paragraph answer to each of these questions:

a. Whom should Riley have contacted when he first spotted the problem? Should he have communicated orally or in writing?
b. Should the junior engineer in engineering design have told Riley to write the memo? Why or why not?
c. Should Riley have waited two months for a response to his memo? What alternatives did he have?

As you answer the questions, refer to the definition of business communication, the communication model, and the definition, control, and maintenance functions of business communication. Each of these concepts will help you to understand the communication situation and to respond to the questions.

For Collaboration

11. Assemble a group of three students from your class. Designate one as a supervisor who has asked for a brief report on the number and type of fast-food restaurants within walking distance of campus. One student should present the results of the study *orally,* and the other should do so in a *written* memo. The supervisor should assess the effectiveness of the two forms of communication, noting the strengths and weaknesses in each. As a group, try to decide which *form* was most effective and why.

3 COMMUNICATING IN ORGANIZATIONS

The Global and Multicultural Environment

What's Ahead

THE GLOBAL ECONOMY
- A Network of Investments and People
- Global Decision Making

GEOGRAPHIC DISPERSION
- Differences in Space and Time
- Overcoming Geography with Technology

CULTURAL DIVERSITY
- Definition of Culture
- Multiculturalism in the United States and Canada
- Language Differences
- Similarities in Organizational Structure
- Differences in Context

BELIEVING IS SEEING
- FYI: A Dinner Invitation in Korea

TALKING AND LISTENING ACROSS CULTURES

WRITING AND READING ACROSS CULTURES
- FYI: Bilingual Publications

SUMMARY

EXERCISES

Do You Know 

- What is the global economy?
- What is culture?
- How does a high-context culture differ from a low-context culture?
- How does what you believe about other people affect how you see them—and how can you see people clearly?
- What should you keep in mind in speaking with or writing to someone of a different culture?

The world of business is growing larger and is shrinking at the same time.

It is growing larger because world trade has expanded dramatically to create a global economy. It is shrinking because the technology of travel and electronic communications provides businesspeople direct and indirect contact with other parts of the world cheaply, quickly, and effectively. Even if you are not currently involved in international business, you cannot avoid the evidence of its existence—and its significance.

In this chapter, you will see how a global economy sets the context for business communication in the 21st century. And you will learn some strategies for communicating within that context—strategies you'll develop further as you read *Business Communication*.

THE GLOBAL ECONOMY

The environment for business, and thus for business communication, is international. Investments across national borders shift daily as companies respond to financial incentives and opportunities, to fluctuations in interest rates and currency strengths, and to perceptions of investment safety. But the trend toward a global economy is clear. Company plants and offices are dispersed around the globe. Work forces are multicultural both domestically and internationally.

A Network of Investments and People

From the U.S. perspective, international business may be looked at in two dimensions: American involvement in other economies and the involvement of others in the United States.[1] In 1990, U.S. plant-and-equipment spending overseas reached $54.9 billion, up 13 percent over 1989. U.S. firms have found production abroad to be efficient, initially in the manufacturing sector, and currently in the service sector. Advances in electronic communi-

[1] Bernard Wysocki, Jr., "The Outlook: U.S. Firms Increase Overseas Investments," *The Wall Street Journal*, 9 April 1990, p. 1, and "Foreign Investment Dip," *The New York Times*, 7 June 1990, p. D5.

cations make it possible for a New York insurer to employ data entry clerks in Ireland to process claims. A California company hires people in Manila to enter citations for a computerized library catalog. U.S. firms also increased overseas spending for research and development by 33 percent between 1986 and 1988 (compared with a 6 percent increase domestically).

At the same time, attracted by relatively cheaper American assets, many foreign-affiliated firms established plants in the United States. By 1990, 10 percent of U.S. manufacturing workers were employed by such firms.[2] Indeed, direct foreign investment in the United States is increasing faster than Americans' direct investment overseas. In 1988, for the first time, the total book value of foreign holdings in the United States exceeded that of American holdings abroad. In 1989, the British were the leading foreign investor; the second was Japan; the third, Australia; and the fourth, Canada.

Global Decision Making

That network of investments and people requires a global perspective in decision making. One chairman of a major U.S. company noted, for example, that if his company had to close a factory, it would not on principle close one in Southeast Asia before one in the United States: "We need our Far Eastern customers, and we cannot alienate the Malaysians. We must treat our employees all over the world equally."[3] The pattern of investments and ownership, then, is international. Few business functions can be carried out in geographic isolation. Local economies tie into national economies, which in turn tie into international ones.

This economic interdependence makes communication critical in the global economy. Such communication fits the frameworks you read about in Chapter 2—with an accent, however, on the *differences* between the sender and the receiver of a message. In an international or multicultural context, you have to communicate across differences in space and time as well as across differences in culture. The challenge—and the reward—in international communication is building a common purpose and a common understanding across those differences.

GEOGRAPHIC DISPERSION

When plants and offices are dispersed around the globe, that dispersion causes difficulties in communicating even within one company. In Figure 3–1, you see the location of the many facilities of one multinational organization: Dominion Textile Incorporated, based in Montreal, Canada.

Differences in Space and Time

First, spatial differences mean that no direct exchange is possible. You can't simply step over to a colleague's desk to pick up a report you need. You have to send a message to get the report. Second, separation reduces

[2] Robert B. Reich, "Everyone Gives, Everyone Benefits," *The Business World*, Part 2 of *The New York Times Magazine*, 1 April 1990, p. 42.

[3] Ibid.

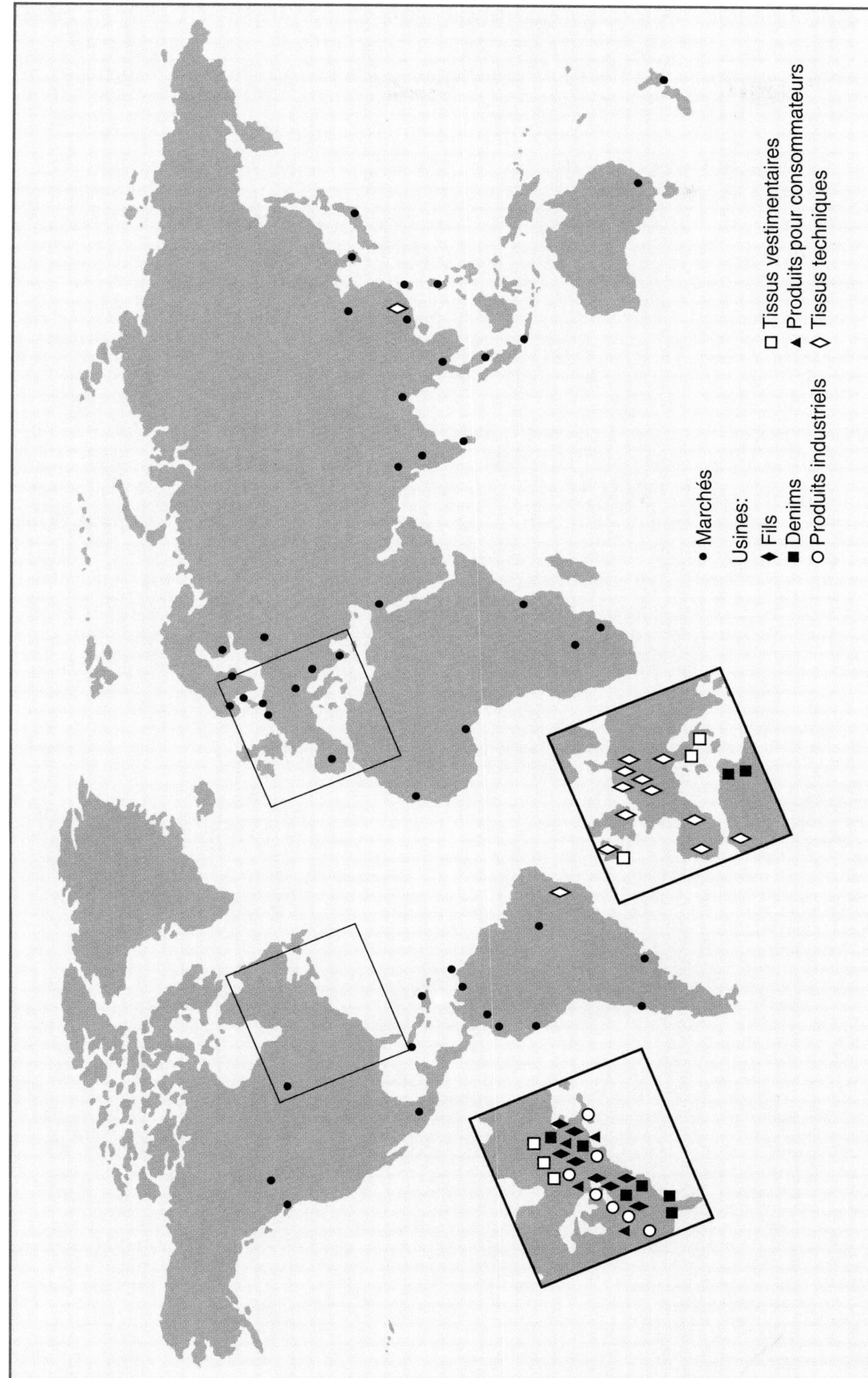

FIGURE 3–1.
This map of the world, with enlarged inserts for the United States and Canada and for Europe, shows the geographic dispersion of Dominion Textile Incorporated's sales offices and plants. It is taken from the French version of the company's annual report, "Une Présence Mondiale" ("A Global Presence"). *(Reprinted by permission of Dominion Textile Inc.)*

the possibility of nonverbal communication, an important element in business dealings, as you saw in Chapter 2. Third, separation usually introduces a delay in getting feedback on a message. That delay, known as *information float,* may hinder decisions and actions.

Fourth, geographic dispersion means that workers often deal across time zones. Your business day and that of the person you are dealing with may not overlap or may overlap for only an hour or two. Figure 3–2 shows the time of day in various parts of the world when it is 9:00 A.M. in Chicago. When you work in the global economy, you need to be aware of more than one clock.

Overcoming Geography with Technology

Advances in transoceanic fiber optics and the satellite transmission of information encouraged the development of the global economy. Those media will aid you, too, in overcoming natural barriers to communication. To reduce information float, you'll use computer networks and facsimile machines to send messages electronically around the globe almost instantly. The recipient's computer or fax can also store the mail for reading at an appropriate point in her or his business day; thus, differences in time zones are overcome. Up-links and down-links from satellites enable participants at remote sites to meet in a teleconference where they can be both seen and heard on video monitors.

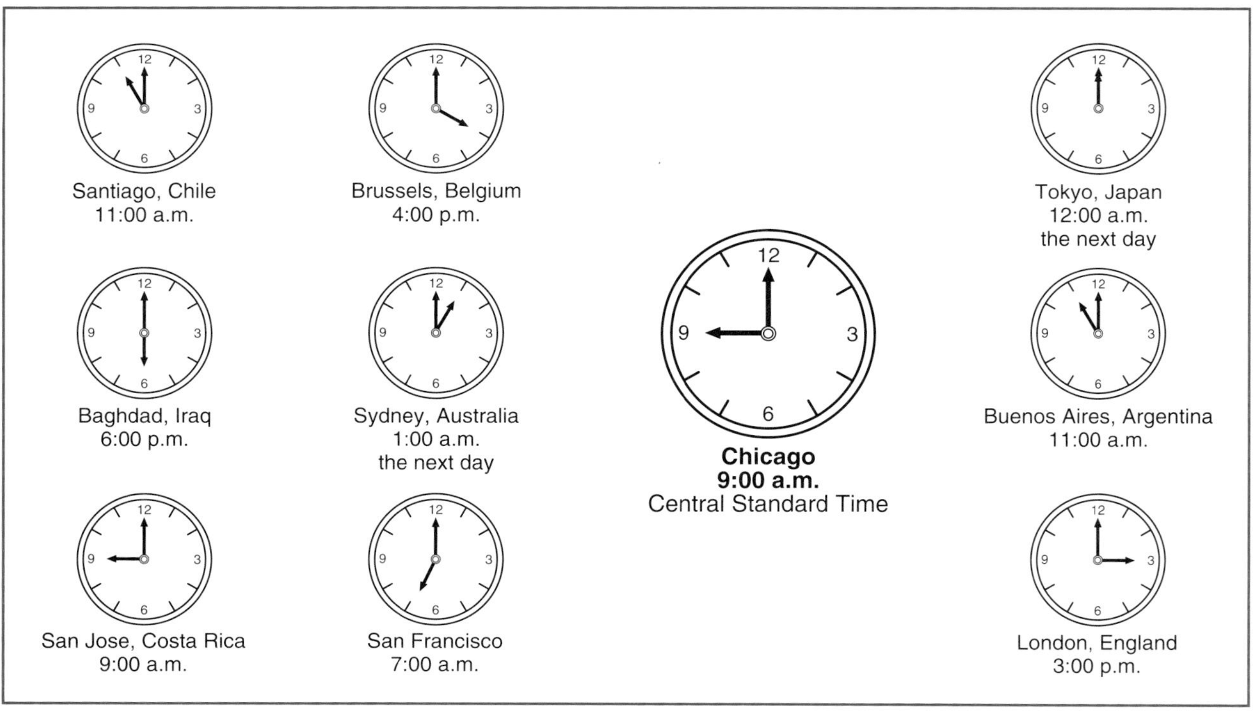

FIGURE 3–2.
Times around the world as Chicago goes to work.

CULTURAL DIVERSITY

Networks of computers and telephones send messages and images swiftly across space and time. But the technology is only a medium. Spanning cultural differences in communication is a more daunting task than spanning mere geography. People communicate differently in different cultures. Documents, for example, *look* different. In writing and reading a business letter, a Spaniard has different expectations from an American concerning the placement of information, the tone, and the acceptable vocabulary, even if both are writing in the same language. The size of the paper also differs. In some cultures, people use few documents, relying mainly on oral and nonverbal communication.

Definition of Culture

How do cultural differences affect how *you* write and talk—or read and listen? First, you need to know what culture is. Here's a simple definition:

Culture is what you need to know to get along in a group.

A group—a culture—shares a common language, along with certain values, attitudes, and patterns of behavior. Within a national culture, organizations also display their own cultures. As a student at a college or university, for example, you participate in its culture. Although the language of instruction and of social interaction may be English or French, within that language you are familiar with certain code words specific to your institution, for example, those designating courses ("E 312," "BU 409") or those describing certain feelings ("I'm pumped," "I'm psyched," "awesome").

What do students at your institution value? Material wealth? Environmental concerns and recycling? Social activism? Athletics? What are the dominant attitudes—toward work, for example, or military service? What is acceptable behavior—in the classroom, in dormitories or fraternities or sororities or apartments, and at sporting events? What is an acceptable level of risk? How trusting are you of other people?

Your answers to these questions will be largely consistent with the answers of those who share the same culture, whether within an organization or within a nation. But a different cultural perspective will lead, of course, to some different answers.

Multiculturalism in the United States and Canada

A long and continuing tradition of immigration has led to a diversity of cultural groups in the domestic work force of both the United States and Canada. Historically, one approach to such diversity has been to educate people of different cultures to adopt the values and behaviors—and language—of the dominant culture. This view is expressed metaphorically in the concept of the *melting pot.* But increasingly, diversity is being cultivated as a national strength, not a detriment.

The role of languages is one example. Spanish is the second language of the United States. Now 8 percent of Americans, Hispanics may become the largest ethnic minority by 2015, surpassing African-Americans.[4] Spanish-language radio and television stations as well as publications are common in such centers as New York, Los Angeles, Miami, and Hartford. Some elementary schools provide intensive instruction in Spanish for both native speakers of Spanish and others. Miami is a capital of Latin American banking, export and import, and culture. Mexican preferences in food, dance, and music flavor the American economy and drive a segment of American advertising.

French is a second language of Canada—and the first and official language of the Province of Quebec. Public signs and official documents in Quebec are printed in French. Telephone operators answer phone calls there in French, then respond to the caller's cue and continue the conversation in either French or English. Organizations based there, like Dominion Textile and, as you'll see, the Centre Canadien d'Architecture, routinely publish reports, brochures, and other documents in both French and English. In your career, you will communicate across different cultures even if you never leave your home in the United States or Canada.

Language Differences

Language is the most obvious mark of cultural differences. National or regional groups separate themselves by their languages or dialects. Language differences are often seen as the most prominent barrier to international communication. That barrier is in part overcome by the use of English, which performs well as an international language of business. English has developed that role in part because it is the native language of so many people, it is flexible in adding new words to match innovations, and it is the language of instruction in American business schools, which have trained many foreign managers.

If you speak only one language, however, (even English), you risk missing out on a good deal of business. Language and culture are interwoven. If you don't understand at least the rudiments of a language, you'll have a hard time understanding the priorities of its speakers.

Similarities in Organizational Structure

Language differences suggest even more fundamental differences in culture. Are such differences decreasing as the economy becomes increasingly global? Nancy Adler, a Canadian authority on international management, sees two opposite effects of the global economy. On the whole, "organizations worldwide are growing more similar, while the behavior of people within organizations is maintaining its cultural uniqueness. So organizations in Canada and Germany may look the same from the outside, but Canadians and Germans behave differently within them."[5] You'll need to understand

[4] "The New America: Hispanics: A Nation within a Nation," *Business Week*, 25 September 1989, p. 144.

[5] Nancy J. Adler, *International Dimensions of Organizational Behavior* (Boston: Kent, 1986), p. 46.

TABLE 3–1
High-Context and Low-Context Cultures

High-Context Cultures
- Homogeneous, with fairly strong distinctions between inside and outside.
- Group-oriented. Individuals identify themselves as members of the group.
- Unwelcoming of deviant behavior. The culture has high expectations for individuals to internalize group norms and behave accordingly.
- People-oriented. The focus is on maintaining relationships.
- Nonconfrontational. Business requires soft-bargaining and indirection to preserve face.
- Humanistic. Control is internal, preprogrammed in each individual as part of the culture.
- Averse to risk.

Low-Context Cultures
- Heterogeneous and generally open to outsiders.
- Oriented to the individual. Individuals seek to fulfill their own goals.
- Welcoming of a variety of behaviors; you "do your own thing."
- Action- and solution-oriented. The focus is on completing the task.
- Able to separate a conflict from the conflicting parties. Conflict in pursuit of a goal is positive. Business requires hard-bargaining with a direct, confrontational attitude.
- Procedural. External rules govern behavior.
- Welcoming of risks.

Source: Adapted from Stella Ting-Toomey, "Toward a Theory of Conflict and Culture," in Gudykunst, Stewart, and Ting-Toomey, eds., *Communication, Culture, and Organizational Process* (Beverly Hills, CA: Sage, 1985), pp. 71–86. Edward T. Hall originally developed this concept.

both organizational similarities (as you read in Chapter 2) and cultural uniqueness (as you'll read shortly) to communicate well in the global economy.

Differences in Context

Think about how you communicate with a close friend. Sometimes just a smile is enough, or a thumbs-up sign. You shrug your shoulders or shake your head, and those gestures convey your message. You may have a few shorthand expressions that summarize a set of ideas between you. A joke about a close group of friends runs this way: The friends share lots of jokes, which they have numbered. When one person says, "Sixteen" to another, the other laughs, thinking about the joke.

Like your communication with a friend, communication in homogeneous cultures reflects strong mutual trust and close feelings. You communicate differently in that context from the way you communicate when people are less well known to each other. Table 3–1 indicates the end points in a range of cultural contexts from *high-context* cultures, like Japan, to *low-context* cultures, like the United States and Canada. Here are some implications of such differences in context for business communication.

Talking and Writing

In a homogeneous or high-context culture, you don't need to say a lot to get a message across; messages are preprogrammed in the context itself. Sometimes silence is even more important than talking. You use your position at a conference table or your facial expressions and other nonverbal means to convey meaning. You don't write much; oral agreements hold.

The wearing of uniforms in many Japanese offices and plants suggests the shared values of the workers. Moreover, Japanese offices tend to follow an open plan. Managers and workers sit side by side. That physical setting encourages direct, immediate, and frequent communication. Groups of employees often share a common telephone and thus are aware of each other's conversations. The limited storage area for documents and the difficulties in writing Japanese may also encourage oral and nonverbal communication.

In heterogeneous or low-context societies, like Canada and the United States, you often write or talk to a stranger. Thus, you must *create* a shared context before you can present information. To cover the distance between you and the other person, you're likely to write down anything that's really important in an explicit statement.

American office layout often encourages individualism and privacy. As people rise in the organization, they separate themselves from others with physical barriers like a wall or a private room. They are likely to send documents to one another. Those documents fill many storage areas, areas that are generally private; in contrast, documents are stored in open and public spaces in most Japanese offices. Currently, there are more secretaries and other support people in United States offices than in Japan, where managers and professionals tend to speak directly to one another.

Making and Implementing Decisions

Decision making also differs. In Japan, groups settle issues collaboratively through the *ringi* process. Proposals for actions or other decisions are circulated among middle management so that consent is gained in advance—a context is built in which the decision then becomes inevitable. In the traditional U.S. company, an executive often imposes a decision made individually. The United States system tends to be "fast-slow-slow-slow": A quick decision may take some time to implement. The Japanese system is "slow-slow-slow-fast" because consent is achieved in the process so that the final implementation is speedy.

In high-context organizations, communication is fostered in all directions. Middle managers especially broker information up and down. Informal and formal meetings and personal contacts dominate. Employees tend to stay with one company throughout their career, so they know one another and the company and can communicate in their own shorthand. Low-context organizations emphasize downward communication and channels are more formal, in part to compensate for higher turnover rates among employees.

Recruiting

The emphasis on relationships in a high-context culture also leads to different recruiting techniques from those in a low-context culture, which values individualism and action. In the United States, recruiters evaluate applicants' resumes and other statements of *credentials* to see what they have accomplished. Japanese hiring practices emphasize character over accomplishments. Recruiters look for the qualities that ensure a candidate's ability to be trusted and compatible with coworkers. In an interview, recruiters ask about a candidate's religion, home life, and upbringing and elicit other personal information. Japanese managers often find U.S. legal constraints against such probing in employment evaluations difficult to deal with.

Trusting

Employment practices reflect the larger issue of collective *trust.* In homogeneous societies, the level of trust is high. One's good name and that of one's family and organization guarantee business agreements, which are often made orally. In a heterogeneous society, the level of collective trust tends to be low; thus, procedures and written contracts are needed to establish concretely the context for the agreement that binds each party. Lawyers are much more numerous in low-context than in high-context cultures.

Maintaining Relationships

In addition to arranging contracts—or while negotiating—lawyers and others in low-context cultures often engage each other as adversaries. People bargain hard in open conflict. Saying "no" means "no": "I don't agree," "I won't comply." In high-context cultures, a premium is placed on maintaining relationships. You use indirection and soft bargaining to save face for the other person in any discussion. "If you want to get along in the world," noted a minister in the Tokugawa shogunate in Japan who died in 1815, "say 'Yes, that's true' and 'That's very reasonable; there's nothing especially difficult about it.' . . . If you don't want to get along in the world, say 'That isn't so' and 'Yes, but . . .' This is not what is wanted; it is unexpected."[6] When a Japanese businessperson today says "yes," that often means "Yes, I understand you." An American counterpart in a negotiation who thinks that means "Yes, I agree" will be misled.

In communicating *across* contexts, then, analyze both the context and the persons you are dealing with.

BELIEVING IS SEEING

In Table 3–1, you read some characteristics of different cultures. If you're Canadian or American, do you feel that the *low-context* description fits you? If you're Asian, do you see yourself fitting the *high-context* pattern? Are these patterns changing as organizations become more similar and as a flat structure replaces a tall hierarchy in many companies in the United States?

The issues of culture are complex—more complex than simple categories can demonstrate. Yet stereotypes and categorical descriptions allow you to organize some of the multiple impressions you receive all at once when you meet someone. Increasingly, researchers point to the role of beliefs in how people see evidence: "Believing is seeing." Put another way, as in *Alice's*

[6] As quoted in Masao Kunihiro, "Why the Japanese Talk English Bad," in "Nippon: The Hidden Treasures of Japan," Advertising Supplement to *The New York Times,* 25 March 1990, p. 15.

Adventures in Wonderland, "Much of what you see depends on how you look."

People in different cultures are different, and they *see* things differently. "A rolling stone gathers no moss" is a proverb that to an American generally means "If you keep active (keep rolling), you won't have to worry that moss will grow on you." Someone from a less action-oriented culture and one that cherishes the past may see an opposite meaning: "The moss, a symbol of stability and longevity, won't grow unless you allow yourself some quiet and inactivity."

Think of how the proverbs you learned taught you about when to talk and how to listen. Several Japanese ones display "active contempt for loquacity and eloquence":[7]

- "Sickness enters through the mouth; misfortune comes out of the same place."
- "When you speak your lips get cold."

Contrast that with an American one that seems to advocate speaking up:

- "The squeaky wheel gets the grease."

Because they are comfortable with silence, Japanese are often seen by outsiders as overly quiet, enigmatic, and inscrutable. In a recent survey in Japan, 76 percent of the respondents thought a taciturn person would be more successful in business than a fluent one.[8] Americans tend to reward fluency and to be uncomfortable with silence—an attribute that sometimes causes them to give in too easily when they negotiate. Faced with silence, they see opposition. They then lower their bargaining position in their eagerness to talk. The silence, however, may have been simply a pause, not an indication of displeasure.

In communicating with people from other cultures, keep in mind at least three cautions about how you *see* them:

- Avoid seeing yourself.
- Think about how they see you.
- Describe what you see. Don't judge.

One phase in understanding is to see everyone as like yourself. But the similarities you see are often more illusory than real, and thinking in such terms causes further misunderstanding. Looking someone in the eye, for example, is a sign of trust and honesty in North America. In other cultures, eye contact is seen as an unwarranted invasion of privacy, and you'll be seen as rude if you look at someone directly. Meet eye-to-eye in the United States and avoid such looks where they are inappropriate.

Think, too, about how others see *you*. To someone from an Arab country, for example, Americans appear impatient. Americans schedule short meet-

[7] Ibid.

[8] This discussion of Japanese language patterns derives from Kunihiro, "Why the Japanese Talk English Bad," p. 15.

ings rather than the day-long ones common in the Arab countries. They look for short-term results. They seek speedy resolutions of problems, or "quick fixes." "Compared with many foreign sources of capital, Wall Street demands faster paybacks—and thus tolerates less experimentation, long-term research, worker training and product development."[9] Americans also interrupt conversations in ways that others feel show a lack of respect, an inability to listen, and inattention to the development of relationships.

Finally, avoid the temptation to use your own culture as an exclusive yardstick for other people's behavior. Learn about other cultures on their own terms. Be able to *describe* differences before you *judge* them.

TALKING AND LISTENING ACROSS CULTURES

Whatever the occasion—a dinner, a meeting, a conference, or a private conversation—be patient and tolerant when you talk and listen to people from another culture. Allow time when you travel. If you're scheduled to arrive in Frankfurt at 9:00 A.M. after an overnight flight from Philadelphia, you may be tempted to arrange a full day of meetings. Resist the temptation. Give yourself a day to recover from jet lag. Drooping eyelids and fuzzy speech are merely symptoms of the disorientation that international travelers experience. Fuzzy thinking is a bigger problem: Communicating with business colleagues requires sharp thinking and quick responses. Similarly, give international visitors to your organization time to adjust.

Arrange discussions with ample time for pauses. Cross-cultural talking takes a lot of energy. When you listen to someone who is speaking in a language that is not her or his own, avoid equating any language mistakes with lack of intelligence. When you talk, enunciate clearly, but don't shout. Avoid jokes and colloquial expressions because these are hard to translate and understand. A "ballpark estimate" of expenses might be useful shorthand for someone who knows about baseball, but it is meaningless to a noninitiate. Aim for simplicity of expression. Use visuals and other channels to reinforce messages. Repeat essential information and summarize periodically to make sure that your listener isn't lost.

In "*FYI:* A Dinner Invitation in Korea," you'll read about one form of cross-cultural talking: a dinner invitation. The author, who was born in America to a family in the German diplomatic corps, describes the invitation from the perspective of a German.

WRITING AND READING ACROSS CULTURES

In writing across cultures, review every document for clarity in a single message. Choose precise words, simple sentence structure, and informative

[9] Reich, p. 42.

A DINNER INVITATION IN KOREA

Lt. Petra M. Gallert
U.S. Air Force

As a German visiting Korea, you will encounter a gregarious, energetic people who are eager to be modern and cosmopolitan. Yet they are also deeply rooted in their customs and traditions. Consider as an example the time a Korean invites you to his or her home for a meal. The manner in which you respond to the offer will tell much about you and your capacity to understand and respect a culture not your own.

Invitations are traditionally offered in what may appear to be a courting ritual. The host will ask, and you'll express your thanks politely but hesitate to accept the invitation. (Were you to accept immediately, a broad-minded Korean would no doubt forgive you; but there would now be a caution in his or her mind that you might perhaps be a little brash and lacking in decorum. As a well-mannered European, however, you are accustomed to polite hesitation, which signals that you are delighted by the invitation but do not wish to impose yourself, and thus, you request further assurance that your company is indeed welcomed.)

Having noted your hesitation, your host will ask again, and you, in turn, will indicate, with perhaps some emphasis, that you're honored by the invitation and that your host is only too kind. In short, you hesitate to accept until the invitation is offered a third time—your cue to accept gracefully and note the time and place. A Korean host may not insist on this ritual, but your acquiescing to it shows your understanding of the need for the buffer of courtesy and politeness.

Much as in Germany, you'll present a bouquet of flowers to your host as you arrive. Unlike in German custom, however, you'll be asked to remove your shoes before entering the main parts of a Korean home. You should also prepare to sit on mats or pillows by wearing clothes that cover your legs. Once you do sit, remember not to show the soles of your feet to anyone, for that gesture is considered an insult.

Your meal will consist of many separate dishes, much like appetizers, and the larger main course, which usually emphasizes meat. Koreans brew some interesting varieties of beer, too, which may surprise you in their strength and acidity. Regardless of any culinary surprises, however, you'll remember never to use your left hand to give something to a Korean, for that, too, is an insulting gesture.

visuals. In "*FYI:* Bilingual Publications," Maurice Boucher of the Centre Canadien d'Architecture (CCA) discusses some of the issues of writing and design when a document is created in two languages. The acronym *CCA,* by the way, was designed to work in both English and French.

Every chapter in this book is a chapter on international business communication. To put it simply, to communicate internationally means to communicate *well.*

BILINGUAL PUBLICATIONS

Maurice Boucher
Coordinator,
Development and
Communications,
Centre Canadien
d'Architecture/Canadian
Centre for Architecture

There is a growing need for bilingual and multilingual publications. More and more regions are composed of important minority groups that represent a large portion of the overall population. Furthermore, growing international cooperation and the increase in the number of multinational organizations have created a need to communicate the same message to diverse audiences. Whatever the reason, the goal remains the same: to make known an idea to two or more groups of people who speak different languages and may have contrasting cultures and ideologies.

Each distinct culture must be known and respected. Since styles and customs may vary greatly from one language to another, important research must go into the study of the differences so that the gap between them can be bridged. This can be accomplished only in direct consultation with the audience that the publication is destined to reach. Certain groups of people may not be familiar with a particular concept or idea. In such a case, additional information may be needed in one of the languages to ensure complete comprehension by all audiences. This additional information may sometimes require a complete reworking of the publication so that it expresses the same message in a totally different way.

Not only must the *content* be reworked, but the *format* of a bilingual publication must also be adapted. Publications should be done in separate editions when they deal with long texts or complex information. However, in smaller publications, different languages can be placed side by side. Although the typesetter may have to compensate for some languages that require longer blocks of text than others to express the same ideas, an adjustment which tends to give the page an unbalanced look, it is more efficient and less costly to have both language versions available in one publication. This format helps the reader find his or her language and also softens the delicate decision about which language is "primary."

Protocol can often be an issue when one is trying to establish the correct *order* in which the languages should be presented. Well-thought-out policies must be established and consistently applied in accordance with laws or established convention.

Although a bilingual publication requires more time and resources, the benefits can be significant. Any target group will react favorably to being addressed in its own language. Whether one is selling a product or communicating an idea, the best results come when care and attention are given to the special needs of the groups addressed.

SUMMARY

- The **global economy** is a web of investments and people across national borders. Companies buy assets abroad and manage offices and plants in different countries because of financial incentives and opportunities, fluctuations in interest rates and currency strengths, and perceptions of investment safety.
- **Culture** is what you need to know to get along in a group. It is the beliefs, values, and attitudes that guide individuals in their choices and their behavior. The most obvious mark of a culture is its **language;** differences in language point to the other differences among cultures.
- One scheme for analyzing cultural differences is to examine the extent of shared values, beliefs, and behaviors. A homogeneous culture like that in Japan displays extensive sharing; a heterogeneous culture like that in Canada and the United States displays little shared context. Japan's **high context** for communication means that oral communication and related nonverbal behavior are stressed. Trust levels and family feelings are high as well. In **low-context** societies, like the United States and Canada, a shared context cannot be assumed. The transmitted message must be overt and complete.
- Having some **stereotypes** in mind can help you see and understand people from another culture. The categories allow you to sort through the many impressions you receive all at once. But in looking at others, be careful not simply to see *yourself.* People do differ. Think about how others see you. And learn about others in a way that allows you to *describe* their culture before you judge it.
- In speaking or writing to someone from a different culture, be patient. Aim for precision in wording and for simplicity in presentation or document structure. Build in redundancy. Summarize often. Use visuals. Enunciate clearly—and write clearly. Don't equate the language mistakes of a non-native-speaker with a lack of intelligence.

EXERCISES

For Discussion

Your readings in this chapter provide the starting point for answering the following questions. In your answers, supplement your readings with information drawn from current newspapers and business periodicals and from your business or other classes.

1. Will multinational organizations always be in conflict with their host countries? Why or why not?
2. Through what institutions, processes, or reward systems are such values as individualism and competition reinforced in North America?
3. When in Rome, so the expression goes, do as the Romans do. How can this advice be misleading? Should a U.S. firm in Japan, for example, adopt Japanese management practices? Should a company let its cargo sit idle on a dock in Algeria because it refuses to pay the "bribe" the dockworkers expect as a culturally acceptable supplement to their pay? Which "gifts" are appropriate business behavior and which ones are "kickbacks"?

4. One mark of a culture is its attitude toward time. That includes ideas about "lateness" or "promptness." What is the right time to arrive at the following:[10]
   a. A class that begins at 1:45
   b. A symphony concert whose tickets note a beginning of 8:30 *sharp*
   c. A play that begins at 8:30
   d. A flight with a 5:50 departure time
   e. A bus with a 5:50 departure time
   f. Your job, which begins at 7:30
   g. A 1:30 meeting
   - For each of these, how late could you be without feeling you have to apologize? Explain.
   - Would people from other cultures answer differently? Explain.
   - In a United States context, how long would you expect a, b, c, or g to last?
5. Many gas stations in America are self-service; that is, the customer pumps the gas. At some stations, you have to pay before you pump. At others, you pump first. How does the difference in when you pay reflect the level of trust between owner and customer? Are you more likely to find pay-first or pump-first stations near a college? Which form are you likely to find at an exit to an interstate highway? Why? You might survey stations near your campus and in other locations to correlate the time of payment and the level of trust in the community.
6. Here are some common business terms in English. Find the equivalent word or words for each in Japanese, Spanish, German, and French. Start with dictionaries of business terms, but don't neglect fellow students from countries where these languages are spoken:

depreciation	chief executive officer
marketing	point of sale
balance sheet	quality circle
inventory	line of credit
spreadsheet	

7. The following letter was written by Alan Lane, who grew up in South Carolina and worked in several textile mills before ultimately acquiring his own, which after twelve years of hard work he built into a small, privately controlled company that operates six plants profitably in the Southeast. To take advantage of the European market, he recently bought a yarn mill in Newcastle, England, whose products can enter that market without the duties otherwise imposed on American goods. Lane spent three weeks in Newcastle following the acquisition and wrote this letter (p. 48) on his return.
   a. What is Lane's view about the criteria for promotion in a plant, and how might that view reflect his cultural values?
   b. What is Martin's likely response in light of traditional patterns of mobility in English factories? What *are* those patterns?

[10] Based on Vern Terpstra, *The Cultural Environment of International Business* (Cincinnati: South-Western Publishing, 1978), p. 92.

CON-TEXT
Office of the Chairman

April 22, 199-

Stanley Martin
Plant Manager, Newcastle

Dear Stan,

I enjoyed my visit to Newcastle and am looking forward to our work together.

I know from the visit that you share the view I have always had of the importance of people in the Con-Text organization. People are always our top priority--the key to our business success. That's why promotion from within has always been our practice. I'm personally very proud of the number of shift supervisors and even plant managers (three, in our six U.S. plants) who have risen through the ranks from the mill floor.

Stan, to make sure that this spirit prevails in our Newcastle operation, I want to start a system of promotion from within that will make sure we develop our management talent from the pool of loyal workers we already have. My managers need hands-on experience and close knowledge of workers, gained from the inside.

I hope you'll bear this in mind as you staff the two new management positions we discussed: director of quality control and accounts supervisor. Let's draw on our own first!

Good to see you! Let me know how we're doing over there.

Warm regards,

Alan

c. What is Lane's tone in the letter? Is it appropriate for an English reader who reports to Lane?

8. You can apply the distinction between *high-context* and *low-context* cultures to communication patterns within organizations in one country. Think of one organization that you know well. Where does communication within it fit in the spectrum? How can you tell?

For Writing

9. Identify a country with a traditional class structure. Read about it. Assume you work for a multinational organization considering building a plant there. For your supervisor, write a brief explanation of how that class system will affect your company's selection of workers for your new plant.
10. Collect information on multiculturalism in your community. Find out, for example, if any local companies are tied by ownership or joint agreements to any foreign concerns. Learn about where the inventory at local stores comes from. Note the presence of foreign students and minorities on your campus. Note any local organizations that participate in international programs. Select a particular aspect of the community to learn about; then write up your results.
11. Review the advertisements in a non-English-language magazine or newspaper. Translate some of them into English (assuming, of course, that you are familiar with the original language). What difficulties do you find in translating? How does the language of advertising reflect cultural as well as linguistic values? Write up the results of your analysis.

For Collaboration

12. Assemble a team to market a new brand of "all-natural" toothpaste to be sold in France. Assign research tasks to the team members. You'll need to find out, for example, about current dental hygiene practices in France; competing products; the French attitude toward "natural" products; and appropriate names in French for toothpaste. Develop some major points in a marketing plan. (Later in the semester, you may write a proposal—see Chapter 17—to present this plan to your company's vice president of marketing.)

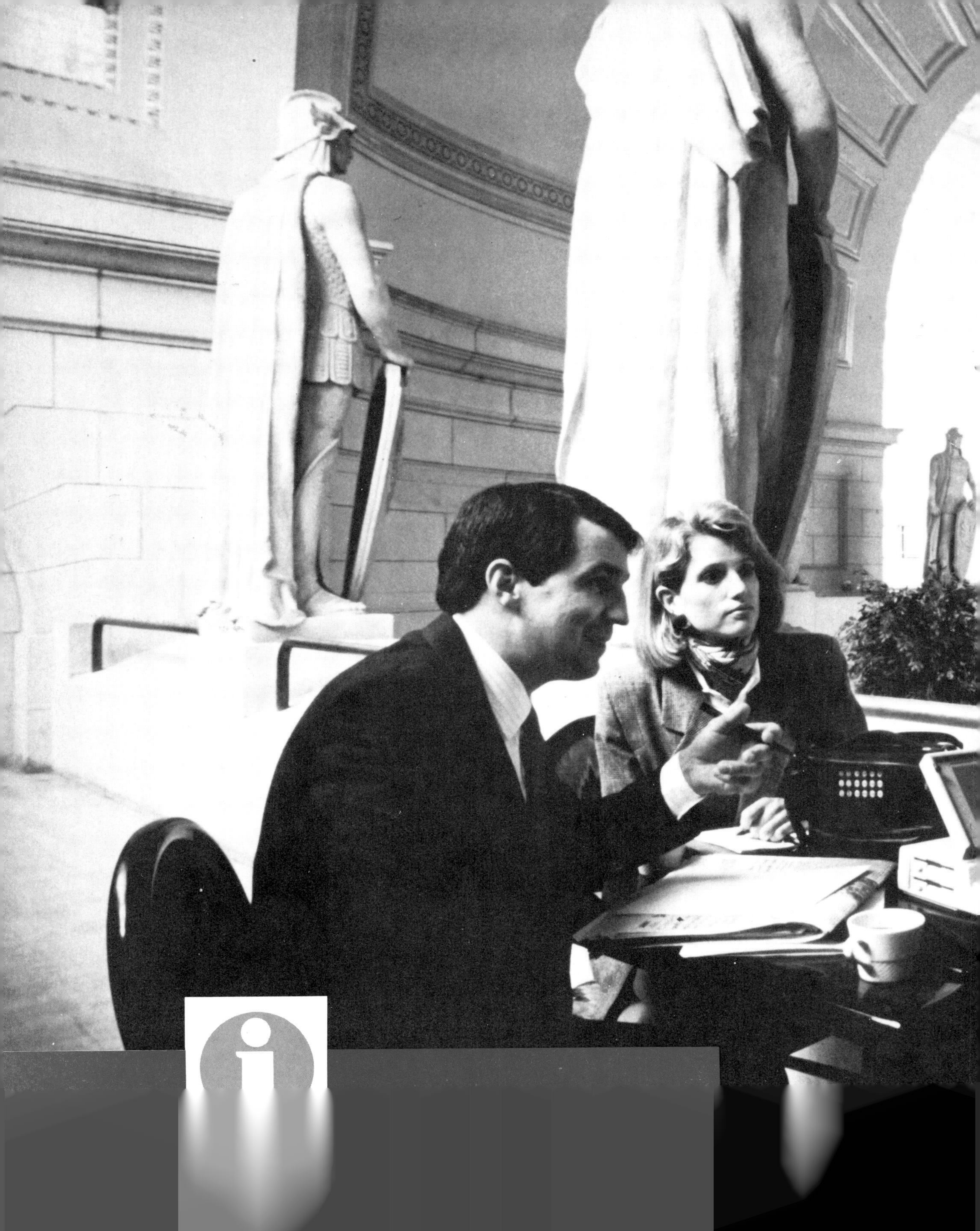

PART II

WRITING IN CONTEXT

4 Macrocomposing: Organizing Yourself to Write
5 Microcomposing: Finding Your Voice
6 Composing with Visuals
7 Revising and Designing
8 Understanding Business Information
9 Accessing the Sources of Business Information
10 Communicating with Electronic Technology
11 Collaboration: Managing Group Communication

INTRODUCTION TO PART II

"Think Globally. Act Locally."

In this part of *Business Communication,* you'll read eight chapters about how to write in a business context. Each chapter slices into the topic at a different angle.

The first four chapters will help you to compose yourself to write and to compose a document—any business document. You'll see two levels of writing. First, you'll learn about the *macro* level, the level of large issues, as in *macro*economics or *macro*management or *macro*marketing. You'll learn how to organize the process of writing and organize your ideas and your evidence. You'll think globally. Then you'll learn about the *micro* level, as when you *micro*market block-by-block and house-by-house. You'll look closely at strategies for shaping words and sentences. You'll act locally to create a voice that clarifies your information and engages your reader. In Chapter 6, you'll learn how to compose in a medium beyond prose: visuals. Such graphic devices will help you both to think through your information and to present it to others. In Chapter 7, you'll learn to look backward at your text and your visuals to revise and design for *readability.*

Chapters 8 and 9 take another slant. In them, you'll learn about finding and using information—an essential currency of business. In Chapter 10, you'll see how electronic technology has changed the means of producing documents as well as the concept of what a document is. Moreover, technology has contributed to a new workplace that promises even more fundamental changes in the way you'll communicate in organizations in the 21st century. One of those changes, as you have seen, is an increased emphasis on flat organizations and enhanced sideways communication and consensus building. Those changes imply even more collaborative writing, a topic covered in detail in Chapter 11. In business, writing is often far from a lonely act.

Writing is not lonely because business writers, even when they are the single authors of a document, always write in a *context:* the context of the organization's and their own goals for writing and the goal of their reader in reading, the context of other documents and talks and videos on the topic, the context of the technology for the document's transfer, and the context of the document's topic as well as other information about the topic.

Especially in a *global* context, to use the meaning of that term used in Chapter 3, your writing may take on meanings you never intended. You have to control the meaning as you build a common ground with the reader. Shaping a document that responds well to the context—that's the challenge you must meet. This part will give you the tools for meeting the challenge.

4

MACROCOMPOSING

Organizing Yourself to Write

What's Ahead

ORGANIZING THE MESSAGE: PRINCIPLES
- Identify the Purpose
- Imagine the Reader
- Recognize Multiple Readers
- Understand the Form

ORGANIZING THE MESSAGE: TOOLS AND TECHNIQUES
- Control Statement
- Direct and Indirect Order
- Introduction–Middle–Ending
- Routine Forms and Formats
- Conventional Patterns

ORGANIZING THE INFORMATION: NONLINEAR TECHNIQUES
- Data Dumping
- Picturing
- Mapping Your Mind
- FYI: Clustering

ORGANIZING THE DOCUMENT: OUTLINES
- The Nonlinear Outline

ORGANIZING YOURSELF: MANAGING THE PROCESS
- Make a Schedule
- Make an Outline
- Warm Up
- Play to Your Strengths
- Be Ready to Change
- Keep Writing

SUMMARY

EXERCISES

Do You Know 

- How does your purpose affect how you organize a document?
- How does your reader affect how you organize a document?
- What is a control statement?
- What conventional strategies can you use to organize information for your purpose and reader?
- How can outlining strategies help you to structure information?
- What routine can you follow to compose a draft?

The commuter train that normally carries you home from a day of work in Philadelphia is delayed—again. It is hot and muggy, and you and your fellow passengers are angry. This is a problem for you, of course; but it is also a *communication* problem for the Southeastern Pennsylvania Transit Authority (SEPTA), the agency responsible for public transportation in the Philadelphia area. SEPTA has to explain what happened and apologize if it is to regain the confidence of its customers—you and the other frustrated passengers.

The problem of presenting information which communicates bad news to customers illustrates the vital importance of *organizing* business messages. SEPTA's solution to the communication problem was an announcement handed out to commuters on the train (Figure 4–1). Let's look at how it organized this message.

The announcement occupies one small page left on the train's seats. Certainly, no longer explanation is desirable. Detailed engineering specifications, maps of the network, and drawings of faulty cable might be needed for another audience, for example, the city's utility oversight group. But such details are unnecessary for the riders.

To solicit rider understanding, the announcement first explains the cause of the delays (overtly stated in Sentence 1 and illustrated in the first paragraph and the next two) and then apologizes (the last paragraph). The author chose to explain *before* the apology, assuming that the explanation would win the reader to SEPTA's side and would strengthen the weight of the apology. The author could have *started* with Paragraph 4, but such a beginning might have seemed weak and uninformative. In structure, the announcement moves from the outcome or *effect* (the continuing delays) to the *cause* (deteriorated signal cables).

Such an announcement is not a routine matter (SEPTA's trains run mostly on time). It's a special, one-of-a-kind document. Its structure, length (even if the delays were long, the company didn't want to take too much of the reader's time in reading), method of distribution, and language all support an informative purpose.

This real business situation illustrates the importance of organizing messages well. Doing so, however, is one of the hardest intellectual tasks in communication because it requires you to address several issues simultaneously. Shortly, you'll look at each of the following issues separately: the principles of organizing messages; the tools and techniques of organizing messages; the techniques of organizing the information that messages carry;

Continuing Media-West Chester delays
caused by defective signal cable

The continuing delays on outbound trains on the Media-West Chester Regional Rail Line are being caused by deteriorated signal cables running from 49th Street Station to Media Station. Sections of the 30,000 feet of signal cable are in poor condition and must be replaced. This has caused SEPTA to instruct train crews to approach two inbound and two outbound signals at reduced speeds, then to stop before proceeding at restricted speed.

While delays on inbound trains have generally been minimal, outbound service is operating 10 to 15 minutes late because of the location of the inoperative signals. Those signals have forced slow train operation over long sections of the outbound railroad between 49th Street and Media.

Because of the condition of the present system, a completely new and modern signal system is under design for the line. However, that system will not be in place until 1995 at the earliest. In the meantime, SEPTA personnel are replacing sections of the defective cable as quickly as possible and restoring the signals to normal or near normal operation. Service delays will continue until all of the cable replacements are made.

We sincerely apologize for the inconvenience this problem has caused. Nevertheless, we hope you understand that the slower service is necessary for a safe operation.

FIGURE 4–1.
Writing in context: An announcement distributed on a train. *(Source: Notice distributed by SEPTA—the Southeastern Pennsylvania Transportation Authority, 10/84–2379–154. Used by permission.)*

the means (outlines) for structuring information to support messages; and the process of organizing *yourself* as a writer to bring all this analysis and understanding to bear on preparing a document.

In writing, you find yourself addressing all these matters at the same time: You think through the structure of the message and the information as you are outlining your document and preparing yourself to write it. But here, we separate out the parts so you can understand and master them.

ORGANIZING THE MESSAGE: PRINCIPLES

To organize a message, you need to identify the *purpose,* imagine the *reader* or readers of the message, and understand the *form* in which the message is to be delivered.

Identify the Purpose

Why you are writing determines to a large extent how you organize what you write. As you saw in Chapter 2, business messages meet one of three general purposes: to record, to inform, or to persuade. Before you begin to organize the message, identify your purpose.

The SEPTA announcement aims both to *inform* passengers of the reasons for delays and to *persuade* them that the agency is doing all it can to correct problems and regain the confidence of its customers. The message is structured to accomplish this dual purpose: Information is provided first to build understanding, then the apology is extended to persuade the reader to accept delays.

Imagine the Reader

To achieve your purpose in writing, you must engage the attention and understanding of the reader—and perhaps move the reader to an action or a decision. The announcement of train delays in Figure 4–1 can't get the reader home sooner, of course, but it can explain the delays in a way that allows the reader to adjust a schedule to accommodate them and to see the long-term advantages of this short-term work. Moreover, in writing the announcement, SEPTA displays a knowledge of the readers (their riders): Many are in a rush, and most are well educated and look for explanations. They would not be content just to sit in ignorance on a delayed train.

To write well, imagine *your* reader, too. Answer these questions:

1. **Will your message be welcome?** If so (perhaps the reader *requested* the message and is eager to read it), then deliver it *directly* and in whatever form and detail the reader suggested.

   If the message is unwelcome instead, as is true with the SEPTA announcement, then you'll need to shape the message to achieve persuasion, providing solid information first, for example, to build the reader's confidence that, despite problems, you (or your organization) is on top of the situation.

2. **What kind of a document does the reader expect?** The forms of business writing are familiar to business readers. That familiarity with the form allows readers to scan and zoom in on points of interest. So meet the reader's expectations about the type and sequence of information in the document. (Using the right form will also make it easier for you to write, as you'll see.)

3. **How much should you say?** The form helps you decide what to say. Writers are often tempted to tell everything they know, which may be more or may be less than is required. Instead, tell readers only what they need—not less than that, and particularly not more. Think of the manuals that document computer systems. Many readers find them frustrating because hefty manuals include a level of detail that ironically may make it impossible to use the system.

4. **What will the reader do with the document?** Few readers in business read word-by-word everything that crosses their desks or screens. Most look at the pictures and read the first or last paragraph. Beyond that, readers

have different styles of reading. They read a lot into and out of a text. Reading style reflects personality and education, of course. It also reflects the conditions in which one reads. A notice distributed as a one-time document on a train can work when it is short and unfancy. Procedures to be used many times—sometimes under harsh conditions, like instructions for changing a tire—require a sturdier medium and pictures to convey information more rapidly.

Recognize Multiple Readers

Imagining your reader is difficult enough when you write one-to-one. The task is compounded when you write to many readers—a common situation on the job—and when some or all of the readers are strangers.

When you must address many readers, first make sure that you limit the list as much as possible. Uncertainty about who should receive a copy often leads writers to send documents to too many people. In the process, they waste paper, reduce the reader's confidence in the writer's ability to target a message, and diminish the prospect for action. *Select* your readers.

Second, clarify for yourself not only who each reader will be but also how the readers relate to one another and whose needs take precedence over the needs of others. Setting priorities in readers is especially important when readers have competing interests.

To establish those priorities, think in terms of three levels, a useful strategy devised by J. C. Mathes and Dwight Stevenson:[1]

- *Primary readers,* who requested the document and whose needs are most important
- *Immediate readers* within the organization, who will approve the document and route it to the primary readers
- *Secondary readers,* who do not have decision-making power but will be affected by the implications of the document

Consider this scene: The president of a bank, concerned because many customers are closing their accounts, asks the vice president of customer relations to report on the causes of the close-outs. The vice president turns the assignment over to his assistant, who writes the report and gives it to the vice president for approval. The *primary* reader is the president. The *immediate* reader is the vice president. If the president passes the report along to the supervisor of personnel, who then provides copies to tellers because they are in part responsible for the problem of customer loss, then the supervisor and the tellers become *secondary* readers.

No matter how well it's written, your message will not work if it addresses the wrong reader or readers.

Understand the Form

Messages, as you saw in Chapter 2, are delivered in *forms* or media—for example, as a memo, a letter, or a speech. How you organize a message

[1] *Designing Technical Reports,* 2nd ed. (New York: Macmillan, 1991).

depends, therefore, not only on its purpose and on its intended readers but also on the form in which it is sent. Letters, for example, follow certain conventions (see Chapter 13). Since they are brief, letters do not allow the writer to present elaborate or complex explanations, whereas reports, which are typically much longer, do allow for such treatment. In a letter you have to get to your main point rather quickly, and you can provide only general supporting information in it.

Oral presentation permits the use of both nonverbal techniques (for example, body language) and immediate feedback between speaker and listener. These are not available to the writer of a written document, and as a consequence the organization of the information in writing will be different from the organization of the same message delivered orally. The SEPTA announcement, for example, is written so that a single message is clearly delivered to each recipient. Had SEPTA chosen to deliver the message through an oral announcement, one made by conductors on the train, the apology would be delivered first, before the explanation.

Selecting the most effective form, and understanding the constraints that form places on organization, will help you organize the message you want to deliver.

ORGANIZING THE MESSAGE: TOOLS AND TECHNIQUES

The principles that guide organization enable you to select patterns based on the purpose, the reader, and the form of the message. This section describes the tools and techniques that are available for you to carry out the organizational scheme you select.

The best starting point is a one-sentence *control statement* that will pull your information together and control its presentation. That presentation follows conventional patterns, as you'll see in the next sections.

Control Statement

You often gather information *inductively,* that is, piece by piece, but you may need to present that information *deductively,* that is, from a main point to its subpoints. In such cases, develop a control statement that either summarizes the main point, describes the plan and purpose of the document, or calls the reader to action. Different purposes for writing dictate different control statements. Different purposes and different readers also determine where you place the control statement in the final document. Here are examples of three types of control statements:

Control Statement: Summary. `The central issue in computing over the next five years can be summed up in one word: connectivity.`

Control Statement: Plan of document. `The analysis is divided into two sections: a description of the 1991 survey and then a detailed presentation of the survey results.`

Control Statement: Call to action. `This report recommends that the`

```
Whistling Abalone restaurant implement a management infor-
mation system to overcome problems in inventory, service,
and bookkeeping.
```

Direct and Indirect Order

When your purpose is to inform or persuade, and when your reader expects and will welcome your message, be *direct.* Start with the control statement, then deploy the evidence that supports it in the order the statement promises.

If, however, you need to build common ground between you and your reader before presenting your main point, especially when you need to *persuade* the reader, consider an *indirect* strategy, as adopted by the SEPTA announcement. Describe the context for your information and the evidence that led to your decision or conclusion before you state it. Establish or confirm the reader's confidence in you. Chapters 12–19 provide detailed advice on direct and indirect ordering in memos, letters, and reports.

Introduction–Middle–Ending

Whether direct (the most common) or indirect in approach, most documents in the European tradition common in the United States follow a three-part scheme for presentation: introduction, middle, and ending. Let that convention help you structure a document.

Introduction. In a *direct* document, the introduction is generally short: just the control statement in a memo or letter, perhaps elaborated in a few paragraphs for a report. It briefly notes the goal and the plan of the document and outlines the context from which the document arose. The introduction to an *indirect* document may be longer and focuses on building the common ground between writer and reader, often with a narrative of the relevant situation or problem and perhaps a statement of authorization.

Middle. The middle provides the proof. Information is divided into segments that support the main points.

Ending. The ending finishes the discussion. A *direct* document ends on the last subtopic promised or recapitulates the main point. An *indirect* document states the main point at the end, often in terms of a recommendation, or a call to action, or a final sales pitch.

Routine Forms and Formats

When the context for your document is *routine,* let the situation itself prompt you to select your information and structure it into major segments, particularly the *middle* of the document. For example, if you are writing a notice about a meeting or an account of an event, use the traditional journalist's prompts for writing an article: *Who? What? When? Where? Why?*

To reconstruct the course of a routine investigation, ask questions like the following:

1. What questions did I ask as I began my work?
2. To find the answer, what method did I adopt?

3. Using this method, what did I observe?
4. From these observations, what can I conclude?

The answers to these questions provide a rough structure for the report itself:

1. Statement of the problem
2. Procedure
3. Results
4. Conclusions

The format for a routine document—a letter, memo, or report—may be programmed into a company's wordprocessing system. You simply enter new information, and the software arranges the final text for printing.

Conventional Patterns

To organize information *within* the segments of a document, or to organize a whole document, use those conventional patterns you've known for years. They'll make your writing easier. Your readers are familiar with them, so they'll make the reading easier, too. You might use one or several of these patterns together. Here are the most common ones in business writing:

- Cause and effect (often, problem and solution)
- Classification and analysis
- Comparison and contrast
- Parallelism
- Narrative

Cause and Effect

You saw how SEPTA developed its announcement in Figure 4–1 from effect to cause. Sometimes you'll need to reason from cause to effect, a pattern that often takes the form of *problem to solution.* Indeed, *problem solving* as a business activity generates many reports. Here's the outline of a problem-to-solution report structured directly to meet the reader's request for the information.

```
1. Current and Potential Problems in Operation at the Whistling
   Abalone Restaurant
   a. Poor inventory control of food and liquor
   b. Inefficient waiter service and floor operations
   c. Added bookkeeping
2. Solution: A Management Information System
3. Advantages of the System
   a. Constantly updated inventory
   b. More efficient waiter service and floor operations
   c. Better bookkeeping
```

Classification and Analysis

When you write to *inform,* you'll often find it useful to show how pieces of information fit into some class *(classification)* or how a whole can be divided into its components *(analysis)*. A report to a textile company that was interested in entering the market for men's ties included an analysis of neckwear trends. Here are the headings for that section:

```
Types
Fabrics
Colors
Widths
Prices
Sales
```

Comparison and Contrast

In analyzing your information, you may find that the best way to understand it and present it is through *comparison.* You can compare the sales picture over several years for ties of different widths. You can compare prices at different stores. You can compare color preferences over several years.

Parallelism

Closely linked to comparison and contrast is *parallelism.* Look for *parallels* in information—that is, sets of like ideas. For example, you might deal with information about *costs:* costs to the buyer or costs to the seller. These two are parallel. But information on demographic models, for example, is not parallel to information on costs. Looking for parallel ideas can help you sort information, and maintaining parallelism in presenting information keeps you from mixing different ideas. (Parallelism is also a powerful concept in constructing sentences. See Chapter 5 and the Handbook for further discussion of sentence parallelism, which is logically related to parallelism in ideas.)

Narrative

A *narrative* retraces an investigation over time. Sometimes, that retracing is framed by a series of tasks. Here's a task-by-task arrangement for a memo about the organization of a competitive swimming program. Just be careful with *parallelism.* Make sure each segment is indeed a *task;* if you were to mix tasks with expenses, for example, you would violate parallelism and confuse the reader. Because all these activities are in fact *tasks,* the list is parallel. (Also note that the ideas are expressed in parallel grammatical form, with verbs ending in *ing.*)

```
Preparing the Pool
Hiring a Coaching Staff
Scheduling Practices
Scheduling Meets
Establishing the Parents' Committee
Selecting the Team Roster
```

Because a *narrative* retraces events chronologically, its structure may be unemphatic, burying a significant result because it occurred on Day 15, right in the middle of an investigation. When you write to *record,* you're likely to use a narrative. But when you write to *inform* or to *persuade,* don't let the clock or the calendar serve as your only organizing device. Instead, arrange information to support a main point.

ORGANIZING THE INFORMATION: NONLINEAR TECHNIQUES

When your assessment of the context for writing shows complexities beyond those you can handle in a routine document, you may need to organize your *information* before you organize your *document.* Inundated by information, or perplexed by your reader, you may find that your purpose dims. Shine a flashlight through the facts to find the main point, the shared purpose with the reader, and supporting evidence that will convince the reader. You need, as one writer puts it, to "break the code." The conventional patterns you've just read about can help you. Or you may try a nonlinear approach:

- Data dumping
- Picturing
- Clustering

Data Dumping

In Figure 4–2, you see one form of *brainstorming,* that is, capturing ideas on the fly. This form is called a *data dump.* On one page, a business communication student dumped words that represented personnel problems where she worked (the Family Deli). Here are some guidelines that she followed—and that you can follow—for creating a data dump:

1. Jot down items on a sheet of paper or in a notebook (or in a new file in your computer) in whatever order they occur to you. Let your associations skip from word to word. Don't censor anything, even if it seems a bit farfetched.
2. Then live with the page or the file for a while. Write in new items as you think of them. Never erase.
3. Reread the list every now and then, and let your subconscious find connections.
4. Sort the items. Try out the conventional structuring patterns you just read about. Underline in a particular color all items that seem to belong in one group. Or circle them and connect them with a line. Or run through the computer file of notes in search of key words; some software will do this automatically, retrieving all items that include the key words. Figure 4–3 shows the Family Deli data dump sorted.
5. Write down a general term that characterizes each of the groupings. Make sure that the items you thought belonged together really do. Account for any items straggling outside a category.

Brainstorming with the help of a data dump is frequently used in collaborative projects (see Chapter 11). Members of a group each cite items to be "dumped." Together they then sort the items to find patterns and connections. Whether you work alone or in a group, data dumping can lead you to identify patterns in the information that can become the basis for organizing it in a document.

```
part-time workers--little motivation
young manager
should we be open 24 hours?
college town crowd and workers at industrial plant
few sales in midnight-6 a.m. range
try to increase sales?
customer survey results--they think employees are sloppy,
   inconsiderate, and inattentive
employee survey: no incentives to work hard, no sense of loyalty to
   the deli
shift schedules
any time everyone could meet?
training
low inventories of needed supplies
customer greeting: ''What are you out of today?''
record of sales over two weeks
   breakout by sandwich types, groceries
   breakout by amount of sales per time period
   breakout of number of customers
night-shift person asleep most of the shift
faulty equipment, especially the fryer
even when we have potatoes, we can't get the fryer to work
peak hours of sales: during the week, 7:30-9; 11-2; 5:30-8
   weekends, 9-2, 5-midnight on Saturday; 11-3, 5-10 on Sunday
preparation tasks: clean grill and fryer, sanitize slicer, cut
   steaks, stock and clean store
motivation: monetary vs. nonmonetary
last person to use an item notes that on an order sheet
   order sheets updated every 2 days
store identification: T-shirts for workers, hats
establish rules for employees
list equipment on sheet--have each shift report on the status of
   the equipment and supplies
employees set own performance standards, review in person with the
   manager
awards program? stars? happy faces? silly? have customers give
   them?
standard ways to increase productivity: automate or change store
   design
sense of belonging and teamwork and accomplishment needed to keep
   employees from just working for themselves
compare the Taber Rd. store with the Nelson St. one?
info about the deli: location, annual revenues, # of employees,
   overview of the menu
better inventory system
```

FIGURE 4–2.
Data dump of information: The Family Deli.

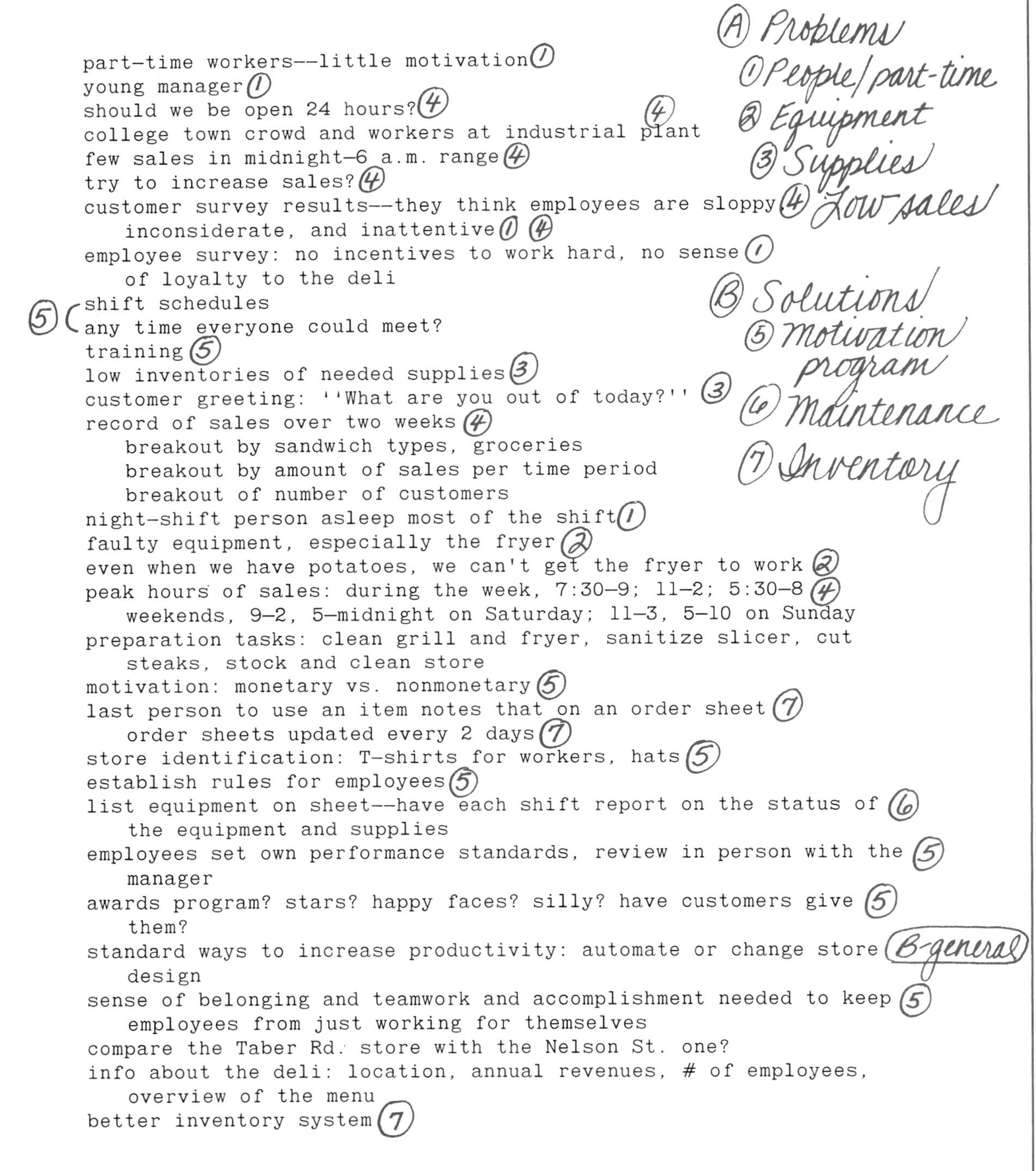

(A) Problems
(1) People/part-time
(2) Equipment
(3) Supplies
(4) Low sales
(B) Solutions
(5) Motivation program
(6) Maintenance
(7) Inventory
part-time workers--little motivation (1)
young manager (1)
should we be open 24 hours? (4)
college town crowd and workers at industrial plant (4)
few sales in midnight-6 a.m. range (4)
try to increase sales? (4)
customer survey results--they think employees are sloppy (4)
inconsiderate, and inattentive (1) (4)
employee survey: no incentives to work hard, no sense (1)
of loyalty to the deli
(5) shift schedules
any time everyone could meet?
training (5)
low inventories of needed supplies (3)
customer greeting: ''What are you out of today?'' (3)
record of sales over two weeks (4)
breakout by sandwich types, groceries
breakout by amount of sales per time period
breakout of number of customers
night-shift person asleep most of the shift (1)
faulty equipment, especially the fryer (2)
even when we have potatoes, we can't get the fryer to work (2)
peak hours of sales: during the week, 7:30-9; 11-2; 5:30-8 (4)
weekends, 9-2, 5-midnight on Saturday; 11-3, 5-10 on Sunday
preparation tasks: clean grill and fryer, sanitize slicer, cut
steaks, stock and clean store
motivation: monetary vs. nonmonetary (5)
last person to use an item notes that on an order sheet (7)
order sheets updated every 2 days (7)
store identification: T-shirts for workers, hats (5)
establish rules for employees (5)
list equipment on sheet--have each shift report on the status of (6)
the equipment and supplies
employees set own performance standards, review in person with the (5)
manager
awards program? stars? happy faces? silly? have customers give (5)
them?
standard ways to increase productivity: automate or change store (B-general)
design
sense of belonging and teamwork and accomplishment needed to keep (5)
employees from just working for themselves
compare the Taber Rd. store with the Nelson St. one?
info about the deli: location, annual revenues, # of employees,
overview of the menu
better inventory system (7)

FIGURE 4–3.
Data dump sorted and classified. Look for *key terms* by which you can *group* information and can select an emphasis for the reader. Here the writer has grouped information to isolate *problems* at the deli and some possible *solutions.*

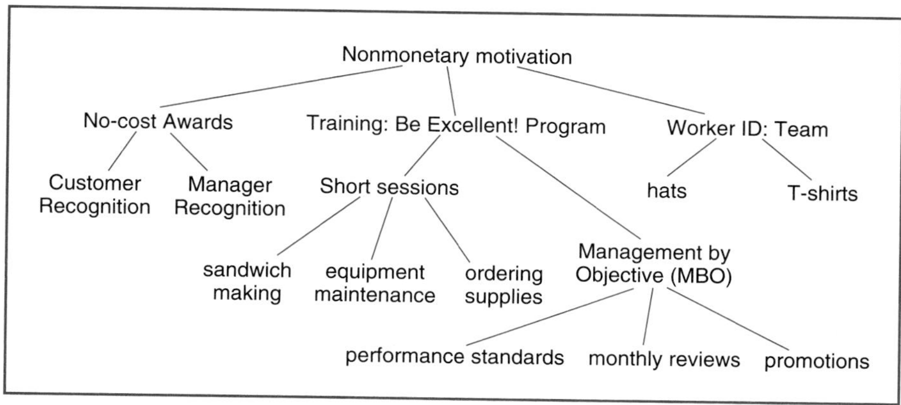

FIGURE 4–4.
A branching of topics from a key word.

Picturing

Try creating a diagram to show relationships among items. For example, sketch the branching of evidence from a key word or statistic, as in Figure 4–4, which shows the implications of the term *nonmonetary motivation* in the situation of the Family Deli. If you find that one branch is very long, you may want to focus your entire discussion on that topic, or you may need to gather more evidence to develop the other branch. Originally, the author began her branching from the term *motivation,* with two branches: monetary and nonmonetary. But the monetary one stopped dead at the second level because the deli had little money for an increase in wages or incentive programs. Therefore, she concentrated on the other side: nonmonetary.

Alternatively, you may want to line up material in rows and columns in a table, as in Figure 4–5. Such a device helps not only to order what you already have, but also, like any structuring device, to predict where more information is needed to fill an empty space.

DELI LOCATION	YEARLY SALES	MARKET SEGMENT	INVENTORY	WORKERS
Taber Rd.	$100 k	50% students 20% factory 10% small business 20% other	supplies: $X equipment: $Y	FT: 1 manager PT: 10 college students
Nelson St.	$150 k	50% neighborhood 20% factory 20% students 10% other	supplies: $A equipment: $B	FT: 1 manager 1 other PT: 4 college students, 3 high school students

FIGURE 4–5.
A tabular form for comparing two delis.

Mapping Your Mind

In "*FYI:* Clustering," Thomas F. Carney of the University of Windsor combines brainstorming with diagramming. Although he discusses a manual system, computer software is also available to create such a cluster.

CLUSTERING

Thomas F. Carney
Professor, Department of Communication Studies, University of Windsor

Capturing the contents of brainstorms isn't easy; we think more than twenty times faster than we can write. Besides, a brainstorm consists of a scatter of words in free association. Brainstorms exist fleetingly in short-term memory. New ideas oust their predecessors. But a simple list of words is meaningless; you need a representational format that fits the brainstorm and allows you to insert words anywhere so that you can write them and remember what they mean—*fast.*

Connections between words provide the context that makes the connections memorable. So write the term that triggered the brainstorm in the centre of a page, and draw a line from it to the first word or idea that comes. If this second idea triggers others, draw lines from it to the new terms triggered. You'll create a chain, or *cluster,* of terms. (Figure 4–6 represents *my* brainstorm around the term *cluster.*)

Another *kind* of idea? Return to the centre-page word; draw a line from it to the new word; then draw lines connecting the latter to its associated terms. It's easy to add words; just join them to associated terms. A link between two different chains? Draw a line between the terms linked in each. Afterthoughts? Add them. You can do this *fast,* capturing the *whole* brainstorm (the best ideas come last) in a form that jogs your memory even six months later.

In clustering, you write out everything *before* you see what you're getting at—unlike what happens in sentence construction, where you're required to be linear and sequential and to know the answer. Sentences are slow, and they cut brainstorms short. It takes a while to grasp a complex message. Rereading the chart of a brainstorm makes it familiar enough for you to see the main point. Then a wordless inner feeling tells you, "*This* is the important chain!" As you look at other chains from this perspective, mentally moving some into the background and others into the foreground, you may see that a *group* of chains should be developed.

To develop the cluster, add numbers to each chain, and turn this visual into an outline. Watch for links between two chains that you can then subordinate to a higher chain.

How should you use such a diagram? Take notes at a lecture. Set out the gist of your ideas when your head's full of the reading done for a project. Use the form to pool expertise for a group project.

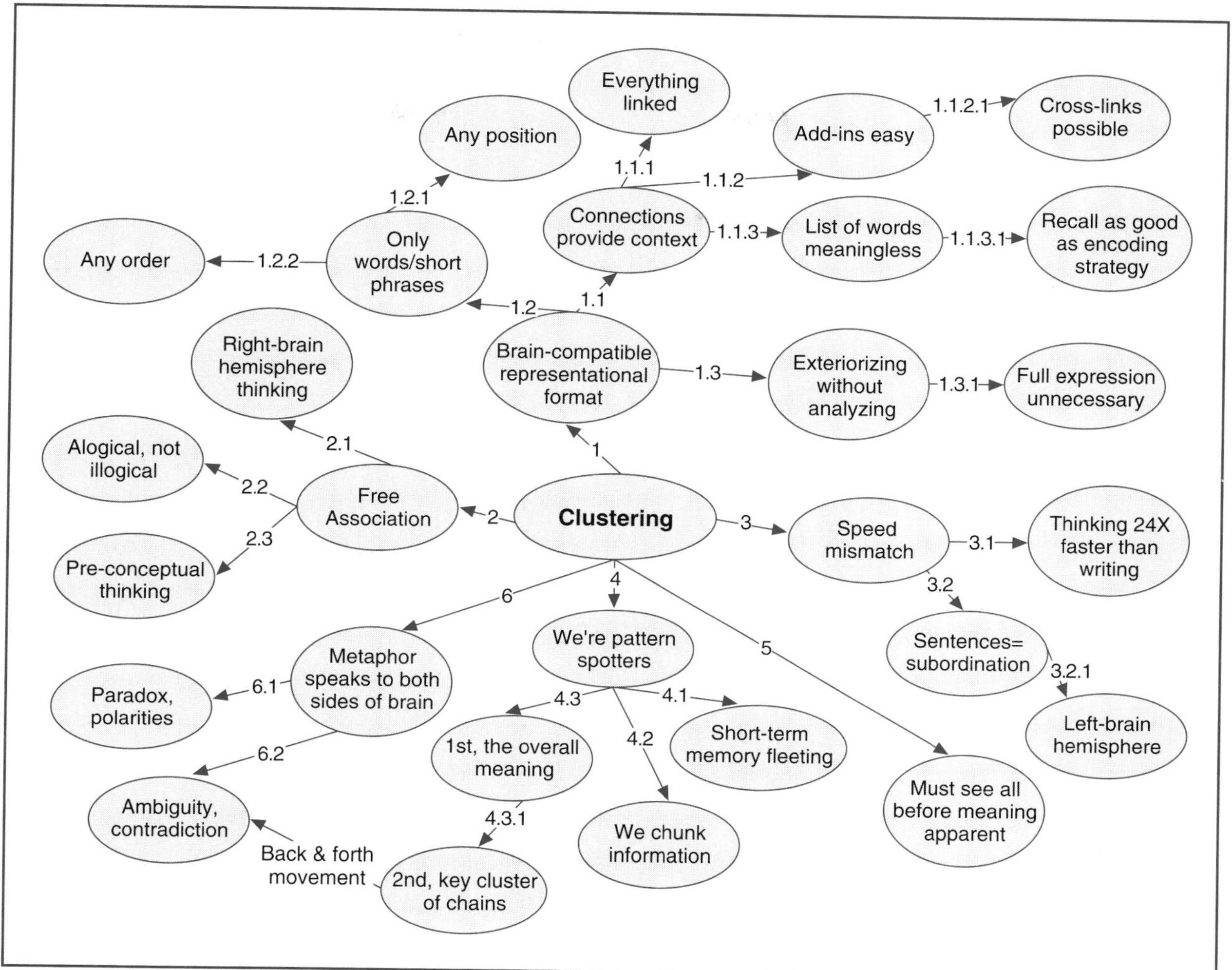

FIGURE 4–6.
A first step in writing: Capturing a brainstorm.

ORGANIZING THE DOCUMENT: OUTLINES

Thinking through the shape of your message and sorting the information that the message will carry move you forward toward writing the document itself. Some writers simply advance to that step: They write. But experienced writers make the transition from analysis to writing through an *outline*. An outline is a sketch of how you want the document to appear when it's written. It shows the form the final product will take: the major sections, key points, general framework.

You're probably familiar with the traditional document outline:

```
 I. Main heading
    A. Subheading
       1. Subsubheading
       2. Subsubheading
II. Next main heading
```

Here each major point is listed as a main heading, with subheadings underneath it, and *sub*subheadings underneath those. Each block fits together to build the overall structure of the final document. While many writers find this form of outlining both logical and helpful, others follow a different approach.

The Nonlinear Outline

If you'd like to try something different, use the form of outline shown in Figure 4–7. With this form, you see an entire document on one side of one sheet of paper, so you can check on the flow and turns of your discussion and ensure that anything suggested in the introduction will be developed later. Work in any direction. When you're finished, you'll create the document by starting at the top of the first column and then moving on to the second and the third columns. The form also works well on a blackboard for organizing collaborative writing projects.

Here's how to create a nonlinear outline:

1. Draw a line across the top of the sheet (or the blackboard) and two lines to form three columns vertically.
2. Place a one-sentence summary of the entire document across the top. That control statement serves as a constant target and as a corrective to wandering thoughts.
3. Distribute your information in the three columns, representing the *introduction, middle,* and *ending.* In distributing your information, you don't need to start with the introduction. You might start by siphoning details off into an attachment to your main document. If the middle of your document is likely to be long, then begin its first heading about midway down the first column and move into the last column as necessary.
4. Consider what information might go into visual form both to convey information and to heighten interest. Note these visuals at the right of each column.
5. Check your emphasis by reviewing the amount of discussion devoted to each topic.

A nonlinear outline can be converted into a linear one as the final form, an approach which some writers prefer to use as a guide when navigating through the actual composing process. Whether you use a traditional (that is, linear) outline or a nonlinear one, the goal is the same: *to provide yourself with a brief sketch of the intended document,* one which guides you through the actual writing of that document.

FIGURE 4–7.
Form for a nonlinear outline.

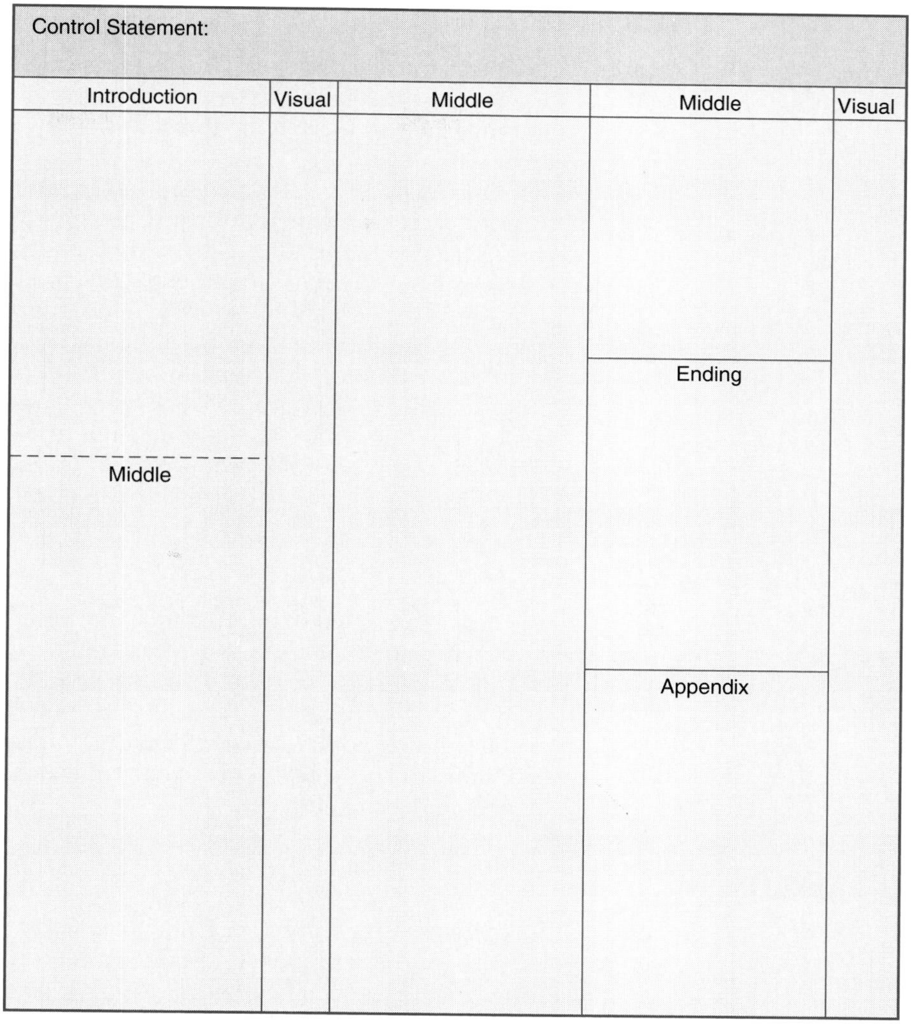

Control Statement:

Introduction
Visual
Middle
Middle
Visual
Ending
Middle
Appendix

ORGANIZING YOURSELF: MANAGING THE PROCESS

The strategies you've learned in this chapter will help you avoid that sinking feeling when you face the blank screen or a blank sheet of paper. Organize the message and the information. You then have to organize *yourself* to carry out the project. Here are suggested steps:

1. Make a schedule.
2. Make an outline.
3. Warm up.
4. Play to your strengths.
5. Be ready to change.
6. Keep writing.

Make a Schedule

First, make a schedule. This is often called a *workplan*. Its purpose is to allow you to relate the tasks to be done to the time in which they must be accomplished so that the final result is ready, in its best form, at the needed time.

Once you have identified the final product and its due date, you then identify each *task* to be performed and the amount of time each will take (or, alternatively, the date by which each task must be accomplished). In other words, you start at the end—the product and due date—and work backwards to the present, showing each component or step along the way. Figure 4–8 presents a simple workplan for the completion of a report. A more detailed workplan could be written to show the many substeps in the process. If the project is a collaborative one (see Chapter 11), the workplan has to show not only *tasks* and *time* but also *assignments*—that is, the work that each member of the group will do to reach the goal by the designated time. Figure 6–14 in Chapter 6 shows a collaborative plan.

Make an Outline

To organize your information and your document, make an outline, either linear or nonlinear. A written outline is particularly important if you draft at a computer or dictate because it will help you keep the whole plan in mind as you work with screens filled with text.

Beginning your writing with writing in hand (your outline) and a clear definition of the elements of communication in your head will help you overcome that blank page.

Warm Up

Stretch a bit before beginning a major writing task, just as you would before a run. If you have to produce a report, warm up by jotting a note. If you slump in the middle of writing, shift to another, easier writing job. When

FIGURE 4–8.
Simple workplan for a report.

TASKS	COMPLETE ON
Gather information	January 3–5
Analyze information	January 6
Outline report	January 6
Compose first draft	January 7–8
Revise	January 11
Submit final report	January 13

that's done, you can return to the bigger project with your pace and rhythm restored.

Play to Your Strengths

Begin to write at a point in the document that you know well. That may be the middle. You may come to the introduction only at the end of a writing session or two. No problem. Think of the report as existing in discrete (though, of course, connected) segments.

Play to your strengths, too, in the time and place you choose for writing and the method of composition you use. Lots of people who hate to write only reinforce the task's perceived drudgery by writing when they are most tired and bored. They schedule the good hours of the day for what they enjoy. Instead, schedule some good hours (the early morning if you're a morning person) for writing, and maybe you'll come to enjoy it. Try dictating into a tape recorder if you think you're better at speaking out your ideas than at committing them to paper. Writing can be difficult enough without opposing your own personality in the process.

Don't think of writing as open-ended ("I'll be here *forever*"). Set a limit in time or in number of pages. But quit writing only when you're ahead, when you know what your next line or section will be.

If you think in terms of *segments,* you'll be able to write in small units without requiring long stretches of time. Most business days are filled with interruptions. Try to segment your writing so that you can work in pieces. Outlines, of course, aid in this process of segmentation.

Be Ready to Change

If the yellow pad you generally write on doesn't seem to come up with prose you like, try the computer. If your outline isn't working, abandon it. Your sentences themselves, spinning out before you, may lead you in an uncharted but potentially profitable direction, and you can create a new outline from that. Be willing to adjust your style of writing a bit if something isn't working.

Keep Writing

As you draft, forget about the rules of composition. Don't cross the page as you would a mine field about to explode with every error. Relax. You'll have time later to fix any problems in expression.

Think of the writing process as a game to be won. It has its rules and routines, but they are less obstacles to overcome than directions to follow. Writing has its moments of frustration and despair, but they can be turned into exhilaration as you break through a conceptual snag or reinterpret a piece of evidence to fit the puzzle. The process of communicating is the process of discovery: sorting through the statistics to find the trend or forcing some vague notion into the precision of words. If you approach the process positively, anticipating the pleasures and emphasizing the accomplishments, you will work with greater speed, less waste in time and energy, and better results than if you view it all as punishment. You can eliminate any false starts, inconsistencies, or dangling modifiers in revision. Revising (which will be discussed in Chapter 7) will make you look good and will make the reading comfortable for the reader—just what you want.

SUMMARY

- Before you write, clarify your **purpose.** Business documents generally meet one (or more) of three purposes: to **record,** to **inform,** or to **persuade.** Identifying the purpose helps you structure the message.
- To make the writing work, learn and meet the **needs of the reader.** Ask questions: Will the reader welcome the message? What does the reader expect in the message? How much should you say? How will the reader use the message? Your answers to these questions determine the information you select to present and the order in which you present it. In addressing multiple readers, aim first at the **primary reader,** the person who requested the document or the individual whom you're trying to inform or persuade. Along the way, meet the needs of **immediate readers,** who will pass the document along, and of **secondary readers,** who will be affected by the document's message.
- A **control statement** pulls together the main idea of your document and your assessment of the purpose of the document for both you and the reader. It appears early in a **direct** document to suggest the topics to be covered and their sequence. It may appear later in an **indirect** document.
- Documents in the European tradition contain three parts: the **introduction,** the **middle,** and the **ending.** Readers who share this tradition expect certain kinds of information in each part. Within the parts, conventional patterns for presentation include **cause and effect, classification and analysis, comparison and contrast, parallelism,** and **narrative.** The format of a **routine** document aids writers in knowing what information to insert where.
- To find the structure inside your information, try **nonlinear** strategies. Try a **data dump** of terms that you then fit into conventional patterns. Try **picturing** the information in diagrams. **Cluster** associations of items as they occur to you.
- Use an **outline,** linear or nonlinear, to convert your thinking and analysis into a sketch of the intended final document. An outline helps you shape the document before you actually write it.
- **Organize yourself** to overcome problems in getting started and to make your time at the screen or with the piece of paper productive. Using a workplan, schedule your writing as a series of discrete tasks. Outline your information. Warm up before a major writing task, play to your strengths in the form and hour you choose for writing, and just keep writing. Save the fine points for revision.

EXERCISES

For Discussion

1. As a class exercise, note on the blackboard the kind of evidence you would need to develop each of the following control statements. Then develop a structure for that evidence.

a. Management, simply stated, is choosing the right people for the job and letting them do it.
b. Here's what to do if your car won't start.
c. You can manipulate statistics to prove anything you want to prove.
d. Follow the old preacher's advice in writing: "First you tell them what you're going to tell them; then you tell them; then you tell them what you told them."

2. Are the following control statements effective? What is the writer's purpose and who is the imagined reader? Do they suggest routine or customized treatment? How should the writer structure evidence to support them?
   a. I think the Taber Road store is in trouble.
   b. As a Bay Area Transit rider, you are entitled to know what the financial condition of your transit system is and why we are forced to propose major fare increases and some reductions in service within the next three months.
   c. Here's the information on the goals, staffing, and costs of corporate fitness programs you asked for in our staff meeting last month.
   d. Let me review for you some of the events of the last several months that have caused our current budget crisis.
3. Choose a topic for a report you are required to write in a business communication (or any other) class. *Limit* that topic and select an approach to writing based on a consideration of *who* would like to read about that topic. Try different strategies for different readers. For example:
   Topic: Corporate fitness programs
   Readers of Your Report:
   a. *Your supervisor.* Assume you are on the staff of a human resources department in a large corporation. Your supervisor is interested in corporate fitness programs, but he doesn't know much about them. He asks you to prepare a statement concerning fitness programs at other companies similar in size and staff to yours. Your purpose is to *inform* the supervisor.
   b. *Vice president for human resources.* You're still in the human resources department, but this time assume that your supervisor asks you to recommend a program for the staff. Your recommendation will be read by the supervisor as the *immediate* audience. But the *primary* audience is the vice president for human resources. The *secondary* audiences will include, for example, the personnel department, which will hire any new staff you recommend. In addition, purchasing would have to approve any expenditures for equipment, and the physical plant staff would have to act on any recommended renovations. Will any other audiences be affected? How would you assess the company's needs? How would you gather the information about equipment and services? What strategies would you need to *persuade* the vice president?
   c. *Human resources directors at several companies.* Assume you are a self-employed fitness consultant to corporations. Write a letter marketing your services to a particular company.

   Think of other situations for writing about fitness. Who would read about the topic? What different kinds of information—and different purposes—would shape your writing?

For Writing

4. Assume that the local Chamber of Commerce (or a campus organization or the student government) has asked you to prepare some literature (a brochure? single sheet?) for new students on the banking services available in your area. Using the clustering, brainstorming, and prompting techniques discussed in this chapter, prepare a data dump of information. Most banks provide free brochures describing their services that you can pick up in their lobbies.

   Select and organize the information in this data dump according to your audience's need for information. Which banking services are students most likely to use?

5. Your purpose in Exercise 4 was to inform. Using the same data dump, prepare a persuasive report on the services that local banks provide for students. Consider the following control statements:
   a. Bank A offers students better checking-account services than Banks X, Y, and Z.
   b. Additional automatic teller machines (ATMs) should be installed at various sites around campus to make banking more convenient for students.
   c. For students, opening a new bank account is a time-consuming, tedious process. (Include a narrative of your own experience.)

6. Answer the following questions concerning your composing process, that is, the way you write.[2] Answer the questions again *after* you finish your business communication course. Have there been any changes?
   a. How often do you write? (Once a week? At the end of a project? Every day in a lab notebook?)
   b. How do you feel about writing? (circle one)
      Enjoy it Neutral Dislike it
   c. What *forms* of documents do you write? (essays, term papers, lab reports, case analyses, marketing surveys, questionnaires, etc.)
   d. What do you do between the time someone asks you to write something and the time you actually start to write? What do you worry about?
   e. Describe any rituals you perform as you sit down to write. (One person we know, for example, must wear a particular green baseball cap to write; others clean their desks or make sure they have adequate coffee.)
   f. How do you decide what information to put where? Do you outline before you write?
   g. How long do you write in any one writing session? If you write for different amounts of time on different projects, describe what determines when you start and stop and how you get going again.
   h. Comment briefly on what you consider the strengths and weaknesses of the *way* you write (your *process of composing*) and of *what* you write (your *style*).

[2] This questionnaire is based in part on Linda Flower, *Problem-Solving Strategies for Writing*, 2nd ed. (San Diego: Harcourt Brace Jovanovich, 1985), pp. 39–40.

For Collaboration

7. As a group project, organize the following topics concerning parking at your college or university. Add topics if you'd like. *Choose* a reader within the university context. *Choose* a situation, either routine or customized. Select a purpose, perhaps to *inform* about the current parking situation, perhaps to *persuade* someone to change the situation.

```
Total number of cars on campus
Total number of spaces in campus lots
Security in the lots: lights, vandalism, theft
Percentage of day and night students, residents, and com-
  muters
Turnover of spaces in an average day
Fees for parking
Distinctions in parking stickers: certain lots designated
  for faculty, others for staff, others for students, etc.
Aesthetics of lots: eyesores? trees to hide?
Convenience of parking near buildings versus aesthetics
  of ring parking lots and a car-free central campus
Costs of a parking garage; relative land values on and
  near campus
Relationships with homeowners near campus on streets
  where students park
```

5 MICROCOMPOSING

Finding Your Voice

What's Ahead

THE ELEMENTS OF VOICE
WORDS
- Concrete and Abstract Words
- Denotation and Connotation
- Content and Structure Words
- Discriminatory Language
- Levels of Usage
- FYI: Acronyms
- Word Play

SENTENCES
- Length
- Parallelism
- Branching

VOICES
- The Corporate Voice
- The Legal Voice
- The Ethics of Voice

AN ENGAGING VOICE
SUMMARY
EXERCISES

Do You Know 

- Why should you prefer concrete terms rather than abstract ones?
- How can you avoid discriminatory language in your writing?
- What are some options to consider when you shape a sentence?
- How do legal and ethical issues affect the voice in which corporations speak and write?

> We wish to take this opportunity to advise you that pursuant to a mutually agreed-upon activity, your mortgage loan has been transferred for servicing from the L & B Mortgage Company to the FBM Mortgage Company. With regard to this matter, please be assured that this transfer of servicing is solely a business transaction based on the data and knowledge obtained in an extensive study to accommodate the servicing of all residential mortgage loans by one company and does not, in any way, reflect any dissatisfaction on anyone's part with your mortgage loan. Effective as of the date of this transfer, your mortgage payments should be forwarded directly to FBM.

The paragraph you just read begins a letter from a mortgage company to its client. Contrast it with this first paragraph:

> To improve service, we have consolidated all our residential loans in one company, FBM Mortgage Company. We have thus transferred your loan from the L & B Mortgage Company to FBM. This transfer is simply administrative. Your loan remains in force exactly as you contracted for it. But beginning on April 1, please send your payments to FBM.

The main purpose of the messages is the same: to inform clients of the need to send mortgage payments to a new company. The explanatory information is also roughly the same. But there the similarities end. Most people find the second opening easier to read and understand. It also makes them feel better about the company. The second opening says *more* with *fewer* words and *shorter* sentences. And it *sounds* better.

In Chapter 4, you learned tools for organizing your information to match the context represented by each of the elements in the communication model: purpose, writer, reader, message, and medium. In this chapter, you will learn how to *express* yourself in writing that matches the context. Choosing words and organizing them into sentences represent the *micro* level of writing. When you write, and particularly when you revise your writing, listen to the sound of your voice as it comes off the page. In this chapter, you will see how to create an engaging voice in your writing, whether you speak for yourself or for an organization.

THE ELEMENTS OF VOICE

Each of the following memos from a manager responds to the same situation: An employee is continually late for work.

```
To:       Donna Spellman
From:     Brian Pierce
Date:     1 June 199–
Subject:  Monthly Tardiness Report
```

You were late in arriving at the office on each of the following dates: May 1, 3, 4, 5, 10, 11, 15, 16, 18, 22, 24, 29, and 30. Such behavior cannot be condoned at this Company. A duty of every employee is to be prompt. The neglect of this responsibility will ultimately affect your performance evaluation and thus jeopardize your stay here at our Company.

```
To:       Peter Hoverson-Smith
From:     Philip Johnson
Date:     1 June 199–
Subject:  Excessive Tardiness
```

In light of our discussion yesterday, let me reiterate the problems caused by your lateness. I'm not sure you appreciate the seriousness of this matter.

Please realize that your tardiness causes other employees to become frustrated because they must carry your work load for this time. Moreover, your staff is left unsupervised. Therefore, they do not know what to do when they arrive in the morning. Many of them, too, have started coming in late. I'm sure you agree that a section head should set a good example for others to follow. I'll look forward to seeing that good example from you.

Pierce sees the primary goal of his memo as recording, for Spellman's personnel record, the details of her lateness. In addition, he uses that formal record to give Spellman fair warning about the ultimate sanction: being fired. He states the rule (promptness) and shows how she has violated it. Pierce sees his role as a hard-line manager who motivates through disciplinary action. His memo is tough. Words like *neglect, ultimately,* and *jeopardize* reinforce the negative voice in this memo.

Johnson sees a different purpose for writing: to persuade Hoverson-Smith to mend his ways. That purpose reflects Johnson's own perception of his role in motivating workers. He appeals to Hoverson-Smith's sense of responsibility as a supervisor in carrying out the goals of the organization. This memo is longer than Pierce's. Although not condoning tardiness, it more clearly describes the organizational purpose for promptness beyond merely meeting the rule. It is part of a continuing discussion between manager and employee, which was conducted earlier in a conversation.

The voices in these two memos—like your voice—reflect, of course, the writers' skills in composition. Moreover, they reflect the writers' attitudes toward the subject of the document and toward the reader. Some managers anticipate resistance from their subordinates and thus structure an assertive message and invoke sanctions to overcome the subordinate's perceived lack of discipline and self-motivation. At the other end of the scale, managers may motivate with reasoning and friendliness when they believe that subordinates do not inherently dislike work, indeed, that they will seek responsibilities and exercise imagination if the conditions are right. Managers who expect heavy resistance may motivate with a stick; those who aim to bring out their subordinates' own best qualities use the carrot. Pierce leans toward the stick; Johnson, toward the carrot.

The *way* you say things often conveys almost as much information as the content of the document. Sometimes, it conveys more. The following sections provide strategies for using words and sentences effectively.

WORDS

A word, like a number, is a symbol, something that stands for something else. What the word stands for or symbolizes is its *referent*.

Concrete and Abstract Words

Figure 5–1 shows the relationship between the word *facility* and one referent for it: a three-story parking garage for 100 cars. At the top of the triangle, the term is abstract; as you move downward, the terms become more concrete. Many referents could be covered by *facility* (a swimming pool, an office building, or a hospital, to name just three); fewer are covered by *building;* fewer still by *three-story parking garage;* and so on.

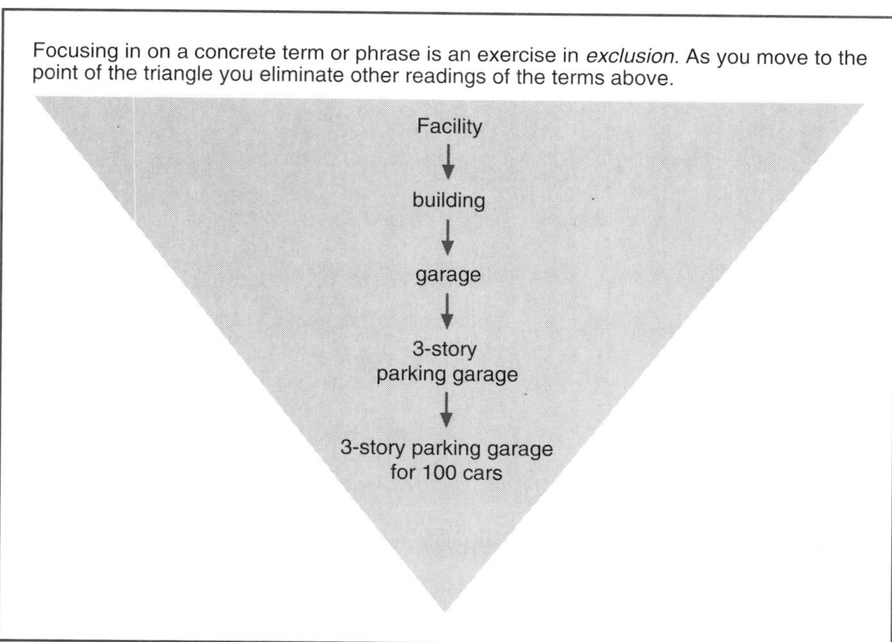
Focusing in on a concrete term or phrase is an exercise in *exclusion.* As you move to the point of the triangle you eliminate other readings of the terms above.
Facility
building
garage
3-story parking garage
3-story parking garage for 100 cars

FIGURE 5–1. Focusing meaning from the abstract to the concrete.

For the business writer, the lesson of the triangle in Figure 5–1 is clear: The possibility of confusion and misreading increases as one moves up the triangle. "Pursuant to a mutually agreed-upon activity" is abstract; "We have consolidated all our residential loans in one company" is more concrete. "Effective as of the date of this transfer, your mortgage payments should be forwarded directly to FBM" is more abstract than "Beginning on April 1, please send your payment to FBM." Use concrete terms to engage the reader and to make your writing vigorous and precise. Avoid overusing such abstract terms as *aspects, factors, things, conditions,* and *areas.*

Denotation and Connotation

Words have two different kinds of meanings: *denotations* and *connotations.* The denotation is the meaning or meanings stipulated in the dictionary, that is, the literal meaning. Connotations are the associated attitudes and images that your words evoke in the reader's mind. Connotations, like electrons, have charges. Authors sometimes use positive words, often at a high level of abstraction (euphemisms), to cover uncomfortable material, like death and taxes. Someone "passes on"; instead of taxes, one pays "user fees." Americans use euphemisms to refer to bodily functions and the places where they occur. Look for "toilet" signs in Europe; look for "comfort facility" and "rest area" in the United States. Here are some other differently charged words for the same referents:

Negative	*Neutral*	*Positive*
huckstering	selling	marketing
broken down	doesn't work	inoperative
kicked the bucket	died	passed on
skinny	thin	svelte

Content and Structure Words

Words can also be classified by their grammatical function into *content* and *structure* words:

Content Words

- Nouns and pronouns (names of persons, places, and things)
- Verbs (names of actions or states of being)
- Adjectives
- Adverbs

Structure Words

- Articles *(a, an, the)*
- Prepositions
- Verb auxiliaries *(have been, could have, will be)*

- Conjunctions
- Expletives *(it is, there are)*
- Qualifiers (which modify adjectives and adverbs: *very, rather, wholly, quite)*

Content words do most of the work of transmitting meaning. Structure words carry some meaning but serve mainly to provide transitions and a framework for other words. To write efficient prose, let the content words dominate. When structure words, especially prepositional phrases and functionless qualifiers, get out of hand, meaning dissipates and efficiency declines.

Verbs

In particular, guard the verb. Be precise: Don't rely simply on the verbs *do, get, use, is* or *are,* or *involves,* the staples of first drafts. Avoid expletives like *there is* and *it is.* Prefer concrete and specific verbs whenever possible. Compare these sentences:

Weak

```
There are many administrative functions that are the kind
that a computer does, but people don't seem to think
about using a computer for them, and so they are wasting
a lot of time.
```

Improved

```
A computer system accommodates many administrative func-
tions now inefficiently completed by hand.
```

In addition to choosing *precise* verbs, choose those that establish the most efficient or tactful relationship between verb and subject. You have two choices: active and passive. In the active, the subject of the sentence *acts.* In the *passive,* the subject *is acted upon:*

Active

```
All five supervisors attended the meeting.
All five supervisors met.
```

Passive

```
The meeting was attended by all five supervisors.
```

When you use the active, you emphasize the actor in a direct statement:

```
The plant manager implemented the plan.
```

When you use the passive, you subordinate the actor. Choose the passive when you want to emphasize the object:

```
The plan was implemented by the plant manager.
```

Choose the passive, too, to be tactful. The passive lets you avoid placing blame and thus reduces the sting of a negative message:

```
   The window was left open, an action that caused dampness
in the room that kept the computer from operating.
```

But the passive requires verbal auxiliaries (like *have been*) and prepositional phrases if the actor is to be named. These extra words may be appropriate, but avoid passives when the context calls for directness.

Verbiage

When structure words pile up, they lengthen the sentence while reducing the sentence's impact. Reduce those pile-ups (excessive verbiage) as in the following phrases with shorter substitutes:

Weak	*Stronger*
at the present time	now
during the time that	while
in the event that	if
due to the fact that	because
for the purpose of	to
on a daily basis	daily
with the objective of	to

Discriminatory Language

Intentionally or not, your words can reflect biases against a different gender *(sexist language)* or culture. Although English common nouns do not regularly show gender as nouns do in, say, French, certain nouns bear a masculine bias, for example, *chairman, spokesman,* and *businessman.* The women's movement has focused attention on how nouns sometimes embed derogatory attitudes toward women. Moreover, documents have traditionally used the masculine pronouns *(he, him,* and *his)* exclusively to stand for all persons. Such usage seems to perpetuate a sense that only men are important.

Sexism, of course, is complex, reflecting deeply rooted cultural attitudes. These biases are more than a matter of language. But they are, in part, a matter of language. Some style guides for writers recommend the use of the pronouns *s/he* or *she/he* or *she or he,* although these forms are cumbersome. Randomly scattering *she* and *he* in a text is also possible. Readers are sometimes brought up short by this tactic, however. In this text, we use both *his or her* and *her or his* as well as *she or he* and *he or she*. Did you notice? Try some of the following tactics:

Eliminate gender nouns and pronouns when possible. Substitute *person* or *people* if necessary:

Inappropriate

```
The average man's decisions are based on his self-inter-
est.
```

More Appropriate

```
The average person's decisions are based on self-inter-
est.
```

Use plural nouns and the various forms of the gender-free plural *they* (being careful, of course, to make the pronoun agree with the noun it stands for):

```
Accountants have found their ranks swelling in the tri-
state area.
```

Use *one* or *you* (*one* is more formal):

```
One has a range of options in choosing a career.
You have a range of options in choosing your career.
```

Replace the third-person singular possessive (*his* or *her*) with an article:

```
Every writer has a method.
Not: Every writer has his method.
```

Not calling attention to gender in nouns and pronouns—or changing them—is fairly straightforward. Avoiding nouns that carry connotations derogatory to women is more difficult. Context is critical. Sometimes it's a matter of parallelism, such as referring to the *men* and the *girls* at the office, even if they are the same age. *Men* should match *women; boy* matches *girl.* Replace *-man* endings: *chair* instead of *chairman, spokesperson* instead of *spokesman,* and *salesperson* not *salesman.* Gender-free titles also help: *flight attendant* rather than *stewardess.* Avoid unnecessary modifiers that add gender to a noun; instead of *lady* doctor or *male* nurse, use only the nouns for both.

As with all the words you use, test your designation of groups against your intent and the reader's perceptions. Avoid using one group as a standard for another. The term *people of color* is preferable to *nonwhite. Asian* is preferable to *Oriental* because the Orient is east only from a Eurocentric perspective. Similarly, *European tradition* is now considered preferable to *Western tradition.*

Levels of Usage

In business, you'll write for a variety of readers. You'll need to select words that match your reader's vocabulary. You also need to match your reader's expectations and the common conventions for language in a document form. As internal documents, memos often include informal language and code words understood by members of the organization. A letter from an organization to a customer is more formal. The relative formality of your language; the degree to which you use insiders' code words, including acronyms (see "*FYI:* Acronyms"); and the relative technicality of your terms—these elements represent different levels of usage.

ACRONYMS

Donna Lee Cheney
Chief Operating Officer,
Patricia Seybold's Office
Computing Group

Writing in the computer industry for most of my career, I have come to realize that I speak in a foreign language when trying to describe computer features and business situations. I speak in WYSIWYG and CPU. (WYSIWYG = What You See Is What You Get and describes a function of software; CPU = Central Processing Unit and describes a component of the hardware.)

How do we reduce the confusion? One suggestion is to recognize that acronyms are a form of speed writing and speaking. It is easier to use three or four letters than to write over and over again the words that those letters represent. Such usage is rather positive. But acronyms can become habit forming and can block more creative thinking. The continual broad use of acronyms results in fewer people understanding business messages. Worse, the use of acronyms makes most people self-conscious and inhibits them from asking what the speaker means.

Successful communicators limit the use of acronyms to those who share the code. For those who don't, good communicators think and write without acronyms—and with a powerful and easy-to-understand vocabulary.

Formal and Informal Language

In a casual encounter, most people use only fragmentary sentences. They also use colloquial expressions and contractions. In a memo from a friend, you'd expect similarly informal language. You'd wonder what was wrong if your friend addressed you stiffly:

> It is expected that you will complete the requested action as soon as possible.

A more formal voice may be appropriate when you address a memo upward in the organization to less well known readers. *Formal* doesn't mean "archaic." It does mean that you avoid contractions and slang and that you revise for precision and emphasis.

Jargon

The term *jargon* refers to the use of code words understood only by one organization or by one profession or technical group. Jargon serves as shorthand for quick communication.

Organizational jargon is a dialect that bonds its users to the group and that distinguishes them from outsiders. At IBM, for example, a *hipo* is an employee on the fast tract to success, that is, someone with "high potential."[1] IBM-speakers don't disagree with their bosses; they *nonconcur.* And anyone who nonconcurs often and abrasively, but constructively, is a *wild duck.* Loyal McDonald's Corporation workers have "ketchup in their veins."

[1] Michael W. Miller, "At Many Firms, Employees Speak a Language That's All Their Own," *The Wall Street Journal,* 12 December 1989, p. 17.

The specialized terms that constitute professional and technical jargon match new ways of observing and manipulating reality. One reason that English is an international language of business and science is the ease with which it accommodates new words. Many English terms in computer operation, management theory, and marketing, for example, have also entered into German, Spanish, and other languages. Use specialized vocabulary when appropriate to convey a message accurately to a reader who understands the terms. But avoid using such terms merely to intimidate or fool the reader.

Word Play

Plays on words and other forms of humor and figurative language are not common in business writing. Why? Figurative language often incorporates double meanings and is not appropriate when you want to convey a single message to your reader. Moreover, word play puts a special burden on people communicating in a second language and on translators. One translator of American documents for European readers, for example, says that his first step is always to change all the football images to soccer images. Use metaphors, similes, and analogies with caution—although you can enjoy the puns for which *The Wall Street Journal* is famous. Here's one example from page 1 of the 18 June 1990 issue (an article by Dennis Farney):

> Unkindest Cut? Timber Firm Stirs Ire Felling Forests Faster Than They Regenerate.

SENTENCES

Choose words that create the right voice for your writing. In addition, shape your sentences strategically, checking them for

1. Length
2. Parallelism
3. Branching

Length

The sentences in the opening paragraph of the mortgage letter at the beginning of this chapter are long: (1) 35 words; (2) 57 words; (3) 17 words. The second letter uses shorter sentences: (1) 16; (2) 13; (3) 5; (4) 11; (5) 10. Although no sentence length is perfect, writers are more likely to lose control of longer sentences. In addition, readers may find them harder to read. In general, vary sentence length to match units of information and reader interest. Follow these guidelines:

- Avoid a succession of either long or short sentences.
- If you write three long sentences, make the next one short.
- Use short sentences to clinch a point.
- In revising, look for opportunities to shorten sentences.

Parallelism

To establish their similarity and build rhythm, you express similar items or ideas in similar form. That's *parallelism.* When speaking about George Washington, lecturers and preachers depend on parallelism to stir their audience:

> He was first in peace, first in war, and first in the hearts of his countrymen.

Businesspersons depend on parallelism for less emotional reasons: to describe a set of components, to list several options or alternatives, or to delineate steps in a process. Whenever you have a series of items to express in a sentence,

1. Make sure that each item belongs to the same logical class of items. Use the term for that class at the head of the list—"options," "steps," "components"—or at least have that term clearly in your own mind.
2. Express each item in the same grammatical form (for example, a single noun or a clause). The first item governs the form of the others.
3. Write the items one after another, or list them with numbers or bullets (•) on single lines. A list takes more space but gives each item heightened attention.

Unparallel

```
The figures were not verified, inaccurate, and they
weren't very convincing, either.
```

Parallel

```
The figures were neither verified, accurate, nor very
convincing.
```

Branching

You shape sentences by their length and by the use of parallelism. In addition, you shape them through your placement of such modifying elements as dependent clauses and prepositional phrases. Not all sentences, of course, have dependent clauses. As you probably know, a simple sentence can be powerful: "Mother died." Value such sentences, especially among longer ones. When you add modifying elements, consider where the sentence *branches* into those modifiers. You have three choices: at the end, after the sentence notes the subject and the main verb; in the middle, by interrupting the subject and verb; or at the beginning, before the subject and verb. Here are examples of each form of branching, designated by right (the most common) and left as you view the sentence:

Right-Branching Sentences

```
1. The market mounted a vigorous rally last Friday
   amounting to 19½ points, despite all the gloom of a
```

budget deficit, higher interest rates, increasing tensions throughout the world, and banking problems.
2. Management must realize certain inevitabilities: that research cannot stay in the lab forever, that there are overall economic timetables to be met, and that a transfer plan is necessary.

Mid-Branching Sentences

1. The market, despite all the gloom of a budget deficit, higher interest rates, increasing tensions throughout the world, and banking problems, mounted a vigorous rally last Friday amounting to 19½ points.
2. Certain inevitabilities—that research cannot stay in the lab forever, that there are overall economic timetables to be met, and that a transfer plan is necessary—must be realized by management.

Left-Branching Sentences

1. Despite all the gloom of a budget deficit, higher interest rates, increasing tensions throughout the world, and banking problems, the market mounted a vigorous rally last Friday amounting to 19½ points.
2. That research cannot stay in the lab forever, that there are overall economic timetables to be met, and that a transfer plan is necessary—these inevitabilities must be realized by management.

The most common pattern in English is the right-branching sentence. Why? Because readers can process it most easily. They have the main thought before encountering the modifiers that qualify it. When all the modifiers come first, readers have to hold them *before* they know what to do with them. They may forget and have to reread the sentence. Left branching, however, builds suspense and anticipation.

Choose the form of sentence that matches your emphasis and your audience's reading sophistication. For straightforward information—that is, most of the time—you'll probably choose sentences that branch right. The other forms tax the reader a bit more—something you'll want to do only with caution. But you may want just that emphasis:

Before you put this annual United Way appeal in the back of your desk drawer, think again.

VOICES

From the general language in which you write or speak, and from the general patterns of sentences within that language, select what sounds like you, what expresses your information accurately and precisely, and what matches your purpose, your reader, and the medium of your message. What do business voices sound like? What *should* you sound like? This section discusses some of the issues of voice in business documents.

The Corporate Voice

In an excellent study, Walker Gibson defines three categories of American voices: tough talk, sweet talk, and stuffy talk.[2] All three can be heard in a variety of prose forms, and each is matched by a prominent pronoun. *Tough talk*, for example, appears in the "I"-based narratives of a certain kind of fiction. For business writers, the most commonly heard voices are sweet talk and stuffy talk.

Sweet talk is "you" talk. It is the language of advertisements and sales pitches. Friendly and familiar, it cajoles the reader, often with chatty images and anecdotes. It assumes a certain intimacy with the reader. Figure 5–2, for example, is an advertisement for a bank that projects an image of close personal attention to customers. The advertisement addresses *you* directly: "If *you* want *your* business to grow." The language is *colloquial*, without technical terms. Note the contractions. Note the use of the name of the banker (Bill Betty) to show that the bank is a group of people and not an impersonal organization. Note, too, all the word play on fish and fishing, beginning with "little fish" and "hooked up" in the headline.

Stuffy talk is "it" and "they" talk. What corporate America and the government write is often stuffy.[3] That stuffiness may derive from defensiveness in the face of perceived objections by and conflicts with the reader. It also derives from group writing, in which writers take little individual responsibility for the voice of the whole. The result is impersonality. Such "official prose" reflects the bureaucratic mind, according to another authority, William R. Brown.[4] He contrasts it to direct speech—the language of power and leadership. The economist John Kenneth Galbraith provides further explanation (his comments, from an "About Men" column, use only masculine references):

> What [the aspiring corporate leader] says is required by the rules and ethics of organization to be both predictable and dull. He does not speak for himself; he speaks for the firm. Good policy is not what he wants but what the organization believes it needs. In the normal case, his speech will be written and vetted by his fellow organization men. In the process, it will drop to the lowest common denominator of novelty. Lindbergh, as has too often been told, could never have flown the Atlantic with a committee. It is equally certain that General Motors could never have written Shakespeare or even a column by Art Buchwald. Executive expression is ignored because, by the nature of organization, it must be at an exceptionally tedious level of organization stereotype and caution.[5]

[2] *Tough, Sweet, and Stuffy: An Essay on Modern American Prose Styles* (Bloomington: Indiana University Press, 1966).

[3] Ibid., p. 91.

[4] "Jargon and the Teaching of Organizational Communication," paper presented at the American Business Communication Association Eastern Regional Meeting, Philadelphia, 22 April 1983.

[5] "About Men: Corporate Man," *The New York Times Magazine*, 22 January 1984, p. 39.

FIGURE 5–2.
An advertisement in "you" talk. *(Reprinted courtesy of Wilmington Savings Fund Society, FSB, Wilmington, Delaware.)*

Phil Di Febo wasn't content to be a little fish, so he hooked up with us.

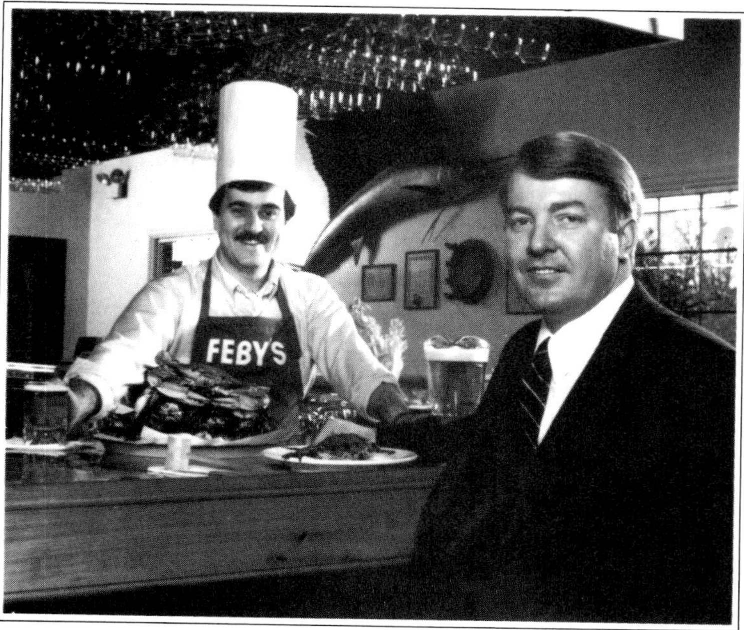

When Phil Di Febo cast about for the capital he needed to open Feby's Fishery, he found out that we were as eager as he was to break new ground. He and Bill Betty of our Commercial Lending team worked out a package of financing for construction, working capital and equipment that helped Feby's grow from a small fish market to a whale of a business on Lancaster Pike.

If you want your business to grow, you need a bank that's as eager to be a big fish as you are. For any type of commercial financing, call our Commercial Lending Department today at 571-7103. Get the attention you deserve and the prompt action you'd expect from a team that's out to catch your business.

Wilmington Savings Fund Society/FSB
Equal Opportunity Lender
© WSFS 1984

Corporate writers, then, often display an off-the-rack style, slipping into phrases and even whole paragraphs from other documents and wearing them for all occasions.

A safe and time-tested voice is not all bad, as many companies have discovered. As a spokesperson, you may well have to write letters and other documents in what one writer calls "Plain Vanilla" style. The style matches an image and an approach codified by your organization. The company's wordprocessing software may provide you with paragraphs of explanation to incorporate into your writing and may check your language and sentence structure against a sample of good prose stored as a standard. When the corporate voice aids in *connecting* you to the reader, use it. When it confuses, abuses, or deceives the reader, avoid it.

The Legal Voice

In the United States, almost anyone who enters into an agreement or certifies information writes in the shadow of a lawyer. The result is often a text that limits responsibility, enforces impersonality, and creates a distance between writer and reader. The text is stuffy. Note the set phrases *(in accordance with)*, the passives *(have been prepared, are based, has been inferred)*, and the expletive *(It should be noted that)* in following statement from a site analysis report of an engineering firm:

```
The above recommendations, which have been prepared according
to the generally accepted soil and foundation engineering
standards, are based on the conditions encountered by the
test borings. It should be noted that, although soil quality
has been inferred from the interpolation of the test boring
data, subsurface conditions between the test borings are, in
fact, unknown.
```

Legal thinking also produces expressions of uncertainty, such as *may, might, seems, appears, we understand that,* and *it is possible under certain circumstances that.* Caution is certainly appropriate, but the language should not get in the way of clarity.

The Ethics of Voice

If the prose of organization life speaks in a voice that is merely obscure, tedious, or dull, then probably no great harm is done to readers. The intended reader may skip the document or may have to compensate for obscure writing by puzzling out an explanation to find what's needed. Consumers have come to expect such puzzlement.

If, however, as sometimes happens, that voice, in its obscurity and caution, *deceives,* then it violates a standard of ethical conduct. What is an acceptable level of deception? Outright lying is rarely condoned. But what about "strategic misrepresentation," a term that covers the use of language to evoke a positive feeling toward some information (as in a euphemism) or to soften the blow to a reader when the news is bad? It's clearly wrong for a company that's had a bad year to report false results in its annual report. But is it wrong to express those results in a lengthy text while diverting the reader's attention with engaging photographs? Is it wrong for companies to use euphemisms? To speak of firings as *downsizing,* or *derecruiting* or to say they run a *lean operation* when that really means they are understaffed?

The answer depends on what the organization intends and whether the language harms the reader. Since 1974, the Committee on Public Doublespeak of the National Council of Teachers of English has presented yearly "Doublespeak" awards that are "an ironic 'tribute' to American public figures who have perpetrated language that is grossly unfactual, deceptive, evasive, euphemistic, confusing, or self-contradictory." The United States State Department, for example, has won the award for redefining the word *kill* as "unlawful or arbitrary deprivation of life." The National Transportation Safety Board has also been nominated—for calling an airplane crash "controlled flight into terrain." The Pentagon was cited for renaming peace as "permanent pre-hostility," combat as "violence processing," and civilian casualties in nuclear war as "collateral damage." Other terms cited: running a *negative deficit* in a not-for-profit program; *therapeutic misadventure* instead of *malpractice.*

Sometimes, you need to put a positive face on things to ease a relationship or to save face for the reader. But language becomes unacceptable when it fails the simple measure of ethical conduct you read about in Chapter 1: to "leave the other person at least as well off."

AN ENGAGING VOICE

Walker Gibson laments the "loss of personality" in corporate writing. His comment raises a significant issue that we should now be ready to address. How much of yourself, of your own personality, should you reveal as you write? Or, more strategically, what personality should you adopt in a document to ensure attaining your goal and engaging the reader?

The answers to those questions can be found only in your close analysis of the context for the document, as you saw in Chapter 4. The working out of that analysis sets you on a particular course in planning the document and in choosing words and sentences that will attract and hold the reader's attention. By "personality," Gibson does not mean mere posturing or self-display. You shouldn't use *I* in every sentence. When the context demands impersonality, back off. When the context suggests a close relationship with the reader, however, refer to yourself and that reader in a conversational style.

For Gibson personality means a *voice* in the prose. To engage the reader, sound like a person, writing to a person, not like a prerecorded message playing on its own. Adjust your voice to the reader. That adjustment determines the details you select to present, the connotations of your words, the shape of your sentences, and the certainty of your stance.

Professionals who know their specialty best are the ones best able to express it in different voices to different audiences: in jargon to technical colleagues, in breezy corporate code to fellow workers, and in simpler expressions, with analogies and other figurative devices, to general audiences. In their style, they accommodate different information and different readers, while still maintaining their own integrity. Particularly where the situation is complex or politically sensitive, allow yourself the opportunity for revision to find the appropriate voice in which to convey your message. Sometimes, you'll want to be forceful; sometimes, personal; sometimes, particularly when the news is bad, rather impersonal.[6] Don't just imitate some document that has been hanging around the office. Exercise a range of approaches, but make sure that the range is tied to *you*.

SUMMARY

- In selecting your words, prefer **concrete** terms to **abstract** ones because they are more precise, less likely to cause misunderstanding and misreading, and more vigorous and engaging.
- The first step in **avoiding discriminatory language** is becoming *aware*. Then, eliminate biased nouns and pronouns when possible; use *one* or *you*, *persons* or the plural. Avoid nouns that carry connotations derogatory to women, for example, "the *men* and the *girls* at the office." Use gender-free titles, for example, *flight attendant* rather than *stewardess*. Avoid using one group as a standard, as in *nonwhite*, or Eurocentric designations like *Oriental*.
- When you shape a sentence, consider three options in form. First, vary sentence **length;** insert a short sentence for emphasis and reader relief in the midst of several long ones. Second, use **parallelism** to build rhythm and to show the logical similarities of the items in a list. Third, control how sentences **branch;** that is, distribute modifiers to connect a series of sentences and to meet reader expectation.
- When they speak for corporations, writers often use a **voice** that is **dull** and **cautious.** The voice may reflect group authorship as well as defensiveness in the face of potential litigation. The prose limits responsibility, enforces impersonality, and creates a distance between writer and reader.

EXERCISES

For Discussion

1. Discuss the ethical implications of "doublespeak." Find current examples in newspapers and reports, and read the *Quarterly Review of Doublespeak* published by the committee you read about in this chapter.
2. Examine your textbooks or publications from your university or another organization to test for discriminatory language. Here are some questions to consider:
   - Is the masculine pronoun *he* used exclusively to stand for nouns?
   - Do any statements carry connotations derogatory to women? To any race or culture?
   - Does the document make any overt attempts to avoid discrimination by including, for example, photographs that show people of color,

[6] For an excellent article on business style, see John S. Fielden, "What Do You Mean You Don't Like My Style?" *Harvard Business Review*, May–June 1982, pp. 128–38.

handicapped individuals, and people from a variety of cultures in the classroom or on the job?

3. Computers have produced many changes in society, including changes in language. Make a list of some terminology from computer development that has entered daily talk (for example, "I'd like to have your *input* on the proposed change," "I'm *programmed* for success," and "One more party and my system will *crash*").
4. Businesspeople, like sports fans, often speak in code. For example, here are terms for a "home run" that Eric Brittingham, a student and baseball player, collected: round-tripper, dinger, gopherball, touchdown, slam, four-batter, tater, blast, rally-killer, grand tour. Take a major event or activity (like a home-run) in your business field or playing field and collect terms that refer to it. Conversely, take a code term, like "bottom line," and consider all its possible meanings in different contexts (for example, "bottom line" may mean "goal" or "gist" or—what else?)
5. Because people may read a variety of business periodicals, each periodical aims at providing a different slant on the news. One of those differences may be the periodical's "voice," including the word choice that its reporters consider appropriate and its sentence structure. Look at the way several business magazines or newspapers—for example, *The Wall Street Journal, Business Week, The Economist,* and *Forbes*—deal with one issue, controversy, or person in the news.
   - What level of usage does each use?
   - What is the common length of the sentences?
   - Is any one form of sentence prevalent in each?
   - Is the voice tough, sweet, or stuffy?
6. Analyze the *voice* in the following letter, which responds to a customer complaint:

   It is with great regret that I am writing this letter to you. Not from regret of any financial loss we may incur as to the outcome of your complaint. Rather, we regret, we fear, jeopardizing your valued patronage.

   I am sick over the damage you have incurred to your beautiful garden because of our faulty sprinkler system, and I propose to do whatever you suggest to make proper restitution.

   Our design engineer, as well as our installation supervisor, feels equally bad, and both admit their error. At this point, anything I say is not enough except that I am very sorry for all your inconvenience due to our error. I will gladly do whatever you feel is just, including monetary considerations for the restoration of your lawn. Of course, this includes installing a new and fault-free system at no charge if you so desire.

   I am currently at the mercy of your desires.

7. The following terms were used to indicate the end points of scales suggesting preferences in soft drinks; the scales were then applied to

particular drinks. Are the terms parallel? Does a pattern of discrimination emerge from the associations in the terms?

Sweet	1	2	3	4	5	Neutral
Salty	1	2	3	4	5	Bland
Expensive	1	2	3	4	5	Cheap
Elegance	1	2	3	4	5	Common
Bubbly	1	2	3	4	5	Flat
Masculine	1	2	3	4	5	Feminine
Smooth	1	2	3	4	5	Rough
Clear	1	2	3	4	5	Cloudy
Light	1	2	3	4	5	Heavy
Popular	1	2	3	4	5	Exclusive
New	1	2	3	4	5	Old

For Writing

8. To analyze your *sentence style,* examine a page or two of a draft document you have written. First, with a colored pencil, place a slash mark at the end of each sentence. Look at the whole page. Is there variety in sentence length? Then count the number of words in each sentence. Next, note how the sentences *branch,* that is, the placement of the modifiers; underline the modifying elements with your colored pencil and note their location relative to the main clause.
9. Assume that you are a supervisor of several clerks in a bank's operation center. One clerk in your group continually parks his car in a space reserved for the vice president of operations. The vice president complains to your supervisor, who complains to you, with the warning, "Get that car out of the VP's space!" You talk to the clerk; the car returns. Now, write a note to the clerk. Perhaps the entire class can write notes. Then, compare your strategies for dealing with the clerk's resistance to behaving as you want him to.

For Collaboration

10. You are a member of a group working on a project in a marketing class. After a month on the job, the group submits a progress report to the professor that analyzes the group's performance. Here is one paragraph from a report written by another member of the group who asks for your suggestions for improvement. Diagnose its problems in voice (that waffling between the stuffy and the informal), organization (review Chapter 4), and sentence structure, and *write* a note to the writer explaining your diagnosis. If your instructor requires, *rewrite* the paragraph with an emphasis on word choice and sentence shape. Refer to the Handbook at the back of the book for advice on style as well as punctuation.

    In any type of project where an individual is involved with a cluster of six diverse people they will encounter many positive and negative attributes. The performance of our group on our initial project was very good; however, the quality of the group members together with the necessary dedication will lead to an improved case analysis the next time around. The members of our group are all friendly and work well together. We all interact and communicate well together. This is vital to a group's performance. Once we started working as a unit we started rolling. A second aspect of our performance that added to our final outcome, was the preparedness of the group members. We all were psyched about the project and did our homework. In each meeting, we voiced our opinions and elicited the most important and relevant facts. The fact that all the members were well prepared for interaction enhanced our total group output. We also kept an eye on the clock at meetings. We specifically implemented a ninety minute meeting maximum. By sticking to this schedule, we had to limit the noncase fraternization during group meetings. No grousing and hanging-out.

6 COMPOSING WITH VISUALS

What's Ahead

THINKING VISUALLY
COMMUNICATING VISUALLY
- FYI: Visualizing the Law
- Consolidating and Recording Information
- Summarizing and Reinforcing a Message
- Unifying the Document
- Providing Dramatic Impact
- Reducing Text
- Crossing Language Barriers

SELECTING THE APPROPRIATE VISUAL FORM
- FYI: Olympic Colors
- Tables and Matrixes
- Line Graphs
- Organizational Charts and Flowcharts
- Schedules
- Bar Charts
- Pie Charts
- Pictorial Charts
- Maps
- Drawings
- Photographs
- FYI: Communicating with Photographs

TESTING THE VISUAL
- Accuracy
- Distortion
- Documentation

THE VISUAL PAGE
- Guidelines for Using Visuals

SUMMARY
EXERCISES

Do You Know ?

- What are some advantages in "thinking visually"?
- Why should you use visuals in a document?
- What are the major forms of visuals in business?
- What tests should you apply to each visual?
- What makes a visual page work?

If you are not in the habit of thinking visually, it's time to begin.

THINKING VISUALLY

Visuals are a major medium—on some occasions, *the* major medium—of business communication. To frame your thinking about visuals, read "*FYI:* Visualizing the Law" (pp. 98–100), which shows how a lawyer thinks and communicates visually.

Like Bertram Wolfson, you can use visuals to help you to analyze and structure information—and to present it to others. Graphics packages that run on personal computers can assist. In Chapter 4, you saw how visuals capture brainstorms. "Window" programs let you juxtapose different graphics and texts. New computer imagery in three dimensions packs even more elements onto a screen. You can, for example, study the complex structure of any system or hierarchy by rotating one item of interest into the foreground and shifting other items into the background.

COMMUNICATING VISUALLY

Think visually. *Communicate* visually. The user of the diagram in Figure 6–1 does both. Often, you'll achieve your goal in writing most effectively not by writing, in sentences and paragraphs, but by expressing your information in visual form.

As you compose a document or presentation, use visuals and color to

1. Consolidate and record information.
2. Summarize and reinforce a message.
3. Unify a document or a series of documents.
4. Provide dramatic impact.
5. Reduce the amount of text.
6. Cross language barriers.

VISUALIZING THE LAW

Bertram Wolfson
Erskine, Wolfson, and Gibbon, P.C.

As a lawyer, I have difficulty dealing with busy executives when the topics we are discussing are emotional (such as death and dying) and complicated (such as estate planning and taxes). To serve clients properly, I need to elicit the right information from them and then aid them in understanding the issues without overwhelming them with such detail and complexity that they become lost in, and frustrated by, the process. I help clients to define their goals and creatively dream with them to explore the many alternatives for accomplishing those goals; I help them understand the advantages and disadvantages of the solutions we conceive; and then I guide them to choosing the best alternative.

For example, assume that Les Busy is president of a large public corporation. He is married to Maura Busy and has a daughter, Bea, and ten grandchildren. Les's total assets are worth $5 million. His goals are to take care of his wife, his daughter, and his grandchildren, now and in the future, and at the same time to minimize death taxes. The Internal Revenue Code, with which we must comply, provides that (1) Les and Maura each have a tax credit at their death equivalent to $600,000, which will not be taxed; (2) funds given to Maura or held in trust for Maura are eligible for the "marital deduction" and will not be taxed on Les's death; (3) Les and Maura each may claim a generation-skipping exemption of $1 million, which may be held in trust and used for Maura's benefit during her lifetime and which, on her death, will pass on to the grandchildren, tax-free.

I have found that the best way to maximize communication with a client is to use a *diagram,* especially when the topics we are discussing are complex. This example, for instance, involves thirteen people, spans three generations, and involves complex legal, as well as very personal and emotional, decisions. The diagram (see Figure 6–1) allows the clients to see the issues clearly; thus, it frees their minds to focus on the important decisions to be made during the planning process. The diagram serves four main purposes.

First, the flowchart format allows me to present legal and tax concepts, and their implications, in a manageable way. Les and Maura can participate with me in drafting a rough version of the diagram on a large sheet of paper and in making changes and additions as we review alternatives and the way the alternatives relate to one another. At the end of the meeting, Les and Maura can look at the rough diagram and, having been through the process of creating the diagram, see and understand what happens on Les's death, on Maura's death, and on Bea's death. As we discuss alternatives, the diagram is revised over and over again until the plan meets Les and Maura's approval.

Second, my staff uses the diagram to draft the legal instruments (wills and trusts) that will embody Les and Maura's estate plan. The diagram reduces the time I must spend explaining how to draft the documents and also serves as a simple blueprint that the drafter can follow while creating the documents; thus, it reduces drafting errors.

(Continued on page 100)

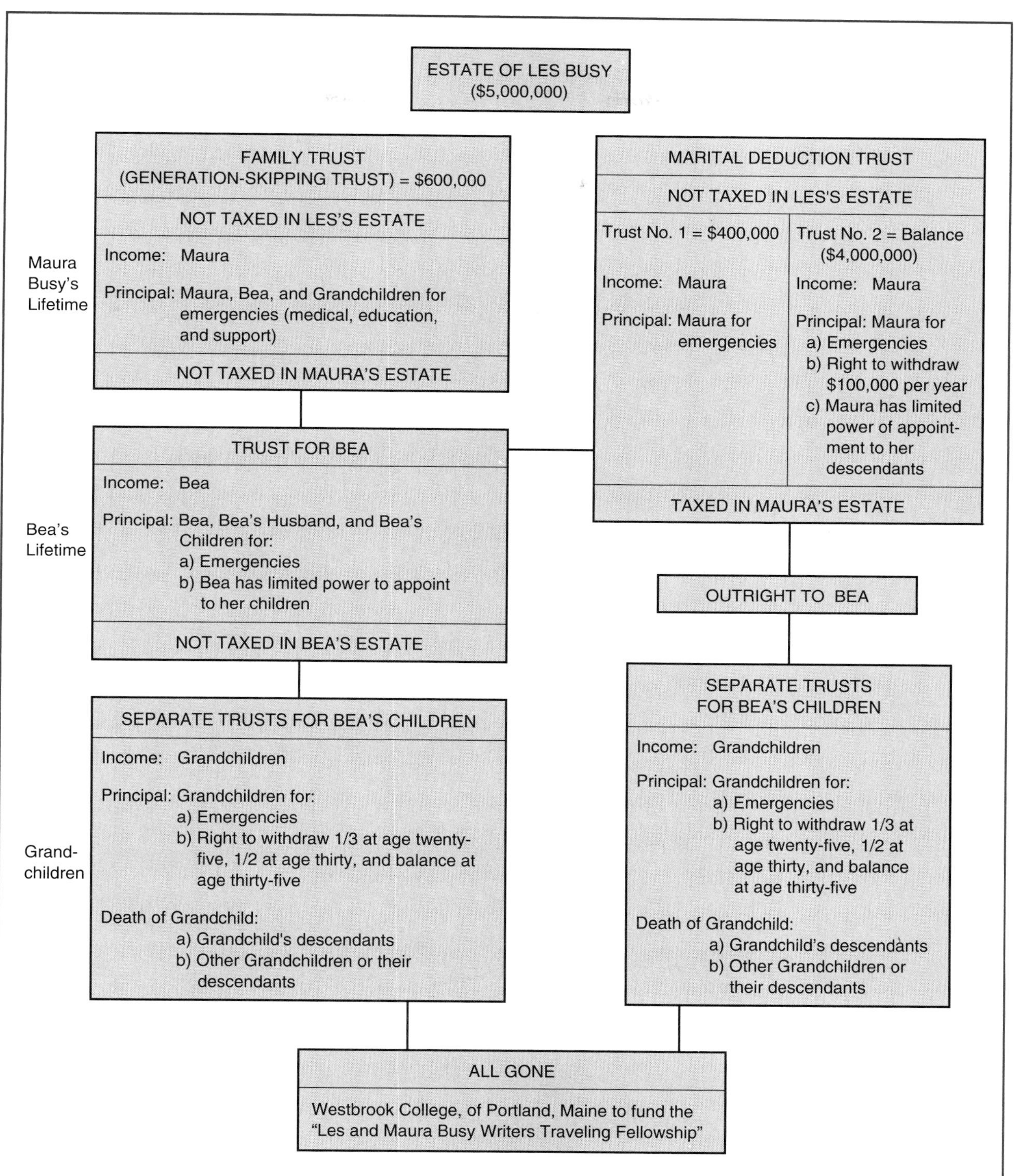

FIGURE 6–1.
A flowchart that frames and documents an analytical discussion.

Third, the rough, handwritten diagram is converted to a computer-generated form, and that version is sent to Les and Maura with drafts of their wills and trusts for their review. It serves as a clear, concise road map to help them understand the lengthy and complicated legal documents.

Fourth, once Les and Maura have approved the drafts of their wills and trusts and have signed the final versions, a copy of the diagram is attached to their signed wills. If, in the future, they wish to review their estate plan or to explain the plan to Bea or her children, or to a financial or other adviser, the diagram will refresh Les and Maura's memories about the contents of the documents and will aid a third party in understanding their complete estate plan.

Visuals in general and color visuals in particular may be expensive and time-consuming to produce. Color may be even more expensive to reproduce.[1] Overused, visual devices may also overwhelm the reader and overwhelm the information. In addition, color sends signals of its own that may confuse and distract, especially on a computer screen. But there are times when only visuals will do, as you saw in Figure 6–1. Here are guidelines for such times.

Consolidating and Recording Information

Use visuals to consolidate and record information. Visuals convey data at high density and in multiple dimensions—greater density and more dimensions than text. Box scores in newspapers record wins, losses, ties, league standing, and other information for sports teams. Even more elaborate score sheets enable team managers and scorers to record the critical events and features of the game. The visual form prompts the user to record certain kinds of information in certain places and provides rapid accessibility to that information for readers who know the code.

People who have to deal with vast quantities of information develop such forms for computer analysis. Figure 6–2, for example, shows you a form that schedulers at USAir developed to display the routings of aircraft.

Summarizing and Reinforcing a Message

Use visuals to summarize the details of interest to a particular reader and to reinforce a message. The Busy family chart in Figure 6–1 summarizes their estate. Sometimes, you need to use a different visual to summarize from

[1] The materials in this chapter were derived in part from A. J. MacGregor, *Graphics Simplified* (Toronto: University of Toronto Press, 1979). See also *The Color Book: Eight Basic Guidelines for Using Color in Business Communications* (Miamisburg, OH: Seiko Mead Company, 1989); Edward Tufte, *Envisioning Information* (Cheshire, CT: Graphics Press, 1990); and L. G. Thorell and W. J. Smith, *Using Computer Color Effectively,* Hewlett-Packard (Englewood Cliffs, NJ: Prentice-Hall, 1990).

```
COPYRIGHT 1990 USAIR          USAIR BOEING 727-200(LONG RANGE) EQUIPMENT ROUTING GUIDE                PAGE   1
                                              FINAL SCHEDULE                              EFFECTIVE DATE 09/05/90
                                              THURSDAY ONLY                                   ISSUE DATE 10/25/90

  GMT 10   11   12   13   14   15   16   17   18   19   20   21   22   23    0    1    2    3    4    5    6    7    8    9   10
  PDT  3    4    5    6    7    8    9   10   11   12   13   14   15   16   17   18   19   20   21   22   23    0    1    2    3
  EDT  6    7    8    9   10   11   12   13   14   15   16   17   18   19   20   21   22   23    0    1    2    3    4    5    6
         |   :    :    :    :    :    :    :    :    :    :    :    :    :    :    :    :    :    :    :    :    :    :    :    :
         |  GSO      CLT                 DEN                 PIT        EWR        ORF       EWR
01 GSO   |    ----------1093----------  -----------1520-----------   -1778--   --343--                                      |EWR
         |   :  2507   55    :    :   :22   00   :    :   00   45   02   50   02   50   02   :    :    :    :    :    :    :
         | EWR       BWI              NAS                 BWI       PVD             PIT     CLE
02 EWR   |    ---------1801----------       ----------1016----------    --------97-------                                   |CLE
         |   :05   03   55    :    : 30 :  30:   :   56   00   10   00   : 32 : 20 08   :    :    :    :    :    :    :
         | CLE      PIT       BWI          BDA               BWI      PIT        DCA      BDL
03 CLE   |    -------------446-------------    ---------451---------   ---99-  -1250--                                      |BDL
         |   :10 51   45  43:  30:    : 35 :  30:   :  41:  30: 35 : 20 :15  59   05   :    :    :    :    :    :    :
         |BDL       PHL              SJU                        PHL      BOS      PHL
04 BDL   |   ------------780-------------    --------------772-------------   --373--                                       |PHL
         |  50   02   50   :    :   : 25 : 20 :    :    :   55    00   11   55   11   :    :    :    :    :    :    :
         |    PHL        BOS        BWI                  DEN                 CLT     MYR
05 PHL   |    -1557--   ---------------683---------------    -----------786-----------                                      |MYR
         |   :   00   11   00   :23  : 15 :    :    :   :15  :05  :    :   00   00   57   :    :    :    :    :    :    :
         MYR    CLT       LGA       BWI            MIA      TPA           CLT     ORF
06 MYR   |  ------1019-------    ---------662---------    -----------1856-----------                                        |ORF
         |  30:16   55   :  37:  25: 27 :05  :    : 36 :  40 33 :10  :  46:   40  40:   :    :    :    :    :    :    :
         | ORF     LGA       BUF        LGA         CLT       MCO             PHL     PVD
07 ORF   |   -------482-------   -------------1039-------------    ----------276---------                                   |PVD
         |   00   :13   55   05   55   00   50   : 33 : 20 :  44:   40    :   06   50  50   :    :    :    :    :    :    :
         |   PVD        PIT          DEN                    CLT        ATL        PIT     AVP
08 PVD   |     -----------1402------------   -----1094------   --586--  --------502-------                                  |AVP
         |   :   40   :15  55   :    :   00   50   :    :  42:  35:  37: 20 :   55   45  39:   :    :    :    :    :    :
         |     AVP       PIT        BWI                 SJU                  BWI      PIT
09 AVP   |    --687-   -------------1555-------------    ------------1554------------                                       |PIT
         |   :   :05   09   : 20 :20  :10  :    :    : 48:   45   :    :   :23   00   02   :    :    :    :    :    :    :
         | PIT      PHL          BDA              PHL      BDL          PHL           MIA
10 PIT   |  --550-   ----551----   -----------770----------   ----------1674----------                                      |MIA
         |   50  52   :10   :   10   :10   :   :14  : 20 :15  : 15 :14  :05  :    :  44:   :    :    :    :    :    :
         MIA          CLT      IND       CLT       MIA             CLT        BOS
11 MIA   |  ---------1050---------  --------1720---------   -----------1447-----------                                      |BOS
         |  30:   :23  :05  :  38: 20 : 36 :  25:   :16  :  35:   : 28 :  30:   : 33 :   :    :    :    :    :    :
         |  BOS              CLT            SJU                       CLT       BDL
12 BOS   |    ---------------1041----------------   ---------------1047----------------                                     |BDL
         |   :10  :    :14  : 15 :    :    : 44:   50   :    :   :13  :  35:   :24  :    :    :    :    :    :    :
         |  BDL          CLT             MIA              PIT      LGA        ROC
13 BDL   |    ---------1055-----------   ------------288-----------   --582--                                                |ROC
         |   :  30:   :18  :10  :   58   :05  :    :  48:   55   11   59   09   :    :    :    :    :    :    :    :
         | ROC     LGA            BDA               LGA      ROC      BOS          CLT     FAY
14 ROC   |   --------1200--------   ---------557---------   -1662-  --------187--------                                     |FAY
         |   00   00   35:   :  40:   40   :   55   40  45:  25: 29 : 15 :   :15  :10 56   :    :    :    :    :    :    :
         FAY    CLT            MSP               CLT           LGA            CLT    GSO
15 FAY   |  --------1547---------   -----714----   --1102---   ----760----  -777-                                           |GSO
         |  2509   50   :   :15  : 20 :   : 34 : 20 :   59    00   :   53  35:15   :    :    :    :    :    :    :    :
         |
  EDT  6    7    8    9   10   11   12   13   14   15   16   17   18   19   20   21   22   23    0    1    2    3    4    5    6
  PDT  3    4    5    6    7    8    9   10   11   12   13   14   15   16   17   18   19   20   21   22   23    0    1    2    3
  GMT 10   11   12   13   14   15   16   17   18   19   20   21   22   23    0    1    2    3    4    5    6    7    8    9   10
```

FIGURE 6–2.
Visual density. This routing guide takes the perspective of the entire USAir system and traces the movement of aircraft across time (read from left to right: GMT is Greenwich Mean Time, the standard; PDT is Pacific Daylight Time; and EDT is Eastern Daylight Time). The three-letter abbreviations are airport codes (GSO, for example, is Greensboro, North Carolina); the abbreviations at the left give the origination airport of the plane; the ones at the right, its termination. Flight numbers are included within the lines of dashes. The form is computer-generated and is one page of a many-page printout. *(Courtesy of USAir, Inc.)*

CITY TIMETABLE

Effective November 1, 1990
Reservations: 1-800-428-4322

Portland, ME

Let USAir Show You Florida, The Bahamas, and Puerto Rico.

© 1990 USAir, Inc. Includes USAir Express flights.

PORTLAND, ME

Meal	Leave	Arrive	Flight No.	Freq.	Stops
To Akron/Canton, OH					
B	7 23a	10 40a	39/E3001		PIT
L/S	12 10p	3 40p	793/E3009		PIT
S	3 25p	8 11p	702/E3011	X6	PIT
From Akron/Canton, OH					
S/	6 50a	10 26a	E3006/720		PIT
L/S	12 05p	2 47p	E3001/349		PIT
	8 25p	11 10p	E3011/466	X6	PIT
To Albany/Schenectady/Troy, NY					
	6 00a	9 45a	E4900/E4912	X67	BOS
	1 05p	3 30p	E4903/E4854	X6	BOS
	4 10p	6 55p	E4904/E4817	X6	BOS
From Albany/Schenectady/Troy, NY					
	7 45a	10 10a	E4911/E4901	X67	BOS
	11 00a	12 55p	E4914/E4902	X67	BOS
	5 00p	9 05p	E4816/E4905	X6	BOS
To Albuquerque, NM					
BB	7 23a	12 15p	39/55		PIT
SD	3 25p	7 51p	702/597		PIT
From Albuquerque, NM					
D	3 40p	11 10p	366/466		PIT
To Allentown/Bethlehem/Easton, PA					
S	6 35a	9 37a	1729/E3540	X67	PHL
S	6 35a	11 44a	1729/E3623		PHL
	11 15a	2 18p	395/E3684	X6	PHL
	6 45p	10 38p	E4905/E3744	X6	BOS
	7 45p	10 50p	137/E3690	X6	PHL
From Allentown/Bethlehem/Easton, PA					
	7 00a	10 10a	E3689/E4901	X67	BOS
S/	7 35a	11 28a	E3764/358	X7	PHL
S/	9 10a	11 28a	E3676/358	7	PHL
S	4 35p	7 05p	E3685/184	X6	PHL
	5 30p	10 02p	E3739/541	X6	PHL
To Altoona, PA					
B	7 23a	10 55a	39/E3403		PIT
L/S	12 10p	3 40p	793/E3425		PIT
S	3 25p	8 00p	702/E3438	X6	PIT
From Altoona, PA					
S/	6 40a	10 26a	E3432/720	X67	PIT
L/S	11 50a	2 47p	E3404/349		PIT
	6 15p	11 10p	E3438/466		PIT
	8 20p	11 10p	E3442/466	X6	PIT
To Atlanta, GA					
SB	6 35a	11 04a	1729/667		PHL
D	11 15a	5 36p	395/1623		PHL
SD	3 25p	7 42p	702/506		PIT
From Atlanta, GA					
B	6 30a	10 26a	490/720		PIT
B	7 00a	11 28a	258/358		PHL
L	12 40p	6 05p	1264/E4904	X6	BOS
D	6 20p	10 02p	1787/541	X6	PHL
D	7 25p	11 10p	2350/466	7	PIT
D	7 25p	11 10p	800/466	X7	PIT
To Atlantic City, NJ					
S	6 35a	9 26a	1729/E3775	X7	PHL
S	6 35a	11 25a	1729/E3711		PHL
	11 15a	2 05p	395/E3618	7	PHL
	11 15a	2 16p	395/E3767	X7	PHL
	7 45p	10 47p	137/E3709	X6	PHL
From Atlantic City, NJ					
S/	7 10a	11 28a	E3691/358	X7	PHL
S	1 50p	7 05p	E3788/184	X7	PHL
S	2 15p	7 05p	E3618/184	7	PHL
	5 20p	10 02p	E3700/541	X6	PHL
To Austin, TX					
SB	6 35a	12 52p	1729/567		PHL
SD	3 25p	11 49p	702/355		PIT
From Austin, TX					
BS	7 30a	2 47p	821/349		PIT
D	2 40p	10 02p	751/541		PHL
To Baltimore, MD					
S	6 35a	9 40a	1729/E3725	X7	PHL
B	7 23a	11 16a	39/1555		PIT
S/	8 10a	11 22a	E4901/384	X7	BOS
	11 15a	2 26p	395/E3635		PHL
L/S	12 10p	3 32p	793/715		PIT
	1 05p	4 27p	E4903/505		BOS
S	3 25p	6 59p	702/136		PIT
S	4 10p	7 03p	E4904/2319	7	BOS
S	4 10p	7 03p	E4904/1911	X67	BOS
	6 45p	10 07p	E4905/680	X6	BOS
	7 45p	10 40p	137/E4400	X6	PHL
From Baltimore, MD					
S/	7 00a	10 26a	351/720		PIT
S	7 05a	10 10a	1049/E4901	X7	BOS
S/	8 15a	11 28a	E3745/358	X7	PHL
S/	10 10a	12 55p	1476/E4902		BOS
Continued next column					
***From Baltimore, MD** (Cont.)*					
L/S	10 30a	2 47p	261/349		PIT
S	1 10p	4 00p	1762/E4903	X67	BOS
S	1 10p	6 05p	1762/E4904	X6	BOS
S	4 00p	7 05p	E3626/184		PHL
	5 20p	9 05p	140/E4905	X6	BOS
	6 30p	11 10p	110/466		PIT
To Bermuda					
SB	6 35a	12 15p	1729/551		PHL
From Bermuda					
LS	1 10p	7 05p	770/184		PHL
L	2 30p	11 10p	451/466		PIT
To Binghamton/Endicott/ Johnson City, NY					
S	6 35a	11 20a	1729/E3476		PHL
	11 15a	3 35p	395/E3598	6	PHL
	11 15a	4 55p	395/E3463		PHL
	7 45p	10 56p	137/E3478	X6	PHL
From Binghamton/Endicott/ Johnson City, NY					
S/	7 00a	11 28a	E3458/358		PHL
S	2 30p	7 05p	E3510/184	X6	PHL
	5 25p	10 02p	E3463/541		PHL
	7 05p	10 02p	E3431/541	X6	PHL
To Birmingham, AL					
L/S	12 10p	6 29p	793/853	X6	PIT
SS	4 10p	8 41p	E4904/1911	X67	BOS
From Birmingham, AL					
Consult USAir Ticket or Reservations Office.					
To Boston, MA					
	6 00a	6 35a	E4900	X7	0
	8 10a	8 50a	E4901	X7	0
	10 45a	11 25a	E4902	X67	0
	1 05p	1 45p	E4903		0
	4 10p	4 50p	E4904	X6	0
	6 45p	7 25p	E4905	X6	0
From Boston, MA					
	7 15a	7 55a	E4900	X7	0
	9 30a	10 10a	E4901	X7	0
	12 15p	12 55p	E4902		0
	3 20p	4 00p	E4903	X67	0
	5 25p	6 05p	E4904	X6	0
	8 25p	9 05p	E4905	X6	0
To Bradford/Warren, PA/Olean, NY					
B	7 23a	10 40a	39/E3021		PIT
L/S	12 10p	5 15p	793/E3028	6	PIT
L/S	12 10p	5 20p	793/E3025	X6	PIT
S	3 25p	7 40p	702/E3083	X6	PIT
From Bradford/Warren, PA/Olean, NY					
S/	7 15a	10 26a	E3020/720		PIT
L/S	11 15a	2 47p	E3021/349		PIT
	7 55p	11 10p	E3083/466	X6	PIT
To Buffalo/Niagara Falls, NY					
S	6 00a	8 28a	E4900/689	X7	BOS
S	6 35a	11 43a	1729/47		PHL
S	8 10a	2 20p	E4901/552	X7	BOS
S	10 45a	2 20p	E4902/552	X67	BOS
	11 15a	4 37p	395/68	X6	PHL
	11 15a	4 42p	395/935	6	PHL
S	4 10p	7 19p	E4904/1671	X6	BOS
From Buffalo/Niagara Falls, NY					
S	6 50a	11 28a	209/358		PHL
S	7 10a	10 10a	1205/E4901	X7	BOS
S	7 10a	12 55p	1205/E4902		BOS
S/	10 30a	12 55p	280/E4902	X7	BOS
S	11 10a	4 00p	348/E4903	X67	BOS
S	11 10a	6 05p	348/E4904	X6	BOS
	5 20p	10 02p	695/541		PHL
S	6 45p	9 05p	1672/E4905	X6	BOS
To Bullhead City, AZ/Laughlin, NV					
BB	7 23a	3 55p	39/E3830	X67	SAN
From Bullhead City, AZ/Laughlin, NV					
Consult USAir Ticket or Reservations Office.					
To Burbank, CA					
Consult USAir Ticket or Reservations Office.					
From Burbank, CA					
SL	10 40a	10 02p	431/541		PHL
To Burlington, VT					
	6 00a	8 45a	E4900/E4811	X7	BOS
	8 10a	12 30p	E4901/E4862	X67	BOS
	10 45a	1 45p	E4902/E4914	X67	BOS
	1 05p	3 10p	E4903/E4825		BOS
	6 45p	9 25p	E4905/E4856	X6	BOS

FIGURE 6–3.
A summary visual. A pocket schedule for passengers concerning the flights to and from one city. *(Courtesy of USAir, Inc.)*

the one you use to record. While the scheduling manager of USAir has systemwide concerns about aircraft routings and connections, the USAir *customer* may want to zero in on the flights to and from one airport, so USAir publishes such a summary guide in table form for ease of reference and remembering (see Figure 6–3).

Where production technology permits, use color to further reinforce a message. If you are publishing a brochure about your company's environmental policy, consider using green paper to underline the message. Reinforce a warning by printing it in red ink or on a red background.

Unifying the Document

Use visuals—and color—to unify a presentation. Consider a series of visuals. To emphasize how the visuals compare with one another, make sure they are consistent in style, size, scale, color, typeface, and the like. Use color coding to place information in categories or to group similar items that are separated on the screen or in a document. Financial information in an annual report, for example, often appears on paper of a different color and texture from the rest of the report for ease of locating and relocating the data.

Corporate publications use the organization's logo to unify their appearance. A logo is a visual signature. Figure 6–4 shows the logo for a historic lodge (and ski area) in Oregon. Such logos reflect an organization's culture and desired image and appear on napkins and walls as well as documents.

Providing Dramatic Impact

Use visuals for their dramatic impact. A well designed visual presentation attracts attention and provides the reader with pleasure in reading. Marketers often develop visual "hooks" for presentations. A college in the mountains, for example, uses photographs of its setting to persuade high school seniors to apply.

As you learned in Chapter 5, your *voice* in words and sentences establishes credibility, entices the reader into your discussion, and fosters understanding and action. Your visual style should achieve the same results. Figure 6–5 shows a notice circulated to students concerning a university writing center. The text appears in paragraph form, in the third person ("the student"). It *describes* the center and its services but buries its appeal to students to visit. Printing the text in all capital letters makes it seem bureaucratic and intimidating.

FIGURE 6–4.
A logo (Timberline Ski Area, Timberline Lodge, Oregon 97028). The logo for this lodge, built by the Works Progress Administration in 1937, is a craftsperson's adaptation of an Indian motif. The logo is seen in a weathervane on top of the lodge. *(Used by permission, Timberline Lodge.)*

UNIVERSITY WRITING CENTER

THE WRITING CENTER IS OPEN FROM 9:00 A.M. TO 12:00 NOON AND FROM 1:00 TO 5:00 P.M., MONDAY THROUGH FRIDAY, AND FROM 6:00 TO 9:00 P.M., MONDAY THROUGH THURSDAY. IT IS LOCATED IN 015 MEMORIAL HALL. THE PHONE NUMBER IS 451-1168.

THE SERVICES ARE AVAILABLE TO ANY UNIVERSITY STUDENT, PART-TIME OR FULL-TIME, GRADUATE OR UNDERGRADUATE. THE MAIN PURPOSE OF THE CENTER IS TO HELP STUDENTS TO INCREASE THEIR WRITING SKILLS IN AREAS SUCH AS GRAMMAR, SPELLING, PUNCTUATION, DICTION, WRITTEN PRESENTATION, AND ORGANIZATION OF THOUGHTS. IT WORKS WITH STUDENTS ON PAPERS FOR ANY UNIVERSITY COURSE. INSTRUCTION IS OFFERED ON AN INDIVIDUAL BASIS AND IS DESIGNED TO DEAL WITH THE STUDENT'S PARTICULAR WRITING PROBLEMS. ONCE THESE PROBLEMS ARE DIAGNOSED, AN INDIVIDUALIZED, FLEXIBLE WRITING PROGRAM IS DESIGNED FOR THE STUDENT AND IS IMPLEMENTED AROUND THE STUDENT'S ACADEMIC SCHEDULE. APPOINTMENTS ARE DESIRABLE BUT NOT NECESSARY. THE WRITING CENTER'S SERVICES ARE FREE. THE WRITING CENTER WILL NOT WRITE PAPERS FOR STUDENTS, CHECK THE CONTENTS OF PAPERS, EDIT PAPERS, OR PROOFREAD.

FIGURE 6–5.
Original notice to students concerning the University Writing Center.

FIGURE 6–6.
Redesigned Writing Center notice. *(Courtesy of Kim Schnitzer and Diane Thena.)*

UNIVERSITY WRITING CENTER

WOULD YOU LIKE HELP WITH YOUR WRITING?

ARE YOU HAVING TROUBLE WITH:

- GRAMMAR?
- ORGANIZATION?
- PUNCTUATION?
- SPELLING?
- WORD CHOICE?

If you are enrolled in a university course, you can receive individualized instruction tailored to your needs at the University Writing Center.

COST:	FREE	
LOCATION:	015 Memorial Hall	
HOURS:	Monday through Friday	9 am—12 pm 1 pm—5 pm
	Monday through Thursday	6 pm—9 pm
APPOINTMENTS:	recommended, but limited walk-in service is available	
PHONE:	451-1168	

We cannot write your papers for you, but we can show you how to make your writing more effective.

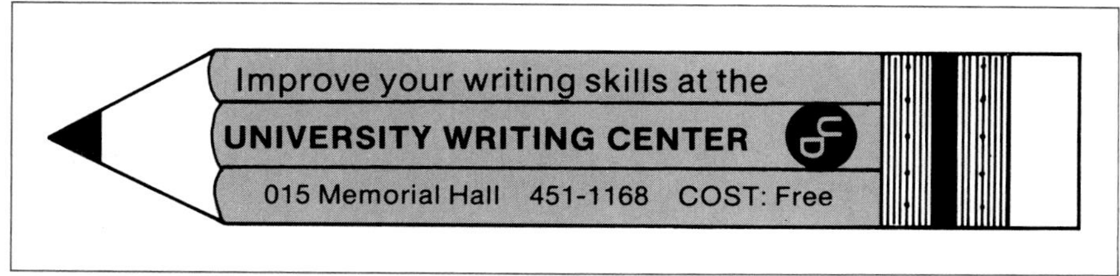

FIGURE 6–7.
University Writing Center bookmark.

In Figure 6–6, you see how two students redesigned the announcement for dramatic impact. The revised notice stresses benefits. Key terms are listed. The student is addressed directly in the opening question. The drawing of the hand and the pencil tugs at the reader's attention and establishes a motif for the writing center that is carried through in a bookmark (in Figure 6–7), reproduced in bright yellow and available in the university bookstore.

Reducing Text

Stretches of text in a draft can often be condensed or made more concrete in a visual:

TEXT

During the visit, I met with representatives of three companies: IBM, DEC (Digital Equipment Corporation), and Zenith. Peter Smith, who represents IBM in the metropolitan region, gave me an estimate of $5,000 per unit for the system. He said a yearly maintenance contract with them would run us about $600. The guy from Zenith (his name is Jeffrey Bowman) quoted me $4,500 per unit for a similar system, and said the maintenance contract with his company would run us $550. I also talked with Kitsel Outlaw of DEC, who gave an estimate of $4,999 per unit. Her estimate of the maintenance contract per year was $550, the same as the Zenith one.

VISUAL

Company	Representative	Per unit cost (in dollars)	Yearly maintenance contract (in dollars)
DEC	Kitsel Outlaw	4999	550
IBM	Peter Smith	5000	600
Zenith	Jeffrey Bowman	4500	550

The visual form—an informal table that might appear as the last part of a sentence—provides the reader with faster access to the information.

Crossing Language Barriers

Visuals are, even more than English, an international language of business. An upward line of profits or return on investment persuades investors across language barriers. Moreover, you can use color, for example, to code information across languages, as you see in "*FYI:* Olympic Colors."

One caution, however, in using color internationally. The connotations of color differ across cultures. An American bride may wear a white gown. A Chinese bride wears red. To an American, blue connotes masculinity; to a Japanese, it may represent villainy; to an Egyptian, virtue and faith.

SELECTING THE APPROPRIATE VISUAL FORM

Your options for communicating visually fall into two broad categories: *tables* or *figures*. A *table* is any arrangement of related information (words or num-

OLYMPIC COLORS

John R. Farquharson
President, ARASERVE

Providing dining services for 10,000 Olympic athletes is a major undertaking. Addressing the unique nutritional and caloric needs of these athletes complicates the mission even more. Add to that mix an environment in which all the languages of the world are spoken, and you have a real communications challenge.

This is exactly what ARASERVE addresses when we serve meals for the Olympic Games. We resolved this entire communications issue at the Seoul, Korea, Olympics by providing a 24-hour-a-day dining service—open to the athletes for self-service.

We communicated all of our offerings visually. First, the items were openly and attractively displayed—beverages, cereals, vast numbers of hot entrees, fruits and vegetables from around the world, breads, and desserts.

Second, caloric and nutritional values were color-coded. We gave each team's trainer a chart listing those values and the appropriate color coding for all options and a bunch of colored dot stickers. The trainer gave each athlete an individualized card with the appropriate stickers on it. The athlete then selected items from that color group.

A 90-pound gymnast might have a card with one green, one red, and one blue sticker, meaning that one portion selected from each of those categories would satisfy her needs. A 300-pound weight lifter might have three greens, four reds, two blues, and two yellows to complete his diet.

Well, it worked. We got awards and praise.

The most popular item served to athletes from around the world at the 1988 Olympic games? The good old American hamburger. The athletes selected thousands of them.

bers) in columns and rows. The term *figure* refers to any other visual form: graphs, charts, maps, drawings, and photographs.

Depending on your purpose, you may display information in one of several visual forms. Here's an example. The U.S. Bureau of the Census notes the following child-care arrangements used by employed parents:

Another's home	40.2%
Child's home	30.6%
Group center	14.8%
At work	9.1%
Other	5.3%

How can you present this information? Consider a pie chart, since you're dealing with percentages, especially if you have a computer program that facilitates pie making (see Figure 6–8). For this chart, as for Figure 6–9, the author entered the pertinent data into a computer program, which then drew the charts automatically.

If you are a social worker writing to a public agency to recommend stringent supervision of people who take in others' children, you may want to emphasize that 40.2 percent figure. Try a *bar chart* (Figure 6–9), the longest bar, of course, being that for "Another's home."

Both charts make the information dramatic, although they deemphasize the precise numbers. An internal corporate document would more likely present the information in a table. Additional columns might provide comparative percentages for other years to show a trend.

In general, complex information addressed to an audience of insiders—that is, people who share an organization's or a profession's code—appears

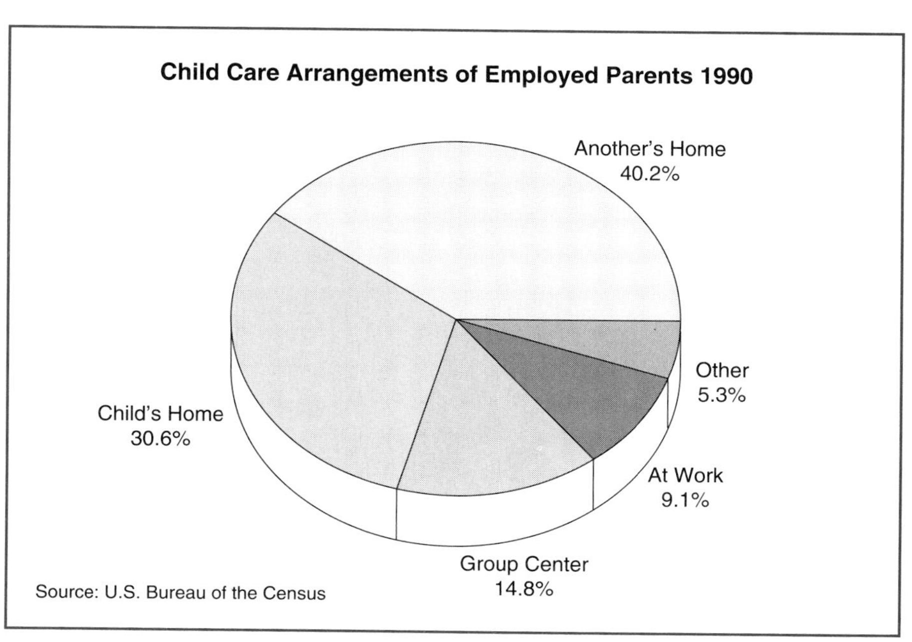

FIGURE 6–8.
Computer-generated pie chart. The pie is angled for a three-dimensional look. *(Courtesy of Rusty Ward and Joanne Drummond.)*

in tables or balance sheets, in line charts that plot equations, or in schedules like the one you saw in Figure 6–2. Financial reports, for example, often have little text—just enough to explain the pages of numbers. Most internal reports are in black and white.

In more broadly disseminated documents, you may motivate readers to understand your discussion with bar charts and pie charts, photographs, and drawings—preferably in bright colors. For insiders, you're likely to compose first with your visuals and to add words later that connect them. For external audiences, you may begin with a theme and a textual discussion and create visuals that reinforce the message and draw attention.

The following sections provide you with a brief overview of the vocabulary of visual forms.

Tables and Matrixes

Use *tables* to compare numbers, as in the financial statements of corporate annual reports (earnings, shareholders' equity, and the like), as well as other numerical information, like the populations of ten cities in 1980, 1985, 1990, and 1995. Tables can combine words and numbers, as in Figure 6–10. What are the advantages of tables? They

- Are produced easily in a typed text.
- Indicate precise data.
- Allow data to be readily compared at many levels.
- Aid researchers in identifying where information is missing because the intersection of a row (horizontal) and a column (vertical) is blank.

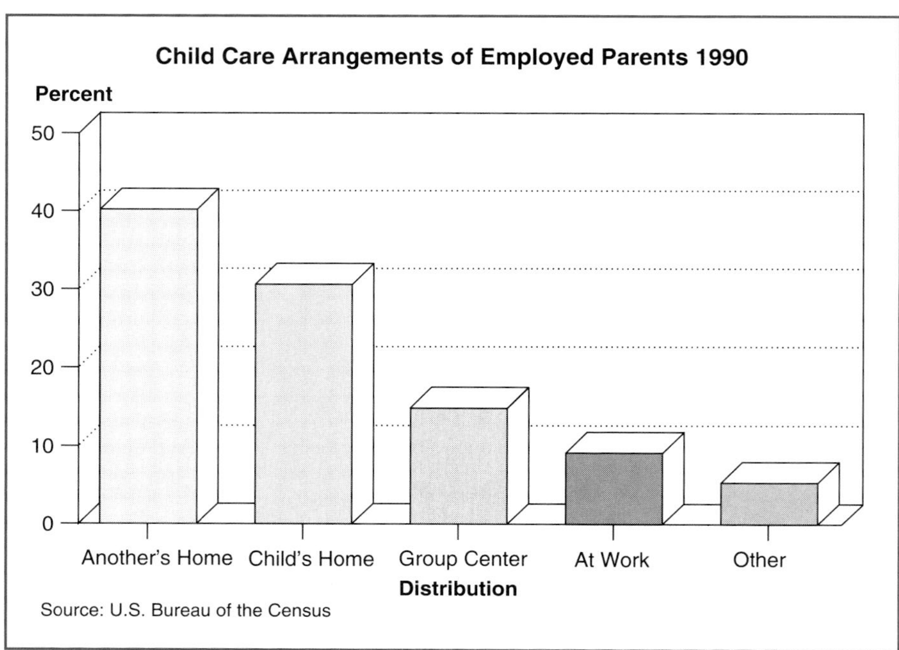

FIGURE 6–9. Computer-generated bar chart showing the same information as in Figure 6–8. *(Courtesy of Rusty Ward and Joanne Drummond.)*

SKI SALT LAKE ALPINE SKI AREA STATISTICS

	Alta 801-742-3333	Brighton 801-943-8309	Snowbird 801-742-2222	Solitude 801-534-1400	Deer Valley 801-649-1000	Nordic Valley 801-745-3511	Park City 801-649-8111	ParkWest 801-649-5400	Powder Mtn. 801-745-3771	Snowbasin 801-399-1135	Sundance 801-225-4107
Average Annual Snowfall	500"	430"	500"	410"	300"	300"	350"	300"	500"	400"	320"
Vertical Drop Serviced By Lift	2,050'	1,445'	3,100'	2,030'	2,200'	1000'	3,100'	2,200'	1,300'	2,400'	2,150'
Base Elevation Top Elevation	8,500 10,550	8,755 10,200	7,900 11,000	8,000 10,030	7,200 9,400	5,500 6,500	6,900 10,000	6,800 9,000	7,600 8,900	6,400 8,800	6,100 8,250
Lift Capacity/Hour	8,500	5,800	8,810	10,350	13,800	1,800	20,900	6,700	4,800	7,425	5,250
Lifts D= Double Chair T= Triple Chair Q= Quad Chair	8D	4D 1T	7D	4D 2T 1Q	1D 8T 1Q	2D	5D 5T 2Q	7D	2D 1T 3 tow	1D 4T	2D 2T
Gondola/Tram/DQ (Detachable Quad)	-	-	Tram	DQ	-	-	DQ & G	-	-	-	-
% Beginner Terrain	25%	26%	20%	20%	15%	30%	17%	22%	10%	20%	20%
% Intermediate	40%	44%	30%	50%	50%	50%	49%	30%	60%	50%	40%
% Advanced	35%	30%	50%	30%	35%	20%	34%	48%	30%	30%	40%
# Runs	39	45	45	60	45	14	83	50	33	39	39
Adult All-Day Lift Pass †	21.00	20.00	28.00* 35.00**	24.00	39.00	16.00	37.00	25.00	18.00	21.00	15.00
Weekend Price (Adult) † Holiday Price (Adult) †	same	same	same	same	same 42.00	same	same	same	same	same	22.00 22.00
Half-Day a.m. Lift Pass (Adult) †	16.00	15.00	22.00* 28.00**	-	-	12.00	-	15.00	15.00	-	12.00
Half-Day p.m. Lift Pass (Adult) †	16.00	15.00	22.00* 28.00**	18.00	29.00	12.00	25.00	15.00	15.00	17.00	16.00
Child All-Day Lift Pass †	-	10.00	15.00* 20.00**	15.00	25.00	8.00	18.00	15.00	13.00	15.00	13.00
Night Skiing †	-	8.00	-	-	-	10.00	8.00	-	8.50	-	-
Skiable Acres	1,750	425	1,900	1,000	725	85	2,200	840	1,600	1,800	400
Onsite Accommodations	X	X	X	-	X	-	X	X	X	-	X
Snowboards Allowed	-	X	X	-	-	X	-	X	X	X	X
Nursery/Child Care	X	X	X	-	X	-	X	X	-	-	X
Distance from Salt Lake Int. Airport	31 mi.	34 mi.	29 mi.	32 mi.	39 mi.	50 mi.	37 mi.	33 mi.	55 mi.	53 mi.	55 mi.
Distance From Salt Lake City	26 mi.	29 mi.	25 mi.	27 mi.	34 mi.	49 mi.	32 mi.	28 mi.	54 mi.	52 mi.	51 mi.
Ski Season	Mid-Nov-April	Mid-Nov-Late April	Nov. 17-Mid May	Mid Nov. Late April	Nov. 23-April 1	Dec.-April	Nov. 16-April 14	Early Dec.-April	Mid-Nov-May	Nov.-21-Early April	Mid. Dec.-April

X = Yes
\- = No
^ = Weekdays
† = Prices subject to change without prior notice

* = Chair lifts only
** = All area including tram
XP = By prior arrangement
Δ = Weekends
Note: 1990-91 ski season statistics

Salt Lake Convention & Visitors Bureau
180 South West Temple
Salt Lake City, Utah 84101-1493
(801) 521-2822/(800)541-4955
FAX (801) 355-9323

FIGURE 6–10.
A complex table. This table condenses abundant information about 11 ski areas near Salt Lake City, Utah. Each column provides numerical information about one area identified in the heading. Each row provides comparative data on one characteristic a skier would like to know about each area—like the average annual snowfall. The legend at the bottom defines symbols used in the table. *(Statistics provided by the Salt Lake Convention & Visitors Bureau.)*

The checklist provides guidelines for presenting data in tabular form:

CHECKLIST FOR TABLES

1. Place units of measurement in the title, not after each entry.
2. Arrange items in a logical order: alphabetical, geographical, quantitative, or chronological.
3. Place numbers in columns rather than rows for ease of comparison and carryover to an additional page. Rows are also limited by the width of the page.
4. Align the decimal points of all numbers in a column.
5. Place long tables (often used for reference) in an appendix.

A common variant of a table is a *matrix,* which plots two sets of data against each other, as in Figure 6–11. The rows indicate levels of membership; the columns indicate benefits (the dependent variables); a dot at the intersection indicates which benefits go with which levels of membership. This matrix is a marketing tool used to sell memberships in the zoo.

Line Graphs

Line graphs are more dramatic than tables. Use a graph to show a trend or a direction rather than actual amounts or separate units. You can compare the degree or rate of change in several variables over time and predict future changes by extending the line. You may draw a simple line across a grid, as in Figure 6–12, or fill in the curves in a surface or silhouette chart as you'll see later in Figure 6–19. The line shows direction vividly but does not have the precision of numbers. You can often convert a numerical table into a

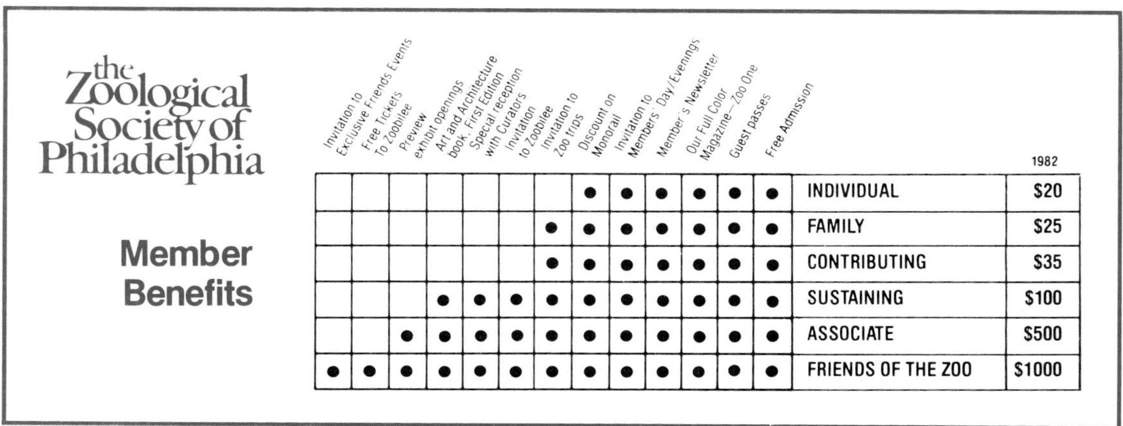

Invitation to Exclusive Friends Events	Free Tickets To Zoobilee	Preview exhibit openings	Art and Architecture book, First Edition	Special reception with Curators	Invitation to Zoobilee	Invitation to Zoo trips	Discount on Monorail	Invitation to Members' Day/Evenings	Member's Newsletter	Our Full Color Magazine—Zoo One	Guest passes	Free Admission		1982
							●	●	●	●	●	●	INDIVIDUAL	$20
						●	●	●	●	●	●	●	FAMILY	$25
						●	●	●	●	●	●	●	CONTRIBUTING	$35
			●	●	●	●	●	●	●	●	●	●	SUSTAINING	$100
		●	●	●	●	●	●	●	●	●	●	●	ASSOCIATE	$500
●	●	●	●	●	●	●	●	●	●	●	●	●	FRIENDS OF THE ZOO	$1000

FIGURE 6–11.
A matrix. *(Used by permission of the Marketing Department, The Zoological Society of Philadelphia.)*

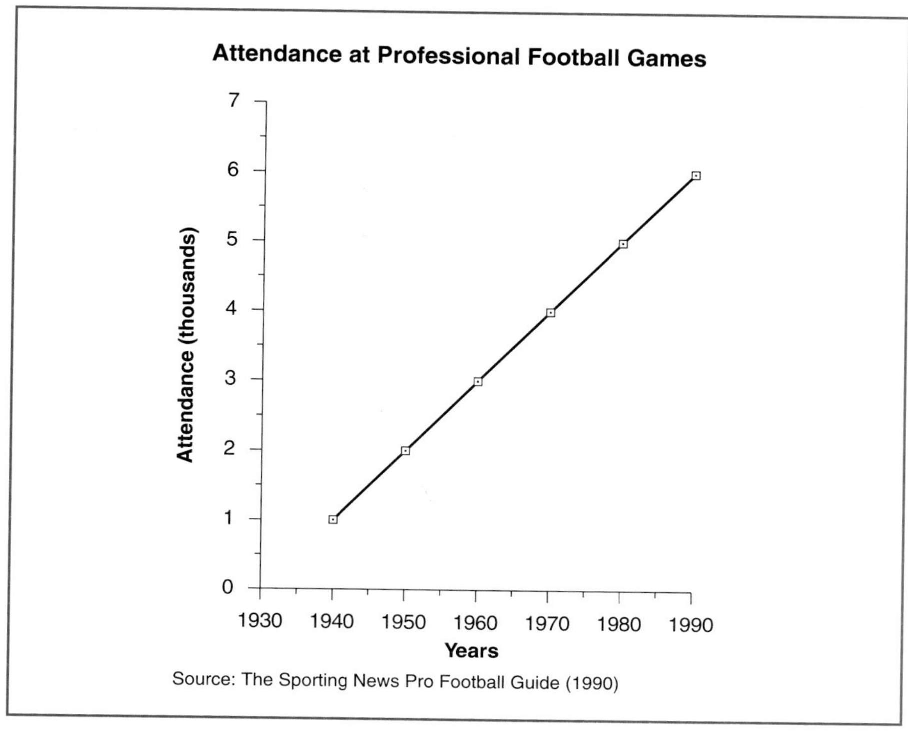

FIGURE 6–12.
A computer-generated line graph. The program that produced this graph labels the vertical axis sideways. Readability is enhanced, however, if all labels read in the same direction. *(Courtesy of Kate McDonald. Reprinted by permission of* The Sporting News.*)*

graph, but unless actual numbers are shown, it's hard to convert a graph into a table.

Use the checklist to help you generate clear line graphs:

CHECKLIST FOR LINE GRAPHS

1. Place the independent variable (often a measure of time) along the horizontal axis and the dependent variable on the vertical axis.
2. Label the vertical axis to the left to keep the area within the grid as free of text as possible.
3. Match the scale to the data and to the reader's ease—preferably in multiples of 2, 5, 10, and so on.
4. If you display several lines on one graph, provide labels to differentiate the lines.
5. To emphasize *each* line, consider using a series of graphs with the same scale.
6. In most cases, keep 0 in the scale. If you need to start the units of measurement on the vertical axis above zero (at, say, 100), then indicate that clearly with, for example, a break in the vertical line.
7. Whenever possible, avoid using a key. Instead, label the curves directly.
8. Keep the line width of each curve equal; distinguish the curves with different colors or with different patterns of dots or dashes. A curve that's wider than the others appears to be more important.

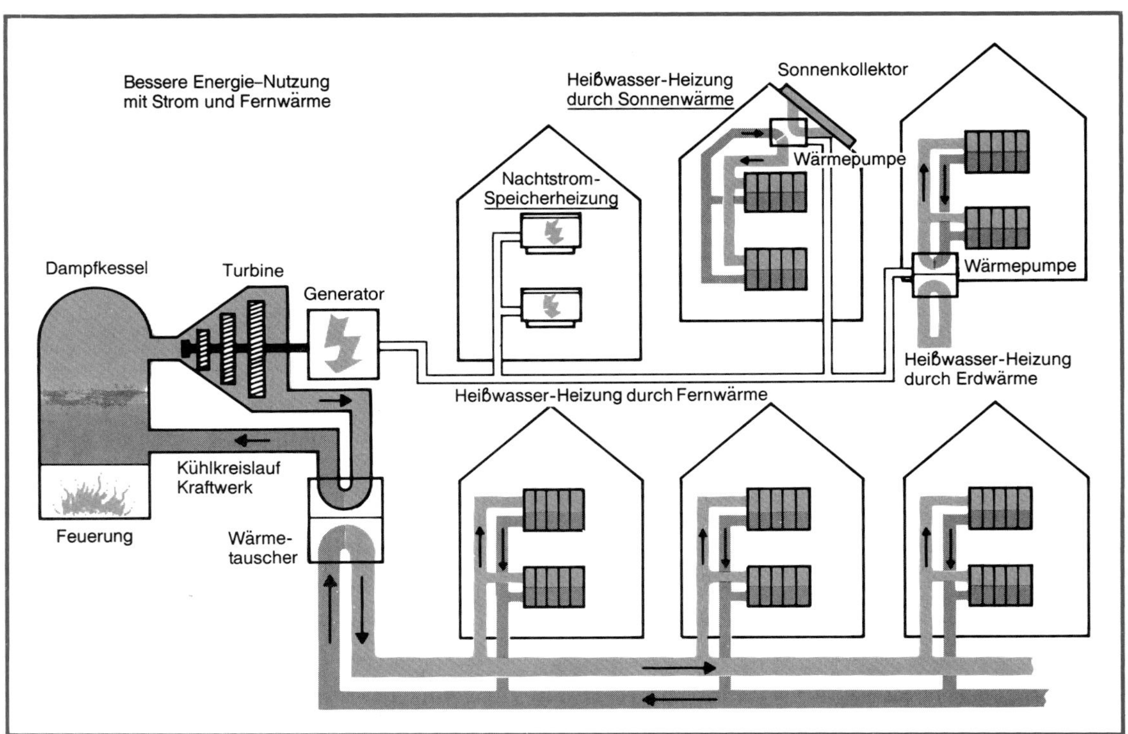

FIGURE 6–13.
A flowchart. Note that the representational system communicates even if the reader does not understand German. *(Courtesy of IZE, Frankfurt, Germany.)*

Organizational Charts and Flowcharts

As the name implies, *organizational charts* show the structure of an organization. The top manager or administrator is usually at the top of the chart. Equal functions read from left to right, subordinate ones from top to bottom. American companies often produce an elaborate series of charts to show an overall structure and the reporting lines within the units. The Xerox Corporation's chart, for example, fills an eighty-page book for just the top 650 positions.[2] The term *tall hierarchy* that you read in Chapter 2 reflects the image in the chart. Such elaboration in charts is common in the United States but less common abroad, especially in Asia. (See Figure 2–2.)

While organizational charts emphasize structure, *flowcharts* show sequence—the steps in a process or a series of activities over time. Symbols, either representational or abstract, are connected by arrows that indicate direction. Figure 6–13 uses representational symbols (houses, a rooftop solar

[2] Andrew Pollack, "Coming Soon: Data You Can Look Under and Walk Through," *The New York Times,* 14 October 1990, p. F9.

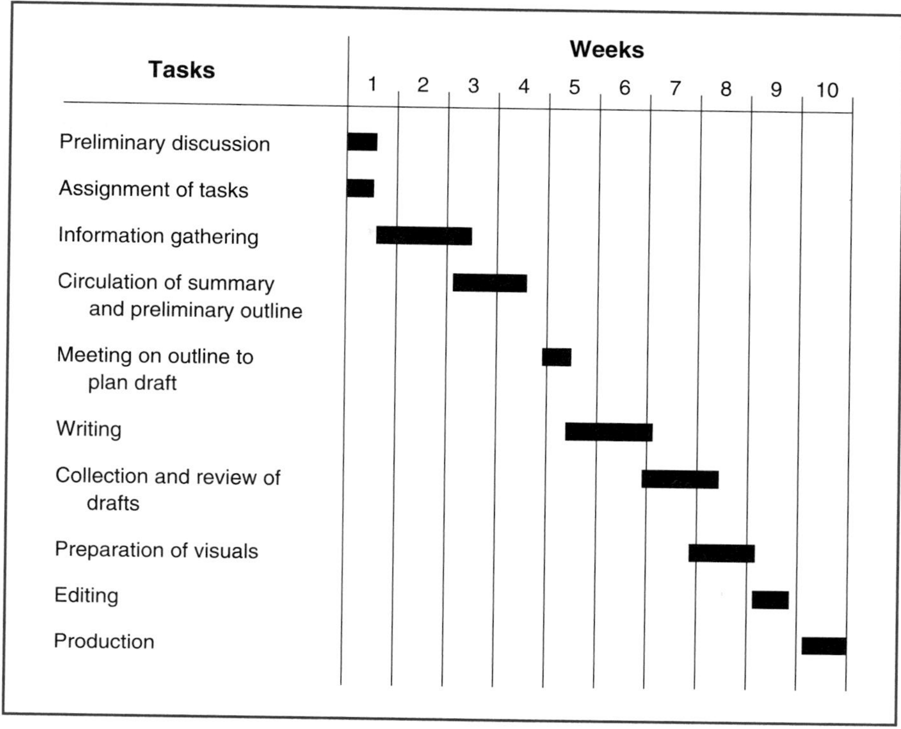

FIGURE 6–14. A Gantt chart for a multiple-author document. In a progress report, the shading in the bars could be changed to cross-hatching to show actual progress.

collector, a turbine) to contrast the improved energy use of solar sources with the use of conventional ones.

Schedules

Schedules display the times for recurring events—like departing and arriving planes or your classes. They also display a sequence of nonrecurring events associated with a particular project. Tracking projects is so important in business that several visual forms have been developed to do the job. The most common is probably the *Gantt chart* (see Figure 6–14). A Gantt chart is a table that notes tasks in the rows and tracks them against time units designated in the columns. Such charts often appear in proposals (see Chapter 17) and aid in controlling and monitoring activities.

Bar Charts

Bar charts are popular devices for showing comparisons. Audiences often find them pleasantly concrete (more concrete than a table or a graph), and writers who have access to graphics software find them easy to create. (See Figures 6–9, 6–15, 6–16, and 6–17.) You simply plug in your information, and the program draws the scales on both X and Y axes and the appropriately sized bars.

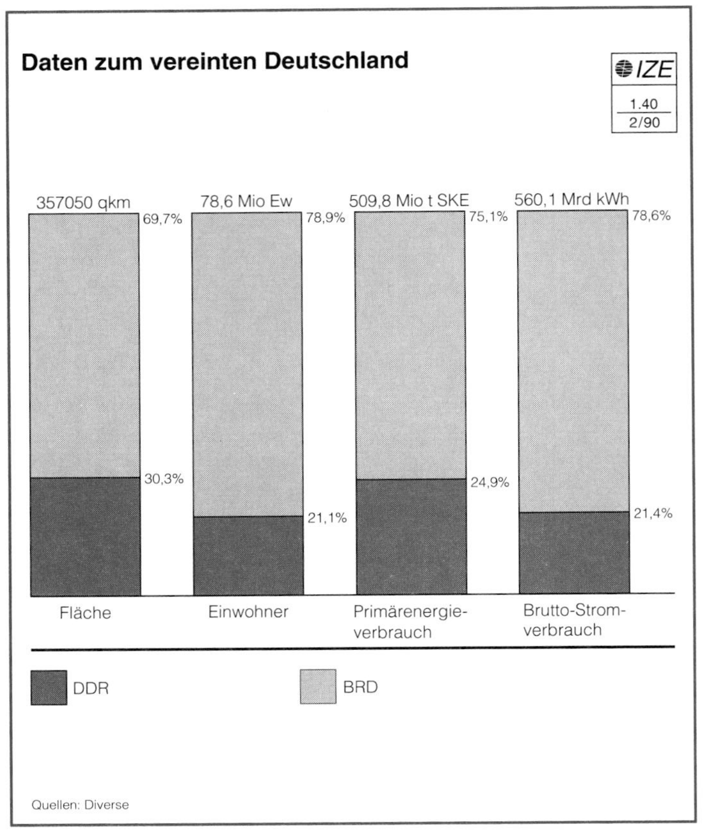

FIGURE 6–15.
Segmented bar chart of information concerning energy use in the united Germany. *(Courtesy of IZE, Frankfurt, Germany.)*

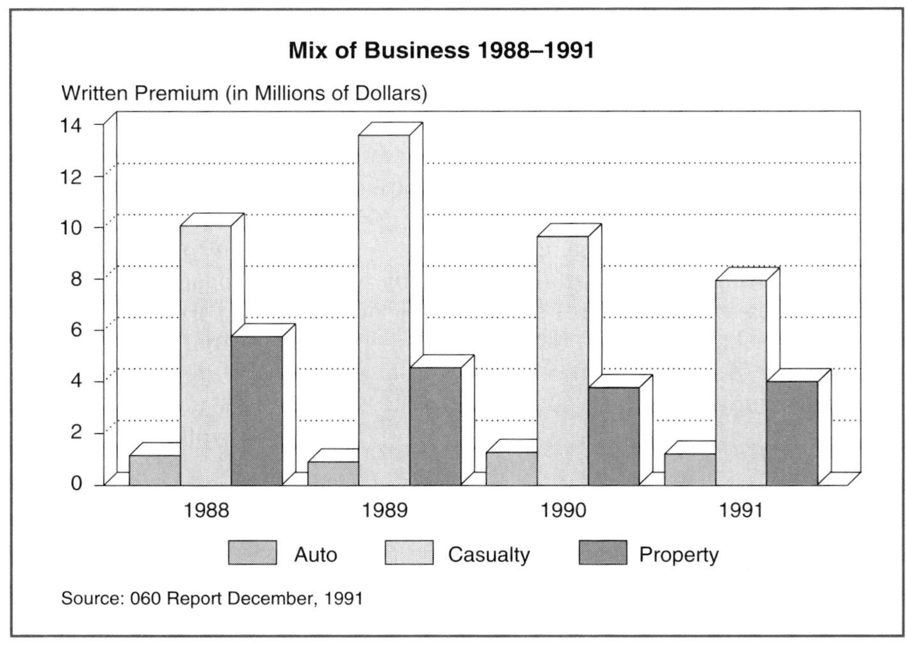

FIGURE 6–16.
A bar chart. The bars are differentiated in patterns keyed to a legend at the bottom. The source (060 Report) is an internal code of the Lincoln Insurance group, which produced the chart for internal distribution. *(Courtesy of Lincoln Insurance Company; designed by Joanne Drummond.)*

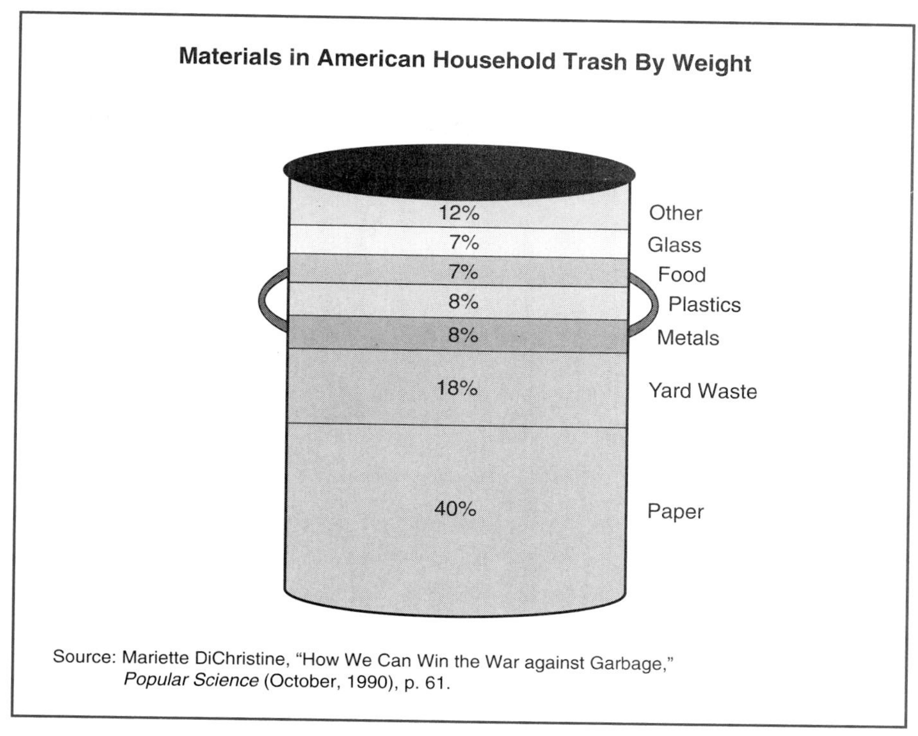

FIGURE 6–17.
A stacked (segmented) bar chart. This chart uses patterns to differentiate trash, and it stacks the amounts in a bar that resembles a trash can (note the handles). Because the amounts are percentages, this information could also appear in a pie chart. *(Courtesy of Joanne Drummond.)*

The checklist provides guidelines for either computer-generated or hand-drawn bar charts:

CHECKLIST FOR BAR CHARTS

1. Arrange the bars either vertically or horizontally.
2. Maintain equal bar width and spacing; a variation would seem to indicate a different quantity.
3. Use solid bars, or differentiate bars with various colors, hatching, or perspective.
4. If you draw the bars to represent something—a hockey stick, people, or bullets, for example—ensure that the representation won't distort the information.

Pie Charts

Use a *pie chart* (as in Figures 6–8 or 6–18) to show the percentages of some whole, like total sales. You divide the pie into pieces that correspond to each product's contribution (see the checklist). Budgets are often shown as pies, as are contributions from different sources to a university's annual fund. As with bar charts, you can plug your information into a computer graphics package that will automatically create the pie.

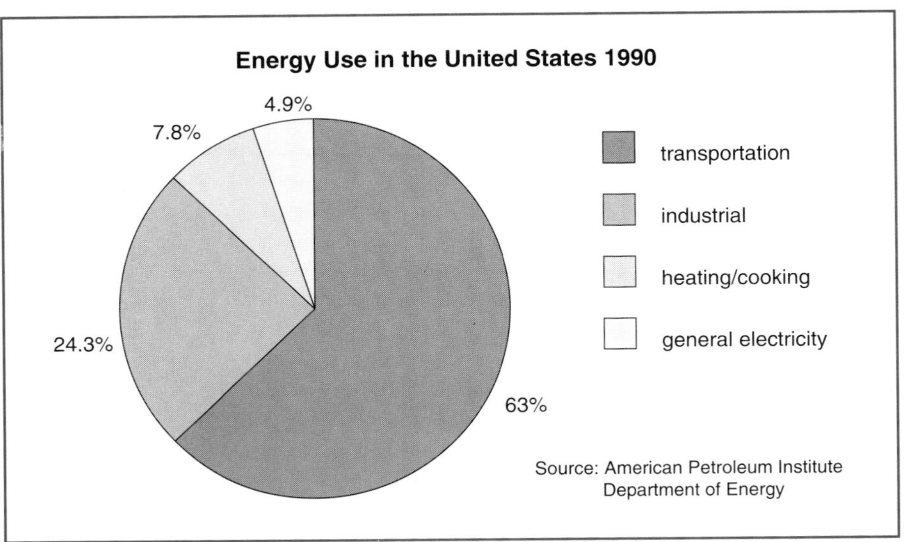

FIGURE 6–18.
A pie chart. Note that the chart makes vivid the amount of oil consumed in transportation. *(Courtesy of Kate McDonald and the American Petroleum Institute.)*

CHECKLIST FOR PIE CHARTS

1. Generally, begin the division of the pie at the top center (''noon''). Most graphics software will not let you begin anywhere else.
2. Arrange the sectors by size, with the largest at the top.
3. Place the labels outside the circle. Don't use dots or a line to connect the label to the pie.
4. Label the slices with percentages, not just words.
5. Try to show no more than five segments.

Pictorial Charts

Pictorial charts, or ''pictograms,'' take advantage of the audience appeal and international understanding of symbols to make abstract concepts concrete, as in Figure 6–19. Follow the guidelines in the checklist to generate pictograms that are clear and readily understood by a wide audience:

CHECKLIST FOR PICTOGRAMS

1. Use symbols that are readily understood.
2. Avoid bias or regionalisms in the symbols.
3. Select symbols that are easily divisible and that contrast well. If you need to use a label, the symbol doesn't work.
4. Keep symbols used as units of measurement approximately the same size.

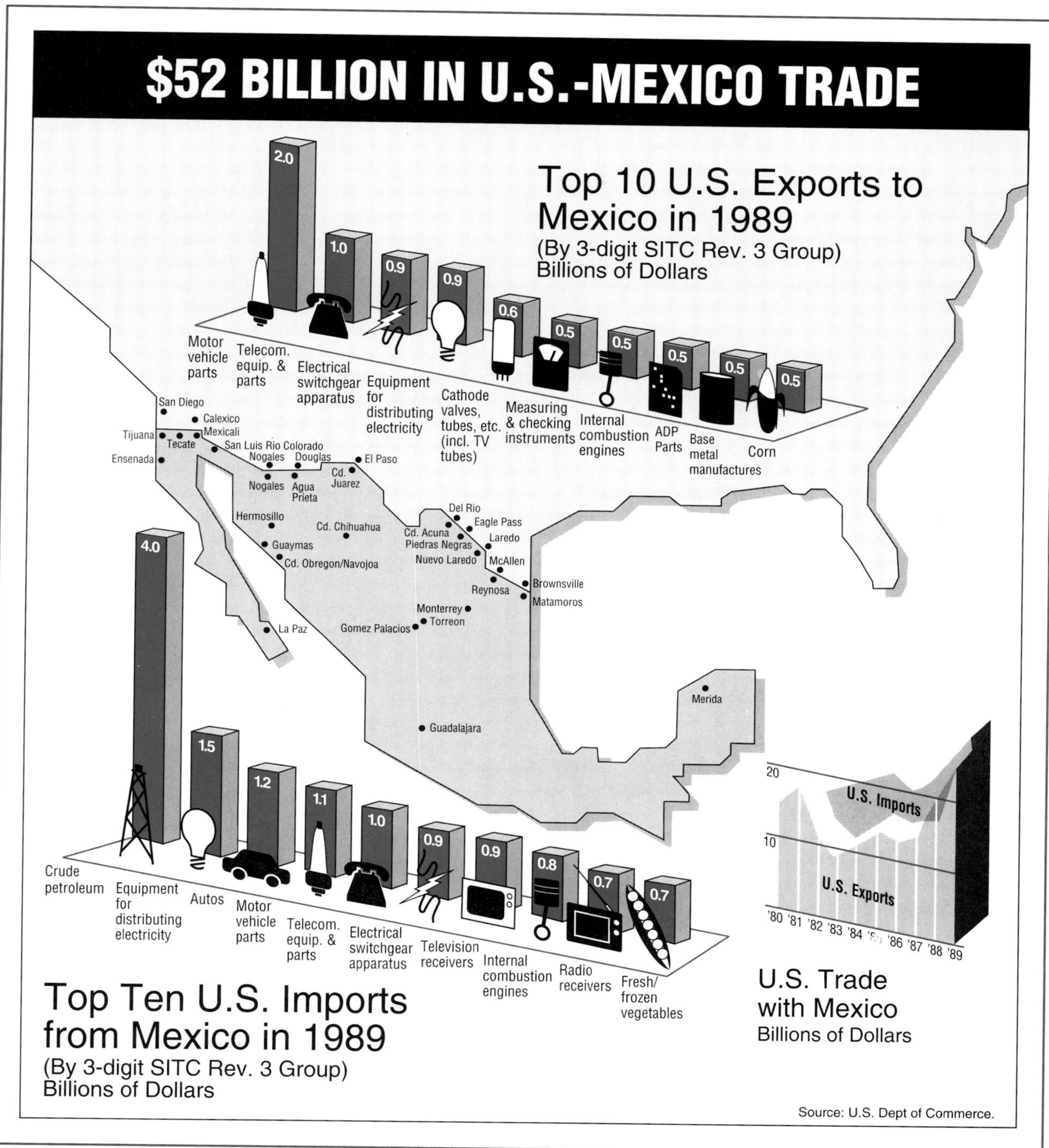

FIGURE 6–19.
A pictogram. This presentation combines four forms: A map of Mexico, two bar charts (with representational drawings), and a silhouetted line graph. It's busy but readable. *(Used by permission of Dow Jones International Marketing Services.)*

Maps

Maps represent a territory that you need to know about for some purpose—getting from here to there, for example, or understanding the geographic dispersion of a multinational organization. Maps show territory at different scales and with different degrees of detail. In Figure 3–1 of Chapter 3, for example, you saw a schematic map of the world that shows Dominion Textile's sales offices and that includes two insert maps, at somewhat larger scale, locating the company's factories in the United States and Europe. Figure 6–20 uses a map of the United States to clarify a strategic plan for the Lincoln Insurance Group.

Drawings

A map is one form of *drawing*. Drawings serve several purposes in documents. One is to make a concept concrete. Another is to instruct. Inter-

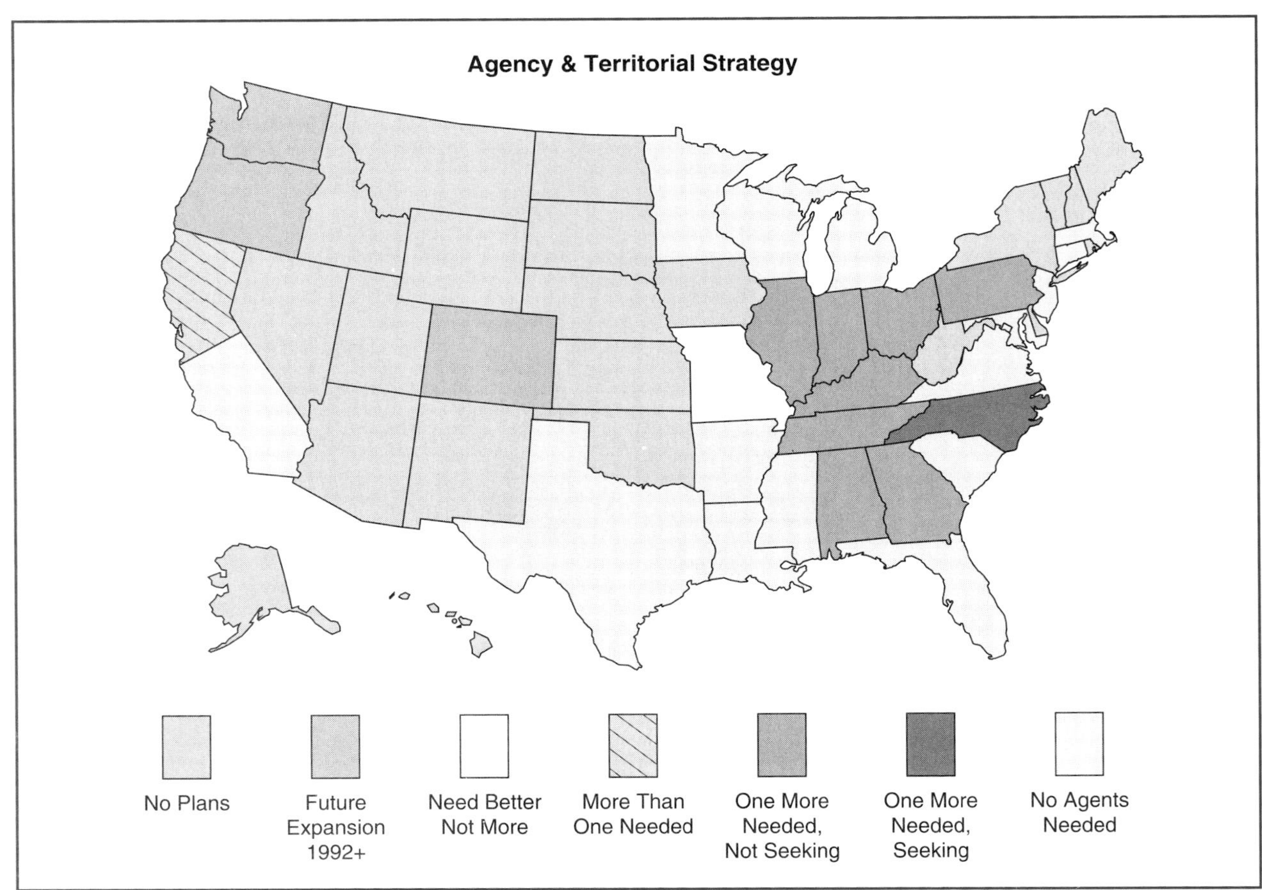

FIGURE 6–20.
A map. This map appeared in an internal report of the Lincoln Insurance Group.
(Courtesy of Lincoln Insurance Company; designed by Joanne Drummond.)

FYI

COMMUNICATING WITH PHOTOGRAPHS

Excerpted from Philip Douglis's May 1990 column for *Communications World,* the monthly publication of the International Association of Business Communicators. Douglis is Director of the Douglis Visual Workshops.

Many organizational communicators still function at the most primitive visual level, even though their audience—employees, shareholders, customers, and community groups—has become more visually sophisticated. The audience no longer really reads, particularly publications that are sent to them at no cost. They look at the pictures, skim the headlines and perhaps the captions, and then move on to other things. Therefore, they must receive an instantaneous message from the images first and then from words as verbal context.

But communicators still think of photographs as mere literal illustrations—something plugged into a hole after the story is written and laid out. The photographs are clichés: the grip-and-grin award picture; the rigid lineups of group shots; the boring view of an employee standing at a machine or sitting at a computer; the ego-gratifying reward for the people who appear in them.

What kind of photographs *should* organizational communicators use? The best photographs juxtapose subject matter incongruously; they are abstract, showing less of the subject and thus saying more about it; and they convey human values—intimate, candid, and spontaneous feelings. They avoid the posed setups and artificial light favored by current commercial photographers. Beyond being mere illustration, they provoke the reader's imagination and feeling.

national symbols aid, for example, in instructing shippers about what to do with boxes. Guides for assembling or troubleshooting devices are often best presented visually (see Chapter 25). Even if the reader doesn't know the name of a particular component, he or she can *see* in a drawing what attaches to what. Moreover, in an increasingly multinational culture, drawings overcome language barriers in the explanation of physical systems. Drawings can also show an "exploded" or "cutaway" view, that is, each component pulled apart in relationship to the whole—a way of seeing both the surface and what's beneath it. Drawings may be presented in different scales, sometimes in a series in which you narrow in on the point of interest.

Photographs

Consider using *photographs* in a document if your budget will cover the cost of taking the photographs and reproducing them. "*FYI:* Communicating with Photographs" provides advice on using photographs well. See the special feature, "Communicating with Photographs in Corporate Annual Reports," for some excellent examples.

TESTING THE VISUAL

Through carelessness or deviousness, you can confuse a reader, you can lie, and you can plagiarize in pictures as well as in prose. Don't. Do test each visual:

1. Is it accurate?
2. Could it mislead?
3. Is the source material documented?

Accuracy

Count. Add. Proofread. Make sure that the segments of a pie chart add up to 100 percent. Make sure that tables of percentages add up to 100 percent—or if they don't add up, explain why. Compare the final visual with your notes. Compare the final visual with your text. Sometimes, text and visuals are prepared at different times by different people. Make sure they agree.

Distortion

A visual can easily mislead. For example, a researcher faced with a scattering of data points that won't line up at a reasonable scale can always *make* them line up if the scale is large enough. Photographs can be retouched to eliminate unsightly trash next to a warehouse. Or labels may deceive. A brochure for a condominium, for example, may carry photographs of a "typical" unit that match only one (if any) unit in the group, and certainly not any that a potential buyer could purchase for the stated price. The bars in a chart can be manipulated so that their size appears to contradict the real numbers they represent. Some software houses, eager to get new packages on the market before they are really ready to run, draw pictures of screens showing effects that the software can't achieve. (One competitor calls this "vaporware.") Don't lie—in either words *or* pictures.

Documentation

Document the sources of visuals or of the information in a visual you've drawn in the same way you document borrowed words and ideas (see "Appendix: Documenting Sources of Information.") Use one of several systems. The simplest is to write a source line at the bottom of the figure:

```
Source: The U.S. Bureau of the Census.
```

Or use a note like those that indicate the source of text in the document. At the end of the visual's title, place an asterisk (*) or a dagger (†). The note then follows the appropriate symbol at the bottom of the visual.

For visuals developed internally in an organization, consider naming the source so that the reader will know the person who may be able to answer questions about it. Date the visual to show its currentness.

THE VISUAL PAGE

How much visual content—or enhancement—is enough? An internal corporate document that's too slick may raise questions about misspent funds. An external document that's too rough may diminish a company's credibility with the audience. The type and number of visuals you use, the paper on which you print them, the resolution of the printer you use to print them, and the method you use to reproduce them—all of these are elements of your *voice* in visuals.

Guidelines for Using Visuals

Check your visual choice on each page of your document, asking yourself these questions:

1. Have you devoted visuals to minor points and neglected major ones?
2. Are the visuals bunched in one section of the document when they might be spread out to lend interest to the whole text?
3. Are the visuals balanced on the page?
4. Is the color contrast appropriate?
5. Are the visuals labeled and integrated with the text?

1. **Have you devoted visuals to minor points and neglected major ones?** A visual framework emphasizes. Make sure that the emphasis is appropriate. Are your visuals effective—or mere dazzle? You can create visuals easily on personal computers. What you create may lead to a more emphatic text or presentation—or to what one visual expert calls "chartjunk." In adding visuals to your vocabulary, you'll also need to add the ability to analyze and edit your visuals.

2. **Are the visuals bunched in one section of the document when they might be spread out to lend interest to the whole text?** Are the visuals near where they are discussed? Gaps between a visual and the explanatory text reduce the reader's understanding and reduce the visual's impact. One exception would be visuals that you'll refer to in several places in the text; a site diagram, for example, for a new shopping mall that your whole report discusses may be reasonably placed in an appendix (see Chapter 19). You might also consider a foldout form for such a visual, or you might make it somehow detachable, so that the reader can place it next to the text while reading. As another exception, visuals that require a certain production technique or type of paper may also appear together rather than spread through the text.

Consider, too, the *size* of your visuals. To fit it on a page, you may have to reduce a drawing or table. Will it still be readable in reduced form?

3. **Are the visuals balanced on the page?** Control the effect of the visuals as they interact and as they are integrated with the text on a series of pages. Balance two or more visuals on a page (see Figure 6–21). Placing a visual off-center may highlight it; but overdone, such asymmetry may disorient the reader and introduce an unwanted element of eccentricity into the presentation.

4. **Is the color contrast appropriate?** Use good contrast in colors; avoid similar shades of the same color—few people can distinguish them—or fluorescent or "hot" colors that clash or cause eye fatigue. For good contrast, use, for example, yellow on blue, white on green, or black on yellow.

5. **Are the visuals labeled and integrated with the text?** Visuals usually can't stand alone. You have to speak for them. The label you choose is

Our 27,000 shareholders and 14,000 employees believe that the more you know about Swissair the better it is for you. And us.

A few words from Swissair in a language all businesspeople understand.

Revenue. Expenses. Profit.
In a highly competitive business, the way to show consistent profits is to provide consistent service.

Passengers Carried, 1973.
Like many other companies, Swissair's traffic has become increasingly diversified throughout the world.

Fleet Size.
Swissair has been purchasing U.S. built planes since 1931. Committing over $500,000,000 in the past six years alone.

Countries We Fly To.
As Swiss business has become increasingly international, so has Swissair's.

Total Number Of Employees.
As Swissair flies to more and more countries we employ more and more people in the countries we fly to.

Inflation vs. Airfares.
In real dollars airfares to Europe are still a bargain.

Protection Of The Environment.
Swissair in its continued efforts towards noise abatement and reduction of pollution has spent over $10,000,000 to date.

Daily Aircraft Utilization.
Efficient scheduling and an investment in maintenance and service facilities pay off in profits.

Total Shareholders.
Swissair is not government run or subsidized. We too have to satisfy our stockholders.

Like you, Swissair is responsible to stockholders. Their dividends are a direct reflection of the quality, efficiency and scope of service we provide our passengers. By maintaining those standards we make sure that both our customers and our stockholders get what they expect from us. Swissair, 608 Fifth Avenue, New York, New York 10020, (212) 995-8400.

SWISSAIR

FIGURE 6–21.
A well-integrated page of visuals. *(Used by permission, Swissair.)*

the bridge between the visual and the surrounding text. The label has two parts: the first part notes the visual's sequence in the document, and the second identifies the visual's content. For the first part, number figures consecutively from 1 throughout the document or by chapter (e.g., "Figure 6–1" means the first visual in Chapter 6). Tables may be either lettered ("Table A") or numbered.

Refer to a visual in the text before you present it. To emphasize the figure itself, make it the subject of the referral sentence:

```
Figure 6 shows the rise in maintenance costs for the sys-
tem over a ten-year period.
```

To emphasize the figure's content, use a parenthetical reference:

```
Maintenance costs for the system rose steadily over a
ten-year period (see Figure 6).
```

The second part of the title that appears on the visual may indicate the topic of the figure in a brief phrase, or it may be a sentence that reinforces the major message of the visual.

Topic: `Capital Spending Overseas by U.S. Firms`
Message: `U.S. firms have increased their capital spending overseas every year since 1987.`

Place the title above, below, or beside a figure—but be consistent in any one document. Label tables at the top above the labels for each column or at the side, as in this text.

In addition to a source note on the visual, you may also include an *explanatory footnote.* For example, a table listing U.S. direct investment abroad compared with foreign holdings in the United States might include this note:

Note: `Inflation causes the book value of these holdings to be far lower than the market value. Because U.S. holdings are on average much older, their value is thus greatly understated.`

You may also use a *caption* to discuss the visual in more detail. In some public relations and marketing documents, as in a special section of photographs in an annual report, captions are the only text on essentially visual pages.

SUMMARY

- **Think visually.** Use visual forms to help you capture thoughts and see a system or object from different points of view. Computer programs can help you to brainstorm, to organize documents and presentations, and to visualize the structure within a vast quantity of information.
- **Communicate visually.** Use visual forms and color to consolidate information, to summarize and reinforce an otherwise detailed message, to provide dramatic impact, to reduce the amount of text in a document, and to cross language barriers.

- Visuals fit into two broad groups: **tables,** which present numbers or words in rows and columns; and **figures,** a term that covers everything else, including charts, drawings, maps, and photographs.
- Test each visual for **accuracy** (no mistakes in recording the data, manipulating them, or spelling them); **distortion** (no lies); and **documentation** (sources properly noted).
- Test the **integration** of the visuals and the text on each page—and in the whole document. Visuals emphasize; make sure you haven't squandered such emphasis on a minor point and neglected a major one. Unless the context or production technique demands it, avoid bunching visuals in one part of a document. Balance the visuals on a page. Check the color contrast. Make sure all visuals are labeled.

EXERCISES

For Discussion

1. Collect a sample of corporate annual reports. Examine the visuals in the reports. Is the consolidated financial information—the balance sheets, income statements, and the like—presented in the same form in each? Or are there differences? What accounts for any differences? How are photographs used in the reports? How does the choice of photographs affect the *style* of the reports and reflect the *image* of the corporation in general?
2. Examine the visuals in popular business publications like *Forbes, Business Week, Fortune,* and *The Wall Street Journal.* What kinds of information do the authors tend to include in visual rather than verbal form? Do you think, for any one article, that the visuals are the *basis* of the presentation or were added as interest-getting devices? In other words, which came first, the words or the pictures?
3. Continue your examination of business publications to look for an example of each type of visual mentioned in this chapter. Is the most effective graphic used in each example? What alternatives are possible?
4. Continue your examination of business publications to look at the use of color. Does color contribute to the message or is it used mainly for decoration? What message does the color convey? Is the color appropriate for only one culture or is it international?
5. Examine the logos of several companies. You may find these on products as well as on stationery and company-produced brochures. Comment on the *image* of the company that the logo seems to project. For example, many people consider the blue IBM logo conservative and understated—and also highly technical and modern.
6. In a full-page advertisement, Mitsubishi Electric showed two items: a piece of pie on a plate and, next to it, chopsticks on a napkin. The picture aims to reinforce the message, stated briefly in the lower left corner, that a blending of cultures—in this case, American and Japanese—can lead to producing the best products. Bring into class or create other simple visuals that reinforce a sales message.*

* Exercise continues after insert.

SPECIAL FEATURE

COMMUNICATING WITH PHOTOGRAPHS IN CORPORATE ANNUAL REPORTS

Corporate annual reports convey to employees, customers, shareholders, and potential investors detailed information about operations and financial results. They also present visual and verbal messages concerning corporate responsibility, credibility, mission, and culture. Photographs are especially powerful tools for capturing and transmitting corporate images, as you see in this dramatic cover of the 1990 annual report of The Travelers Corporation, whose marketing symbol is the red umbrella.

The following pages display more photographs that both inform the reader and elicit a mood in which to read. The subjects vary: places (corporate headquarters, locations served), products, people (employees or customers). To frame your review of these photographs, you'll read how photographer Douglas Johns approached an assignment and how several reports describe their covers (page SF-2). The shape of the headquarters of the Transamerica Corporation shown on page SF-3 sets the theme for its report: "The Power of the Pyramid: Financial Integrity."

These photographs, of course, are of the highest professional quality—in perspective, composition, and definition. All are in full color. How do you respond to each photograph? What message about the company do you see? How does the visual image create a positive attitude toward the company and what it does?

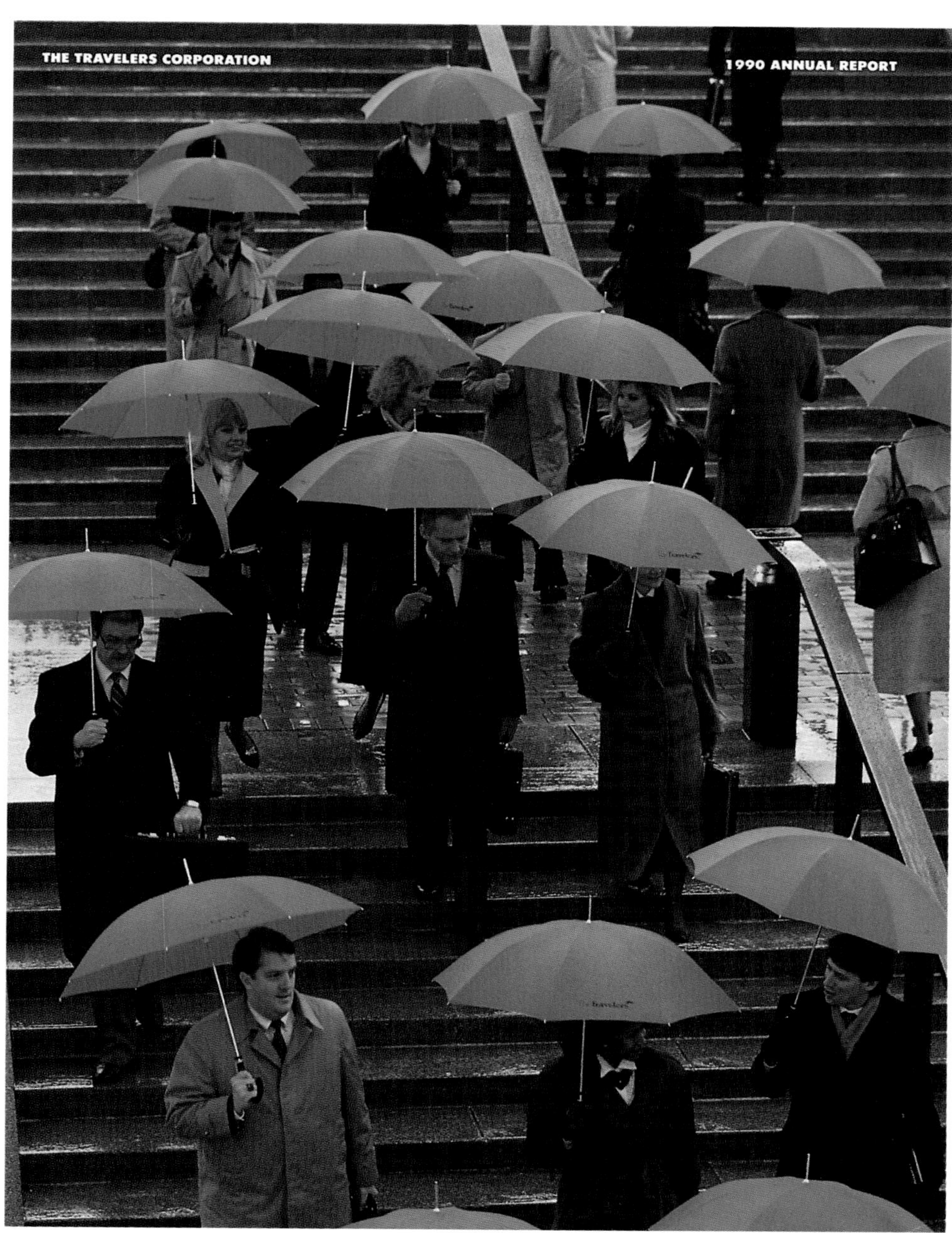

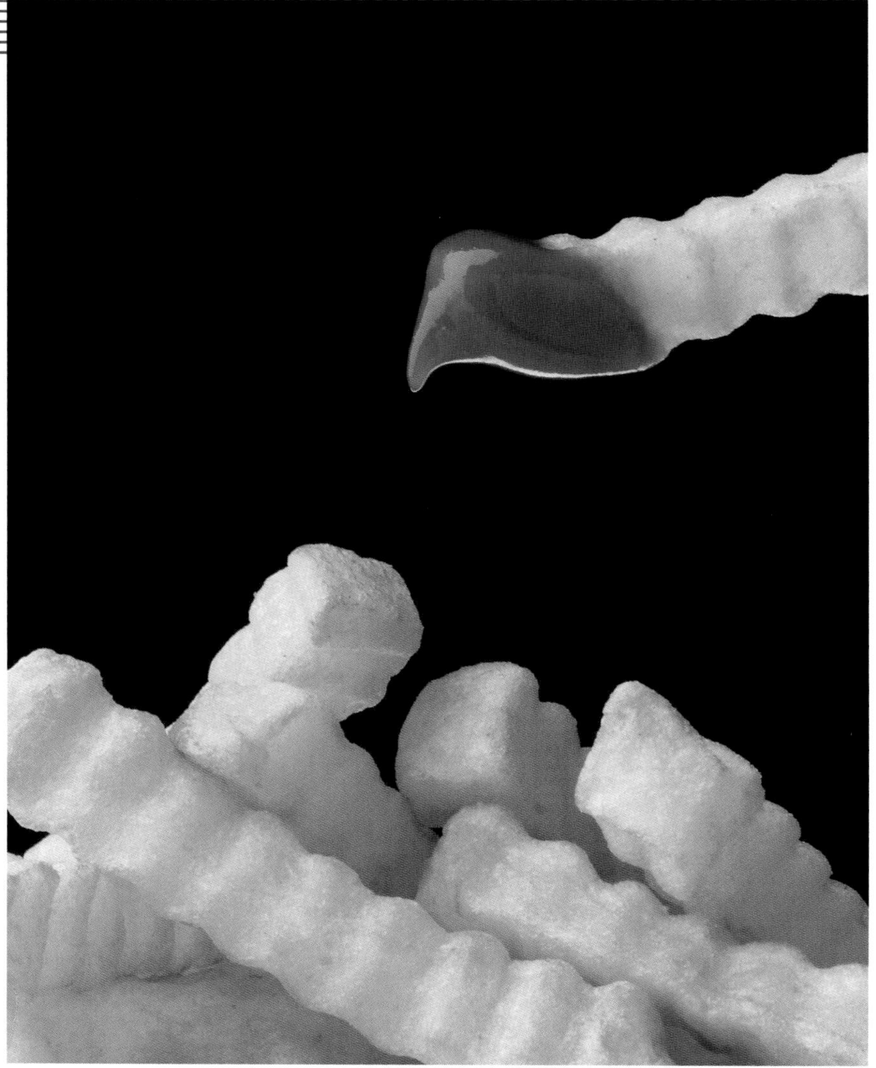

The art director/designer for the 1985 annual report of the Paradyne Corporation, Wendy Sherman, decided to focus on using "icons" to depict the various clients that used Paradyne telephone, voice, and data communications equipment in their day-to-day operations. Wendy reviewed the client list and chose those who were well recognized and whose products and services were used frequently by consumers and businesses across the country.

After she narrowed the field, she and Doug [Johns] looked for distinguishing icons for each customer. They sought fairly simple elements that could be incorporated into an image with a diagonal thrust. Of course, all had to have potential for interesting graphic shapes, color, and texture as well. The final series included a gas pump nozzle, a thermometer, a telephone receiver, and a cowboy boot. Each shot is an extremely close study of the object—like this study of Heinz ketchup on a french fry. The lighting for all was very directional and abstract; shadows are as much an element as highlights.

The images were shot in 8″ × 10″ format to allow for the greatest clarity in detail and color rendition. The product shots were printed as varnish tints so they would be extremely subtle and suggest the "behind the scene" impact that Paradyne products had on these companies. For enhanced texture, the photos are printed on a smooth, coated stock, and the text and financial information is on a rougher stock with a speckle tone. The photographs worked; the report was one of four "Top of the Top 60" award winners in the 1986 competition in graphic design sponsored by Mead Paper.

—Kathy Johns, the Douglas Johns Studio

1990 Annual Report

Transamerica Corporation

The Power of the Pyramid: Financial Integrity

Here's what Phillips says about the cover:

Now in its third decade as an environmental model, Phillips' Bridger Lake lease in Utah's Wasatch National Forest is proof that searching for energy and safeguarding the environment can go hand-in-hand. This year's cover shows blades of grass stretching through the crystal waters of Henry's Fork, a creek that makes its way through the 3,800-acre lease site. Production from Bridger was the first ever allowed in a national forest when it began in the middle 1960s.

Here's what Pfizer says about the cover:

Outside of the U.S., Japan is the largest single Pfizer market. In June 1989, we successfully launched Diflucan, our pioneering antifungal agent, there. Mr. Shoki Imoue, a 45-year-old Japanese teacher, shown here among his students, was cured by Diflucan of a serious fungal infection.

Here's what General Motors says about the cover:

The 1991 Park Avenue Ultra presents America with a redesigned motor car that is the most sophisticated six-passenger vehicle ever offered by Buick. An extensive list of standard equipment includes an advanced V6 engine, an electronically controlled transmission, and a new ConforTemp dual climate system.

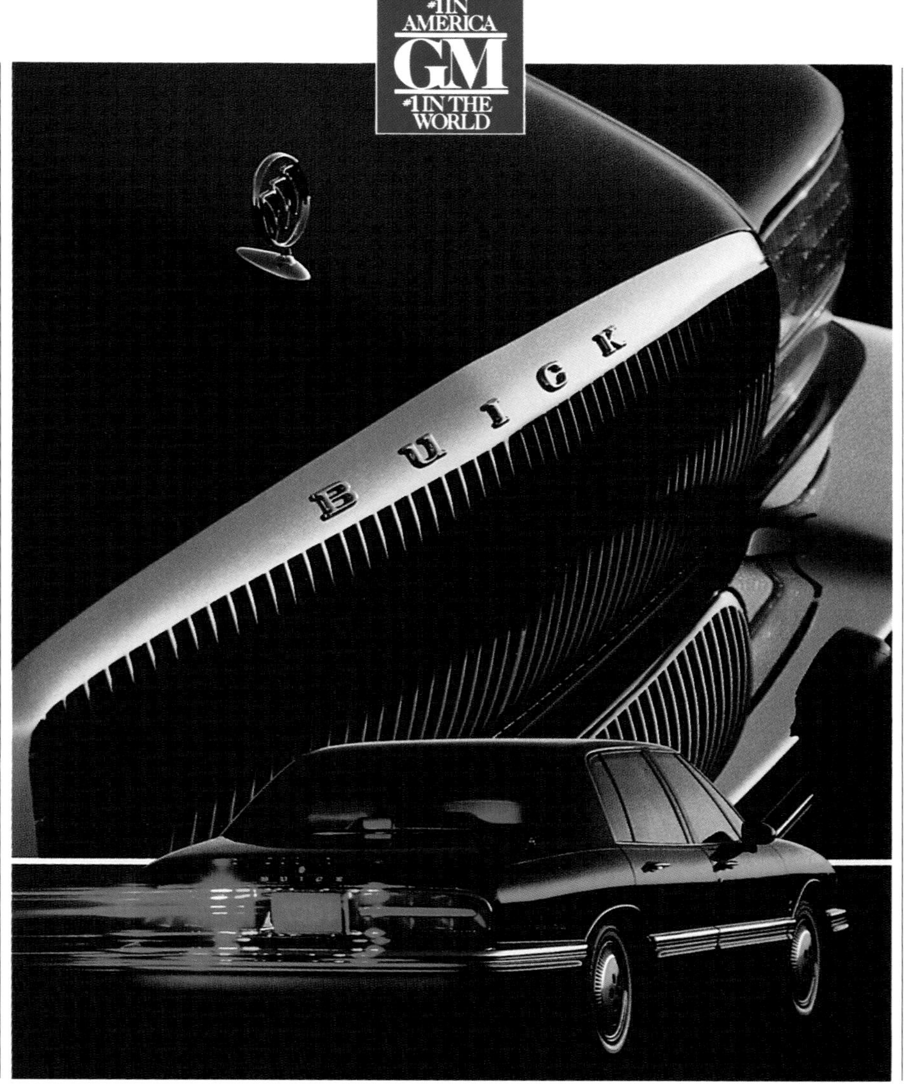

1989 ANNUAL REPORT
GENERAL MOTORS
#1 IN AMERICA
GM
#1 IN THE WORLD
BUICK

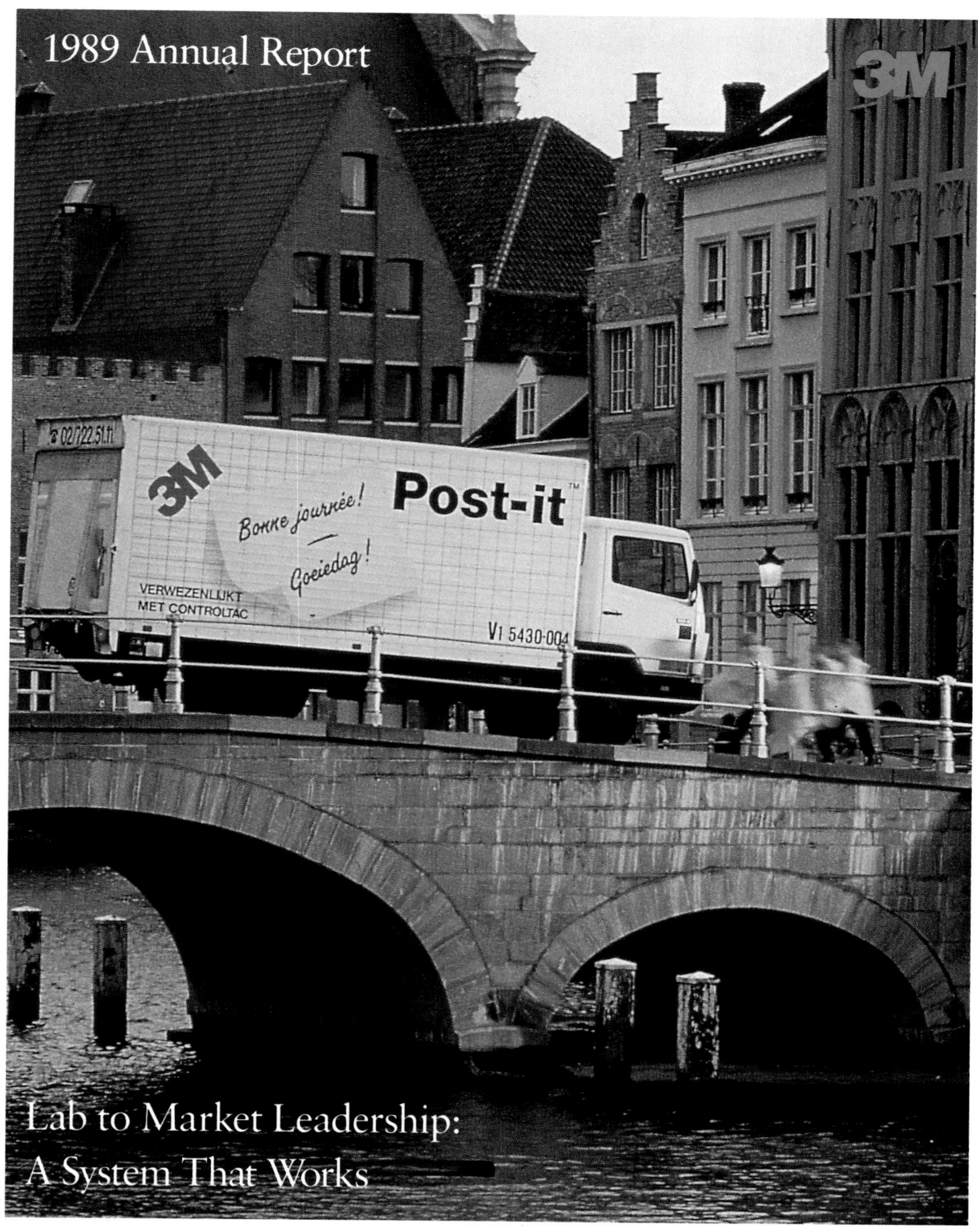

Here's what 3M says about the cover:

In Bruges, Belgium, a 3M truck advertises popular Post-it brand notes. Graphics on the truck employ 3M's own Controltac brand fleet-marking films. Like many 3M products, both are successful worldwide, producing more than half their sales outside the United States. Post-it notes, a whole new product category pioneered by 3M, celebrates its 10th anniversary in 1990.

1989 Annual Report

THE WILLIAMS COMPANIES, INC.

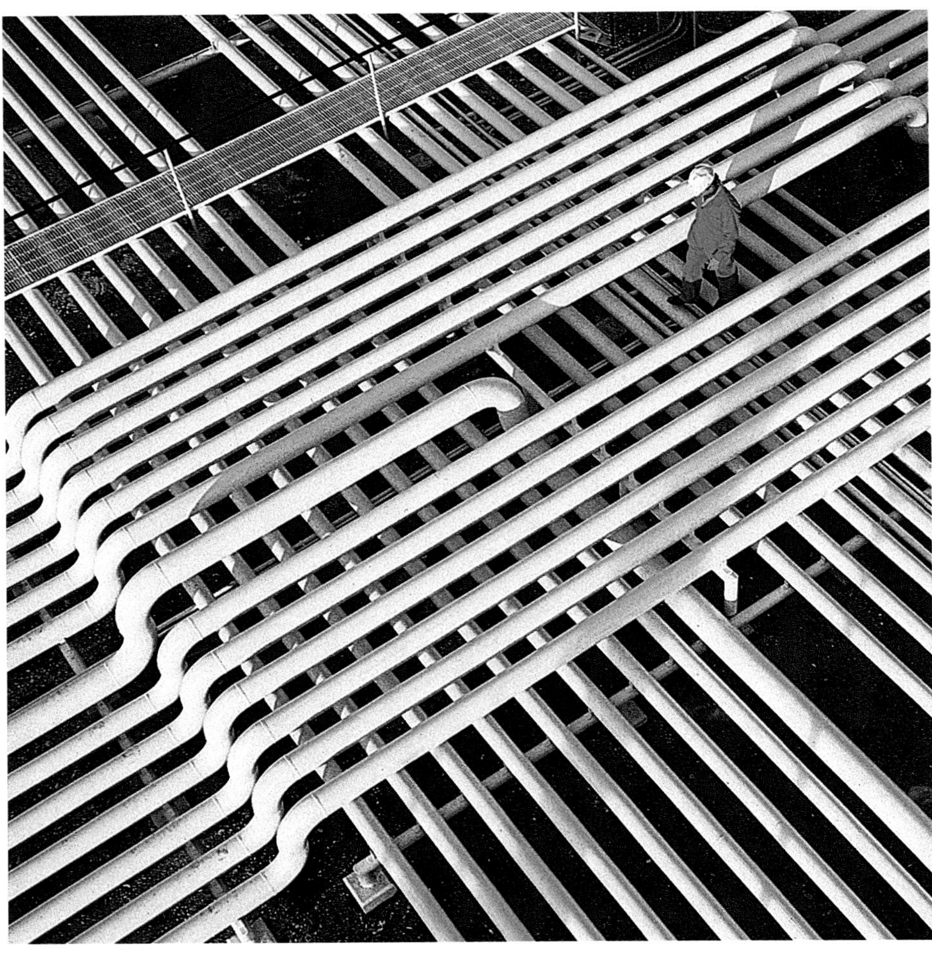

Here's what The Williams Companies, Inc., says about the cover:

Williams Pipe Line Company's Alexandria, Minnesota, terminal provides this symmetrical view of pipelines serving the facility. The pipelines of The William Companies not only provide transportation of petroleum products and natural gas but also serve to protect the transmission of digital telecommunications. Williams Telecommunications Group pioneered the concept of installing fiber-optic cable cross-country in pipelines removed from traditional service.

7. Obtain copies of instructions for assembling or operating equipment intended for a multilanguage readership. Examine the use of visuals to carry the bulk of the instructions. Note particularly international visual symbols for shipping and handling that are contained on the packaging. How easy are the symbols to understand? How much of the instruction copy can you understand from the visuals alone?

8. What's wrong with this picture? (The information for this figure was taken from Lester Thurow, "The End of the Post-Industrial Era," *Business in the Contemporary World,* Winter 1990, 2.)

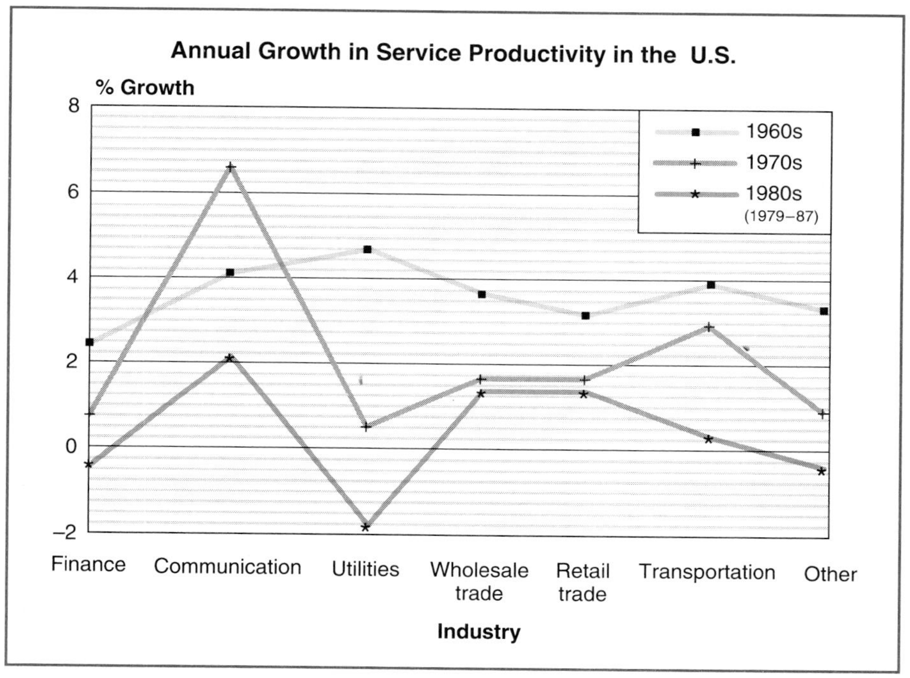

For Writing and Drawing

9. Arrange the information in the following paragraph in a *matrix.* Is anything missing?

```
In our survey we examined the hiring practices of four
companies. We were chiefly interested in whether they in-
terviewed on campus or not, whether they hired only busi-
ness students or were interested in talking with other
majors, whether they offered starting salaries over
$20,000, and whether they had a training program for new
hires. Groliers Inc. hires only business students; their
starting salaries are over $20,000, and they are inter-
ested in talking with only business majors. They inter-
view on campus. Micromessages Ltd. believes that new
hires should start with fairly low salaries and work up
fast, so they start at under $20,000. They interview on
```

campus for all majors and have a training program. The Kermit Factory, which interviews on campus and pays more than $20,000 in starting salaries, offers training programs and hires only business majors. The last people we talked with were from Bowman Inc., which interviews all majors and interviews on campus. They offer a training program and start at over $20,000.

10. The following information is displayed in a table. Convert it to at least two other visual forms:

U.S. Dollar vs. International Currency

New York Rates (3 P.M.)	Wed.	6 Mo. Ago	1 Yr. Ago
Australian dollar	1.2027	1.3405	1.2661
British pound	0.5343	0.6107	0.6202
Canadian dollar	1.1535	1.1755	1.1772
French franc	5.2600	5.7565	6.4180
German mark	1.5680	1.7110	1.8815
Italian lira	1,173.50	1,257.75	1,355.00
Japanese yen	137.10	159.15	140.60
Mexican peso	2,892.00	2,764.03	2,565.00
Spanish pesata	98.05	109.40	119.40
Swiss franc	1.3015	1.5175	1.6317

11. Design a visual for your college newspaper that shows the percentage of total ticket sales from these men's sports: football, 50%; basketball, 25%; soccer, 10%; baseball, 7%; other, 8%.

12. Here's some information about the number of heart attacks suffered by men and women in different age groups in Harborville in one year. Design a visual to display these figures. Pick an audience and a document form for the visual. Discuss your visual in class; compare it to the visuals prepared by others in the class.

    Heart attacks in Harborville: MEN: age 30–40, 4; age 41–50, 8; age 51–60, 17; age 61–70, 35; age 70+, 42. WOMEN: age 30–40, 1; age 41–50, 3; age 51–60, 8; age 61–70, 20; age 70+, 29.

For Collaboration

13. An advertisement for a gun control group provides the following statistics concerning the number of deaths caused by handguns during one year: United States, 8,915; Switzerland, 53; Israel, 25; Sweden, 19; Australia, 13; Canada, 8; England, 7. Assemble a team to design a visual (or several visuals) to dramatize this information in a brochure advocating gun control. Support this information with further research and visuals to bolster this picture.

    Another team in the class should design a visual to *deemphasize* this information in a brochure for an organization advocating the individual's right to purchase guns. That team should find other information to support the importance of the open purchase of guns.

14. The *Statistical Abstract of the United States* is an excellent source of detailed information about industrial production and individual behavior. As a group, decide on a topic and gather information on it from the *Abstract.* Then each member of the group should develop a few visuals to display the information. Compare these visuals and decide in the group which one is the best, and why. Present the visual(s) to the class.

7 REVISING AND DESIGNING

What's Ahead

RESEEING
A REVISING ROUTINE
- Guidelines for Revising
- Revising with a Computer

MACROREVISING
- Use Conventional Formats
- State the Controlling Idea
- Use Parallel Headings
- Develop Strong Paragraphs
- Design the Text as a Visual

MICROREVISING
- Focusing
- Emphasizing
- Proofreading

READABILITY
- FYI: Measuring Readability

SUMMARY
EXERCISES

Do You Know 

- What routine should you follow in revising?
- How can you make the macrostructure of your document easy for the reader to follow?
- What is the role of paragraphing?
- What elements contribute to the look of a document on the page?
- What makes a document readable?

In Figure 7–1, you see a draft of a letter whose purpose is to address misunderstandings concerning two invoices and to inform the recipient of the need to pay in full. The letter is real, although the identifying information has been disguised. In Figure 7–2, you see a revised version of the letter. In this chapter, you will learn strategies for turning a weak draft into a strong revised text—for getting from Figure 7–1 to Figure 7–2—in your own writing.

RESEEING

How would you feel if you received the letter in Figure 7–1? It is long: one and a half pages single-spaced when typed on letterhead. The structure of the letter responds to the client's own letter enclosing the check. It deals with two invoices (dated 1 and 3 April) and two issues: the lack of written approval of the work plan and the padding of charges. Are those issues adequately differentiated? Should the author *say* that the company had already reduced the total of the second invoice? Do the following statements from the last paragraph of the letter add to the credibility of the author's company or, in protesting too much, damage it?

```
We try to be "up-front" with our clients. . . .
We are not accustomed to having our integrity and
sincerity questioned.
```

The letter sets up an opposition between "we" and "you"—with the "you" often set in an accusatory framework:

```
You state that you will not pay the 1 April
invoice. . . .
. . . you felt that we "padded" our charges.
You have stated that you are a reasonable individual.
```

"You have stated" sounds legalistic; so does the indication of weeks and months in both the verbal and the numerical form and the use of phrases like "the said work." Do these legalisms suggest a threat? "We take strenuous

We are in receipt of your 14 April letter and check in the amount of $7,000. We would like to respond to the reasons you cite for not paying the full amount of your invoices.

You state that you will not pay the 1 April invoice because this expense was incurred as a result of our not having the original work plan approved by A. J. Sampson prior to proceeding with the said work. We indeed contacted Ms. Sampson prior to proceeding with the work. Because of the urgency of the project and your settlement schedule, we verbally discussed the work plan and approach to be used on this evaluation. We also requested that a Dixwell representative be present during the proposed work. Ms. Sampson verbally agreed with our proposed work.

We have successfully completed numerous projects of this nature using verbal authorization. Also, the availability of drilling contractors was limited because of the work demand for drillers at that time of year. Being sensitive to your time constraints, we decided to proceed with the work. Getting written approval of the work plan from Ms. Sampson and rescheduling a driller could have delayed the work two (2) to four (4) weeks.

The first indication from you of any problems came almost two (2) months after the field work was completed. We had verbal approval on the work to be performed, and we attempted to expedite our services to conform with your time constraints.

Your reason for not paying the full amount of the 3 April invoice was that you felt that we ''padded'' our charges. You stated that as no regulatory meetings were required, the amount invoiced appeared to be totally out of line. In your review you failed to recognize that we provided a work plan and a summary report of findings and recommendations regarding the site, which were required by the EPA.

We take strenuous exception to the comment that our invoice was "padded." Our invoices have reflected <u>actual time</u> spent on your project. They are not "padded" in any way. Prior to billing and based upon prior discussions, we had already reduced our total invoice amount by more than 10 percent of the total actual fees associated with completion of your project. We hope you take into account the fact that we have saved you tremendous costs associated with this problem. Many other firms may have taken less of an aggressive posture with the EPA and performed unnecessary work and recommended costly remediation measures.

We try to be "up-front" with our clients and we aggressively represent our clients' best interest. We are not accustomed to having our integrity and sincerity questioned. It is especially surprising coming from someone in a senior position at Dixwell. We value our relationship with the professionals at Dixwell and have attempted to serve you with that relationship in mind. You have stated that you are a reasonable individual. In that light, we ask that you reevaluate the amount of your final payment.

FIGURE 7–1.
Draft of a letter collecting payment.

We received your 14 April letter and check for $7,000. We would like to respond to the reasons you give for not paying the full amount.

1 April invoice. As you note, we did not receive written authorization to proceed with the work billed in the 1 April invoice. We did, however, receive oral authorization from A.J. Sampson on 1 January. The availability of drillers at that time of year was limited. Ms. Sampson agreed that writing a new work plan would unnecessarily delay the project. We then went ahead with the field work, at which your representative was present. We completed the work on 10 January. Only two months later did you tell us that that approach had not been appropriate. The invoice represents completed work.

3 April invoice. The bill is not padded. You are correct in noting that no regulatory meetings were required. But we did provide a work plan and a summary report of findings and recommendations regarding the site, documents required by the EPA. The preparation of those documents necessitated the extensive study represented in the invoice. That study, however, provided evidence that the storage tanks can be removed without the much more costly remediation measures that other firms might recommend. The study saved the need for regulatory meetings and extensive reconstruction.

We hope that these remarks clarify any misunderstanding concerning the invoices. We look forward to receiving your check for $1,500, which represents the difference between your 14 April check and the total of the invoices.

FIGURE 7–2.
The revised letter.

exception to the comment that our invoice was 'padded' " is tough. Is the last sentence, then, inconsistent? Should the writer say, simply, "Send us the full payment"?

As you saw in Chapters 4 and 5, issues of *what* to say and in what order (macrocomposing) and how to sound (microcomposing) frame your thinking as you plan your writing, as you write, and as you revise what you've written. This chapter focuses specifically on revising—literally re*seeing* the text, to fit its structure and voice to the context. The chapter also discusses conventional format and design. Sometimes, it's best to start with format and design; recognizing that a well framed business letter does not exceed one page and that headings help mark the text might have aided the writer of Figure 7–1 in shaping his response.

Figure 7–2 shows how the writer revised the letter after talking with some colleagues and his supervisor. It's shorter—one page. It's tighter in its explanation, yet it provides more details to support the company's position.

It uses underlined headings to sort the two bills. It avoids legalisms. It's not accusatory. The voice is confident, accommodating, rational—and unwavering.

A REVISING ROUTINE

With a broad plan in mind, experienced writers write, then perhaps replan on the spot if the writing leads them in an interesting new direction. They reread as they go along, letting the text on the page or screen help them see where to go next. When they finish a whole draft or a section, they then review it to see what can stay ("stable text," one writer calls it) and what needs to be changed. They revise at various points in the process, but especially at the end, when they test the document against their goal and their readers' needs.

Inexperienced writers often write before they have even a glimmer of a plan. They just write. They may also edit too soon, and that editing kills their creativity. They revise at the wrong level; they concentrate on spelling (not a bad thing in itself) when their whole argument lacks definition and proof. They let a document go when they are tired—not when the document is right—and send raw prose off to the reader.

How do you revise? Start by acknowledging that you *will* have to revise whatever you write. The task may be light or heavy depending on the simplicity or complexity of the context and of what you have to say. Revising gives you the opportunity to look good, to look as if you think only clear thoughts and always write well. You spend hours drafting a text that you then spend hours changing, time that may seem wasteful. That time, however, is a price you often have to pay for quality.

Guidelines for Revising

Here are some guidelines for an effective revising routine:

- **Write with revising in mind.** Double-space on paper or, better, write with a computer so the revising process will be mechanically easier.
- **Just keep writing.** Revise only when you've finished a segment or the whole.
- **Allow time between writing the draft and revising.** This way you can see old text with fresh eyes.
- **Don't start every revision session on page 1.** Give fresh perspective to other segments.
- **Share the text.** Ask others to read and comment, as you read and comment on their documents, to check on structure and voice. Ask someone to outline your text, and check that outline against your intentions.
- **Keep a record of drafts.** This way you'll know which is the current and authoritative one. Collate comments on one master copy and label it with a date and a version number. If you use a computer, make sure that the title of your file indicates both the *document* and the *version,* and keep a list of which documents are on which disks and

what represents the current—and thus most authoritative—version.

- **Test the document.** Especially with instructions or training material, develop a procedure for testing the document with a sample of users before issuing it widely.

Revising with a Computer

Computer programs for wordprocessing, as you probably know, allow you to write and revise without a mess. You can write rapidly and then easily add, delete, and move things around as you resee things. The new instantly replaces the old.

The software can also help you revise. It can check spelling. One caution, however: If the program recognizes the word as a word it will accept it, even if you use the word in the wrong sense, as in a confusion of *affect* and *effect* or a misplacement of *when* for *went.* Many programs also include "search-and-replace" features. If you discover, 100 pages into a document, that you've misspelled a company's name perhaps twenty-five times, you can tell the program to substitute the correct for the faulty spelling, and it will find and correct each instance. Sophisticated programs can also act as your alter ego and electronic reader with advice on grammar and style.

Revising on a networked computer—one that allows you to send a draft electronically to another writer—also aids in sharing the revising tasks. Having someone else look at your work is often an essential phase in your ability to resee the draft, and that phase can be eased by electronic transmission.

Revising at a computer, however, also entails risks. First, because of its very ease, and because of a certain hypnotic quality of a computer screen, revision there may become pathological. You may exhaust your energies on frivolous details and rearrangements that keep you from really reseeing the text. You may also spend energy in computer housekeeping, playing with files and commands rather than text.

Second, playing around may also cause you to *lose* text if you don't save it properly in the system's memory. Back up all files at the end of a work session.

Third, some writers also complain of eyestrain at the terminal if they use one for more than a few hours at a time. You'll read more about the physiological effects of computers in Chapter 10.

Fourth, the computer may cause you to waste paper. Either because they don't trust the system or because they need to see paper to know they've written prose, many writers print out frequently. They edit on the page and then transfer the edits to the screen. In effect, they use the computer as a smart typewriter. But all this printing takes time and paper. Consciously try to accommodate to the screen and to print out only near the end of the whole writing project.

MACROREVISING

Develop a *routine* for revising, then within that routine, look back at the macrolevel and the microlevel you learned about in Chapters 4 and 5. At the macrolevel, revise to make sure that the document as a whole works;

think globally about your purpose and organization. Then make that order obvious to the reader with the following techniques that map a route through the document:

1. Use conventional formats.
2. State the controlling idea.
3. Use parallel headings.
4. Develop strong paragraphs.
5. Design the text as a visual.

Use Conventional Formats

Think about a fast-food restaurant. A seasoned visitor knows how to handle one. You know where to look for the menu. You know that you'll need to approach a cash register to order. You know when to pay. You know where to look for napkins and straws. Similarly, in entering a conventional business document, a reader has certain expectations about how to get what's needed. This textbook provides descriptions of the most important of these document formats in Parts III, IV, VI, and VII: memos, letters, bids, proposals, reports, resumes, procedures, and special corporate forms. Businesspeople share a knowledge of these forms. Identify the format, and the reader will know how to respond. When you violate a routine form, the reader has greater difficulty in reading.

When you revise, check to be sure that you have adhered to the conventions. If you discover that the document you are writing requires a specialized form, you'll need to incorporate a statement about the *form* before you can present new information.

State the Controlling Idea

A conventional format helps readers feel that they are on familiar ground. A control statement near the beginning also sets up the reader's motivation to read and provides a framework on which the reader can assemble the information that follows. Especially in routine documents—the bulk of business writing—such an overt statement clarifies the context for the reader by establishing the terms of the writer's and the reader's shared purpose in the document. In general, revise to give the overview before the details; give the familiar before the new.

If you think the reader may not understand your shared purpose or may resist your message for some reason, you may withhold that control statement until you develop a shared purpose and understanding. That is, you may try an *indirect* plan. As you revise, make sure that any indirection is strategic rather than accidental.

Use Parallel Headings

The control statement, as you saw in Chapter 4, controls not only *what* you will discuss but *how* you will divide the discussion. Those divisions must be *parallel,* that is, logically matched units of the whole. That parallelism is shown in the heading that begins each segment. In Figure 7–2, the "1 April invoice" is matched by the "3 April invoice." In this chapter, a unit on "macrorevising" is matched by a unit on "microrevising." Each of the five items in "macrorevising" is a "method" for mapping the text.

Headings aid readers in skimming and remembering main points. Most business documents use them to break up the page and to alert readers to turns in the discussion, just as highway signs alert drivers. Your draft should include headings from your outline; if not, add them in revision. List them in the table of contents of a report or in the introduction of less lengthy documents.

Headings come in two varieties: descriptive and informative. Descriptive headings name the segments of conventional documents:

```
Introduction
Results
Conclusions
Recommendations
```

Informative headings are specialized and derive from the subject matter of the document itself. All the headings in this chapter, for example, are *informative* ones. Check their informative value by looking again at the "What's Ahead" section at the start of the chapter. Sometimes, *all* headings in a document are informative. Or informative headings may appear within the larger segments identified by descriptive headings.

In indicating the levels of discussion, headings show what fits within what. The level is usually differentiated typographically. Use the style appropriate for your organization or client. Here is one technique.

0-ORDER HEADING

(Chapter title--centered, bold, underlined, capped)

FIRST-ORDER HEADING

(Major heading in chapter--centered, bold, capped)

Second-Order Heading

(Heading within a major segment--centered, underlined, upper- and lowercase)

Third-Order Heading

(Heading within a subsegment--at the left margin, underlined, upper- and lowercase)

Fourth-Order Heading

(Heading within a subsubsegment--indented, underlined, upper- and lowercase)

Fifth-Order Heading. The heading is run in at the beginning of the paragraph of text.

In revising headings, follow these guidelines:

- Keep to one line of type.
- Look for ways to minimize the number of levels.
- Keep headings at the same level parallel in expression.

Develop Strong Paragraphs

Paragraphs are probably the chief mapping device for readers. Paragraphs are a function of print. We don't speak in paragraphs. The paragraph indentation (or a double space above and below the paragraph) distinguishes that text as a unit. When you divide your text into paragraphs, you mark components of the discussion and you help pace the reading.

Marking Components

What is a component? In your outline, you note topics and subtopics. You may find as you write that each subtopic fills one paragraph. Or you may, like some writers, just keep writing as you draft. When you revise, you look for the *component* discussions. Often, you'll turn a rambling narrative into something more logically structured, as in Figure 7–2. In revising the document, the writer decided to peg the middle paragraphs of the letter to the two invoices—one paragraph for each.

Paragraphs, then, show the divisions of the text. But they also must *connect* with one another. In the *introductory* paragraph, you set up both the division and the connections. You preview the document. In such a paragraph, you may pose questions that you will answer, or you may explicitly state your intentions, as in the following introductory paragraph:

Predicting Term
Adding Terms

This report on the preferences of workers over fifty-five years old in planning for retirement is divided into <u>two</u> parts. <u>First</u>, the report details the results of our survey of a sample of 150 employees. <u>Second</u>, the report suggests some implications of that survey for corporate retirement policy.

You can also set up the topics that will be discussed. The following paragraph previews the "roles" of a university. Note, by the way, the use of parallelism. Each sentence begins with a role, expressed in the same form: "As a . . . ." Such parallelism is carried through in the report, each segment of which is devoted to one role, in the order given and with the noun as heading:

Repetition

Pronouns

The university is a big organization that performs many roles in addition to teaching and research. <u>As an entertainer</u>, <u>it</u> stages dramatic events, musical events, and athletic events. <u>As a restaurateur</u>, <u>it</u> feeds fifty-five thousand students and faculty every day. <u>As a hotel keeper</u>, <u>it</u> houses thirty thousand students in many varieties of accommodations.

As a security force, it maintains order and discipline among all the constituents. And as a transportation department, it maintains the roads, the parking lots, and the garages.

In the middle of the document—the longest stretch—you use *supporting* paragraphs that develop the components of your controlling idea. The following supporting paragraph begins a segment on the topic of managing conflict. The opening sentence engages attention with a familiar notion: It's good to avoid conflict. But the paragraph then turns around to show that *avoiding* conflict is ineffective; the last sentence sets up the topic for the segment, that is, managing conflict:

Repetition

Pronoun/Adding Term

Contrast

Many executives are skillful at avoiding conflict with coworkers. But that very skill may cause organizational problems. When different people hold conflicting opinions about something, those differences can inhibit action, of course. But they may also be the source of innovation. Moreover, smoothing over conflict may only postpone inevitable difficulties. The real skill, then, is not avoiding conflict, but managing conflicts to advance the goals of the organization.

The next supporting paragraph balances a contrast between Americans and Europeans. The *also* in the first sentence reminds the reader that the previous paragraph provided another point of comparison. The comparison is parallel. Americans are treated first, then Europeans, as announced in the opening sentence:

Adding Term

Repetition

Pronoun

Contrasting Phrase

Pronoun

Contrasting Phrase

Americans and Europeans also differ in how they assess someone's credentials. Americans are apt to judge people by their accomplishments. In response to a question like "Tell me about yourself," they list primarily their education and work experience: "I went to college at . . . ," "I worked for . . . ," "I am a (and then they name a profession or other occupation)." On the other hand, Europeans are often judged by, and judge others by, their family connections and their professional associates. When asked about themselves, they tend to respond more indirectly with information that connects them to people: "My mother, Frau Doktor Wilmanns of Munich, has had an important influence on me."

Concluding paragraphs aid the reader in reconnecting the topics developed in each component, as in the concluding paragraph of Figure 7–2.

Within each paragraph, sentences, too, must be connected. Parallelism of sentence form is one strong connector. In addition, as Figure 7–3 shows, certain terms can aid in signaling connections. You can also connect sentences in a pattern of cross-linking in which the first part of the sentence restates familiar information from the sentence before; the end of the sentence provides new information, as in the following sequence:

FIGURE 7–3.
Road signs for the reader: Signaling terms in paragraphs.

- Pronouns that substitute for earlier nouns ("The balance sheets. . . . *They* . . .")
- Summarizing terms (*these delays, those signals, these issues*)
- Repetition of key terms
- Connecting words or phrases
  - To add: *and, in addition, moreover, also*
  - To contrast: *but, on the other hand, however*
  - To cite: *for example, as an illustration, for instance*
  - To change scale: *more broadly, specifically*
  - To show a result: *thus, therefore, consequently*
  - To restate or clarify: *that is, in other words*
  - To sum up: *finally, in conclusion*

```
But we did provide a work plan and a summary report of find-
ings and recommendations regarding the site, (documents) re-
quired by the EPA. The preparation of those (documents) neces-
sitated the extensive (study) represented in the invoice. That
(study), however, provided evidence to show that the storage
tanks can be removed without the much more costly remediation
measures other firms might recommend.
```

Once you have established a pattern in a paragraph, stick to it. Don't for the sake of variety, or by accident, send the reader mixed signals about how to read.

Pacing the Reading

Paragraphing paces the reading. As you have seen, paragraphs serve a *logical* function in designating the components of a discussion. They also serve a *psychological* function in dividing the text into units that match the reader's reading style. A paragraph adjusts the amount of material which is to be delivered during any one moment of concentrated attention to the capacity of the reader for such attention. That means, for example, that you should use short paragraphs for difficult information and less motivated readers. Use longer paragraphs for easier material and the motivated.

Break up a sequence of long paragraphs with a short one for emphasis. Look for such sequences in revision. Look for whole pages without paragraph divisions. If you see such a page, rethink the text so that you can insert a paragraph break.

When your discussion is complex, reward the reader with a short *transitional* paragraph that allows some breathing room. Such paragraphs provide no new information but pull a discussion together before you plunge the reader into the new material:

```
Having examined three problem areas in our operation--in-
ventory control, waiter service, and bookkeeping--let's turn
to a description of the solution for all of these: a manage-
ment information system.
```

Design the Text as a Visual

In your revising, focus on identifying clear blocks of text; then provide a map for readers that helps them both to know which blocks are coming up and to remember which blocks they've seen. As you've seen, you'll create that map by using conventional formats or explaining a new format; by clearly stating the controlling idea; by using parallel headings to preview new sections, to show the relative levels of different sections, and to aid readers in remembering; and by developing strong paragraphs. In mapping the text, you are also designing it to work for the reader. As you wrestle the text into shape, consider as well how it will look on the page or the screen. Appearance alone cannot substitute for clear presentation, and merely fussing with typefaces won't solve structural problems in the presentation. But well designed prose *looks* good. Its appearance reinforces the clarity of the text and adds pleasure in the reading.

With a wordprocessing system connected to a laser printer, and especially with a *desktop publishing* program that includes multiple features for text and graphics, as you'll see in Chapters 10 and 19, you can call up many options in page design. Such options should serve your information and your reader; they should not simply draw attention to themselves. Here are a few of the options to consider in shaping your text:

- **Type.** Figure 7–4 shows examples of different typefaces (for example, Chicago, Geneva, and New York), type sizes (designated in points), family branches (bold, shadowed, outlined), postures (roman or italic), and composition (upper- or lowercase).
- **Margins.** Wordprocessing software allows you to justify the right margin, that is, line up all the words at the right edge, as in this textbook. But most authorities suggest a "ragged" (un-lined-up) right margin in all but typeset documents.
- **Lines.** You can adjust the width of the lines on a page and the space between the lines (as in single and double spacing).
- **White space.** Designers emphasize the need to think about *active* white space, that is, using the space to distinguish the components of a discussion (like the indentations that open a paragraph). Check that every page has at least one paragraph break. Currently, a wide left margin is popular in books and brochures. Sometimes the margin contains headings or brief items of text.

In addition, consider the design of the document as a whole. Memos *look* like memos and letters *look* like letters, as you'll see in Chapters 12 and 13. Particular organizations may set standards for appearance. You yourself may decide on the answers to other questions about design, or you may need to conform to standards set by the reader. Ask these questions:

This sentence is set in Chicago typeface at a 12 point size.
This sentence is set in Chicago typeface at a 12 point size with an italic effect.
This sentence is set in Chicago typeface at a 12 point size with a bold effect.
This sentence is set in Chicago typeface at a 12 point size with an outline effect.
THIS SENTENCE IS SET IN CHICAGO TYPEFACE AT A 12 POINT SIZE WITH ALL SMALL CAPITAL LETTERS.

This sentence is set in Venice typeface at a 10 point size.

This sentence is set in London typeface at a 16 point size.

This sentence is set in Monaco typeface at an 18 point size.

This sentence is set in Geneva typeface at a 9 point size.

This sentence is set in Athens typeface at an 18 point size.

This sentence is set in New York typeface at a 20 point size.
This sentence is set in New York typeface at a 16 point size.
This sentence is set in New York typeface at a 14 point size.
This sentence is set in New York typeface at a 12 point size.
This sentence is set in New York typeface at a 10 point size.
This sentence is set in New York typeface at an 8 point size.

FIGURE 7–4.
A sample of the type possibilities available in a personal desktop publishing system.
(Courtesy of R. John Brockmann.)

- Is the *size* appropriate—both the size of the page and the length of the text as a whole?
- Is the *binding* effective? Handbooks of procedures that will be updated, for example, are probably best presented in a loose-leaf binder.
- Have you used *special features* appropriately, for example, sections of text differentiated by different-colored paper?
- If appropriate, are there *section dividers* bearing the title of each section on a tab?
- Do the *graphic devices* or *logos* on the title page and section dividers reinforce the controlling idea of the document or its producer, and are such devices parallel to those in any other documents in the series?

MICROREVISING

At the macrolevel, as you have seen, you look globally at your document to focus its main point, to restructure and reconnect as necessary the blocks of evidence that support that point, and to design a route through the text for the reader.

At the microlevel, you check your form of expression within that framework. You make sure that your *voice*—in words, sentences, and visuals—is appropriate and correct. Keep in mind what you learned in Chapter 5. Look once more at the voices in the original and the revised letters of Figures 7–1 and 7–2. How do they differ? Obviously, the revised version is shorter. *Shortening* is not always a goal of revising, since a discussion sometimes needs to be expanded with more evidence, but often what we draft uses more words than necessary to tell its tale. Look for ways to cut the words and intensify the meaning. Here are some brief guidelines for focusing and emphasizing. Check the Handbook at the end of the book for further advice in editing out errors in grammar, punctuation, and word choice.

Focusing

The revised letter in Figure 7–2 focuses clearly on the two invoices, which are identified in underlined headings in the text. On average, sentences in the revised version are shorter, reduced in verbiage, and strengthened in the area of relationships among subject, verb, and object or complement. Words are used more economically:

Original: `We are in receipt of . . .`
Revised: `We received . . .`

Original: `Availability of drilling contractors was limited because of the work demand for drillers at that time of year.`
Revised: `Availability of drillers at that time of year was limited.`

Original: `We take strenuous exception to the comment that our invoice was "padded". . . . They are not "padded" in any way.`
Revised: `The bill is not padded.`

The revised version is also more direct and concrete, telling more in fewer words:

Original: We hope you take into account the fact that we have saved you tremendous costs associated with this problem. Many other firms may have taken less of an aggressive posture with the EPA and performed unnecessary work and recommended costly remediation measures.

Revised: That study . . . provided evidence to show that the storage tanks can be removed without the much more costly remediation measures other firms might recommend. The study saved the need for regulatory meetings and extensive reconstruction.

Emphasizing

While focusing the text more precisely, the revised version also omits information about the 10 percent reduction in the bill as well as the protests about the organization's integrity and sincerity. Those items unnecessarily diluted the argument. It uses a five-word sentence for a major point: "The bill is not padded." The ending, too, is clearer. Note the difference between "In that light, we ask that you reevaluate the amount of your final payment" and "We look forward to receiving your check for $1500. . . ."

The revised version achieves appropriate emphasis and a professional tone. Accusations and nit-picking in the original give way to simple declarations of fact.

Proofreading

At the end of your revising, before you hand in or mail or fax or e-mail the message to the reader, *proofread.* That means, for example, check word use. In Figure 7–1, the writer uses *verbal understanding* incorrectly; Figure 7–2 is correct. *Oral* means *not in writing. Verbal* simply means *in words*—either spoken or written.

Check spelling. Check punctuation. Check consistency in content between visuals and text. If you've noted in your control statement that you will discuss five topics, check that there are still five and that each is numbered properly. For letter-perfect copy, proofread backward, the last word in the document first, and so on. Or have someone read the text aloud as you check another copy. Check compliance of your format with requirements for the document: line spacing, total number of pages, margins, type of paper, and appropriate elements. Don't lose the easy points by omitting some item or required design feature.

READABILITY

The goal of your revising is to enhance *readability,* that is, the reader's ability to understand and use the document to achieve your common purposes. Not all readers, of course, read in the same way, and one reader may use different strategies for reading different documents. According to Gibson and Levin's Adaptive Process Model of Reading, readers adapt their strategies to[1]

- Different types of information they're reading about
- The difficulty of the concepts they're reading about
- The style of writing
- The rate of understanding as reading proceeds
- The newness or oldness of the material to them
- Their personal interest in the subject
- Their reason for reading
- The instructions given about how or why to read

They also try to read as little as they can to get their work done, skimming and zooming in to find what they need. The strategies you've been reading about in this chapter will help you to map a variety of routes through the text for different readers.

Moreover, although early measures of readability focused on the need for short words and short sentences, current research emphasizes the need for the document to match its *context:* the document develops a shared understanding between writer and reader, it meets its goal, and it shows the reader *how* to read as well as gives the reader *what* information is necessary. Readability is not tested arbitrarily through a count of syllables and words but realistically with a sample of users actually using the document. In "*FYI:* Measuring Readability" (pages 144–145), the head of the leading U.S. organization concerned with readability, the Document Design Center, summarizes the issues.

SUMMARY

- Experienced writers mix drafting and revising effectively, now creating text to fill the **outline,** now **reviewing** the text to see if the sentences and the plan itself work. If not, these writers make a new plan. Inexperienced writers mix drafting and revising ineffectively, either **revising too soon** and killing the text or **not revising enough.** Wordprocessing programs facilitate the mechanics of revising: adding, deleting, and moving text and checking on spelling. But working at a screen brings risks in the form of the wrong kind of revising and, ironically, excessive printing.
- To make the macrostructure of your document easy to follow, **map a route** through the discussion for the reader. Use a **conventional format** that matches the reader's expectation for the structure of the document. State the **controlling idea** that governs the content. Use **parallel headings** to provide an advance organizer for new information, to point to turns in the discussion, to show the levels of segments, and to aid the reader in remembering main points. Develop **strong paragraphs.** Design the text **visually** to reinforce the central message.
- Paragraphs mark the **components** of a discussion: They divide and connect. Each paragraph develops a component or a subcomponent of the

[1] This summary is adapted from a presentation by Daphne O. Jameson at the Association for Business Communication, Midwest and Canada Regional Conference, April 1990.

MEASURING READABILITY

Janice C. Redish
Vice President, American Institutes for Research

What Is Readability?

You want what you write to be readable, but what do you mean by *readability?* You could mean "Is it legible?"—Can readers see the words and pictures without straining? You could mean "Is it understandable?"—Can readers grasp your message quickly and easily? You could mean "Is it useful?"—Can readers use the document to accomplish both their purposes and yours?

What you really want is a document that works. Therefore, you must consider all three meanings of *readability.* An effective document is legible, understandable, and useful.

Can Formulas Measure Readability?

Formulas that give you a number or a reading grade level take an extremely limited view of readability. They measure only sentences and words. Readability formulas can mislead you for at least two reasons:

1. They don't measure most of the important factors in readability.
2. Short sentences and short words aren't always easier to read.

What Readability Formulas Don't Measure

Because readability formulas can look only at words and sentences, they don't tell you whether

- The content is appropiate for your readers.
- The tone is appropriate to accomplish your purposes.
- Your document is organized logically for your readers.
- Your sentences make sense together.
- The headings in your document help readers find information quickly.
- The page design helps your readers find information quickly.
- The type is legible for your readers.
- You have enough examples to help readers.
- You have illustrations (pictures, charts, etc.) when needed.

controlling idea of the document. A paragraph must also connect with the one above and the one below. **Introductory** paragraphs preview the document. **Supporting** paragraphs elaborate the details. **Concluding** paragraphs bind off the discussion. Within paragraphs, the sentences must connect with one another. Paragraphs also pace the reading and match the reader's capacity for paying attention. **Transitional** paragraphs add no new information; they summarize one segment and point ahead to another in a lengthy document.

- In your planning, and especially in your revising, think of the text as a **visual.** Consider such elements of design as typeface, layout, and white space. Keep documents in a series parallel in design.

Yet all of these elements are critical to readability.

Why Short Sentences and Short Words Aren't Always Easier to Read

Not all short words are easy words. Readability formulas that count syllables can't tell the difference between these two sentences:

> We waved our hands.
> We waived our rights.

You may be using simple words in a specialized way. Readability formulas can't tell the difference between these two sentences:

> Enter your living room.
> Enter your gross income.

What Can Style Checkers Do?

Many of the computer programs that give you readability scores also give you advice on style. They can be useful if you consider them advisers, not arbiters of style. Like readability formulas, they can react only sentence by sentence and word by word. If you concentrate on sentences and words, however, you may be missing the most serious problems in your document. If you change sentences and words in isolation, you may be destroying the coherence and continuity of your text.

Then, How Can You Tell if Your Writing Is Readable?

When you have a draft, the best way to measure its readability is to have a sample of your audience try it out. In a "usability test," you address all the aspects of readability. You not only learn how legible, understandable, and useful the document is, but find out just where and how it needs to be fixed.

- The ultimate goal of revision is to ensure that your document *sounds* like you—has an effective and engaging voice—and presents the right information in a structure that is as easy to read as possible. Although most measures of readability focus on words and sentences (short is better than long in each category), current research points to a more important measure: The document should match the reader's style of reading and its **context;** that is, it should develop a shared understanding between writer and reader, meet its **goal,** and show the reader *how* to read as well as give the reader *what* information is necessary. Readability is not tested arbitrarily through a count of syllables and words but realistically with a sample of actual potential users of the document.

EXERCISES

For Discussion

1. What is your own revising routine? Answer the following questions. Watch yourself as you revise a document, although such self-consciousness may temporarily reduce the impact of your revising.
    a. If you use a computer for writing, do you write a draft longhand first and then type it in? If so, do you *change* the text as you type it? Or do you write directly at the keyboard? Do you edit at the terminal, or do you print out your text and revise on paper? How many changes do you need to make in the text before you print it?
    b. Once you get going on a draft, when do you start to look back to revise? After every sentence? After every paragraph? Not until you have written for a specific period or filled the screen? If your routine varies, describe your approach to looking back.
    c. What cues do you look for in the text that tell you what to revise?
    d. Do you consider your routine effective?

2. Compare how different people in your class or office respond to the questions in Exercise 1.

3. Based on your instructor's comments on your assignments and any discussion you have heard by your instructor or by other students about your work, create your own revising checklist. Note the *strengths* of your writing that you'll need to maintain in future documents. Note any *weaknesses* you'll need to correct.

For Writing

4. The best writing exercise is to *revise* a document. Choose a document, preferably your own. As you revise it, look for ways to *map* the text for the reader, to design the page, and to ensure that your voice will be engaging.

5. Each of the following sentences is ineffective. Some are simply wrong; they include errors in punctuation, faulty agreement (of subject and verb or of pronoun and referent), lack of parallelism, misplaced or dangling modification, and shifts in subject or in point of view. Some use words imprecisely and inefficiently. Some drag the reader through cumbersome twists of thought in the writer's mind. In such sentences, the writer *thinks* that an idea has been conveyed when the reader is actually missing essential terms or concepts. Use what you learned in this chapter and Chapter 5 to revise these sentences. If your knowledge of grammar and punctuation is rusty, refer to the Handbook at the back of the book for specific advice.
    a. To develop solutions to the stated objectives we will solicit ideas from students and faculty.
    b. Several of the dimmers are no longer working as well as many of the dimmer switches.
    c. Many of the house lights are burned out or are missing, this fact led to an incident of an elderly woman slipping on the stairs because she could not see in the darkness.
    d. If it is not feasible for either of these methods because of monetary

limits, grants and or donations will be looked into in order to rectify this growing problem.

e. These estimates, which, averaged over two or three semesters, would become very accurate, would enable us to determine our service program earlier in the semester, because we would know our spending limit.

f. Because the restaurants most important goal is customer satisfaction, it must be sure to give them the proper attention that they need.

g. The incidence of child abuse in this country is rising. There is also a rise in the number of mental problems diagnosed among preschool and elementary school children—some are a result of child abuse—some are not.

h. Compare the grades of students who were counseled in private schools, with those comparable problems in public schools who have not yet been counseled.

i. For example, the lack of adequate planning before launching into a project might cause efforts to be redone or revised before the project can be successfully completed thereby causing more time and money to be spent than would have been necessary if proper planning took place in the beginning.

j. The system test work load in terms of staff days required is itemized below. This estimate is contingent upon timely completion of the activities, on which the processor testing is dependent, according to the schedules in the processor testing milestones.

k. The problems which concern most businesspeople are those of communication, activists' lack of misunderstanding of how business operates, the role of profits and profit margins, and what are perceived (among the minority) as the unrealistic, unreasonable, or even hostile attitudes of consumerists.

l. It is extremely important, in delegating, that the manager take whatever steps are necessary to assure complete understanding of the assignment on the part of subordinates.

m. Much information should be passed on to your staff, but quite often it is not important enough to reproduce a copy for everyone.

n. Even despite the honest efforts of all parties involved to fully understand their objectives you will probably still experience instances where trial and error will occur.

6. For each of the following paragraphs, determine
   - How the paragraph represents a *component* of the larger discussion
   - How the sentences are connected

   Then *revise* the paragraphs into more efficient and connected prose.

   a. During the summer months at the bank a number of deposit accounts were closed. Since that period of transition, our bank has been continuously losing an alarming amount of customers. The percentage of accounts that are closed each year is 3 percent. This figure is the average for the industry. The rate of closed accounts for our bank is 18 percent.

   b. At the end of this past winter term, many students moved back to the dormitories and found they needed to make mid-year room changes. As these changes were attempted to be made, much confusion and inconvenience began to be felt by the students, the Resident Assistants, the Hall Director and many frustrated parents. Piles of students' belongings were left crowding hallways and lounges as students were forced to wait (sometimes as long as two hours) to move into their new rooms.

c. To test my proposal, I will gather and survey the opinions of my coworkers, both buyers and clerks. This will show the consensus of the department. This will be finished within the week. Also, research will be gathered on the cost of the terminals. As we have the system already, the terminals are the only equipment that is needed. This will be completed by 2 May.

For Collaboration

7. A key element in revising, as you read in "*FYI:* Measuring Readability," is "usability testing," that is, testing how a document works with a sample of people who need to use it. As a group project, obtain a document that tells you how to do something, for example, how to register for classes, how to assemble or operate a device (the instructions for using a VCR might be particularly fruitful), or how to accomplish a procedure in a laboratory class. The group should all be familiar with the process in general but should not be experts in it. Then review the document in terms of what you have learned in this chapter and in Chapter 6 on visual presentation. Brainstorm about the document's content and method of presentation. Then revise the document for greater *readability.*

8 UNDERSTANDING BUSINESS INFORMATION

What's Ahead

THE ROLE OF INFORMATION IN BUSINESS COMMUNICATION
TYPES OF BUSINESS INFORMATION
USING DIFFERENT TYPES OF INFORMATION
CHARACTERISTICS OF GOOD BUSINESS INFORMATION
- Accuracy
- Timeliness
- Relevance
- Reliability
- Sensibleness

PATTERNS OF INFORMATION USE
- Using Information to Record
- Using Information to Inform
- Using Information to Persuade

SUMMARY
EXERCISES

Do You Know 

- What purpose does information serve in producing business documents and presentations?
- What kinds of information are available to business communicators?
- How can you distinguish good from bad information when you are preparing a business document or presentation?
- How do you use information in business communication to make sure you achieve your goals?
- When you interpret information, what rules and procedures should you know and apply?

"The only thing as bad as too little information is too much information."

Although it's easy to imagine having too little information about an issue or problem, many people don't realize that it's often just as bad to have too *much*. In fact, businesspeople frequently complain about "information overload"—that is, being smothered in reams of data, often produced simply because someone (probably using computerized information systems) *could* produce it rather than because it bears on the problem at hand.

In business, information is a vital commodity. It provides the basis for decisions and serves as the *content* of all business communication. It is the material that is carried within your communication message. Good information is highly valued. Bad information is dangerous.

In this chapter, you'll see why information is so important to business. You'll learn how to classify and assess it and how to interpret it effectively for use in various forms of business communication. You'll discover the difference between good and bad information—and thus see why too much information, particularly if it's bad, can create as many problems as too little.

THE ROLE OF INFORMATION IN BUSINESS COMMUNICATION

Commercial organizations and nonprofit institutions daily produce, file, process, shuffle, and try somehow to stay on top of a wealth of information: sales projections, audit data, personnel policies, judicial decisions, stock quotations, figures on the gross national product, purchase orders. Indeed, the vast amount of information that large organizations have to deal with causes an information overload that can prevent effective decision-making and can obstruct clear communication.

However, information plays a vital role in business—and therefore in business communication. Its communication role varies according to the purpose of the document or the talk in which it is used. In Chapter 2, you learned the three broad purposes of communicating in organizations: to record, to inform, and to persuade. Sometimes, as you saw, these purposes overlap. If you are writing a memo "for the record" or an informative letter, information is dominant but plays a *passive* role. Let's say you are asked to get bids on a new television set for your fraternity and are to present a report to the finance committee at next Monday's meeting. Your report will obviously be centered on information, but the information will play a passive role: It's just there. Of course, you will try to present it clearly, concisely, simply, and attractively—perhaps in a table or graph that will aid understanding. But you will really just be presenting the information so it can do its job.

On the other hand, in communication that is meant to persuade, information plays an *active* role: It helps you to convince someone of something. If your original fraternity assignment had been to recommend which new television set to buy, you would be making a persuasive report. You would gather the information just as you did for the informative report, but then you would use it as a tool in persuasion. This doesn't mean that you will manipulate the information in any devious way, only that you will structure and shape it to fit the purpose at hand.

To summarize, the role that information plays in business communication depends on whether you are communicating principally to record or inform, or principally to persuade. If recording or informing is your goal, the information will be passive, that is, presented for its own sake. If persuading is your goal, the information will be active, that is, used to advance an argument or support a recommendation.

TYPES OF BUSINESS INFORMATION

Regardless of the specific goal of your document or talk and hence of the role that the information plays in it, you must understand information in a broad sense. What is information? One useful way to classify it is according to its internal characteristics. We can identify four types:

Fact: Undisputed or accepted knowledge
Observation: A record of sensory perceptions
Interpretation: An explanation of an event or a characteristic
Opinion: A statement of a preference or viewpoint

These four types of information differ according to the extent to which they are "accepted": Facts are most widely accepted, and opinions are least widely accepted. For example, if we say that water freezes at 32 degrees Fahrenheit, we are stating something that is widely accepted. Indeed, this is a fact by definition, a universally agreed-on position (assuming, of course, the use of the Fahrenheit scale). If we say that we prefer snow to rain, this is a statement of personal preference and applies only to us; others have different views.

These examples are simple. What about the statement "It rained in Seattle yesterday"? This is an observation, the record of a sensation. If you were in Seattle yesterday and got wet, then you observed that it was raining. When the National Weather Service records the weather in Seattle as rain, then the observation really turns into a fact because it achieves a kind of official status. It is written down, recorded in retrievable form, and set above debate. But note that the fact is based on an observation.

Now let us look at this statement: "It rained in Seattle yesterday because a cold front passed over a warm front." We call this statement an interpretation because it explains a phenomenon. Is it a fact? Meteorologists hold that the collision of warm and cold air masses produces rain. But there are other interpretations. Primitive peoples believed that rain came in response to supplications to the gods, and even today rainmakers perform ritual dances to bring relief to drought-stricken areas. Who is to say that one interpretation is better than another?

As you can see, we are getting into tricky territory here because if we pushed logic to its limits we might argue that all facts, observations, and interpretations are merely opinions. If we go too far in this direction, we begin to call into question a lot of views that civilized people have a great stake in keeping settled. It just doesn't make sense to debate every "fact," because we need to have broad agreement on many matters simply to get along in life. In sports, it's a settled point that the official is always right. If the homeplate umpire calls the pitch a strike, it is a strike. If each call were debated endlessly, the game would never proceed. If the batter or the spectators have a different opinion, they are welcome to it, but the game must go on.

USING DIFFERENT TYPES OF INFORMATION

To see how classifying information can help us understand and use it in business communication, let us suppose that you are asked to send your supervisor a memo reporting on the progress you are making on your assignment to develop a new benefits package for assembly-line workers in the Houston plant. In preparing to write the memo, you gather the following information:

1. The average benefits package for similar employees in the Houston labor market, according to the Texas Department of Labor Statistics, amounts to 42 percent of their base salary.
2. The benefits package in place at your company's Houston plant costs an amount equal to 48 percent of base salary, according to the personnel office.
3. A survey you conducted of workers in the Houston plant reveals that 66 percent are "satisfied" or "very satisfied" with the current benefits plan.
4. The general manager of the Houston plant has written in a memo to

you that he regards the existing package as "unnecessarily costly" and "not appreciated by the workers themselves."

5. Several people in the Houston personnel office have told you that imposing a new benefits package that reduces contributions from the employer may lead to pressure for unionization among the workers.

Here you have five pieces of information. Before you pull them together for your memo, you need to assess them and to determine the usefulness of what you have available to work with in composing your memo. Here is where understanding the types of information helps.

It's pretty easy to see that the first two items on the list are facts as we have defined them: information that is agreed on. It is possible, however, to imagine disputes that could arise over them. For example, the question of what constitutes "similar" workers might be raised to call into doubt the

Information, provided through both printed and electronic media, serves as the raw material of business communication.

data from the Texas Bureau of Labor Statistics. Exactly what benefits are included in calculating the company's contribution ratio might also be questioned to discredit the 48 percent figure that was given by the personnel office. But, as in baseball, at some point you have to agree on what is accepted as a fact—or at least on who gets to make the final call that will be considered official.

If we look at the fourth and fifth pieces of information, we would probably agree that these are not facts but either interpretations or opinions. They are subject to disagreement depending on who looks at them. This doesn't mean that they are useless, only that they are not recorded facts of wide acceptability, as the first two are. We simply need to classify them as separate from facts so we can use the information with maximum effectiveness.

The third piece of information is trickier to classify according to our scheme. In one way, the level of satisfaction among the current workers might be called opinion because the responses to the survey are obviously expressions of personal viewpoints. However, the statement that 66 percent of those surveyed consider themselves "satisfied" or "very satisfied" can be regarded as a fact, that is, presumably, undisputed data obtained in the survey. If the results are accurately reported, then it's a fact that the satisfaction level, according to this particular survey of those particular workers at that particular time, is 66 percent. We might want to call this piece of information an observation rather than a fact because it is the record of a perception.

When you assemble information in preparing to write a memo or other business document, you should not spend an undue amount of time separating that information into fact, observation, interpretation, and opinion. But using the classification scheme as a tool can help you see the differences among the kinds of information available to you. The more you understand about information, the more effectively you can use it to communicate to others. (The section below on "Patterns of Information Use" provides specific advice on different ways of using business information.)

CHARACTERISTICS OF GOOD BUSINESS INFORMATION

Another characteristic of information that you need to assess is its quality. What is *good* business information?

Quality is a difficult concept, but it's a practical one. People often ask, "How good is your information?" They want to know its quality. There are many ways to measure quality in information. Here are five common sense tests that information you use in communication should meet. Information should be

- Accurate
- Timely
- Relevant
- Reliable
- Sensible

Accuracy

Information should always be *accurate.* If you are presenting data on sales at five branch stores over a two-month period, make sure that the numbers are correct: Verify that they were properly gathered, check them against the original sources where possible, perform the arithmetic correctly, and so forth. And of course, don't forget to check the numbers in your memo against the numbers on the printout from which you worked; copying accurately is part of meeting the test of accuracy. Similarly, if you are quoting somone, you can't prove the accuracy of what the person said, but you can be certain that you are quoting her or him correctly. Whatever the information you use, make sure that it is accurate. People can still disagree with you, but give them correct information to disagree with.

Timeliness

Information should be *timely.* The debt owed by less developed countries to U.S. banks should be reported from the latest available figures, not from the ones you happened to run across in an old newspaper. If you want to value the assets of a company, find out today's receivables, not last month's. If you are quoting the views of an economist on the relationship between the federal deficit and interest rates, be sure you are quoting her most recent writings or speeches. What she said last August may not be what she believes today. Always aim for the most recently available information, unless, of course, historical comparisons are required. The more up to date the information you cite, the more willing your audience will be to believe it.

Relevance

Information should always be *relevant* to the question at hand. Relevance is, of course, relative. In examining the investment attractiveness of a new software company, for example, you may not at first consider its stock option plan for executives relevant, but that information might indeed be quite relevant to determining the nature of the firm's commitment to its personnel, the future liabilities it may incur, and the prudence of the management. You have to gauge relevance according to the issues you are addressing and the point you want to make. Citing the views of an astrologist on the movement of the stock market illustrates an extreme of irrelevance that few serious persons would entertain. But few situations are so clear. If the astrologist's record is better than your broker's, you might want to reconsider. In general, though, relevance is fairly easy to determine.

Reliability

Like relevance, *reliability* is a test that you have to apply with care. The simple question to ask is "Can I rely on this information?" Answering it means evaluating the source. The daily *Wall Street Journal* is a reliable source of information on new debt offerings, stock prices (from yesterday, of course), and management changes at large corporations. Your hometown newspaper might cover in greater detail the problems of your local utility in bringing on-line its newest nuclear reactor. But a phone call from a friend hinting that a merger may occur soon between two oil companies clearly doesn't meet the test of reliability. Whenever possible, use standard, recognized sources of information, preferably printed ones. When you are quoting unpublished sources, reliability is harder to measure, but if you always aim for the highest level of dependability you will seldom go wrong. At the very least, you can always flag a dubious source or piece of information by indicating that it comes from "usually reliable sources" (if it does) or is "speculative" (if it is). The golden rule of being honest with your reader applies here as it does everywhere in communication.

Sensibleness

Finally, the best test of information is its *sensibleness.* If you are quoting a source that says the world will end next week, you should certainly be aware that many people will regard that prediction as silly. If your computer printout shows that sales of frisbees increased 500 percent in the Cherry Hill store every day for five days, you should be alerted to the possibility of error. Maybe sales did exhibit that pattern for some logical reason—if the International Frisbee Contest was held in southern New Jersey that week, for example. But information that looks odd to you may, in fact, *be* odd. It will certainly look that way to others, and it will therefore reflect poorly on you and may undermine the goal of your memo or report.

Be wary about major changes in data over time that don't have obvious explanations. Reread quotations carefully if a surprising statement appears: "The President said yesterday he doubted that his wife would support his campaign." Be on the lookout for the startling or the bizarre. Sometimes, truth is startling or bizarre, but you are skating on thin ice if you report information that just doesn't make sense.

Information that is accurate, timely, relevant, reliable, and sensible is, of course, not perfect. Your tests for these qualities may lead you to conclusions different from those that someone else would reach. These are subjective matters. The final test of information is its particular usefulness in a given document or presentation.

PATTERNS OF INFORMATION USE

Because information is the content and not the goal of business communication, you need to be aware not just of its internal characteristics but also of how it is used. The "how" varies with the goal—with why you are using it.

Suppose you are tracking stocks with the aim of potential investment. You jot down pertinent data in a table each day; that is, you *record.* Now suppose you are a broker whose client asks for a list of ten stocks in the retail industry that have a price–earnings ratio under 10, a yield of at least 6 percent, and a price under $35. You might prepare a simple list with the stock names in the left column and the pertinent information in three columns to the right of the names. The client can then run down the list and find what he or she wants. Your goal here is to *inform.*

If you are asked not just to inform the client but to make a recommendation on a stock to purchase—that is, if your goal is to *persuade*—you might present the same simple table but also include a paragraph or two in which you advance reasons why one or several issues are more desirable than others. Or you might include data, within the text of a letter rather than in a table, on the one or several stocks you recommend.

In these examples, the same information assumes a different form depending on the goal: recording, informing, or persuading.

Using Information to Record

If you write to record, the criterion for information use is ease of access. The presentation of the information is determined by the characteristics of the information itself. Writing to record often calls for tables and other visual forms of presentation to make the information most accessible. You want the information to be there for use when a need arises. Writing the minutes of a meeting, keeping a log of telephone calls, and noting the activity of a stock are typical examples of the use of information to record.

Using Information to Inform

Writing to inform requires added attention to the reader's needs. Visual forms of presentation are useful, but you need to pay attention to potential problems in accessibility. Uncommon or ambiguous terms may require explanation. Grouping of data may be appropriate. You need to help the reader understand, but because you are not making a case, the information itself is still dominant and plays a passive role, as in recording. Writing to a supervisor to inform her about an important sales prospect and sending a letter to customers to let them know of a new service are illustrations of the use of information to inform.

Using Information to Persuade

If the communication goal is persuasion, the criterion for information use is support of the point or recommendation being made. The presentation of information is governed by the writer's goal and perception of what the reader needs to understand to accept the argument being made. Information therefore plays an *active* role: It is there to advance the writer's intention and to persuade the reader to adopt the writer's point of view or suggestion for action.

To support arguments in persuasive writing, you need to answer questions in the reader's mind. Chief among these questions are always "What?" and "Why?" The reader wants to know facts and reasons: what happened, and why it happened. Therefore, the information you use to persuade will have to answer one or the other of these two questions. Facts, as we have seen, are undisputed or agreed-on statements in numerical or verbal form, such as dates, numbers, or names. Interpretations, or reasons, are explanations of the facts and the relationships that may exist among the facts. For example, it may be a fact that the sales of Product Y increased 18 percent in June over May, and another fact may be that advertising expenditures for the product increased 10 percent in June over May. To say that there is a direct causal link between the two facts—that the increase in sales resulted from the increase in ad spending—is an interpretation, an explanation of the relationship between the two facts. Because most business problems concern *why* rather than just *what,* when you prepare documents or talks you will frequently find yourself interpreting information.

Different arguments can often be made based on the same information. This is true not because of error or fraud on the part of those making the different arguments but because of the way in which the information is *interpreted.* As you assess and use information in business documents, you need to interpret information carefully.

Guidelines for Interpreting Information

Here are four common sense guidelines for interpreting information:

1. Make sure that specific details adequately support your generalizations.
2. Test cause-and-effect relationships carefully.
3. Avoid oversimplification and exaggeration.
4. Use all the available information, not just those parts that support your own conclusion or argument.

1. **Make sure that specific details adequately support your generalizations.** Generalizations are drawn from specifics and should be adequately supported by them. Sometimes, when you interpret information, you reach conclusions that are not properly supported by the details that you have analyzed.

The owner of the RapRock Music Store surveyed 200 customers one Saturday. Here are two of the results:

- Fifty percent of the customers had shopped at RapRock before.
- Thirty percent of the repeat customers made purchases on Saturday of $15 or more, and 20 percent of the new customers did so.

Based on these data, the owner drew this conclusion: Because repeat customers buy more than new customers, we should work on getting more customers to return to the store.

Is the generalization adequately supported by the details? If the 30 repeat customers who each made purchases of $15 or more in fact averaged $15 each, the total sales for that group would be $450. But if the 20 new customers made *larger average* purchases—of, for example, $30 each—then the total sales for that group would be $600. In this case, the owner's generalization would be inadequately supported by the details, and the opposite course of action—trying to encourage *new* customers—would be more appropriate.

It's easy to raise other questions: Was the Saturday on which the survey was taken a *typical* sales day—or even a typical *Saturday?* What specific purchases were made by both groups? Perhaps a new compact disk by a hot group was introduced that day and constituted the bulk of the sales to both groups. That fact might change the generalization.

2. **Test cause-and-effect relationships carefully.** It's often hard to know whether an apparent *cause* really leads to an observed *effect.* Ascribing an outcome to a specific cause can often lead to problems when one interprets information.

The owner of RapRock Music found from his survey that 60 percent of the women who came to shop on Saturday made a purchase, whereas only 35 percent of the men did. He concluded that because women bought more than men, he should target his advertising to women.

Is this a reasonable conclusion? Is gender the *cause* of this effect (that is, of greater purchases)? Another factor might play a role, for example, age. Suppose that *all* the purchasers were aged fifteen to nineteen, whereas *all* the nonpurchasers were twenty or older. The *cause* of buying might more logically be considered age rather than gender.

Seventy percent of those who made purchases at RapRock on the day of the survey paid by credit card, and the rest used cash. Does this fact make valid the conclusion that the store's acceptance of credit cards *causes* greater sales?

The test of a causal conclusion is whether another, equally plausible explanation exists for an event. In this situation, neither gender nor method of payment may be the *cause* of greater or smaller purchasing; they may instead be coincidences, phenomena that appear with another phenomenon but do not cause it. Sorting out causal links is always difficult. Sometimes, a cause is clear, but complex phenomena of the type that businesspeople deal with—like sales decisions—can rarely be reduced to single cause-and-effect relationships.

3. **Avoid oversimplification and exaggeration.** Seeking a single cause for an event can lead to oversimplification and exaggeration. Although sometimes simple explanations are correct, in analyzing complex situations you should be prepared to expect multiple—and sometimes unknown—causes and should therefore avoid looking foolish by insisting on simple explanations.

The owner of RapRock found that customers who drove to the store bought less than those who came by bus. He concluded that the advertisements he had placed on buses must be successful. His conclusion obviously oversimplifies: The advertisements might indeed be successful, but that conclusion cannot be reached based solely on the evidence at hand. He would need to survey his customers more carefully, asking, for example, if they had read the ads, what they thought of them, and what other ads they had seen. It might turn out that the customers who came by bus share other characteristics that better explain their higher levels of purchases. More information and deeper analysis are needed before one reaches a simple conclusion like the owner's view that his bus advertisements had succeeded.

4. **Use all the available information, not just those parts that support your own conclusion or argument.** When the information you have gathered seems to support a conclusion that makes sense, you face a natural temptation to stop your analysis. However, you need to review the information to make sure that you are not overlooking details that contradict your conclusion. And you need to be sure that you have *enough* information available. It's easy to overlook details that don't seem to fit the conclusion

you have reached or to stop looking before you have examined all the relevant information, as the owner of RapRock Music did when he jumped to hasty conclusions based on inadequate information.

SUMMARY

- **Information** is the content of business communication: It is what you communicate when you write a memo or a report or give a talk.
- Information can be classified into four types: **facts** (agreed-on or undisputed points) **observations** (what one perceives—sees, hears, etc.); **interpretations** (explanations of how facts or observations are related); and **opinions** (viewpoints or preferences). Distinguishing among these types when you assess business information helps you to meet communication goals.
- Good business information is always **accurate, timely, relevant, reliable,** and **sensible.** Apply these standards to your information before you use it in preparing business presentations and documents.
- The way in which you use information will vary according to the goal of your communication. Ease of access is crucial when you write or speak to record or inform; support of the argument being made is the main test when you communicate to persuade.
- In interpreting information, you should be certain that the specific details support the larger generalizations, that you understand the difference between cause and effect, that you avoid oversimplification and exaggeration, and that you use all the available information and not just the information that supports the conclusion you want to reach.

EXERCISES

For Discussion

1. A survey on alcoholism included this question: "Have you ever been closely associated with someone who was an alcoholic—either a family member, or a close friend, or someone you worked closely with?" The results varied dramatically according to the region of the United States in which the respondents lived. The following are the percentages of "yes" answers by region:

   West, 71
   Midwest, 62
   South, 56
   East, 41

   Here are some conclusions that different people drew from the results:

   a. Westerners are more likely than Easterners to have alcohol problems.
   b. Westerners are more likely than Easterners to discuss personal problems.
   c. It's safer to drive in the South than in the West.

   Label each of these statements as fact, observation, interpretation, or opinion. Discuss the techniques (and the potential dangers) of drawing inferences from survey data.

2. Study the data in the following table:

Country	Health Expenditure in $ per Capita	Life Expectancy at Birth	Deaths from Heart Disease per 100,000
United States	1,500	75	435
Germany	900	73	584
Japan	500	77	266
Great Britain	400	74	579

Answer these questions:

a. Are these facts? Why or why not?

b. Can you infer that there is a direct relationship between health-care expenditures and life expectancy? Between health-care expenditures and deaths from heart disease?

c. Is there an *in*direct relationship? Any relationship at all?

3. The average cost of purchasing an existing 2,000-square-foot home with three bedrooms, two baths, and a two-car garage was calculated for the following cities in July 1989 and January 1990:

City	July 1989	January 1990	Percentage Increase/(Decrease)
Reno, Nevada	$100,000	$115,000	15.0
Houston, Texas	105,000	95,000	(10.0)
Columbus, Ohio	93,000	89,000	(0.3)
Raleigh, North Carolina	78,000	85,000	9.0

On the basis of this information, a student wrote a report indicating that housing costs are directly linked to the health of the local economy. She noted that Houston's economy was in decline because of problems in the oil industry, which reduced housing costs. Does this seem like a valid inference? Are there other possible explanations?

The student had difficulty interpreting the data for Columbus because its economy seemed to have remained healthy. A friend who lived in Columbus advanced this explanation: Less affluent buyers had begun to enter the market, and thus more homes in the lower brackets were selling in January 1990. Specifically, she pointed out that before July 1989, people had been moved into Columbus from the New York area by American Electric Power Co., which had relocated its headquarters from New York City to Columbus. These people had owned relatively high-priced property in the New York area and so were able to buy Columbus houses in the higher price ranges. By January, additional workers were moving in from the company's Canton, Ohio, offices. Because prices in Canton were lower than prices in New York, this new wave of people were buying lower-priced houses in Columbus. Does this explanation help account for the apparent conflicts in the interpretation? Are there other possible explanations? In addition to the basic information presented, would you advise the student to gather more details before making any inferences? What might she look for?

For Writing

4. Using the information provided in Exercise 1, write one paragraph on "geographic differences in alcoholism." Use only the information given. (Do you feel that you have enough information of the right sort to complete the assignment? Why or why not?)
5. Using the information provided in Exercise 2, write a one-page statement on one of the following topics:
    a. Greater expenditures would improve health care.
    b. The quality of health care is *not* related to the amount of money spent on it.

For Collaboration

6. Assemble a team of four students from your class. Each member should gather information on one of these topics:
    a. The cost of tuition and room and board at three colleges.
    b. The cost of breakfast (establish the specific items) at three area restaurants.
    c. The cost of an oil change at three area service stations.

    As each member presents his or her information, carefully evaluate the *information* itself. Does it meet the characteristics of *good* information? Why or why not? After you have discussed these characteristics, review how you might *use* the information differently for recording, informing, and persuading purposes. As you discuss patterns of use, pay attention to the guidelines for interpreting information given in this chapter.

9 ACCESSING THE SOURCES OF BUSINESS INFORMATION

What's Ahead

SEARCHING FOR INFORMATION
SOURCES OF BUSINESS INFORMATION
- **Personal Observation**
- **Interview**
  - Guidelines for the Interview
- **Survey**
  - Guidelines for Developing the Questionnaire
  - Guidelines for Selecting the Population
- **Literature**
  - Primary Materials
  - Print Indexes
  - Electronic Indexes
- FYI: Find It Fast

SUMMARY
EXERCISES

Do You Know 

- What is the best way to find the information you need to produce a business report or presentation?
- How can you obtain information from your own observation and experiment?
- How can you obtain information from interviewing others?
- How can you obtain information from surveys?
- How can you obtain information from published sources?

• It's 11:30 P.M., and the college library closes at midnight. Your paper on major trends in banking is due tomorrow afternoon. You have most of the paper done, but you still need to find some statistics to support one of your conclusions. Where do you start?

• You're at your desk putting the finishing touches on the memo that your supervisor requested on which three cities to use as test market sites for the new frozen dinners that your company has developed. You need to be sure that each city is as representative as possible of the national population in race, gender, and income patterns. How can you find family incomes for Omaha, Baton Rouge, and Tampa?

Business communicators—students writing papers that simulate their future roles or working professionals already involved in complex assignments—need a lot of information. How do they go about finding it?

SEARCHING FOR INFORMATION

The search for information begins when any search begins: when you know what you are looking for. Without a clear goal, your search will almost certainly dead-end. Your search is under way when you can complete this sentence: "I need ____________ so I can ____________."

Let's look at three statements that students made to launch their search for information:

1. I need a book on accounting.
2. I need an article on Japanese management.
3. I need a newspaper story on auto sales.

Note two qualities of these statements. First, they fill in only one of the two blanks, omitting the one on the purpose ("so I can ____________"). Second, they specify the object of the search not as information but as a *source* of information: a book, an article, and a newspaper story. Let's improve the statements:

1. I need to understand government accounting practice so I can

write a paper on how the Town of Newry presents its financial statements.

2. I need to know the basic elements of Japanese management so I can write a paper contrasting it with American practice.

3. I need a list of auto sales by manufacturers so I can write a memo that compares the sales of American-made and imported cars by month for 1991.

You can see that the three revised statements are not just more precise but specifically directed toward information rather than a source and related to the intended use of the information in a communication. This difference points to the most important rule of setting up an information search: Know exactly what *information* is required and why. If you phrase your objective in terms of a *source,* you have already directed the search in a way that may prove unproductive or wasteful. For example, the best information on Japanese management may be not in an article but in a book. You must also indicate clearly to yourself the *reason* for the information—to write a memo, a paper, whatever. Knowing that can help you discover the best source of the best information rather than limit you to something that may not answer your questions.

Once you know what you are looking for, you can establish a process that will aid you in finding it. First, relate the need to the source that can meet that need. Then, identify the steps required to access the source. Here's a sample process, based on the second example above:

Need: I need to know the basic elements of Japanese management so I can write a paper contrasting it with American practice.

Sources:
- Books on Japanese management
- Articles on Japanese management in professional and scholarly journals on management
- Newspaper and magazine articles on Japanese management and how it works
- Views of American management professors and American businesspersons about Japanese management and how it contrasts with American management

Steps:
- Check library catalog for books.
- Check indexes to periodical literature in library to find articles.
- Interview professor of management at my college and president of a local company.

Of course, this is a simplified scheme, but it does illustrate the basic procedure you should follow:

1. Identify the needed information.
2. Identify the likely sources.
3. Identify the steps that you have to take to locate and use the sources that will supply what you need.

The more complex the task, the more care you have to take in identifying the pieces of the process. For example, if you are writing a doctoral dissertation on a subject, you need much more information than if you are writing a three-paragraph story for your school newspaper. And if more information and sources are involved, you need to develop the steps of the process of searching more fully and with attention to the time you will need to carry out the search. You might have to block out the work into units and to assign weeks or months to each, being sure to allow enough time for each and connecting them in the right order. Preparation will make your research more productive. For example, you should survey the published literature before you interview a professor or businessperson so you come to such an interview well armed and in control of the basic information.

SOURCES OF BUSINESS INFORMATION

As we saw in Chapter 8, information can be classified into various types and can be assessed for internal characteristics and methods of explanation. We can also classify the *sources* of information. The four basic sources of business information are

- Personal observation
- Interview
- Survey
- Literature (published material)

The type of information that will be produced varies with the source. Table 9–1 relates these four basic sources to the types of information described in Chapter 8.

Let's now look at each of the four sources to see its strengths and weaknesses and to find out how to use it to get the information needed to solve a communication problem.

Personal Observation

If you want to find out how long it takes to assemble the individual components into a stereo system, one way is to time yourself as you assemble the system. In doing so, you make a direct or personal observation. Many problems in business require information that comes from direct observations: What is the total of accounts receivable this month? What is the average length of time a customer must wait in line at the checkout counter? How large should the new desk be to accommodate a microcomputer? How long does it take to walk from the desk to the men's room? Each of these questions can be answered with information that comes from direct observation.

An obvious problem with such information is that it is subject to dispute. The time it takes me to assemble a stereo system may differ from the time it takes you, depending on our experience and dexterity. The size of the new desk can be measured, but what standard should be used? You may want a desk that just accommodates the new computer, whereas the person who will sit at the desk may want one a foot longer to accommodate a telephone

TABLE 9–1
Different Sources Yield Different Types of Information

Sources of Information	Type of Information Obtained
Personal Observation	Fact Observation
Interview	Fact Observation Interpretation Opinion
Survey	Opinion (and under certain circumstances, also fact, observation, and interpretation)
Literature	Fact Observation Interpretation Opinion

and an ashtray. It may take you five minutes to walk to the men's room from your desk, but your boss may make the trip in just two minutes.

Thus, the information that results from personal observations must always be presented with an explicit recognition of the source: "Such-and-such an experiment yielded such-and-such a result," or "Under the following specific conditions, the following results were observed." Making clear the origins of the information will alert the reader or hearer to the potential problems that accompany experimental data and will allow you to interpret the information to meet your communication goal without worrying endlessly over its acceptance.

Interview

The purpose of an interview is to gather facts, observations, interpretations, and opinions from a single individual, usually an expert on a particular topic or a specialized part of a topic. Which of the types of information you gather (facts or opinions, for example) will depend, of course, on what you want and should not be left up to the interviewee. If you're after facts, don't settle for the person's opinions. The interview should be used only to gather information that is not readily available in another form. Don't interview an expert as a substitute for doing basic research in the library. Go to an expert to supplement general information or to get specialized views or facts that cannot be found in published works.

It should be noted here that we are discussing interviews as a source of information, not as ends in themselves. Doing a profile of the company's oldest retiree or youngest vice president or most athletically proficient accountant requires an interview, but the purpose of such interviews is to flesh out the character of the individual rather than merely to provide information. Some of what is said here may be relevant to that approach, but "doing an interview" for the company or school newspaper is really a different topic.

Guidelines For the Interview

Here are seven basic guidelines for maximizing the effectiveness of interviews as a source of information for business writing or speaking:

1. Select the interviewee carefully.
2. Arrange the interview in advance and at the interviewee's convenience.
3. Prepare for the interview.
4. Have a plan for the interview, including specific questions.
5. Make a record of the interview.
6. Thank the interviewee orally and in writing.
7. Treat the interviewee with the utmost respect.

1. **Select the interviewee carefully.** Picking at random the name of a management professor to interview for your paper on Japanese management style probably won't produce satisfactory results. Have a reason for selecting the person you select, if only because you're likely to be asked. If possible, you should interview someone who not only is recognized as an expert in the subject you are studying but is also known to be both helpful and available. It will help if he or she is a reasonable person, who will answer your questions carefully and concisely and send you on your way, rather than a fanatic, who will try to convert you to some viewpoint. Finding out as much as you can about the prospective interviewee before requesting a meeting will help you avoid unpleasantness or wasted time.

2. **Arrange the interview in advance and at the interviewee's convenience.** Don't ask the CEO of a Fortune 500 company for an interview on Friday at 4:15 because you will be in town and free then, and don't corner your professor after class and demand an immediate meeting so you can gather information for the term paper that's due tomorrow. Always write or phone to request an interview (with an explanation of the reason, of course) as far in advance as possible, and offer a number of possible days and times to suit the person's schedule. Interviewing only persons you know is best, but that is rarely possible. The next best thing is to have an intermediary, someone who knows both you and the interviewee and can arrange a meeting or supply a reference. But in the absence of such good fortune, you just have to call or write—perhaps both if you want to be sure of getting on a busy person's calendar.

3. **Prepare for the interview.** You shouldn't rely on an interview to supply basic information that is otherwise available. Instead, use the interview to obtain the specialized viewpoints or knowledge of the expert. This means that you should be thoroughly versed in the basics of the topic before you go. Interview the expert only when you have made yourself as expert as possible so you have something intelligent and important to ask.

4. **Have a plan for the interview, including specific questions.** Don't go into an interview with a vague sense of what you want—"some information on" Topic X, for example. Jot down questions in a logical order and make every effort to proceed through your list. Don't be rude, pushy, or impatient, but politely try to keep the interview focused on specific questions and to move it along toward the goal you have set. Sometimes, the interviewee's asides or apparently irrelevant comments will turn out to be gold mines, but you should not count on it. The person being interviewed will respect you more for having specific questions and a clear sense of direction.

5. **Make a record of the interview.** Take notes or record the interview

on tape, being sure, of course, to secure the person's permission in advance in either case. Don't rely on memory to get the "drift" of the conversation, and don't think that the most important points will automatically stick with you. Of course, simply jotting down answers or even recording the whole meeting won't guarantee that you will understand all that was said or will emphasize the right points. However, you will have something to look over or listen to afterward to jog your memory or to confirm what you thought was said.

6. **Thank the interviewee orally and in writing.** Common sense dictates that you thank the person at the time, and it should be equally obvious that every interview requires a written acknowledgment. Even if the person was cranky and useless, a prompt note of thanks is absolutely required.

7. **Finally—and above all—treat the interviewee with the utmost respect before, during, and after the interview.** Don't badger, fawn, or show your own feelings. Don't get into a debate, even though that's what the interviewee may really want. Don't expect too much (and of course, don't settle too quickly for too little). Remember that the person who grants you an interview is giving you a gift: his or her time, skills, and knowledge.

Survey

Whereas the interview elicits specialized knowledge from an individual, the survey gathers collective viewpoints from groups of persons. It thus provides opinions. Surveys are frequently used in business to determine consumer and employee opinions. Under certain circumstances, a survey also yields information that may be classified as facts, observations, and interpretations. For example, demographic data gathered in a survey may be thought of as factual (within the conditions of surveys that we will discuss shortly): age, marital status, educational level, income, home ownership, and so forth. If you ask respondents about their views of how certain events are connected, you might say that you have gathered interpretations. For example, a question asking for a respondent's level of agreement with the statement "High deficits cause high interest rates" would yield interpretations—or, more precisely, opinions about interpretations. Because, as we saw in the last chapter, these distinctions get tricky, it is best as a practical course to think of surveys as providing collective opinions.

The value of surveys in achieving this purpose is generally described in terms of two qualities: validity and reliability. *Validity* refers to the degree to which a survey yields the information that you want. A survey is said to be valid if it measures what it sets out to measure. For example, a survey might ask people to indicate which of three products they are most aware of based on TV advertising. It would be invalid to claim as a result that the product that people are most aware of is the one that they will actually buy, because their awareness may not be directly related to their decision to purchase. Validity is a question of the internal characteristics of the survey, that is, what it measures.

Reliability has to do with the predictive power of a survey. A survey is said to be reliable if its results can be replicated to a reasonable degree among a different group of respondents. If 54 percent of your respondents say they prefer sugarless soft drinks, the results can be considered reliable only if a similar response is obtained from other groups. If your first group included only dieters, you might suppose that the results would not be replicated among a group of people who are not dieters. Hence, the survey would not be considered reliable for a broad range of the population, although it would be reliable within the given group if three versions of it administered to three groups of dieters produced the same results in each case. Reliability, then, is a function of the persons surveyed rather than of the internal characteristics of the survey instrument.

Surveys are complex and are properly the subject of treatment by social scientists and statisticians. We cannot cover all aspects of survey research here, but within the two broad categories of validity (the internal characteristics of the instrument) and reliability (the characteristics of the group surveyed), we can provide some rough guidelines to aid you in using surveys to gain the information you may need to solve a business problem.

Guidelines for Developing the Questionnaire

Follow these guidelines as you develop the questionnaire you will use:

1. Limit the number of questions you ask.
2. Phrase the questions clearly.
3. Aim for responses that can be readily tabulated.

1. **Limit the number of questions you ask.** If you construct a questionnaire that asks everything you want to know, chances are that your respondents won't cooperate, or if they do, they will get bogged down and begin to answer too quickly. Select your questions carefully to balance your need to get answers with your respondents' tolerance of being involved. Some very useful questionnaires ask only one or two questions, and often those answers are all that is really needed.

2. **Phrase the questions clearly to prevent ambiguity, confusion, tricks, or automatic responses.** A respondent might readily be confused by a question like this: "If the presidential election were held today, and if your income were 20 percent higher than it is now, and if a third-party candidate were running, would you consider voting for a Democrat?" A question that a respondent might feel obligated to answer in only one way is also useless: "Should executives be ethical?" You have to construct questions that are simple yet elicit useful information.

3. **Aim for responses that can be readily tabulated to yield meaningful information.** The simplest questions require "yes" or "no" answers, but sometimes you need to measure degrees. That's why scales of response are generally used in surveys. For example, you might want to know whether persons who have used a product like it. Instead of having a yes–no choice, you should offer a range of possible responses that will better capture the reality of consumer attitudes. A five-part scale is typical: "Agree strongly," "Agree somewhat," "Neutral," "Disagree somewhat," or "Disagree strongly." Although you may also want to make room for comments, you should try to pin down the responses to specifics that can be measured. An open-ended questionnaire is useful if you want people to speculate and make free asso-

ciations, but it presents enormous difficulties in tabulation. Whenever possible, construct response categories that can be easily converted to numbers.

Guidelines for Selecting the Population

Before we provide specific guidelines, it is necessary to discuss briefly the concept of *sampling*. Surveys gather representative opinions, and if the group surveyed is well selected, it is then possible, within certain constraints, to make generalizations about the larger population that the group represents. Of course, if there are thirty people in your class, you can, in fact, ask each of them to respond to certain questions and then say that this is what the class thinks. You have surveyed the entire population of that class. But if you want to find out what the entire school of 1,500 people thinks, you probably cannot survey them all. You have to choose a smaller group: a *sample*. That sample should be representative of the characteristics of the population and large enough in total number to allow you to make generalizations about the population it represents. Our guidelines, then, relate to sample size and sample composition:

1. Select the largest practical sample.
2. Use random sampling techniques to select the sample.

1. **Select the largest practical sample.** *Practical* is the operative term here. A practical sample size for a survey you are doing to write a paper for your marketing course will be smaller than the sample that Procter & Gamble can use to test a new product. Although sample *composition* is more important than sample *size* in determining a survey's reliability, a good rule of thumb is that the minimum size of a sample is 50, simply because descriptive statistics for smaller sizes lack meaning.

2. **Use random sampling techniques to select the sample.** A random sample is not a haphazardly selected one but one in which the probability of inclusion of all the elements of the population is known. Random sampling techniques vary, but the three most common are *simple, stratified,* and *systematic.*

- *Simple random sampling* gives every element of the population from which the sample is drawn the same chance of being selected. Drawing names from a hat is a common technique of simple random sampling because every name in the hat has an equal chance of being drawn.
- *Stratified random sampling* puts all elements of the population into relevant categories or strata and then uses simple random sampling to identify the sample. The result is that the gross characteristics of the sample reflect the gross characteristics of the population. For example, if the population is 60 percent female, you would separate men from women and randomly sample each group so that the total sample is 60 percent female.
- *Systematic random sampling* requires you to select the sample in a systematic or fixed way, for example, to select every fifth name from a list. Again, this method ensures that every element of the population will have a known probability of appearing in the sample.

Sampling technique is a specialized branch of knowledge with its own texts, experts, debates, and issues. If you use surveys as a source of information for business communication, you must become familiar with sampling technique so the information that you use will be acceptable to those to whom you are communicating. Our discussion here should be considered merely an overview.

One other issue that you should weigh in using surveys is the process by which the questionnaires are administered. You can conduct a survey by phone, in person, or by mail. Each approach has advantages and disadvantages, and the choice depends on convenience, time, and cost. The most direct method is obviously to administer the survey in person, but this is often not practical. Again, you should become familiar with the specialized knowledge in this field if you expect to rely on surveys to identify information that you will use in documents or talks.

Literature

The most familiar source of business information is literature. This does not mean poetry or fiction, of course, but publications. *Literature* refers here to documents that are external to the firm. Plenty of information is published internally in a variety of forms; reports and memos are particularly useful internal information sources. These are accessible through corporate libraries and often through computerized information systems. Here we will concentrate on public literature.

This public literature can be classified into two types: primary material and secondary material, or indexes. The latter are tools that provide access to the former. Because the primary material actually supplies the information, we start with a brief description of various types of primary published materials and then look at the indexes that help you to access the primary materials. In a search, of course, the indexes are the first items you use.

Primary Materials

Primary materials include periodicals (or serials), books, and reports. *Periodicals* are commonly called magazines and newspapers, but the terms *periodicals* and *serials* are more inclusive and also suggest the key feature of these items: They are published on a regular basis—daily, weekly, monthly, or whatever. We can further divide periodicals into the popular and the professional. Popular magazines and newspapers are meant for a wide audience of lay readers; professional journals are for specialists. Many so-called popular business periodicals do, however, carry quite specialized information, but the articles tend to be broader and they are written for a nonspecialist audience. Table 9–2 lists a number of popular business sources. *The Wall Street Journal,* for example, is a business newspaper of wide circulation that is read by many people for its excellent political and social coverage, but it is a particularly useful source of detailed economic and financial news: daily stock and bond reports, news about executive changes, and other company information of all sorts.

Books differ from periodicals in that they are published only once (although, of course, they can be reissued in revised editions). Books are obviously less timely than periodicals, but they are usually more definitive.

TABLE 9–2
Some Common Business Periodicals

Popular	Professional
Barron's	*Academy of Management Journal*
Business Week	*Accountancy*
The Economist	*The Accounting Review*
Forbes	*Administrative Science Quarterly*
Fortune	*Harvard Business Review*
The New York Times	*Journal of Accountancy*
The Wall Street Journal	*Journal of Business*
	Journal of Business Communication
	Journal of Finance
	Journal of Marketing
	Journal of Marketing Research
	Journal of the Academy of Marketing Science
	Management Science
	Managerial Communication
	Personnel
	Personnel Journal

Studies of specialized topics, general works on subjects like marketing practices and management techniques, and reference volumes (dictionaries, encyclopedias, and factbooks) are all books that can provide information about business topics. Table 9–3 lists some important reference works, all handbooks, on international business.

Reports fall somewhere between periodicals and books in their publication characteristics and definitiveness. Reports are issued by government agencies, foundations, universities, and professional societies. They are generally quite specialized, dealing with a limited topic. Census reports, for example, are rich sources of demographic data that marketing specialists must be familiar with. The reports of accounting societies set the standards for the field. Reports on wages, unemployment, exports and imports, and other government documents are often valuable for business topics.

Print Indexes

Getting at the information you need in periodicals, books, and reports requires a knowledge of *indexes*. Be aware that indexes are secondary materials, that is, not the source of information but *guides* to finding the information. Table 9–4 lists some common indexes.

The New York Times Index, for example, indexes that newspaper. If you want to find information about leveraged buyouts, you will consult that

TABLE 9–3
Handbooks on International Business

Export Documentation Handbook
Foreign Business Practices
Foreign Commerce Handbook
Handbook of International Business
Handbook of International Management
International Marketing Handbook

TABLE 9–4
Some Common Indexes to Business Information

General Indexes and Literature Guides
Business Information
Business Information: Applications and Sources
Business Information Sources
Directory of Business and Financial Services
Encyclopedia of Business and Financial Services
Indexes to Specific Periodicals
Barron's Index (published with *The Wall Street Journal Index*)
The New York Times Index
The Wall Street Journal Index
Indexes to Multiple Periodicals
Accountants' Index
Accounting Articles
Business Periodicals Index
Insurance Index
Personnel Management Abstracts
Public Affairs Information Service Bulletin
Readers' Guide to Periodical Literature

listing and from it get the titles and dates of articles in the *Times* on the subject. You would *not* get listings of what appeared in other publications—only those in the *Times.* The *Business Periodicals Index* is probably the best general guide to materials on business topics appearing in a great many popular and specialized periodicals. The *Readers' Guide to Periodical Literature* is broader than the *Business Periodicals Index* and is useful for topics of more general interest relating to business; for example, the growth in two-income families and the effect of this phenomenon on marketing might be treated more broadly, with attention to its social dimensions, in periodicals other than those surveyed in the *Business Periodicals Index.* Here the *Readers' Guide* would be a helpful complement. The more specialized indexes, like *Accounting Articles* or the *Insurance Index,* will help you access information on relatively narrow topics.

Probably the most familiar "index" is the catalog of a college or public library. Every student is familiar with this tool, and it is indeed a great one.

TABLE 9–5
Some Computerized Search Services for Business Information

Databases (available through online vendors)
ABI/Inform
Management Contents
Online Vendors (which search databases)
BRS
CompuServe
DIALOG
Dow Jones & Co.
Dunsprint
A. C. Nielsen
SDC Search Service

Online library catalogs offer fast and effective access to the wealth of information used by students and practicing businesspeople.

If you look up "Footwear—imports" in your college library catalog, you will probably find books and government reports on that topic, and if you are using a large research library, you can have confidence that you are getting a good sample of the available literature. But the catalog is limited to the books and other separately published items that the specific library holds. More information, and perhaps better and more timely information, is likely to be available from other sources. Don't stop with the library catalog.

Electronic Indexes

You should be aware that many indexes are published electronically and are available in computerized search services. Table 9–5 lists some common reference services accessible through computers. Most college and large public libraries provide such services, sometimes for a fee. They scan large databases according to search words that you provide, and they print out citations (author, title, and place and date of publication) for items that you then secure directly through the library. They also often give short summaries, called *abstracts,* that let you know whether the article or report in question covers the topic you are researching. Computerized databases speed the literature search, but they really offer nothing generically different from what you can find in published indexes.

Using computerized indexes takes some initial experimentation and, if possible, help from knowledgeable librarians or other experts. In "*FYI:* Find it Fast" (pages 174–175), information expert Marie Flatley offers advice on how to use "Boolean operators"—English words that help you narrow and refine information searches.

The enormous quantity and range of literature on business topics make a complete survey out of the question here. You should simply be aware of the types of publications available and then develop a more specialized familiarity as you research particular topics.

FIND IT FAST

Marie Flatley
Professor, Department of Information and Decision Systems, San Diego State University

In business it is not always what you *know* that is important, but what you can *find out*. Some of the most useful sources of business information are bibliographic databases. These databases are available both online and on CDs. Whether you are searching for information through your computer connected to a remote computer or on a library's CD database, you can use some simple search strategies to make your search more efficient and effective.

Through the use of Boolean operators—such as AND, OR, and NOT—you can search large databases quickly and accurately. The operators allow you to combine concepts rather than using single concepts. For example, if you are looking for information on print or radio advertising by physicians, you might ask the computer to find all information in its database on *physician OR doctor AND advertising NOT television*.

Occasionally, a tight, clearly defined search will produce either too many or too few results. When you have too many citations, narrowing the topic often pares down the list to a manageable size. Adding another concept is usually the best way to proceed. Some searchers add a concept that narrows the time period searched, perhaps to the last one

SUMMARY

- To begin a search for information, you need to know not just *what* you need but *why* you need it, that is, what communication purpose it will serve. As you define your needs, think not about *sources* of information but about the *types* (**fact, observation, interpretation,** and **opinion**) that you need. You need to plan the search process so that it will lead you to find what you want.
- Information can be obtained through **direct observation.** For example, you can count the number of cars parked in the employee lot or experiment with different billing procedures to determine which is best.
- **Interviewing** others provides useful business information. For example, you can ask a researcher for specialized information that he or she has developed.
- **Surveys** are common means of obtaining business information. They are used especially to determine customer and employee attitudes and opinions. If you do a survey, you must carefully design the questionnaire and select the population to be surveyed.
- Business information is published in books, periodicals, and reports. You access this information through indexes, both in print and electronic.

EXERCISES

For Discussion

1. By using only the card catalog of your college library, how many sources of information can you locate on the following topics:
   a. Productivity in the U.S. auto industry

to five years. Other searchers add another concept, such as geographic region, industry, or even a specific name. Some searches, on the other hand, produce too few results. One of the most common problems with these searches is misspelling or plurals. For example, if the word *physician* were misspelled, the computer will only find any article where it was misspelled the same way—an unlikely event. Perhaps using the plurals *physicians* or *doctors* yielded only a few results. By truncating the search with *physician** and *doctor**, telling the computer to find anything with the root and wildcard ending, you can expand the search to include both the singular and plural forms.

You can also expand a search by using broader terms, additional spellings, or more synonyms. In searching for articles on *databases*, try expanding with the OR connector by adding *data base OR data-base OR databank*.

One of the best sources of help in analyzing search results is your librarian. Not only will librarians have access to the controlled vocabulary of the database, but they are also highly experienced searchers.

By using good search strategies with a clearly defined concept, you will be able to gather information fast.

b. Capital investment in the United States by foreign governments and private investors
c. ERISA
d. Operations research
e. Theory X and Theory Y management
f. Computer manufacturing in Germany

Is each topic listed in the catalog as it is here? Or did you have to do some sorting and shifting to find the entries?

2. Look up the same topics as in Exercise 1 in the most recent year's edition of *Business Periodicals Index*. What differences in the number and type of sources do you find? Which approach yields the "best" information? Why?

3. Which of the topics below should you look up in (a) the card catalog; (b) *Business Periodicals Index;* (c) *The New York Times Index?* Why?

	a	b	c
"Employment at will"			
U.S. trade deficits			
J. M. Keynes			
Westinghouse			
Inventory control			
Griggs v. Duke Power			
Apple, Inc.			
Cotton production in China			
U.S. Steel			

For Writing

4. Prepare a reading list of what you consider the five most useful published items you can find on one of the following topics:
   a. Quality circles
   b. Nonprofit accounting
   c. Zero-based budgeting
   d. Investment in municipal bonds
   - How did you identify the items? That is, what *sources* did you use to locate them?
   - What standards did you use to determine their usefulness?

5. A survey of 100 students at Montgomery County Community College revealed that 60 were aware of their advisers. Of these, 50 percent felt that their advisers did a "good" or "excellent" job in providing academic information. There are 4,200 students at the college. The 100 respondents to the survey were interviewed as they came out of the registrar's office during the drop–add period. Answer each of the following questions:
   a. Is it *valid* to conclude that "60 percent of the students at the college know their adviser"? Why or why not?
   b. Is it *valid* to conclude that "half of the students at the college think their advisers do a "good" or "excellent" job in providing academic information"? Why or why not?
   c. How could you test the *reliability* of the survey results?
   d. Comment on the size and selection of the sample.
   e. Suggest additional kinds of information that you might want to gather (by survey or other means) to complement the data from this survey in the preparation of a report to the dean of students on academic advising.

6. Prepare a preliminary listing of sources on one of the following topics by conducting a computerized information search. Be sure to employ the advice offered in "*FYI:* Find It Fast."
   a. Expenditures on advertising by nonprofit organizations like the Red Cross and Project Hope
   b. Employee performance evaluation
   c. Yarn manufacturing in South America
   d. Restaurant preferences among people over age sixty-five
   e. The cost of hotel accommodations in Hong Kong

For Collaboration

7. You and three other students are members of the College Research Corporation. You have been hired by the Office of Student Life at your college to gather information on the attitude of new students toward social life in the dorms. You must construct a simple survey to get the information. Follow these steps:
   a. List the questions you will ask.
   b. Identify the sample of whom you will ask the questions, and explain how you chose that sample.
   c. Decide what you should do to assess the validity and reliability of your survey.
   d. Explain what information you will gain from the survey and how you will use it to make a report.

   Now do the survey and write the report.

10 COMMUNICATING WITH ELECTRONIC TECHNOLOGY

What's Ahead

THE ELECTRONIC MEDIA PRODUCTION
- Wordprocessing
- Desktop Publishing
- Electronic Paper

THE ELECTRONIC CONTEXT FOR COMMUNICATION
- Hypertext
- FYI: Hypermedia
- The Merging of Oral and Written Media
  - Facsimile Transmission
  - Electronic Mail
- FYI: Local Norms in E-Mail
  - Electronic Bulletin Boards and Conferences
- The Electronic Workplace
  - The Pancake Organization
  - Decentralization

THE COSTS OF COMPUTING
- Privacy
- The 24-Hour Workday
- Physiological Effects
- Psychological Effects

SUMMARY

EXERCISES

Do You Know 

- How can wordprocessing systems help you to produce a document?
- What is "desktop publishing"?
- How have computers expanded the options that writers can select in organizing material for readers?
- How has electronic technology contributed to the merging of oral and written media?
- What's new about the "electronic workplace"?
- What personal costs accompany the benefits of computing?

For Sheila Griffin, corporate advertising director for Motorola, the day begins when she

> clicks on her cellular phone at 5:30 A.M. as she sets off from home in St. Charles, Illinois, for the hour drive to work. First, she checks her "voice mail," the recorded messages people leave on her phone. "Then I make calls to Europe," she said. "I get to the office and check the faxes. I get Europe out of the way and then work on things in our own time zone." Ms. Griffin gets home to her husband, a civil engineer, and two young children 13 hours after she left and spends three hours with them. "Then at about 9:30, the phone rings," she said, "and it's Japan."[1]

Electronic technology is changing where and how people work. Advances in transoceanic fiber optics and enhanced satellite links expand the abilities of people around the world to communicate with each other in a 24-hour business day. The number of personal computers has also expanded; it is currently estimated to be forty million in the United States, compared with fewer than one million in 1980.[2]

How people use their telephones and computers reflects their personality as well as their organizational and cultural context. For example, in an interesting study, the Stanford Business School found a striking difference among top executives: In Brazil and Mexico, such executives use the technology to analyze and plan strategies, especially for dealing with their unstable economies. By contrast, U.S. executives use the computers for accessing the reams of production and other data available to them and for simple wordprocessing and electronic mail. One explanation is that computers entered U.S. firms mainly as secretarial tools and percolated upward only

[1] Peter T. Kilborn, "The Work Week Grows: Tales from the Digital Treadmill," *The New York Times*, 3 June 1990, Section 4, p. 3.

[2] John Markoff, " 'Talking' on the Computer Redefines Human Contact," *The New York Times*, 13 May 1990, p. 1.

gradually. Computers entered at the top in Brazil and Mexico; from the beginning, executives considered them management tools.[3]

THE ELECTRONIC MEDIA

How you use computers and how computers themselves function will change as you pursue your career. Computers will become smaller and more powerful; they will be enhanced even more by video and audio technology for multimedia computing; computers and telephones will merge in extensive global networks that create, disseminate, display (probably in three dimensions), and print information.

Because of these changes, and because companies adopt technology at different rates, you don't need to know the details: They will change anyway. But you should be familiar with the technology in general. Such technology serves as a medium of communication that will not only reflect but also shape your message. In this chapter, you'll learn about the role of electronic technology in the context of writing in the global economy. You'll read first about the use of computers to produce documents and presentations. Then you'll read about how electronic technology is changing even more fundamentally the concept of what a document or presentation is. You'll also see how such technology is changing the concept of the workplace in general and some of the personal costs of these changes.

PRODUCTION

You're probably familiar with techniques for producing a document on a computer. If not, or if you'd like to read more about the basic process, the next section, on wordprocessing, is for you.[4]

Wordprocessing

If you're not already a committed user of computers for wordprocessing, give them a try. They're not that difficult. Not everyone will find writing at a screen either pleasurable or efficient, and few people will write exclusively on a computer. But for many writers, the computer offers another strong weapon against what are seen as the terrors of prose.

The term *wordprocessing* covers a variety of kinds of *hardware* (the physical equipment) and *software* (the programs that tell the equipment what to do). You'll need to learn how to operate whatever system is available to you. Your writing will have to wait while you learn.

That writing will be made easier, however, once you're underway. How? First, as you saw in Chapter 7, wordprocessing programs enhance revision;

[3] Pamela Sebastian, "Business Bulletin," *The Wall Street Journal*, 17 August 1989, p. 1.

[4] For other information on electronic technology, see Chapters 6 and 22 for computer graphics; Chapter 7 for revising with a computer; Chapter 9 for computerized information-retrieval systems; Chapter 13 for dictating letters; and Chapter 21 for voice mail.

you can add, delete, move things around, and check your grammar and your voice. Specialized programs can even take a sample of model letters, for example, from one organization, develop a set of standards from them (like format, length of sentences, and key phrases), and match any new letters you create against the standard.

Second, for many documents, the computer can serve as an automatic writer. You simply draw together blocks of prose stored in memory, particularize them for the reader and the document at hand, and press "Print." The software can also create automatically some elements necessary in reports, such as an index, a table of contents, footnotes, and bibliographies. And it can hold standard formats for such documents as memos, resumes, manuals, and letters. You simply insert new information in a general file, and the computer takes care of lining up items as required.

Third, you can integrate research, analysis, and writing at the terminal. The citations and text you collect in an online search can be merged directly (with proper documentation) into your own text. You can also merge information from electronic spreadsheets—programs that sort financial information in rows and columns—and graphics programs. *Window* programs that split the screen into different pages make this work easier.

Desktop Publishing

An enhancement of wordprocessing programs directed to the design and printing of documents is called *desktop publishing* (DTP). Such programs give extensive formatting, graphics, and printing capabilities to individual writers. As you saw in Chapters 6 and 7, business writers today are paying increased attention to the *look* of their documents. Visual appeal is essential to motivate readers, to convey complex information, and to enhance readability. You need to think about visual display within the text and to think of the text itself as a visual on the page or the screen. Desktop publishing aids you in achieving good design, as you see when you compare Figures 10–1 and 10–2. For an example of a newsletter prepared on a desktop publishing system, see Figure 26–8 in Chapter 26.

Electronic Paper

Wordprocessing and desktop publishing *add* to the amount of paper produced in organizations. You'll read shortly about using nonprint media for transferring messages. The likelihood is not great that such media will replace paper. Indeed, the evidence supports the opposite conclusion. America's consumption of paper multiplies yearly. Why? First, computers are creating *more* information, not just providing another way to store existing information. Second, industrial psychologists estimate that reading on a screen is 20 to 30 percent slower than reading on paper. It's also harder to skim information. So people often prefer paper. Paper can also be more secure, both for privacy of access and durability of record keeping. Third, the number of information *workers* has increased; each produces a large number of documents—and photocopies of the documents.

QUESTION

article titled "The way to abolish the Senate, or at least muzzle it, is to white-ant it from within," and later attacked as a "spurious conception" the Senate's role as a "defender of States' rights." The Treasurer, Mr. Keating, described the Senate as "the swill of Australian politics," after it opposed the ID card.

WHY YOU SHOULD VOTE 'NO'

1. This proposal will not guarantee fewer elections.

The proposal is for a maximum, not a fixed, four-year term for both Houses of Parliament.

There is nothing in this proposal to prevent the Prime Minister calling an early election whenever it is to his political advantage. In fact, this proposal would almost certainly mean more elections, not less, because it actually gives the Prime Minister more power to call elections at whim.

2. This proposal includes another attempt to introduce simultaneous elections, a further device to reduce Senate powers.

The Australian people wisely rejected this idea in referendums in 1974, 1977 and 1984. It was wrong then and it is wrong now. In fact, in 1977 Labor's Senator John Button admitted that simultaneous elections reduced the power of the Senate. He said the Labor Party wanted to see the proposal passed because, in his words, "it limits the significance and influence of the Senate."

3. This proposal is a direct attack on the fundamental purpose and structure of the Senate.

At present, the House of Representatives has a maximum term of three years, while the Senate has a fixed term of six years. By turning the Senate into a mirror image of the Lower House with an identical four-year flexible term, the whole purpose of the Senate would be fundamentally undermined.

This proposal would strip the Senate of its powers and independence. A Prime Minister would be able to sack the entire Senate whenever it disagrees with the Government or votes against bad laws like the ID card. The Prime Minister could do this by immediately sending the whole Parliament to a new election.

This proposal, under the guise of a four-year term, is an attack on the integrity and independence of the Senate. This integrity and independence provides the fundamental checks and balances necessary to a truly democratic Parliament.

4. This proposal would undermine our bi-cameral Parliamentary system.

A bi-cameral system provides two separate and distinct chambers with the Lower House controlled by the Government and with the Upper House providing the essential checks and balances of a House of Review under our Westminster system.

The proposal will place the Senate constantly under the hammer of the Prime Minister, reducing its ability to act fearlessly in the public interest.

5. This proposal would give the Federal Government more power over the Senate.

It would allow the Government to push laws through the Senate under the threat of an early election. This was admitted by the Minister for Justice, Senator Tate, when he told the Parliament that the proposal for simultaneous elections contained in Question 1 means that it would be in the Senate's self-interest "not to push to the brink too many propositions too early in the Government's life."

DON'T BE DECEIVED BY CANBERRA.
KEEP THE STATES AND THE SENATE STRONG.
VOTE 'NO.'

FIGURE 10–1.
This figure and Figure 10–2 are from a brochure authorized by the Australian Electoral Commission to provide information concerning a referendum. This figure presents reasons to vote "no." It is filled with text in small print. The one column format allows for little white space.

Question 1—The YES case

WHAT A YES VOTE DOES NOT MEAN

While a four year maximum term offers Australia many benefits there is one thing it does not do—

• A YES vote will not touch the powers or independence of the Senate.

• On many occasions Australians have indicated they want to retain the role and power of the Senate. The proposal for four year terms was very carefully drawn up to ensure the Senate retained all its powers. A YES vote will not weaken the Senate's powers in any way.

A YES vote for four-year maximum terms will have many other benefits

The Senate will have the same four-year term as the House of Representatives under this proposal.

• As the whole Senate will be elected at the same time as the House of Representatives it will be more accountable.

• Eight year terms for the Senate would be too long. Such a long term for any elected representative would isolate them from the people they represent. All politicians should be accountable for their actions.

A yes vote will not touch the powers or independence of the Senate

• The watchdog role of the Senate will not be affected in any way. Just as it can now, the Senate will be free to review, amend or reject legislation.

• The Senate's powers over Supply bills will not be changed.

• The changes mean the Senate will still be able to force a Government to elections but will be accountable to the people for its performance at the same time.

The arguments for a YES vote are simple and sensible.

• A YES vote will mean more stable government.

Australia has too many elections

FIGURE 10–2.
Less text and the enhanced design elements possible with a desktop publishing system make this page more readable and more emphatic than that in Figure 10–1. The page presents reasons for a "yes" vote. Design elements include the two-column format, boxes with screens behind white lettering, bullets, active white space, and a larger typeface with more variations in size than in Figure 10–1. See Chapter 7 for more information on design.

THE ELECTRONIC CONTEXT FOR COMMUNICATION

Computers offer a speedier and often more comfortable way to write a document. They also enhance the look of the output. But more than being simply *production* tools, electronic media have fostered fundamental changes in the context of communication itself:

- New ways to see and organize information
- The merging of oral and written media
- New structures and relationships in the electronic workplace

Let's look at each of these changes.

Hypertext

A document on paper is by definition linear. The writer creates a structure, and the sentences march line after line. Much thinking, however, is associative: We wander, often productively, from idea to idea, not always in a straight path. In Chapter 4, you saw examples of such productive wandering in the planning of a document. In a new computer-based method for organizing information, *hypertext,* the writer divides information into individual units and creates an overall structure. The reader can then access the information in an associative way, linking item to item in a personal text that matches an individual's purpose and reading style. Moreover, an extension of the *form* for communicating information—*hypermedia*—enhances the number of channels through which an audience can receive information. "*FYI:* Hypermedia" (pages 186–187) provides you with an introduction to these new media.

The Merging of Oral and Written Media

Although in- and out-boxes have not disappeared from the office scene, office mail increasingly circulates in forms that can't be put in a box. One such form is *voice mail,* the transfer of messages via telephones with memories. An answering machine is a simple voice mail tool; more sophisticated, computer-enhanced systems can lead a caller through some procedure, like registering for classes or making an airline reservation. Chapter 21 provides advice on using voice mail.

Facsimile Transmission

Another form is *facsimile transmission.* "Fax" machines scan a document and convert text into digital pulses, which in turn are transmitted across phone lines as audible tones and are then reconverted by the receiving machine. Transmission across the country or around the world takes about twenty seconds. The Japanese have been major developers of such machines. The technology is well suited to the easy visual reproduction of a language with thousands of characters. It also accommodates Japanese culture, which emphasizes consensus building and last-minute decision-making, as you saw in Chapter 3.

A fax number has become an expected piece of information on business

HYPERMEDIA

Rebecca B. Worley
Director, Business and Technical Writing Internships, University of Delaware

Hypermedia is a new computer technology that links information through three major communication media: print, audio, and video. With a hypermedia system, you can sit in front of your computer screen and read text, listen to an audio tape, and watch a video or an animated graphic, all at the click of a mouse.

But hypermedia is more than a new technology; it is a different way of gathering and organizing information. Traditionally, information is organized by a writer or an editor and is presented in a linear sequence. For example, reference books generally present information alphabetically or chronologically. To some extent, even textbooks and business reports are arranged as a series of chapters or sections that the author expects the reader to follow.

With a hypermedia system, however, information is packaged as separate, independent modules, and each module is linked with others to form a complex web. You enter the system at any point that you select, and you choose your own path through the information according to your interests or need for information. In this sense, you have become the author. With a hypermedia system, you decide how much information you want and what sequence you want it presented in.

Although hypermedia is an evolving technology, it is already being

cards, on stationery, and even on the name and address page of pocket calendars. Companies use faxes to speed the transmission of documents, to prevent the loss or delay of mail, and to reduce long-distance telephone charges. Because of the necessary courtesies in calling, phone calls abroad often last at least 20 minutes, whereas a detailed fax can be transmitted in three or four minutes. Because faxes end up on paper, they also give the recipient visual cues to the level of formality of the document, for example, typing versus handwriting, stationery versus memo sheet.[5] And they provide a text for translation, unlike a phone call in a foreign language.

Faxes are not without problems, of course. If you dial the wrong number and that number happens to reach a fax machine, your document will end up in the wrong hands. Another risk is the false positive: Mere confirmation that the intended recipient's machine received the transmission does not necessarily mean that the document was properly transmitted or that the recipient received and read it. Unsolicited advertising is another problem; advertisers tie up the recipient's phone lines and use the recipient's paper and printing capacity. Eventually, experts predict, fax machines will yield to enhanced direct connections among computers for sending documents and printing them out at the receiver's end.

Electronic Mail

Electronic mail, or ''e-mail,'' is the sending of a message composed on one computer to another computer. Even though the message appears on a screen and is therefore ''written,'' it often reflects the more casual voice of

[5] Jolie Solomon, ''Business Communication in the Fax Age: Machines Foster Speed, Clarity—And Impatience,'' *The Wall Street Journal,* 27 October 1988, p. B1.

used in a number of applications. In the classroom, for example, students can access text describing a biochemical process, watch the video of a laboratory experiment, and access an audiotape giving step-by-step instructions for performing the experiment. In business, hypermedia is being used mainly by professional communicators and training directors to promote business campaigns, to explain company policies and procedures, or to instruct new employees, all using multimedia.

The concept behind hypermedia has been around since 1945, when Vannevar Bush proposed a system for organizing information that would approximate the way in which the human mind works.* People gather information, explore concepts, make decisions, and create new ideas by a process of association. One thought triggers another, which in turn triggers a third, through random association. Therefore, hypermedia approximates the way people think.

Technology has made Bush's idea a reality, and new developments will enhance the speed, the ease of use, and the memory capacity of the computer systems that make hypermedia possible. Hypermedia is truly changing the way people know and learn.

* "As We May Think," *Atlantic Monthly,* July 1945, 101–8.

conversation. One student who kept sending messages in capital letters received this response from the recipient: "Stop shouting at me!"

E-mail systems are fast and relatively inexpensive compared to letters and long-distance phone calls. A trade group, Electronic Mail Association, estimates that six million Americans sent or received e-mail in 1988, up from five million in 1987. The total U.S. market for e-mail services and software is expected to be $1.2 billion in 1992, according to Frost & Sullivan, a New York consulting firm.[6]

If your college or university has an e-mail system, try it out. The system may be a *local-area network* (LAN) that connects the terminals within one computer laboratory or building. Over a wider area, computers are often connected through telephone lines or fiber optics. To become a part of the network, you'll need an account that will allow you to log on. You can then send and receive messages. Many universities have such e-mail systems, as do companies. Your terminal may be wired directly to a larger computer that powers the network, or you may need a *modem* that connects your terminal through a telephone line.

As a private user, you can subscribe to one of several commercial e-mail services, including CompuServe in Columbus, Ohio, and those provided by such telecommunications organizations as MCI, AT&T, US Sprint, and British Telecom's Dialcom Group. "*FYI:* Local Norms in E-Mail" (pages 188–189) provides advice on using e-mail.

The medium of e-mail often loosens inhibitions. People "say things via computer that they wouldn't dare utter in person or on paper. They hurl

[6] Jeffrey A. Tannenbaum, "Speed, Cost and Cachet Aid Growth of Electronic Mail," *The Wall Street Journal,* 27 July 1988, p. 29.

LOCAL NORMS IN E-MAIL

JoAnne Yates
Associate Professor, Sloan School of Management, Massachusetts Institute of Technology

Because e-mail is a relatively new communication medium, norms for its use are still emerging and may vary significantly among organizations. For example, norms for the formality of messages vary. In some organizations, e-mail is viewed as a very informal channel, often replacing telephone calls. Messages are generally brief, informal, and unformatted, and users do not worry about occasional errors in spelling and grammar. In other organizations, e-mail is also used for longer and more formal communications. In such messages, the norms of formality, formatting, and mechanical correctness that apply to written memos are more likely to be applied to e-mail messages.

Norms for genre conventions also vary among and within e-mail communities. Is an e-mail message the equivalent of a memo (an e-memo?), a letter, or a handwritten note? Most e-mail systems provide a standard memolike header with "To," "From," "Subject," and "Date" information. The sender fills in the subject line and the system identification (ID) of the receiver (sometimes shortened names such as JYATES and sometimes random strings of letters or numbers), and the system automatically adds the date and the sender's ID. The system may also provide the real names of the senders and receivers. Because

insults. They let off steam. They breach bureaucratic protocol. Then they push the 'send' button."[7] The tendency toward insults and otherwise emotional messages is called *flaming.* The speed of e-mail approximates the quick response of conversation—in a form, however, that is *received* as writing and can be preserved, sometimes to the sender's regret.

Electronic Bulletin Boards and Conferences

E-mail users can participate in *electronic bulletin boards.* Like a speedier and bigger version of a board on a wall, these message systems are edited at one location and collect and disseminate messages throughout the world on topics of interest to subscribers. A more interactive form is the *electronic conference.* In an electronic conference, several individuals, often at widely scattered locations, log onto their computers, access the conference, read others' comments, and type their own in response. The activity may occur simultaneously or over time. Such conferences connect, for example, the followers of popular musicians like the Grateful Dead. The electronic conference can also serve as a town meeting; Santa Monica, California, opened a network in 1989 to allow residents to comment from their homes on city affairs. Through conferencing, specialists throughout the world can share information in a faster and friendlier form than through newsletters and other publications.

The role of these changing media was demonstrated vividly in the communication surrounding the events in Tiananmen Square in Beijing in 1989:

[7] Jolie Solomon, "As Electronic Mail Loosens Inhibitions, Impetuous Senders Feel Anything Goes," *The Wall Street Journal,* 12 October 1990, p. B1.

of the heading, some people view the message as a memo and omit any salutation or sign-off. Others see the system heading as very impersonal and often uninformative, and they add a greeting and sign-off to make the message more like a personal note or a letter. Thus, the message may start with "Hi, Joan" or "Joe—" and may end with "Bill" or "Take care/Mary." Still others treat messages sent internally as memos and those sent externally as letters.

Other norms that vary from system to system or community to community concern formatting devices and symbols. Because e-mail systems generally lack most formatting tools (such as underlining, boldface, and tabs), users have to find other ways of indicating structure and emphasis. For example, in many e-mail communities, word emphasis (indicated in hard copy by **word** or <u>word</u>) is indicated by _word_, *word*, or WORD. In addition, some specialized symbols such as (-: (a sideways smiley face) and (-; (a winking smiley face) have come to be used in some e-mail communities to indicate that a passage is to be taken as a joke. When you start to use e-mail, or when you change e-mail communities, ask about or observe the local norms so that you can use the medium properly.

In the first days of the uprising, Western journalists transmitted their video feedback home via satellite without interference from Chinese authorities. But as things heated up, these normal channels were closed down, and journalists turned to the microcomputer. Enterprising reporters from ABC News, using scanners and personal computers, were the first to digitize video pictures and transmit them as electronic mail back to the States. Many of these pictures were then retransmitted to China via fax, where they gave many people outside Beijing, including illiterate peasants, shocking evidence of what had happened.

Meanwhile, students were doing their own transmitting, sending a barrage of fax transmissions to strategic locations around the world. When the authorities finally caught on and silenced the fax machines, the democracy movement, too, turned to the personal computer. Though authorities were monitoring the phone lines and censoring radio and televison transmissions, they weren't able to identify the flood of digital messages that went out via telephone lines to personal computers in the United States and Europe.[8]

The Electronic Workplace

The changes in technology that you have been reading about—changes that are indeed revolutionary—contribute to a reshaping of the structure and management of organizations. In this section, you'll see how electronic media have contributed to two major changes you read about in Chapters 2 and 3:

[8] Bernard R. Gifford, "Technology and Change in China: A Retrospective," advertisement in *The Chronicle of Higher Education*, 5 July 1990, p. A18. Used by permission.

the flattening of corporate hierarchies (pancake organizations) and decentralization.

The Pancake Organization

"In 2010, the typical large business will have half as many management levels and one-third as many managerial positions as it does today."[9] Reinforcing this tendency, electronic communication within organizations is blurring the lines of authority. In communicating with e-mail, you can reach anyone on the system, at any level in the organization. The form *seems* conversational, but it does not provide the clues to status that you'd find in someone's private office or in her or his feedback—like a silence—on the phone. For example, William Gates, chairman of Microsoft Corporation, is connected on one system with most of the company's fifty-two hundred employees. Decisions are debated and then announced on the network. Employees contact one another—and Gates, who "receives and dispatches hundreds of electronic notes a day."[10] The ease of sending electronic messages encourages lower level workers to contact superiors—and vice versa—for enhanced communication and diminished barriers among levels.

Decentralization

The ability to connect with others electronically has encouraged the development of *virtual* rather than *physical* work groups. Employees who are separated physically at widely scattered locations can still collaborate through electronic conferences and mail so as to share information and build a consensus on project teams. At IBM, for example, employees throughout the world participate in conferences on specific topics; if a production problem arises at one plant, scientists from several others can read the description on the screen and add their comments. "Problems get solved in minutes that might otherwise never get solved," noted the director of computing systems for IBM research.[11] Studies have found that employees who can exchange messages on a computer system often work better together than those who must rely on personal meetings or phone calls.

Work, then, can move to the workers. A New York firm employs clerks in Ireland. It may also employ managers in Darien, Connecticut; Portland, Maine; and Laramie, Wyoming—all of whom work in their homes and "telecommute," that is, link themselves electronically. Some twenty million people are estimated to be working at least part time at home—a number expected to grow by 7 percent a year.[12] By some estimates, one third of American employees will do part-time or full-time work from their homes by the year 2000.

The satellite office or neighborhood work center is another step in decentralization. Southern California companies have been in the forefront in America in setting up such centers so that workers can work in cluster offices near their homes—all connected to a central office and each other through computer links—and can avoid long commutes in cars.

[9] Kerry Pechter, "Workplace Openers," *The Wall Street Journal,* 4 June 1990, p. R5.

[10] Markoff, p. 1.

[11] Markoff, p. 20.

[12] Calvin Sims, "Coast-to-Coast in 20 Seconds: Fax Machines Alter Business," *The New York Times,* 6 May 1988, p. D5.

Specialists from different departments of an automobile company are brought together through interactive computerized conferencing to design new systems.

The structure and management of organizations are predicted to become so dependent on electronic media that on/off switches will simply disappear. Computers will be on continuously. Whereas today an office worker has to take steps to connect to the systems, tomorrow's worker will have to take steps to *dis*connect. The workstation will surround the worker. Cellular technology will find anyone anywhere. "You'll be reachable, no matter when it is, no matter where you are," says Norman Weizer, senior consultant at Arthur D. Little Inc. "The problem will be how much privacy you want."[13]

THE COSTS OF COMPUTING

The question of privacy leads to the final issue you'll read about in this chapter: the personal costs of computing. The results of electronic technology are mixed.

Privacy

How much privacy do you want? How much privacy will electronic technology *allow* you? These are serious issues. Within organizations, e-mail systems open the lines of communication. They also enlarge the potential for control from the top. Many companies routinely keep a copy of all e-mail conversations—a record that managers can read to control the actions of employees.

Indeed, it isn't always clear whether an e-mail message is intended solely for one recipient or is addressed to the larger public as part of an electronic

[13] Laurence Hooper, "Future Shock: Your Office Will Look Different 10 Years from Now, but You May Not Like It Any Better," *The Wall Street Journal,* 4 June 1990, p. R19.

conference. The 1986 Federal Electronic Communications Privacy Act requires the operators of public electronic communication systems to protect the privacy of messages, and it places some restrictions on private systems. But interpretations of the act can be difficult.

That issue was central to a political controversy in Colorado Springs, Colorado, in 1990.[14] For more than a year, the mayor read the e-mail circulated by city council members from their home computers on a system purchased by the council. Several council members, curious about the mayor's knowledge of the issues they had discussed on the system, raised the question with the city manager, who decided that the messages were, in effect, telephone calls and should be private. The mayor confirmed that he was reading the council's e-mail by complaining to the council that his access had been curtailed.

The mayor defended himself by saying that he was monitoring council members' actions to make sure that they were not holding illegal caucuses through the system. He saw the system as an electronic conference to which he had the right of access because Colorado law requires that city council business be conducted at public forums. The council members said that the mayor's reading, even if technically legal, undermined the political system and at the least was "bad manners."

The 24-Hour Workday

The issue of privacy has another face: the incentive that computers and a global economy provide for 24-hour workdays—as you saw at the beginning of this chapter. Managers report that they are working harder and longer. But analysts say that such workers may be achieving more "throughput" without enhanced output. For example, Ronald E. Kutscher, Associate Commissioner of the Bureau of Labor Statistics, can now write seven drafts of an economic analysis with his computer in the same time that he took to compose two or three before. "Can I argue that the article is better?" he said. "I don't know. It isn't being measured."[15]

Some recipients of faxes feel that the speed of transmission must be matched by a speedy response. That speed intensifies the pressure and makes it harder to take time to deliberate. A further intensification of pressure comes from corporate support for the purchase of personal computers. Although having a company buy you a computer seems like a benefit, some employees then feel a not-so-subtle pressure to put in extra hours of work at home.

Physiological Effects

Various studies show that working at a computer terminal presents some dangerous side effects. One effect is called *repetitive motion syndrome* (RMP). When you write with a pencil or pen and you move around physically to file and retrieve sheets of paper, you vary your physical motions. You're also likely to take breaks in the activity. Writing at a terminal allows no such variety. You retrieve files and enter data and text continuously with the same

[14] John Markoff, "Furor Erupts from Computers in Politics," *The New York Times*, 4 May 1990, p. A12.

[15] Kilburn, p. 3.

motion, a repetition of motion that may lead to inflammation of the hand and arm tendons.

The screen also can provide a kind of hypnotic attraction. People blink less, eyes are strained, and eye muscles have difficulty focusing, conditions that contribute to myopia. Birth defects, miscarriages, and even some cancers have also been associated with the low-frequency electromagnetic waves emitted by video display terminals.

Psychological Effects

Other potentially damaging side effects may be considered psychological or intellectual. In their ability to digitize information, computers can lead to an emphasis on individual items. Seeing discrete modules can enhance readability, as you saw in Chapter 7. But undue emphasis on bits of information may draw attention away from the context that gives that information significance. The *accumulation* of facts becomes more important than *interpretation* or *coherence.* With hypertext, for example, a savvy reader can follow a productive personal route through information. Less able readers, however, can immerse themselves in item after item unproductively until they are hopelessly out of touch with what they were looking for, a condition known as being *lost in hyperspace.*

Digital information can cause you to get lost. In addition, the computer's speed may contribute to a shortening of your attention span. You may come to believe that *all* information can be transferred in short, discrete units—like "sound bites," the pithy expressions that politicians formulate for television.

SUMMARY

- A **wordprocessing** system helps you to enter text rapidly and then to delete and move around chunks of text in revision without the mess of pencil and paper. You can also connect to other programs—like spreadsheets and information systems—to merge research and writing on one screen. Producing a document on a screen is fast and frictionless.
- **Desktop publishing** is an enhanced wordprocessing program that runs on personal computers. It allows you to integrate graphics and print texts that rival the output of professional printshops.
- Traditional documents are linear; the writer imposes an order on information, and the reader must read in that order. With **hypertext** programs, you can mark individual units of information so that the *reader* can order them in a way that matches her or his personal purpose and reading style.
- Telephone lines—traditionally used for *oral* communication—now carry essentially *written* forms through **facsimile transmission** and **electronic mail.** Facsimiles are printed out as documents; e-mail appears on a screen and often displays a conversational style and informality.
- E-mail systems have encouraged a flattening of reporting levels in the "electronic workplace" and more collaboration through *virtual* as opposed to *physical* work groups. These work groups are often **decentralized.** Workers in their homes and in satellite offices—here or abroad—are connected

with each other and with a central office through computer and telephone links. Workers can work almost anywhere. They can also work at almost any time. Any hour of the day is work time somewhere on the globe; electronic technology spans time zones.

➧ The results of computing are not unmixed. The privacy of transmission is an issue, as are the stresses of the 24-hour workday, the physiological effects caused by work at a terminal, and the psychological effects of a shortened attention span as information content takes precedence over its significance and the speed of computers makes people think that all messages should be speedy.

EXERCISES

For Discussion

1. If you have access to individuals in large organizations, survey their use of electronic media. Make up a questionnaire for your survey (see Chapter 9). Here are some questions to start with; add others as appropriate:
   - Which form of electronic communication do the respondents use most frequently?
   - What are its advantages and disadvantages?
   - What kind of message or information do they most frequently send?
   - How has electronic communication changed their daily routine of doing business?
   - How has it changed the messages they send?
2. As a cautionary project, collect stories about what can go *wrong* with computers, especially with wordprocessing programs. You may have had some encounters with lost text yourself; start with those. If not, survey other students or faculty—the computer lab would be a good place for such a survey—for their tales. Then discuss these in class. Write a list of the problems on the board (see Chapter 4 for advice on brainstorming); *classify* the kinds of errors and the frequency of each; then create an outline for a brief guide to such problems—and ways to avoid them.
3. Computing has its own language, some of which has been presented in this chapter. Here are some terms. What do they mean?

central processing unit	laser printer
CD-ROM	local-area network
database	mainframe
desktop publishing	minicomputer
disk drive	modem
electronic spreadsheet	monitor
groupware	shareware
hardware	software
WYSIWYG	

For Writing

4. Find out what methods of electronic communication—voice mail, e-mail, fax, and teleconferencing—are available on your campus. Using any two of the methods, prepare a message for transmission. Is the message you prepared for e-mail different from the one you prepared for voice mail? How are they different from a message prepared for fax transmission? At your instructor's direction, discuss your messages in class.

5. Assume that you are in the market for a personal computer. Collect information about various systems (check with the salespeople at a local computer store and read the popular periodicals on computing, for example, *Byte, PCWorld,* and *MacWorld*). Establish your requirements. Then make a chart (see Chapter 6) that compares all the information you've collected and that will aid you in your decision.
6. Educators often say that students should be "computer-competent" or "computer-literate"—although the meaning of those terms is slippery. Assume that you are a student consultant to your college or university's computer planning committee. One issue to be addressed in the committee's report is the level of computer competence among the students on campus. The committee has asked you to compile information about computer literacy. You should include the following:
   - A definition of computer competence
   - A list of *goals* for achieving computer competence (perhaps directed to each major or specialty) over the next five years
   - A brief plan for implementing those goals
   - A recommendation about how progress toward those goals can be measured

   To prepare your information, *survey* a sample of other students. Your instructor will set the number of people to be surveyed. Ask them, for example:
   - What kinds of software and hardware for computing, if any, do they use?
   - Where do they do their computing? In the dormitory? At home? At a campus computer site? In a laboratory?
   - How did they learn about computers? In classes? In tutorial sessions at computer sites? In short courses? In high school? On their own?
   - How much computing service, and of what kind (access to personal computers, to printers, to e-mail, and to powerful software), should be provided by the university? By the students themselves?
   - What is their own definition of "competence," and do they meet it? In wordprocessing only? In numerically intensive computing? In business applications?
   - What recommendations do they have for enhancing computer instruction and use on campus?

   Compile your results. Use visual forms (see Chapter 6) wherever appropriate.

For Collaboration

7. With others in the class, survey a wider sample of students and create a more comprehensive file of information about computer competence on your campus.

11 COLLABORATION: MANAGING GROUP COMMUNICATION

What's Ahead

COLLABORATION: THE ORGANIZATIONAL WAY
- Forms of Collaborative Writing
- Advantages of Collaborative Writing

WHO'S RESPONSIBLE?

HOW GROUPS FORM AND FUNCTION
- Formation of Groups
- Group Processes

GROUP WRITING
- Guidelines for Group Writing
- FYI: Collaborating to Write This Textbook
- FYI: Making Assignments

GROUP ORAL PRESENTATIONS
- Guidelines for Group Oral Presentations

REVIEWING AND EDITING THE WORK OF OTHERS
- Guidelines for Editing the Work of Others

SUMMARY

EXERCISES

Do You Know 

- How much writing and speaking in businesses is done collaboratively and is collaboration more or less effective than individual work?
- When you work in a group to produce a business document or presentation, who is responsible for getting the work done? Who gets credit for it?
- How are groups formed to complete collaborative communication projects? How can groups work most efficiently and effectively?
- What special skills and techniques are needed in group writing projects?
- What special skills and techniques are needed in group oral presentations?
- What should you do when you are working in a group and you need to review and edit the work of other members?

When Maria Alvarez began the M.B.A. program at the University of Pittsburgh, she was surprised to discover that every Wednesday she had to spend the entire afternoon working with six other students in a team project on marketing. Because she was the only one of the seven who had been an undergraduate marketing major, she felt that she spent more time teaching basic principles to her fellow team members than in getting the assignments done. Her frustration turned to anger when the team had to write the final report. How, she asked her adviser, can a group of people *write* a report? She wanted just to do it herself, even if that meant the others would get credit for her work. Her adviser explained that "business *is* teamwork," a thought that Maria had never really considered before.

Maria is not alone. Many students undervalue the collaborative nature of business. But even those who know that teamwork is important in business sometimes exclude business *communication* from the list of business functions that are typically carried out in groups.

This chapter reviews the collaborative nature of business communication and presents guidelines for working in groups on communication projects, both written and oral.

COLLABORATION: THE ORGANIZATIONAL WAY

Collaborative communication is important because the work of organizations is done in and by groups. Some people think of writing as a private, even a lonely, act. Of course, sitting down to face a pad of paper or a computer screen is a private act and can be lonely, but in an organization, writing is usually a group process. Although one person may in fact "write" the text of a report or proposal—that is, put the words together to form the text—many others may be directly involved. For example:

- A supervisor makes the assignment and ultimately approves the document.
- A colleague gathers the data.
- A staff designer prepares the graphs.
- An editor oversees production and prepares the final copy.

In large projects—for example, preparing a 200-page proposal for the U.S. Department of Defense—dozens of individuals may be involved directly—and still more, indirectly—in collecting information and securing internal approval for the project. Even a relatively short and apparently simple document like a memo asking permission to hire a new computer programmer may involve several persons, even though one individual—the person initiating the request—actually "writes" the memo.

Forms of Collaborative Writing

Collaborative writing takes three basic forms:

1. **A single writer follows a plan that is collaboratively developed.** For example, a group studying potential new markets for breakfast cereal may prepare all the material and agree about how it is to be written in report form; however, one member of the team is the single writer for the project and is responsible for all editorial functions.

2. **Multiple writers follow a plan that is collaboratively developed.** For example, the report on new markets for breakfast cereal might be written in parts after the whole group has made decisions about the final product; each member writes his or her part.

3. **Multiple writers follow a plan that is developed by one person.** For example, the marketing manager may take all the information developed on markets for the cereal, outline his or her own plan for the final report, and then assign parts to be written by each member.

You may already have encountered one or all of these forms of collaborative communication; if not, you will as you pursue your business career.

The third form is the least effective in promoting true collaboration; it is most common in a formal project in which professional communication experts work under the direction of an editor who makes assignments to writers, designers, proofreaders, and other professionals. This form is also occasionally used in large projects—for example, preparing proposals (see Chapter 17)—in which a supervisor typically takes charge of the work and assigns group members to work on those parts for which they have special expertise.

The first and second forms are the most common among businesspeople who write as part of their job but are not hired as communication professionals. In the first form, a group meets to plan the work and then agrees to have one person—because of his or her familiarity with the topic and/or perceived communication ability—actually compose the text. The whole group reviews this work and jointly edits and makes suggestions to the single writer.

The second form is the hardest to manage but can be the most fruitful because it taps all the talents of group members. In it, the group collaboratively develops the plan and assigns parts of the project to each member. Bringing together all this work requires group editing. Depending on the complexity of the project and the skills of group members, this form of collaboration often calls for one manager or editor to monitor all work and to take responsibility for keeping each person on track.

The choice among the three forms depends on company practices, the nature of the specific project, the nature of the group, and the skills and experience that the team members bring to the project. No single form is inherently better than the others. Indeed, selecting the form is itself often a collaborative decision.

Advantages of Collaborative Writing

How common is collaboration in business communication? Surveys of on-the-job writing differ, but one suggests that nearly 90 percent of business professionals sometimes write as part of a team.[1] That's not surprising, and it's safe to assume that whatever your specific business position, you can expect to do a great deal of your writing through groups.

Research also indicates that group writing is "better" than individual writing in business, that is, that the products of group work achieve better results. Why? We can list at least four reasons why collaborative communication can be more successful than individual writing on the job:

1. Work produced in a group benefits from the broader base of information and experience that the group brings to the project. When several people collaborate, the pool of what they know and have done is bigger than when one person completes the assignment. Of course, this is not always true since one expert may know more than several novices. President John F. Kennedy once greeted a group of eminent scholars dining in the White House by saying that never before had so much genius been represented in one room there—except when Thomas Jefferson dined alone. But Jeffersons are rare—in politics and in business.

2. Group projects tap more perspectives and viewpoints than individual ones and can therefore be more truly representative of the whole organization. When you bring together a marketing manager and a production engineer, for example, you may get two quite different perspectives on how to develop and promote a new product. Differing points of view from people in different parts of the organization can result in a more realistic approach to solving a communication problem.

3. Groups can work faster by dividing tasks. This advantage is not always obvious because the opposite can occur: Too many participants can

[1] A. Lunsford and L. Ede, "Why Write . . . Together: A Research Update," *Rhetoric Review*, 5 (1986), 71–81.

Working collaboratively, the typical practice in modern business, requires understanding of group dynamics and recognition of the unique contributions that groups make to problem-solving and communication.

slow a project. But properly managed, a group can get its work done faster because the total work to be done can be divided up and assigned to individuals according to their experience, expertise, and talents.

4. A group project becomes a mini-version of the communication situation being addressed. Because communication within the group duplicates the process of communicating by the group to its intended audience, it speeds the final work and makes it easier. For example, when the accountant on the team has to translate her expertise into understandable language for the human resources specialist, the final job of producing an understandable report for the board of directors is made easier.

WHO'S RESPONSIBLE?

Students sometimes find the corporate emphasis on group projects unsettling. Since first grade, teachers have stressed the importance of doing your own work, of being individually responsible, and of not sharing information with your classmates. Now someone tells you that in business most work is done through groups, and that even writing is, in an organization, a group endeavor.

The chief problem that students perceive in group projects is the assignment of responsibility. It's obvious that if Mary Jones has a report due Friday, the failure to meet the deadline is hers. But what if Jones is a member of a four-person group? Whose fault is it if the deadline passes? Can she blame the others for failing to submit drafts of sections to her on time? Should she?

These are tricky issues of ethics, corporate citizenship, and politics. We can't answer them specifically here; instead, we will establish two basic guidelines on responsibility in group projects:

1. Every member of the group is responsible for the group's actions.
2. The designated leader of the group bears the principal responsibility for its action as long as he or she has the authority to match that responsibility.

These two guidelines may seem slightly contradictory. How can everyone be responsible for everything when one person is more responsible than others? That snare is inherent in organizational life. Each person working in the group must feel personal responsibility not just to complete his or her own portion of the work well and on time but also to see that the group assignment is completed, even if that means assuming extra duties. Membership in the group extends responsibilities. At the same time, each group has a leader, someone who assumes the role because of his or her corporate position (because that person is the boss) or because of his or her special skills and talents in managing a group communication project. That person has a special responsibility to see that the group's assignment is completed.

However, the added responsibility exists only in proportion to the authority given to accomplish the task. If your position within the corporate hierarchy is such that you can't compel actions from others in your group, then by definition you shouldn't have to assume increased responsibility for the outcome. That's why it's a poor idea to put a junior person in charge of a writing project that depends for its successful and timely completion on the work of people senior to him or her. As in all aspects of corporate life, in a group writing project, authority must match responsibility.

We approached the issue of responsibility here negatively, emphasizing the blame attached when something goes wrong. The issue should also be considered from the opposite perspective: In a group writing project, who gets the credit for a job well done? The answer should be obvious. All members of the group share in the credit. The group leader may be singled out for special praise, but that should be limited to his or her unique contributions and should not detract from the praise earned by the whole group. Credit is shared in direct proportion to work done.

HOW GROUPS FORM AND FUNCTION

Groups may have as few as two members or as many as several hundred. Collaboration is really a continuum, a range of situations. At one end is the simple situation of a supervisor assigning one person to write a memo with the understanding that the supervisor will read and modify it to suit her needs in communicating to someone else. A more complex situation, further along the continuum, might involve a planning group of four or five participants who brainstorm a situation and devise a strategy that will actually be put in writing by only one or two of the members.

The most complex situation on the continuum is that of the integrated communication group in which several or many persons really function as one in assessing the communication issue, identifying goals, searching for information, planning the document, crafting the text and visuals, and editing and producing the final product. Although individual members carry out one or more of the separate parts of the project, the work is done in an integrated fashion, and each member bears full responsibility for the results rather than only for his or her discrete part.

Formation of Groups

Sometimes writing projects are carried out by groups that already exist in an organization, such as the staff of the accounting department, the proposal support group, or the marketing division. Sometimes people are brought together from several divisions to form a special group to complete a writing project. Managing the process of group writing differs depending on whether the group already exists or has been created especially for the project.

The chief advantage of working with an existing group is that the members are all known to each other and probably have experience in working together on other projects, even on writing projects. The disadvantage is that the pool of talent is fixed; you have to exploit the strengths and overcome the weaknesses of the group as it already exists. The advantage of creating a special group is that you can, within reasonable limits, get what you need. If, for example, the work at hand requires a good many graphs and charts, you can make sure that you have a graphics specialist to handle these. On the other hand, creating a group to do a specific project often means that the people haven't worked together before. You may thus be starting at the top of the learning curve and may be forced to spend seemingly unproductive time just forging the team and developing good interactions among the members.

Group Processes

Regardless of how the group is formed and where it is located on the continuum of collaboration, its work must be accomplished with concern not just for the final product but also for the way the group itself functions. Hundreds of studies of group process provide clues to how groups function and suggestions for how to make groups function well. We can distill this information into five simplified rules:

1. Understand and accept the goals of the group.
2. Understand and accept the process of working together—with all the frustrations as well as pleasures that come from being on a team.

3. Clarify roles, responsibilities, and assignments at the beginning of the project.
4. Communicate openly and fully with all group members all the time.
5. Provide for a regular review not just of the substance but also of the process of the group's work, including periodic feedback and any necessary correction as well as a final evaluation of how the work came out.

Working collaboratively requires group consciousness, that is, a constant awareness of the group as a group. Sometimes this means putting the group's substantive goals in a secondary position while you give attention to how the group itself is functioning. Consider these questions:

1. Does everyone know where you are headed and why?
2. Are people talking to each other regularly and openly and not just when a problem occurs or the process appears to be breaking down?
3. Does each participant know his or her assignment and stick to it, but without ducking responsibility for the overall purpose?
4. Do the members point fingers or draw a too-fine line between roles?
5. Does the group regularly evaluate its way of working together and look for even better ways to function smoothly and efficiently?
6. When the job is done, does the group rate itself *as* a group and identify better ways to proceed in the future?

Many observers of group processes see collaboration as group *learning.* We acquire knowledge and experience jointly and—as philosophers say—construct reality together. Groups are therefore extraordinarily powerful tools of learning and of communicating. Keeping a high level of awareness of how the group itself is functioning will make it easier for the group to work together to achieve its communication goals. "*FYI:* Collaborating to Write This Textbook" (pages 204–205) gives you a glimpse of how one collaborative effort worked.

GROUP WRITING

An awareness of the writing group as a group must of course blend with an awareness of the communication goals that the group is formed to meet. That blending produces three general guidelines for group writing:

1. Make sure that the *entire* group understands the assignment at the outset.
2. Evaluate the capacities, talents, and special strengths and weaknesses of each member of the group, and assign tasks accordingly.
3. Monitor both group and individual progress to keep everyone focused on the outcome—and the deadlines.

Guidelines for Group Writing

Let's look at each guideline in detail.

COLLABORATING TO WRITE THIS TEXTBOOK

William D. Andrews
Deborah C. Andrews

The textbook you are reading is the product of collaboration. Some of the advice in this chapter originated from this collaboration. We want to tell you a bit about how we collaborated to write *Business Communication*.

We are quite different people. Debby is a full-time teacher, a professor of English and coordinator of the concentration in business and technical writing at the University of Delaware. In addition to her regular teaching of undergraduates and graduate students, she consults with corporations and agencies on business communication and teaches professionals in on-the-job courses on various aspects of writing. Although Bill was a full-time college teacher and business consultant, for the past twelve years he has been a college administrator and is currently the president of Westbrook College in Portland, Maine. In that job he is more of a "businessperson" than an academic; running a small college involves management, marketing, and financial skills and experience similar to those required in any business. Our education, experiences, and day-to-day responsibilities are therefore quite different.

As writers, we are also very different. That's why we decided six year ago, when we wrote the first edition of *Business Communication*, to follow this approach: We conceived and planned the book jointly, assigned ourselves chapters to write according to our interests and strengths, and then edited each other's chapters so that we achieved a single focus. We followed the same approach with this, the second edition.

Most of the collaboration was therefore not directly related to actual writing, or putting words together. Doing that, we sat at separate computers in separate studies and "wrote" alone. The real collaboration came at the thinking and planning stages, both for the book as a whole and even for individual chapters that one of us had the primary responsibility for writing.

The fun of the collaboration came as we sat around the table in our house in the mountains of western Maine. We debated, praised, criticized, and sometimes had to stop talking about a topic because our points of view were so different. Sheets of paper from our computers

1. **Make sure that the entire group understands the assignment at the outset.** It is sometimes difficult for an individual writer to grasp completely the full dimensions of an assignment, and that difficulty is magnified in a group writing project. Like sports teams, writing groups must function together to achieve goals because the result must be more than the total of each individual's performance. But unlike sports teams, writing groups do not operate within fixed rules. The group leader or manager of a writing project must be both coach and umpire at the same time, inspiring and coaxing the group toward the goal and also developing and enforcing the "rules" as the game proceeds.

The questions that the individual writer must ask and get clear answers

piled up on the floor. Diagrams and notes were scattered among the coffee cups. Outlines and *many* revised tables of contents vied for space among our books, articles, and correspondence.

From this year-long effort in writing the second edition of *Business Communication,* we learned the importance of two guidelines for effective collaboration:

1. **Play to your strengths.** Whether you're working with a coauthor to whom you happen to be married or in a large work group in a corporation, assign tasks according to who is *best* at doing them. Don't expect the collaboration to be a learning experience that will make a poor editor great or a sloppy writer precise. Don't expect great changes in people working collaboratively. Find out what tasks each person in the group does best and assign the work accordingly.

2. **Respect differences and avoid judgments.** Everyone is uniquely talented. Give the members of a collaborative group the opportunity to show their talents, and don't rush to slap "good" and "bad" labels on either the approach or the outcome. Find ways to truly work *together,* to make the whole better than the sum of the parts.

Students and friends who have lived through this collaborative project with us typically ask two questions: Is it hard to write a book with your spouse? Can you tell who wrote which chapters?

We can answer the first question easily: Collaborating with a spouse on a writing project combines the joys and frustrations of *both* marriage and professional work. Both in marriage and on the job, personality differences grate, habits can become the source of tension, and values can be in conflict. But both marriage and work can be satisfying, engaging, and joyous. It all depends on how you collaborate.

The second question—Who wrote which chapters?—is one we want you to try to answer. Can you tell which of us "wrote" this chapter on collaboration? If you figure that out, test your analysis on other chapters. If you write to us (in care of College Division, Macmillan Publishing Company, 866 Third Avenue, New York, New York 10022), we promise to answer. Then you'll be our collaborators.

to are equally appropriate in a group situation: Who is the audience? What is the purpose? What form should the writing take? How long should it be? When is it due? But now the trick is to ensure that every member of the group understands the questions and can work within the limits that the answers establish. If four members of a five-member group think that the report is being written for the merchandising vice president and one thinks it's for the sales manager, serious problems can develop. The levels of language, the use of details, the categories of material to be included, and the form of presentation all vary according to the perception of the audience. Hence, it is critical that from the beginning everyone in the group know the exact goal.

The best way to promote clear understanding is to bring everyone together at the beginning of the project to discuss it in detail. The group leader must take charge, establishing the parameters of the project precisely and responding clearly to every question. The meeting should be informal and open so that everyone with questions gets a chance to ask them—and gets a direct, unambiguous answer. Everyone should leave the meeting with a strong grasp of the overall assignment that can be focused in a single statement, for example, "We are writing a 50-page report due on 20 September on sales of women's accessories in our branch stores in the Newark area to inform the merchandising vice president of our current operations." No one in the group should misunderstand and think that the purpose of the project is to persuade the reader to drop this line of merchandise, even though that may be the opinion of one member of the team.

Everyone should leave this first meeting with a clear view of the project, but to reinforce it, the group leader should follow up with a written statement like the one just given. At the end of the meeting, it may seem that everyone understands, but if that understanding is not confirmed in writing, you leave open the possibility of later confusion.

At the initial meeting, when the assignment is clarified it may also be possible to assign specific tasks. Or it may be necessary to have a separate meeting or even several to delegate the tasks. At the very least, the first meeting must end with a consensus about the group's assignment and a

MAKING ASSIGNMENTS

Jone Rymer
Associate Professor, School of Business Administration, Wayne State University

Although you may not always write with a team during your career, you will always interact with others as part of getting your writing done, especially in assigning writing tasks. Participating in classroom groups can help you develop the collaborative skills critical to *giving* assignments. You and your peers may discuss your plans, for example, and then each can go off to draft a section of the team report. When you come back to share your writing, you might discover that each member interpreted the group consensus differently, or that your individual drafts didn't work out exactly as you anticipated. In short, the group's assignments to the members resulted in drafts that require numerous revisions. What went wrong with giving the assignments?

Assigning writing may sound easy to you since you have been on the receiving end of so many school assignments in which *completing* the assignment, not *making* it, seemed like the hard part. However, getting a subordinate to write a draft that meets your needs is no simple matter.*

Assigning a draft may mean that you have some definite ideas about how you want that writing to sound, and about what you want it to say—and maybe what not to say. How can you tell someone else all that without practically writing it yourself? Or giving an assignment

* See Barbara Couture and Jone Rymer, "Dyadic Interaction during Composing: The Primary Collaboration in Workplace Writing," in Mary M. Lay and William M. Karis, eds., *Collaborative Writing in Industry: Investigations in Theory and Practice* (Farmingdale, NY: Baywood Publishing Company, 1991).

precise statement of it orally and, immediately after, in writing. "*FYI:* Making Assignments" provides practical advice on this topic.

2. **Evaluate the capacities, talents, and special strengths and weaknesses of each member of the group, and assign tasks accordingly.** At either a first or a follow-up meeting, the overall project should be divided into discrete tasks to which deadlines are attached. Again, the group manager has a special responsibility because he or she must take the lead in segmenting the project, always being flexible and open to suggestions and criticisms. All members of the group should participate in this step, but the group leader has the final authority for seeing that the project is completed effectively and on time.

In an individual project, the writer has to identify the separate parts and put deadlines on each. In a group project, individuals must be assigned to each task. Here is where the manager's "people skills" are called on. As the manager of a group project, you must realistically evaluate each member's abilities and assign the tasks to those best equipped to complete them. If you are working with an existing group, you probably already know quite a bit about the members and what they can and cannot do. This knowledge makes it easier to come to a meeting with a preliminary assignment list that can serve as a basis for group discussion and final assignment. If Jaworski is a superb stylist, the group's writer-in-residence, then you can reasonably assign him to the job of composing the draft. If Hughes is an instinctively good

may mean that you don't have a clear idea beforehand about what you want in the finished product, but you expect that somehow the subordinate's draft should meet your requirements. What do you tell the writer then?

Often managers who assign writing don't collaborate effectively with their subordinates. They may take the approach of a manager for an American automotive manufacturer with whom I worked. He claimed that he didn't have time to explain to his subordinates how he wanted things written. "It's their job to figure it out!" he insisted. His approach of giving a writer the task without explaining the audience's needs and his own purposes typically ended with dissatisfaction on both sides, lots of revisions, and even rewriting by the manager himself.

For this manager, learning to collaborate meant learning to think about the task beforehand to figure out what he wanted—something that is difficult to do if you "think on paper." Collaborating also meant discussing the projected draft in some detail, ensuring that the manager's ideas were well understood by the writer. Furthermore, if that kind of collaboration were impossible, the manager had to recognize the increased need for and had to assume some responsibility for revision after drafting. For him to treat it as solely the writer's fault was unfair because nobody else can get inside his head to know how he wanted the draft done. In short, assigning writing means collaborating with the writer so that revision will not become an unnecessarily time-consuming, unpleasant process.

editor who can pull together the drafts of several persons into a seamless whole, then you can give her that job. And so forth.

When a group is being specially formed for a project, it may take several meetings—and some private conversations with the individuals and others who have worked with them before—to determine who is best at what. It's worth spending a meeting or two simply talking out the issues and discovering who wants—and is able—to handle what parts of the overall job. Although respecting individual preferences is obviously desirable, once again the group leader is finally responsible and must make the assignments in the way that is most likely to lead to the intended outcome. Both Jones and Marvin may consider themselves whizzes at compiling tables of numbers, but if you need only one person to produce tables, you will have to choose between them—and keep both happy and productive in the assignments that they do receive. Not everyone can be goalie on a hockey team. Several may want to be, but someone—the coach—finally has to decide and has to implement the decision in a way that keeps everyone working together efficiently as a team. Tact and common sense are helpful.

Once the assignments are made, they should be recorded in writing and circulated to everyone in the group so that each member understands his or her role, its relationship to the roles of the others, and the deadlines that everyone must operate under. For a large project, a scheduling chart is desirable. If warranted, a less formal approach can be taken. In any case, it is important that everyone know his or her assignment *and* all the other assignments. You don't want people to feel that they are operating in a vacuum, and you do want them to know who else is doing what so they can informally seek assistance and coordinate efforts.

If, as is sometimes necessary, several persons have responsibility for the same task, it's important to clarify the boundaries that exist within that task. Say that you have assigned Levine and Hardy to "writing the draft." Make sure that Levine knows he is responsible for Sections 1 through 4 and Hardy

Team sports, which corporations often sponsor, develop skills useful in all areas of business, especially in communication.

for 5 through 8. Or if one is to write and the other to edit and rewrite, make sure that they understand. The clearer the division of responsibility, the more effective will be the result—and the less the energy and goodwill lost along the way.

3. Monitor both group and individual progress to keep everyone focused on the outcome—and the deadlines. In group writing, a good control system is even more necessary than in an individual project. You can always check with yourself to see how it's going. It may be harder to check with others, who may be located elsewhere in the building, who may keep different hours from yours, or who may not feel obliged to inform you of problems as they occur. Controlling a group project requires a good balance between involvement and delegation. Don't be a nag, stopping by someone's office every few hours to ask, "How's it going?" But don't disappear and assume that all's going well unless someone tells you it's not.

You will be aided in retaining control of the project and keeping everyone focused by periodic group meetings at which brief and informal progress reports are given (see Chapter 21 for advice on conducting such a meeting). Meetings keep all members informed about the project and remind them that it is a continuing responsibility. Preparing for a meeting gives each member the opportunity to consolidate the work to date and to think about how and where it's headed. A meeting of this sort is a form of social control in that it maintains a consistent but gentle level of peer pressure. If necessary, interviews with individuals can be scheduled to follow up in detail on particular issues or to prod those who don't appear to be making good progress. The group meetings should not be used to discuss everyone's work in detail, but they serve the important function of keeping everyone's attention focused on the group's work and preventing individuals from drifting too far into their own activities as ends in themselves.

GROUP ORAL PRESENTATIONS

Preparing oral presentations offers different challenges from preparing written documents. When the oral presentation is to be done collaboratively, the challenges multiply. The three guidelines for writing in groups apply to preparing presentations, as do the general tips on group process.

What differs, of course, is the *medium* of communication. (See Chapter 22 for general advice on business presentations.) In a presentation, the message is conveyed orally (and almost certainly with visuals). The receivers are physically present or at least connected electronically through closed-circuit television. Feedback can be instantaneous. The look and sound of the sender(s) of the message carry great weight and may either reinforce or undermine the message itself. All these special characteristics of oral presentations require attention when the work is being done collaboratively.

Guidelines for Group Oral Presentations

Here are three guidelines for preparing group oral presentations:

1. Establish the format of the talk early in the preparation process and stick to it unless circumstances change.

2. Assign speaking parts with great care.
3. Aim for a single impression without submerging individual differences.

Let's look at each point in some detail:

1. **Establish the format of the talk early in the preparation process and stick to it unless circumstances change.** Questions of format include how much time is to be scheduled, how many speakers there will be, what the balance will be of speaking and visuals, and when and how questions and answers (that is, communication feedback) will occur. These matters must be addressed at the outset of the project, not left to the hours or minutes before the presentation is to be made. The work of the group in assessing the communication issues, identifying the audience's needs, and assembling the necessary information depends on the format. Once the format has been set, collectively, it should not be changed unless, of course, the overall circumstances of the presentation change. For example, if at the last minute you learn that members of the board of directors have been invited to join the audience, which you thought would consist of senior management, you may well modify the planned presentation.

Time may be assigned, or you may ask for it. Either way, the length of the presentation should be known and accepted at the outset by every member of the group. The number of speakers is another variable over which you may or may not have control (more on this below), but either way, it's vital to know this at the beginning so that no one is disappointed by finding out that she or he won't be speaking—or terrified at the last minute by finding out that she or he *will be*.

The balance of speaking and visuals will be determined by the group with reference to the subject itself, the audience, and the physical setting of the talk (for example, whether the room can be darkened to permit slides). If more than one person is to speak, it's especially important to have an understanding about how visuals and talk will be balanced and integrated. Sometimes the first speaker will not use any visuals, whereas subsequent speakers will rely nearly exclusively on them.

Finally, setting the format requires you to determine whether, when, and how audience questions will be addressed. Will your approach be to say, "Stop us at any point to ask questions," or "Please hold all questions to the end," or "Please see us after the talk if you have questions"? Each of these three approaches is legitimate, depending on the subject and the audience, but a decision about which rules will apply should come early in the group process—and should be maintained.

2. **Assign speaking parts with great care.** If you think of a business presentation as a dramatic production, you realize that speakers need to be assigned their parts not randomly but with great care. You don't assign parts of a group presentation alphabetically any more than you would cast the parts in *Othello* alphabetically.

The most important question is, obviously, how many persons will actually speak. Groups sometimes like to select one of their members to "speak for them." Or they sometimes prefer to have every member speak, even if only briefly, as a way of showing that everyone worked on the project.

Neither of these is a good decision in its own right. The decision needs to be made according to the subject, the audience, and the circumstances of the presentation. For example, if the project itself was long and involved many persons but resulted in a relatively simple final point to be made (buy the telephone system from Company A, stop producing compact cars, or open a new office in Denver), it may be appropriate to assign one person to do the talking so that the focus will remain clear.

On the other hand, a complex project may have drawn on the specialized knowledge of several experts, each of whom really needs to present his or her part because of the level of understanding needed to convey the information and arguments. It undermines the credibility of your presentation to have a presenter stumble through the arcane language of a discipline that he or she doesn't understand. It's even worse to have to refer questions to another member of the team because that person prepared the material that the speaker is only reading. In cases like this, the speaker becomes an actor reading a script that he or she doesn't understand—and the results can be unsatisfying and sometimes embarrassing.

Assigning speaking parts in a group presentation requires an assessment of each member's technical understanding *and* speaking ability. Avoid extremes: on the one hand, the technical expert reading tables of complex data; on the other, the smooth talker mouthing words that he or she clearly doesn't understand.

3. **Aim for a single impression, without submerging individual differences.** The members of the team are individuals and will and should appear individual in a group presentation. But the presentation should make a clear, unified impression. You don't want the people viewing the presentation to perceive a hodgepodge of information coming randomly from all directions, nor do you want them to think that so much control was imposed that the team members aren't really saying what they think.

Balancing the need for a single impression while allowing for individual differences is not easy. Keep that goal in mind as you assign responsibilities and speaking parts and prepare the presentation. It also helps to answer two of the biggest questions that businesspersons have about group presentations: How should we dress? How should we orchestrate the physical arrangements?

Dress should not be an overwhelming concern, but people making group presentations wonder if they should dress alike and sometimes give more emphasis to that issue than to more important ones. A simple rule is for everyone to dress in accordance with the audience and the purpose, not with a dress code imposed by the group. For example, a formal presentation to senior management obviously requires formal business attire, but it doesn't mean that everyone should coordinate the color of blouses and shirts. A presentation to persons from another culture requires an understanding of appropriate dress in that culture. Thus, it may be hot and humid in Cairo when you make your formal presentation, but Egyptians assume that all the members of your group will wear suits, not shorts. Or if the presentation is to be a "shirtsleeve" meeting at the boss's summer home, you don't want to be the only member of the presenting team to arrive in a suit.

Nothing mars a good group presentation more than poor control of the physical arrangement of the talk: presenters bumping into each other as they move back and forth from the podium, the passing of the microphone to different speakers along the table every three minutes, awkward pauses while everyone looks to see who is to speak next—or even worse, members of the group asking each other who wants to go next. Give some thought to how the presentation will be orchestrated. And give an overview of the answer to your audience at the beginning:

```
I will present the general issues here and then call on Jen
to describe the background of the problem and Larry to pres-
ent our proposed solution. After that, any of us will be
happy to answer your questions, but if something comes up
during any part of the talk, don't hesitate to interrupt. We
want to be sure to explain this complex issue clearly. We
will each limit ourselves to ten minutes.
```

Understanding and observing these three general guidelines should help your group presentation to achieve its goal—and should help all of you on the team to enjoy the job and do it well.

REVIEWING AND EDITING THE WORK OF OTHERS

Whether the outcome of a group process is an oral presentation or a written document, all the members participate by reviewing and editing each other's work. This is part of what makes a project truly collaborative. Even though sometimes a single "editor" is assigned, everyone gets involved in reviewing and editing.

Guidelines for Editing the Work of Others

General principles of revision (see Chapter 7) apply, but the special nature of group projects makes some additional advice helpful:

1. Control the impulse to rewrite.
2. Let the writer do his or her own rewriting.
3. Be specific in criticism.
4. Don't nitpick.
5. Remember to praise good work and to cite places where the writer handled the material particularly well.

1. **Control the impulse to rewrite.** Editing is repair work, not construction. If you add new paragraphs or sections, you may introduce errors or change the writer's point. You may also introduce a new style or tone that clashes with the original. Take the broad perspective. Try to see what the other person is doing and why—and be faithful to it.

2. **Let the writer do his or her own rewriting.** This approach will reinforce patterns of appropriate prose and make your job with subsequent drafts or projects easier. Suggest changes. Let the writer carry them out according to the original intention and style.

3. **Be specific in criticism.** Don't just turn the draft back with such generalizations as "I just don't like it" or "It's not what I had in mind." Write a summary of your comments for a long report. Use consistent notations. Make clear both what your criticism *is* and *is not*.

4. **Don't nitpick.** The writer has only so much energy for revision. Don't waste that energy by presenting too many minor criticisms. Focus on main points. Put yourself in the shoes of the person whose work you are reviewing: Would you want someone to say *that* to you?

5. **Remember to praise good work and to cite places where the writer handled the material particularly well.** Those places will provide the writer with models for shoring up less good ones. And being appreciated helps one forge ahead. Everyone needs praise, and groups need to be nurtured, encouraged, and led forward. Making review and editing positive experiences reinforces healthy group processes.

SUMMARY

- Both scholarly studies and the experience of practicing professionals show that nearly all businesspeople write **collaboratively** on the job. The reasons are that organizational work generally builds on group effort and that collaborating on writing and speaking tasks can make the final product both better and easier to achieve. By working in a group, you can tap more information and experience than by working individually, you can get a broader view of the whole organization and its needs, you can divide the work for greater efficiency, and you can simulate the overall communication process.
- Group projects raise political and ethical issues about **responsibility.** Generally, all members of the group share responsibility and credit. The greater one's level of authority in the group, the greater the responsibility.
- Sometimes collaborative projects are carried out by existing groups and sometimes by groups formed specifically to do the job at hand. In either case, members must pay regular and serious attention to the group *as* a group and must work hard to nurture and encourage the group itself by clarifying the group's goals and processes as well as all assignments and responsibilities, communicating openly, and monitoring and evaluating the work and the process frequently to gain feedback and to set course corrections as warranted.
- You can enhance group writing by making sure at the outset that all members understand the assignment, by assessing the skills and talents of all members and assigning tasks accordingly, and by monitoring group and individual progress at all times.
- Preparing and delivering group presentations require early establishment of the presentation's format, careful assignment of speaking parts, and achievement of the goal of a single impression without submerging natural differences among members.
- Reviewing and editing the work of others in a group can improve both the group process and the final product if you avoid rewriting others' work, allow them to be their own writers, are specific in criticism, stay away from nitpicking, and praise good work.

EXERCISES

For Discussion

1. You are assigned to head a team that will analyze the success of your company's promotional campaign to introduce a new brand of running shoe. You are to produce a formal report for the marketing vice president. You can select three people to join you on the team. Briefly describe the qualities, experience, and organizational position of the people you want, and explain why. Assign specific duties to each.
2. Anne Behnke was a new assistant buyer in the shoe department at a large Kansas City department store. She and her supervisor, the chief buyer, Mary Landers, went to Chicago to preview the new summer lines. When they returned, the merchandising manager to whom Landers reported asked for a detailed memo report on what the two had seen so the store could prepare a coordinated fashion promotion for the summer, linking clothes and accessories. Landers told Behnke to write a draft of the memo. When it was done, Landers liked the draft so much that she had it typed up under her own name and sent it to the merchandising manager. If you were Behnke, what would you do? Discuss the situation with respect to the ethics of group writing projects.
3. Harry Lloyd assigned three junior auditors under his supervision to prepare reports on the adequacy of the documentation used by the company's purchasing department. He asked them to work independently and submit their reports to him. He told them that he would "edit" their reports and produce a draft version of the final report, which he planned to submit to the head of the purchasing office. He told them that he would incorporate the "best" of each report in the draft and then ask them each to comment on the draft before he submitted it. Discuss this approach as a form of group writing. What are its strengths and weaknesses? If you were one of the junior auditors, how would you react to the assignment? If Lloyd asked for your suggestions, what would you tell him to do to improve the process?

For Writing

4. Think of a group of which you are or have been a member (for example, a youth group like Boy or Girl Scouts, a sports team, a public service club, a fraternity or sorority, a work group, or a neighborhood association). Write three or four paragraphs describing how the group was formed and how it operates (for example, leadership selection, establishment of goals, formality of procedures, and methods of change).
5. You have been asked by the dean of students at your college to form a group of commuter students called Road Runners to encourage greater participation in campus life by students who live off campus. Write a memo to the dean outlining how you propose to organize the group. How will you select the members? Why? How will they be officially invited to join? What leadership structure will be created? What rules of operation will be followed? How will the group's goals and activities be identified?
6. You have been assigned by your supervisor to lead a group of three people to examine the physical appearance of the fast-food restaurant where you work and to present an oral report to her and to the district manager.

Write a memo to the group outlining the procedures for the presentation itself. Consider such matters as who will speak and in what order, how the group will dress, and the amount of time that will be allotted to each speaker.

For Collaboration

7. You and two other students in your class are assigned to produce a report on student participation in the running of your college or university. It is due in three weeks. Set up a schedule of activities assigned to each of the three of you that will bring the project in on time. Show exactly *who* will do *what* and *when*. Be prepared to explain and justify the assignments and the schedule.

8. Do Exercise 4 or 5 above. Now form a group with three other people from your class to review and edit the document. Follow the guidelines given in this chapter for reviewing and editing the work of others. After you complete the assignment, discuss within the group which guidelines were easy to follow and which were hard. What *other* suggestions would you make for such a collaborative task?

PART III

MEMOS AND LETTERS

12 Memos
13 Elements of Letter Writing
14 Managing Routine Letters
15 The Routine and Beyond: Negative Situations
16 Customized Letters to Persuade

INTRODUCTION TO PART III

"Went out. Be back later."

—Full text of a refrigerator-mounted message from a teenager to his parents.

In Part III of *Business Communication,* you will learn strategies for composing the most common forms of writing in organizations: memos and letters.

Chapter 12 discusses memos, documents that circulate internally in an organization. They are so prevalent that some companies and government agencies suffer from "memo mania." Strategically written memos, however, perform an essential role in achieving the control and maintenance functions you read about in Chapter 2.

Letters carry messages externally: from organizations to other organizations, from organizations to customers and clients, and from individuals to other individuals and to organizations. You will write memos and letters to request something and to respond to requests, to inform the reader, and to sell the reader on an idea or an action. Chapter 13 discusses some basic elements to get you thinking about letters. Then, in Chapter 14, you'll learn to apply those elements in preparing letters to meet routine business situations. In Chapter 15, you'll learn to deal with bad news and to say no. In Chapter 16, you'll focus on the sales opportunities in letter-writing situations.

Other specialized forms of memos and letters are covered elsewhere in the book:

Chapters 18 and 19: Memo and letter reports and letters of transmittal
Chapter 23: Letters of application for a job
Chapter 24: Letters accepting and refusing job offers
Chapter 26: Letters to shareholders and investors

As you immerse yourself in the different situations for writing memos and letters that you'll read about in this part, be careful not to lose sight of what all memos and letters have in common. As you read in Chapters 2 and 4, each correspondence has a goal. It aims to get something done. When it works, whatever the situation that bred it, it works for the same reasons: It balances the needs of writer, information, and reader. It is accurate and useful. It meets the conventions of the format.

Moreover, as you read in Chapter 5, a letter should sound crisp, an engaging voice coming through the page. Even in routine memos and letters, but especially, as you will see, in more customized ones, pay particular attention to how you sound. Write as one person writing to another person. That probably sounds like pretty pat advice, like always brushing your teeth after meals. But it's simply a matter of getting into the habit. Don't pose. Don't settle for worn-out phrases. When the situation is more than simply routine, don't copy memos and letters from a book—this book or any other book. Instead, use these memos and letters to help you develop your own strategies. Don't sound like a book. Sound like *you.*

12 MEMOS

What's Ahead

DEFINING MEMOS
- FYI: The One-Page Memo

THE FUNCTIONS OF MEMOS
- Meeting Organizational Goals
- Meeting Personal Goals

GUIDELINES FOR WRITING MEMOS
- Identify the Context
- Review Your Communication Options
- Determine the Structure
- Distribute the Information
- Conform to Conventions
- Edit and Revise
- Evaluate Against All Goals

WHEN MEMOS GO AWAY

SUMMARY

EXERCISES

Do You Know 

- What do people in businesses, government agencies, and other organizations mean when they talk about—and write and read—memos?
- Why do organizations produce so many memos? What purposes do they serve?
- How can one write memos efficiently and effectively to meet goals?
- Will memos disappear as electronic means of communication grow in business offices?

"Cut a Memo, Not a Tree"

This slogan appeared on the desk of an employee of the federal Environmental Protection Agency. His protest seems particularly apt; saving paper both protects trees and reduces bureaucracy.

Memos, the most common form of internal written business communication, are easy targets for critics of bureaucracy precisely because they are produced in such vast quantities by businesses, colleges, and government agencies. Writing and circulating fewer of them is a worthy goal. But there is a good reason for the popularity of memos: They document the many maintenance and control activities (see Chapter 2) that all organizations require. Memos are sent to advise employees of new safety procedures, record changes in company policies and practices, invite staff to summer picnics, announce changes in benefits, summarize sales and inventory data, verify compliance with regulations, and otherwise keep organizational wheels turning and monitor activities to help meet goals.

Although the vast majority of memos serve maintenance and control functions, memos can also help define corporate missions and images and communicate these to employees. The adoption of a new logo and instructions for its use in documents, for example, are appropriate topics for a corporate memo.

Although memos typically *record* and *inform*, they can also *persuade*. For example, a memo might be written to request permission to reschedule a meeting or to undertake a project. You might want your supervisor to allow you to study building trends in Oak Park to determine if a new convenience store should be located there, or to increase your secretary's salary, or to take Friday off. A memo is an appropriate tool for each of these requests.

Memos *can* be bureaucratic. Organizations probably do produce too many of them. And every memo, like any other form of business writing, can be made better: sharper, clearer, more engaging and persuasive, more to the point. Trees can be saved if memos are produced and sent electronically, through e-mail and other versions of networked computer systems—a trend that is increasing.

But memos are necessary to advance organizational and personal goals.

In this chapter you will see what memos are, why they are needed, and how to write them efficiently and effectively.

DEFINING MEMOS

The word *memorandum,* of which *memo* is the shortened and most common form, derives from the Latin word for "remembering." It is the same root as for the word *memory.* We write memos so that something will be remembered. Here is a definition:

> A memo is an internal document that is generally short, focuses on a single topic, is clearly directed to achieving a purpose, and follows conventions or formulas in form and content.

Study the three sample memos (Figures 12–1, 12–2, and 12–3) to find their common characteristics. Do they fit our definition?

The first memo (Figure 12–1) is a fill-in-the-blank form. The memo informs Meyer Comisky, a supervisor in the manufacturing department, that

SUN-RAY, INC.

INTEROFFICE MEMO
PAYROLL FORM/23a
2 SEPTEMBER 199-

ATTN: Meyer Comisky
1st Shift Supervisor
Manufacturing-4

This notice confirms the hiring of John Dreys in your department, effective 15 September 199-. Please verify the following information and return an initialed copy of this memo to the Payroll Office immediately. Note any changes in black ink.

Wage rate (hourly)	$7.75
Account reference	4-23C
Employee social security number	083-38-5667
Personnel Office reference	09/92/455

Confirmed ____________________
Date ____________________

FIGURE 12–1.
A fill-in memo.

the hiring of John Dreys at a particular salary is confirmed as of a particular date. Further details are supplied (for internal accounting, personnel records, and so on). As a recipient of the memo, Comisky must return a signed copy to the payroll office so the new employee can be entered on the company's payroll and personnel-information system. The objective of this memo, then, is to *record* so that the recording itself will activate a system and cause good things (like payroll checks) to happen. This memo serves an important *maintenance* function; personnel matters must be properly handled if the organization and its people are to survive and prosper.

The second memo (Figure 12–2) is a bit more complicated. It's more than a fill-in form, but it is quite short and is meant to inform. The writer is informing employees in the Emergency Services group about a new procedure to follow in admitting patients to the Intensive Care Unit. Note that the writer uses abbreviations (ES, ICU) that the audience would readily understand. Although her purpose is mostly to *inform* (that is, to make sure all appropriate employees know that a new system is in place), it is partially also to *persuade* (that is, to solicit the compliance of the recipients with the new procedures). The memo serves an important *control* function, helping to make sure that the hospital's ongoing activities are proper.

CENTRAL FLORIDA COMMUNITY HOSPITAL

Interoffice Memo

TO: All Employees, Emergency Services
FROM: Marianne Majesky
Director, Patient Services
DATE: 17 September 199–
SUBJECT: New PRO Procedures

Effective December 1, 199–, new procedures will be implemented in the Patient Records Office to ensure that patient admissions from ES to ICU will be handled quickly.

After that date, ES personnel must complete new Form ES-27 for any patient transferred to ICU. A copy of this form should be sent to ICU and to Patient Records.

All ES employees are asked to cooperate with this new procedure. Address any questions to me at ext. 7881.

FIGURE 12–2.
A simple memo to inform.

SPRINGDALE VALUE CENTERS, INC.

TO: Marvin Mapes
Controller
FROM: Joan Leutens
Staff Accountant
DATE: 15 March 199-
SUBJECT: Suggested Software Purchase

The cost of providing auditing services to the divisional offices has always been a major concern of yours. When you mentioned at our last staff meeting (3-4-9x) that you wished we could automate some of the functions now performed by staff accountants, I looked into the cost and effectiveness of software that I thought would be available to maintain certain divisional records and perform basic audit functions on the data.

The result of my search is the recommendation that we purchase Act-II, a software package produced by CorpRec, Inc. The package will cost $2,125, and we will have to pay a semiannual maintenance fee of $75, which includes all updates.

Enclosed is a description of Act-II and its capabilities, along with a list of firms currently using it. Herb Burns and I visited one installation (at Letts Manufacturing), and we both think the system will be just what we need.

I'll be happy to discuss this with you at any time. I do think the proposed software will help us meet your goal of reducing the cost of auditing in the divisional offices.

Enclosure

cc: Herb Burns

FIGURE 12–3.
A memo to persuade.

The third memo (Figure 12–3) is more explicitly persuasive in intent. It is meant not to record information but to persuade the audience to do something. Joan Leutens, of course, supplies information (name of package, supplier, cost, and so on), but the information is marshaled toward persuading her supervisor to purchase a particular software package. Notice how carefully the memo is oriented toward its specific audience. The first two sentences refer to Mapes's interest in cost savings. The last paragraph is aimed directly at him again, reiterating the fit between this software and his long-standing interest in saving money. Unlike the memo in Figure 12–1, this is not a fill-in form. It is a tailored memo, clearly aimed at its recipient and clearly intended to persuade the recipient to make a specific response. The memo serves *control* functions because it is aimed at improving the firm's operations.

Despite their obvious differences, these three memos are well executed to achieve goals. If we look at what makes them effective, we can identify the key features of the memo form described in our definition:

• Each memo is an *internal* document, sent within an organization. Shorthand expressions can thus be used (abbreviations, for example); complex matters can be briefly and generally mentioned (the provision of auditing services to divisions, for example, which would surely have to be explained and expanded upon if the audience were outside the organization); and polite expressions and ingratiating phrases can be dropped in favor of directness ("This notice confirms" and "Address any question to me at ext. 7881"). These are not messages aimed at customers or others outside the organization. Their shape, style, and content fit their internal audience.

• Each of the memos is *short.* Although 5-page or even 20-page memos do exist, most people equate the memo with brevity. (See "*FYI:* The One-Page Memo.") When he was president of Ford, Robert McNamara had a rule that a good many other chief executive officers (for example, at Procter & Gamble) have adopted: No memo can be longer than one page. This is a good rule; but even when the one-page memo is not formal corporate policy, the memo is still among the briefest of business documents.

• The brevity of the memos presented here results from their focus on a *single topic.* Each deals with one topic (and related subtopics, of course).

• Each of the memos is clearly directed to achieving a *purpose.* An identifiable outcome is obvious: the confirmation of a hiring, a change in operating procedures, and the approval of a software purchase. The purpose can be to record, inform, or persuade.

• Each of the memos is highly *conventional.* A heading begins each memo, providing a structured way to indicate audience, writer, subject, and date. The first example is the most conventional, since it is really a fill-in form. The second follows the conventions but is structured by the writer without the benefit of blank spaces to be filled in. The third is customized in structure, use of evidence, and language. The degree of conventionality in the format and content of memos depends mostly on the organization in which the writer works. Many large companies, hospitals, universities, and government agencies have rigid standards. Even when the content of the memo is left to the writer's control, the heading, use of abbreviations, persons to receive copies, and so forth are firmly set. If the company you work for has rules about memos, you may find that writing is made easier as a result. After all, it's simpler to fill in a form than to establish your own pattern of organization and weigh evidence and language at each step. On the other hand, the open form does allow you to be creative and flexible and to respond more concretely and directly to your audience's needs and your own purpose.

THE ONE-PAGE MEMO

William Cheney
Environmental Engineering Consultant and former President of PACE International

The average person's concentration span can be measured in seconds, the attention span in a few minutes. Engineers, usually somewhat more cautious and objective than the average employee, tend to wax lawyerlike in their memos. This tone can lead to obfuscation if not boredom for the recipient.

As a manager and the eventual president of an engineering firm, I was dismayed by the time taken to write a simple memo on one subject, to say nothing of the time taken to make sense of many of the well-intentioned memos which were circulated daily. I sent the following memo to my staff:

> From this date, no interoffice memo shall exceed one page. If it is necessary to overrun that limit, a summary sheet must preface the memo.
>
> Any memos that violate this rule will be returned for revision. Please promulgate this policy to your staff.

The response was positive. Interestingly, the "ghost writers" for those managers who delegated their memo writing to others were soon apparent in staff meetings. The result of such revelations was the promotion of some whose light had been hidden under the bushel of their bosses' inability to communicate well.

My memo had a threefold effect. More precise wording was used, paragraphs were shortened, and repetitive statements were eliminated. These changes, in turn, made work easier for everyone and more rewarding for many. Through shortened memos, the cream came to the top.

THE FUNCTIONS OF MEMOS

People write memos to meet goals. Memos help meet both organizational and personal goals. Ideally, the goals of the organization and the goals of the individual employee should be met simultaneously, but in practice conflicts do occur. You can minimize these conflicts by understanding the difference between organizational and personal goals.

Meeting Organizational Goals

Regardless of their organizational function or communication purpose, memos should provide the right information in the right form at the right time to the right people. Determining what's "right" in each case depends on understanding the goal or goals to be met.

• The right *information* is the information required (whether the assignment is implicit or explicit) to get a job done, to reach the intended goal. Sales data or personnel policies or fund balances may be needed, and the writer of the memo has to provide what is needed in response to a particular assignment.

• The right *form* is the form that makes the information most readily useful to the person receiving the memo. A simple fill-in-the-blank memo may supply what is needed to activate a payroll entry, whereas a description of the workings of some auditing software may be needed to persuade someone to purchase it.

• The right *time* is the time at which the information can be used most effectively to make the decision. The January receivables report will help more in early February than in early March. The interview schedule for a job candidate should be on everyone's desk before the person arrives, not the next day.

• The right *people* are those who request or routinely need the information. Does it make any sense to send the monthly sales figures to the director of security? Should the vice president of manufacturing get copies of all memos reporting on the performance of the company's retirement-fund portfolio?

Using a Memo to Record the Minutes of a Meeting

One of the most common uses for the memo, the recording of minutes, provides a good illustration of these four *rights*. Because meetings (see Chapter 21) are so frequent and important in organizations, recording their substance as minutes is standard practice. The memo is the usual tool. Examine the following memo:

The results of the many meetings that fill a businessperson's day are usually recorded in *minutes* written in memo form.

INTEROFFICE MEMO

TO: Promotion Task Force
FROM: Jack Fidman
DATE: 18 August 199-
RE: Minutes of 17 August Meeting

All Task Force members were present (Serbin, Hartogh, Lane, Gimache, Spiller, Fidman).

Nancy Serbin reviewed our charge from Cory Anderson: to evaluate current promotion practices and make recommendations for changes. This evaluation is needed because Level III employees have complained that promotion to Level II is taking too long, and new hires with less direct experience are being placed at II, ahead of loyal employees who are trying to work their way up. Staff morale is affected. Everyone agreed on the problem and issues and understood and accepted our assignment.

It was felt that the Task Force needed more information on the following:

1. Profile of Level III employees (especially time in grade)
2. Profile of Level IIs hired within last two years
3. Same data for Level IIs and IIIs at all branch sites

Chris Hartogh also suggested that we do a survey of attitudes among Level IIIs here and at branches to see if the morale problem is real, but after discussion it was decided not to "rock the boat" at this point and perhaps raise expectations until more hard data are available for review. Nancy Serbin will get the information and circulate it before the next meeting.

Copies of current position ratings were distributed and briefly reviewed. Because the group needs the information on current IIs and IIIs before deciding if a real problem exists, the meeting was adjourned, and the next meeting was scheduled for Monday, 8 September, at 8:00 in Conference Room C.

<u>Distribution</u>

K. Gimache   N. Serbin
C. Hartogh   R. Spiller
W. Lane

cc: Corey Anderson, Director of Human Resources

This memo provides the right information: a brief, simple account of the discussion, its outcomes, and what comes next. The memo is in the right form: Each paragraph captures a key part of the meeting, and the conventions show clearly the pertinent information, including the distribution. The memo is written and circulated at the right time: the day after the meeting, when people can recall what happened and so make notes on anything that should be added or restated, and sufficiently in advance of the next meeting, for which the memo also serves as an announcement. And the right people get the memo: all those who participated and the person who initiated the group and needs to be kept informed of its progress.

Getting it all right in writing the minutes of a meeting means capturing all pertinent points in brief form and putting them together effectively for the right people in a timely way. Good minutes help an organization keep on track, pursuing its goals and monitoring progress.

Meeting Personal Goals

Writing good minutes—or any other form of memo—also serves personal goals. First, writing memos is an expected part of the job. You do it because you are supposed to. Second, you do the job in a way that reflects best on you. Writing a good memo can help you look good. This doesn't mean that memo writing is showing off, only that a job well done reflects favorably on the person doing it.

Unfortunately, almost everyone with business experience can recall examples of memos that don't seem to serve any purpose beyond glorifying the writer, calling attention to what he or she did or knows or can do. Here's an example:

MEMORANDUM
INTERFAX SERVICES

19 August, 199-

TO: Doris Ryan
Employee Benefits Supervisor
FROM: Marcia Henderson
Retirement Coordinator

The Bay Area Gerontological Society meeting last Thursday was the occasion for presenting this writer with the third annual Gordon Puff Award for contributions to better understanding of the needs of senior citizens. The award recognizes the work done to promote community awareness of the problems and challenges of retirement.

During the presentation many references were made to the preretirement program developed at Interfax and described in several articles in major trade publications. It was very good publicity for Interfax and reflected highly on our entire employee benefits program. Representatives of the local press were in attendance and will probably write a story that will provide further publicity for the company.

This kind of openly self-serving memo is not uncommon in organizations. Its sole purpose seems to be to make the writer look good. We easily recognize such memos for what they are. However, other kinds of self-promotion through memo writing are also common and a bit more subtle. Consider the following example:

INTEROFFICE
CORRESPONDENCE

TO: Production Office/ATTN: Records
FROM: Larry Connors
DATE: 3 March, 199-
SUBJECT: Production Report for February

I am happy to report record production figures for the Box Division for February. We completed 62,000 units, compared to 59,500 units in January and 58,700 in February of last year. That represents an increase of 4.2 percent over January and 5.6 percent over the prior-year period.

This dramatic increase was accomplished despite poor weather conditions early in the month that forced us to cancel the evening shift one day and curtail the day shift another day.

I am proud of the work done by my men. We will continue to work at our highest level to improve production even further in the future.

CC: J. R. Folsom, VP, Operations
K. Munoz, General Manager
F. W. Fairless, Plant Operations Coordinator
T. Shimada, Supervisor
W. Rindle, Foreman
T. Post, Foreman
J. P. Burleigh, Foreman

This memo serves a simple but important organizational purpose: to report monthly production figures of the box division. It accomplishes this aim, though the narrative (as opposed to tabular) presentation of the data may be less than efficient. The language of the memo reflects its underlying function, namely, to glorify its writer. Note that the first word of the memo's text is *I*, and that the recurrent use of the first-person pronoun draws the reader's attention more to the writer than to the subject.

Phrases within the document also highlight the accomplishments: "happy to report," "dramatic increase," "proud of the work done by my men," "work at our highest levels," "improve production even further." (One wonders if the writer owns "his" men.) The language is intended to focus attention not on the production numbers but on the writer.

One additional sign of this intention is the distribution list (the persons named to receive copies of the memo). Many large companies have a fixed distribution list for certain routine documents, and many managers require subordinates to "copy" them on any document sent out of the division or section. The seven-member copy or distribution list in this memo reflects the writer's effort to spread his fame far—from foremen to the vice president for operations. Persons knowledgeable about corporate politics say that you can gauge the political (as opposed to purely functional) nature of an internal document by the length of the distribution list.

When you send a memo "down" the organization—that is, to those who report to you—the distribution list is not likely to be a political concern. (See Chapter 2 for a thorough discussion of horizontal and vertical communication.) But when you write "across" (to your peers) and especially "up" the organization (to those to whom you report), lengthening the list often serves political purposes. In this instance, sending copies to one's organizational superior is an obvious effort at self-promotion. In general, when you wield a big copy list, people will guess that you're more interested in impressing your superiors and peers than in getting the work of the company done.

By considering the possible conflict between organizational and individual goals in memo writing, we don't want to imply that you will always or even frequently confront that problem yourself. But you should be aware that quite legitimate personal goals (to be seen as having done a good job, for example) can coexist with organizational goals. As always, the best way to bring credit on yourself is to do a good job. Collecting or discovering the right information and conveying it in the right form at the right time to the right people—in other words, writing a good memo—can be one mutually beneficial way to serve the company's and your own goals.

GUIDELINES FOR WRITING MEMOS

We can identify seven guidelines that help shape the writing of good memos—memos that simultaneously meet organizational and individual goals:

1. Identify the context.
2. Review your communication options.
3. Determine the structure.
4. Distribute the information.
5. Conform to conventions.
6. Edit and revise.
7. Evaluate against all goals.

Identify the Context

Why is this memo being written? Who will read it? What can or should the reader do after reading it? What do you as the writer want the reader to do? Answering these questions is a way of fixing the context for a memo (see Chapter 4). You need to review the audience, the subject, and the specific purpose of the memo. The audience is the person or persons to whom the memo is addressed, including (as secondary readers) those who receive copies. The subject is the topic of the memo. The specific purpose is the outcome the writer desires: to record? to inform? to persuade? If the purpose is persuasive, what is the specific action you want the reader to perform?

Memo conventions help define audience, subject, and purpose. The "To" line requires you to identify the audience. The "Re:" or "Subject" line forces you to state the subject succinctly, and sometimes even the purpose, as this example shows:

```
     To:  Kei Okada
Subject:  Recommendation to Change Starting Hours in Unit Y
```

Review Your Communication Options

Should you write the memo in the first place? Or should you just pick up the phone and call the woman in real estate and ask for the information directly? If you have been specifically assigned to write a memo, then of course you must: That's your job. But if you have a choice, consider whether an alternative form of communication (probably oral rather than written) would serve the same purpose more effectively and efficiently.

Putting a request or an answer in a written memo makes sense if

- The information is complex, lengthy, or subject to misunderstanding.
- More than one person should receive the information or the request.
- It's important to document for later use (even legal requirements) that the request was made or the information supplied.
- Company policies require written documentation.

Here's a simple rule that seems obvious but requires frequent attention: If there is no good reason to write the memo, don't. "Cut a Memo, Not a Tree."

Determine the Structure

Memos take shape from their writer's perceptions of subject, specific purpose, and audience. The skeleton, the overall structure, is determined by the material and by what the writer aims to do and thinks the audience needs and wants.

Like all communications, the memo ordinarily follows a three-part division: introduction, middle, ending (see Chapter 4). The length and content of each part depend on the audience, subject, and purpose. A memo should begin with one clear sentence that states the subject and, ideally, provides a summary overview. This is the *introduction,* and of course it may take more

Gathering and analyzing data are important steps in the production of an effective memo.

than a single sentence. The *middle*, or body, may take the form of a simple table or a sentence or two of explanation of data. But if the subject is complex, much more will be required. The *ending* may be brief, even abrupt, in a memo requesting information from a subordinate:

```
Please supply the information requested here by Friday of
next week.
```

A more complex memo may require a longer ending, as in this example:

<u>Conclusion</u>. The data briefly summarized here lead to several possible conclusions. It is obvious that more resources must be placed behind the marketing effort if we are to gain significant consumer response to the product. This means an increase in the advertising budget by as much as 50 percent. Likewise, it is obvious that quality control must be improved. Finally, I believe that a further study of the effectiveness of the current advertising campaign would help us assess our situation and plan for a strengthened marketing program.

Distribute the Information

The information that a memo conveys cannot be randomly or thoughtlessly distributed within the document. The writer must place it to achieve the intended outcome and to meet the expectations of the audience. Within the typical three-part division of a communication, the core of information belongs in the middle. One would not usually begin or end a memo with the key information, though it is possible to preview or summarize it at the beginning or end.

The following two sample memos were written to answer a specific request for information about the attractiveness of the stock of the Ice Chip Company. Notice how differently the basic information is distributed.

MEMO A

To: Clarence McGhee
From: Betty Silvers
Date: 17 August 199-
Subject: Investment Analysis of Ice Chip Company

This is in response to your request for a report on the attractiveness of Ice Chip Company as an investment prospect. The table below summarizes the basic information you desire:

Bid range	4 to 12
P/E	18
Dividends	$.09 quarterly
Current yield	8% (current price of $7.50)

Based on my review of various advisory-service reports and discussion with analysts who follow the stock, it seems that Ice Chip is a well-managed company developing and effectively marketing ice-cream sandwiches and related novelties with high margins and excellent prospects for growth in the Sunbelt markets it serves. Its financial position is sound, and it has been favorably recommended for long-term capital appreciation.

My recommendation is that we take a substantial position in Ice Chip Company. I will be happy to supply additional information or answer any questions you may have.

MEMO B

To: Clarence McGhee
From: Larry Downs
Date: 17 August 199-
Subject: Ice Chip Company

Ice Chip Company is currently paying dividends of $.09 per quarter and yields 8%, based on a selling price of $7.50 per share. The P/E is 18, a little high but probably justified by their growth prospects in southern and southwestern cities. The stock has traded in the $4 to $12 range over the past six months, which shows that it is a relatively volatile stock, a bit speculative. Management seems good. It looks like a nice investment prospect for us. Please call if you want to know more.

The memos supply the same information, but the organization of that information in Memo A makes it more accessible to the reader. Memo A follows a clear division into introduction, middle, and ending. Memo B throws the information at the reader at the outset, with no context, and with little effort to relate the parts and to separate data from interpretation.

As this comparison illustrates, a good memo

- Exhibits a clear structure that helps the reader through it.
- Distributes information within that structure in a way that highlights key points.
- Keeps recommendations clearly separated from the evidence on which they are based.

Conform to Conventions

Memos are especially conventional: Most businesses, colleges, hospitals, and government agencies have rules or at least guidelines about how memos should be prepared. These generally relate to format, but they may also prescribe style. Two conventions usually covered are the *heading* and the *distribution list.*

The **heading** includes the "To," "From," "Date," and "Subject" lines. There are many combinations for these. You simply need to know which combination is required by your employer and to follow the rules carefully.

The **distribution list** may be set by corporate policy. For example, some firms require that immediate supervisors be included on the distribution list for all memos, on the assumption that one's boss should always know what one is up to. Sometimes the convention is that all members of a department or unit get copies of all memos sent outside it. These requirements, of course, vary greatly from organization to organization—and from unit to unit within organizations. But there are usually clear enough guidelines to make it possible to know to whom copies must be sent. You can of course add to the list if there are substantive (nonpolitical) reasons to do so.

Conventions can also govern a host of lesser points of style. Here are some typical examples:

Dates. Military organizations and those who work with them generally write dates this way: 17 September 1973. This form is also typical in Europe and is becoming accepted as proper style in U.S. organizations as well.

Names. Some organizations use the first or first two initials to designate all employees in memos: W. W. Baxter or K. Ryan, rather than William Wainwright Baxter or Kathleen Ryan.

Position or title. In some organizations, conventions dictate that the position or title for each person be specified after his or her name: George Blake, Head of Records; Maryanne Clark, Facilities Supervisor.

Abbreviations. The government is not alone in making much of abbreviations. Many companies encourage the wide use of abbreviations, especially in memos. If they are common in your organization, by all means use such abbreviations, as they make communication simpler and more direct.

Appearance. Memos simply look different from other documents in most organizations because of conventions that dictate spacing (single or double), placement on the page (large or small margins, and so on), and even typeface (boldface for the "To," "From," "Date," and "Subject"/"Re:" lines, for example, or fill-in forms with these items already printed).

Edit and Revise

Before you hand the final draft of your memo to the typist or enter it into your word processor, you should subject it to close scrutiny and edit and revise carefully. Revising should follow the guidelines applicable to all documents (see Chapter 7). In addition, you might ask yourself these questions that relate to the memo form itself:

1. **Can I tighten the prose?** Because it's an internal document, a memo can use abbreviations, shorthand expressions, and inside phrases known to those who will receive it. It can be abrupt and to the point, less ingratiating than a letter to a customer or other person outside the organization. In editing, look for ways to cut formality and exploit the opportunity for succinctness provided by the internal nature of the memo. Prune, cut, and shrink the prose. Chop out long and cumbersome expressions ("it is believed to be desirable to," "based on a thorough review of all available evidence, this writer recommends," "owing to the unusually long and difficult process of collecting, analyzing, and verifying the data," and so forth). Make one word do the work of two or three. Shorten sentences and express ideas directly.

2. **Is the message clear?** The exclusive focus of a memo on a single topic means that in revising you should look for stray comments, points that diverge or suggest side tracks. Focus on a clear single message. Most writers end up knowing more about their subjects than they can or need to communicate, especially in memo form, where brevity and directness are at a premium. Use the revision process to identify sentences or even paragraphs that don't clearly support the *central* point of the memo, no matter how interesting the information may be in its own right.

3. **Will my reader understand?** As you revise, measure all aspects of the memo against your perception of the audience's needs: Is this word known to my reader? Will he or she understand that concept without definition? Is this much detail really necessary, or can I condense to a few generalizations?

4. **Have I followed company format?** Because a memo is conventional, during revision you need to give special attention to whether it uses conventions effectively. Is the subject line specific and helpful? Does the distribution list include everyone who must receive a copy—and no one else? Company style and format guidelines exist to make communication easier. In memos they are particularly helpful and should be used as standards to guide revision.

Evaluate Against All Goals

The only reason for writing a memo is to reach some goal. Thus it is reasonable that the last step in the process is to compare the document you've written with the goals you set for yourself to see whether you have achieved them. Of course, the memo's final goal is to accomplish something within the organization, but you can't really evaluate your final draft that way because you won't know what response it will elicit.

However, when you wrote the memo you should have clearly stated to yourself both the organizational and the personal goals you designed it to achieve. These are useful and final standards for checking the draft before it is produced and sent out into the system. Let's say you determine that the organizational goal of your memo is to request your supervisor's approval of the purchase of a new printer for your office. You can ask, in reviewing the final draft, whether the specific purpose is absolutely clear, whether the supporting evidence is strong, whether the advantages to the company are made evident, whether the benefits are shown to exceed the cost, and so forth. Asking these questions is a way of checking to see if the organizational goal (or goals) of the memo are likely to be met. Such questions help you to focus on the purpose, and that focus gives you a different angle of approach from simply looking for comma faults or misspellings or long-winded phrases.

You should also ask if the memo appears to meet the personal goal you set for yourself. Does it present you in a good light—without reaching too far or overstating? Does it show you as an accomplished, capable employee? Does it reflect full credit on you without detracting from anyone else?

WHEN MEMOS GO AWAY

Some students of business practice predict that memos, like dinosaurs, will go away. Where? Into electronic impulses. In the "paperless office," where information is transferred electronically, memos will disappear.

This prediction is silly. Memos won't disappear just because the medium for sending them changes. Electronic means of communication in the office do offer many advantages for speeding and making more effective the production and circulation of all sorts of business communications, as you saw in Chapter 10. Electronic mail is particularly useful for memos. Because they are internal documents, memos can be forwarded throughout the organization to anyone on the network. Each recipient gets her or his copy immediately. Responses, corrections, or comments can be made quickly. The received memo can be stored or dumped. Memos that convey changes in corporate practices, for example, can be moved into appropriate files that come to constitute an electronic policies and procedures manual, always kept up to date by the inclusion of the latest changes. Memos that announce events (company picnics or early closings) or personnel changes (a new receptionist or a promotion in Section 83) can be read and dumped. Decisions on the storage of memos sent through e-mail are not different from those that must be made on paper documents—just easier to carry out.

Electronic means of interoffice communication used to write, distribute, respond to, and store memos will increase in frequency and capacity. As that happens, writers cannot lose sight of the need to produce clear and simple documents that get the company's and their own jobs done. But it may save some trees.

SUMMARY

- The **memo** is the most common form of written business communication. It is an internal document that is generally short, focuses on a single topic, is clearly directed to achieving a purpose, and follows conventions or formulas in form and content.
- Memos serve both the organization's and the writer's purposes. For the organization, memos **record** information, **inform** others about information, and **persuade** others to do something. They can serve all three of the organizational functions of **definition, control,** and **maintenance,** but the vast majority of memos are aimed at maintenance and control. For the individual writer, memos offer the chance to perform successfully, to show what she or he can do. Occasionally conflicts arise between organizational and personal goals, but these can be minimized if you are sensitive to their possibility.
- To write a good memo, you should know the **context** for it; consider all communication options, including not writing at all; determine the structure; distribute available information into that structure; conform to company **conventions;** edit and revise carefully; and check the final memo against the original **organizational** and **personal goals.**
- Although electronic communications, especially electronic mail systems within offices, can speed the writing and circulation of memos, the memo as a form will continue because it meets urgent and important organizational goals.

EXERCISES

For Discussion

1. Ask several friends or relatives to define *memo* based on their work experiences. How do their definitions compare with the one given here? Is there a commonly accepted understanding of memos and their functions?
2. Secure a memo from a relatively large organization (your college may be a good choice), and analyze its use of conventions: headings, distribution list, physical appearance, and so on. Note any ways that you think the conventions contribute to or detract from the overall presentation and the effort to achieve a goal. (You'll have to start by deciding what you think the goal is, that is, what the memo is trying to accomplish.)
3. Which of the following topics seem to be appropriate for memos? Explain why the others are not.
    a. A request to your supervisor to purchase new chairs for the reception area of your office
    b. Your proposed vacation plan, for approval by your boss
    c. Your company's affirmative action policy and procedures, for review by the top managers
    d. A change in the reimbursement policy for employees using their own cars on business trips
    e. A proposed restructuring of the firm to be considered by the board of directors

f. Price updates for the toy section of a department store
g. Company policy on unsolicited gifts from vendors

For those topics that are appropriate for memos, identify which of the three communication functions would be served: definition, control, or maintenance.

For Writing

Here are some typical business situations that call for memos. Write a brief memo on each, using appropriate headings and distribution lists. In each case, note whether the organizational purpose is definition, control, or maintenance.

4. A new secretary, Anne Weiss, has been hired in your department starting on 12 January at a salary of $18,500 a year. Notify Lorie Griscom, director of payroll services.
5. You slipped on the ice on the parking lot as you were entering the building. You need to report this accident to the director of buildings and services, to your supervisor, and to the director of personnel (because of possible insurance claims).
6. You were asked by your supervisor in the marketing department to examine the sales figures for the southwestern region for the past quarter and to compare them to the year-earlier period. In the past quarter, sales were $54,898, compared to $53,900 for the year earlier.
7. The three word processors in your office are not under service contracts. Time and parts charges for service for the past year amounted to $824. Service contracts for the three machines would cost $250 a year for each machine. Write to Harold Jansky, your supervisor, recommending that the department purchase service contracts for next year for the three word processors.
8. You traveled to Omaha on company business and have to submit a trip report detailing your expenses: airfare, $345.00; taxi and parking, $12.50; hotel, $165.00; meals and entertainment, $87.50. Your supervisor, Mary Landers, must approve the reimbursement, and Harold Wallace, the assistant controller, has to have the report to write you a reimbursement check.
9. Here is an example of an ineffective memo:

```
TO:    All Employees
FROM:  Harrison Locke, President
DATE:  28 August 199-


   Beginning next Tuesday, all employees who use Parking
Lot B will need to place stickers on the rear window of
their cars. These are available from Security. Please
comply with this directive.

   Parking Lot B will be closed for two weeks for repair.
Employees who cannot find space in Parking Lot A should
discuss this problem with Security.
```

```
    The company picnic, originally scheduled for next Sat-
urday, is postponed until after Labor Day. Details will
be available next week from the Personnel Office.

    I hope you all have a safe and happy Labor Day holi-
day.
```

Refer to the guidelines for writing memos when you consider such questions as conventions (Where is the "Subject" line?), audience (Does everyone receiving the memo have the same interest in all of its topics?), focus on a single topic, distribution of information, and tone. *Rewrite* the memo (you may want to write several rather than one) to convey the same information more effectively.

For Collaboration

10. Write a brief memo in response to this communication situation: Your department has just been moved to a different floor of the building, but the door locks were not changed and the people in the group that used to occupy your new offices still have keys. You are concerned about security and want the former occupants to turn in their keys. Write to them requesting the keys without offending them.

    After you've written the memo, compare it to several written by others in your class and note any differences in tone, structure, and use of conventions. Discuss the differences and identify successful strategies in trying to meet the goal of the communication.

11. The director of food service at your college is eager to understand how students regard the quality of the services she offers to the campus. She is particularly interested in (a) quality of food; (b) practicality of hours; (c) appearance of the dining room; and (d) friendliness of the help. Form a team of four persons from your class to undertake this investigation, and then prepare a memo to the food service director responding to her request.

13 ELEMENTS OF LETTER WRITING

What's Ahead

LETTERS AND PHONE CALLS
CONNECTING ETHICALLY WITH THE READER
- Be Honest
- Value the Reader's Time
- Use the Reader's Code
- Consider the Reader's Self-Interest

PLANNING LETTERS
- Timing
- Organizing: Routine and Customized Letters
- Dictating
- Writing Within the Law

THE LETTERLY VOICE
CONVENTIONS
- Standard Elements
- Format

WRITING LETTERS INTERNATIONALLY
SUMMARY
- FYI: Communicating with a Japanese Partner

EXERCISES

Do You Know 

- When should you write a letter rather than telephone?
- What ethical concerns should you keep in mind in connecting with a reader through a letter?
- What makes a situation for letter-writing routine? Customized?
- What are some legal issues in letter-writing?
- What is the "letterly voice"?

Figure 13–1 on page 242 is a letter on the letterhead of the CCA. The two-column format is not common in most letters but serves well the bilingual audience this letter addresses. In this chapter, you'll learn about the basic elements of letter writing in a range of organizational settings and styles. Unlike the memos you read about in Chapter 12, which are forms for writing within an organization, you'll write letters most frequently to the *outside:* as a corporate representative to a client or customer, as an individual to an organization, or as one organizational spokesperson to another.

LETTERS AND PHONE CALLS

As you saw in Chapter 10, electronic technology is rapidly changing the way people in business communicate. The traditional letter sent through the mail is becoming rarer. Especially in the United States, you'll often handle routine inquiries and information transfer over the phone. You may also leave a message on a voice-mail system to await the intended recipient, who can then respond by leaving a message in your voice-mailbox. Facsimile machines allow you to send a written message with the speed of a phone call. Although such messages now often take the form of letters, the mode of transmission is changing the form, as you'll see. Currently, e-mail systems are often limited to internal communication within organizations, but systems are expanding to serve external communication to vendors, clients, and customers.

You may also prefer a phone call to writing. You can handle sensitive or controversial information without worrying about a paper trail. Calling often takes less time than writing (unless the person you are calling is talkative).

You'll probably still need to *write* rather than telephone, when

- The information is complex, lengthy, or subject to misunderstanding.
- The information is being sent across one or several time zones. Writing consolidates information, negotiates differences in business hours, and saves on the long-distance charges for a phone call.

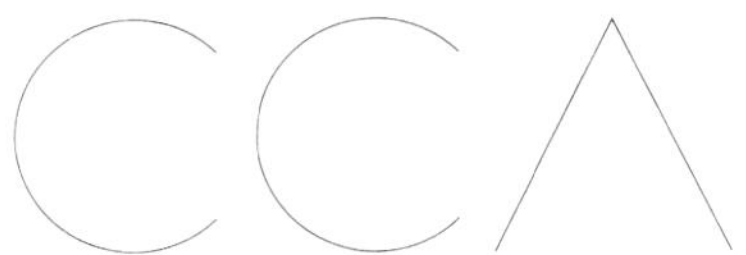

Centre Canadien d'Architecture/Canadian Centre for Architecture

Le Centre Canadien
d'Architecture et
le Réseau de développement
Aga Khan
ont le plaisir
de vous inviter à
une présentation spéciale du

**Prix Aga Khan
d'architecture 1989**

le jeudi 30 novembre 1989
de 18 heures à 20 heures
au Centre Canadien
d'Architecture.

La cérémonie officielle de
remise de ce prix a eu lieu
à la mi-octobre au Caire.
C'est à Montréal que les
onze projets gagnants du
prix Aga Khan seront
présentés pour la première
fois en Amérique du Nord.
Ils le seront à nouveau en
décembre au Museum of Modern
Art de New York.

Deux membres du jury du
concours,
le professeur Oleg Grabar,
titulaire de la chaire Aga Khan
au département des beaux-arts
de l'Université Harvard, et
le professeur William L. Porter,
titulaire de la chaire Aga Khan
au département d'architecture et
d'aménagement du Massachusetts
Institute of Technology,
présenteront les projets.

Une réception suivra la
présentation.

R.S.V.P.
939-7000
Sophie Hébert

The Canadian Centre for
Architecture and
the Aga Khan Development
Network
have the pleasure of
inviting you to
a special presentation of the

**1989 Aga Khan Awards for
Architecture**

on Thursday, 30 November 1989
from 18:00 to 20:00
at the Canadian Centre for
Architecture.

The official prize-giving
ceremony was held in Cairo in
mid-October. The Montreal
session is the first North
American presentation of the
eleven winning projects. A
second takes place at the
Museum of Modern Art in New
York in December.

The presentation will be
undertaken by two members of
the Award's Master Jury:
Professor Oleg Grabar,
Aga Khan Professor,
Department of Fine Art at
Harvard University, and
Professor William L. Porter,
Aga Khan Professor,
Department of Architecture
and Planning at the
Massachusetts Institute of
Technology.

A reception will follow the
presentation.

R.S.V.P.
939-7000
Sophie Hébert

1920, rue Baile, Montréal, Québec, Canada H3H 2S6
Téléphone 514 939-7000 Télécopieur 514 939-7020

FIGURE 13–1.
A letter of invitation in two languages. *(Courtesy of the Centre Canadien d'Architecture.)*

- The information is being sent across a language barrier. A written text eases translation.
- The message needs to be recorded against potential legal action.
- The letter requires a signature or other mark of authorization.
- The letter is a personal statement intended to make the reader feel good. A letter can be treasured; phone calls disappear.

In addition, of course, you may simply prefer writing. You have time to work out an argument, to establish a case, and to revise a bit before you make yourself vulnerable to a reader. You have more control over the conversation.

CONNECTING ETHICALLY WITH THE READER

''I am a junior at Midwestern University.''

Faced with writing a letter requesting information or applying for a job, students often begin with a flat announcement of themselves, as in this quotation. But think about that. Why should a reader be interested in your status in school? Does that statement *connect* writer and reader? Does such a sentence *encourage* a reader to read? When you write a letter, and especially when you *revise* a letter, open on a point that is *shared* with the reader. Refer to or establish common ground. Then gradually move to new information within that shared framework.

Traditional books on letter writing stress the importance of shaping a letter from the reader's point of view, a perspective that's called the *you attitude.* Such advice is a good beginning as you plan a letter. But it may lead to the artificiality and excesses of sweet talk you read about in Chapter 5. Instead, think about what you and the reader need to accomplish together *through* the letter—something you might call a *we attitude.* In thinking of that common purpose, remember the simple measure of ethical behavior you learned in Chaper 1: In all your dealings, leave other people at least as well off as you found them. To behave ethically when you write a letter:

- Be honest.
- Value the reader's time.
- Use the reader's code.
- Consider the reader's self-interest.

Be Honest

As with any form of communication, you should not use letters to deceive. Assess the limits of your information carefully. Do not promise what you can't deliver. Letters of application for a job and (other) sales letters provide multiple opportunities for deception. Don't deceive.

Value the Reader's Time

Letters look for answers: information to be sent in another letter or some action or decision. Make it easy for the reader to respond. Increasingly, letters seeking information leave blanks or list questions so that the reader can fill in the blank or respond to the question on the original letter. If the reader faxes the letter to the sender, the original still remains with the reader, because the facsimile machine copies the letter electronically as its method of transmission. The high cost of letter writing and the decreasing availability of secretaries make responses on original letters increasingly common. In 1990, the average cost of a business letter was $11.71 plus postage.

In addition to making your letter easy to respond to, make your letter *short.* Most letters should not exceed one page. If you have more to say, consider writing a brief cover letter that presents the main points on one page, and then attach a sheet with the details.

Use the Reader's Code

One feature of memos, as you read in Chapter 12, is the use of organizational code words and acronyms to keep messages brief. Inside correspondence uses insider's language. When you write *outside,* write in the reader's terms. Name items as the reader would. For example, a writer at a textile company addressing a letter to Running Gear, Inc. began:

```
As you are aware, the Running Gear, Inc. account is $250,000
in arrears.
```

That's the textile company's name for the account. But Running Gear, Inc., of course, labels the account with the name of the textile company. Thus the letter should have begun:

```
As you know, your account with us is $250,000 in arrears.
```

Pay attention to forms of address. Americans are generally casual. It's conventional, however, even in the United States, to address someone formally in the first letter. If the letter in response is signed with a first name, use that name in future correspondence. Sign your next letter with your first name, too, unless you want to send a specific signal that the reader's informality is inappropriate.

Watch the *connotations* of your language as well as its direct meaning. The *writers* of the following statements saw them as merely informative:

1. Please send us your correct social security number.
2. If the shirts are not properly washed, then their useful life is reduced.

But the *reader* in each case took offense:

1. Do you think that I would send you the *wrong* social security number?
2. Are you accusing me of *not* washing the shirt properly?

Scout out any veiled attacks in the drafts of your letters and revise to eliminate them.

Consider the Reader's Self-Interest

What will the reader derive from the message you present? Sometimes, that self-interest is clear. When you write to order a product or service, the reader, who is in business to provide that product or service, completes a sale. When you write a letter of recommendation for a job candidate, the reader gains valuable insights that aid in selecting the right candidate—and the candidate's status is enhanced.

Sometimes, however, the reader's self-interest is less clear. How does a reader gain when you ask for information from him or her? You have to think in broader terms. The reader's *role* in the organization may include answering such requests. You and the reader may share a friendship with some third person who makes the bridge. Or you may phrase your request in a way that enhances the reader's self-esteem, and that compliment provides motivation.

When the situation calls for negative information, you often have the opposite problem: writing in a way that does not *diminish* the reader's self-esteem, that is, writing to save face for the reader. You have to tread a fine line between tact and honesty. Some evasion may be needed to smooth the relationship. You may use the passive voice, for example, to avoid placing blame:

`The washer had been overloaded, a condition that strained the motor.` (Rather than, `"You overloaded the washer."`)

Be sensitive. But don't go overboard. For particularly significant letters, share your draft with someone who can ferret out stuffiness or excessive evasion.

PLANNING LETTERS

Before you write a letter, consider these questions:

1. When should I write?
2. Can I use a routine formula, or do I need a customized letter?
3. What technology can I use to aid my writing?
4. What is my authority for writing?

Timing

Most correspondents seek immediate replies to their letters, and your credibility is enhanced by promptness. But if you have lots of correspondence, assess each item to see what to do first and what can wait. Observe the fixed deadlines of financial filings. Be sensitive to key players who can't be kept waiting.

Organizing: Routine and Customized Letters

You can't give each letter the same attention. Sort the situations for writing into those that are routine and those that deserve a customized response.

Ordering and responding to orders, requesting and responding to requests—these situations make up the bulk of day-to-day business communication. Many such situations are uncomplicated and repetitive. In such *routine* situations, first exploit options for *not* writing. Use a phone call to an 800 number, voice mail, and other electronic technology, as you read in Chapter 10, to place and receive orders or to complete other simple procedures. Major vendors and major customers are often connected in a computer system that automates the sales and billing.

When you need to *write* a letter, check to see if a form letter is available to meet the need. One insurance company, for example, estimates that 70 percent of its correspondence is routine. If you worked in their customer relations department, you would write letters to explain new policies and procedures, to respond to common customer inquiries concerning account status and benefit eligibility, or to acknowledge new policies. To do so, you would simply call up the appropriate letter form on the screen; choose, insert, and arrange paragraphs from the system's memory; insert the specific customer information; and send the text to a personal printer or to the wordprocessing center for final printing. Although the customer may see the situation as unique, for you and the company, it fits a common pattern, and thus calls for a routine response.

Companies use forms and standard text to reinforce a corporate image, to speed up the writing process, to control the quality of letters, and to minimize discrepancies in the corporate story when several writers are responsible for creating letters. Ironically, too, wordprocessing has allowed writers to make the letters *look* more personal with the easy inclusion of personal identifiers about the reader throughout the letter.

Unlike routine letters, one-of-a-kind situations demand *customized* (or "customer-ized") letters. Identifying such situations can be tricky, because some occasions that demand special treatment *look* routine. You will learn more about routine letters in Chapter 14. You'll read about customized letters in Chapters 15 and 16.

Dictating

A good wordprocessing program is probably your best tool for creating letters efficiently. Another tool is a dictaphone or other form of dictation machine to create letters that will later be transcribed and sent. Dictating is simple if you keep in mind the general strategies for preparing *any* document you read about in Chapter 4. You may dictate directly to a secretary; more frequently, you will use either a personal dictation machine or a company's central dictation system, usually accessed through your telephone—perhaps even a cellular phone in a car. If you are not familiar with the machinery, practice with it.

Guidelines for Dictating

Follow these steps for effective dictation:

1. Clarify the logistics.
2. Dictate.
3. Proofread.

1. **Clarify the logistics:**

- Note your name, department, billing code, and the like.
- Specify the layout and the type of stationery to be used.
- Clarify whether this is a draft or a final copy. If it's a final copy, note the number of copies to be made and the name(s) of the recipient(s).
- Provide instructions for dealing with any enclosures.
- Establish the priority and deadlines for each letter.

2. **Dictate:**

- Spell out the name of the addressee, along with any other unusual or ambiguous words or punctuation.
- Indicate paragraph breaks (by saying, "New paragraph") and special typography, capitalization, and the like.
- Speak in a normal tone. Don't shout; don't mumble or speed.
- Take advantage of a stop or pause button if one is available when you need time to think. Take the time.

3. **Proofread:**

When the copy is returned to you, **proofread.** When you sign a letter, you take personal responsibility for the contents, spelling, and the like. Mistakes reflect *you,* not the typist.

Writing Within the Law

Letters often serve as contracts binding an organization to some course of action or establishing the terms of a transaction between writer and reader. Employment contracts are usually in letter form. Sales contracts and commitments for delivery of products also appear as letters, sometimes called *letters of intent.* Letters concerning credit and the collection of debts also commit writer and reader to certain actions and to sanctions when the actions do not occur, as you saw in the opening letter of Chapter 7.

When you write a letter, then, first confirm the range of your authority. Should you check the letter with someone else? Should you write the letter but have someone else—who has more authority or who knows the reader—sign it? Much business correspondence is not actually written by the person whose signature appears at the end.

Second, include the appropriate language. Your organization's lawyers may place constraints on what you can say. Certain standard agreements require standard language; you can deviate from that only with further legal advice. When you write to complain about a product or service, make sure your complaint is clear. You may receive an immediate adjustment and close the correspondence. But if not, a record of your letters and the company's responses can become central to court action against the company.

If you write a letter evaluating someone, that letter becomes part of a case for hiring or promoting—or perhaps firing or not promoting—that person. You must be careful to avoid *libel,* that is, malicious and false statements that might injure another's reputation or character. Chapter 16 provides advice on writing letters of recommendation.

THE LETTERLY VOICE

Undue emphasis on the legal implications of letter writing is one source of a problem in the way many letters sound. Letters display a variant of the corporate voice (see Chapter 5) that we can label the *letterly voice.* It's hard to say *why* letter writers revert to stuffy and obsolete language when they write, but the fear of committing themselves on paper may be one reason. Speaking on behalf of an organization may be another. And some writers assume that readers will take them seriously only if the letter sounds ponderous. Figure 13–2 is an example of such a letter (a real letter with identities masked). If you have problems deciphering it, don't feel you are alone; the intended recipient had trouble, too. Figure 13–3 shows some letterly phrases and their direct equivalents.

The voice in most routine and direct letters should be pleasant but somewhat impersonal: The information is key. In persuasive letters, however, voice carries more weight; sometimes the voice is even more significant than the information as you'll see in the following chapters.

FIGURE 13–2.
The letterly voice creates confusion.

Pursuant to the Reference (a) telecon, the Contractor hereby requests that the addressee contact his cognizant designated group leader in writing to establish proper procedures for the shipment of deliverable items under the subject contract.

I am advised by my group leader that a letter of delegation from your unit's transportation officer stating the appropriate prime contract number, transportation funding/appropriation citation and billing office, together with copies of the relevant contract pages containing this information, is required. This letter should be addressed to Mr. John Paul Jones, Purchasing Services, c/o this Contractor at mail stop B-80, and copied to Mr. Mike Smith, Transportation Office, c/o HELLO, San Francisco.

My understanding is that once this has been done this Contractor's shipping department, under a "procedure A" authorization, can then obtain the required funding/billing data from HELLO, San Francisco, to issue its own order.

Any questions regarding this matter may be addressed to the undersigned at (415) 111-2222 or (415) 111-3333.

LETTERLY	DIRECT
Please be advised by this correspondence that . . .	I'm writing to . . .
We wish to advise you that . . .	[Omit. Just begin.]
The undersigned	I
Thanking you in advance for your kindness and attention to this matter I remain,	Thank you
Your recent communication relative to . . .	Your letter about . . .
I am in receipt of your letter of recent date	I received your letter
As per your correspondence of X date	Your letter of X
In regard to the matter above referenced	Concerning X
Attached hereto please find	Attached is
Enclosed herewith please find	Enclosed is
Pursuant to your request As per your request	In response to your request
Forward your payment to	Send your payment to
extend an invitation	invite
being of service	serving

FIGURE 13–3.
The letterly voice and the direct voice.

CONVENTIONS

In writing letters, you'll reinforce your professionalism and match reader expectations by adhering to the conventions of presentation you'll see in this section. These conventions work most of the time in an American setting, although advertising and marketing correspondence may play with them to gain attention.

More significantly, electronic technology is changing the concept of a letter. For example, many companies place a cover sheet before letters to be sent by facsimile machine to a reader; the traditional letter then becomes the second page of the transmission. Those two sheets will certainly merge into a new form whose elements accommodate faxing just as the current elements now accommodate mailing. Electronic mail systems are also becoming more common. Coding information that designates the originator, the receiver, the electronic pathway, and the time of transmission (date *and* time of day) is formatted automatically. The traditional letter, then, is becoming less common. You should be aware of the standard elements and standard formats, but be ready to change as the occasion demands.

Standard Elements

Here's a brief review of the elements you are likely to see—and thus likely to write—in a traditional letter.

Sender's Address

The letterhead provides the sender's address and thus tells the reader where to reply. A mark of some status in a company is to have a letterhead that also includes your name and title. Printed letterhead has traditionally been reserved for organizations, but desktop publishing programs are encouraging a profusion of letterhead. Now, divisions and departments often create their own stationery, as do individuals, in an attention-getting typescript and with graphic enhancement (see Figure 13–4 on page 253).

Date

Always date letters. The date establishes the correspondence as a matter of record and provides a reference point for future correspondence.

Inside Address

It may seem silly to tell the reader his or her name and address. But again, because letters are a matter of record, you include the name of the recipient, title, and address (with zip code), as well as mail stop numbers for large corporations. Avoid abbreviations, unless the company's formal name is an abbreviation. Proofread the inside address particularly carefully: No organization likes to have its name misspelled.

Attention Line

An attention line flags the letter for a particular reader. Generally, you use such a line when you designate the reader by role rather than by name:

```
Attention: Personnel Director
```

If you know the name (and you should), then use a salutation. The only exception is a letter aimed primarily at the *organization;* the attention line emphasizes that the individual is subordinate to the larger unit, as in the military or other bureaucracies.

Subject Line

Subject lines are not as common in letters as in memos, but they serve the same purpose: to announce the subject of the letter or to refer to the number of an account or a date of prior correspondence. Such a designation is particularly useful in letter reports and in project-related correspondence.

Salutation

The salutation is the greeting that begins the letter. Commonly, the salutation begins with *Dear* (although that's a bit obsolete). A formal salutation includes a person's title and name, followed by a colon:

```
Dear Professor Smith:
```

An informal salutation uses the person's first name, followed by a comma:

```
Dear Jim,
```

Never use a semicolon at the end of a salutation. If you are unsure of the gender of the reader—if, for example, you are replying to a letter signed "D. H. Carlisle"—don't take a chance with *Mr.*, a designation that might offend D. H. if she's a she. Instead, use the salutation

```
Dear D. H. Carlisle:
```

As you'll see, the simplified letter format (see "Format" below) omits a greeting. Such an omission is becoming common when a letter addresses a role rather than a person, as in a customer complaint or correspondence concerning an account. Avoid "Dear Sir or Madam" as just another cliché in the letterly voice.

Complimentary Close

Like the salutation, the complimentary close is gradually disappearing as routine correspondence takes the simplified form. You may use a last line, "Thanks," and then sign your name. When you do begin the letter "Dear __________:" end with one of the traditional closings: "Sincerely yours," "Yours truly," or "Sincerely." They differ little in meaning or tone. "Respectfully" implies a certain deference on the part of the writer. "Cordially" and "Best regards" are informal.

Signature

Type your name several spaces below the complimentary close or the end of the text. Your company name may come either above or below your typed name. Although you type your full name, you may sign the letter with your nickname if your relationship with the reader warrants it.

Other Notations

Beneath the signature you may include other notations, for example:

Enc(s).	Enclosures. Note the number if there are more than one: "Encs (3)." Note the title if you'd like: "Enc: ACS Compendium."
Initials	If someone other than the writer typed the letter. The writer's initials come first, then the typist's: "DCA:dtd."
Copies	*cc* (or *pc* for photocopy) and then the names of the recipients of the copies (after a colon).
P.S.	Don't use this, except perhaps in sales letters. Organize your letter to include what you need—and don't resort to afterthoughts.
Signed in absence	As a matter of record, let the reader know if the sender of the letter is different from the signer: "Peter Smith for Mary Jones" or "Signed in Mary Jones's absence by Peter Smith."

Subsequent Pages

On rare occasions, you may write a letter of more than one page, particularly in letter reports and contract letters. Head each page after the first with the recipient's name, the page number, and the date. Use paper that is of the same quality as the first page, but not letterhead.

Format

How these letter elements are placed on the page is a matter of *format*. The most common business format is the *block* letter. Two others are the *modified block* (with indented paragraphs) and the *simplified*. Figure 13–4 shows you these different formats.

WRITING LETTERS INTERNATIONALLY

Letters are artifacts of a culture. The conventions you just reviewed say something about how Americans address each other (or avoid addressing each other, as in the simplified format) and how management practices developed in the United States and in England while the United States was a colony. They also reveal information about the U.S. mail system and our way of designating addresses. They reflect how we transact business: briefly, with a minimum of courtesies.

Such standards are hardly universal. The size of stationery differs (a problem sometimes in filing international correspondence). Conventions differ. More significantly, the approach to readers through letters differs among cultures. Some cultures consider American letters, in their simplicity and directness, rather brusque. Traditional Japanese business letters, for example, open gently. A literal translation of the salutation may read, "Allow us to open with all reverence to you." That greeting is followed by a formulaic remark about the seasons or the weather:

```
The season for cherry blossoms is here with us and everybody
is beginning to feel refreshed. We sincerely congratulate you
on becoming more prosperous in your business.
```

The traditional letter then takes an indirect approach in which explanations precede statements about actions taken and in which information is presented chronologically.[1] It uses stock expressions and ritualistic approaches. As you learned in Chapter 3 and will see in more detail shortly and in Chapter 20, much business in Japan is conducted orally or in faxes or telexes that simply provide statistical information. Some small companies employ one person to write all letters. Even at large companies, one person often writes all sales or "official apology" letters.

[1] Saburo Haneda and Hirosuke Shima, "Japanese Communication Behavior as Reflected in Letter Writing," *The Journal of Business Communication*, 19:1 (1982), 19–32. For further information on writing letters internationally, see also John Hinds and Susan Jenkins, "Business Letter Writing: English, French, and Japanese," *TESOL Quarterly*, 21:2 (1987), 327–50; William V. Ruch, *Corporate Communications: A Comparison of Japanese and American Practices* (Westport, CT: Quorum, 1984); and David A. Victor, "Franco-American Business Communication Practices: A Survey," *World Communication*, 16:2 (1987), 157–75.

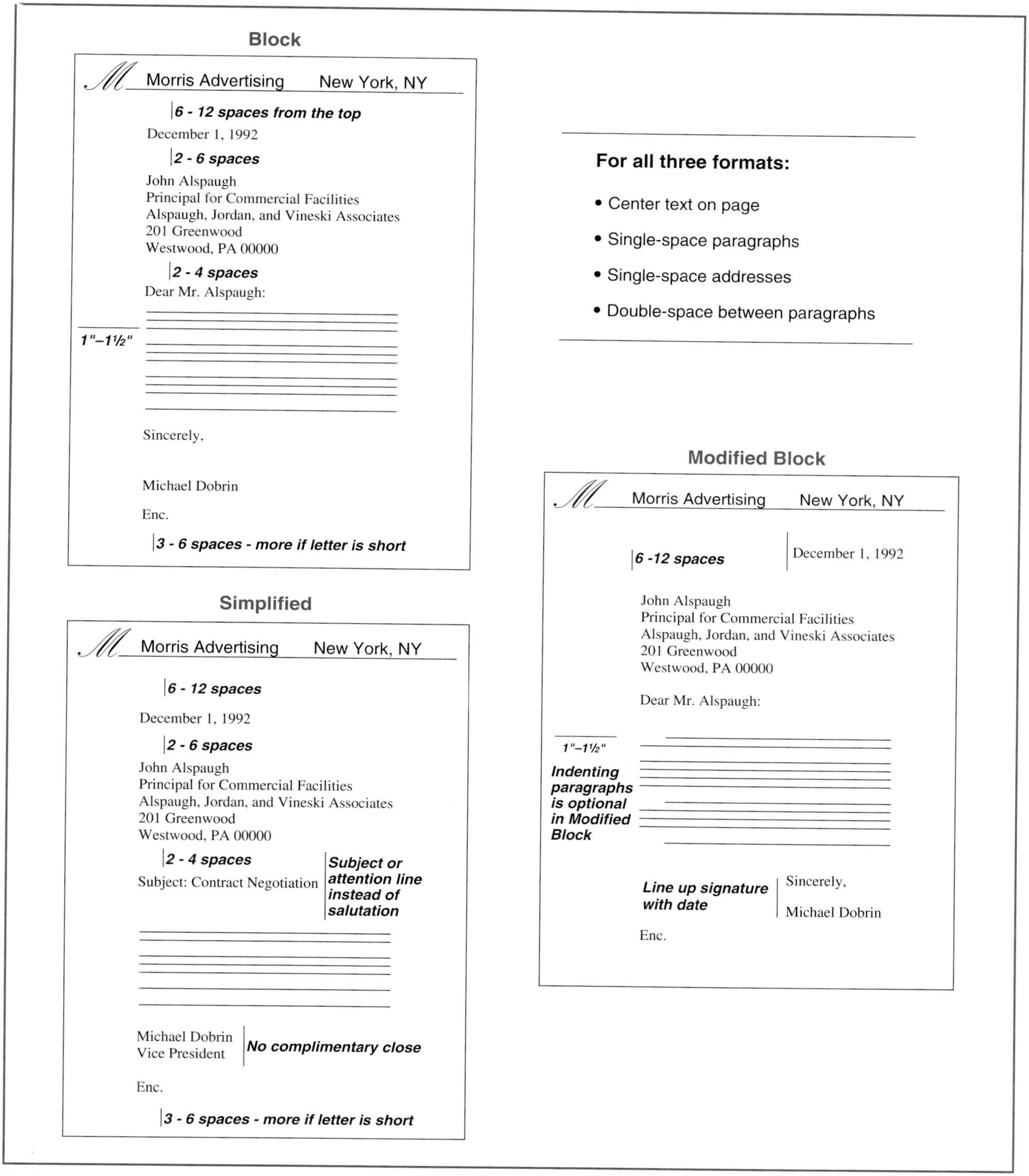

Block

Morris Advertising New York, NY

6 - 12 spaces from the top

December 1, 1992

2 - 6 spaces

John Alspaugh
Principal for Commercial Facilities
Alspaugh, Jordan, and Vineski Associates
201 Greenwood
Westwood, PA 00000

2 - 4 spaces

Dear Mr. Alspaugh:

1"–1½"

Sincerely,

Michael Dobrin

Enc.

3 - 6 spaces - more if letter is short

For all three formats:

- Center text on page
- Single-space paragraphs
- Single-space addresses
- Double-space between paragraphs

Modified Block

Morris Advertising New York, NY

6 -12 spaces December 1, 1992

John Alspaugh
Principal for Commercial Facilities
Alspaugh, Jordan, and Vineski Associates
201 Greenwood
Westwood, PA 00000

Dear Mr. Alspaugh:

1"–1½"

Indenting paragraphs is optional in Modified Block

Line up signature with date Sincerely,

Michael Dobrin

Enc.

Simplified

Morris Advertising New York, NY

6 - 12 spaces

December 1, 1992

2 - 6 spaces

John Alspaugh
Principal for Commercial Facilities
Alspaugh, Jordan, and Vineski Associates
201 Greenwood
Westwood, PA 00000

2 - 4 spaces

Subject: Contract Negotiation *Subject or attention line instead of salutation*

Michael Dobrin
Vice President *No complimentary close*

Enc.

3 - 6 spaces - more if letter is short

FIGURE 13–4.
Three common formats for letters: block, modified block, and simplified. *(Courtesy of Michael Dobbins.)*

Some Canadians object to the hale, "cheerleaderish" tone in American letters. Their letters tend to be more reserved. Before you write to someone in another culture, then, learn about that culture's—and that person's—priorities and conventions for letters. Talk with other people in your organization who have experience writing letters abroad. If your command of your reader's language is good, then use that language. Otherwise write in English. To accommodate translation, emphasize the use of terms in their denotative senses, that is, their direct dictionary meaning (see Chapter 5), and avoid any anecdotes or other stories of merely local interest.

In "*FYI:* Communicating with a Japanese Partner," Ken Charhut, Director, Automated Distribution Systems at the Baxter Healthcare Corporation, comments on communication issues in the two facsimile transmissions shown in Figures 13–5 and 13–6. Joint ventures and partnerships call into question the traditional designation of *inside* and *external* correspondence, as these figures show in their mix of memo and letter elements. Like much business correspondence, these documents update the status of a project; they also follow up on a meeting.

SUMMARY

- Although telephones and electronic technology are replacing letters for some communication, you will write a letter when the information you need to present is lengthy or complex, when you are writing across time zones and language barriers, when a routine letter may seem faster than a phone call, and when you need a paper trail for legal purposes. You will also write when a personal relationship can best be maintained through a letter.

COMMUNICATING WITH A JAPANESE PARTNER

Ken Charhut
Director, Automated Distribution Systems,
Baxter Healthcare Corporation

Time differences between our home office outside Chicago and the office of our Japanese partner, Tokyo Sanyo Electric Co., Ltd., as well as the cost of travel, mean that written communication is the major channel for maintaining our business relationship. By far the most popular method of communicating is through the fax machine. We usually send between three and seven faxes a week to the Japanese. We may receive one to three faxes from them.

The difference between the number of faxes sent and received and the content of those faxes reflect cultural differences. U.S. companies tend to be comfortable with individual contributions. Someone works on a project, uses his or her own judgment on decisions, and sends along periodic updates to management, who then oversee the progress of the work. The updates document time lines and hold the project team accountable for meeting each milestone. Management expects frequent updates to keep control of individual actions.

Japanese companies, by contrast, use a communal system of accountability. Time lines are not written. Instead, a team meets frequently and discusses goals and progress orally. Only the end goal is documented in writing; the intermediate steps are assumed to have happened.

- To connect well with the reader, think of the **common ground** between your self-interest and the reader's self-interest. Take a **"we-attitude"** that emphasizes what's shared and familiar and that treats the reader **ethically.** Be honest. Value the reader's time. Use the reader's code. Consider the reader's self-interest, and, if necessary, save face for the reader.

- **Routine** letters are those that match simple and uncomplicated situations for ordering and responding to orders and for requesting and responding to requests. They follow a standard form in response to a common, frequently repeated situation. A **customized** letter is needed when the situation requires special concern for the reader or is in some other way unique. Conveying negative information or attempting to persuade the reader of something often demands a customized letter.

- Because letters, by virtue of being written, form a record of a project, make sure you are **authorized** to write a letter, particularly one that holds the company to promises concerning project work and delivery dates. Confirm employment contracts and policy statements in letters with a company lawyer, if necessary. Be careful to avoid libelous statements in letters evaluating people.

- Feeling the shadow of a lawyer as you write a letter is one cause of the **"letterly voice,"** that ponderous sound that often emanates from letters. Another is the temptation to write the obsolete language of traditional letters rather than to think of letters as current forms of communication requiring the language of the 1990s.

The two faxes (Figures 13–5 and 13–6) illustrate those differences in style. We were introducing a new piece of equipment into the U.S. market and had set several goals for a successful project launch.

As the launch date approached, we were determined to meet our schedule. During the week of 22 April, we went to Japan to talk with representatives from Sanyo to confirm the schedule. On 29 April, we received a follow-up facsimile from Sanyo reiterating what we had discussed (Figure 13–5). The fax was really a favor to us. Sanyo assumed that the discussion itself confirmed their intention to deliver the product and appropriate accompanying information at the right time.

However, we tend to believe that nothing is happening unless someone documents the action. Having not heard from Sanyo for a week, the project leader sent a desperation fax assuming the worst and pleading for a response. In fact, the schedule was met, as Sanyo had been working diligently but did not feel compelled to take time from that work to write us an update saying so. The desperation was caused by a difference in form as opposed to any substance in the communications process.

TELEFAX

April 29

TO: Beth Frampton LCE-2N
Pharmaceuticals Technology Group
Travenol Laboratories Inc.

FROM: K. Kashiwa
2nd Technology Dep. Refrigerator Div.
Tokyo Sanyo Electric Co, Ltd.

Thank you very much for your trip to Japan and had fruitful meetings with us.

The shipping schedule of repair parts

A; May 9 repair parts for RMH
new cutter unit, new brake unit (may be without solenoid) new conveyor, lo2T modified PCB

B; May 26 #ATC machine for UL submission,
Entire new mechanism & PCB for RMH,

C; June 9 4 Entire new mechanism & PCB for No,4,5,6 and U of Il

D; June 25 3 Entire new mechanism and PCB for No,7,8 and 9 machine

We will send you the idea concerning about cost separations and our proposal of repair parts cost tomorrow. Please wait one day.

TO; Ken Charhut
This concerns the UL application for the seal motor and the conveyor motor brake pack, We are changing the brake pack to the SS21-UL, But, it is controlled by a relay.
The relay maker will guarantee this model for up to 500,000 cycles. We believe that the conveyor motor will last for 1/2 a year and the seal motor is guaranteed for 2 years, Therefore, these parts will eventually have to be replaced. For the time being, we will apply for UL approval with these specifications. Also, we will try figure a way to eliminate the relay from the brake pack.

Regards;

Kiyoshi Kashiwa

Kiyoshi Kashiwa

FIGURE 13–5.
Fax from Sanyo confirming the schedule. *(Courtesy of Ken Charhut.)*

TELEFAX

May 6

To: K. Kashiwa
ME Group, Refrigerator Div.
Tokyo Sanyo Electric Co., Ltd.
Gumma-Ken, Japan

From: B. Frampton LCE-2N
Pharmaceuticals Technology Group
Travenol Laboratories, Inc.
Deerfield, IL

Regarding the shipping schedule to which we agreed, we are expecting Sanyo to ship ''problem parts'' replacements (repair parts) for Riverside and modified 102T PCB on May 9. Will Sanyo be shipping to us directly, or will you ship through Travenol, Ltd.? Please respond--if you are shipping through TL, we want to contact them and urge them to expedite the shipment. You (or TL) must inform us of all pertinent shipping information. If for any reason you are unable to meet the May 9 shipping schedule, please inform us immediately, and let us know when you will ship. Please remember that we will only be able to begin marketing the ATC July 1 if we restart Riverside on May 19, and if we submit for UL approval in early June. Receipt of UL documentation is critical. We have been discussing this documentation with you since December (5 months), and we were expecting the documentation on April 14th.

Regarding our shipments to you of 6 units (point 3 of April 30 fax). What dollar value should we assign to the units? As you know, we must assign a value for customs purposes. Please respond, so that we can ship as early as possible.

Regarding your April 30 proposal for sharing the ATC improvement costs, we agree to pay XXXX yen per new PCB, for 9 new PCBs, for a total of XXXX yen. We will pay after we receive the PCBs.

The label copy in your May 6 fax, point # 5, looks ok as long as it is centered on the label.

Ken is reviewing the spare parts list and will get back to you in a few days on your point # 6.

We look forward to your prompt reply to the questions above. Thank you.

Regards,

Beth Frampton

Beth Frampton slw

BF/slw/3232A

FIGURE 13–6.
Desperation fax to Sanyo. *(Courtesy of Ken Charhut.)*

EXERCISES

For Discussion

1. Interview friends or other people you know who write letters on behalf of organizations. What is their process for composing the letters? How much time do they spend on a letter? If the times for different letters vary, why? Do the letters go through an approval route before being mailed?
2. Ask non-American students at your university or ask individuals in a company that does business abroad for examples of letters written in other than an American context. How do they differ from the general American business letter? Do they use different conventions? Different strategies for lining up material?
3. Comment on the *voice* in the following first two paragraphs of a letter sent to season ticket holders after the start of the baseball season had been delayed by a strike. How does the writer *connect* with the reader in the opening?

   We would like to take this opportunity to thank you wholeheartedly for your patience and support throughout the recent labor–management contract negotiations. The notion of a prolonged absence of baseball left us all beleaguered and dispirited. Fortunately, we can now look forward to home runs, great catches, and wins in the headlines instead of discussions and uncertainties.

   We are well aware of the inconveniences that these negotiations may have caused you. We have always felt that "the game," in its purest form, belongs to the fan, and thus we have decided to dedicate ourselves to honoring you this season. We are going to go all out, all season long, to let you know how important we feel you are to baseball. This season will be the "Year of the Fan."

For Writing

4. Books of sample letters appear frequently on the best-seller list of business publications. Purchasers of the book then select a letter for the occasion and fill in the blanks with their own information. Although such letters may sound as canned as they are, the principle of *imitating* a good model as you write is a valid one. Select from your mail—or from letters distributed in class—one you think is particularly effective. Imitate its style and approach as you write another letter with different information. Note particularly both the *conventions* of the letter—inside address, complimentary close, and the like—and its organization and style. Under what circumstances would you need to *deviate* from the model?
5. Write a straightforward letter. Then ask someone who is fluent in another language to translate it into that language. As that person translates, or when the translation is finished, interview the individual about how such a message would be conveyed in that culture and about any difficulties encountered in translating. Then turn in to your instructor your original letter, the translated letter, and a brief report on your interview. Perhaps discuss these translations in class.

For Collaboration

6. In the accompanying figure, you see a one-page letter that a photographer sent to high school seniors. You may have received such a letter when you were in high school. In a group, analyze the voice in the letter (review Chapter 5) and the letter's organization (review Chapter 4). Review Chapter 7 and the Handbook at the back of the book for advice on revising. What *assumptions* does the letter make concerning what the reader knows—has been told earlier—about senior portraits? What is the main point of the letter—the photographer's sales pitch? *Rewrite* the letter to make that point more obvious—and appealing. You may rewrite one draft together or draft a letter individually and then meet to decide on one final joint draft. Discuss each group's letter in class.

Dear member of the Senior Class of 1993:

First of all, you do **not** have to have your portraits made by the **contract** school photographer.
Here are a few reasons why we feel you should have your Senior portraits taken by our Studio.

We will not rush you in and out of the Studio. We take at least 30 minutes and take 10 poses.

We have a fully equipped Studio but we do not take environmental photographs. (Given the uncertainty of the Minnesota weather it would mean too many cancelled appointments, wasting your time and mine. It would mean that we could not offer the low prices that we do. Remember, some schools will not use that **type** of Photograph.)

We do **not** require a deposit on your proofs, in fact, at **your** option we will mail them to you.

We believe for the best protection, that all color Photographs should go into frames not folders, so we sell the folders separately.

For the sake of economy, we do not send you an expensive brochure with either our Portraits or someone else's put out by a film company.

Modern retouching* can do wonders, it will remove blemishes and soften harsh lines underneath the eyes. If you have a clear complexion there is no need to pay extra for retouching. Other studios do not give you a choice. We do. Some Studios offer you low prices but do not tell you that it is for unretouched Photographs. Be sure to ask.. With our Studio you are given a choice..

(cont.)

We offer a 10% **discount** from our print prices if you have your portraits taken during the months of **July** and **August**..

Sitting fees - due at time of the sitting
Regular - 10 poses 30 minutes no retouching - - - - - - - - $20.00
Deluxe - 10 poses 30 minutes with retouching - - - - - - - $30.00
Additional 10 poses - $15.00
Retake charge - $7.00 Retouching additional pose - - - $ 5.00

Our Packages - - includes yearbook glossy
50% of the cost of your order is due at the time the order is placed

	no retouching	**with** retouching
1-8 × 10, 2-5 × 7, 4-3 × 5, 16 wallets	$ 79.00	$100.00
1-8 × 10, 2-5 × 7, 8-3 × 5, 24 wallets	$ 95.00	$120.00
1- 11 × 14, 1- 8 × 10 2-5 × 7, 8-3 × 5, 48 wallets	$160.00	$200.00
Additional wallets - 16 - wallets - $15.00	24 for $20.00	

Folder prices - 3 × 5 & 5 × 7 -.50 each 8 × 10 -.70 each
11 × 14 - $2.00 each

For those who cannot find a package to their liking we have a-la-carte prices comparable to the above.

As some schools require Yearbook glossies by the 1st of October and summer appointments fill fast don't delay, call 667-2841 today for your appointment.

*Retouching cannot correct hair or clothing imperfections.

14 MANAGING ROUTINE LETTERS

What's Ahead

PLANNING ROUTINE LETTERS
REQUESTING
- Placing an Order
- Inviting
- Requesting Information

INFORMING
- Confirming and Thanking
- Responding to a Request for Information
- Writing About a Policy or Procedure
- Writing About an Account
- Covering an Enclosure

SUMMARY
EXERCISES

Do You Know ?

- How do you know a situation is "routine"?
- What strategy should you use in writing a routine letter?
- How should you write a request?
- What approach should you take in informing a reader?

Many business functions are repeated, day after day. When you write to accomplish one of these functions, your writing often fits a form or formula—one set by your organization or one you create for yourself. The situation is not emotionally charged, and the message is relatively uncomplicated. Your self-interest and the reader's self-interest are well matched. Your purpose is to *inform.* Your approach should be simple and direct. Your letter should be short. In this chapter, you will learn how to write such letters.

PLANNING ROUTINE LETTERS

You'll conduct much routine business on the phone, as you saw in Chapter 13. When you need to *write,* however, organize your information to fit a three-part plan:

Beginning. A short first paragraph (preferably one or two sentences) that connects you and the reader. Include the control statement that announces your shared purpose and that provides an overview of the content of the letter.

Middle. Subsequent (short) paragraphs that include any necessary explanation and details.

Ending. A courteous closing that states any action required, along with deadlines.

This approach works well for most routine letters. If, however, you realize as you plan that you need to *establish* common ground with the reader, or if you think the reader may object to the information or otherwise take offense, or if you need to *sell* the reader on an action or decision, then a more customized approach may be necessary. Such situations often dictate a more indirect strategy for organizing information and even greater attention to courting or saving face for the reader and to creating an effective voice in your prose. The categories of "routine" and "customized" are not watertight. Assess each situation.

Keep routine letters to one page. If you have additional details or facts to send, attach separate sheets. The letter is more likely to be read if the reader can see the beginning and the end of the message at once.

Figure 14–1 shows a form letter that thanks contributors to the Animals

ADOPT
Animals Depend On People Too

February 26, 199X

Frank and Paula Muzopappa
RD#2, Box 2490
Hamburg, PA 19526

Dear Friends of the Zoo:

On behalf of the Zoological Society of Philadelphia, it is my pleasure to acknowledge your recent contribution to the Adopt-An-Animal Program and to welcome you as an ADOPT parent. Your contribution of $50.00 to support Petal the African elephant is evidence of your commitment to the Philadelphia Zoo and the animals that comprise its world-famous collection. We are grateful for your generous support.

As you know, the ADOPT program is essential to the Zoo, as it provides direct support to combat one of our most pressing problems--the rising costs of feeding the more than 1,600 animals that comprise our collection. The Zoo's bill for meat, vegetables, crickets, mealworms, hay, and zoocakes continues to increase and makes up a substantial percentage of our annual operating expenses. Thus the faithful support of individuals such as you has become especially valuable.

Enclosed are your ADOPT materials for the current year. Each year when you renew your adoption, we will send you a gold sticker reflecting your year of participation in our program. This will serve as your record of sponsorship.

Again we thank you for your support of the ADOPT-AN-ANIMAL Program. I hope you will be able to come to the Zoo in the near future to visit your adopted animal.

Sincerely,

Wm V. Donaldson

William V. Donaldson
President

WVD:mlh
Enc.

The Zoological Society of Philadelphia
34th Street and Girard Avenue
Philadelphia, Pennsylvania 19104
215 243-1100

FIGURE 14–1.
A routine letter. *(Used by permission of the Marketing Department, The Zoological Society of Philadelphia.)*

Depend On People Too (ADOPT) Program at the Philadelphia Zoo. Note its approach.

Beginning. The first paragraph connects writer and reader through the mention of the gift and announces the topic of the letter: information about the ADOPT Program.

Middle. Paragraph 2 expands on the importance of the gift to make the reader feel good about having given—and to encourage more support. The statement is concrete (down to the crickets and mealworms). Paragraph 3 notes that material is enclosed and mentions a "gold sticker" that may appeal particularly to children.

Ending. The last paragraph closes the letter on the best point of connection between writer and reader: "Come to the Zoo." And it does so in personal terms, inviting the reader "to visit *your* adopted animal."

For the routine transfer of information, directly structured letters, often form letters like this one from the zoo, are exactly right.

REQUESTING

When you write to *request* something—to order an item or service, to invite someone to attend something, or to ask for information or advice—*think in the reader's terms.* How does the reader refer to or file that item, service, information, or document? What will the reader gain from attending the event? Anticipate questions.

Placing an Order

When you place an order, either in writing or on the phone:

1. Identify catalog numbers, sizes, colors, material of construction—whatever the seller requires to complete your order. Use lists.
2. Specify the shipment method and deadline.
3. Specify the method of payment (enclosed? send a bill? bill to credit card?). Calculate subtotals and totals.

Fill in the pertinent information on a preprinted order form, or write a letter like the one in Figure 14–2.

Inviting

When you invite someone to do something—to attend a meeting, to come to dinner, or to join an organization—consider the reader's motivation to accept the invitation as you draft your letter. Often, accepting is a function of the reader's role or clearly in the reader's self-interest—and may be just what the reader is looking forward to in a pleasant occasion. In those circumstances, your letter should be simple and direct:

1. Cover the logistics (who, what, when, where, why, and how much). If necessary, note who pays.
2. Anticipate any problems, like difficulties parking.

Perry Associates Inc.
1515 Tutweiler
Houston TX 77251

October 18, 199-

Watson-Jones Incorporated
PO Box 2347
Oakland, CA 94623-0704

Attention: Creative Gifts Department

Please send me the following items advertised in your Fall 199- catalog:

Quantity	Item	Cost ($)
5	2-pound selection of The Squire's Cashews	125
3	Hawaiian Macadamia Cakes	30
9	Chilly Cheese Assortments	45
	Total	200

So that I may distribute these to my staff before Chanukah and Christmas, I need to receive them by December 11.

Enclosed is a check for US $200. I understand that you do not charge shipping on orders over $150, so I have not included an amount for that.

Manuel Ramos
Vice-President/Operations

FIGURE 14–2.
A letter placing an order. The letter is in the simplified format.

3. Specify the means of responding and the deadline. Make the response easy: Provide your telephone number and address or enclose a response card.

A printed invitation may include such information within a design that gains the reader's attention and sets a theme. A design in the invitation may derive from the event itself and may be repeated on brochures or other documents, like an exhibition catalog available at the event. Figure 14–3 is a bilingual invitation from the Centre Canadien d'Architecture.

Requesting Information

The purpose of many letters, both personal and corporate, is to *request information.* Your first task in planning such a letter is to find the right person to write to if you have not already identified him or her. Sometimes you'll write to a role or an office, for example, to the "Admissions Office" at law schools you'd like to learn about. You may need to check standard business directories or make phone calls to companies to find out who is responsible for the information you need.

If you're requesting printed material, refer to it by the title, stock number, or other code created by the reader. The letter in Figure 14–4 uses a routine approach to ask for information that the reader should be prepared to give easily.

INFORMING

The purpose of many business letters is to *inform.* You can often insert your information into the three-part structure of the routine letter. Select information to match a reader's request or your organization's priorities in providing the information. Keep in mind the four requirements for ethical letters you read about in Chapter 13: Be honest, value the reader's time, use the reader's code, and consider the reader's self-interest. Here are some common situations for writing letters that inform.

Confirming and Thanking

The expected confirmation of an order, of course, is receipt of the product or service ordered. Some companies encourage further purchases by enclosing a brochure, another order blank, or a form letter of thanks.

As an individual or as a company spokesperson, you may also write to confirm the receipt of a payment, a product, a service, or a document. Your confirmation assures the sender that the item is in good hands. As a routine matter, just say, "Payment acknowledged" or "Invitation accepted"—often on a form. Be sensitive, however, to how the occasion for acknowledging receipt may suggest a more customized approach. That initial contact may provide an opportunity to explore to an even greater extent the shared territory with the reader.

BACK

Ernest Cormier, *Élévation et coupe longitudinale du vestibule d'honneur et de la tour de l'Université de Montréal*, 5 avril 1929 et 17 janvier 1930. Encre sur toile, 130,0 x 65,5 cm.

Ernest Cormier, *Elevation and longitudinal section of the entrance hall and the tower of the Université de Montréal*, 5 April 1929 and 17 January 1930. Ink on drafting cloth, 130.0 x 65.5 cm.

(CCA AR01: 2402-00001)

FRONT

Phyllis Lambert
Président et Directeur du
Centre Canadien d'Architecture/Canadian Centre for Architecture
a le plaisir de vous inviter à
une avant-première pour les Amis du CCA
des expositions

Ernest Cormier et l'Université de Montréal

et

Passages à l'Université de Montréal
Photographies de Gabor Szilasi

à 17 h 30
le lundi 30 avril 1990

Les expositions marquent le
Centenaire de l'Ordre des architectes du Québec

INSIDE LEFT

Phyllis Lambert
President and Director of the
Centre Canadien d'Architecture/Canadian Centre for Architecture
has the pleasure of inviting you to
a preview for the Friends of the CCA
of two exhibitions

Ernest Cormier and the Université de Montréal

and

Sighting the Université de Montréal
Photographs by Gabor Szilasi

at 17:30
Monday, 30 April 1990

The exhibitions celebrate the
Centenary of the Ordre des architectes du Québec

INSIDE RIGHT

FIGURE 14–3.
A bilingual invitation from the CCA. *(Used by permission of the Centre Canadien d'Architecture. Photograph, Collection Centre Canadien d'Architecture/Canadian Centre for Architecture, Montréal.)*

12 Garden Court
Houston, TX 77036

November 20, 1990

Mr. K.L. Wolfe, President
Hershey Foods Corporation
100 Mansion Road East
Hershey, PA 17033

Dear Mr. Wolfe:

I recently purchased shares of the common stock of your company for my IRA. My purchase was based on Value Line Investment Survey's high evaluation of your stock.

Please send me a copy of your 1989 annual report and your third quarter report for 1989.

What is the duration of the Milton Hershey Trust? How many shares are outstanding of Class A and Class B, and how much of each does the trust own?

Thank you for your response to my questions.

Sincerely,

David Rittenhouse

FIGURE 14–4.
A request for information.

Responding to a Request for Information

Use the request to structure your response. With some letters, you'll merely write "yes" or "no" or other short phrases or numbers in the margin next to the question and return the original. Other occasions require more information in a new letter, as in Figure 14–5, which responds to the letter in Figure 14–4.

Writing About a Policy or Procedure

You may write a letter to customers or vendors to remind them at certain intervals about a long-standing policy or to announce changes in policies or procedures. Figure 14–6 is a reminder.

Hershey Foods Corporation
Corporate Administrative Center
P.O. Box 814
Hershey, Pennsylvania 17033-0814
Phone: (717) 534-7552
Telex: 6711079 HERSH UW

JAMES A. EDRIS
Director, Investor Relations

November 30, 1990

Mr. David Rittenhouse
12 Garden Court
Houston, TX 77036

Dear Mr. Rittenhouse:

Thank you for your recent letter and for your interest in Hershey Foods Corporation. We always appreciate receiving comments and inquiries from our stockholders. Mr. Wolfe has asked me to reply.

Enclosed are the 1989 Annual Report and the Third Quarter interim report as you requested. In response to your question regarding the duration of the Milton Hershey School Trust, it is perpetual.

There are currently 74,907,932 shares of Common Stock and 15,278,404 shares of the Class B Common Stock outstanding. Of these, the Milton Hershey School Trust holds 22,928,493 shares of the Common Stock and 15,153,003 shares of the Class B Common Stock.

Thank you again for your continued interest in Hershey.

Sincerely,

James A. Edris

James A. Edris

JAE/jmf

Enclosures

FIGURE 14–5.
An informative response to the letter in Figure 14–4. *(Used with the permission of Hershey Foods Corporation.)*

E. I. du Pont de Nemours & Company
Incorporated
Wilmington, Delaware 19898

November 30, 1990

To All Vendors

GIFTS, FAVORS, AND ENTERTAINMENT

As the Holiday Season approaches, it is timely to express our appreciation to you, our valued suppliers. We wish, also, to remind you of a long-standing Du Pont Company policy.

We take pride in the business relationship with our suppliers, but in the interest of proper business relations, our employees are not permitted to seek or accept for themselves or others any gifts, favors, or entertainment without a legitimate business purpose, nor seek or accept loans (other than conventional loans at market rates from lending institutions) from any person or business organization that does or seeks to do business with, or is a competitor of, the Company.

This policy is not intended to eliminate those entirely ethical and traditional common courtesies usually associated with customary business practices such as business lunches, nor does it preclude the giving of token promotional or advertising items of nominal value.

We believe our policy provides clear guidelines which are well understood by our employees. We solicit continued cooperation in observing that policy by your firm and its representatives. If you have any questions concerning this policy, please call L. F. Rattigan, Jr. at (302) 774-9005.

W. E. Tatum

W. E. TATUM
SENIOR VICE PRESIDENT
DU PONT MATERIALS, LOGISTICS AND SERVICES

WET/bn

Better Things for Better Living

FIGURE 14–6.
A form letter stating company policy. *(Courtesy of the Du Pont Company.)*

The following letter announces a new policy at a discount department store. It also educates the reader about the new procedure and shows how her or his self-interest will be served.

To provide you with better check-cashing service through our new electronic checkout system, we are implementing a new Customer Check-Cashing Courtesy Card System. An application form is enclosed.

Your new card will allow you to cash personal checks in the amount of purchase up to $250. No preapproval will be required. You will also be allowed to purchase merchandise with payroll checks (not to exceed $250) issued by local employers.

Jones Department Stores Inc. will continue to honor your current check-cashing card for 90 days from the date of this letter. To avoid interruption of your current check-cashing privileges, we ask that you complete the Jones Customer Courtesy Card application as soon as possible.

New Courtesy Card applications are processed daily. Therefore, you can expect to pick up your new Courtesy Card approximately two weeks from the date your application is submitted.

We appreciate the opportunity to serve you.

Writing About an Account

You may be bombarded with phone and mail solicitations to apply for credit cards, to join record clubs, to subscribe to magazines, and to open checking accounts. Communicating about the accounts you open often occurs over the phone. In a corporate setting, too, much account information is requested and responded to in phone calls. When you need to confirm a statement or an action, however, you may write, as in the following letter closing a checking account:

I am leaving the Houston area and thus closing my checking account, 856-67-6682, as of October 1, 199-.

Please send a check for the account balance to me at the following address:

246 Cherokee Rd.
Pontiac, MI 48053

Thank you.

DUFFIELD ASSOCIATES
Consulting Geotechnical Engineers
5350 Limestone Road
WILMINGTON, DELAWARE 19808-1296

(302) 239-6634

LETTER OF TRANSMITTAL

DATE	JOB NO.
ATTENTION	
RE:	

TO ______________________________

____

____

WE ARE SENDING YOU ☐ Attached ☐ Under separate cover via ______________ the following items:

☐ Shop drawings ☐ Prints ☐ Plans ☐ Samples ☐ Specifications

☐ Copy of letter ☐ Change order ☐ ______________

COPIES	DATE	NO.	DESCRIPTION

THESE ARE TRANSMITTED as checked below:

☐ For approval ☐ Approved as submitted ☐ Resubmit ______ copies for approval

☐ For your use ☐ Approved as noted ☐ Submit ______ copies for distribution

☐ As requested ☐ Returned for corrections ☐ Return ______ corrected prints

☐ For review and comment ☐ ______________

☐ FOR BIDS DUE ______________ 19 ______ ☐ PRINTS RETURNED AFTER LOAN TO US

REMARKS ______________________________

____

____

____

____

____

____

____

____

____

COPY TO ______________________________

SIGNED: ______________________________

PRODUCT 240-2 NEBS Inc., Groton, Mass. 01471

If enclosures are not as noted, kindly notify us at once.

FIGURE 14–7.
Form for a letter of transmittal. *(Courtesy of A. Ingrid Ratsep, Ph.D., Duffield Associates.)*

Covering an Enclosure

When you send a document to a reader, you may simply attach your business card or a note on a removable sticker saying "Here's what you requested." If you're including several items, you might enclose a "letter of transmittal" that lists the items and the intended recipient. That letter, often a form, as in Figure 14–7, may serve two readers: an *immediate* reader in your organization who will assemble the documents and a *primary* reader elsewhere to whom they will be sent.

In transmitting documents, be particularly careful to sort routine occasions from those that could serve a more customized purpose. "Here it is" may be your entire message. Or you may find a selling opportunity in the occasion, as when you apply for a job in the cover letter that accompanies your resume (see Chapter 23).

SUMMARY

- A situation is **routine** when (1) your purpose and your reader's are well matched; (2) the purpose is a common business function—like ordering and responding to orders, requesting information, and informing; and (3) the situation is not emotionally charged and the message is uncomplicated.
- Be **simple** and **direct** in a routine letter. Begin with a statement about your shared interest with the reader, elaborate with any necessary details, and close courteously but briefly. Don't belabor the letter.
- When you write to **request** something—to order an item or service, to ask for information or advice, to request application blanks or brochures, or to invite someone to attend something—*think in the reader's terms.* Use lists. Value the reader's time and make it easy to respond.
- When you write to **inform,** consider first whatever request the reader made. Confirm an order by sending the item. Acknowledge receipt of whatever a reader may have sent. Be sensitive to an opportunity to thank the reader that may also provide an opportunity for a more customized sales approach.
- In writing any letter, meet the four requirements for ethical letter-writing: Be honest, value the reader's time, use the reader's code, and consider the reader's self-interest.

EXERCISES

For Discussion

1. Review your own mail. Perhaps bring in a sample to class. Note which items seem to take a relatively routine approach. How are the letters organized? How readable are they (review the guidelines for readability in Chapter 7)?
2. An insurance agency that offers a full line of personal, business, and life insurance has developed a series of form letters to match routine situations for writing. Three samples of their letters appear on page 274. (Their name is masked there, but the letters are real.) Discuss the ap-

proach in each. What is the situation? Why is it *routine?* Do you see any need to revise the letter? If so, what would you suggest? (For more letters from the agency, see Exercise 3 in Chapter 16.)

Letter A

Thank you for providing me with the expiration date(s) of your ________________ insurance.

I will be in touch with you approximately sixty days prior to the actual renewal date of your current policy. At that time, we will conduct an analysis of your insurance needs.

In the meantime, please remember that we are a full-service insurance agency. Should you have any questions regarding your present insurance protection, please contact us. Our professional staff is ready and eager to serve you.

Letter B

Thank you for taking time from your schedule so we could review your insurance needs for the future. We are obtaining quotations from several insurance companies to assure you a thorough insurance program that meets your criteria and is competitively priced.

I will call for an appointment to present our proposal the week of ________________.

Again, thank you for the opportunity to quote your insurance package. I look forward to presenting our recommendations to you.

Letter C

Thank you for the opportunity to present our proposal on your insurance coverage. It was a pleasure making our presentation at your (________________) office on (date).

Because of your interest in how insurance affects your business, Thompson Insurance will work to keep you informed of developments and to keep you updated on trends in the insurance industry.

As a full-service agency, Thompson Insurance is ready to serve you. Should the need arise, please give us a call.

For Writing

3. As human resources manager of Christos, Inc., a large, regional insurance broker, write to Creative Connections (12 West Temple Ave., Pomona, CA 91768) concerning their gift selections for corporate and

customer awards programs. You heard about them from a friend, John Sloan, who manages an agency in Los Angeles. Describe your employees (20 agents: 12 men, 8 women; and 55 clerks: 50 women, 5 men) and your customer base, some 1,000 fairly affluent individuals. Ask about the gifts they sell and their consulting services for advice on gift giving.

4. Order by mail from Rizzoli Bookstores (31 West 57 St., New York City 10019) the catalog from the "Traum und Wirklichkeit" show you saw in Vienna, Austria, in 1990. You've heard that Rizzoli has the catalog. You don't know how much it costs, and you'd like an English edition if that's possible—and if the English version contains the complete text of the German one. Arrange shipping and payment.
5. In preparing a report for a business communication (or other) class, write to some company or individual for information. *Select* the right person to give you the information you need. Find the address of the company in a standard business source (see Chapter 9). Use specific questions, in list form, within the letter.
6. Write a letter closing out your checking account (number 809-94-51) with the First National Bank of Colorado (3243 East 5 Ave., Durango, CO 81301). You've had some problems balancing your account and are thus unsure of the amount remaining in it. In addition, two checks (#3066 for $85 and #3088 for $50), written last year, have failed to clear. Explain to the bank personnel that you'd like them to check on the checks and then to send the balance to you at your new address.
7. Assume that you are turning over the responsibilities to someone else for a job you've held. Write a letter to that person *describing* your duties.
8. As the secretary of a campus organization, write to someone to invite that person to speak to your group. Note *why* you are writing to that individual. Assume the reader is not familiar with your group; describe it briefly. Provide information on logistics and expenses.
9. Assume that the person you invited to speak to your group (in Exercise 8) accepted your invitation and gave a good talk. Write a thank you note to him or her.

For Collaboration

10. Assemble a group to write a letter that matches each of the following situations. Each member of the group may write one letter, and then the group may meet to compare drafts and draft a composite group letter. Or you may write together. The product of your group, however, should be one letter acceptable to all.
    a. You are in charge of calendar sales for a printer. Every year, you send a reminder to your customers to reorder their calendars. Write the text of the form letter.
    b. You're in the accounts receivable department of the Goodall Worsted Company. Your company is changing its payment terms from 60 days on all accounts to 30 days. Write a form letter to your customers announcing the change in policy. With the new policy in place, the company hopes to reduce prices across the board.

15 THE ROUTINE AND BEYOND: NEGATIVE SITUATIONS

What's Ahead

A ROUTINE APPROACH TO NEGATIVE SITUATIONS
- Refusing an Invitation
- Writing About Problems with an Order
- Refusing a Claim

WRITING BEYOND THE ROUTINE
- Have the Right Person Sign the Letter
- Place the Explanation Strategically
- Check the Sound of Your Voice

ANNOUNCING BAD NEWS

REFUSING REQUESTS

DEALING WITH PROBLEMS IN A PRODUCT OR SERVICE
- Writing the Complaint
- Responding to the Complaint
- FYI: Rudeness Never Works

SUMMARY

EXERCISES

Do You Know 

- Why do letters about negative information sometimes require a customized approach?
- What questions should you ask in writing such a customized letter?
- What strategies can you use to encourage readers to read bad news?
- What should you keep in mind in refusing a request?
- Why are customer complaints important to businesses as well as to customers?

> We have read your manuscript with boundless delight. If we were to publish your paper it would be impossible for us to publish any work of a lower standard. And as it is unthinkable that, in the next thousand years, we shall see its equal, we are, to our regret, compelled to return your divine composition, and to beg you a thousand times to overlook our short sight and timidity.[1]

If you were the author of the manuscript rejected in this letter, would *you* feel rejected? The rejection is clear—the journal is returning the manuscript—but it is embedded in layers of statements intended to save face for the reader.

That's the challenge: to achieve a *positive* response in the reader when you deliver *negative* information—without being dishonest or otherwise changing the information. How people say no to each other strongly reflects both cultural and personal styles. Asians, for example, rarely say no directly. The rejection letter you just read, from a Chinese economics journal, is one example. Americans are more comfortable with negative information and denials, but bad news can still sting. Thus writing in negative situations may require special sensitivity to the reader. In this chapter, you will learn to write both routine and customized letters with negative information, and you'll learn to gauge the situation to know which response is appropriate.

A ROUTINE APPROACH TO NEGATIVE SITUATIONS

Announcing bad news, refusing a request, complaining about a product or service, or responding to a complaint—such situations may be simple or complex. When they are simple, don't demean the reader by writing anything other than a routine letter. As you learned in Chapter 14:

[1] "Sweet Rejection," *The Editorial Eye,* 13 (February 1990), 5.

1. State the main point.
2. Elaborate with subpoints and supporting evidence.
3. Define any requested action.
4. Close briefly but courteously.

These guidelines operate in the following routine responses in negative situations.

Refusing an Invitation

Here's a routine refusal of an invitation sent to someone who understands the situation:

> Unfortunately, I must say no to your kind invitation to speak with the Toastmasters group about business presentations. On that date I have to give one of those presentations to the Chicago Board and thus cannot join you. Thank you for thinking of me.

Writing About Problems with an Order

The following letter from a garden store alerts the customer to a problem with shipping an order:

> We're sorry, but our Day Lily Portfolio is not yet ready for shipment.
>
> We anticipate that the bulbs will be at a proper growth stage about November 1. We will ship them to you on that date.
>
> In the meantime, please let us know if we can supply another of your gardening needs. Enclosed is our current catalog, for your perusal. Please note our special sale on swoes, the ultimate garden tool.

If the customer's order is unclear, you may need to phone or write for clarification. If you no longer carry the product, then write to tell the reader about whatever equivalent product you do carry or to suggest where the customer may find the product. Don't automatically send a substitute; the customer may want only the item ordered. Explain the problem to the reader if you find that you are unable to ship what you had promised or if a back order continues well beyond a reasonable time.

Refusing a Claim

In Figure 15–1, you see a response from United Air Lines to a customer who had requested frequent flyer credit for a flight taken two years earlier. The answer is a simple reference to the rule concerning a time limit on retroactive flight credit.

MileagePlus®
UNITED

March 23, 1992

Ms. Gloria Bigelow
1840 Sea Spray Lane
Foster City, CA 94404

Dear Ms. Bigelow: Account: 99415 323 324

Thank you for contacting us regarding your Mileage Plus account.

As stated in program materials, retroactive flight credit in Mileage Plus is limited to travel occurring within the last twelve months. Therefore, we have credited your account with the mileage for flights you took during that period and are returning the remaining flight information you submitted should you wish to retain it for your records.

If you have a question regarding the above, or any other aspect of the Mileage Plus program, you may want to call our toll-free information number, (800) 421-4655.

We appreciate this opportunity to clarify our policy and look forward to serving you on your next United Airlines flight.

Sincerely,

John Carr
John Carr
Customer Service Representative

JC/jh
Enclosure

United Airlines Mileage Plus Service Center • P.O. Box 6233 • Carson, CA 90749-6233

FIGURE 15–1.
A routine refusal of a customer's claim. *(Courtesy of Mileage Plus, Inc.)*

WRITING BEYOND THE ROUTINE

Negative information, however, sometimes creates a distance between you and the reader, introduces something unusual into the business situation, and requires more complex information and explanations. Treating the negative situation as routine might cause the reader not to read or might offend the reader. Under such circumstances, you deliver the information, perhaps. But you've lost the reader. To both deliver the news *and* keep the reader, consider a more customized approach.

In planning such a letter, be sure you:

- Have the right person sign the letter.
- Place the explanation strategically.
- Check the sound of your voice.

Have the Right Person Sign the Letter

Negative information gains credence and acceptability—and stings less—if its source is an authority, that is, an expert on the subject at hand, a person with leverage and rank in an organization, a leader. A letter to guests at a hotel whose air-conditioning isn't working is better signed by the general manager (as you'll see shortly) than by the head of building services. The marketing manager may provide shareholders with statistics on sales during a good year. Poor sales and the resulting poor financial performance may require a letter from the vice president of operations or the chief executive officer. An executive may well ask a subordinate to call or write someone to accept an invitation or an assignment. *Refusing* may require a more personal touch to avoid offending.

That source in a higher rank indicates that the reader is taken seriously and that the information is also taken seriously. Such concern suggests a greater likelihood of control and correction.

Place the Explanation Strategically

If the negative information you need to deal with is obvious (perhaps too obvious) to the reader, open with that shared knowledge and move on to the explanation. You see that approach in the following letter written by the general manager of a hotel during an unusual April heat wave when the air-conditioning wasn't working. The letter was slipped under the door of each occupied guestroom.

As most of you are aware, the hotel's air-conditioning system is not currently operating. I would like to explain to you why we have not been able to resolve the problem.

Calgary is experiencing record-breaking heat that came much earlier in the year than normal. The Royal Arms Hotel has a 25-year-old HVAC (heating, ventilation, and air-conditioning) system that requires two weeks to convert from heating to air-conditioning. In past years, the mild weeks of early spring have allowed an easy conversion.

> But not this year. The conversion should be completed by early next week, and with its completion temperatures in the hotel will be immediately reduced.
>
> We realize that you may be leaving us before then. We are indeed sorry for the inconvenience to you in the meantime, and we appreciate your patience with us as we resolve this problem.

If the negative information or decision is *new* to the reader, however, seeing it in the first sentence might simply cause the reader to stop there. To establish your credibility as the writer of the letter and to save face for the reader, you may use an *indirect* plan, as you read in Chapter 4.

You'll open with some positive or at least neutral statement that can connect you and the reader. That statement shows your understanding of the reader's self-interest and your ability to describe the situation from the reader's point of view. In the opening statement, often called a *buffer* before the negative news, think less in terms of your *position* in the matter and more in terms of *description.* The length of the buffer depends on the complexity of the situation and your sense of how much is needed to overcome the reader's resistance and to treat the reader ethically, as you'll see in the section on "Announcing Bad News."

Check the Sound of Your Voice

Hearing a voice in the letter that's too blunt or too casual or seeing an explanation that's cursory or unclear might offend the reader. When there is trouble, confirm your credibility and good character by writing especially *well.* Your voice coming off the page should engage the reader and inspire confidence. At a minimum, of course, such a letter must contain no errors in grammar or spelling; such errors undermine your professionalism. Moreover, to convince, your voice should sound crisp and individual, not stuffy or canned. Here's a canned paragraph—an example of the corporate voice you saw in Chapter 5. The paragraph formed the bulk of a response to a customer complaint. Can you tell what the complaint was about?

> Please accept my apologies for any inconveniences you may have experienced as a result of the problems you encountered. There is no excuse for the type of service you received, but rest assured, this is not our normal standard of service. I have passed your letter on to my department heads so that they can investigate and make corrections. I appreciate your bringing these matters to my attention, for it is through feedback such as yours that I am better able to monitor our operation and make improvements where necessary.

The Major Appliance Consumer Action Panel confirms the importance of good writing in its annual "Silver Pen" award for the best response to a customer complaint. The panel

> considers such qualities as sensitivity and responsiveness to a consumer's situation and complaint. Clear and concise language and proper writing style also are de rigueur.
>
> What the letter doesn't have to do is give the consumer what he or she wants.
>
> Indeed, say experts in the field of consumer relations, it's not what you tell consumers that counts, but how you tell it.[2]

That "how" means writing well.

ANNOUNCING BAD NEWS

In delivering negative information, corporate spokespersons need to exercise a certain amount of "damage control." They also need to be honest. The following letter announces the bad news—the auction of a boat slip that the reader of the letter has rented for several years—in the second paragraph after a brief buffer in the first. The fourth paragraph states an action required of the reader (the removal of his boat from the slip). That information might have begun the letter:

> IT IS CRITICAL THAT YOU REMOVE YOUR BOAT FROM YOUR SLIP BY 31 OCTOBER.

But such an approach might seem too strident. Instead, here's what the property manager wrote:

> Manassas Wharf Investment Associates, the owner of your marina slip, has recently made a difficult marketing decision. Because we value you as a slip renter, we want to notify you immediately of this decision and related upcoming events.
>
> After careful consideration, Manassas Wharf Investment Associates is auctioning your marina berth and 22 other slips we own. The auction will be held on Saturday, 20 October 1992, beginning at 11:00 A.M.
>
> The Taylor Auction Company will conduct the auction. Before the auction date, the auctioneer will hold several open houses for prospective purchasers to preview the slips. They will occur on the following dates: October 7, 8, 11, 12, 14, 17, 18, and 19.
>
> All slips are intended to be sold at auction. Closing will occur approximately 45 days after 20 October 1992. For that reason, it is especially important that you remove your vessel from the berthing space at the Marina on or before the date of your lease's expiration, 31 October 1992.

[2] Robin Goldwyn Blumenthal, " 'Dear Buyer: Sorry Your Widget Broke, but It's a Nice Day and . . .'," *The Wall Street Journal*, 23 July 1990, p. B1.

As you know, the hired managing agent for Manassas Wharf Investment Associates is Global Management. If you have questions regarding your rental situation or the auction, please call or write directly to them:

Global Management
16 Aft St.
Portland, ME 04101
207-772-1234

In a culture that looks to progress and the future, you can control the damage of negative information by evoking a larger context, as in the signs that accompany highway construction: "Temporary Inconvenience, Permanent Improvement." The following letter, from a municipality to a homeowner, takes such an approach to announcing a 24-hour curtailing of water service. The explanation precedes the announcement:

During the week of 28 March, probably on that Monday, the sanitary sewer outside your home will be reconstructed.

Explanation with emphasis on minimal disruption

The particular process to be used allows for the complete reconstruction of sanitary sewers through existing street manholes without any excavation and with minimum disruption to the homeowner.

Specific request

A new structural pipe can be installed within the existing sewer pipe in approximately 24 hours. During this period, we ask for your cooperation in minimizing your use of water, as the process will block the end of your service connection. Please postpone such activities as clothes washing, baths, and showers during this period. Excessive water use could cause a backup that would flood your basement.

Extra attention to notification of temporary inconvenience

At least one day before the reconstruction of the line directly in front of your residence, we will notify you in person of that action. We hope such specific notice will minimize your inconvenience during this necessary sewer replacement.

Figure 15–2 takes a similar approach in announcing a reduction in the company's dividend to stockholders. It explains the need for the reduction as one of several steps the company is taking to improve its larger financial picture. Note that the letter bears the signature of the Chairman and CEO, Edward H. Budd, which enhances the credibility of the information.

REFUSING REQUESTS

Finding or creating neutral territory between writer and reader, as in all negative situations, is the key when you need to refuse a request.

As the owner of a business or as a spokesperson for a supplier or financial institution, you may have to write a letter denying credit to someone who

Edward H. Budd
Chairman and
Chief Executive Officer

The Travelers Companies
One Tower Square
Hartford, CT 06183

October 8, 1990

Dear Shareholder:

Last Friday The Travelers announced the addition of $650 million to our real estate reserves and the Board of Directors declared a dividend of $.40 on the common share, a reduction of $.20 from last quarter. I am writing to tell you why we took these actions.

The commercial real estate market has deteriorated sharply in the last few months. This has been caused by a number of factors, led by tight credit and generally weaker prospects for the economy. The impact of these conditions on Travelers is significant because of our concentration in mortgage loans and real estate investments, made primarily in the mid-1980s. With the actions announced today, our real estate reserves total $1.150 billion and our balance sheet will fully reflect the deteriorating environment we anticipate.

Reducing the dividend is one of the most difficult decisions a company can make. I am fully aware that the dividend paid on our stock is an important reason many people have invested in The Travelers. However, we are confident that these actions will improve the company's long-term value for our investors.

To do this, we must be certain that the resources are available to support the growth in our core businesses. The company has restructured its businesses and reorganized operations to pursue aggressive strategies in Managed Care and Employee Benefits, Commercial Property-Casualty, life and pension products.

The dividend reduction, combined with the $800 million of net proceeds from the sale of non-strategic businesses and over $200 million in recent cost reductions, will provide additional capital to support the growth of our core operations.

FIGURE 15–2.
A letter explaining a reduction in a company's dividend. *(Reprinted courtesy of the Travelers Companies.)*

October 8, 1990

Page 2

While the reserve addition will cause a net loss for the year, we are making excellent progress with strategies and operations in our core businesses. Managed Care and Employee Benefits Operations are producing record sales and substantially increased profits. Our property-casualty national accounts business continues to earn excellent returns. Major programs are underway to focus ongoing attention on cost efficiencies and quality service.

We now forecast a 25 percent increase in operating profits for 1990 over 1989. We are determined to sustain that momentum.

I appreciate the support that we have received from so many shareholders. I pledge to you that the entire management team will do everything possible to justify your confidence as an investor in The Travelers.

Edward H. Budd

Edward H. Budd
Chairman and
Chief Executive Officer

has requested such a privilege. Be particularly careful to be *accurate* in stating the grounds for the denial. Establish criteria for credit and measure the applicant objectively within them. Suggest alternatives, like cash payment, partial payment plans, and perhaps discounts for cash transactions. The structure of the following letter denying credit is indirect, with a three-paragraph buffer before the denial statement. That explanation may seem a bit self-serving for the hardware store, but it does set up how the store maintains low prices and it invites a later application:

Neutral ground between writer and reader: the order

Thanks for the order you sent on the 15th. We'll have it ready for you when you stop by on Tuesday.

Need for limited number of credit accounts

Like you, many carpenters, painters, and plumbers in the Springfield area find all their supplies here--when they need them and at the right prices. Our prices are competitive largely because we buy with cash ourselves from *our* suppliers and take advantage of their discounts while we avoid interest charges. We pass those savings on to you.

Criteria for credit. The reader meets one of two (local residence).

So to keep the cash flowing and avoid too much extra bookkeeping, we maintain very few credit accounts. We limit these accounts to local residents whose annual gross income from contracting is at least $35,000. You obviously meet the first criterion. As for the second, you mentioned that your current income is $25,000. What I hear from your customers suggests that figure will be rising. As soon as it does meet the minimum, we'll be glad to reconsider your application.

Alternative payment plan and resale

In the meantime, we hope you'll continue to purchase your supplies here on a cash basis. Let us know, too, if you have special orders for us to fill. We pride ourselves on an ability to find one-of-a-kind hardware items to suit the one-of-a-kind houses and carpenters in our community.

Sometimes the "temporary inconvenience, permanent improvement" approach works when you refuse a request, as in the following refusal stated as a postponement:

Neutral ground between writer and reader: tough job. Sense of mystery.

This is a tough letter to write, and you will see why in a minute. First I have some news to please you. You have been selected to attend the supervisory management program offered by the EISE.

Explanation

But we have a complication. Five hundred people applied for the program. Each session can accommodate only 15. We held to rigid standards for selection--standards I'm pleased to say you met--and compiled a list of 200 qualified applicants. In fairness to these applicants we have given priority for enrollment on the basis of years with the association. We'd like to serve first those who have been members of the Management Institute longest.

Decision

Thus we cannot grant your request to attend the session on 11-12 April.

Alternative

Your two years of membership place you in the group scheduled for Sessions 60–70, tentatively, 18 July–15 August of next year. We are currently negotiating with the consultant offering these programs to increase the number of sessions we can schedule. Should the increase go through, we'll make every effort to move you closer to your preferred dates.

Reaffirming common ground and personal connection

Thank you again for your interest in our supervisory management program. I'll be in touch with you concerning the schedule for future seminars.

Resale: another alternative

In the meantime, I've enclosed a brochure about other programs we offer and would be happy to discuss ones you would like to attend.

DEALING WITH PROBLEMS IN A PRODUCT OR SERVICE

As a customer, you talk with or write to a company representative when something goes wrong with a product or service. You show how what you received failed to match what you expected, and you seek an adjustment to close that gap. Your communication aids you in achieving satisfaction and provides important information for the companies you're corresponding with. The significance of customer complaints is underlined by Marcus Sieff, former chairman of Marks & Spencer, Britain's largest retailing company:

> Our customer liaison department receives about 2,500 letters, parcels and phone calls a week. Many of these letters and calls praise our staff and sometimes our goods; but the majority are critical. They complain, for instance, that our goods have turned out to be unsatisfactory; the ranges are inadequate; we are short of sizes or our colors are poor.
>
> If a customer is constructively critical, perhaps covering a wide range of goods, we invite him or her, sometimes a couple together, to the head office as our guests for the day. There we show them around the departments concerned so they can see what we are doing and make their views known to the relevant executives. In the old days, we replied to a letter with a letter, but we have found it is more efficient and economical, as well as much appreciated by the customer, to phone (if we have the number) as soon as we receive the letter, particularly if it is a complaint.
>
> When someone has been poorly treated in a store, we arrange for the store manager to invite the customer in, apologize and give the customer tea and whatever recompense is justified. It is imperative to deal with complaints politely.[3]

As Sieff makes clear, organizations and their customers need one another. Customer comments can pinpoint trouble spots in a product or service and provide tips for marketing. Moreover, it's more efficient to keep present customers happy than to abandon them and seek new ones. Dissatisfied customers tend to talk about their dissatisfaction and thus hinder new busi-

[3] Marcus Sieff, "Give the Customer What He Wants," *The New York Times*, 29 July 1990, p. B11.

ness. Customer relations staff at many companies, like Sieff's, thus call people in response to a letter of complaint; the call is prompt and personal. Inviting customers into the company is probably less common, especially in the United States. (Serving tea with the adjustment is uncommon.)

Dealing with problems in products and services is a critical communication task for both the customer and the company. Here are guidelines for writing on both sides.

Writing the Complaint

If you run into trouble with an order, or if something goes wrong with a product or service, you may phone the company to seek a correction. Many companies maintain toll-free numbers for such occasions. You may also return the item to where you bought it for exchange, repair, or credit. Service industries also encourage comments; many hotels, for example, leave "guest response questionnaires" in the room. You simply fill in the blanks.[4]

In writing or phoning to make a claim, adhere to whatever form or procedure the company suggests in the inserts that may accompany a product package or on the packaging itself. Clarify in your own mind what is wrong. Poor or discourteous service? Faulty merchandise? Problems in posting a credit? Note the details:

- The time, date, and place of the purchase
- The merchandise or service purchased, including such pertinent data as serial numbers, the model, and the warranty information
- The cost (with invoices and receipts)
- A brief narrative of the problem

Decide what you want the company to do: Refund your money? Substitute an item? Make a repair? The following letter establishes the writer's general loyalty to Matson products as the common ground with the reader and then shows how one product failed to meet either the writer's or the company's standards:

To ease the pain of the end of the soccer season, I recently bought my son a long-sleeved red Matson soccer shirt with three white stripes down each sleeve, a white neck band, and white cuffs. He loves the shirt.

There is only one problem: The middle stripe on each sleeve ripped out on the first washing. Only one side of each middle stripe is now stitched onto the shirt.

[4] Customer relations departments generally keep logs of complaints and *complainers*. They record the names in part to spot people who may write frequently only, it would seem, as a way of obtaining free coupons for products. Most companies still respond cordially to such people—but omit the coupons.

Clearly, that's not how you intend the shirt to be worn. Torn stripes make my son feel bad and look bad next to the Matson logo.

I asked the salesclerk at Marshall Field's, where I purchased the shirt, for an exchange, and he referred me to you. Please send me a new, long-sleeved red soccer shirt (size M 12–14). I'll be happy to send you this one in exchange, if you would like. Or send me my money back (receipt copy enclosed: $45.15).

Thank you. We're avid soccer fans, and thus avid Matson customers, and know you'll want to correct this problem.

The letter in Figure 15–3 (page 290) shows a different voice in its complaint. It is more direct in its narrative of cause (misfiling of the tapes) and effect (closing the account). The letter was sent following discussions with store clerks, and it documents the request to cancel the account.

In any letter addressing a problem with a product or service, clarify the complaint without alienating the reader. Everyone makes mistakes. Show your understanding of that fact, and appeal to the reader's self-interest in correcting the mistake. Write on the assumption that the reader is honest and fair.

Responding to the Complaint

As Sieff makes clear, well run companies take customer complaints seriously. You may not be in a position to respond to complaints, especially if you work in a large company where such matters are handled by a specialized department. But knowing strategies for handling negative information positively can aid you in any communication situation, as you see in "*FYI:* Rudeness Never Works." (See pages 292–93.)

Writing a letter in response to a customer complaint provides an opportunity to address the writer directly. You can neutralize the specific negative information presented by the writer that might cause resistance to buying company products or services. As in any response, structure your letter to meet the complaint. Remember that your own credibility and that of your company are questionable when someone issues a claim against you. Use your response to rebuild that credibility. Stress the positive first. Then deal with the particulars of negative information. Use the last line to resell the customer. Figure 15–4 (page 291) provides a brief and effective response to the complaint you read in Figure 15–3.

Although most companies agree to adjustments whenever possible, sometimes companies refuse a claim if the failure was clearly caused by the customer or otherwise resulted from conditions not under the company's control. The best of these letters educate the customer in understanding the reason for the rejection.

16 Papermill Road
Newark, DE 19713
9 October 1992

Peter Trumpethouse
Store Manager
Popcorn Video
123 College Square
Newark, DE 19713

Dear Mr. Trumpethouse:

In June, I applied for and received a Popcorn Video membership card. Throughout the summer, I used this card frequently. Twice during my membership period, video tapes that I returned were unaccounted for by the store. This resulted in unsubstantiated late charges to my account. It also prevented me from renting other tapes during subsequent visits to the store.

On both occasions, the tapes were eventually located on the shelves and the late charges were deducted from my account. Although I appreciate these gestures, I am afraid that at some point a temporarily misplaced tape may become permanently misplaced. If this were to occur, I would be unable to prove that I had returned the tape. I cannot afford to take that chance.

Enclosed is my membership card. Please take the necessary steps to close my account. Thank you.

Sincerely yours,

Kerri Weidner

Kerri Weidner

FIGURE 15–3.
A complaint that leads to a request to close an account. The letter is in the modified block format. *(Courtesy of Kerri Weidner.)*

123 College Square
Newark, DE 19713

13 October 1992

Kerri Weidner
16 Papermill Road
Newark, DE 19713

Dear Ms. Weidner:

I agree. You have not received from us the service a valued customer deserves. I can understand why you want to cancel your membership.

Accordingly, we have closed your account. But please reconsider. In fact, if you would like to rejoin within the next month, please see me personally at the store and I will give you a coupon for five free rentals.

We value you as a customer and hope you'll return to Popcorn Video soon.

Sincerely,

Peter Trumpethouse

Peter Trumpethouse
Store Manager

FIGURE 15–4.
Response to the letter in Figure 15–3. The letter is in the block format.

RUDENESS NEVER WORKS

Jean Bohner
President, Writing at Work

Your department is packed with sale shoppers. Two customers choose that day to return mismarked shirts. One customer begins, "I'm never shopping here again. The service is terrible. . . ." The other customer begins, "You must be going crazy today. I'm sorry to add to your problems, but I do need this shirt to take to a birthday party in an hour." Which customer are you going to go out of your way to help?

It's Saturday night and because the cook is having another "bad" night, you're getting orders that are late and often wrong. As you apologize, one table becomes increasingly rude, threatening to leave—forever. The other table is understanding, but the people there ask if you think they'll be able to make their eight o'clock curtain. Which table will get dinner first?

In both these scenarios, the problem is not your fault; it is in fact beyond your immediate control. You're doing your best in difficult situations. And your customers' rudeness does nothing to make you try harder. If anything, it puts them at the bottom of your list. As one customer service representative said, "When back orders become available, you can be sure which customers will get theirs last—the ones who gave me the most trouble."

And what do your customers want? To irritate you? To make you feel inadequate? To have to find another store to shop in? To go to another restaurant and begin again? Probably not. They certainly want their problems solved—new shirts, their orders. But as your own reaction shows, rudeness doesn't solve problems. It merely slows down solutions.

So if you're writing to complain about a problem, remember your own reaction to rudeness and remember what you want—to solve the

SUMMARY

- You write a **routine, direct** letter when your self-interest and that of the reader overlap, when the business situation is a standard one, and when the information is unemotional. If your need to announce a problem, refuse a request, or otherwise say no fits that pattern, then use a routine approach even with negative information. But negative information sometimes creates a **distance** between you and the reader, introduces something unusual into the business situation, and requires more complex information and explanations. For those situations, you may need to develop a **customized approach.**
- In writing a **customized letter,** consider your **authority** to write, the **placement** of your explanation, and your **voice.** First, hearing negative news from an authority or someone with leverage and rank in the organization sometimes softens its blow for the reader, shows the reader that the information and the reader have been taken seriously, and suggests control of the situation and possible correction. Second, using an **indirect approach**—with the explanation before the conclusion or decision—and detailed treatment also may aid the reader in accepting the message. Finally, make sure that your **voice** coming off the page is unhackneyed, professional, and appropriate.

problem. Consider this first paragraph in a letter to a sales representative:

```
    Your new, supposedly high-tech communication system
is filled with bugs. You said you had over three-hundred
successful installations (which we now doubt). If it
isn't fixed soon, we're taking our business somewhere
else.
```

Writing this way may make you feel better, but does it get your phones working? What would get them working?

- Acknowledge your reader's difficulty—say you understand that implementing a new system is not easy.
- Stick to the facts of the problem—list the bugs. They can't be corrected if no one knows what they are.
- Show how the problem affects your business—describe briefly but in detail your potential loss of customers.

And, of course, just as being rude when making a complaint doesn't solve problems, being rude when answering a complaint doesn't solve them either. You want the problem solved as much as your customer does, no matter who is at fault. Say you're sorry the problem exists or apologize immediately if your company is at fault, and get on with the solution.

Your letter isn't just going into an envelope or a fax machine or ending up at a computer terminal. It's going to another human being who, just like you, doesn't respond gladly to being yelled at.

- To encourage readers to read bad news, frame it in a context of **shared understanding.** Show the reader you can see the situation from her or his point of view. Concentrate on *describing* rather than formulating positions. Whenever possible, show a neutral or positive side, perhaps as a function of a long-term gain: "Temporary inconvenience, permanent improvement." But don't lie.

- In **refusing** a request, create a neutral ground between you and the reader that allows both of you to maintain your self-interests. Try to offer an alternative, if appropriate. Avoid the patronizing or detached language of the **corporate voice;** negatives sting more when they are delivered in such language.

- Businesses depend on customer complaints. They use this feedback to learn about problems in products and services and to develop marketing strategies, and this criticism provides them with the opportunity to address the customer directly and thus **neutralize any opposition** to buying from the company in the future. It's best to keep current customers satisfied. **Customers** need to **alert businesses** when what they receive in a product or service doesn't match their expectations.

EXERCISES

For Discussion

1. Because a large group of conventioneers was scheduled to check out of the hotel the next morning, the "Executive Assistant Manager/Rooms" wrote the following letter and slipped it under each guest's door. Comment on the letter. Was it sent by the right person? Is the explanation in the right place? Does it *sound* credible and welcoming?

   We would like to take this time to thank you for staying at the Quality Courtyard Inn/Downtown. We hope that your stay with us has been an enjoyable one, and it has certainly been a pleasure to have you as our guests.

   Tomorrow, we will experience a very heavy checkout. Although checkout time is 12:00 noon, we would like to encourage you to checkout before 11:00 A.M. to avoid long lines and delays at the front desk.

   So that your checkout can be as fast as possible, we will have a full complement of cashiers beginning at 7:00 A.M. We will also have a full complement of bellmen to store your luggage for you until it is time to leave. Additionally, if you presented a credit card upon check-in, please take advantage of our express checkout, which is detailed in the information guide on the bedstand in your room. As a reminder, any room checking out late will be charged a half-day rate.

   Again, we hope your stay with us was enjoyable, and we wish you a safe trip home or wherever you next travel.

2. Discuss the *voice* in this letter from a customer to her broker.

   Exactly what the hell do I have to do to get you to transfer my account to the Boston office?

   I've written to you and to Poopsey (or whatever you call the head of your office). Next it will be to the Chairman of the Board.

3. Bring to class a sample of letters that report negative information or refuse a request. Note whether the letters use a routine or a customized approach. Does the approach work? How do the letters *sound?* Could a reader take offense at what is said?

For Writing

4. Revise the following letter. It displays errors in both its approach and its expression and spelling. (Check Chapter 7 and the Handbook at the back of the book for advice on correcting errors in sentence structure and word use.)

   I ordered an electric antenna for a 1972 mustang. The first problem was, it took six weeks to finally get to my address. I ordered the electric antenna back in the middle of February. The salesman that I talked to on the phone told me that your company strived on prompt service and also informed me that I would be receiving my electric antenna in one week. The second problem I encountered was when I opened the item I ordered. It was not the correct model.

I understand that salesman get a large number of phone orders and can make mistakes. I can also understand a few days late, But five weeks late and completly the wrong item ordered. I disagree with your system.

I am sending this item back to your company COD. I also expect a full refund within two weeks due to your large mistake. If I have not received my full refund the Better Business Bureau will hear from me.

5. The following letter smacks of the corporate voice, although its approach and content are otherwise probably appropriate. Review the letter and revise particularly so that it *sounds* better.

   Thank you for your recent communication relative to your dissatisfaction with a purchase of MICROCHIPS. Your comments have been forwarded to our production specialists for their immediate investigation and whatever corrective action is required to prevent a recurrence.

   We sincerely regret the concerns you have expressed and appreciate your bringing this matter to our attention. We continually strive to satisfy all our customers and are disappointed when this is not achieved.

   In appreciation of your interest, we would like you to have with our complements a copy of our latest recipe booklet and a refund in the amount of $1.61.

   We hope in the future you will continue to be our valued customer and that our products will meet your fullest expectations.

6. You are the personnel director of The Big Company, Inc. Richard Short, the son of a friend, has applied for a sales associate job. He's a likable person, but he has no sales experience (your advertisement specifically stated "5 years' experience minimum"). Moreover, you are looking for someone with a strong background in pharmaceuticals (your product); Richard is a sociology major and has had no technical courses. His letter of application emphasized his strong communication skills. Such skills are certainly important to the job, but they are not enough. Write a letter to Richard Short (address: 120 Clark, Laramie, WY 82070) that rejects his application.
7. You work for a photographic studio. The studio's policy is firm: no returns on portraits except for *technical* problems. Your own quality control generally screens those out anyway. Steven Smith wants to

return his portrait and get his money back. He doesn't think it *looks* like him. But there is nothing technically wrong with the prints. Write to Mr. Smith refusing his claim. Or, while noting the "no-returns" policy, offer Mr. Smith the chance for a retake of his portrait.

8. You are a broker with Jefferson/Anderson Inc. You have been assigned to manage the portfolio of Amos R. J. Brock. Among other suggestions, you advise that he buy into WaterBoard Associates, a manufacturer of sailboards. Purchased at 17½, the stock declines steadily. After a year of ownership, Brock, against your judgment, decides to sell at 9. His sell order is accompanied by a letter implying that you recommended WaterBoard Associates only because you *use* their products and not because you understood their position as a business. Brock is a solid investor. You want to keep him as a client. Write a letter responding to his criticism.

9. You are the coach of a soccer team for boys 10 to 12 years old. Jeff Sprinter, a 12-year-old seventh grader, has attended each tryout and wants to be a goalie. He has extensive (and expensive) goalie clothing, purchased by his father, who has also attended each tryout. By the rules of the league you compete in, you can carry only 16 boys on the team. Twenty-two boys have tried out. Your policy is that each player must be capable of playing *each* position. That means that all players must be runners. Jeff clearly hates to run and is slow in the field. He also hates the field. He's smart and a decent goalie; but he's not the *best* goalie (that's Peter Smith), and you don't want to carry a player on the roster whom you can't play. So you cut Jeff. His father is upset. He writes to you and asks for a response *in writing* about why you cut Jeff. Write to: Dr. Jeffrey P. Sprinter, 12 The Circle, Randolph Estates, Brattleboro, VT 05301.

10. Fortunately, you came out of an auto accident unscathed. But your car, a 1990 Chevrolet, did not. You took it to the Body Works auto repair shop, whose estimate for repair was reasonable. You, the shop, and the insurance adjuster all agreed on a price. You paid the bill and picked up the car two weeks later; now, two months later, the paint is peeling and you can see old rust on what was to have been a new part. Write a letter asking the shop to make an appointment with you to redo the work. You're writing rather than calling, by the way, because you want a record of your claim and because you are at school now; the shop is in your hometown, 150 miles away.

11. You are the customer relations manager for the Maison Blue shop in Columbus, Ohio. Amy Persons, who has had a credit account with the store for nine years and is a frequent customer, charged a formal dress and then returned it after it had obviously been worn for a social occasion.[5]

    Mrs. Persons (whose address is 2814 Sycamore, Columbus, OH 43220) obviously expects the charge for the dress to be removed from her account. The store manager has directed you to write her a letter telling her that this cannot be done because the dress is no longer salable.

[5] This exercise and Exercise 14, courtesy of William R. Brown.

   a. Indicate the goals of the letter you are planning to write in a brief list.
   b. Write the letter.

12. On pp. 288–89 and in Figure 15–3, you read two letters of complaint. In Figure 15–4, you read a response to Figure 15–3. Assume you are in customer relations with the Matson Shirt Company. Write a response to the complaint on pp. 288–89.

For Collaboration

13. You and some fellow students have become increasingly concerned about the noise level in the library on campus. You are all commuter students and depend on the library as a place to work between classes. You also must do your library research at busy hours; you can't wait for a late-evening lull. Plan a strategy for decreasing the noise level. As part of your plan, decide *who* should receive letters from your group about the problem (the director of the library? the dean of students? the student council president? the vice president-operations?). Then, write the letters, tailoring each to the appropriate reader.
14. You are the chairperson of the Academic Standards Committee at your university. With your committee, you need to draft a new letter to be sent to students who have been placed on academic probation. Academic probation means that they will have two semesters to raise their GPAs to 2.0, will be excluded from participation in intercollegiate sports and leadership positions in student organizations, and will be expected to take the steps necessary to improve their academic performance. Failure to improve in the time allotted may result in being dropped from the rolls of the college. Students on probation are urged to use the remediation resources of the college, the counseling center, and the tutoring services.
    a. Indicate the goals of the letter you are planning to write in a brief list.
    b. Write the letter either in your group or individually. If you write as individuals, then meet to agree on one final text.

16 CUSTOMIZED LETTERS TO PERSUADE

What's Ahead

ESTABLISHING COMMON GROUND
SELLING
- Know What You Are Selling
- Know the Reader You Are Selling It To
- Show Why the Reader Needs What You Are Selling
- Treat the Reader Ethically

PLANNING THE SALES LETTER: THE AIDA APPROACH
- Attention
- Interest
- Desire
- Action

WRITING THE SALES LETTER
WRITING A PERSUASIVE INVITATION
REQUESTING A RESPONSE TO A QUESTIONNAIRE
ASKING FOR A LETTER OF RECOMMENDATION
WRITING A LETTER OF RECOMMENDATION
WRITING LETTERS WITH COMPLEX INFORMATION
SUMMARY
EXERCISES

Do You Know 

- What four guidelines should you consider in preparing a sales strategy?
- What is the AIDA plan, and how can it help you to structure a letter?
- What should you keep in mind when you need to make an invitation *persuasive?*
- What should you include in a letter of recommendation?

When Procter & Gamble launched Ace detergent in Mexico in the early 1950s, the local competition ran rings around it. The product had a low-suds formula that suited it well to American washing machines. But many Mexicans at that time washed clothes in the river or in a basin of water; an abundance of suds was the measure of a good soap.

"P&G assumed that what was good across the Rio Grande should be good here as well," says Claude Saloman, the general manager for P&G Mexico.[1] A change in the formula led to vastly increased sales. As did a change in the packaging: Instead of the large cardboard boxes common in the United States, P&G packages the soap in plastic bags (cheaper and better for keeping the soap dry) and in smaller units (100 grams—enough for one wash). Purchasers often shop every day; the small amount is easy to carry and doesn't require a large expenditure at any one time.

To sell a product or service, you have to know your customer. Put another way: You can *buy* in any language; you *sell* in the language of the market. This chapter discusses letters that customize an approach to the reader.

ESTABLISHING COMMON GROUND

As you read in Chapters 14 and 15, you use a routine approach to letter writing when your self-interest and that of the reader overlap, when the business situation is a standard one, and when the information is uncomplicated and unemotional. Orders are placed and sales completed, information is requested and answers supplied—every day. Such transactions are completed routinely, often over the phone or in the direct, unfussy letters you saw in Chapter 14.

However, when there is a *distance* in interests and purposes between writer and reader, or when the information is complex, you may need to customize your approach. That distance may be cultural, as in the P&G example or in the letters you'll see in Figures 16–5 and 16–6. Or the distance

[1] Alecia Swasy, "Foreign Formula: Procter&Gamble Fixes Aim on Tough Market: The Latin Americans," *The Wall Street Journal,* 15 June 1990, p. 1.

may be simply one of style or imagination. Plan and write in a way that establishes a common purpose and creates the desired action or understanding in the reader. In the rest of this chapter, you will see first how to develop an approach in a letter that sells the reader on a product, an idea, or an action. Then you will learn a customized approach to dealing with complex information.

SELLING

When your purpose is to *persuade,* plan your approach in a way that establishes a common ground with your reader and gains the reader's compliance in purchasing your product or acting in the way you request.

Follow these strategies:

1. Know what you are selling.
2. Know the reader you are selling it to.
3. Show why the reader needs what you are selling.
4. Treat the reader ethically.

Know What You Are Selling

Clarify your idea or product and your goal. That selling is an *art* signals the intangible quality of being able to see a product in itself as well as from someone else's point of view. Remember the bank safe company in Chapter 2. When they thought of their product as *safes,* they faced a shrunken market. When they thought of their business as *bank support,* that market broadened to encourage them to produce a new item: automatic teller machines. When P&G thought of its product as a low-suds detergent, they cut out Mexico. A reformulation opened a new market. Analyze the product you have. Measure it against the competition; elaborate on special features; figure out what's newsworthy about it. Then imagine what the product could be.

Know the Reader You Are Selling It To

The potential for your product may reveal itself best when you consider target markets. Move back and forth between these first two steps. In the information-gathering phase, get demographic information about the market: gender, age, occupations, income, education, and the like. Find out its psychographics, too: its values, beliefs, and attitudes; its activities and its ambience. Too narrow a concept of the market may hinder effective sales.

Show Why the Reader Needs What You Are Selling

This is the trickiest step. You have to convert information about the *product* into a sales strategy for the *customer.* There is no mysterious formula. That's another reason why selling is an art. You need to find or develop an interest in the reader for something you have an interest in selling. In the rest of this chapter, you'll see how several writers found or created that interest. The approach requires imagination. It also requires self-control against unethical manipulation of the reader, as you'll see shortly.

Treat the Reader Ethically

When you write to sell a product or to encourage the reader toward some action, remember once more the simple measure of ethical behavior: In all your dealings, leave other people at least as well off as they were before. Remember, too, the guidelines for ethical letters in Chapter 13: Be honest, value the reader's time, use the reader's code, and consider the reader's self-interest, that is, the reader's *appropriate* self-interest. In creating a false desire for a product, heavy-handed sales campaigns may entice and then trap a reader. The stereotypical supersalesperson is someone who can sell air-conditioning to residents of Antarctica, that is, someone who can *create* a desire where there is no real need. Avoid such unethical manipulation.

PLANNING THE SALES LETTER: THE AIDA APPROACH

Sales letters consume a good deal of money and attention, particularly in the United States, where direct-mail campaigns fill mailboxes in homes and offices every day. Unless you have managed to remove your name from every list, you probably receive such letters. The letters sell magazines, insurance, credit cards, photography services, seminars, and the like. They sell colleges to high school seniors and continuing education courses to professionals. The letters aid consumers in finding out about a range of products and services—*if* they are honest and accurate and deliver what they promise.

Direct mail is a highly specialized business whose products can provide tips for writing the less glossy letters that you are more likely to write more of the time. Check your mailbox. One four-part plan you'll see in many of the sales letters you find in the box is the AIDA approach: attention, interest, desire, action.

Attention

You cannot convey your message, of course, unless the reader *reads* the message. You gain attention with something familiar to the reader. That point of familiarity may be an earlier purchase (thus, as you saw in Chapter 14 and will see again in this chapter, thank you notes often turn into sales letters). It may also be an appeal to the reader's membership in an elite group. One direct-mail letter begins, "Are you one of the new breed of powerboat captains?" Presumably, you'd like to consider yourself one of the elite "new breed."

Fund-raising organizations often ask individuals to write to their neighbors or colleagues to build credibility and thus engage the reader's attention. That same approach, by the way, operates in the network of home sales for such products as clothes, vitamins, and household equipment. You're more likely to listen to—and buy from—someone you know and trust.

The attention getter may appeal to the reader's emotions: nostalgia about shared days in college at the beginning of an appeal for the alumni fund, shared fear about the deterioration of the environment in an appeal for contributions to a wilderness society, or pride in the possibility of owning a new powerboat. "You may already have won!" on an envelope has encouraged many readers to open that envelope and get into the message.

Glenn McAllister, President, Citibank (Maine) N.A., begins a letter about the United Way to local businesspeople with this attention getter:[2]

```
Seeing clearly and straight talking are personal qualities I
see every day in Maine people.
```

Interest

McAllister follows up on his theme of clear sight and straight talk in the next paragraph to create *interest* in the reader:

```
On a crisp fall day in Maine, we can see clearly for miles.
But sometimes it's harder to see things close at hand: chil-
dren in need, families in crisis, or a lonely elderly person.
```

The interest segment introduces the benefits—to the reader or, as in this letter, to society.

Desire

With the reader's interest awakened, the next segment provides more detailed evidence. In it, you line up the argument to predispose the reader to agree to the action you will request. McAllister's letter creates a desire to contribute with these concrete examples:

```
Straight talking . . . there are people who need help in our
community, and the United Way needs your help to do something
about it. I believe this is the best way to personally make a
difference. That's because the United Way systematically
identifies critical community needs, ensuring that your con-
tribution will go where it's needed most. Preventing child
abuse, caring for the elderly, counseling teens against sub-
stance abuse, sheltering homeless families--these and dozens
more vital services will be made possible by your contribu-
tion to the United Way.
```

Action

Finally, close the sale. Identify clearly what decision or action you want the reader to take. Make the action easy. Set deadlines, too, that encourage prompt action, lest the reader forget. In his letter, after noting that he will be sending the reader further material about the United Way, including pledge cards, McAllister closes:

[2] Letter courtesy of Glenn McAllister.

```
Remember what our community has given to you, and please con-
sider giving back generously.
```

WRITING THE SALES LETTER

To see further examples of the AIDA plan in action, look at Figures 16–1 and 16–2. Jon Bailey, the author of the letter in Figure 16–1, sells pet food door to door. He thought at first that the organic and scientifically balanced diet his pet food provided was his greatest selling point. He drafted a letter on that basis when he took over the company's delivery service. But the more he looked at his customer base, the more he realized that *delivery* was his chief appeal. He also realized that most of his customers are elderly. Younger people tend to buy their pet food in grocery stores; handling 20- or 30-pound packages is not a problem for them. It *is* a problem for the elderly.

His letter, then, focuses (but not exclusively) on an elderly audience: The pet food is delivered *for free,* and they can save on large orders without having to heft them. That focus is reflected in the discount for customers over 65. He originally thought of beginning his letter this way:

```
If you are over 65 you can save on food for your pet!
```

But that seemed unnecessarily discriminatory. He felt it was more important to reaffirm his own credibility in the opener as someone who was caring—about people and pets. That approach acknowledges a side issue of home delivery: security. To provide a service, he needs to enter the houses and place the bags of food in the appropriate storage space. That won't work if people are afraid of him. Moreover, he recognized on his first round of visits that many current and potential customers were housebound and might look forward to his visit. So the letter takes a personal approach in saying that he enjoyed meeting them and looks forward to a continuing relationship.

Figure 16–2 also follows up on an earlier contact; it thanks a current subscriber while soliciting a further contribution to public radio and television. The photographs taken from popular programs gain the reader's attention. Short paragraphs that detail the importance of the subscriber's contribution develop interest. The naming of programs and reference to *Applause* magazine create desire. The final appeal is underlined; the station eases the reader's path to contributing by enclosing a WHYY-addressed envelope.

WRITING A PERSUASIVE INVITATION

The AIDA approach is obvious when you are soliciting a contribution or selling a product or service. It may also be appropriate for other kinds of requests and other kinds of sales. How can you sell someone, for example, on agreeing to give a talk when that talk will take time and energy—and especially when you can't pay the speaker? The unsuccessful letter of invitation on page 306 gets the information off the writer's chest. But it's written strictly from the *writer's* point of view. The beginning is flat—and probably of little interest to the reader. The logistical details come *before* the reader has

7 October 1991

Dear Customer:

Attention

We're eager to serve you and your pet!

The top-quality Canine Caterers food products and supplies you have come to rely on will now be delivered to you with even greater savings by Pet Care Caterers, your exclusive home delivery service.

Interest

We'd like you to know that the following remain unchanged:

- Regular, dependable, free home delivery
- In-house charge accounts
- Handsome gift certificates for your friends
- Expert, professional nutritional advice

In addition, we would like to introduce you to the following new benefits:

Desire

- 5% discount for any pet owner over the age of 65 with a purchase of $25 or more a month
- Acceptance of all manufacturer's authorized coupons for all products that we carry
- 5% discount for the purchase of 100–300 pounds of dry pet food
- 10% discount for the purchase of more than 300 pounds of dry pet food
- Monthly specials

Action

Fill in the enclosed product list for October and call me with your order today. I'll begin delivery immediately and bill you next month. If you need a product that is not on the list, call anyway. The list is too short to cover all the products we carry--and we keep adding products as you suggest them.

We've enjoyed meeting you and your pets and look forward to continuing our service as Pet Care Caterers, your total pet care supplier.

Sincerely,

PET CARE CATERERS, INC.

Jon Bailey

Jon Bailey
President

FIGURE 16–1.
A sales letter. *(Courtesy of Jon Bailey.)*

TV12
WHYY
INDEPENDENCE MALL WEST
150 NORTH SIXTH STREET
PHILADELPHIA, PA 19106

Dear Subscriber,

Attention

Thanks!...for your support of TV12 during the past year.

Through your contribution, we were able to present an outstanding schedule of programs. Please accept the enclosed certificate as a sign of our appreciation.

Interest

Without your commitment and concern we simply couldn't exist -- your support makes possible the TV12 programs you enjoy every week.

Desire

Your subscription is coming up for renewal soon. Your renewed support today says "Yes!" to THE CIVIL WAR, MASTERPIECE THEATRE, WILD AMERICA, MYSTERY!, THE BRITISH COMEDIES, THE METROPOLITAN OPERA PRESENTS, NOVA, SESAME STREET, THE MACNEIL/LEHRER NEWSHOUR, NATURE, WALL $TREET WEEK, THIS OLD HOUSE and more.

And, you'll receive another full year of Applause, our attractive and informative program magazine. In addition to the program listings and repeat schedules, there are many interesting feature articles for you.

Action

Renew your commitment to the station you depend on for TV programming of uncommon quality and variety by returning your check in the enclosed envelope today.

We look forward to hearing from you.

Sincerely,

Willo Carey

Willo Carey
Director of Development

WC:kq

P.S. Please consider increasing your support this year.

THIS LETTER IS PRINTED ON RECYCLED PAPER.

FIGURE 16–2.
A letter soliciting a contribution. *(Used by permission of Willo Carey, Director of Development, WHYY Inc.)*

any reason for knowing them. They can only bore the reader. Moreover, the invitation itself is phrased in stuffy language ("We would like to extend an invitation") and is not specific. It provides no reason for the reader to feel engaged in reading and accepting the invitation; it's easy for the reader to say no.

The Unsuccessful Invitation

The student chapter of the American Management Association will hold its monthly meeting on Friday, January 6, in 206 Bennett Hall.

Refreshments will be served at 3:30, and then the meeting will begin at 4:00. We would like to extend an invitation to you to be the speaker at the meeting.

You could talk about any aspect of management you'd like.

Please let me know your decision as soon as possible.

Contrast that letter with the following one, which uses the AIDA plan. The student who wrote the letter shows his sensitivity to the professor's research interest and preference in cookies.

The Successful Invitation

When I asked at the December meeting of the student chapter of the American Management Association for suggestions concerning speakers in the new year, your name was at the top of the list.

Logically enough. Your classes are favorites. Now, we'd like to hear more--particularly about your work on the long-range plan for Yugoslavia that you keep hinting at in class.

Could you discuss that strategic planning process at our January meeting?

The meeting will be held in Bennett 206; refreshments (your favorite Oreos brought in just for the occasion) at 3:30; talk at 4:00.

I'll stop by during your office hours on Wednesday to learn your response (and twist your arm, if necessary).

REQUESTING A RESPONSE TO A QUESTIONNAIRE

As you collect data for a project, you often need to ask people to respond to a questionnaire. If the reader shares your interest in the results, a brief note may get you your response. But sometimes responding is not a matter of course; you need to *sell* the reader on responding. First, value the reader's time. Make the questionnaire itself short, unambiguous, physically easy to answer, and easy to return to you (see Chapter 9 for guidelines on creating questionnaires). Then, in the covering letter, appeal to whatever connects you and the reader and to the reader's self-interest. Note in particular the *voice* in Figure 16–3, which solicits a response to a questionnaire. The writer's own infusion of personality aims to engage the reader. Do you find it engaging?

ASKING FOR A LETTER OF RECOMMENDATION

While you are a student, and again perhaps after you've been out of college a year or two, you may write to a professor or a supervisor to ask for a letter of recommendation. You know the reader is busy; you want to set yourself up for a strongly positive recommendation (anything less is usually not effective). If you know the reader well, use a routine approach. Writing such letters may be a normal part of your reader's business day.

However, if you need to cover some distance—in time or lack of familiarity—with the reader, use the AIDA plan. Begin by reestablishing your identity in the reader's context; speak positively about the reader or what you've learned from him or her, to gain *attention:*

> In the two years since I took your organization and management behavior course in the fall semester of 199–, I've enjoyed putting the ideas you taught me into practice. I've really felt ahead of the game because of that class.

Then create an *interest* in yourself as related to the reader. Include a brief work history:

> I have been designing software systems for a small producer, Alfa Inc. Their major product is Alfabet, a file management system (don't blame me for the name). It's particularly targeted to small firms, like insurance brokerages, that handle a lot of paperwork.

The *desire* phase becomes trickier. How can you persuade someone to take the time to write a letter? You can't, of course, pay them—one way to accommodate a reader's desire under other circumstances. Instead, in such a letter, consider *your* future success a measure of the *professor's* success. Assume that he or she will want you to do well. Show that the letter will contribute to your advancement along a direction set in college:

> I've enjoyed my work at Alfa. But I'm ready to move into a job with greater diversity and more responsibility. I'm particularly attracted to a position at CompuTemps, a large software house in Vancouver, BC. The description seems to suit me (see the enclosed). I hope you'll agree.

Digital Equipment Corporation
Continental Boulevard
Merrimack, New Hampshire 03054-9987

digital™

Tereza Takile
Plimpton - Smith Inc.
6674 Skyline Drive
Salt Lake City, UT 84101

Dear Digital Computer User:

You've never heard of me, but frequently you hear from me. I'm the copywriter who pens many of the letters, brochures, and catalogs sent to you describing the products and services that complement your Digital computer system.

The purpose of this letter is to determine whether you wish to remain on the Digital Peripherals and Supplies mailing list. We don't want to annoy you with undesirable mail...material you may consider junk because you're plain not interested in the subject matter.

Frankly, we both lose if the mail is considered junk: we lose on printing and postage costs; you lose valuable time in poring through your business mail. So please do me a favor, and I'll do you one in return.

There's a questionnaire on the back of this letter. If you fill it out as completely as you can, and send it back to Digital in the reply envelope, I'll use the information to control what mail gets sent to you in the future.

The more I know about your system...and you... the better job I'll do. Take your title. It's important because it tells me something about your "system connection." A systems manager has one set of interests, a data communications manager a different set, a programmer yet another... and so forth. If I know your title, and it accurately characterizes your interest, you'll receive only relevant information from me.

Is it a deal? Hope so. Otherwise, I'll keep sending you junk mail and you'll keep tossing it.

Sincerely,

Your copywriter correspondent
at Digital Equipment Corporation

P.S. Please don't toss this questionnaire. My job depends on the number of returns. Thanks.

FIGURE 16–3.
A persuasive letter requesting information and enclosing a questionnaire. *(Copyright, Digital Equipment Corporation 1987. All rights reserved. Used by permission.)*

Finally, state the *action* you seek. Clarify the logistics: where to send the letter, to whom, and by what date. Balance insistence and excessive modesty; don't provide a lazy reader with an excuse, but don't force someone who is lukewarm toward you to write anyway. Note your follow-up to confirm the reader's decision concerning the letter:

```
    If you agree, I hope you'll write me a letter of recom-
mendation. I've enclosed a copy of my current resume, along
with a brief statement of my goal in this position. Please
send the letter to:

    Antonio P. Brizzolara
    Personnel Director
    CompuTemps Inc.
    100 Fleming St.
    Vancouver, BC V5P 3G2

    Could you also please write before December 12? I'll un-
derstand if your schedule does not permit you to write at
this time. But your word would carry a lot of weight with
CompuTemps. I'll call you next week to see if you have any
questions about my request.

    Thanks for any assistance you can give me as I try to put
what I learned at State into practice.
```

WRITING A LETTER OF RECOMMENDATION

Although a letter of recommendation is a fairly routine document that aims to *inform* the reader about a candidate, usually the recommender wraps that goal within a more important goal of persuading the reader to hire (or promote) the individual. To write a *negative* letter of recommendation is a contradiction in terms.

A solicited letter of recommendation is thus always positive. The chief problem in such letters is that the writer's enthusiasm may not translate into something convincing to a reader. Writing about people often bogs down in abstractions ("dependable, responsible, sincere, honest, forthright, kind to animals, gets along great with people"). The abstractions fail everyone. The writer is shown to be uninsightful, the person the letter is about remains in the shadows, and the reader doesn't get the information he or she needs to make a decision.

In the letter, you'll need to establish your own credibility first—if that is not already known to the reader. Discuss how long and in what capacity you have known the person. Establish criteria for your evaluation (or use any criteria given in the form requesting the recommendation), and measure the person against those criteria. Your own credibility is enhanced—and the person's case strengthened—when you write well. Convince with concrete, picturable evidence.

If you are asked by a third party to *evaluate* someone, then your oral report or letter may balance negative and positive information or may even concentrate on the negative. (Chapter 24 discusses personnel evaluations.) Although such letters have traditionally been held confidential, recent court actions have confirmed employee access to such records. For that reason, many companies telephone people listed as references.

The following is a letter of recommendation that evaluates the candidate against what the writer considers the standards for the fellowship (AAAS is the American Association for the Advancement of Science):

Announce the topic of the letter.

I am pleased to recommend John Phillips for the Mass Media/Science and Engineering Fellows program.

Show how long and in what capacity you have known the candidate.

Establish criteria for evalutions, and measure the candidate.

Mr. Phillips was my student in "Rhetoric for Business and Technical Writers," a course that examines the purposes and structure of writing in different disciplines, particularly in management, science, and engineering. We looked at how professionals communicate with each other and with the public. Mr. Phillips's work in the course was outstanding. Because of his background, first as an electrical engineering major and now in economics, he was comfortable with the technical content of the texts we read. But more than that, he was sensitive to the devices authors use to encapsulate technical information and convey it to various audiences.

Mr. Phillips is also a first-rate writer himself. In several papers concerned with technology and organizational structure in an office environment, he proved his ability to observe well, to select critical information from his readings, and to build a cogent, clear, and engaging discussion.

Measure the candidate against the criteria of the new position.

I am somewhat familiar with your program from discussions I've attended at AAAS meetings and from colleagues who are science journalists. John Phillips seems to me to fit well into the framework and goals you have established for the program. I recommend him highly.

Please call if I can provide any further information for you as you select candidates for the program.

WRITING LETTERS WITH COMPLEX INFORMATION

As the Director of Investor Relations at Hershey Foods Corporation, James A. Edris responds to many requests for information. In Figure 14–5, you saw one of his routine responses. In Figures 16–5 and 16–6 (pages 312–315), you see more customized responses to the more complex questions shown in Figure 16–4. Edris deals with cultural differences as well as differences in levels of understanding about economic systems in these letters sent to a professor and a student at the Academy of Economics in Wroclaw, Poland. He presents Hershey Foods in an honest and accurate as well as a positive light.

Jerzy Czupial

- How many of your workers are employed in R&D?
- Do they have their laboratories in every plant of the corporation or do they work in a special central unit/ laboratory, or division?
- How much does the Corporation spend for its R&D?
- Do you assess the profitability of this spending? If yes, what is the method of these assessments?
- Have you ever considered the possibility and profitability of joint venture operations with Polish firms?

Darek Garczynski

- How is the total amount of dividends determined?
- How is the corporation's net income divided?
- When is the decision to increase the dividend per share taken?
- Is the corporation interested in the stock market price of the common stock and Class B common stock and does it make any efforts to control the level of this price?
- What is happening with the restructuring of Hershey Foods?
- What's the role of the Research and Development staff and how do they work?
- Are there any unique products that are produced only by Hershey Foods (Hershey's kisses are lovely!)?
- What's the development program for employees about?
- When will Hershey's products be available in Poland?
- Is it possible to receive Hershey's 1989 Annual Report or other materials about Hershey Foods?

FIGURE 16–4.
Questions asked about Hershey Foods in letters from Jerzy Czupial, a faculty member, and Darek Garczynski, a student, at the Academy of Economics in Wroclaw, Poland.

Hershey Foods Corporation
Corporate Administrative Center
P.O. Box 814
Hershey, Pennsylvania 17033-0814
Phone: (717) 534-7552
Telex: 6711079 HERSH UW

JAMES A. EDRIS
Director, Investor Relations

March 23, 1990

Dr. Jerzy Czupial
ul. Prosta 2m. 15
53-509 Wroclaw, Poland

Dear Dr. Czupial:

Thank you very much for your recent letter and for your interest in Hershey Foods Corporation. We are glad you like our products. All of us in the United States have been following the events in your country with a great deal of interest. We wish you well in your endeavors to overhaul your economic system.

I may not be able to answer all your questions precisely, but I will do my best to give you meaningful answers.

1. There are approximately 200 people involved in the Corporation's research and development function. This includes a corporate engineering group. Most of these people are professionals with a university degree. Many are PhD's.

2. Our research and development efforts are centralized in a Corporate Technical Center which we opened in 1979. There are quality assurance laboratories in each plant, however, to test products to make sure we are delivering top quality. There is also a Corporate Quality Assurance Group which sets the standards and oversees the divisional efforts to assure quality through our Product Excellence Program (PEP).

3. In 1989 Hershey Foods spent $16.1 million on research and development. Please see footnote number 11 on page 35 of the enclosed 1989 Annual Report for a comparison with prior years' expenditures. By the way, our research and development expenditure in 1989 was .0066 of sales. Other food companies probably spend similar amounts whereas a pharmaceutical company, for example, would spend at a higher rate.

4. It is very difficult to measure the profitability of the total category because much of the R & D staff's work is done to support operating divisions. For instance it is difficult to measure the return on our quality assurance program, on the other hand we know intuitively that the cost of poor quality products would be devastating to our consumer franchise. One area where it would be easier to measure effectiveness is new product development. Here one could assess the

FIGURE 16–5.
A customized response to complex questions: James Edris's letter to Jerzy Czupial.
(Used with the permission of Hershey Foods Corporation.)

Page 2
Dr. Czupial

success rate and profitability of new products as they are introduced and establish a record of performance. Again it would be difficult to measure the efforts of the engineering group to formulate more efficient manufacturing processes except in the overall productivity measurement of the Corporation (Operating divisions have a target of productivity savings which are equal to at least one percent of sales annually).

5. We have only recently begun to look at the European market in a general sense and need to do a lot of homework before becoming involved there. Joint ventures are certainly attractive vehicles for establishing business relationships in a new market, and I am sure we will consider that a viable avenue for entry into European markets.

Hopefully my comments will be of some use to you. Good luck in your efforts. We certainly are living in exciting times.

Sincerely,

James Edris

James A. Edris

JAE/jmf

Enclosures

Hershey Foods Corporation
Corporate Administrative Center
P.O. Box 814
Hershey, Pennsylvania 17033-0814
Phone: (717) 534-7552
Telex: 6711079 HERSH UW

JAMES A. EDRIS
Director, Investor Relations

December 3, 1990

Darek Garczynski
ul. Sliczna 56/16
50550 Wroclaw
POLAND

Dear Mr. Garczynski:

Thank you for your recent letter and for your interest in Hershey Foods Corporation. It appears as if Mr. Minsker has been a good publicist for our company.

I shall attempt to answer your questions:

1. The dividend policy calls for the company to pay approximately one-third of its earnings to stockholders in the form of dividends. In recent years the dividend has ranged from 35 percent to 40 percent of our net income. We try to strike a balance between the needs of our stockholders for an adequate dividend payout and our need to reinvest in new equipment to keep our business growing.

2. Net income is divided by the total number of shares outstanding to determine earnings per share. $171,054,000 - 90,186,336 = $1.90 per share.

3. Over the last 15 years the dividend has been increased during the third quarter. Our Board of Directors normally considers the amount of the dividend at the August board meeting.

4. The Corporation is very interested in the price of its Common Stock because the market price determines the value of our company. While we cannot and should not control the price of our stock, we try to maximize the price through a program of consistent, appropriate information dissemination. We feel that investors should know as much as possible about the company (without giving away trade secrets or competitive information), so that their investment decisions are properly made.

5. Our restructuring is going very nicely. We are happy to be out of the restaurant business which has been declining in recent years due to too much supply and not enough demand (the market is saturated, that is, the U.S. has more restaurants than it has consumers). Our purchase of the U.S. operations of Peter Paul/Cadbury has gone very well. We have quickly integrated their operations into ours, and the operating margins have improved nicely, a bit ahead of schedule.

FIGURE 16–6.
Another customized letter: James Edris's response to Darek Garczynski. *(Used with the permission of Hershey Foods Corporation.)*

Mr. Darek Garczynski
Page 2

6. The role of our Research and Development Staff is varied and vital. They must make sure that none of our ingredients can be detrimental to the health of consumers, they must develop and test new products, they must help us continually improve the quality of our products, and they must help us work more efficiently to ensure greater profits. These profits help provide resources to reward shareholders for investing in our business as well as to reinvest in the continued growth of our business.

7. HERSHEY'S KISSES chocolates are the best example of a truly unique product. In September we introduced a new version of the KISS with an almond inside of it. That required a new technology to shell mould the KISS instead of dropping or depositing it on a metal sheet, as we do with the regular KISS.

8. The development program for employees takes many forms. There are in-house training programs for employees to gain new job skills. There are programs for managers to become better managers, there are programs for all employees to become more productive and more conscious of quality. There are also programs to reimburse tuition for people who want to get a university education, provided that the major course of study is business related, i.e. accounting, business administration, etc.

9. Currently we are trying to establish some form of business base in Western Europe. Hopefully as we become better established in the Common Market, we can become more involved in the Central European market. I guess it will take us as much as it takes to get a soccer team which can beat Italy in the World Cup tournament.

10. Enclosed are copies of our 1989 Annual Report, as well as recent quarterly reports, a financial fact book, and some graphs, which I hope you will find interesting and useful.

Thank you again for your interest in Hershey Foods Corporation. Good luck in the future.

Sincerely yours,

James Edris

James A. Edris

JAE/jmf

Enclosures

SUMMARY

- In establishing common ground with the reader in a sales strategy (1) **clarify** what you are **selling** and your goal; (2) **analyze the market** and find your target audience; (3) **show why** the reader needs what you are selling; and (4) **treat the reader ethically.** The product or service may take on new meanings when you consider different demographic groups as potential customers. The sales message should show how the audience's self-interest requires your product or service. That self-interest, however, should not be merely a manipulation of your own thinking.
- The **AIDA** plan can help you structure a sales letter. First, grab the reader's **attention.** You'll try to find some common ground with the reader to open on a familiar note, or you may otherwise appeal to the reader's emotions. Then, in the middle, provide the evidence that **interests** the reader. With that interest awakened, provide further details of the product's benefits to create a **desire** to buy. Finally, close by moving the reader to **action:** the decision to buy. The AIDA approach makes the sale both easy and inevitable (or so the writer hopes).
- When an invitation or other request is *routine*—when the function is a standard one and the reader is predisposed to accommodate you—use a routine approach. But when you are asking a favor, consider more **persuasive strategies. Engage** the reader's **self-interest. Interest** the reader. Use a **personal** and **appealing voice.**
- A **letter of recommendation** aims to persuade the reader to hire or promote the subject of the letter. It builds the case. First, establish your own credibility if that's necessary and show how long and in what capacity you have known the candidate. Then **establish criteria** for your evaluation and measure the person against those criteria. Your own credibility is enhanced—and the person's case strengthened—when you write well.

EXERCISES

For Discussion

1. Here are several opening paragraphs of letters. Each is at best flat. Some actually may create resistance in the reader when the opening should, as we have seen, create a connection with the reader. Discuss other ways of starting these letters.
    a. Could you please send me copies of the costume and property plots that you devised last spring for Angels Academy's production of Cole Porter's *Anything Goes?*
    b. [In a letter to the university registrar] The present process of registering for classes is aggravating for both the students and the faculty. With the input of the student body, the registration process may be made simpler, which would serve to benefit the university itself. Please fill in the enclosed questionnaire.
    c. My name is Mindy Jones.
2. Collect the direct-mail letters and other advertisements you receive over several weeks and bring them to class. In class, analyze the letters to see if they use the AIDA plan or some variant of it. How do the letters open?

What connection does the writer make with the reader? What benefits are shown? What details are provided to support the reader's interest? You might also bring in the *envelopes,* as the appeal often begins there.

3. Here are three sales-oriented form letters used by the insurance agency whose routine correspondence you saw in Chapter 14, Exercise 2. Letters A and B below apply a more obvious selling technique to two standard business occasions. Letter A resells the customer who has purchased insurance coverage. Letter B uses a note of congratulations to introduce the agency. Letter C is a follow-up after attempts to phone have failed (note the AIDA approach in this letter). Do you think the letters work?

LETTER A

Thank you for placing your ____________ insurance coverage with Thompson Insurance.

We appreciate the trust you have placed in us. Thompson is committed to giving you the finest service available. Please contact us immediately should you need any support and/or service.

You can reach any of us between the hours of 9:00 A.M. to 4:30 P.M., Monday through Friday. We're proud of our staff. We think you'll see why as they provide the service that we promised you.

Again, we thank you for your business and look forward to working with you.

LETTER B

Congratulations on your decision to go into business as ____________.

We're sure you did some careful planning before you made your move. Insurance planning is also important to your success. That's where Thompson Insurance is ready to serve you.

Thompson Insurance is a successful full-service agency. We offer a wide range of insurance coverages and services. We know our business. Our clients understand that when we work, we work for them.

You can be assured that Thompson Insurance will work hard for you. We'll call to arrange an appointment, or if you prefer, you can call us--right away.

LETTER C

We're not trying to keep up with the Joneses--we're trying to keep up with you, to assure you the best coverage possible!

We know you are a busy individual because we've been trying to reach you to discuss a matter which can directly affect your personal situation, especially your home's insurance. We would like to discuss these questions with you:

- How can you make sure your insurance coverage realistically reflects the current value of your house and possessions?
- How much money can you save on your insurance premiums if you install smoke detectors and/or home security devices?
- How can the changes in your children's ages and even the type of cars you own affect your insurance premiums?

The Thompson Insurance Agency would be happy to provide you with answers to these questions and any other issues regarding your personal insurance which may concern you. Just fill in and return the enclosed postage-paid card, and I will get right back to arrange a meeting that's most convenient for you. Or, if you prefer, you can call me directly at Thompson Insurance: 555-1122.

For Writing

4. Revise the following letter and questionnaire. You'll see many problems in approach, in organization, in the writer's voice; and in sentence structure, capitalization, punctuation, and spelling. Use your understanding of letters gained from Chapters 13, 14, 15, and 16, and the Handbook at the back of the book to analyze and revise.

Attention: Spanish Department Chairperson

As a communications major, I am interested in studying ways to improve communication problems between cultures. A problem that language departments are concerned with everyday.

In an effort to help study the problem, I am doing a report on the difficulties that occur between american culture and various other cultures. Will you please give me your opinion on the interactional problems between spanish culture and american culture.

I have enclosed a questionnaire with some general questions. Any other opinions would be greatly appreciated. Your input would be a great help and very useful in the study of improving intercultural communication.

QUESTIONS

1. What values are most important to the spanish culture?
2. In a spanish culture, what are the most annoying things that americans do in a conversation (if any)?
3. What would you say is the general attitude of Americans when in a spanish culture?
4. Are there any major differences in the communication habits between spanish and american culture? If so, please explain.
5. What do you feel is most important to remember when in a communication exchange between americans and the spanish?
6. Is there anything that you would like to add?

5. You've been employed in an entry-level job for two years after graduation from college. Now you're ready to move on. Write a letter to a former professor asking him or her to write a letter of recommendation for you.
6. As the secretary of a campus organization, write a persuasive letter to invite someone to speak to your group. Note why you are writing to that individual. Assume the reader is not familiar with your group, so describe it briefly. Provide information on logistics and expenses.
7. The son of a friend of your mother is interested in working for the company where you work. He is a marketing major in college and someone the company would be strongly interested in hiring. *Sell* the company to the individual. Describe its advantages: the people who work there, the working conditions, the location, the benefits, and the like.

For Collaboration

8. You and some friends have decided to start a painting company part time while you attend school and in the summers. You'll do both exterior and interior painting of residences. In a group, write a sales letter and design a flyer that you'll distribute in your neighborhood soliciting business. Give your company a name. Develop a theme and a major selling point: your rates, your experience, your caring attitude, whatever. Develop follow-up letters to send after you visit homes to give estimates.
9. As a group project, devise a sales strategy for some organization. You may use a real organization you are familiar with, for example, a campus group. Or work with a public-service agency that might like your assistance in putting together a fund-raising campaign. If you have corporate experience, devise a strategy for a real or imagined product or service. Define your target market population. Develop a series of letters or brochures establishing your central sales point and backing it with evidence. Remember: Know your product, know your reader, show why the reader needs the product, and treat the reader ethically. If you have access to a computer graphics package, incorporate both visual and verbal elements.

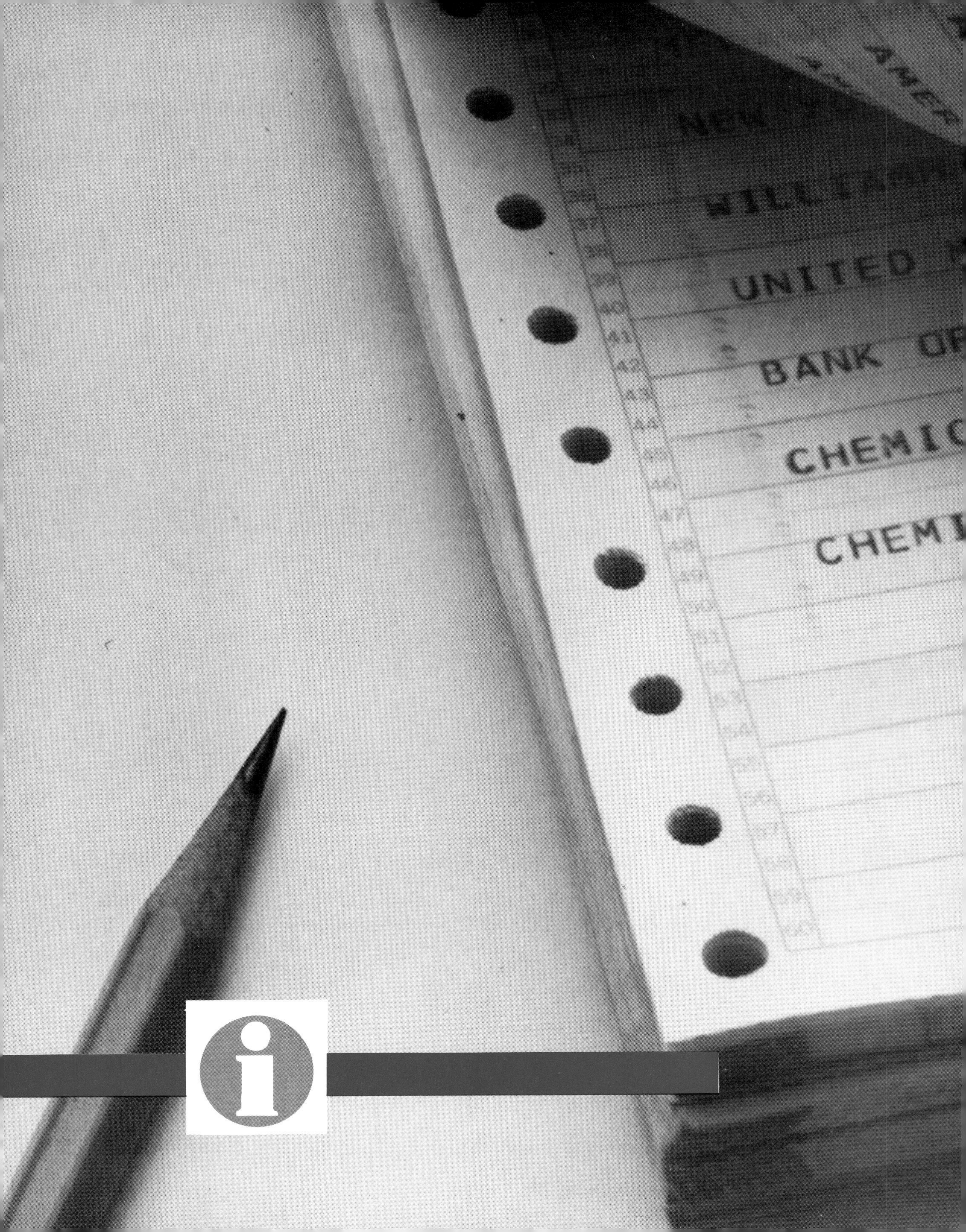
NEW
UNITED
BANK

PART IV

PROPOSALS AND REPORTS

17 Bids and Proposals
18 Elements of Business Reporting
19 Formal Reports

INTRODUCTION TO PART IV

When businesspeople talk about reports, they cover a lot of territory. The root meaning of the term *report* is simple: "to carry back." *Reporters* carry back messages to the people who need them, often at regular intervals. They provide accounts based on observations and investigations.

The simple act of reporting, however, has given rise to a variety of forms of reports. Reports can be conveyed orally or in writing. Written ones can be conveyed on paper or electronically. Reports appear as memos or letters or in full dress: text bound in a cover and surrounded by special elements. Reports may thus extend for one page or many. They may be written by one author—or many; they may be read by one reader—or many.

The concept of carrying *back* messages also points to a cycle of reporting in which some people request information and others provide it. When people in an organization identify a problem, that problem triggers an investigation to find a solution. As you will see, complex investigations are *documented*: in a proposal that sets the plan, in progress reports that monitor the work, and in a formal report that incorporates the answer. In Chapter 17 you will learn how to analyze an organizational problem, how to design an investigation into solving that problem, and how to write a proposal to present that plan to a supervisor, client, or sponsor of research.

In Chapters 18 and 19, you will learn how to write reports: the routine reports that are the stuff of everyday life in an organization and the customized reports that respond to more extensive one-of-a-kind investigations. To write reports, you will need to call on all the strategies you learned as you read Part II of this textbook:

- Planning writing tasks and structuring the report (Chapter 4)
- Wording your material in a voice that suits the occasion and the readers (Chapter 5)
- Presenting appropriate material visually (Chapter 6)
- Revising and designing the report (Chapter 7)
- Accessing and interpreting the business information which is the content of the report (Chapters 8 and 9)
- Writing and disseminating reports electronically (Chapter 10)
- Writing collaboratively (Chapter 11)

The following chapters make frequent cross-references to Part II. In writing a report, you apply all those techniques learned and practiced separately in earlier chapters.

17 BIDS AND PROPOSALS

What's Ahead

SOLVING BUSINESS PROBLEMS
REQUEST FOR BID
BIDS
- Guidelines for Solicited Bids

INVESTIGATIONS: PROBLEMS OF FACT, MEANS, VALUE
- Problem of Fact: Informative Report
- Problem of Means: Interpretive Report
- Problem of Value: Persuasive Report

REQUEST FOR PROPOSAL
PROPOSALS: A CASE STUDY
STRATEGIES FOR PROPOSALS
- Clearly Identify the Problem
- Describe a Reasonable Approach to Solving the Problem
- Show that You Can Carry Out the Proposed Approach
- Present One Clear Message

THE STRUCTURE OF PROPOSALS
- FYI: Proposal Writing
- Introduction
- Problem Statement
- Objectives
- Solution
- Justification
- Budget

SUMMARY
EXERCISES

Do You Know 

- What kinds of problems do businesses need to solve, and what role does communication play in solving them?
- What are bids, and what kind of business problems do they solve?
- What kinds of investigations are carried out to help businesses solve problems?
- What are proposals, and what kind of business problems do they solve?
- How do you prepare proposals?
- How do you structure proposals?

''Don't give me problems. Give me solutions.''

Businesspeople face many problems, but they prefer solutions. The boss who instructs subordinates to provide solutions rather than problems expresses this preference. Identifying problems and finding solutions to them are common and routine business functions—so much a part of the job that few people explicitly label and consider what they are doing. Sometimes, however, the process of problem solving is made formal and carried out through written documents. Four documents that businesses use to solve problems are discussed in this chapter:

Request for bid (RFB)
Bid
Request for proposal (RFP)
Proposal

As the name implies, a *request for bid* leads to a *bid,* which is an offer to supply a good or service at a specified price. A *request for proposal* leads to a *proposal,* which is an offer to undertake an investigation that will solve a problem. The immediate outcome of a proposal is a report that presents the solution.

To write any of these documents, you must understand the role each serves in solving business problems. You therefore need to understand the nature and types of problems businesses encounter. Reports are tools for problem solving. You will see in this chapter that reports, especially customized reports that solve specific problems, originate in proposals.

SOLVING BUSINESS PROBLEMS

Some problems can be solved directly. Recall the example in Chapter 2 of the student who was cold because the window was open. She could simply get up and close the window—a direct response. However, few business problems lend themselves to such direct solutions. Working with others to meet organizational goals requires you to communicate to solve most problems. Even reasonably direct solutions often call for some communication with others.

Table 17–1 classifies business problems into four types according to what is known about the problem, the solution, and the method of getting from problem to solution. Different outcomes result from different combinations. For example, when both the problem and the solution are known and the method of solution is at hand, you take direct action: You simply implement the solution. All the other types of problems, as you can see in the "Outcome" column, require some form of communication.

If both the problem and the solution are known, but you cannot carry out the solution, the required communication is a request for bid, in which you solicit one or several others to provide the solution. You know what needs to be done or provided, but you want someone else to do it. For example, if you run out of drawers for filing correspondence (problem), and you decide that you want another filing cabinet (solution), you ask a supplier to quote a price for the desired model (request for bid). He or she does so (bid). When you purchase and install the filing cabinet, the problem is solved. Specific suggestions on writing RFBs and bids are given below.

Problems solved through the bidding procedure are relatively easy. More interesting are those that require investigations. When you investigate a business problem, the solution comes through a report, but the process starts with a request for proposal and then a proposal. This type of problem is one of the most challenging in business practice and is discussed in detail later in this chapter.

REQUEST FOR BID

Some problems do not require investigations because the solution is known. When this is so, you turn to someone else to provide the solution. You issue a request for bid. An RFB might seek

- A new copier for the accounting department.
- An improved benefits package for employees.
- A service contract for maintaining rotors on the navy's helicopter fleet.

TABLE 17–1
Business Problems Classified

Problem	Solution	Method of Solution	Outcome
Known	Known	Available	Action: implement solution
Known	Known	Unavailable	RFB, leading to bid
Known	Unknown		RFP, followed by solicited proposal offering investigation
Unknown			You may receive an unsolicited proposal offering an investigation

The RFB must specify

- The item or service sought, including as many details as possible.
- Price constraints if any.
- The time when the good or service must be available or installed.
- Details about the bidding process (to whom the bid is to be submitted, when, and where).
- An offer to answer questions or supply additional information about requirements.

Government agencies, which purchase most goods and services through competitive bidding, have elaborate forms, procedures, and even staffs to carry out this function. Large corporations are similar, but even in some of those—and certainly in small firms—preparing an RFB falls to the individual who needs the good or service to solve a business problem. Figure 17–1 presents a sample RFB from a consulting firm in Scotland.

BIDS

Responding to a bid requires careful attention to the specific requests made in the RFB. All items must be addressed. Additional information, if relevant, can be supplied, but it is critical to answer all questions or requests posed in the RFB. If you are uncertain, always seek clarification.

In some cases bids are *unsolicited.* That is, they are not prepared in response to a specific RFB but are sent to a firm because you want to sell a good or service. Unsolicited bids are similar to sales letters (see Chapter 16). If your bid is unsolicited, you have to make a special effort to get the reader's attention and to sell *the problem.* Whereas the recipient of a *solicited* bid already recognizes the problem, someone receiving an *unsolicited* bid first needs to be told that she or he has a problem that the bid is designed to solve.

Guidelines for Solicited Bids

When you respond to a request for bid, you must

1. Be responsive to the recipient's needs by answering all questions, explicit or implicit.
2. Structure information strategically to ensure ease of access.
3. Verify the accuracy of all numbers.
4. Use an appropriate format to achieve a neat and polished appearance.
5. Explicitly justify substitutions.

1. **Be responsive to the recipient's needs by answering all questions, explicit or implicit.** Ignoring any aspect of the RFB signals lack of concern or simple carelessness, neither of which improves your chances of acceptance.

2. **Structure information strategically to ensure ease of access.** Tables, graphs, and other visuals are especially helpful, particularly in presenting

Sylvan Associates
198 The Broadway
Edinburgh EH9 3JG
Telephone 031-662-4593

1 February 199-

Request for Bids for Travel Services

Sylvan Associates, a management consulting practice employing 35 professionals, seeks to contract with a travel agent to handle all corporate travel arrangements and ticketing. Travel expenditures are currently £300,000 yearly, and we anticipate growth of 10% a year over the next five years.

The firm we contract with will be our exclusive agent for air, car, and hotel bookings and will be expected to provide fast service at the lowest possible rates. The firm must deliver tickets directly to Sylvan, often on very short notice.

To be considered for selection as Sylvan's exclusive travel agent, please send a written bid containing the following:

1. Firm history, number of employees, annual billings.
2. Corporate clients currently served (with contact name and phone number).
3. Specific details of making arrangements and delivering tickets.
4. Fees.

Bids must be received at our corporate office (attention Leslie Arrows; Fax: 031-662-8876) by Friday, 18 February 199-. Questions may be addressed to Ms. Arrows.

FIGURE 17–1.
A request for bid.

price information. Visuals may well carry the central message, with text to explain or qualify.

3. **Verify the accuracy of all numbers.** Because bids are essentially price quotations, you must make sure that all numbers are right and add up. Many bids fail simply because the arithmetic is wrong.

4. **Use an appropriate format to achieve a neat and polished appearance.** Neatness promotes ease of access and reinforces your image as a professional. If a format for response is specified (as usually occurs in government bidding), follow it scrupulously. If none is specified, follow the form

used by your organization. (Information on memo and letter formats is given in Chapters 12 and 13 and on report format in Chapter 18.)

5. **Explicitly justify substitutions.** If what you offer differs in any way from what is requested, explain why the substitution is better in quality, price, or both. Recognize that your response is not direct, and explain why what you offer is superior to what was requested.

INVESTIGATIONS: PROBLEMS OF FACT, MEANS, VALUE

When you face a business problem for which you don't know the solution, the bidding procedure will not work. You need to have someone investigate the problem to identify the best solution. Such an investigation calls for a request for proposal. To understand how to write an RFP and how to respond to one as the writer of a proposal, you need to know what sort of investigation is required to solve the problem at hand. Problems requiring investigation can be classified according to what you need to find out to solve them:

- Some require you to find out *what*. These are problems of *fact*.
- Some require you to find out *why* or *how*. These are problems of *means*.
- Some require you to find out the *best* way. These are problems of *value*.

Each type of problem leads to a different type of investigation, requires different types of information, and results in a different report. Some examples follow.

Problem of Fact: Informative Report

The sales manager of the Niblex Company wants to know the sales of its salted snacks (pretzels, chips, and nuts) in the United Kingdom, Germany, and Japan. This is a *what* problem, a problem of *fact*. Your investigation requires you to obtain facts: the relevant sales data. The result is an *informative report*, presented as a simple table:

Sales of Salted Snacks for 199- (in Units)

	Pretzels	Chips	Nuts	Total
U.K.	50,000	65,000	38,000	153,000
Germany	52,000	60,000	44,000	156,000
Japan	21,000	18,000	10,000	49,000

Problem of Means: Interpretive Report

Assume that when the sales manager sees the report, she asks *why* sales are better in the U.K. and Germany than in Japan. You must now deal with a problem of *means*. Your investigation goes beyond facts to interpretations and opinions (see Chapter 8). You may seek more facts first, for example, on production, distribution, advertising, the sales of other brands, national preferences, and price. You may do market surveys of consumer interests and price sensitivity in making snack purchases. From all this information you draw inferences; you explain. You write an *interpretive* report. Let us say that you conclude that U.K. and German sales are higher than Japanese sales because other brands also sell better in those two countries; in other words, there is higher overall consumption of salty snacks in the U.K. and Germany than in Japan. The reason, you conclude, is that national tastes in Japan don't favor salty foods and national customs don't include snacking.

Problem of Value: Persuasive Report

A third type of investigation now arises because the sales manager, reading your interpretive report, agrees with your conclusion but asks, "How can we improve sales in Japan?" She has raised a *value* problem: What's the *best* way to do something?

You use the facts and interpretations from your first two reports, but now you make a recommendation, for example: Through advertising try to persuade the Japanese to try pretzels, chips, and nuts to add a new dimension to their taste. You write a *persuasive* report in which information is used actively, to support a recommendation.

The kind of investigation you pursue, the kinds of information you use, and the kind of report that results from the investigation depend on the problem to be solved. If you understand the difference among problems of fact, problems of means, and problems of value, you can shape the investigation at the beginning to produce the right answer to the problem at hand.

REQUEST FOR PROPOSAL

You solicit an investigation through a request for proposal, which identifies the problem. A solicited proposal is written in response to an RFP. It outlines the investigation that will lead to solving the problem. A report, based on the proposed investigation, presents the suggested solution.

Figure 17–2 presents a request for proposal, sent in letter form, to several insurance brokers.

PROPOSALS: A CASE STUDY

Jennifer Friedman, of Reimbursement Services, received the letter in Figure 17–2 and called Simpkins. The letter itself, although formally a request for proposals, is intentionally quite general. Simpkins thought it would be useful to announce his company's desire to review its health care program to several brokers and then respond with more details in individual phone conversations with those who expressed interest. After her conversation with Simpkins, Friedman responded with the proposal presented in Figure 17–3 (page 331).

As you can see, JFS Manufacturing has a problem to which it does not

JFS Manufacturing Company
3645 West Broad Street
Camden, NJ 09064

26 October 199-

Dear <broker's name>:

JFS Manufacturing Company would like to improve its health care program for employees. Rising costs and growing employee complaints about inefficiency have caused us to consider changing our plan.

If you would like to review our current program and offer alternatives to meet our need for cost containment and improved efficiency, please phone me to discuss the services you can provide.

Sincerely,

James Simpkins, Sr.

James Simpkins, Sr.

FIGURE 17–2.
A request for proposal.

know the answer. Through a request for proposal it seeks help: an investigation that will lead to a solution. Friedman responds with a proposal: an offer to study the problem and recommend a solution. Notice that the first four steps under "Procedure" require the collection and analysis of information. These constitute the investigation. The fifth step is the presentation of the results in a report that reviews the results of the investigation and makes recommendations based on it.

STRATEGIES FOR PROPOSALS

Jennifer Friedman prepared a proposal that would lead to an investigation and report. She followed four strategies for effective proposal writing:

1. Clearly identify the problem.
2. Describe a reasonable approach to solving the problem.

REIMBURSEMENT SERVICES

P.O. Box 74
Moorestown, NJ 08057
609-636-3588

1 November, 199-

James Simpkins, Sr.
JFS Manufacturing Company
3645 West Broad Street
Camden, NJ 09064

Dear Mr. Simpkins:

I enjoyed our telephone conversation yesterday concerning the trouble you are having with the benefits program at JFS. The enclosed brief statement shows how Reimbursement Services can improve the package to benefit both you and your employees.

The proposal outlines the specific services we offer and indicates our experience. It also provides a schedule of activities we would conduct for you.

Please feel free to phone me if you have questions about the proposal. I look forward to working with you.

Sincerely,

Jennifer Friedman

Jennifer Friedman
Benefits Counselor

Enclosure

FIGURE 17–3.
An insurance brokerage proposal. The cover letter. *(Courtesy of Jennifer Friedman.)*

3. Show that you can carry out the proposed approach—indeed, that you are the best organization to do so.
4. Present one clear message.

REIMBURSEMENT SERVICES

PROPOSAL FOR JFS MANUFACTURING COMPANY

Proposal

Reimbursement Services proposes to design an employee benefits program that fits the needs of the JFS Manufacturing Company and costs less than the plan currently in use.

Statement of Problem

In today's market, health care costs are continually on the rise. As a result, employee benefits programs are becoming more important to an organization's efforts to maintain the highest quality employees. Too often these benefits plans are not properly designed and are thus both too costly and of insufficient appeal to employees.

Objective

By first understanding your needs in a health care program, we can develop one that will be most beneficial for JFS Manufacturing. We will then search for this particular type of program at the least possible cost. In addition, we aim to improve the employer/employee relationship through our service of the program. We orient employers as well as employees to the new plan, assist with claims, and educate employees on how their benefits can best serve them.

Procedure

1. We will meet with either you or your benefits coordinator to
   --assess your specific areas of interest in an employee benefits package
   --discuss your philosophy of compensation

2. We will collect information about the JFS Manufacturing Company, including
   --an employee list
   --employees' birthdates and dependent status
   --copies of bills and enrollment books from present carriers

1

FIGURE 17–3 (continued).
The enclosed proposal.

3. We will contact insurance firms that can
   --provide the program you are looking for
   --insure you at the lowest rates

4. We will analyze the information we receive from insurance carriers.

5. We will present to you
   --an analysis of your present program
   --our suggestion of a less expensive and more effective employee benefits program.

6. We will visit your firm monthly following adoption of a program. We will conduct a claims assistance meeting with employees and provide each employee with a printout detailing his or her benefits.

Record of Service

Reimbursement Services has successfully designed effective benefits programs for over one hundred South Jersey firms. A list of clients will be provided on request. We are experts in the field of analysis and design. In addition, we have a twenty-four-hour phone number as well as a staff experienced in handling claims and problems.

Cost to JFS

Our suggestions for a more effective program are free. You pay the normal cost of the plan to the insurance company, and we receive from the carrier the usual agent's commission. All of our service of the plan is also done without charge to you or your employees.

Schedule

Week 1--initial interview
--collection of data
--survey of insurance firms for information
Week 2--analysis of results
Week 3--presentation to JFS

2

Clearly Identify the Problem

All proposals address problems. In a solicited proposal, the problem is already known, but the proposer must still clearly state the nature of the problem. In an unsolicited proposal, the writer must first establish the problem—*from the reader's point of view.*

An illustration: A large consulting firm responded to an RFP from a university hospital. The management of the hospital had solicited proposals to develop a master plan to guide the hospital's development over the next decade. The management was convinced that it faced a serious space problem and needed a rational plan for integrating a new building into its overall scheme. The consulting firm analyzed the hospital carefully and concluded that the real problem was a cumbersome organizational structure, which led to overlapping responsibilities and massive confusion about who reported to whom. This problem, the group felt, had to be addressed before the space issue could be considered.

The consulting firm's proposal, however, was rejected. The hospital board saw it as unresponsive to the perceived need for more space. A rival proposal team, which also saw the organizational problems, wisely subordinated the need for organizational change within a plan for physical development and thereby met both the perceived needs of the board and its own (and the other consulting firm's) analysis of management problems.

Car salespeople understand this principle. If a customer is interested in high performance, talking about fuel efficiency is fatal to making the sale. If the customer wants "basic" transportation, emphasizing the plush interior won't do. Understanding what the customer wants and pitching the message to that perceived need are as important in writing proposals as in selling cars.

For your own sake, as you undertake the investigation, be sure that you know whether you are dealing with a problem of fact, means, or value—or some combination of these. Although you do not specifically state this identification in the proposal, you must be sure yourself about what type of problem you are dealing with so you can seek the appropriate information and produce the appropriate kind of report. Remember:

- A problem of fact requires facts and leads to an informative report.
- A problem of means requires facts, opinions, and interpretations and leads to an interpretive report.
- A problem of value requires recommendations based on facts and interpretations and leads to a persuasive report.

Describe a Reasonable Approach to Solving the Problem

Once you have identified the problem (the right one, of course), you must propose a reasonable way to solve it. Note carefully that the proposal does not present the solution itself. That will come later, in a report (see Chapters 18 and 19), after you have carried out the work described in the proposal. What the proposal provides is a *method,* an approach that will reasonably lead to a solution or answer.

Here is one example. A large insurance company wanted to help the suburban municipality in which its headquarters were located to overcome the pressure on highways created by morning and evening rush-hour traffic. Almost 1,200 workers arrived at the office for a 9:00 A.M. start and left at 5:00 P.M. One way to solve the problem was to adopt flexible work hours to stagger traffic. The company identified the problem clearly and solicited a proposal from a consulting firm for a study to evaluate the effectiveness of flexible hours in solving the problem. Here is the relevant section of the proposal, labeled "Approach to the Problem":

> We will administer to all hourly and salaried employees a simple questionnaire (see Appendix A) that will determine the likely impact of flexible working hours on the flow of traffic to and from the office. The questionnaire will ask each person to list his or her most likely times of arrival and departure (with information on car pooling) under the proposed policy. We will then code and process these data to prepare a master schedule showing the number of employees arriving between 7:30 A.M. and 9:30 A.M. and leaving between 3:30 P.M. and 6:00 P.M. Using this schedule we will evaluate the likely effectiveness of the policy on traffic patterns around the headquarters building.
>
> Our final report will make a recommendation to guide you in deciding whether or not to adopt flexible work hours as a way of solving the traffic problem.

The approach defined here is relatively simple but has the advantage of yielding a good deal of concrete information on which a recommendation can be based. Note that the "approach" section is addressed exclusively to the *means* and suggests not a solution to the problem, but a reasonable way to *reach* a solution.

Show that You Can Carry Out the Proposed Approach

A reader legitimately wonders: Can this person (or organization) pull it off? Having accepted the existence of the problem and the viability of the proposed method of attack, the reader now wants to know if *you* are the one to do the job. Do you have the experience and education? The physical resources? The contacts with experts needed to get additional help? The time and money it will take?

Sell yourself and your organization: people, time, equipment, money, facilities. Convince the reader. Show any related experience that proves your track record on similar projects.

Present One Clear Message

Proposals are sales documents that must make a single point and make it clearly and repeatedly, just as advertisements carry to the consumer a single strong image or theme. To work, a proposal must have a pitch; all elements have to repeat, restate, and emphasize that pitch. In the absence of a clear pitch or message, the proposal dissolves. It loses effectiveness as its discrete parts deliver multiple (and perhaps contradictory) messages.

The unifying theme of the proposal can be stated as a simple phrase, as in these examples:

```
   Cost reduction through improved quality control
   Improvement of employee morale through benefits packages
tailored to individual needs
   A better environment that increases worker productivity
```

These are unifying themes around which proposals can be shaped. The theme can be announced first in the title, previewed in the introduction, and reiterated through the problem, solution, and justification sections.

As Brent Worley shows in "*FYI:* Proposal Writing," a clear and unified theme helps *sell* your proposal.

THE STRUCTURE OF PROPOSALS

Conventional formats help proposal writers control and effectively deploy information. Company practice on format varies, and as always you should follow the conventions prescribed by your employer or by the sponsoring

PROPOSAL WRITING

Brent Worley
Agent, Gallen Insurance Agency

Last week, a friend who's been working in sales and presenting proposals for more than 35 years inadvertently reminded me of the importance of written proposals. Two days before, he had presented a proposal on property and casualty insurance to the owner of a small business. "I must have told him five times in our meeting that this was the most complete coverage for the price," said my friend, "and then today he phones me, says he's looked over the proposal and is going to buy because, as he said, for the price, this policy offers the most complete coverage. He practically repeated my own words to me." More to the point, he quoted from the proposal.

Whether your proposal involves products, services, or ideas, it's unlikely that the persons you want to decide in your favor will do so just because your oral presentation sparkles. Your written proposal remains after you have left the meeting and speaks for you when they're discussing a decision. Remember this when you start writing.

As the cliche goes, you can't fit a square peg into a round hole. So, as best you can, fit your proposal to the needs of your target person or organization. In other words—most likely those of your business communications professor—analyze your audience.

agency to which the proposal is submitted. Here we discuss a generalized structure applicable to all proposals: short or long; memo, letter or other; internal or external; solicited or unsolicited. This generalized structure includes three components: the front matter, the proposal core, and the back matter.

The *front matter* in a formal proposal is similar to that included in a major report (see Chapter 19): cover (with title, date of submission, name of sponsor, name of proposer, and the like); executive summary or abstract; and table of contents. *Back matter* is also similar to that for a report: bibliography and appendixes.

The proposal *core* focuses on the three guidelines we mentioned: problem, approach, and qualifications or justification. Here is a typical list of headings, similar to those in the JFS Manufacturing Company benefits proposal:

```
Introduction
Problem Statement
Objectives
Solution
Justification
Budget
```

Introduction

The introduction briefs the readers on the main points of the whole proposal and prepares them for the reading. It provides an overview of both the substance and the process of the proposal. It aims at a broad audience,

Here's what I mean. Like the people who read them, proposals come in different sizes, shapes, and lengths. Suppose you had to make a proposal on workers compensation insurance to a Type A entrepreneurial spirit. A lot of detail will merely slow this person down. As a business owner, he or she knows that workers compensation is a legally mandated requirement, so in this case you're selling price and service. If you can't do it in four pages tops, you're wasting not only the client's time, but also yours.

On the other hand, some organizations seem to thrive on bulk. They favor lengthy, more formal proposals with massive appendices, especially if committees are involved. The more people on a committee, the longer your proposal will likely be. But companies have different corporate cultures and therefore different styles and expectations. A long proposal could be just as much off target with some companies as it would be with our entrepreneur.

So prepare your thoughts and plan your proposal carefully. If you have a solid proposal presented in a clear, concise, well-reasoned format, it's like looking over the decision-maker's shoulder and suggesting "Do it."

both in management and in any technical specialty on which the proposal draws.

Problem Statement

The problem statement conceptualizes the basic problem to be addressed. For example, the problem statement in a proposal for analyzing and improving the quality control system of a thread manufacturer might be:

> The Matthews Thread Company has experienced a 32 percent increase in returned shipments from customers based on unacceptable quality, and this increase is eroding profit margins. An improved quality control system is needed.

A complex problem may lead to a longer and more detailed problem statement. To show that the problem is recognized within a profession or discipline, you may also refer to published literature, as in the following:

> Economists have been unsuccessful in determining the price elasticity of demand in higher education, a problem that makes tuition setting difficult for colleges and universities that want to predict the impact of tuition on enrollment.

In a solicited proposal, the writer essentially repeats—with appropriate modification and elaboration—the problem as defined in the RFP. You can assume familiarity with the technical field: A proposal to accountants can freely use the language of accounting. However, because in an unsolicited proposal the writer must first convince the audience that a problem exists, the problem statement in such a proposal is less easy to compose. Often you have to move toward the problem through a series of statements you know the reader will agree with until you can bring the proposal around to the core of the problem and induce the reader's agreement with that. Here is the problem statement for an unsolicited proposal. It is part of a *sales letter* (see Chapter 16). It tries to promote a service to someone who doesn't know he needs it:

> Industrial spying costs American business millions of dollars a year. Research is expensive, and when research results are passed to competing firms, the short- and long-term losses can be substantial. Why should your competition gain the benefits of *your* research? To prevent such illegal "leaking" of industrial research results, Securitech has developed a program to (a) audit your corporate research security policy and practices and (b) recommend improvements that will protect your costly investment in research. Our approach is described in Section III below.

The problem is defined generally, but in terms designed to make the recipients of the proposal see its applicability to them. Once they accept the problem as real for them, they are prepared to read further about the means of solving it.

Objectives

The objectives section is a transitional element between the problem and the solution segments. It establishes specific objectives for the proposed work that will lead to the solution of the problem. For example, in the proposal dealing with price elasticity of demand in higher education, the objective might be:

```
To develop an equation based on historical enrollment and
tuition data at XYZ University to predict the effects of tui-
tion changes on enrollment.
```

Proposals may have one or more objectives. Generally, the objectives should be measurable, for example, to increase the profit margin to 14 percent, to reduce the deficit to $3,000, or to decrease employee absenteeism by 2 percent a month for two years. Whenever possible, make the objectives quantitative, in numbers of people, dollars, machines, or whatever.

Solution

The solution section defines the method of attack that will be followed to solve the problem, for example, a review of the existing literature, an experiment or a set of controlled observations, a "what if" simulation, or an in-house survey. This section answers the reader's question: "How are you going to solve my problem?" It must therefore be detailed and authoritative, stating clearly the actual work that will be done.

It is also desirable to provide a schedule linking the parts of the work to demonstrate that everything will indeed come together in the end. For example, you might schedule three weeks to review the published literature and interview company executives, three weeks to design an appropriate survey instrument, two weeks to interpret the collected data, and one week to summarize and make recommendations. Most schedules are displayed in visual form (see Chapter 6).

A schedule serves two good purposes: It helps the proposer structure the work to be done, and it convinces the client that the proposer knows his or her business and has a realistic grasp of the problem and the time and energy required to find a solution. The absence of a detailed schedule not only may leave you with an unstructured task to be performed but may also leave the reader feeling that you are vague and unorganized.

Justification

The justification section proves that you can do the job. It shows your track record and details your resources. Some of the needed information is considered "boilerplate." For example:

- Prepared data plugged in as needed
- Current detailed resumes of principal investigators and others
- Lists of past customers, clients, and sponsors
- Inventories of computer hardware and software available in your business

- Statement of finances bearing on the project
- Management structure

In short, informal proposals much of this information may already be known and can therefore be quickly summarized. But even when the resources are not detailed in full, you must still persuade the audience that you can do the job.

Budget

The budget gets serious attention from reviewers of proposals because it is really the quantitative abstract of the whole document. The budget expresses in the medium of money everything contained in the proposal and therefore represents a brief summary understood at a glance by expert reviewers. In analyzing the budget, they assess the value they will obtain from you. Reviewers look not for the cheapest proposal but for the one promising the greatest *value.* An unrealistically low budget is often regarded as a sign that the proposer doesn't understand the problem and may therefore not be able to reach the solution quickly and effectively. An inflated budget, of course, can also be a reason for rejection. In the proposal business, it's a commonplace that noticeably low or high budgets are equally destructive to a proposal's chances of being accepted. The "right" budget is the one that realistically assesses and presents costs.

In organizations that deal extensively with proposal preparation, budget specialists handle the details, and customers or sponsors likewise have budget analysts who review that segment. But the person responsible for the overall proposal still has the responsibility to see that the budget is appropriate and well integrated with the whole package. Even though financial experts may prepare and review the budget, it should be understandable to nonspecialists and not a maze of figures requiring the translating capabilities of a CPA.

The components just described may lead you to think of proposals as collections of discrete pieces. In some proposal-oriented companies, that observation may be true, as the paste-and-scissors approach dominates when time is short and the pressure is high. But proposals really are unified documents that should, as you saw earlier, present one clear message.

Centering the proposal on one clear message—and making that message explicitly apparent to the audience—allows the writer to unify the segments that comprise an effective proposal. An effective proposal is one that is accepted. When it is accepted, you can get on to the investigation it proposed and, following that, to the report that presents the results and recommendations from the investigation. The solution is in sight.

SUMMARY

- Business problems can be classified according to what is known about the problem itself and the solution and whether or not the solution can be carried out directly. Table 17–1 classifies business problems.
- **Bids** are aimed at situations in which both the problem and the solution are known, but the method of carrying out the solution is not immediately available. Bids are offers to supply a good or service at a specified price.

If they are produced in response to specific requests, they are called **solicited bids;** otherwise they are **unsolicited.**

- When a problem is identified and someone is asked to investigate it through the writing of a proposal, it is helpful to distinguish among three types of problems:

  Problems of fact require you to find out *what* happened or is true. They lead to informative reports presenting factual information.
  Problems of means require you to find *how* or *why* something happened or is done. They lead to interpretive reports containing explanations.
  Problems of value require you to find out the *best* way to do something. They lead to persuasive reports containing recommendations.

- **Proposals** address situations in which a problem is known but the solution to it is unknown. Proposals are offers to undertake an investigation leading to the solution of a business problem. If they are written in response to a request for proposal, they are called **solicited proposals;** otherwise, they are **unsolicited.** Proposals do not present recommendations; they do not present the solution, only the approach to be taken in reaching the solution. Solutions are recommended in reports that are written based on the proposed investigation.

- To write a proposal you must clearly identify the problem to be solved, describe a reasonable approach to solving it, and show that you are the best person or organization to carry out the approach.

- Effective proposals follow a format that parallels the strategies of identifying the problem, describing the approach, and justifying your ability to carry out the approach. The proposal can contain sections labeled "Problem," "Objectives," "Solution," "Justification," and "Budget." These sections can be further divided depending on the length and complexity of the proposal.

- A successful proposal is a sales document that carries to the reader one clear message. All the components of the proposal must advance that message. A successful proposal that makes its point clearly will be accepted. Once that happens, the proposer carries out the investigation and reports back to the sponsor with information and, if appropriate, recommendations.

EXERCISES

For Discussion

1. Using the scheme given in Table 17–1, classify each of the following business problems as briefly described by the people who face them. Determine whether the problem and solution are known or unknown and whether the method of solution is available or unavailable.
   a. Our end-of-the-month profit-and-loss statement takes too long to produce because our computer system is slow.
   b. We need more parking space behind Building K.
   c. Something is wrong with our hiring system because new employees don't seem to fit the needs of the individual departments.

d. My sales force in Florida can't find out how long it will take to make delivery on the orders they take.
e. Our air conditioner is broken.

2. For each of the problems in Exercise 1, determine, again using the classification scheme in Table 17–1, what *outcomes* are needed. Which problems can be solved through direct action? Which will require communication, that is, a bid process or a proposal process?
3. Label the following as problems of fact, means, or value:
   a. What is the best way to get from Munich to Vienna?
   b. How many employees work in the Minneapolis store?
   c. Why is the corner office on the first floor of Harrison Hall always seven degrees warmer than the middle offices?
   d. Who sold the most flannel shirts last week in the men's department at the Johnstown store?
   e. Why does it take four weeks to process a purchase order?
   f. How can we save money on airline tickets?
4. Go to the purchasing office (it may be called the business office) at your college and ask if you can have a copy of the guidelines used for preparing requests for bids. Examine them to see what effect on the *writing* of an RFB such organizational policies and procedures have. If your college is government-supported, look in particular for the *legal* requirements, and try to gauge their impact on the writer of an RFB.

For Writing

5. Write a request for bid (RFB) for three new filing cabinets for your department.
6. Write a bid responding to the RFB you prepared for Exercise 5. How easy was it to prepare the bid based on the RFB? Could the RFB have been more precise—and thus easier to respond to?
7. A chain of grocery stores in the St. Louis area sent your consulting firm a request for proposal for a study of its employee benefits package. Before you submit the proposal, you are asked to send a one-page outline as a preproposal so the chain can get an early sense of the extent of the project and its likely costs. Write an outline showing each of the major headings you expect to include in the final proposal.
8. Here are some topics on which students in business communication courses have written proposals:
   a. The organizational structure of a fraternity
   b. Campus parking facilities and regulations
   c. Computerization of the inventory system in a sporting goods store
   d. Selection of fire-retardant wall coverings for a new motel
   e. Financial impact of two-for-one promotions at a video store
   f. Effect of colors on the buying habits of men in clothing stores
   - For each topic, complete this sentence, which will serve as an introduction to the proposal: "This is a proposal to . . ." Be precise in phrasing the sentence, as it will *control* the entire project and the final document that emerges from it.
   - For each topic, using the one-sentence control statement, prepare an

outline of the proposal showing the major elements that the final document will contain.

- What kind of information (see Chapter 8) will you need to complete the proposal? Examples are a review of the professional literature, observation and experiment, a survey, and books and reports.

For Collaboration

9. As part of a proposal to the U.S. Department of Commerce for a study of the impact of foreign-car imports on employment in the U.S. steel industry, you and the three other members of your team must include a schedule of tasks for the 18 months you expect the work to take. Prepare the schedule in as much detail as possible. Don't forget these tasks: data collection, progress reports, final editing, and production. There are many others, of course. Try to get them all into a form that is easily understandable to the sponsor, to the members of your team, and to you as project director.

18 ELEMENTS OF BUSINESS REPORTING

MEASURES OF ACCOUNTABILITY
CONTEXT FOR REPORTING
GATHERING INFORMATION
FYI: Electronic Reporting on Spotted Owls
Fact Sheets
ROUTINE REPORTS
The Progress Report
The Trip Report
A Routine Site Evalua
SUMMARY
EXERCISES

Do You Know ?

- What is the purpose of reports in an organization?
- How does writing a report aid the author?
- How does a routine report differ from a customized one?
- What is the function of a progress report?
- What is the function of a trip report?

> One of the most important reasons for writing reports is because it forces the experimenter to review the project to see whether it is getting anywhere and to reorient the attack if it isn't. What you carry in your head and have in your notebook will generally turn out to have big holes in it when you once get it down on paper in orderly fashion. Without writing it up, you are not likely to realize the existence of these gaps.[1]

Writing a report clarifies your thinking, as this comment from H. W. Gillett, former president of Battelle Memorial Institute, the international contract research organization, emphasizes. You force yourself to be precise and complete. The report also carries your message to others: to readers inside your organization or to government regulatory agencies, other corporations, shareholders, customers, clients, or sponsors outside. You'll prepare reports to finish off the investigations you read about in Chapter 17. You'll also write less complex reports to conduct the day-to-day routine of the office. Sometimes the reporting may seem to take on a life of its own. But properly conducted, reporting enhances your own life and the life of the organization. In this chapter you will learn some basic elements of business reporting.

MEASURES OF ACCOUNTABILITY

Reports measure accountability. Within an organization, they are written upward through the *reporting lines* implicit in the organizational chart (see Chapter 2). Report writers "carry back" messages to their superiors. Reports account for things, such as inventory on hand, orders, production rates and output, and expenses. They also account for people's activities, such as sales visits and other travel, work to date on projects, and any accidents or illnesses. And they measure things and activities against standards and projections. At regular intervals, internal reports serve to monitor and control the operation of the organization.

Reports written to readers outside the organization measure other kinds

[1] H. W. Gillett, "The Psychology of Report Writing," *Battelle News* reprint.

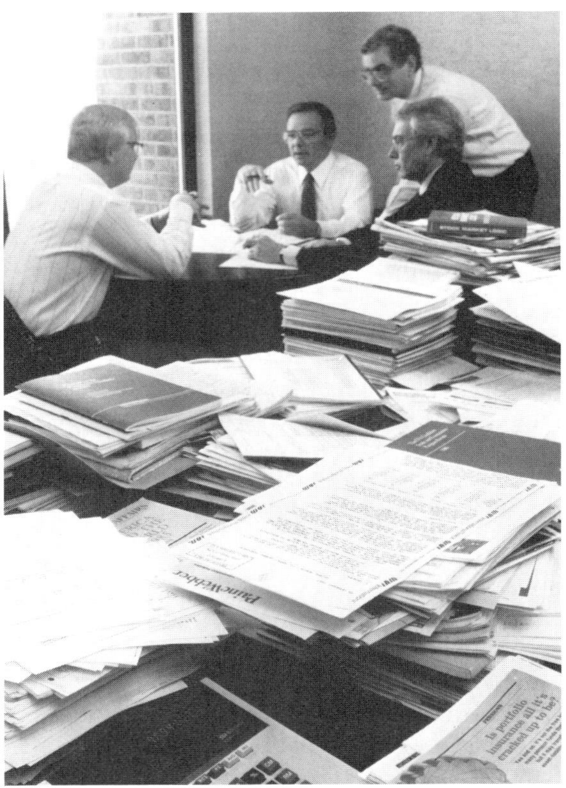

Reports proliferate in business because they provide the information upon which decisions are made.

of accountability. For example, companies "carry back" messages to government agencies concerning compliance with policies and regulations. Especially in the United States, and particularly in the defense industry, the preparation of compliance reports is a major corporate expense. Periodically, corporations report on their compliance with affirmative action agreements, with industrial and office safety practices, with statutes governing retirement and benefit programs, and the like. Publicly owned companies also must, as a legal requirement, report certain basic financial and marketing data to shareholders every quarter. Such reports are one cost of doing business in a democracy.

Finally, you write reports to enhance your (positive) visibility in the organization. In a large company, supervisors more than one level above you may know you only by your reports.

CONTEXT FOR REPORTING

All reports provide information. The *context* for reporting that information may be routine or customized. A *routine* report is appropriate when you and your reader share a lot of common ground, as in an internal report; when the information, at least from the reader's point of view, is uncomplicated;

and when the business situation is a common one, often represented in a form submitted at regular intervals. You gather the necessary information to answer the questions implied in the form, and you present that information directly. Figure 18–1 shows a *routine* computer-generated internal report in the form of a *fact sheet.* It is dense; it uses insider's code for readers who share that common ground. The report aims to record information and to inform the reader. Many of the problems of fact you read about in Chapter 17 result in such routine reports.

When you need to *interpret* information for the reader, that interpretation, too, may fit a general pattern that has become routine in an organization. You will read suggestions for preparing such a report shortly. Beyond interpretation, you may need to *persuade* the reader toward some action or decision. Such persuasion may require a more customized approach when you need to *establish common ground* with the reader. You may take a page or two—perhaps more—to set up the context for the report in a description that builds a common understanding. Under such circumstances, too, you may present more complex information. A one-of-a-kind situation imposes a demand for a one-of-a-kind investigation and customized organization of the information in a formal report.

DOMINION Industrial Fabrics Co. SLOW MOVING AND OBSOLETE INVENTORY

WHSE	STYLE	P.C.	DESCRIPTION	QUAL	AGE(mth)			TOTAL	SOLD	AVAILABLE	REMARKS
					'7–12	'13–18	'19+	METERS	NOT AVAL	TO SELL	
M.I.W	A-162/92	103000	GREIGE	1	77,689			77,689	0	77,689	
M.I.W	A-166/92	103800	GREIGE	1	1,055			1,055		1,055	
M.I.W	A-204/153	108800	GREIGE	1	0	0	300	300	0	300	
M.I.W	A-232/165	103500	GREIGE	1	345	339		684		684	
M.I.W	AJ-162/97	10VR00	GREIGE	1	414			414		414	
C	B-333/93	13VB01	BLEACH PURE	2	490			490	0	490	
M.I.W.	B-340/101	138300	GREIGE	1	719			719		719	OFF STD
M.I.W.	BJ-335/122	13VD00	GREIGE	1	1,064			1,064		1,064	
C	E-153/150	293415	UNBL. S/N	1	473			473	473	0	
M.I.W.	E-198/116	290200	GREIGE	1	17,197			17,197	17,197	0	
M.I.W.	FR-151/135	310200	GREIGE	1	9,417			9,417	9,417	0	
M.I.W.	K-90/126	452600	GREIGE	1	2,997	5,048		8,045	8,045	0	
C	K-90/161	453000	GREIGE	2		677		677		677	
C	L-375/153	478904	UNBL. D/N	1	3,461			3,461	0	3,461	
Z	MP-839/102	554001	SING. BL. SCHR.	1		0	658	658		658	
M.I.W.	MP-839/112	554000	GREIGE	1	7,559	0	0	7,559	0	7,559	
C	MS-372/114	575918	BLEACH PURE	2	492			492	0	492	
C	N-103/115	605001	UNBL. ANTIS.	7	2	3,139	131	3,272		3,272	
C	N-103/115	605001	UNBL. ANTIST.	3	14	1,835		1,849		1,849	
C	N-103/115	605001	UNBL. ANTIST.	2	1,607			1,607		1,607	
C	N-103/115	605001	UNBL. ANTI.	1	256			256	0	256	
C	N-103/153	606001	UNBL. ANTI.	3	102			102	0	102	
C	N-103/153	606001	UNBL. ANTI.	7	41			41	0	41	
C	NS-1/156	6003CA	NATURAL H-S	7	29			29		29	
C	NS-103/155	604001	PL. ANTIST.	7	111			111		111	
C	NS-103/155	604001	PLN. ANTIST.	2	51			51		51	

T. STOROZUM, I. NAGY, C. MCGEE, S. DELUCA Page 1

FIGURE 18–1.
A routine inventory report. *(Courtesy of Sirio DeLuca, Dominion Textile, Inc.)*

GATHERING INFORMATION

In Chapters 8, 9, and 17, you read about strategies for conducting an investigation. Some reports require little research; others demand extensive reading, interviewing, surveying, and observing. In "*FYI:* Electronic Reporting on Spotted Owls," one writer describes strategies for drawing evidence together for an interpretive report. The description emphasizes *electronic* means of retrieving and presenting the evidence.

An important feature of professional training is knowing what reports in the profession look like. What may seem like a one-of-a-kind situation to an outsider is routine to a professional. A routine form for reporting aids in conducting the investigation as well as presenting the results. At Duffield Associates, Inc., a firm of consulting engineers, professionals prepare reports that evaluate the impact of development on the natural environment. A. Ingrid Ratsep, Ph.D., Senior Project Manager, prepared the guidelines shown in Figure 18–2 (page 350) for field investigators who examine a site and interpret its potential for development. Later on you will see these guidelines applied—in Figure 18–7, which shows a preliminary report, and in Figures 19–4 to 19–7 (Chapter 19), which show segments of a longer report.

ELECTRONIC REPORTING ON SPOTTED OWLS

Henrietta Nickels Shirk
Assistant Professor
Department of English
Northeastern University

Imagine this scenario: You are responsible for a team of researchers who have been studying the influence of the logging industry on the endangered spotted owls in the federally owned forests of Oregon. You must prepare an environmental impact statement for your manager, who heads a federal agency and who will pass the report on to a high-level committee in your agency.

You are working late at your home computer. You decide on the information you need, and you bring that into your report:

Current statistics on your region. You need some facts—about characteristics of the forested lands, about counts of spotted owls. Your team has been tabulating and storing this information in a database on the office's computer, which you dial up. You download the appropriate files.

Comparative statistics nationally and internationally. To bring the picture home to some of your audience, you decide you should compare current data with previous studies in Oregon, in the United States as a whole, and internationally. You dial into appropriate databases, read abstracts and then entire articles or fact sheets as pertinent, select the information that supports your points, and download that and citations for the information into your document.

Visual and oral information on the region. Your team of researchers has been photographing the forests, videotaping the activities of spotted owls, and interviewing owners of logging operations as well as nature conservationists. You have organized all this material on a videodisc. You browse through it, identifying and pulling out relevant pictures,

Although information is increasingly generated electronically, it still tends to be presented on paper—unlike the report on the spotted owl. The myth of the paperless office is just that: a myth. Computers have increased the use of paper, and much of that paper is reports. Sirio DeLuca, Director of Marketing in the Industrial Fabrics Company of Dominion Textile, Inc., notes that the introduction of computers at his company led to a "surge of information." There are, he said, "too many issues of too many reports to too many people." The present challenge is *consolidation*. The goal of reporting is to simplify, to create categories for just the right information.

Fact Sheets

Often, the way to simplify the collection and presentation of information is to create a visual form that defines the categories in which to record results. Sirio DeLuca sees as a major managerial task the development of such reporting forms. Figure 18–3 (page 351) shows one form he developed: a weekly "reconnaissance report." The form allows sales representatives to capture important factual information quickly: sales visits, amount sold, and progress toward targets. From these snapshots DeLuca can compile an aggregate picture of activity during the week. Because the form is maintained

video segments, and interviews that expand on the statistical information.

At this point, you have assembled a lot of information. How do you organize it? Your manager and you have decided that the report should be an on-line document rather than a printed one. Text is harder to read on a screen than on paper, but computer presentation allows you more alternatives with sound and pictures and with arrangement. You choose a hypermedia authoring tool that allows you to mark pieces of information for the reader to link them according to individual choices and needs. For example, you can mark the term *spotted owl* in your statistical presentation. A reader who knows about the owl reads on by. A reader unfamiliar with the owl can click on the term and go to a screen that asks if more information is desired on the owl's required habitat, nesting locations, or food sources. By clicking on one of these terms, the reader can then view video segments or photographs of pertinent information.

Creating an on-line report allows you to embed a good deal of information that is available for the reader who needs it but that is out of the way of the more knowledgeable reader. You then create a menu of all the components. The menu is the first computer screen the reader sees. You also create individual menus for each major section of the report. Your readers can then select the order in which they will read the whole report and each section. You'll send the report to them at their e-mail addresses at the agency.

GUIDELINES FOR WRITING A WETLAND REPORT

Use these guidelines to compile your bits of information in a standard wetland report. The minimum required information for each section is indicated under each heading, along with the preferred order of presentation for that section. Use the headings, noted in bold, as your table of contents. Let the guidelines help you work in short periods of time on each segment in between all the interruptions that break up your day at the office.

List of Figures

List of Tables

Executive Summary

–Name project, location, and owner of project site
–Name consultant, retained by whom, for what (project name and purpose), where (township, county, and state), and when (date of site evaluation)
–In brief, present the main results of site evaluation
–Provide an overview of any additional applicable work that is required

Section 1.0 Introduction

–Name project, location, and owner of project site
–Name consultant, retained by whom, for what (project name and purpose), where (township, county, and state), and when (date of site evaluation)

Section 2.0 Methodology

2.1 Desktop Review
–Educate the reader on the importance of a desktop review
–Cite material reviewed (maps, reports, photos, etc.)

2.2 Field Reconnaissance
–Educate the reader on the importance of the field reconnaissance and how it differs from the desktop review
–Name and cite the methodology used
–Provide a brief overview of the methodology and problems that may be associated with the methodology

Section 3.0 Results

3.1 Desktop Review
. . . . .
3.2 Field Reconnaissance

Section 4.0 Conclusions and Discussion

References
Appendices

FIGURE 18–2.
Guidelines for writing a wetland report. *(Courtesy of A. Ingrid Ratsep, Ph.D., Duffield Associates, Inc.)*

Salesperson Weekly Bookings										
	UNIT:	[000]$								
	FOCUS:	6 Months								
	END MONTH	Jul–Sept 23	October	November	December	January	February	March	April	May
	Report Date:	29/9/89	28/10/89	25/11/89	22/12/89	27/01/90	24/02/90	24/03/90		
	Report #	DT25R59D	25-M-06	25-M-06	25-M-06	25-M-06	25-M-07	25-M-07		
	Salesperson #	71								
	Target	3650	3650	3650	3650	7300	7300	7300		
	INVOICED YTD	1772.7	2476.5	3183.3	4026	4639.4	5471.3	6323.5		
	Future Bookings	1657.9	1604.4	602. [50]	0	2804.7	1454.5	1118.2		
	Unconfirmed Ord.	63.4	104.8	27.3[50]	0	54.24	83.6	73.8		
	OVERDUE							392.2		
	Target Gap	[156.0]	536 +	162.6 +	376 +	198.34	[290.6]	607.7		
	Of Plan	104%	115%	104%	110%	103%	96.00%	108%		
WK	Booked	Booked	CXL	TOTAL	CUM	WEEKLY	TARGET			
No	First	2nd	ORDERS	WEEK	[000 $]	TARGET	STANDING			
40	26.3	4.4	**	30.7	30.7	12.0	18.7			
41	42.75	0.38	**	43.13	73.8	24.0	49.8			
42	18.3	0.38	19.2	19.2	93.0	36.0	57.0			
43	4.56	**	**	4.56	97.56	48.0	49.6			
44	59.1	16.7	**	75.8	173.36	60.0	113.36			
45	29.0	**	**	29.0	202.36	NO GAP	NO GAP			
46	16.6	**	**	16.6	218.96	NO GAP	NO GAP			
47	0.9	**	[50,2]	[49.3]	169.66	NO GAP	NO GAP			
48	3.5	10.0	**	13.5	183.16	NO GAP	NO GAP			
49	7.4	**	**	7.4	190.56	NO GAP	NO GAP			
50	5.2	1.2	**	6.4	196.96	NO GAP	NO GAP			
	11 Weeks to Go			[$ TILL JUNE 90]						
8	32.3	1.0	**	33.3	33.3	IN TALLY	NO GAP			
9	8.8	1.3	**	10.1	43.4	IN TALLY	NO GAP			

FIGURE 18–3.
A weekly "reconnaissance report." *(Courtesy of Sirio DeLuca, Dominion Textile, Inc.)*

electronically, DeLuca can read each salesperson's report as a whole or compile his own report on one topic—like visits—across all these reports.

"Taking the customer's pulse" is another critical reporting function for which DeLuca developed a one-page, fact-sheet form (see Figure 18–4). It, too, is computer-generated and thus easy to update. Pertinent sheets can be faxed quickly worldwide. Salespeople review this sheet before a visit and update as necessary afterward. The text is in English (although DeLuca's Italian origins are reflected in his designation of *Milano*).

ROUTINE REPORTS

Fact sheets are useful in reporting the solution to a problem of fact. Many routine reporting requirements may be met with such a single sheet. Or you may include such sheets *within* a longer report for a more complex investigation.

Beyond fact sheets, you may report your information in a memo or letter. You write at pre-set intervals or when the writing is triggered by certain events, like a visit to a customer or participation in a conference. Such reports

COUNTRY: ITALY
CUST. NAME: CRESPI
ADDRESS: ADDRESS
CONTACT: MS. GALI
TITLE: MERCHANDISER

HISTORICAL BACKGROUND

PARENT CO.	Crespi
MFG. FACILITIES	1 Plant In Milano
TYPE OF BUSINESS	Coaters, Coagulators, Laminators, for the Footwear Industry
MARKET SEGMENTS	Ladies, Men, & Childrens Footwear
FABRIC REQUIREMENTS	Cotton, Poly/Cotton, & Rayon/Cotton Sheetings, Osnaburg, Twills

FABRIC SPECIFICATIONS	A	B	C
WIDTH (CURRENT)	158 cm	155 cm	155 cm
WIDTH (IDEAL)	158 cm	155 cm	155 cm
YARN SIZE	20's × 20's N.M.	16's × 16's N.M.	20's × 20's N.M.
COUNT (CURRENT)	24 × 24/5cm	18 × 18/5cm	20 × 20/5cm
COUNT (ACCEPTABLE)	?	?	?
WEIGHT	150g/m2	140g/m2	110g/m2
WEAVE	1 × 1	1 × 1	1 × 1
FIBER CONTENT	Cotton	Cotton	45/55 Rayon/Cotton
FINISH REQUIRED	None	None	None
FINISHED SPECIFICATION	None	None	None
PUT UP (CURRENT)	Bales	Bales	Bales
PUT UP (IDEAL)	1800m Max.	1800m Max.	1800m Max.
AVG. PIECE LENGTH (CURRENT)	130+	130+	130+
AVG. PIECE LENGTH (IDEAL)	130+	130+	130+
TYPE OF SEAMS	To Be Adv.	To Be Adv.	To Be Adv.
CORE SIZE	?	?	?
TENSILE	50kg/5cm	40 × 36kg/5cm	30kg/5cm
TEAR	?	?	?
VOLUME (ANNUAL)	720000	720000	720000
COMPETITORS	?	?	?
CURRENT PRICE	?	?	?

PURCHASING CRITERIA			
PRICE CONTENT	?	?	?
TERMS	?	?	?
DELIVERY INCREMENTS	?	?	?
MISC.	?	?	?
TRIALS REQUIRED	None	None	None
SAMPLES REQUIRED	Closest Available Style	Closest Available Style	Closest Available Style
MISC. NOTES	Being Costed	Being Costed	Will Suggest Poly/Cotton

FIGURE 18–4.
A customer profile with some missing elements to be added. *(Courtesy of Sirio DeLuca, Dominion Textile, Inc.)*

often fit a formula established by your organization or negotiated between your organization and your client or customer. In writing such a report, develop information that answers the questions implicit in the form. Here are two of the most common: the progress report and the trip report.

The Progress Report

To control and monitor the complex projects you read about in Chapter 17, principal investigators usually communicate with their clients or sponsors at predetermined intervals. The form of communication is the *progress report,* sometimes called an *interim report* or a *status report.* The report helps in validating approaches (and assessing any need to change them) and outcomes. Dates for submitting reports are established in the proposal. Progress reports usually follow a simple three-part formula, reporting

1. What has been accomplished.
2. What remains to be done.
3. What (if anything) requires special attention—any problems.

Within those parts, progress is measured against the statement of tasks and the schedule in the proposal. Figure 18–5 is a progress report on the JFS Manufacturing Company project you read about in Chapter 17. The first section measures the work accomplished against the tasks defined in the proposal. The second evaluates the schedule. The third section describes the work remaining. The last section summarizes the project.

The JFS project is going smoothly. The report is factual and direct. Many progress reports are similarly direct. If there is some trouble, however, you may need to use a more customized approach. The occasion of the progress report allows you to give fair warning. You negotiate corrections in the scope of the work, the cost, or the schedule with the client or sponsor to ensure that there won't be any surprises in the final report. An honest assessment of where the project stands is desirable for everyone's sake. Figure 18–6 on page 356 is an internal status report that explains an overage in monthly expenses.

The Trip Report

When your work requires you to leave the office, you may have to document your time away through another common form of routine report: the *trip report.* Such reports can focus either on the trip itself or on the information you gained from the trip. In focusing on the trip itself, you document expenses as part of audit requirements and personnel practices. Most companies have forms for such reporting. Cover these topics:

1. Reason for the trip
2. Logistics (date, time, locations, and people met with)
3. Expenses (with attached receipts)
4. Results (sales made, contacts developed, and future actions needed to reach the intended goal)

REIMBURSEMENT SERVICES

PROGRESS REPORT FOR JFS MANUFACTURING COMPANY

Work Accomplished

Here is an overview of the work to date. I have completed one third of the work on this project.

Task 1: Initial Interview

On November 14, I met with Janet Cunningham, the benefits coordinator for JFS Manufacturing. Janet informed me that the administration is dissatisfied with the high costs of the present group-insurance plan. In addition, JFS is interested in maintaining the best employees through a comprehensive benefits program. They prefer a 100 percent plan but would accept an 80 percent plan if the cost were considerably less and there were other benefits of some significance.

Task 2: Collection of Data

Janet Cunningham also provided me with certain data necessary to our project. The JFS Manufacturing Company's present major medical carrier is Blue Cross of New Jersey, and the present group life carrier is Phoenix Mutual. A copy of the October billing from Blue Cross provided the names, birth dates, and dependent status of employees. Unfortunately, Janet could not find a copy of the latest billing from Phoenix, but she promised to mail me one when the November billing arrives.

Task 3: Information Sent to Insurance Companies

I sent census information to four insurance companies asking all to follow a minimum life schedule and to show me their suggestions for a dental program. I have also asked each insurance firm for specific information as outlined on page 2 of the report.

1

FIGURE 18–5.
A progress report on a project that's going smoothly. *(Courtesy of Jennifer Friedman.)*

CIGNA–Standard wraparound on Blue Cross with a variety of surgical schedules and deductibles.

Guardian Life–100 percent plan superimposed on Blue Cross 14/20 series and Rider J. with a $100 deductible.

New York Life–Standard 100 percent wraparound plan.

Metropolitan–Comprehensive program with a $100 deductible and a $500 out-of-pocket maximum, both with and without first dollar coverages.

Schedule Status

At the end of the first week, work on this project is on schedule. I am waiting for proposals to come in from the various carriers that have been solicited.

Future Work

When I receive proposals from CIGNA, Guardian Life, Metropolitan, and New York Life, I will analyze each to determine which firm can provide the most effective package at the least cost. Next, I will put together a presentation folder and report to explain my recommendation. This report will cover an analysis of both JFS's present plan and the recommended plan. I will then meet with you to explain the programs and answer any questions you may have.

Schedule

Completed------Week 1--initial interview
--collection of data
--survey of insurance carriers

Entering-------Week 2--analysis of results
Week 3--presentation

Niblex, Inc.
Production Department

To: C. Blake, VP Operations
From: J. Saunders, Production Supervisor
Date: April 2, 199-
Subject: Manufacturing Cost Data, March

Units produced	897,000
Labor Costs	$322,800
Material Costs	$135,600
Average Unit Cost	$ .511

Both labor and material costs per unit exceeded division goals, resulting in a 1.1-cent-per-unit overage. Labor costs were increased by the snow emergency on March 7, which reduced the work force by three persons that day. Material costs were affected by an increase in the price of salt. Both these problems were one-time and should not recur. We are making every effort to lower direct unit costs this month to compensate for the performance during March. Our year-to-date figures remain within the 50-cent-per-unit goal, despite the March problems.

FIGURE 18–6.
A status report that explains a problem.

A Routine Site Evaluation

Whereas progress reports and trip reports are *generic* forms (that is, forms of reporting common at most organizations), other forms are routine only in one company or profession. In Figure 18–7 you see a "preliminary wetland evaluation" prepared by Duffield Associates for a developer who had retained an architect to construct an office building on the site. Both federal and state laws regulate construction on sites that contain wetlands, an area usually found between uplands and open water. Duffield Associates surveyed the site to determine the presence of such wetlands and the applicable regulations for construction if wetlands were present. The report is real, although client identities and locations are masked. Figure 1, a map of the site, is omitted to protect the client's identity.

DUFFIELD ASSOCIATES, INC.
5350 LIMESTONE ROAD WILMINGTON, DELAWARE 19808-1296 302-239-6634
CONSULTING GEOTECHNICAL ENGINEERS

PRELIMINARY WETLAND EVALUATION
Smithfield Site
New Castle County, Delaware

3 October 1991

1. Desktop Review

Duffield Associates, Inc., reviewed maps and other documentation to characterize the project site in general. Here are the results of that review.

Location and Topography. The Smithfield site map prepared by HMC Architects/Planners, Job No. 1111 (14 September 1991) shows that the project site is located adjacent to the Pewterford Estate and bounded by Johnson Run and the Daniels Building to the southeast, Hardscrapple Road to the northeast, and Thompson Road to the southwest. The elevation of the project site varies between approximately 316 and 218 feet above mean sea level. The highest elevation occurs in the northern corner of the site; the lowest, near the southern corner. The site map and the Wilmington North, Delaware USGS Quadrangle both show topography in the wooded area of the south central portion of the site that may indicate a stream channel, although no channel is marked.

Wetlands. The U.S. Fish and Wildlife Service's National Wetland Inventory (NWI) map does not show any wetlands on the project site. The NWI map, however, provides only a general evaluation of wetlands that are usually larger than 0.5 acres. It thus does not preclude the presence of wetlands that may contain less acreage or that may consist of more than 0.5 acres situated along small topographical depressions.

Soil. The USDA Soil Conservation Service's (SCS) Soil Survey of New Castle County maps the following soil series on the project site:

Aldino	Montalto
Glenelg	Neshaminy
Manor	Montalto

1

FIGURE 18–7.
A professional report. *(Courtesy of A. Ingrid Ratsep, Ph.D., Duffield Associates, Inc.)*

The map shows the site as covered mainly by the Neshaminy and Montalto series. None of the soils listed appears on the hydric soil list prepared by the National Technical Committee for Hydric Soils. The Aldino soil series, however, is characterized by a seasonal high groundwater table within one to two feet of the surface. Such a high groundwater table can sometimes be indicative of hydric soil inclusions.

2. Field Reconnaissance

On 25 September 1991, Duffield Associates conducted a field reconnaissance of the site. The Federal Manual for Identifying and Delineating Jurisdictional Wetlands (Federal Interagency Committee for Wetland Delineation, 1989) was used for the evaluation.

Wetlands. We noted an intermittent stream and adjoining wetland in the wooded area in the south central portion of the site. The total wetland occupies approximately 20 percent of the site. The intermittent stream and adjoining wetlands were situated in the Aldino soil series as mapped by the New Castle County Soil Survey and were located where suggested by the topography of the site map and the USGS Quadrangle. Numerous seeps were observed within the wetlands.

Vegetation. The forested wetland adjacent to the intermittent stream was dominated by box elder (Acer negundo), green ash (Fraxinus pennsylvanica), red maple (Acer rubrum), spicebush (Lindera benzoin), and greenbrier (Smilax rotundifolia). The small fringe of upland forest noted was dominated by tulip poplar (Liriodendron tulipfera), ground pine (Lycopodium complanatum), and Japanese honeysuckle (Lonicera japonica).

3. Regulation of Wetlands

Federal Permits. The U.S. Army Corps of Engineers (COE), under Section 404 of the Clean Water Act, regulates the deposition of fill or dredged material into "waters of the United States," including wetlands. The COE permits applicable to the Smithfield site are the Nationwide Permits (NP).

NP 26 allows you to fill up to 0.99 acres of headwater, nontidal wetlands without prior notification to the COE. This site is applicable. However, once a project requires the filling of more than 0.99 acres, you must request predischarge approval from the COE. This request is then subject to review by other federal agencies including the U.S. Environmental Protection Agency and the U.S. Fish and Wildlife Service. To increase the likelihood of

2

FIGURE 18–7.
Continued.

approval, you must demonstrate that the site layout minimizes the impact of the fill on wetlands and that no other alternative is economically feasible. Even then, the review for this permit can be subjective. Filling more than 0.99 acres of wetlands generally requires creation of wetlands to replace those being filled (wetland compensation) on a 1:1 basis. Occasionally, even higher replacement-to-loss ratios are required. Failure to apply for the necessary approval prior to filling more than 0.99 acres would violate federal regulations.

NP 12 authorizes the placement of utility lines in wetlands as long as the area is returned to preconstruction grades on completion. NP 14 allows for the construction of minor road crossings in wetlands if the stream channel they cross has a defined bed and bank and if the wetlands "do not extend beyond 100 feet on either side of the ordinary high water mark of that water body." Further evaluation would be necessary to determine if this permit is applicable to the project site. The acreage of wetlands filled or impacted under these two permits is not added to that filled under NP 26.

Delaware Permits. Delaware's Department of Natural Resources and Environmental Control (DNREC) does not currently regulate nontidal wetland areas of less than 400 acres but does regulate subaqueous lands. Subaqueous lands are defined as public and private lands that occur below the mean high water mark. A Subaqueous Lands Permit from DNREC would be required for any activities within the intermittent stream.

4. Recommendation

If you decide to proceed with the development of this project site, Duffield Associates, Inc., recommends that you initiate the following steps:

- Conduct a wetland delineation to flag wetland boundaries in order to determine wetland acreage.
- Prepare a report documenting the wetland boundary delineation.
- Identify all potential impacts on wetlands or the stream and obtain the necessary permits.
- If the project requires the filling of more than 0.99 acres, present the proposed plans and wetland report to the Joint Permit Process (JPP) meeting in Dover. JPP meetings are held every month. Representatives from federal and state agencies comment there on the site layout and the likelihood of permit approval.

3

SUMMARY

- **Reports** "carry back" information to people who need it. They serve as **measures of accountability.** Internal reports measure things and people as they contribute to productivity. External reports measure compliance with regulations and assignments. Both internally and externally, complex reports present the results of an investigation.
- As with all writing, good reports enhance a writer's visibility in the organization and thus her or his reputation. Writing reports also disciplines the writer's thinking and encourages better work. Such self-educational reports don't need to be distributed to be useful.
- Some reports are **routine:** you share a common purpose and context with the reader; the information is, within that context, uncomplicated—often, a matter of facts; and the form is well established. Follow the form as you select the content. Some reports, however, require **customized** treatment: You may be dealing with a problem of means or value; you may have to create the reader's awareness of your purpose; your information may be complex; or you may have to develop a structure for information to match a one-of-a-kind situation.
- One of the most common forms for reporting is a **fact sheet.** The sheet condenses abundant information, often numbers or other discrete items, into a table or a series of short sentences grouped in brief sections with headings that point out key words.
- A **progress report** monitors work on a project against tasks and deadlines established in the proposal. It discusses what has been accomplished, what remains to be done, and what may require any special attention.
- A **trip report** meets one (or both) of two purposes: It may focus on the trip itself to document expenses for the record, or it may focus on what was learned. It can become an informative report for management.

EXERCISES

For Discussion

1. The report in Figure 18–7 is a *routine* evaluation of a site. Can you tell which elements in it are "canned" (that is, common to all such reports), and which are particular to this investigation? How might the recommendations lead to more business for Duffield Associates?
2. The following questionnaire was used as the basis for a study of worker motivation in a small retail store. It was administered to all salespeople. Are the questions biased? How reliable and useful would the information derived from this questionnaire be? What *scale* would be appropriate for answering each question? Here's one suggestion:

```
Suggested scale for answers:

_____ About half of the day or more
_____ About one quarter of the day
_____ About one eighth of the day
_____ Time never seems to drag
```

   Revise these questions or develop alternative ones to measure motivation (see Chapter 9 concerning questionnaires). How might you present the results in a report?

EMPLOYEE MOTIVATION SURVEY

1. On most days on your job, how often does time seem to drag for you?
2. Some people are completely involved in their jobs. For others, the job is just one of several interests. How involved are you in your job?
3. When you don't like some policy or procedure on the job, how often do you tell your opinion to one of your supervisors?
4. How free do you feel to disagree with your supervisor to her or his face?
5. Which of the following two statements comes closer to your opinion about our store:

    - The relations between management and employees are not very strong because management's interests are different from the employees' interests.
    - The relations between management and employees are strong because both groups are working together toward a common goal.

3. In Chapter 17, you read about problems of fact, means, and value. For the following questions, analyze the *type* of problem the question represents. Then suggest *who* might read a report that answers the question; you may have several different readers for different circumstances. Define the kind of information you'd need to answer the question and decide under what circumstances (if any) a report delivering the answer would be *routine* and what circumstances would require more *customized* treatment.
    a. What mix of stores is appropriate for a new shopping mall in X community?
    b. Should the ABC Company move its offices to X?
    c. What is the best car for X customer?
    d. What stocks and/or bonds should X client buy?
    e. Who works for Z Corporation?
    f. What programs are needed to improve productivity at X Inc.?

For Writing

4. Create a *fact sheet* on some topic of interest to you. You may develop your facts from personal observation, interviews, or surveys. You may also use secondary sources; if so, be sure to document them. Review Chapter 6 for advice on presenting evidence in tables. Develop an appropriate *form* for the sheet. Perhaps create a logo or other graphic device in its heading. Here are some suggested topics:
    - Your college or university
    - The nutritional content of the offerings at several fast-food restaurants
    - Recycling programs at your college or in your town
    - Computers at your college or university

- Career opportunities in your major field
- Fitness programs for people of different ages

For Collaboration

5. Write a progress report on a group project you are completing for your business communication class or another class. If you are not already engaged in such a project, then form a team to write a progress report on what you are learning in the class itself. Define your goal—for the project or the class. Can you agree on a common goal? Then define a standard to measure your progress toward that goal. If your project included a proposal, measure your progress against the standards set there. If not, establish standards. Measure your progress, too, against the calendar.

19 FORMAL REPORTS

What's Ahead

- DEALING WITH COMPLEXITY
  - FYI: Objectivity in North American and Chinese Reports
  - Introduction
  - Middle
  - Ending
- SPECIAL FEATURES OF THE FORMAL REPORT
  - Front Matter
  - Back Matter
- READABILITY
  - Text
  - Visuals
  - Design
- A STUDENT REPORT: A MANAGEMENT INFORMATION SYSTEM FOR A RESTAURANT
- SUMMARY
- EXERCISES

Do You Know 

- What information should you include in the introduction to a formal report—and how should you organize it?
- What is the role of the middle of the report?
- Should the ending always summarize?
- What is the role of an executive summary?
- How can you enhance a report's readability?

In Figures 19–1 and 19–2, you see the cover and contents page of a report that informs Canadians who are about to be posted to Zimbabwe about the country of their future residence. It is one of many such reports that the Canadian International Development Agency (CIDA) prepares about different countries in the world.

DEALING WITH COMPLEXITY

When your information is complex and lengthy—as in a report describing a country—even if the business situation is routine, you'll probably create a formal report. Such a report includes features that address in particular the needs of multiple readers. Some formal reports aim mainly to *inform,* like the CIDA reports. Some *interpret* information. Some aim at *persuasion.* The student report (pages 383–394) aims to persuade the reader to accept its solution to a problem of value: selecting the *best* approach to improving service and bookkeeping at The Whistling Abalone restaurant.

In preparing a formal report, be particularly aware of your reader or readers. Often, the writer of a formal report must create common ground with a reader who is external to the organization or is otherwise unfamiliar with the material being presented. In addition, formal reports frequently must balance the needs of diverse readers. Review Chapter 4 to refresh your thinking about meeting reader needs. In addition, Figure 19–3 suggests some implications of your analysis of the audience for how you write the report. Readers in different cultures also have different expectations about the function of reports, as you can see in "*FYI:* Objectivity in North American and Chinese Reports" (pages 368–69).

In the standard formal report in North America, preliminary elements, also called *front matter,* provide a series of overviews and maps to engage attention and send multiple readers on their multiple ways through the text. Material that follows the text *(back matter)* provides the most detailed evidence (in an appendix), documentation of secondary sources, and an index for quick reference. You'll see such elements shortly. First, you'll learn to create the three main segments of the report itself: the introduction, the middle, and the ending.

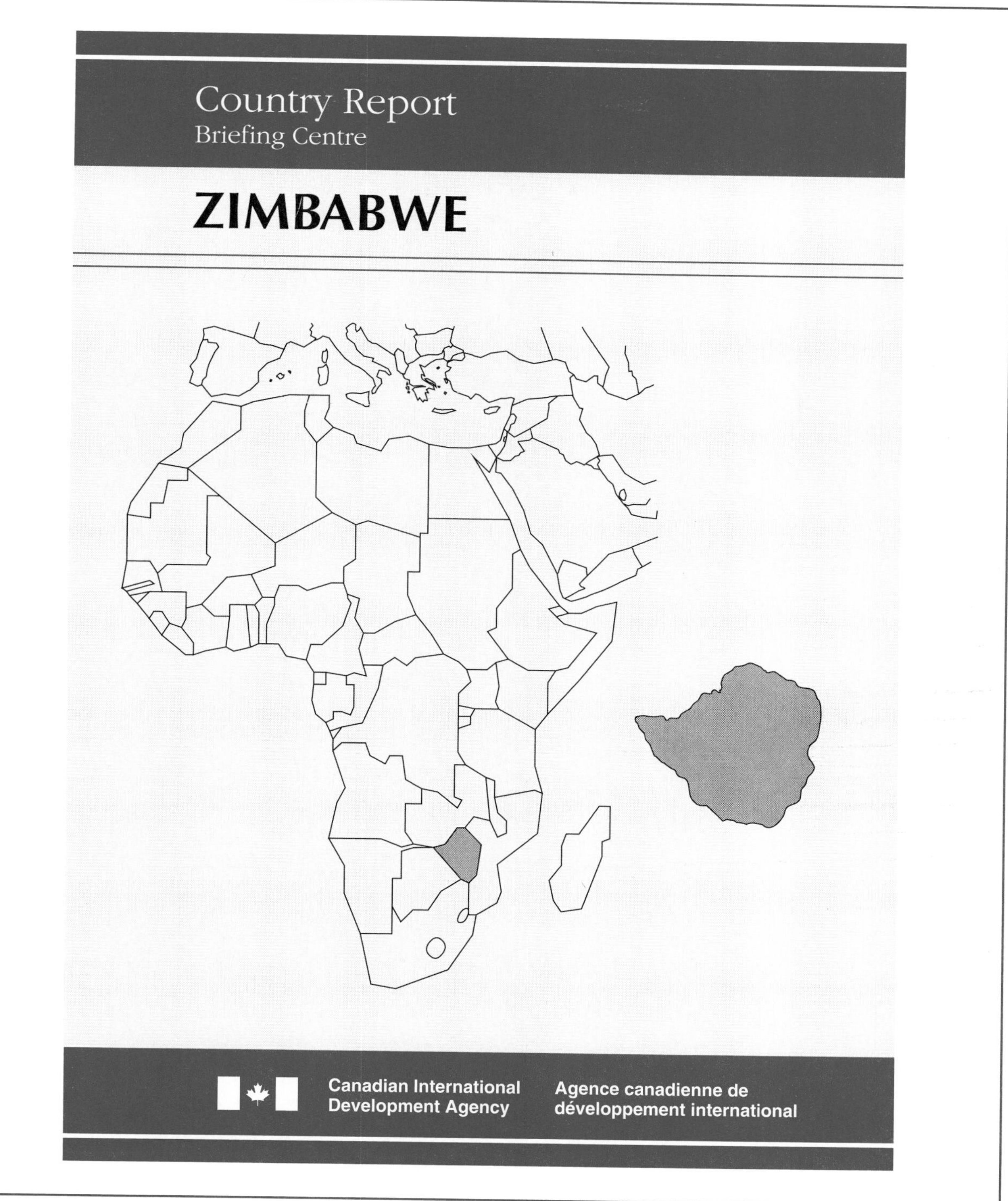

FIGURE 19–1.
The cover of a government report. *(Courtesy of the Agence canadienne de développement international; Canadian International Development Agency.)*

TABLE OF CONTENTS

PART I: GENERAL INFORMATION

1 *GEOGRAPHY*

1.1 Location and Size
1.2 Physical Features
1.3 Climate

2 *HISTORY*

3 *POPULATION*

3.1 Size
3.2 Ethnic Origins
3.3 Religion
3.4 Language
3.5 Cultural Aspects

4 *POLITICS*

4.1 Government
4.2 Political Parties

5 *INTERNATIONAL RELATIONS*

5.1 Foreign Affairs
5.2 Canada and Zimbabwe

6 *ECONOMY*

6.1 Overview
6.2 Development
6.3 Agriculture
6.4 Mining
6.5 Energy
6.6 Industry
6.7 Trade
6.8 Tourism

7 *EDUCATION*

8 *HEALTH*

BIBLIOGRAPHY

FIGURE 19–2.
A contents page of the government report. *(Courtesy of the Agence canadienne de développement international; Canadian International Development Agency.)*

Question	Answer	Implications
Why is the audience reading this report?	Has to, but isn't really interested.	Make it lively and brief; use introduction to attract interest.
	Will have to summarize its contents for someone higher up.	Write a clear, precise executive summary.
	Loves the topic and can't read enough on it.	Provide all the relevant details and don't hesitate to elaborate on interesting points.
What is the audience's level of technical understanding?	High—at least up to yours.	Don't hesitate to use specialized language, and don't overexplain.
	Low—lay audience.	Simplify discussions of technical matters; translate specialized language into clear English.
What can or will the audience do as a result of reading this report?	Take some action.	Clearly focus on the conclusions and the recommended actions; say what should be done and why.
	File the report for reference.	Be sure all aspects of the issue are covered adequately; don't worry about specific recommendations.
Are there any unique "political" implications that you should be aware of?	Yes—the sponsoring agency already did a study showing contradictory results.	Downplay the differences between the conclusions—but make your own clearly apparent.
	Yes—the sponsoring agency doesn't normally use the approach you did.	Make a special effort to explain why you chose the approach you did—its advantages and so on.
	Yes—Congress has expressed doubts about this project.	Give special attention to the secondary audience (Congress) and try to be especially persuasive.
	Yes—public opinion seems to be against this idea.	Write, for a lay audience, a well developed defense or explanation of the idea.

FIGURE 19–3.
Writing implications of your profile of the audience.

OBJECTIVITY IN NORTH AMERICAN AND CHINESE REPORTS

Linda Beamer
Crosscultural Communication Consultant

Reports written by North Americans nearly always purport to present information as objectively as their writers can manage. Progress reports, status reports, trip reports, trouble-shooting reports—even personnel evaluations—all attempt to relay observed facts with a minimum of personal bias. But such objectivity is not the goal of business communicators in all cultures.

For a recent class in the People's Republic of China, graduate students wrote consultants' reports on a Chinese product or market addressed to fictitious English-speaking readers. The reports were intended to inform the readers. But the students wanted instead to exhort them and to paint a glowing picture. One student's topic was an overview of government programs offering preferential treatment to overseas Chinese (citizens of another country but racially Chinese) who choose to move to China. The student, however, found herself unable to limit her report to statistics. Instead, she urged "returning" Chinese to understand their duty to help build the motherland.

Another writer analyzed the refrigerator market in China for a Japanese manufacturer. For 13 pages, the writer boasted about China's economy and the millions of households demanding refrigerators. Only

Introduction

When do you write the introduction to a report? You may start there as a way to build momentum for composing the whole draft. If so, you'll probably want to come back to the introduction at the end of your drafting to incorporate whatever changes in structure and information you've made while writing. Many authors, however, start writing in the middle, comfortably expressing familiar material, and compose the introduction at the end, when they've confirmed how the story comes out.

Whenever you write the introduction, however, remember that readers often form an impression of an entire project on the basis of the first page or two of the report. Although different readers may read the report itself selectively, *every* reader will probably read the introduction closely. Those pages are critical. You must immediately pull the readers away from whatever occupied their thoughts before reading and set their thoughts on your cause. Reaffirm your goal before you write. Is it to

- Provide neutral information?
- Arouse interest?
- Influence an attitude?
- Convey the solution to a problem?
- Urge someone to take an action?

Begin with a statement of your common ground with the reader and gradually move the reader toward the new. Most business reports use a direct structure, at least in an American context (see Chapter 4). In the introduction, you cover these topics:

in the last two paragraphs, however, could the writer bring herself to note the government's freeze on imported refrigerators—a freeze that would eliminate the market for that manufacturer. In the middle of an analysis of pending legislation to restrict silk imports, another student wrote: "Since currently there is no quota, before the bill is adopted let your company grasp this opportunity and try to enter the U.S. market!"

Questioned about the lack of objectivity in their own reports, the students looked, in turn, at the degree of objectivity in the sources they had used. Although objectivity is necessarily hard to define (and culture-bound), of some 160 sources consulted by the class the group identified only three as objective. The difference stems in part from how documents are used in the two cultures. In North America, decision makers believe they make better decisions when they have as many facts, impartially presented, as possible. In China, decision makers rely less on published sources for their information. They *discuss* the facts and issues; they *write* to persuade readers of the correctness of a decision already taken by the leaders. Objectivity may be sacrificed for that persuasive purpose.

1. The main point (your conclusion or recommendation or the answer to the reader's question)
2. The context (Who requested the report and when? What problem necessitated the report? What specific questions were asked?)
3. The scope and plan of the discussion that will follow

The announcement of the report's framework makes it easy for readers to know what to do with the details that will come in the middle.

If you anticipate that the reader will need to be sold on your conclusion or will find a bald statement of your conclusion either threatening or pushy, you may be *indirect.* Announce the context for the report—who authorized it, what problem necessitated it, what information you were assigned to discover, what limits were placed on your search, and what the plan of the report will be—but withhold your conclusion. Perhaps begin with a narrative of the project. Then gradually, as the middle develops, you'll bring the reader through the analysis and into your main point.

Here's the introduction to a directly structured report. It's an internal report at a shirt manufacturer aimed to *inform:*

> At the request of Ana Pappas, President, the Marketing Department prepared this report to furnish the Executive Committee with the information necessary to aid them in deciding whether to diversify into the manufacture of ties.
>
> To provide this information, we conducted a detailed study of trends in men's neckwear. The primary sources were articles from industry publications and interviews with Philadelphia manufacturers and retailers.

The report covers types, fabrics, colors, widths, prices, and sales of neckties. It looks particularly at the influence of specific designers.

Two limits on the report should be mentioned. First, because the majority of neckwear manufacturers are privately owned, few financial reports and industry sales figures are available, and thus the report does not cover costs. Second, the information compiled from interviews derives from manufacturers and retailers only in the Philadelphia area, one of several segments within Brooks's total market.[1]

The writer of this report was a fashion merchandising student who worked part time at the shirt manufacturer. She wrote an informative report that aimed at comprehensiveness and objectivity and that avoided making a recommendation. Her writing assignment came from her supervisor, who had in turn been assigned the investigation by his supervisor, the vice president of marketing, who received *his* assignment from the president. All three people became *immediate* audiences for the report and made comments on the draft that were then incorporated into the final version, which was submitted by the president to the executive committee, which constituted the *primary* audience.

The report could, of course, have developed differently. The marketing vice president, for example, might have objected to the idea of diversification into ties and biased the report accordingly. Or he might have favored developing a line of ties and encouraged his staff to develop a strongly persuasive report to that effect. In assigning the report, the president might have been responding to a board member she thought was foolish in suggesting ties. She might then have told the vice president, in effect, to come up with a negative report.

The following introduction begins a *persuasive* report. In Chapter 17, you saw the proposal that initiated this investigation; you saw the progress report in Figure 18–5. The approach here is more *indirect.* It begins with a statement of the problem (rising costs); it then announces the authorization and topic of the report and the five objectives; it then gives the plan of the report. The *recommendation* of a specific benefits package, however, is saved until the end of the report itself.

With the rising costs of health care, employee benefits programs are becoming more important to an organization's efforts to maintain first-rate employees. Too often, however, these benefits plans are not properly designed and are thus ineffectual.

In response to a request from JFS Manufacturing Company, Reimbursement Services has prepared this report, which analyzes the company's present benefits program and presents the design of a new and more effective plan. The new plan addresses the firm's objectives and needs in a health care program.

Five major objectives comprise the ideal benefits program for the JFS Manufacturing Company:

[1] Courtesy of Jane Bacal.

1. Provide ample protection for the employees while being cost-effective
2. Improve employee morale through the plan's serviceability
3. Use a fair and uniform rate of contribution for the employees
4. Incorporate a master plan to improve and add benefits over time
5. Lend itself to effective communication to the employees

This report is divided into two main parts: a description of the present program and then an analysis of the recommended program. Each program is analyzed in terms of the firm's objectives for an ideal health care package.[2]

The introduction in Figure 19–4 begins a formal report on a wetland evaluation (client identities and locations are masked). The standard approach to such a report is shown in Figure 18–2.

Each of these introductions eases the reader into the report by forecasting both the *content* and the *structure* of the whole document.

Middle

The middle gives the proof. The middle is further divided into smaller *segments.* The segments must be clearly identified because not all readers will read every segment. For *routine* reports, the segments follow a predefined course. You fill in the information required, as in Figure 19–5.

Whether the report is routine or customized, exploit the conventional patterns for organizing information you learned in Chapter 4:

- Cause and effect
- Classification/analysis
- Comparison/contrast
- Narrative

The student report at the end of this chapter is a customized one organized by cause and effect, that is, problem to solution. The table of contents in Figure 19–2 shows that the country report *classifies* its information. The Ratsep report in Figures 19–4 and 19–5 develops a *comparison* between the desktop review and the field reconnaissance.

Although words are important in presenting evidence, the middle of a report often contains a good deal of *visual* presentation. To write the middle segment, you may *start* with those visuals and then develop text to explain them. Routine reports often rely completely on the visual presentation of information. More customized reports mix presentation forms. Match reader expectation; some readers are uncomfortable if too many pages pass without a table or figure. Avoid using a narrative, for example, for financial information that belongs in rows and columns. Make sure that the information in visuals is consistent with that in the text.

[2] Courtesy of Jennifer Friedman.

Identification of the site and proposed site plan

Scope of the Duffield project

Purpose of the project

In-depth description of project location

General overview of wetlands to provide background for the client. The section defines and cites the function of wetlands and tells the client briefly how wetlands on the site were identified. Usually this section is expanded to two pages of text; it is a "canned" section used in all such reports.

SECTION 1.0
INTRODUCTION

The Morits site, owned by Maks Development Corporation, is located approximately 4 miles northwest of the City of Wilmington, in New Castle County, Delaware (Figure 1). Maks Development Corporation plans to develop the site as a condominium retirement community.

In July 1991, Duffield Associates, Inc., was retained by Maks Development Corporation to evaluate the Morits site for federal and state jurisdictional watercourses and wetlands.

The purpose of this evaluation was as follows: (1) to delineate the U.S. Army Corps of Engineers' (COE) area of jurisdiction, which includes all areas identified as "waters of the United States," including wetlands; (2) to identify jurisdictional areas regulated by the State of Delaware as subaqueous lands; and (3) to provide documentation to support the location of the delineated wetland boundaries.

1.1 Site Information

The Morits site is a 34.4± acre irregularly shaped site located approximately 4 miles northwest of the City of Wilmington. The development in the surrounding area is a mixture of zoned commercial and residential properties characterized by remnant woodlots and fallow fields. The Morits site is bounded by Downard Lane to the north; a fallow field owned by Kline and Associates to the east; and a mature woodlot to the south and west owned by K. Kangur. The northern three quarters of the Morits site is a fallow field; the remainder is a mature woodlot that is contiguous with the adjacent woodlot to the south and west.

1.2 General Introduction to Wetlands

In general, wetlands can be considered a transitional area between uplands (land areas characterized by well-drained soils) and deepwater areas. The COE defines wetlands as "those areas that are inundated or saturated to support, and that under normal circumstances do support a prevalence of vegetation typically adapted for life in saturated soil conditions. Wetlands generally include swamps, marshes, bogs and similar areas" (33 CFR 328.1 (b)). Wetlands are a unique natural resource characterized by a number of beneficial wildlife and socioeconomic functions. . . .

FIGURE 19–4.
Introduction to a formal wetlands report. *(Courtesy of A. Ingrid Ratsep, Ph.D., Duffield Associates, Inc.)*

Keywords that reiterate the project proposal submitted to the client

Introductory paragraph to this section—shows client what to expect

SECTION 2.0
JURISDICTIONAL WATERCOURSE IDENTIFICATION AND WETLAND DELINEATION METHODOLOGY

A two-step evaluation was conducted for the Morits site for the identification of jurisdictional watercourses and the delineation of wetlands. First, a desktop review was initiated to provide a general site characterization and to determine potential areas subject to federal and state jurisdiction. Second, a field reconnaissance was conducted to verify the presence of these jurisdictional watercourses and to delineate existing and functional jurisdictional wetland areas.

Documentation of the methodology employed for the desktop review

2.1 Desktop Review

The desktop review involved the study of available topographic, wetlands, and soils documentation of the area. References utilized included the United States Geological Survey's (USGS) topographic quadrangle mapping; the United States Fish and Wildlife Service's National Wetland Inventory (NWI) mapping; the United States Department of Agriculture Soil Conservation Service's (SCS) county soil survey; existing site plans; and other available documentation relating to the project area.

Documentation of the methodology employed for the field reconnaissance

2.2 Field Reconnaissance

The field reconnaissance involved an evaluation of the Morits site by a team of Duffield Associates' environmental scientists. The purpose of the field reconnaissance was to field-evaluate all areas that were determined in the desktop review to be characteristic of a potential watercourse and/or wetland area.

To identify existing federal and state jurisdictional watercourse areas, all depression areas capable of conveying water were evaluated for the presence of a defined streambed and streambank.

To identify and delineate existing and functional jurisdictional wetland areas, the "Routine On-Site Determination" was utilized as defined in the Federal Manual for Identifying and Delineating Jurisdictional Wetlands developed in 1989 by the Federal Interagency Committee for Wetland Delineation. This methodology involved the three-parameter approach for the identification of wetlands, which includes the examination of vegetation, soils, and hydrology. Since the site was not characteristic of prior anthropogenic disturbance or atypical natural conditions, no additional evaluation was required.

FIGURE 19–5.
Part of the middle segment of the wetlands report introduced in Figure 19–4.
(Courtesy of A. Ingrid Ratsep, Ph.D., Duffield Associates, Inc.)

Ending

In the ending, you can once more expect heightened reader attention and a wide readership. Don't waste that moment. Bring the reader back up out of the bog of detailed information with a reminder about the main point. In a probem-solving report, state the conclusions and recommendations drawn from the evidence, as in pages 7–8 of the report to the owner of The Whistling Abalone restaurant (pages 393–394). Circle back to any questions posed in the introduction and show that you've given the answers.

SPECIAL FEATURES OF THE FORMAL REPORT

To provide a variety of access points and to streamline the presentation of information at different levels, the formal report often includes several special features. Some come *before* the report as front matter:

Letter (or memo) of transmittal	List of figures and list of tables
Cover	Executive summary and abstract
Title page	Preface
Table of contents	Foreword

After the text you might include other elements. If you have a good deal of raw data or calculations to present, you may siphon that information off to an *appendix*. You may also include a *bibliography* or *references* if you consulted printed or electronic sources in your research. An *index* is essential for a long report. The student report at the end of the chapter includes a memo of transmittal, a title page, a table of contents, an executive summary, and a list of references.

Front Matter

The elements that precede the report help to orient the reader.

Letter (or Memo) of Transmittal

The *letter of transmittal* (a *memo* if the report is being circulated *within* an organization) gives you a chance to talk about the report in perhaps a more informal and personal voice than the report itself allows. Figure 19–6 shows such a personal letter of transmittal (contrast this with the routine form for a transmittal you saw in Chapter 14, Figure 14–7). It's also useful in directing the report to each of several readers.

In writing the memo or letter, imagine that you are handing over the report in person. What would you say? In that cordial conversation

- Review the logistics and authorization for the work, with particular thanks to the reader for assigning the report and to any others who assisted in its preparation.
- Highlight the content of the report, emphasizing what's of interest to this reader.

Acknowledgment of project completion

Project results in brief

Marketing pitch: further services Duffield can provide

Thanks to the client and offer to clarify or rectify any outstanding issues the client may have regarding the contracted work

DUFFIELD ASSOCIATES, INC.
5350 LIMESTONE ROAD WILMINGTON, DELAWARE 19808-1296 302-239-6634
CONSULTING GEOTECHNICAL ENGINEERS

July 30, 1991

Peter Maks
Maks Development Corporation
1128 Sweetgum Lane
Wilmington, Delaware 19808

W.O. 73252.WA
RE: The Morits Site
Jurisdictional Watercourse
and Wetland Evaluation Results

Dear Mr. Maks:

On July 27, 1991, Duffield Associates, Inc., completed the jurisdictional watercourse and wetland evaluation for the Morits site. This evaluation was conducted in accordance with our June 29, 1991, proposal.

During our July 1991 field evaluation, we identified 2.6± acres of wetland associated with three small tributaries that traverse the wooded southwest section of the site. The results of this evaluation are documented in the enclosed report.

We would be pleased to be of continued service to you as you develop the site design plan for the Morits site. We can assist your project architect and engineers in the development of a site plan which avoids or minimizes the impact on jurisdictional areas, and we can also provide assistance in preparing all applicable Federal and State permits required for any proposed impacts on these documented jurisdictional areas.

If you decide to continue with our services, we can prepare a proposal for the additional services.

Thank you for this opportunity to serve you. If you have any questions, please contact us.

Very truly yours,

DUFFIELD ASSOCIATES, INC.

Ingrid Ratsep

A. Ingrid Ratsep, Ph.D.
Senior Project Manager

AIR:lmh
Enclosure: Report

FIGURE 19–6.
A letter of transmittal. *(Courtesy of A. Ingrid Ratsep, Ph.D., Duffield Associates, Inc.)*

- Cite any deviations in the report from the original plan for the project.
- Offer to answer questions about the report.
- Note any need for further study.

Cover

Many organizations have standard covers for their reports. The cover is instantly recognizable to the reader in a stack of other reports and confirms a certain consistency and polish that enhances a company's image through its documents. Specialized reports may be graced with well designed covers whose artwork reinforces the central theme of the text (as in Figure 19–1). As a practical matter, the cover holds the pages of the report together.

Title Page

Every formal report has a title. It may appear directly on the cover. Or it may be included on a title page inside the cover. Some report covers have windows onto the title page through which the title shows. In general, routine reports have routine titles that denote the *function* of the report, for example, "Second Monthly Progress Report." Such a descriptive title may be all that's necessary. Customized reports, however, require more substantive titles, like the one in Figure 18–7.

An informative title, like the informative headings you read about in Chapter 7, alerts readers to the content and approach of the report. It allows the report to be filed in an information retrieval system and enables readers to refer to the report.

Although you may be tempted to leave the title to the last minute, don't. The reader reads it *first* and forms an important impression of your report from it. Develop a tentative title early in your writing, and let it shape the structure of your draft. Then revise the title with the following thoughts in mind:

- **Enrich the title.** Instead of merely noting the topic—"Avalanches"—note your approach:

  "Avalanches: The USDA Forest Service's Role in Forecasting, Control, and Public Education."
- **Place key terms at the beginning.** And don't include anything in the title that's not covered in the report.
- **Avoid dual titles,** like "Computers and Inventory Control." Instead, show the *relationship* between these terms: "A Computer-Based Inventory Control System for the Family Deli."
- **Scrutinize for possible misreadings** and for unwarranted connotations or misplaced modifiers:

  "Comparison of Dried Milk Preparations for Babies on Sale in Seven European Countries" (*Problem:* The milk is on sale, not the babies, but the title is misleading.)

  "Views Men Have of Women in Labor" (*Problem:* This report deals with women in the labor force; the term *labor* has an alternate connotation for women.)

  "Mothers and Such: Views of American Women and Why They Have Changed" (*Problem:* the meaning of *they;* how "women" have changed or how "views" have changed?)

Table of Contents

The table of contents lists headings from the report and notes the page on which each appears. It thus quickly reveals the report's structure. Preparing the table of contents gives you an opportunity to check on the logic of the report, to see if the segments follow rationally and if the headings indeed give realistic cues to the reader about what's to be found in each section. Make sure all headings are parallel.

List of Figures and List of Tables

As the name implies, the list of figures collects titles of the report's figures. If you have tables, make a list of tables, too. Give both the figure or table *number* (or letter) and the *title*.

Executive Summary and Abstract

An *executive summary* condenses the report for a decision maker interested in the main lines of the discussion. The summary tells what the report is about: the context for and significance of the work and the main point or points. If action is called for, it names the required action. The term *executive summary* usually refers to the summary of a corporate or government report or proposal in a business setting. Another term, *abstract,* is usually used for scientific and technical summaries in academic settings as well as in professional journals or the proceedings of meetings. Abstracts rarely exceed 200–300 words; summaries for short reports may occupy one page (as in Figure 19–7). But a longer document may require a 10- to 15-page summary, perhaps separately bound.

Most writers create the summary last. But others find that creating a summary *before* they settle in to write a whole document aids them in the final writing. They know how the story comes out. A summary also helps direct a team in a multiple-author project. Keep these suggestions in mind:

1. Write from the table of contents. Flesh out those topics.
2. Include the report's control statement.
3. Include the most important statements in support of the control statement.
4. Make sure that the summary is readable without reference to the report itself.
5. Use complete sentences.

The summary is a major business tool. Everyone who receives the report will probably at least skim the summary; many will not ever read the whole report.

Preface

Some reports, and many books, include an introductory statement from the author called a *preface.* The preface serves some of the same functions as a letter of transmittal; it allows the author to converse with the reader of the report, perhaps more personally than in the report or book itself. The preface often includes an overview of the author's intention for the document and a statement thanking those who assisted in the task.

Project scope

Project context and client plans for the site

Purpose of the evaluation

Results

Recommendations to client based on the results

EXECUTIVE SUMMARY

In July 1991, Duffield Associates, Inc., evaluated the Morits site for federal and state jurisdictional watercourses and wetlands for the Maks Development Corporation.

The Morits site is located in an area zoned as mixed commercial and residential, approximately 4 miles northwest of the city of Wilmington, in New Castle County, Delaware. Maks Development Corporation plans to develop this 34.4± acre site as a condominium retirement community.

The purpose of this evaluation was as follows: (1) to delineate the U.S. Army Corps of Engineers' (COE) area of jurisdiction, which includes all areas identified as "waters of the United States," including wetlands; (2) to identify jurisdictional areas regulated by the State of Delaware as subaqueous lands; and (3) to provide documentation to support the location of the delineated wetland boundaries.

The evaluation indicates that three small tributaries and 2.6± acres of wetland exist on the Morits site. The wetland areas are associated with the tributaries that traverse the southwest corner of the site. The wetland areas identified are characteristic of a palustrine forested wetland area.

Any proposed development of the site should attempt to avoid and, if not possible to avoid, then minimize the impact on identified watercourses and wetlands. A Federal 404 Permit will be required for any proposed impacts on watercourses and wetlands. A State Subaqueous Lands Permit will be required only for any proposed impacts on watercourses.

FIGURE 19–7.
An executive summary. *(Courtesy of A. Ingrid Ratsep, Ph.D., Duffield Associates, Inc.)*

Foreword

Some reports, particularly those providing potentially controversial or otherwise value-laden information, include *forewords.* These statements are written by authorities (not the authors of the report) who validate the importance and credibility of the report.

Back Matter

Three elements to consider placing *after* the report are *appendixes,* a *bibliography,* and an *index* if the report is long.

Appendix

As the name implies, an *appendix,* sometimes called an *attachment* or *exhibit,* contains material appended to the report. The appendix is often highly technical and documents conclusions and raw numerical information for the record. Include such information as

- The full text of a questionnaire whose results are summarized in the report itself.
- The complete derivations of formulas highlighted in the text.
- An earlier report on the project that this report modifies.
- Detailed rules and codes that served as the legal basis for applications discussed in the text.
- Figures that form the basis for discussion in several places in the text or that are foldouts or otherwise unusual in size.
- A glossary of terms, abbreviations, or symbols used in the report.
- Letters to the author concerning the information covered. The letters may be quoted in part in the report.

You may include one or many appendixes. Label and number (or letter) each one. Include the titles of all appendixes, along with page numbers, in the table of contents.

References and/or Bibliography

When you write up your own observations and conclusions, you don't need to document them. But when you use other sources, cite where you found both visual and verbal information. Chapter 6 provides guidelines for citing a visual; the appendix on documentation at the back of this book provides guidelines for citing a prose discussion.

Index

Create an index for a long report intended for multiple readers. Many computer programs can compile an index of key words automatically. If you need to work by hand, then read through the text with note cards by your side. Jot one key term on each card as you go through, alphabetize the cards as you jot, and note the page number of each page on which the term occurs. The process is rather slow and tedious. But remember that you want readers to find what they need by the term under which *they* will look for it.

READABILITY

In reviewing the draft of any report, and particularly a long and complex report, insert cues in the text so that your organization is obvious and multiple readers will be able to find multiple paths through the information—and reminders about where they have been and where they are going. In addition, look for ways to streamline the text by expressing appropriate information in *visual* form (see Chapter 6) and design the whole report for clarity and impact.

Text

To ensure readability in the text of your report, clarify and simplify its organization. In addition, look for ways to insert special statements that tell the reader how to read. Long reports may lose readers. Follow these suggestions to keep readers on track. Review Chapter 7 for more details about revision.

1. **Check your organization.** Review the table of contents to make sure that you have presented the right information in the right order. Lack of parallelism in headings, for example, may signal a lack of logic in the segments themselves.
2. **Provide overview statements** for the whole report and for each segment, for example:

```
This section discusses a third task required in establishing
a competitive swim team: making up the practice schedule.
```

3. **Provide checklists,** where appropriate, of topics you will discuss, for example:

```
The committee analyzed public transportation systems in each
of the following cities:

   San Francisco
   Miami
   New York
   Houston.
```

4. **Use headings strategically** to enable readers to skim and zoom in on specific segments.
5. **Periodically summarize a discussion** before moving on to the next topic.
6. **Enrich** the discussion with selective *cross-references.*
7. **Refer to the main point** in each major segment, for example:

```
A second problem that can be solved by the incorporation of a
management information system is the added bookkeeping that
resulted from our expansion.
```

8. **Avoid surprises.** Where you have, for example, a *finally,* make sure that you've earlier cued the reader to expect a series. Check for casual references early in the document that depend on the reader's having read an extended discussion later on. Bring in the extended discussion earlier, or delete the reference. Don't present new information as though the reader were familiar with it.

9. **Play to reader expectations.** In a list of items or systems from which the reader is to select one, *start* or *end* with the one you are recommending; don't bury it in a middle position, which is unemphatic.

Visuals

Much of the factual information in your report is best presented visually, as in Figure 19–8, a table from the country report on Zimbabwe referred to at the beginning of this chapter. As you draft your report, and as you revise, look for ways to enhance the visual presentation.

Design

Desktop publishing systems have enhanced your ability to incorporate visuals in reports and to design appealing pages of text and other appealing elements, like the cover and contents page you saw in Figures 19–1 and 19–2. Use whatever systems are available to you. Just be wary of overdesign. Slickness may reduce a presentation's impact. Assess the reader's expectations and taste.

For any reader, select an appropriate typeface and page layout (see Chapter 7). For each page, be sure that you have

- Adequate white space and consistent margins.
- At least one paragraph break per page.
- No single last lines of a paragraph carried over to the next page.
- Adequate space around figures.
- No heading as the last line of a page.

Make sure, too, that every page is accounted for. Sometimes, to ensure completeness, page numbers are given in the form, "page 2 of 15," the first number indicating the sequence of pages and the last indicating the total number of pages in the document. Most commonly, the number is printed at the top right of the text on the page, with the number for the first page of the introduction centered below the text of the first page. But practice varies. Again, adhere to the standards of your organization. Here is one common system:

Title page	i [not printed]
Subsequent front matter	ii, iii, etc. [printed]
First page of report proper	1
Subsequent pages	2, 3, 4 . . .

If your report includes an appendix, number its pages in sequence with the body of the report. Every appendix page is numbered. Sometimes appendixes are numbered separately by appendix, for example, A–1, A–2.

Profile

Comparative Data

	Zimbabwe	Canada
Area	391,109 km^2	9,976,000 km^2
Population (1986)	8.5 million	25.1 million
Population density, per km^2	20.2	2.5
Urbanization (1984), %	27	75
Average annual growth of population (1973-84), %	3.2	1.2
Life expectancy at birth	57 years	76 years
Infant mortality rate (per 1,000 live births)	77	9
Daily calorie supply per capita as percentage of requirement	82	129
Adult literacy rate, %	70	99
Number enrolled in primary school as % of age group*	131	103
males	136	105
females	127	102
Percentage of work force (1980) in:		
agriculture	53	5
industry	13	29
services	34	65
Percentage of population under the age of 15 (1983)	30	23.2
GNP per capita (1984)	$760 US	$13,280 US
Average annual growth rate of GNP (1965-1984),%	1.5	2.4
Inflation rate (1973-84), %	11.4	9.2
External public debt as % of GNP	28.4	1.35
Debt service as % of GNP	5.4	4.96
Current account balance (1984)	-$97 million US	$1,974 million US

Source: World Development Report, 1986, World Bank

* Figures can exceed 100 per cent because pupils above or below the official primary school age (generally 6 - 11 years) are included in the calculation.

FIGURE 19–8.
A table presenting comparative information about Zimbabwe and Canada. *(Courtesy of the Agence canadienne de développement international; Canadian International Development Agency.)*

A STUDENT REPORT: A MANAGEMENT INFORMATION SYSTEM FOR A RESTAURANT[1]

The owner of The Whistling Abalone, a resort-area restaurant, moved his operation to a larger space to accommodate increased business. But he was afraid that the move might exacerbate some already existing operating problems and might bring on other problems as well. So he asked Tom Puglisi, who is a waiter at the restaurant in the summers and an accounting student during the school year, to identify the problem areas and to recommend procedures to streamline operations. (Tom Puglisi's report is reproduced on the following pages.) The owner decided to install the system recommended by the report.

3 March 1991

To: John Bossacco
From: Tom Puglisi
Re: MIS System Report

I am happy to submit to you the attached report, "A Management Information System for Better Inventory, Service, and Bookkeeping at The Whistling Abalone." It presents the results of the project I proposed to you on 14 November 1990 to investigate the feasibility of implementing a management information system at the restaurant.

The report identifies areas of potential improvement and notes specific features of MIS that meet each need. It should enable us to solicit bids from manufacturers of specific systems to determine the most cost-effective one for The Whistling Abalone.

The three area managers, Becky Anderson, David Smity, and Ann Wu, provided valuable insights during the investigation. I appreciate their assistance.

I've enjoyed working with you on this project. Please let me know if I can be of any further help.

[1] Courtesy of Thomas E. Puglisi.

A MANAGEMENT INFORMATION SYSTEM FOR BETTER INVENTORY, SERVICE, AND BOOKKEEPING AT THE WHISTLING ABALONE

Submitted to John Bossacco
The Whistling Abalone
12 Ocean Street
Monterey, CA 93940

Submitted by Thomas E. Puglisi

3 March 1991

TABLE OF CONTENTS

Executive Summary iii
Introduction 1
Current and Potential Problems in Operation 1
    Inventory Control: Food 2
    Inventory Control: Liquor. 2
    Waiter Service and Floor Operations 2
    Bookkeeping 3
The Solution: A Management Information System 4
Advantages of the System 4
    Constantly Updated Inventory 4
    More Efficient Waiter Service and Floor Operations 7
    Better Bookkeeping. 7
Conclusions. 7
Recommendation 8
References. 8

LIST OF FIGURES

Figure 1. Some Reports Available from a Restaurant MIS 5
Figure 2. System Overview 6

EXECUTIVE SUMMARY

The Whistling Abalone recently moved to a new location in Monterey, California. The transition to a larger space, with doubled seating capacity, has already revealed problems in the current pattern of operations and will undoubtedly create further problems when we move into full capacity this summer. John Bossacco, owner of the restaurant, asked me to identify these problems and to recommend a solution.

The increased volume of food and liquor has resulted in poor inventory control. Moreover, the large size of the restaurant has impaired waiter service and floor operations in general. Another problem is the added amount of bookkeeping that has come with expanded operations.

These problems must be resolved before the vacation season begins in May. The purpose of our move is to expand our business and to improve our already good reputation. Problems like those mentioned will undoubtedly hurt our reputation if not corrected immediately.

I recommend the use of a management information system (MIS) at The Whistling Abalone to correct our problems. A simple system can solve all those problems mentioned and provide other useful features for our bright future.

INTRODUCTION

Our move over the winter to a larger building has greatly expanded the operations of The Whistling Abalone. In making this move, we cannot compromise the quality of our service and thus our reputation.

As is common in any business expansion, we have been experiencing some operating problems, particularly poor food and liquor inventory control, less efficient waiter service and floor operations in general, and added bookkeeping.

John Bossacco, owner of the restaurant, requested that I identify the problems caused by our expansion. This report summarizes the needs we identified and recommends the installation of a management information system (MIS) that will make our operations more efficient, will lower costs, and will enable us to provide even better service. Such a system should allow us to be in top condition when we begin our busy tourist season in May.

This report is divided into three sections. The first section details the problems caused by our expansion. The second provides an overview of a management information system. The third shows how the system can solve each of the problems identified.

CURRENT AND POTENTIAL PROBLEMS IN OPERATION

To identify the needs resulting from our expansion, I interviewed the kitchen manager, the bar manager, and the bookkeepers. Each commented on changes in his or her specific operation. I also observed floor operations in the dining room to determine problems with waiter service. After the interviews and observations, I researched MIS in current trade periodicals to determine the features of MIS that are applicable to The Whistling Abalone.

Inventory Control: Food

Our new restaurant has twice the seating capacity of the former one; thus we have been serving about twice as many dinners compared to this time last year. The increased number of dinners served has greatly increased the volume of food inventory that we handle. Becky Anderson, the kitchen manager, has found keeping track of the inventory manually to be inefficient. Items are often either understocked or overstocked. If the restaurant runs out of an item, that dinner cannot be served, and guests complain. If an item is overstocked, it often spoils, increasing costs. Becky also suspects that certain kitchen employees have been stealing food. The present system is not accurate enough to indicate the amount of pilferage or the identity of the pilferer.

Inventory Control: Liquor

Our present system lacks any control over the inventory of liquor at the bar. David Smity, the bar manager, has a running count of the liquor delivered to the restaurant, but he has no way of determining the quantity that should be left at the close of business each evening. He spends over 10 hours weekly attempting to keep an accurate total of the amount of liquor we have in storage. He suspects that the waiters may be giving away drinks to friends and regular guests. He also thinks that the bar boys may be taking a bottle now and then after work. The information provided by the present manual system is often inaccurate and is usually available too late to indicate any causes of shortages.

Waiter Service and Floor Operations

Since our move to the new restaurant, some of our guests have complained of poor service. The waiters note that the increase in size has required them to walk much farther to do their jobs. The bar and the kitchen are distant from each other and from the dining room. Waiters have to walk more than three times as far to the bar and the kitchen as at the former restaurant. These added steps can slow down even the best waiters and greatly impair their service. The extra time spent walking is spent away from the table. As a result, there is less time to provide the personalized service The Whistling Abalone is known for.

The waiters and the cooks have also had problems communicating. The waiters try to minimize the number of trips to the kitchen; as a result, they are often late in picking up their dinners. The cooks get angry when the food cools; the guests aren't happy, either. Moreover, if the cooks aren't sure about the order, the waiter is rarely around to clarify it. This lack of access to the waiters also causes the cooks to be angry. The animosity between cooks and waiters is getting worse. Both parties have individual objectives, and neither is willing to compromise.

These problems decrease the quality of our service and of our food. The Whistling Abalone's reputation is based on gourmet dinners and excellent service. We cannot afford to blemish our reputation at such a crucial time as our recent move.

Bookkeeping

The increase in the size of our business has also increased the amount of bookkeeping. Ann Wu, bookkeeper, figures that the accounting tasks involved in payroll, inventory invoices, and accounts payable alone are enough to keep her and her assistant busy all week.

In addition to these tasks, she is responsible for recording all the information from dinner checks each night. She must record the numbers of each dinner, appetizer, dessert, and drink served by manually going through each dinner check. While she does this, she also checks for waiter mistakes in calculations. This method was adequate at the former restaurant, but with the increased size this method has become tedious and inefficient. Ann and her assistant are both working overtime.

THE SOLUTION: A MANAGEMENT INFORMATION SYSTEM

A reading of several restaurant journals and discussion with experts in MIS have turned up several systems used by other restaurants to meet many of the needs that The Whistling Abalone now faces. Two excellent sources are cited at the end of this report. Figure 1 shows the variety of reports available from such a system.

For purposes of explaining the features of MIS, assume that our system will be composed of an electronic cash register (ECR), a small personal computer, and two remote-site printers. (Specific software and hardware for The Whistling Abalone will be selected in the second phase of this research, but this setup is common in restaurants of our size.)

When the waiter receives an order, he or she takes it to the cashier. The cashier punches the order into the ECR. The following then occurs:

1. The drink order is automatically sent to the bar and is printed on the remote-site printer there.
2. The food order is sent to the kitchen and is printed on its remote-site printer.
3. The entire order is sent to the computer, and each food and drink item is recorded in its memory.
4. The ECR neatly prints the dinner check to be presented to the guests when they leave.

Figure 2 illustrates this process.

ADVANTAGES OF THE SYSTEM

The system aids in solving each of the problems we identified.

Constantly Updated Inventory

When the order is entered into the ECR, the computer records each food and drink item. The computer automatically subtracts from inventory the items

FIGURE 1 Some Reports Available from a Restaurant MIS

About Menu Items

- Current inventory
- Breakout of ingredients used and their availability
- Shopping list (continuously updated) of ingredients needed
- Comparison of vendor prices per ingredient
- Total sales
- Sales recorded by hour, day, week, month, year
- Recipes

About Customers

- Individual tally for each check
- Demographic information
    - peak meal times
    - table turnovers
    - percentage of guests ordering from each menu category
    - total number of guests broken out by hour, day, week, month, year, or by menu category

About Operations

- Sales and profit figures
- Waiter scheduling
- Spread sheet scenarios for setting menu item prices and categories to achieve a profitable menu mix

FIGURE 2 System Overview

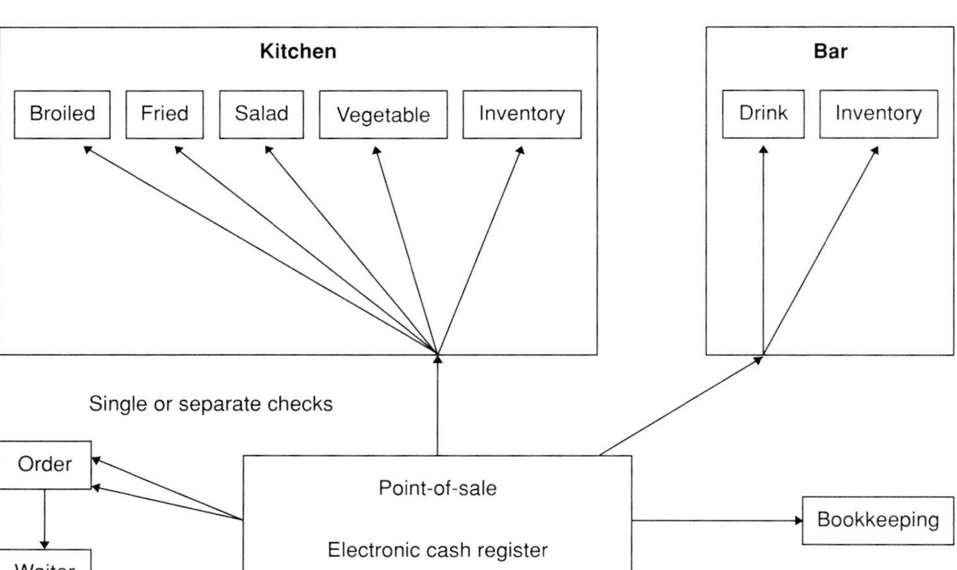

that are ordered. Moreover, the computer can be programmed to know every ingredient of each dish. When a certain dinner is ordered, the computer subtracts from inventory each ingredient in that dish, right down to the last half teaspoon of salt.

The computer can also be programmed to subtract a certain number of ounces of liquor or mixer for each drink. If a Beefeaters and tonic is ordered, two ounces of Beefeaters and four ounces of tonic are reduced from inventory totals.

The system thus provides a constantly updated total of food and liquor inventory. At any given time, a bar manager and the kitchen manager can compare the computer's inventory total with the actual totals in storage. These tighter controls will facilitate inventory reordering and will help to prevent overstocking, understocking, and pilferage.

More Efficient Waiter Service and Floor Operations

The waiters make only one trip to the ECR, and their entire order is placed. After that, they simply have to time their orders and pick them up when they are ready. The time saved can be used to provide better service for their guests.

Communication problems between the waiters and cook are also eliminated. The order is printed in detail in front of the cook; thus discrepancies and potential confusion are prevented. The waiters need not enter the kitchen to place their orders.

Better Bookkeeping

Many of the bookkeepers' tasks can be facilitated with the use of this system. Because each item order is recorded in the computer, Ann need not record information manually from the dinner checks each night. Mathematical errors are eliminated because the electronic cash register prices each item and totals the bill. Elimination of these tasks alone will save the bookkeepers at least twenty hours per week.

Programs are also available to compute the payroll, to keep records of accounts payable, and to keep track of invoices. These features will greatly reduce the bookkeepers' burden and will save on labor costs. We are now paying Ann and her assistant for twenty hours of overtime per week.

CONCLUSIONS

This investigation has led to the following conclusions:

1. *Inventory.* The most crucial and costly problem we face right now is poor inventory control. The costs of overstocking, understocking, and pilferage can cut into profits considerably in the restaurant business. A management information system can substantially improve our inventory controls. The availability of updated inventory totals is crucial to prevent unnecessary inventory costs.
2. *Service and floor operations.* The service at The Whistling Abalone is one of our main attractions. The recent decrease in the quality of our service must be corrected. An MIS will allow waiters to spend less time on the logistics and more time on service to customers.
3. *Bookkeeping.* The amount of additional bookkeeping associated with our recent expansion has been a great burden on Ann Wu. Keeping accurate records of operations is crucial in any business. An MIS can alleviate a large number of small but time-consuming bookkeeping tasks. Eliminating the manual recording of items served will be a major benefit to the bookkeeping operations. Computerizing other accounting functions will also reduce the work load.

RECOMMENDATION

Based on these conclusions, I recommend that The Whistling Abalone implement a management information system that has the following capabilities:

1. Keeping accurate and updated inventory records.
2. Providing automatic ordering of both drinks and dinner items to ease the waiter's ordering tasks.
3. Providing record-keeping and accounting functions to facilitate bookkeeping.

REFERENCES

Farrell, Kevin. "Skeeter's Restaurant: A push-button operation," *Restaurant Business,* 1 June 1989, 148–50.

Farrell, Kevin, and Denise M. Garbedian. "Banking on Management Information Systems," *Restaurant Business,* 15 May 1990, 69.

SUMMARY

- Use a **direct** structure for most **introductions** to customized reports. Announce the main point, review the questions and context that led to the investigation, and describe the plan of procedure of the report itself. If you expect reader resistance, however, then proceed **indirectly.** Line up the evidence first, or review the context in more detail. Perhaps provide a narrative of the work to set the stage for your conclusion.
- The **middle** of the report provides the evidence that supports your main conclusion. You may start your draft by gathering the visuals that represent your results and that you'll explain in the middle. The middle should be **segmented** according to a **conventional pattern,** such as cause to effect or effect to cause (problem to solution), classification and analysis, comparison and contrast, or narrative.
- The **ending** of the report may summarize your main points, but a full summary is not always necessary. You may draw a conclusion. You may recommend a further action. Certainly, you'll answer any questions posed in the introduction, and you'll draw the reader back out of the details of the middle onto a more general plane as you show what all the details add up to.
- An **executive summary,** one of the elements of a formal report, provides a brief summary of the main points. All readers will probably read the summary, although they may read other sections selectively. Sometimes the text itself is meant only for the record, and the executive summary is all that the decision makers will go on.
- To ensure **readability,** look for ways to insert special text that tells the reader how to read. Long reports may lose readers. To keep readers on track, use headings, overview statements, checklists, and cross-references. Insert transitional paragraphs that summarize one section and forecast the next. Repeat the main point in each major section. Exploit the use of **visuals** to streamline the text and highlight factual information. **Design** each page and the report as a whole for clarity and impact.

EXERCISES

For Discussion

1. Review the guidelines for readability in this chapter and apply them to the professional report in Figure 18–7 in Chapter 18 and the student report in this chapter. Does each follow the guidelines? Can you recommend any alternative forms of presentation?

2. Here's the table of contents from a report advising American businesspeople about appropriate behavior at meetings in Japan. Are these headings parallel? Does the way that the headings are expressed point to any problems in the report's organization or approach?

   Executive Summary
   Introduction
   Greetings
      The Bow
      Third Party
      Presenting the Business Card
   Gift Giving
   Nonverbal Behavior
      Body Movements
      Silence is Golden
      Gestures
   Developing a Relationship with the Japanese Businessman
   Before, During, and After the Meeting
      Investigate the Japanese Company
      Detail is Important
      Group Dominance
      Ethics
      Negotiating
      After the Meeting
   Conclusion
   References

3. Read this draft of the introduction to a report dealing with a common problem on college campuses (and elsewhere): too few parking spaces. Determine *who* the reader might be for the report and what the report's purpose is. Review the guidelines for an introduction. Then analyze this draft to advise the writer on how to revise.

   Over the last 16 years, the university has undergone significant changes. Enrollment has doubled and the number of buildings on campus has also increased. Consequently, the university has had to increase its classroom facilities. New buildings such as McKinley Lab, Johnson Lab, Hobson, and the extension of Gates Library have been added to accommodate the students. However, with the increase in classroom facilities there has been a substantial decrease in university-provided parking.

   The parking development plan for the university is a viable plan and once in operation will alleviate the current parking problem.

SIGNIFICANCE AND PURPOSE

As at most thriving universities, parking problems are common. Due to current parking problems the community is suffering in terms of inconvenience and expense. Therefore, to continue growth and stability at the university, an action-oriented plan must be undertaken.

The purpose of this report is to recommend our parking-development plan to alleviate current parking problems. These recommendations will alleviate the current parking deficiencies.

LIMITATIONS

This report is limited to current parking deficiencies and a proposed recommended parking-development plan. This plan indicates what needs to be accomplished but does not give an economic analysis. For these reasons, a cost-income summary is not submitted.

PROGRAM CONSIDERATIONS

Among the many important factors to be considered in formulating the plan's parking facility are location, accessibility, land cost, and site geometry. The new parking facility should be conveniently located with respect to campus, thereby, keeping walking distances to a minimum. The site's accessibility to major streets is necessary to maintain efficient facility operation and keep congestion at a minimum.

In selecting locations for the new parking facility, primary consideration must be given to the accessibility of the site to major arteries. The public transportation system must be made readily accessible, convenient, and inexpensive. Among the many important factors to be considered in formulating an incentive plan to entice commuters to utilize public transportation are accessibility and expense.

For Writing

4. The best exercise in learning *how* to write a report, of course, is to *write* a report. Here are some possible topics—each with an international flavor. Select one to write on, or let these inspire other topics of greater personal interest to you.

- International differences in how a soft-drink manufacturer packages its product
- A review of the market strategy of X Company in Y country
- A comparison of the food relief programs of several countries as they provide foodstuffs in one country in Africa
- A survey of the causes or possible means of control of fan violence at soccer matches in the United Kingdom and Europe
- A review of corporate day-care programs and maternity leaves in Sweden and the United Kingdom as background for determining the feasibility of a day-care program at XYZ Company
- A profile of X country for students from an American university studying there for a semester
- An overview of laws that students should be familiar with when traveling in Europe
- Review of drug-testing programs and methods in international sports competitions

For Collaboration

5. Here is a list of topics to consider when planning to locate a plant in a foreign country or otherwise invest there. Assemble a team to investigate one country. Develop information on these topics and report your results. You may use a *fact sheet* for reporting (see Chapter 18). Or you may develop an *interpretive* report that draws together the information into a profile of the country. Or you may write a *recommendation* report that advises a manufacturer or an investor about prospects in the country.[3]

Profile of the Country

The country's gross national product
Type of government
Natural resources
Manufactured products
Culture: Religion, languages, literacy rate
Size of foreign debt and rate of growth
Population and rate of growth

Additional Questions

What American companies are already there? (competition or support)
Any trade restrictions on exports?
Any problems with import-based industries?
What percentage of your work force can be American? What role for foreign nationals?
Investment structure: Can your company be a wholly owned subsidiary or must a certain percentage be owned by people within the country?

[3] Based on Sally E. Parry, "Using Foreign Investment to Structure Assignments for a Business Communications Class," *The Bulletin of the Association for Business Communication* (June 1987), 30.

Taxes: Any tax or investment breaks?
Prohibitions on certain types of investment?
Services: Banks, shipping, delivery, telephones, export processing zones (infrastructure)?
Corruption?
Inflation rate?
Can you repatriate profits?
Any moral or ethical reasons for investing or not investing?

PART V

LISTENING AND TALKING

20 Elements of Oral Comunication
21 Telephone Calls and Meetings
22 Business Presentations

INTRODUCTION TO PART V

"Talk to each other."

—A coach, to the team

In Parts II, III, and IV of *Business Communication,* you read chapters that focus on *documents.* Some business occasions demand writing. You write to create a permanent record because writing transcends time and guards against the fragile and potentially variant memories of individuals involved in an activity or decision. In addition, readers can skim a document as their interests and attention spans vary and can refer to it as they puzzle over details. When you write, you can revise a document: You can reexamine statements to make sure they say exactly what you want. However, when you talk, you can't take back your words.

But when you talk, you enhance the emotional setting of your words, enrich the amount of nonverbal communication supporting the words, give heightened visibility to an idea or issue, forge teamwork and group feelings, and speed the process of gaining information from other people. In this part of *Business Communication,* you will learn about the risks and rewards of oral communication in a business context.

Chapter 20 provides an overview of the *elements* of listening and talking and includes guidelines for reading nonverbal cues—for listening not only to words but to environments—and for conveying messages orally. It further focuses on the ethics of such messages and strategies for managing conflicts.

Chapter 21 looks at two common occasions for listening and talking: phone calls and meetings. How these occasions *merge* (in teleconferences) and how writing and oral communication merge (in electronic meetings) are described briefly at the end as hints at a future direction for oral communication, hints you saw earlier in Chapters 1 and 10.

Finally, Chapter 22 looks closely at the formal presentations you may make at a meeting or on such other occasions as a training program, a press briefing, or a government hearing.

Through talking to each other, and listening to each other, managers demonstrate their accountability on the job. Management *productivity,* like the productivity of the team, depends on communicating well. You may already be an avid telephone user—many Americans are; the advice in this part will help you to capitalize on the time you spend on the phone. If you feel meetings are a waste of time—many Americans do—then the advice will help you to make the ones you participate in more effective.

20 ELEMENTS OF ORAL COMMUNICATION

What's Ahead

CHOOSING BETWEEN WRITING AND COMMUNICATING ORALLY
- Guidelines for Choosing Speaking over Writing

NONVERBAL ELEMENTS
- Body Language
- Setting

STRATEGIES FOR EFFECTIVE LISTENING
- Recognizing Barriers
- Getting the Message
- Getting the Intent
- Listening to a Different Culture
- FYI: Meishis in Japanese Business
- Listening to the Other Gender

STRATEGIES FOR EFFECTIVE TALKING
- Guidelines for Talking

ETHICS OF ORAL COMMUNICATION
- Gaining Compliance
- The Rogerian Strategies for Managing Conflicts
- Taking No for an Answer

SUMMARY

EXERCISES

Do You Know 

- What factors shape a decision to talk out a situation on the job?
- What are some advantages of talking over writing?
- What nonverbal elements send messages in a conversation?
- What are some barriers to effective listening?
- What strategies will help you to listen effectively?
- What should you keep in mind in talking effectively?
- What are the Rogerian strategies for managing conflicts?

Consider these situations:

- You're concerned about a coworker's attitude toward her job. You start to draft a note, but you reconsider and walk down the hall to talk with her.
- You're not sure which of several marketing strategies would be best for a new product your company has developed, so you ask the product developer to join your marketing team in a brainstorming session.
- You've submitted a proposed reorganization plan for your division. Your boss asks you to come in and talk about it.
- You're a broker for an investment firm. You've bought a list of potential clients, and you're going to call them to solicit business.
- Your division's sales have been lagging. You call in the salespeople to motivate them to sell more.
- Every quarter, you present a five-minute overview of the financial standing of your group to the group's administrators at their quarterly meeting.
- You've applied for a job, and now the company's college recruiter wants to talk with you about your application.
- You're a banker, and your former fifth-grade teacher asks you to visit his class because they are studying banks.

In each of these situations, someone has decided that writing will not accomplish the communication goal. That goal requires oral communication, either in addition to writing or instead of writing. In this chapter, you will learn strategies for determining when to talk and when to write. You'll also learn about the nonverbal elements that enrich messages conveyed orally. Such enrichment, however, comes at the cost of potentially greater misunderstanding than in writing. Before you can talk effectively, you need to listen effectively—to nonverbal cues as well as to the words in the message itself. You'll learn how to recognize barriers to effective listening and how to overcome those barriers. Finally, you'll read about strategies for talking effectively and ethically.

CHOOSING BETWEEN WRITING AND COMMUNICATING ORALLY

The choice between writing and talking—and between talking and silence—reflects the norms of your culture, the policy or procedures of your organization, and your own personality. In a recent study, nearly half of 432 corporate buyers surveyed said salespeople are "too talky." When asked what most impressed them about salespeople, respondents placed at the top of the list the skill of "really listening." The next skills, in order, were "Answer questions well," "Don't waste their time," and "Have good presentation skills."[1]

As you saw in Chapter 3, Americans are indeed known worldwide both for their ability to talk and, perhaps ironically, for their insistence on written confirmation of agreements. People from some other cultures are known worldwide for their ability to be comfortable with business agreements made orally and for their ability *not* to talk. Experts caution that American impatience with silence often leads to costly compromises in business negotiations while counterparts from other cultures profit from their ease at not talking and their skill in listening.

The culture of your organization, either indirectly or in written policy or procedures, also affects your choice between writing and talking. As you have seen, U.S. companies often measure accountability in written reports. The document codifies and confirms information or a decision and provides a unit for measuring success: You count the number of contracts signed. Some companies, however, make more use of face-to-face meetings as a parallel and unwritten way of measuring accountability. Because of their flexibility, talking and listening in meetings are more attractive in turbulent times and in the midst of corporate changes. Documentation may not change fast enough to keep up with new realities of the workplace.

Finally, your own personality may lead you to choose talking over writing. Some people like to talk and seek occasions for doing so. Others find that the prospect of a face-to-face discussion sends them to their pencil or computer. You may avoid discussions, preferring to write from the sidelines.

Guidelines for Choosing Speaking over Writing

Within the constraints of your culture, your organization, and your personality, you'll probably choose talking

1. To speed communication when you can achieve an immediate response to an immediate request.
2. To test an idea and foster consensus.
3. To enhance personal relationships.

1. **To speed communication.** You pick up the phone or walk down the hallway when a brief discussion will convey some simple information or

[1] Communispond Inc. study as reported in Timothy D. Schellhardt, "Managing," *The Wall Street Journal*, 22 March 1990, p. B1.

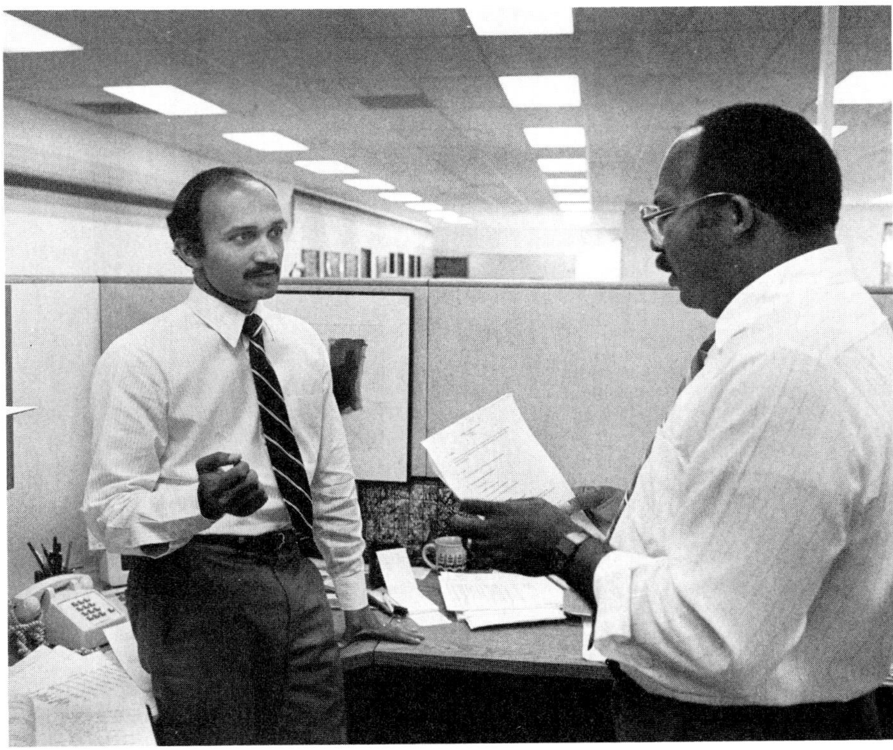

Face-to-face conversations are typical instances of business communication and require attention not merely to words but also to body language.

gain a quick response. A memo may languish in someone's in-box for days (someone calls it his "here-to-stay" box). Your call or direct request could encourage a prompt answer.

2. **To test an idea and foster consensus.** Talking through an idea with the intended audience of a document before you write often enhances the document—in at least two ways. You test your approach and priorities in a context that allows the audience to help shape the direction of the presentation. That testing then increases your confidence as you write and predisposes the audience to accept the report because it reflects her or his own thinking.

Moreover, gathering people to talk through a problem or situation can encourage the synergy and innovative solutions you read about in Chapter 11. The meeting also fosters consensus as different points of view accommodate each other in a plan for action.

3. **To enhance personal relationships.** You talk, and especially listen, to build and enhance personal relationships. In writing, you address a real reader, of course. But as you write, the reader is only a fiction, someone you imagine. You may have a picture of the reader or readers in your mind (even in a frame on your desk), but the picture is only a representation. As you talk, however, you share a room or a hallway with the person or persons you are talking with, and you can exploit the full range of nonverbal communication that the setting allows. Emotionally charged messages are often

best conveyed personally—like firings and hirings—with written follow-up later.

You may need a personal meeting to *persuade* someone to buy something or believe you. Your presence lends credibility. You meet with your boss to convince her of the appropriateness of the proposed divisional restructuring you described in a memo earlier. The college recruiter wants to see how a potential applicant acts, how he presents himself. Bosses want to see how their subordinates think on their feet. Fifth-graders may want to *see* a banker. The salespeople in your division may want to shake your hand.

NONVERBAL ELEMENTS

Shaking hands is one of many forms of nonverbal communication that enrich discussions. In giving directions, you point and perhaps draw blocks or landmarks in the air. Such gestures intensify or clarify a message delivered simultaneously in words. Shaking hands and pointing at landmarks are intentional; an observer can probably read such signals easily, especially if the observer shares your cultural background. Much body language, however, is relatively unconscious. Its meaning depends on how an observer interprets it, and the interpretations may vary widely, especially across cultures. Businesspeople increasingly study nonverbal techniques that will help them demonstrate credibility and leadership. As you learned in Chapter 2, both an individual's body language and the setting of the discussion are significant forms of nonverbal communication.

Body Language

A gesture may be enough to convey a message. In giving the "thumbs-up" sign to a pilot, a mechanic indicates that the aircraft is ready for departure. On the way into school, a child waves to say good-bye to a parent. The soccer team captain raises his index finger to indicate, "We're number one. We've won." Such gestures are useful shorthand among people who agree about what the gestures mean.

Eyes and Facial Expression

In enhancing a verbal message, you send signals, for example, with your eyes and facial expressions. To "look someone in the eye" as you talk in the United States is to show honesty and reliability. On campus and in small towns, people may smile and say hello to strangers passing on the sidewalks. Smiling when you are introduced to someone is a sign of interest and welcome.

Appearance

You also send signals with your appearance. The role of appearance is, of course, complex. When you *feel* attractive, either because you are naturally so or because you cultivate attractiveness in your manner and attire, that feeling tends to encourage you to act in a way that makes others also find you attractive. Thus, career advisers counsel job seekers in the proper dress and behavior during interviews, and presenters at major meetings consider what they'll wear as well as what they'll say.

Movement

How you *move* and how you sit send additional signals. Tapping your fingers in a meeting may indicate to others that you are bored—or nervous. A frenzied walk may show the walker's lack of control over projects and time; a leisurely walk may show a lack of energy or direction. When people cross their arms as they talk, that action is often interpreted as a barrier against the listeners. Positioning your arms at your side is a more open posture. In the United States, a comfortable distance between two people engaged in a conversation is around 17 inches. Some people are more comfortable with less distance and move toward the other person; others need greater personal space and back away. Each movement can lead to misunderstandings, as you'll see.

Touch

You also send signals in the way you touch others. Your style of touching is constrained by your own personality, by the occasion, by the norms of the culture you were brought up in and the one you work in, and by law. Quite apart from all the intimate means and meanings of touch, touching in more public circumstances may be perceived as a sign of warmth, good feeling, and comfort. Cultural norms on touching, however, vary greatly. In European cultures, and especially in the United States, touching persons of the other gender during business occasions, except in handshakes, is unacceptable. In a business setting, physical contact of any kind can be interpreted as sexual harassment. In other cultures, or in nonbusiness settings like sports events, touching, even between genders, is often encouraged. Indeed, the absence of touch can signal hostility. You need to be aware of the great communication power of touch—and also of the cultural and legal norms that control it.

Setting

Architects talk about how a building *reads,* that is, how easily people can orient themselves within the building to find what they need. You've certainly had to find your way through such buildings as classrooms, offices, and gyms. You look for cues, some in the structure itself and some in signs, both verbal and visual. Think of the nonverbal signs which orient visitors, whatever their native language, to the layout of an airport.

Similarly, you need to read cues in the settings for conversations and meetings. In remaining behind her desk when other seating is available, a manager conversing with a subordinate may be interpreted as defensive and not welcoming of new ideas. The person who sits at the head of the table is traditionally the leader of the meeting. The person who has a private office on the corner of an upper floor of the building may well be the head of the company.

As you saw in Chapter 3, spatial privacy accompanies a rise up the hierarchy of most U.S. organizations. Several years ago, the chairman of an

Communicating across language communities often requires the use of visual symbols that convey recognized meanings.

insurance company developing plans for a large new corporate headquarters tried to counter the trend toward segregating managers from workers. He also thought the home-office system for writing insurance was like any manufacturing operation and wanted one low building with vast open spaces. The rest of the upper management wanted a separate wing for executives who would enjoy private offices and greater luxury in the building materials. At a review of the design, the chairman was heard to say to the executive committee, "Gentlemen, there will be no wing." The wing was built, however, a tribute to the power of structural symbols of authority.

STRATEGIES FOR EFFECTIVE LISTENING

Nonverbal elements intensify and clarify a verbal message. They may also contradict the message, as in the building of the office wing. To communicate well orally, develop strategies for listening to verbal and nonverbal messages. Then you can talk effectively based on that productive listening.

Recognizing Barriers

To listen well, you need to overcome several barriers. One barrier is the tendency to talk too much, the subject of the advice in Figure 20–1.

The *setting* may also distract the listener. The room may be noisy. It may be excessively cold or hot. You may be sitting in an uncomfortable chair or standing uncomfortably.

The *speaker* may create barriers. You may find the speaker's gestures or mannerisms distracting—the way keys are jingled or glasses pushed up on the nose or hands waved. If the session is being translated, you may lose attention between languages. Repeated phrases like "OK" or "you know"

When's The Best Time To Stop Talking?

Probably
now.
A story is
told about
FDR when he
was a young
lawyer.
He heard his
opponent
summarize
a case before
the jury
in eloquent,
emotional,
but lengthy
appeal.
Sensing the
jury was
restless,
FDR is reported
to have said,
"You have heard
the evidence. You
have also listened
to a brilliant
orator. If you
believe him, and
disbelieve the
evidence, you
will decide
in his favor.
That's all I have
to say."
He won.
Overstate
and bore.
Understate
and score.
When a baseball
umpire says,
"Strike three!"
He doesn't have
to add "Yer out."
That's what
strike three
means.

A message as published in the *Wall Street Journal*
by United Technologies Corporation, Hartford, Connecticut 06101

FIGURE 20–1.
Overcoming a major barrier to listening—talking. *(© United Technologies Corporation 1985.)*

or "eh?" may bother you. You may find the other's clothing or general appearance distracting.

The *listener* may create internal barriers. It's hard to listen when you are absorbed in your own problems or issues, or when you are indifferent or preoccupied. You may only pretend to listen. If you are uninformed about or uninterested in the subject of the discussion, that lack of understanding and motivation also reduces your ability to listen and respond well. You may dismiss the message because it's too difficult. Moreover, you may filter the speaker's remarks through excessive anticipation: You hear what you expect rather than what is said. Or you hear only enough to frame your response, and you concentrate on that response rather than listening. If anticipation has prepared you for an argument, your defensiveness may filter out the real message. Some of the defensiveness may derive from your negative attitude toward the speaker.

Finally, *differences in culture* and *a difference in gender* between you and the speaker may create barriers to listening, particularly a lack of sensitivity to nonverbal cues. For example:

- If you back away from a Latino or Italian, who is used to standing closer to another person in conversation than you are, that move may be interpreted as rejection. If you move to your comfortable distance in a conversation with a Japanese, who is used to more space, that move, too, may be misinterpreted.
- In a discussion, Japanese executives sit up straight, arms balanced on a chair's armrests, as befits people of good education. They may find offensive the slouching posture that an American feels is appropriate.
- Arab men—heads of state, heads of large families—often hold hands in public and may be pictured doing so in the press. Such hand-holding is a sign of trust and friendship. An American businessperson in a Gulf country may misinterpret the gesture.

Getting the Message

To listen well, you'll need to understand both the verbal and the nonverbal messages. In trying to interpret, remember, and respond to the verbal message, poor listeners move from detail to detail as the speaker presents them—then generally give up as the accumulation of details overwhelms their memory. Effective listeners identify or create the controlling idea of the talk and let it aid them in constructing a framework in which to place the details. As you listen,

- Sift out the core message.
- Identify the organizational structure.
- Take notes and paraphrase.
- Define key terms.
- Make connections to what you already know.
- Anticipate the information's uses and applications.
- Reconfirm any controversial points or evidence with the speaker.

Getting the Intent

Listen also for the speaker's *intent.* Your ability to interpret nonverbal behavior is important in understanding intention. Such behavior, along with the tone of voice, may either reinforce or contradict the verbal message.

Analyze particularly any *covert* intents. Intending to find out about your extracurricular activities, an interviewer asks, "What sports do you participate in?" You are active in clubs, the theater, and musical groups, but not sports. If you assess the real intent as "extracurricular activities," then you'll respond, "I'm not too active in sports, but would you like to hear about other extracurricular activities I participate in?"

Sometimes, of course, what people say *is* what they mean. As a listener seeking covert intents, you may misread a signal. Someone who says, "People like you impress me with your ability to get work done," may intend a compliment. A listener sensitive about her age may hear, however, "You're surprised because you think someone my age can't do *anything.*" In looking for covert intent, be aware enough of your own biases and pressure points so as not to attribute to others any self-confidence you lack.

A speaker's intent is often signaled by the connotations of the words he or she chooses. Analyze, for example, a speaker's use of jargon. If a speaker drags out terms from a professional language different from yours, is he trying to impress you? To intimidate you? Or is he just displaying his own laziness in not adjusting the language to your needs? In addition, analyze a speaker's choice of slang or coarse usage. Is she deliberately trying to offend you? Is she trying to signal her own toughness? If the speaker is evasive, weigh the evasion on the basis of your feel for the context of the discussion and for the speaker to assess whether to let the evasion go or to question it.

Listening to a Different Culture

It's easiest to communicate with someone you like who is like you. However, as you read in Chapter 3, you are likely to spend your career in a multicultural workplace. Interpreting both verbal and nonverbal messages across cultures and languages can be difficult right from the first introduction, as you see in "*FYI:* Meishis in Japanese Business."

Here are some other scenarios to consider, as pointed out by consultants on intercultural communications:[2]

- A U.S. manager seeing two Arab-American employees arguing decides to value their privacy and not intervene. But their Koran and Bedouin tradition led these employees to expect the intervention of a *wasta,* or intermediary, who would negotiate a win-win result to preserve group harmony. Lacking such intervention, the two employees let the argument escalate.

[2] The following examples are cited by Jolie Solomon, in "Learning to Accept Cultural Diversity," *The Wall Street Journal,* 12 September 1990, p. B1.

MEISHIS IN JAPANESE BUSINESS

Mohammed Ahmed
Head, English Language Program, International University of Japan

Many Japanese are hesitant to introduce themselves to strangers. That reticence, whether personal shyness or expected polite behavior, is overcome by presentation of the "meishi," or business card. American businesspeople, too, often exchange cards when they meet, but the timing and the mode are different in Japan. There's a ritual. Exchangers bow to each other. They hold the cards in a prescribed manner while passing them. They scrutinize each other's card silently. Only after this procedure has been slowly completed do they begin to talk.

In addition to name, address, and phone and fax numbers, the meishi contains an even more vital piece of information: the individual's exact position in the company he or she belongs to. In reading the meishi, the exchangers are determining who is senior or junior or whether they are equal. Based on that determination, each can select the proper level of language for addressing the other. The language a junior uses in addressing a senior differs in Japanese from a senior's language in addressing a junior.

In Japan's hierarchical society, how one talks, not what one talks about, is important. One does not want to lose face or feel embarrassed by adopting an inappropriate or rude tone in front of a senior person. Conversely, one needs to maintain an authoritative voice in front of a junior. The beginning point of the entire Japanese business culture is hierarchical, personal relations. There is no such thing as a direct, pure exchange of messages, at least not right away. Often, a third party is engaged to arrange introductions between businesspeople and to smooth any potential conflicts in advance. As such, business communication is often indirect and mediated. When no third person is around to introduce them, the meishi plays this important role of mediating between two individuals when they come face-to-face for the first time.

The Japanese derive their sense of importance less from their sense of individuality and more from their membership in a group. On the rare occasion when a Japanese introduces himself without a meishi, he is apt to say, for example, not "I am Saito" but "I am Sony's Saito."

• "A Latino manager starts a budget-planning meeting by chatting casually and checking with his new staff on whether everyone could get together after work. His boss fretted over the delay and wondered why the manager didn't get straight to the numbers. Latino culture teaches that building relationships is often critical to working together, while the dominant American culture encourages 'getting down to business'."

• A white American male interviewing an Asian woman looks for eye contact. Her lack of such contact leads the interviewer to think she's hiding something or is insecure. She sees the persistent eye contact as "domineering, invasive, controlling." The two don't trust each other.

Anne B. Forrest, Senior Vice President and Asia Regional Director in Hong Kong for Hill and Knowlton Asia Ltd., International Public Relations Counsel, describes other problems that occur when supervisors from North America listen only within the context of management strategies from home:[3]

• "When one of our department assistants was given an opportunity to fill in for his supervisor, the assistant came to me in a state of distress. 'You Americans are always trying to get people to do your jobs,' he said. There lay the basic misunderstanding. While I'm constantly encouraging staff to grow and take on more responsibility, some Asians, if they are happy with their jobs, are content to stay there and develop that skill thoroughly. 'For me, I have no desire to have my boss' job,' the department assistant explained."

Reading signals about worker satisfaction and knowing how to praise or criticize can cause confusion, according to Forrest. An American senior secretary placed in charge of a battery of secretaries, most of them Chinese, wanted to be helpful and thus toured the office frequently. The secretaries, however, thought their performance was being questioned. "And when we proudly announced we had hired additional secretaries to spread the workload, the hardest working ones made plans to quit their jobs. They were proud of their ability to handle so much work and thought we didn't think they were efficient or doing their jobs properly."

• After a Chinese member of a design group gave a particularly fine presentation to a weekly staff meeting at Hill and Knowlton, the American staff members led the group in applauding her. British members of the group noted later that they found the applause embarrassing, an example of the "American cheerleading mentality" that is inappropriate in a professional environment.

Listening to the Other Gender

In addition to cultural differences in attitudes toward achievement and work, gender differences also pose barriers to listening. In the preceding scenario, for example, is it significant that the speaker was a woman? Would the American staff have applauded a man? Researchers are characterizing differences in how men and women talk and in how they respond to each other's talking. When a female manager, for example, says to a male colleague, "Do you think we should invite X to the meeting?" she may well mean, "We *should* invite X." Her colleague, however, may think he's heard a question.[4]

In general, women's speech tends to be descriptive and polite rather than direct and informative. Women use more questions and signs of uncertainty. Men tend toward an adversarial style of conversation; they question and challenge. Women tend toward a supportive style; they agree and empathize. As one expert summarizes, perhaps glibly, men *report;* women seek

[3] "The Continental Divide: Coping with Culture Gaps," *Communications World,* June 1988, 20–22.

[4] Solomon, p. B-1.

rapport.[5] In discussions, men tend to interrupt women and to set the agenda more than women interrupt men or establish discussion topics. Women's interruptions, moreover, are more likely to be seen as violating a norm of subservient behavior, whereas men's interruptions are encouraged.

Patterns in speech and discussion behavior will probably change, however, as women and minorities increase their share in the labor force in the United States. The Department of Labor estimates that the white male share will drop to 39.4% by 2000, from 48.9% in 1976.[6] But awareness of such differences remains essential to effective listening.

STRATEGIES FOR EFFECTIVE TALKING

Cultivating a sensitivity to the diverse ways of communicating and to the range of interpretations of messages is the chief element in strategic listening, in addition to overcoming distractions in the environment and self-absorption. Many people deny diversity. Under the assumption that human nature is universal, they look for success in communication by treating everyone alike. Although seemingly fair-minded, such an approach may backfire, as you have seen. Instead, listen to differences. Seeking eye contact isn't a universal characteristic, nor is the need to move up in an organization. Withhold judgment. Allow for individual preferences and idiosyncracies. Ask people how they would like to be treated, and incorporate that answer into your behavior.

Guidelines for Talking

Listen first. And then, as you talk,

1. Use nonverbal elements appropriately.
2. Be literal with people you don't know well.
3. Repeat and summarize.
4. Use visuals and writing where necessary to foster understanding.
5. Take turns in discussion.

1. **Use nonverbal elements appropriately.** As you have seen, you may deliver one message with your words and another with your gestures. To enhance understanding, avoid cross-signals. When you communicate internationally, be particularly careful with gestures. Making a fanning motion in front of your face in the United States usually means something smells bad; to a Japanese, the motion means the person is refusing something or doesn't understand.

2. **Be literal and direct,** at least until you know the other person's conversational style. Use questions for questions, statements for statements, imperatives for imperatives. What's the meaning of the following sentences?

[5] For a popular discussion of how men and women differ in their conversational style, see Deborah Tannen, *You Just Don't Understand: Women and Men in Conversation* (New York: William Morrow, 1990).

[6] Solomon, p. B-1.

a. You can clear the table.
b. Are you the turkey?
c. You make a better door than a window.
d. Do you know what time it is?
e. You think I like having classes at eight every morning.

The first example reads like a statement but is really an imperative: "Please clear the table." In (b), the context would help in determining the sense, but what's being asked is "Did you order the turkey dinner?" In (c), the statement is an imperative obscured in a metaphor; it means, "You're blocking my view. Please move." The question in (d) is also an imperative: "Please tell me what time it is." Depending on *how* it is said, (e) might sound like a question or a statement about what you think. It means, however, "I don't like having classes at eight every morning."

For clarity, use the appropriate form to deliver the message. In addition, avoid irony and humor; both may easily be lost on a listener or may cause misunderstanding. And avoid insider's code, especially in international settings and with multilingual audiences.

3. **Repeat and summarize.** Because listeners will be distracted no matter how compelling your talk, give them the opportunity to catch up on main points. You need more redundancy in oral communication than in writing, which allows readers to retrace their steps if they lose their way.

4. **Use visuals and writing** to augment a discussion and aid in remembering, especially when you are delivering difficult or highly technical information. Use multiple channels to convey your message.

5. **Take turns.** Linguists and psychologists study the cues people provide in discussions to indicate that they have finished their remarks. The cues often differ among cultures and between genders, even in the same language. The British, for example, are apt to end a statement with a tag question ("Don't you think?") that returns the conversation to the other person. Interrupting another person is a sign of aggressive behavior. Finishing off another person's remarks may represent nervousness. Looking at your watch while another talks indicates impatience and may be considered rude. Americans are often uncomfortable with silence between remarks, as you have learned. In other cultures, the end of one person's remarks does not necessarily signal the need for another to begin.

ETHICS OF ORAL COMMUNICATION

When you talk and listen, you provide information, as you do when you write, and that information should conform to standards of honesty in intent and should not deceive. Moreover, your talking is often meant to influence others toward complying with you in meeting your personal or organizational goals. In influencing others, keep in mind the simple measure of ethical behavior: Leave them at least as well off as they were. In this section you'll learn briefly about strategies for gaining compliance and for resolving conflicts when other people resist your appeals.

Gaining Compliance

In a recent study, Sullivan, Albrecht, and Taylor looked at how managers in a wide spectrum of organizations tried to gain compliance from their subordinates.[7] The goals for persuasion fall into three main categories: (1) to attain change in the business environment; (2) to maintain a relationship; and (3) to maintain one's self-image. The authors found that the type of resistance expected or actually offered by subordinates was the major determinant of the strategies managers used to gain compliance. To overcome resistance, most managers used reasoning, especially in more formal organizations with established rules and procedures. They established a friendly atmosphere to create a favorable impression, and they rewarded compliance. Managers who perceived themselves to be highly powerful and dominant over subordinates, however, turned to the more assertive strategies of making demands and setting deadlines. They invoked sanctions against those who did not comply.

The strategy you adopt reflects both your personality and your training and results in different voices—both in writing and in speaking—as you saw in Chapter 5. You may begin in a friendly vein but become increasingly assertive in follow-up situations as resistance increases. Persuasion often takes time. It also takes attention, particularly if the resistance is strong. It takes an ability to deal with people as the individuals they are, not as myths or stereotypes, and an ability to perceive situations as subject to intervention and change. Two consultants offer this advice:[8]

- In a heated discussion, get on the other person's physical level: Sit if the other person is sitting; stand if she or he is standing—about six feet apart.
- Avoid taking the other person's tone if that might lead to a shouting match. "Bring screamers down to your emotional level; don't rise to theirs."
- Don't defend yourself until you've heard the other person out.
- Prepare whatever information may be necessary to investigate the conflict *before* you talk. If you don't have the proper authority to resolve the conflict, then avoid an unproductive discussion and refer the person to someone who can.

The Rogerian Strategies for Managing Conflicts

Traditional European rhetoric sees arguments in terms of winners and losers. The result is a victory (or a loss) and a score. You aim to dominate the other person, your opponent, and to bring her or him around to what you know is right. Any investigation of the other's position is merely tactical; you are looking for vulnerabilities.

[7] Jeremiah J. Sullivan, Terrance L. Albrecht, and Sully Taylor, "Process, Organizational, Relational, and Personal Determinants of Managerial Compliance-gaining Communication Strategies," *The Journal of Business Communication,* 27 (Fall 1990), 331–55.

[8] Sam Deep and Lyle Sussman as quoted by the "Executive Memo," *Marriott Health Care Services,* 12:8 (1990), 1.

A newer approach to conflict that reflects multicultural values is *Rogerian argument.* This technique is based in the client-centered therapy of the American psychologist Carl Rogers.[9] The essential strategy is a sensitive and thorough exploration of the other person's view—not simply to find its weaknesses, but to understand it and to use that understanding as a basis for further discussion. The process seeks to discover shared values and to avoid threats. You aid the other person in reshaping opinions without losing face. You may also change *your* mind as the other position convinces you. To discover a resolution that injures no one

- Agree on an objectively phrased statement of the issues to be discussed. The statement should separate the *people* from the *problem.* Probe the issues. Conflicts rarely have only a single cause or a single resolution.
- Construct an impartial and balanced statement of the other person's opinions and values.
- Develop an impartial statement of your position.
- Listen to and read (if they are written) all statements.
- Analyze the common ground between your positions as measured by objective criteria.

Such a discussion takes agreement in advance to enter into this kind of negotiation. In the end, the goal is to arrive at an innovative resolution that accommodates each side.

Taking No for an Answer

Rogerian strategies will help you conduct discussions to solve conflicts. Moreover, a sensitive and descriptive approach will also help you to accept negative news while maintaining a positive business relationship.

When someone says no to you, weigh the importance of that information. If the no is firm and the issue is trivial, let it go. Avoid a spiral of ever-escalating conflicts on trivial issues.

If the issue is important, review the situation from the other person's point of view to test how inflexible that no is. With some people, the first answer to all requests is denial. Does the other person want to be convinced? If so, accepting that first no will result in a double negative: You won't get what you asked for, and the other person will think less of you for your easy acceptance. Try one attempt to convince. Be careful in that attempt not to sound self-serving. If a potential speaker tells you she can't accept your invitation, for example, don't respond by saying, "But today is my deadline for submitting the list of talks." Such self-interest may only reinforce her feeling that her denial was appropriate. Instead, emphasize, perhaps, the interest of your division in hearing the talk or the importance of the speaker's credentials, which led you to her in the first place.

When someone tells you no, the manner in which the no was delivered or your own biases sometimes keep you from hearing it. Place the message

[9] In *Rhetoric: Discovery and Change* (New York: Harcourt, Brace & World, 1970), R. E. Young, A. L. Becker, and K. L. Pike adapt Rogers's principles to rhetoric and use the term "Rogerian argument."

in the context of its source. When you are criticized, for example, ask yourself these questions: Does the critic have a hidden agenda? What does he or she have to gain in criticizing? What's the critic's track record in sizing up other situations? Evaluate the no, being careful to strip it from any defensiveness you feel against its deliverer. Don't shoot the messenger; that is, don't think you can eliminate negative realities simply by getting rid of the bearer of negative information. Listen.

SUMMARY

- How much you talk—rather than write—on a job reflects **cultural norms** and preferences, the **policy and procedures** of your **organization** concerning the necessary documentation of an activity, and your own **personality.**
- Because talking is interactive, you choose oral communication to encourage a speedy response to a request, to test an idea and foster consensus before and during the creation of a document, and to enhance a personal relationship. At one extreme, writing is needed to *record* information; talking doesn't last. At the other extreme, the strongest persuasion often comes in personal discussions.
- **Nonverbal** elements are often as important as the verbal ones in intensifying and clarifying a conversation—sometimes more so. You send messages with your body language: how your eyes make contact with others, how you register expressions on your face, how you move, and how you touch someone else. Your tone of voice may also alter the meanings of the words you use. And the setting of a conversation sends signals. The observer gives meaning to these signals, sometimes a meaning not intended by the speaker, especially because so much nonverbal behavior is unconscious.
- Four major barriers to listening are **talking too much; distractions** in the environment or the speaker; your own **indifference,** preoccupation, or lack of knowledge of the subject being discussed; and **differences in culture or gender** between you and the speaker.
- To listen effectively, listen to the message itself and to the speaker's intent. Cultivate **diversity;** don't assume that everyone is alike.
- To talk effectively, **listen first.** Then use nonverbal elements appropriately; be literal with people you don't know well; repeat and summarize; use visuals and writing where necessary to foster understanding; and take turns.
- As opposed to traditional strategies for gaining compliance that emphasize winners and losers, **Rogerian strategies** emphasize finding common ground among disputants. Through the process of developing objective statements of each point of view, you develop an innovative solution that saves everyone's face and gains consensus.

EXERCISES

For Discussion

1. Obtain from your college business or personnel office or from the dean of students a copy of the college's statement on sexual harassment.

Examine the section on "touching" or "physical contact." Discuss the following:

a. Is the policy clear, that is, easy to understand and practice?
b. Does following the policy *improve* or *impede* communication? How does it affect the use of nonverbal elements of communication?
c. Can you suggest any improvements to ensure a harassment-free environment that also allows appropriate nonverbal communication?

2. Talk with some international students at your school about their expectations in conversations and particularly their sense of what's *different* about talking with Americans. Report on your findings in class.

3. In this chapter you read that you should be literal with others whose conversational style you don't know well. Listen carefully for several days to collect instances where statements that were not literal or direct may have caused confusion. Listen for code words; in a restaurant, for example, saying "I'm OK" when a waiter brings around coffee means, "I don't want any more coffee." Write the statements and discuss your collection in class. How might a more literal approach have fostered better understanding? Note, too, any irony or humor that may similarly have backfired.

4. One management consultant advises, "Eat sushi in Japan; serve the Japanese a barbecue in Texas." When you are entertaining visitors, how should you use nonverbal behavior to make them feel at home? What are some techniques for anticipating needs and avoiding potential conflicts?

5. In Chapter 13, you read four guidelines for ethics in letter writing: Be honest; value the other person's time; use the other person's language; and consider the other person's self-interest. The discussion of ethics in this chapter takes a different approach to the subject. But those four guidelines also pertain to oral communication. Using your reading of this chapter and your own experience, discuss in class the validity of those four guidelines in talking and listening.

For Writing

6. For two weeks (or more), keep a listening journal in which you analyze your listening skills, identify those you want to improve, and measure your progress toward improvement.[10] Use, for example, the HURIER analysis of listening components developed by Judi Brownell of Cornell University to identify listening components: *h*earing, *u*nderstanding, *r*emembering, *i*nterpreting, *e*valuating, and *r*esponding.[11]
   - **Hearing**—Overcoming distractions and concentrating on the speaker.
   - **Understanding**—Recognizing main points and the structure of the talk and subordinating details.

[10] At the 1990 annual convention of the Association for Business Communication, Thomas L. Means of Louisiana Tech University described in detail a course unit on listening that includes a listening journal based on the Watson-Barker Listening Test.

[11] Courtesy of Judi Brownell.

- **Remembering**—Connecting new knowledge with old and recalling important information.
- **Interpreting**—Listening to intent and nonverbal cues as well as verbal ones.
- **Evaluating**—Hearing a speaker out even if your points of view are different and resisting premature closure on an opinion or belief.
- **Responding**—Encouraging others to speak and providing effective comments.

Rate yourself on each skill. Decide on one or two to improve in. Record your progress each day as you listen—in classes or in informal discussions.

For Collaboration

7. Listening and talking are, of course, collaborative enterprises. How you rate yourself as a listener may differ from how others rate you. Using the HURIER scheme described in Exercise 6, ask someone who talks with you—and thus someone you listen to—to rate you. Does her or his perception of your strengths and weaknesses match your own? Exchange ratings in class and discuss them with your raters.
8. Divide the class into groups of three to five people. Each group will then investigate one of the topics presented in this chapter. A group looking at nonverbal communication might prepare guidelines to understanding the gestures used by Americans in conversation. Read about the topic (review Chapter 9 for hints on sources), and observe conversations. What, for example, does a raised eyebrow or a shrug of the shoulder or a look at the ceiling mean? Another group might read about and observe differences in the way men and women talk and listen and present those findings. Another might look at the cues people give that indicate they have finished talking in a conversation and that invite or forestall comments from others.

   When the research is complete, each group should present its results orally in class. In presenting the results, comment both on the topic and on how your group collaborated on its research (review Chapter 11).
9. Take notes on the presentations prepared in Exercise 8. Return to your groups to compare your notes on other speakers. Then assemble everyone's notes on *your* presentation, and evaluate whether the main points you thought you had presented did indeed come through.

21 TELEPHONE CALLS AND MEETINGS

What's Ahead

PHONE CALLS
- Outgoing Calls
- Incoming Calls
- Voice Mail

MEETINGS
- The Risks in Meetings
- The Rewards of Meetings

ROUTINE AND CUSTOMIZED MEETINGS
- Regular Meetings
- Task Forces

THE MEETING PROCESS
- Group Dynamics
- Conducting a Meeting
- Attending a Meeting
- Using Meetings to Solve Problems

MEETING INTERNATIONALLY
- Preparing
- Participating

FYI: Deciding to Meet Abroad

MEETING BY PHONE AND ELECTRONICALLY
- Teleconferencing
- Electronic Meetings

SUMMARY

EXERCISES

Do You Know 

- How can you make a phone call *productive?*
- What risks and rewards do meetings offer to organizations?
- How do *routine* meetings differ from *customized* ones?
- What are the stages of group dynamics in a meeting?
- What should you keep in mind in conducting a meeting?
- How should you prepare for a meeting abroad?
- How has technology changed the meeting process?

Pharmaceuticals Division

Baxter Healthcare Corporation
1425 Lake Cook Road
Deerfield, Illinois 60015
708.940.5746
Fax: 708.940.5635

Baxter

Ken Charhut
Director of Marketing
Automated Distribution

薬品部門

バクスター ヘルスケアー コーポレーション
米国イリノイ州ディアフィールド
レイク クック ロード 1425番地
電 話 : (708) 940-5746
ファックス: (708) 940-5635

ケン チャーハット
マーケティング ディレクター
自動化配送部

Ken Charhut's business card is printed in English on one side, Japanese on the other. In Chapter 13, you read his comments on two faxes sent between his company and Tokyo Sanyo Electric Company, a partner in Japan. Later in this chapter, you'll read some of his thoughts on meetings in Japan. Like many businesspeople, Charhut spends much of his day on the phone—speaking directly, using a modem that connects his computer to an e-mail system, retrieving voice mail, or sending faxes—and in meetings. In such forms of oral communication, managers demonstrate their accountability on the job. Management *productivity* comes from using such forms *well.* In this chapter, you will learn strategies for productive phone calls and meeting.

PHONE CALLS

You don't need to be told that the telephone is a critical tool of the modern office. You use it often—to find out information from a person or a database, to get a quick response to a question, to confirm a date for a meeting, to encourage a sale, to place an order, or to maintain a relationship. Americans are particularly comfortable using phones (and uncomfortable in locations remote from telephones). From 1980 to 1987, "the time Americans spent on the telephone increased 24 percent, from 3017 trillion minutes to 3754

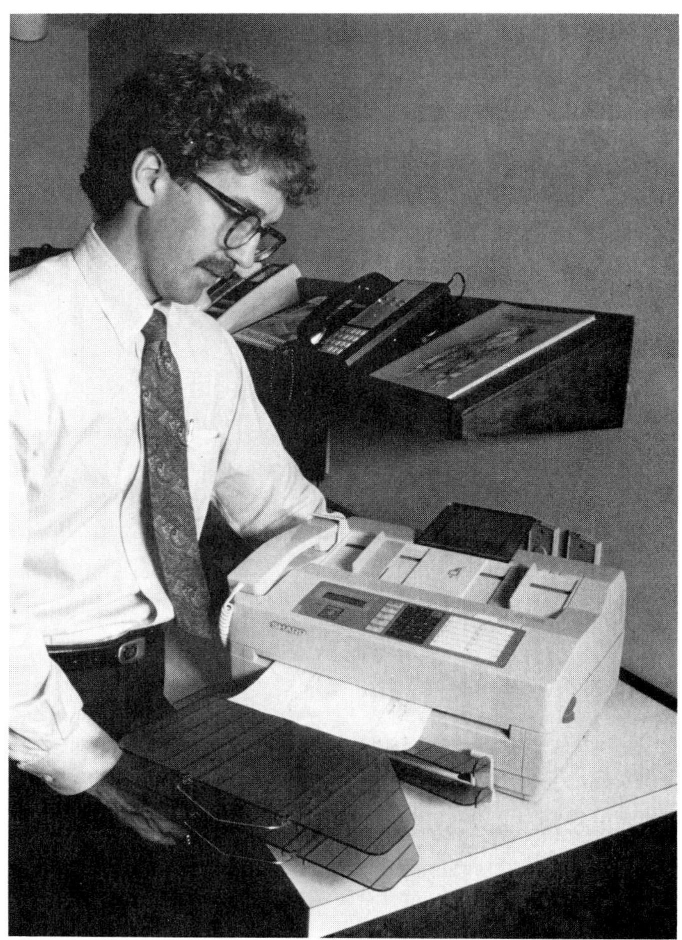

Electronic means of communication enhance the potential of communication.

trillion minutes, while the population grew only 7 percent,'' according to the Federal Communications Commission.[1]

Some of the growth reflects telephone links among computers and facsimile machines, as you read in Chapters 10 and 13. But a Federal Communications Commission economist estimates that such usage accounts for only perhaps 10 percent of the increase. People are just talking more to each other. The aim of some of that talking is simply to maintain a bond between the callers. But in an office setting, communicating by phone is another means of achieving organizational goals. Such use requires that you *manage* phone calls—both those that you make and those that you receive.

Outgoing Calls

Because telephoning is often faster than writing, it is useful when you need to convey or request information quickly or to place an order. Toll-free

[1] Trish Hall, ''With Phones Everywhere, Everyone Is Talking More,'' *The New York Times*, 11 October 1989, p. 1.

numbers, for example, are encouraging the growth of telephone shopping. L. L. Bean, the outdoors outfitter in Freeport, Maine, received 60 percent of its orders by phone in 1986 (the remainder by mail). In 1988, telephone orders accounted for 70 percent. Some organizations are also using *telemarketing* (sales calls) instead of letters in marketing drives. The call is interactive and more personal and thus aims toward greater persuasion and a quick response. For reference checks and other potentially controversial discussions, telephoning eliminates a paper trail when such a record may be undesirable.

Guidelines for Calling

Whenever you call someone, follow these steps:

1. Know the outcome you seek.
2. Get through to the intended recipient.
3. Complete your plan.
4. Close the call decisively and courteously.
5. Follow up as necessary.

1. **Know the outcome you seek.** Why are you calling? To place an order? Check a reference? Make a date for lunch or a meeting? Convey important news? Phoning just to "keep in touch" is common and often desirable, but you should clearly identify the goal of your call before you place it. If there is an instrumental purpose, label it. If you're just keeping in touch, be aware of that. If the goal is, as is often the case, mixed—that is, an objective outcome along with a generalized desire to maintain contact—be sure you identify both goals so that you can achieve each.

2. **Get through to the intended recipient.** This can be a tricky step. Rather than spending their own time dialing and redialing, some managers have secretaries place calls for them. This practice, however, often annoys the recipients, especially those at the same organizational level as the caller. It's best to place your own calls. If necessary, arrange with the recipient's secretary for a time to call as you would for a meeting time. You can then call with some assurance that your call will be received. When you find yourself in a game of "telephone tag" with someone, you may decide to *write* or to try to meet your goal some other way—perhaps with a call to someone else who is easier to connect with. Electronic-mail and voice-mail systems solve some of the tag problems. At the least, let the phone ring long enough for someone to answer, especially if the intended recipient is elderly or works some distance from the phone.

When you've got through, establish your identity briefly but in adequate detail to alert the respondent. Ask if this is a convenient time for a call. People often pick up the phone on the run—few people are capable of leaving a ringing phone unanswered—and they may be unable to talk with you at that time. Arrange another time if necessary.

3. **Complete your plan.** Convey your message or ask your questions, again briefly. Take notes on the person's responses while you talk and verify any potentially controversial or ambiguous information at once. If, for example, you have called to clear up a dispute on a bill, and the respondent

suggests that you skip the payment and wait for the next bill, then note that suggestion, along with the name of the person at the company who made that decision. Your notes will support you in any further dealings.

4. **Close the call decisively and courteously.** Confirm the next step in the project under discussion or otherwise indicate that the call is at an end. Don't just stop. Listen for cues from the respondent. It may be hard to get out of a phone call if the other person wants to keep talking. Peg the closing to some comment of your own or the respondent's that finishes off at least this segment of a continuing discussion.

5. **Follow up as necessary.** After you hang up, take any further notes, including those about activities you committed yourself to in the call. You may also have to write a confirming document to the recipient.

Incoming Calls

Telephoning, of course, is a two-way street. You need to call effectively. You also need to be an effective receiver of phone calls.

Think of the calls you receive. Although many may be welcome, others, particularly sales calls, may tie up your time ineffectively. You may want to screen your calls. Secretaries use courteous but decisive tactics to block unwanted ones. The essential tactic is asking the callers to identify themselves and their purpose. A salesperson may be asked to *write* a message; people unwilling to identify themselves will usually hang up. Answering machines are useful in screening calls, even when the recipient is near the phone. Some 28 percent of the homes in America had answering machines in 1989.[2]

If you don't have a secretary or a machine to screen your calls, then do your own screening in the first few minutes. Ask for further identifying information from someone whose name you don't recognize. Don't hesitate to end an unwanted sales call abruptly. If you suspect that the call may be controversial or that you may want to look up some information before you continue a discussion, find out the caller's number, arrange a time to call back, and do so. Returning the call aids in verifying the identity of the caller when, for example, you have been asked to evaluate a job candidate.

Avoid revealing too much in a phone call, particularly to a stranger. Don't be too hasty to point out shortcomings in your company or in people you're being asked to comment on. Determine the proposed use of any information that you'll give before you give it.

After the call, follow up. Some companies have forms for recording notes and action items sparked by phone calls. Keep a record (see Figure 21–1).

Voice Mail

When you call an American office you're increasingly likely to reach a voice-mail system. A recording welcomes your call; your responses on a touch-tone phone move you through a sometimes complex process to reach the "mailbox" of the person you're calling. At that point, you can leave a

[2] Ibid., p. C10.

```
Thomas Barnes, VP, DataCom, 1/23/92. 11:30 a.m.

--Ellen worked there as account mgr for 3 yrs, left to get MBA
--Always punctual, organized, easy to deal with--"A real pro"
--Supervised 6-8 accounts; all grew under her control; hands-on
   when problems occurred
--Sorry to see her leave but supported her decision to go to
   grad school; would hire her back anytime
--"You'll be lucky to get her"
```

FIGURE 21–1.
Effective record of a phone call that provided a reference check.

message in your own voice. The system screens calls for the recipient, cuts down on telephone tag, and allows you to leave your message. You can specify an order, acknowledge the receipt of a document or other item, confirm a date for some meeting—carry on routine business without having to write and without the time delay writing usually requires.

You'll need even more preparation for leaving a message on voice mail than for an ordinary call. A real-life respondent can guide you through your information; a machine may not offer such prompts. On the other hand, talking to a voice-mail system saves the time spent in small talk and politicking that otherwise go along with telephoning. You can get into and out of your message faster.

In leaving a voice mail message:

1. Establish the logistics: the time of the call, your name, and your organization (if that's not known to the recipient). The system may record the date and time automatically, but it's courteous to note this information yourself.
2. Speak clearly.
3. Be brave. Some callers find speaking with a machine daunting. The tape records what they say; they can't correct or change the message (although some sophisticated sytems do allow for editing). Just move ahead.
4. State the purpose of the call.
5. Provide your information or questions.
6. Give a time frame for the person to return your call, or otherwise suggest how that person can leave a message for you.

As a recipient of voice mail:

1. Check your mail frequently, particularly after a period when you have been either away from the phone or on the phone. Most systems can take messages from other calls while you talk with one person.

Callers assume that you'll check in periodically and act on that assumption. Take notes as you listen.

2. Keep your recorded message short and up-to-date. A simple message identifying the phone number reached is often adequate for personal machines. In an office setting, it's best to include information about when you will be available to receive or return calls and who might assist the caller in the meantime.
3. Avoid cute messages or ones that might be misunderstood. Think of the person listening to your message. One student, echoing a popular television show, began her message with her name and then asked, "And who the hell are you?" A potential employer returning her call, offended by the message, indicated that the company was no longer interested in her application. (She changed the message.)

MEETINGS

In addition to using the telephone productively, managers need to achieve productivity in another major form of oral communication: the meeting. A meeting may engage two people or thousands. You've probably participated in meetings: of campus organizations, of a sports team, or of a group at work. Meetings serve multiple purposes that fit within the general goals for business communication you have been reading about: to inform and to persuade toward a decision or action. Moreover, meetings, like documents, serve *maintenance, control,* and *definition* functions in organizations, as you will see.

The Risks in Meetings

In serving goals, meetings also entail risks. They can derail in personal squabbles and power struggles. The politics of who calls the meeting and who is called may override more instrumental purposes. Someone may call a meeting as a vote of confidence. Anyone left off the invitation list may read that snub as a sign that her or his days at the company are numbered. Because of their public nature, meetings may discourage the participation of those who are bright but lack good presentation skills and may unduly reward slick but empty performances. The potential for embarrassment is high. Too many like-minded people in a meeting can encourage the "groupthink" that fails to explore the problem or uncover options or see flaws in a plan. Groupthink can result in speedy closure on a weak decision. It can also lead to the "corporate voice" in the document that presents the decision. Too much diversity, on the other hand, may cause a breakdown in the group. People may reject an idea simply because they are in a turf battle with its presenter.

Meetings also take time: the time to arrange a merging of several persons' schedules, the time everyone spends together, and the time to follow up. According to one study, senior executives spend about 17 hours a week in meetings and 6 hours getting ready for them. And meetings may be easily diverted. One meeting called to formulate a major restructuring at a West Coast manufacturing company degenerated into a 90-minute discussion

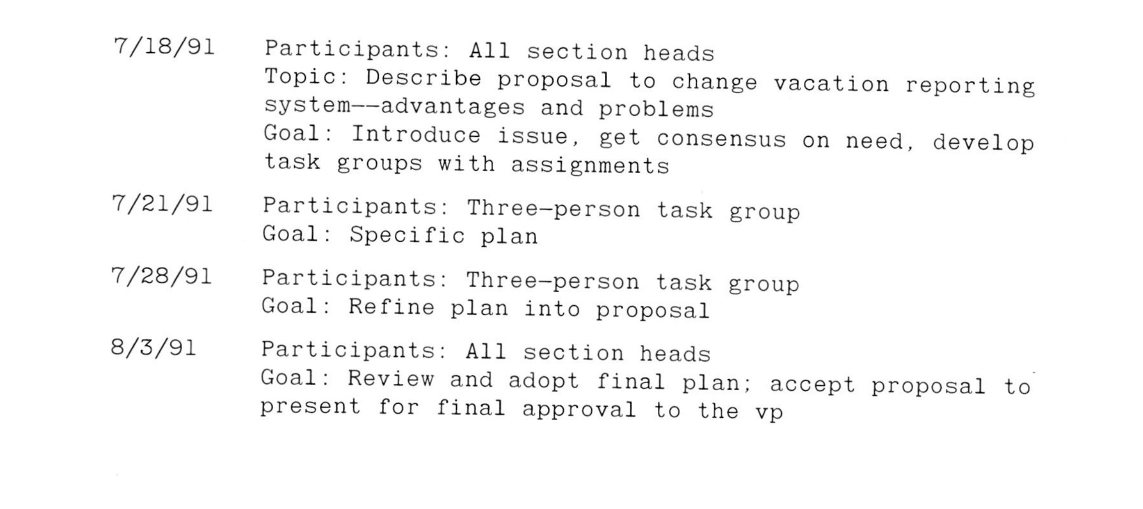

7/18/91	Participants: All section heads Topic: Describe proposal to change vacation reporting system--advantages and problems Goal: Introduce issue, get consensus on need, develop task groups with assignments
7/21/91	Participants: Three-person task group Goal: Specific plan
7/28/91	Participants: Three-person task group Goal: Refine plan into proposal
8/3/91	Participants: All section heads Goal: Review and adopt final plan; accept proposal to present for final approval to the vp

FIGURE 21–2.
Log of meetings on one issue.

about the food to be served at the office party. That conversation among 18 executives cost the company $2,200 in salaries.[3]

Given such risks, you should think at least twice before bringing several people together in a room. Assess whether a memo or e-mail might work as well.

The Rewards of Meetings

Getting a group together, however, may be just what's needed

- To solve a problem.
- To give visibility to some information or an issue.
- To forge teamwork and a group feeling.
- To form a consensus and encourage people to buy into an agreement.

You saw some of the elements of such group processes in Chapter 11. Many companies initiate and control their work through a series of meetings, what one expert calls a "meeting system."[4] Figure 21–2 provides a log of such meetings.

Given a project or a problem, the manager assigns tasks in an initial meeting. After the meeting, individuals conduct the necessary work, which

[3] Carol Hymowitz, "A Survival Guide to the Office Meeting," *The Wall Street Journal,* 21 June 1988, p. 41.

[4] "Making Meetings Matter: A Report to the 3M Corporation," prepared by Lynn Oppenheim, Wharton Center for Applied Research, Inc., 1987.

they report on in the next meeting. In that second meeting, then, the situation is assessed, directions are evaluated, and further work is assigned to be reported on in a third meeting. The meetings serve to monitor the work that occurs in the intervals between meetings, to profit from group responses, and to build momentum in the group.

Written reports may serve as a parallel form of accountability, as you learned in Chapter 18. Well established companies sometimes need fewer meetings and rely more on documents for control. Newer companies may require more meetings. Such meetings provide more flexibility than documents in measuring accountability when issues are murky and authority patterns are less clear. In encouraging decisions by consensus, meetings also diffuse the risks each person must assume for the decision. Similarly, in turbulent times, companies turn to meetings to develop new control methods.

In addition to *controlling* activities and measuring accountability, meetings help companies *define* their mission and priorities. They provide a platform for directing the company's resources to reflect changing values in a rapidly changing business environment. Meetings also serve as a forum for announcing those new directions in a way that builds consensus and agreement.

ROUTINE AND CUSTOMIZED MEETINGS

Like written reports, meetings can be classified on a scale from *routine* to *customized*. Routine, or regular, meetings often serve the maintenance and control functions you read about in Chapter 2. They keep the routine of the company going. They occur at scheduled intervals, generally with the same attendees. Customized meetings are called to match a particular one-of-a-kind need. They are often set up to solve a problem or to deal with issues of corporate definition and policy.

Regular Meetings

A finance committee may meet every quarter, a division staff every month, a fraternity every Tuesday evening. Standing-committee chairs or individuals assigned particular projects report on their progress. The meetings monitor activities, provide early warning of problems, keep people informed, develop consensus on a group decision, and build team spirit. Their main purpose is thus *informative,* although sometimes, of course, they lead to action. They also enhance the sense of identity and common purpose in the group.

Such formal meetings as the annual meetings of stockholders of publicly held companies are also *routine.* Controlled by senior management, such meetings aid in shaping the company image and in redirecting or reinforcing organizational priorities. They give visibility and heightened attention to major issues. Minutes of the annual meeting and of company board meetings become part of the record examined by auditors in evaluating the company's performance. Formal meetings adhere to Robert's Rules of Order for procedures on voting and other matters.

Task Forces

Whereas regular meetings follow the chain of command and foster organizational control, other meetings, like customized reports, reflect one-of-a-kind occasions, a more open structure, and greater diversity. The most significant of these are the meetings of "task forces" or other specially selected teams assigned to define aspects of the company, to solve a particular problem, or to gather information for a decision. A task force may, for example, design a new corporate logo or product, establish new policies or procedures, or develop a strategic plan for growth, acquisitions, and mergers. People may be pulled from all over the company to brainstorm in such a group. They profit from good visibility in the company and a chance to meet new people with less risk—and more potential for gain—than in staff groups.

Determining who should participate on a task force or other specialized problem-solving team can be difficult, as you saw in Chapter 11. Group success requires a mix of intelligence, creativity, and practicality among the members. For informative sessions, or when the goal is to have everyone do the same thing, as in a training session, it's wise to gather people who think alike. However, when the goal is innovation, a recommendation for something new, or a decision that requires broad investigation, it's wise to gather a diverse group. It's important that people in the group have roughly the same levels of assertiveness and ability to express themselves and persuade others. If one member is much stronger, that imbalance can undermine group success.

Politics also enters the selection process. It's easier to manage a group representing the same organizational level. In a mix of levels, rank may dominate over other factors. Task forces should be small to be workable—no more than seven or eight people—and such exclusivity may grate on those not selected.

THE MEETING PROCESS

Whereas meetings differ in what they aim to accomplish and in who attends, the *process* by which the meeting achieves its goals has certain common elements, primarily the dynamics of group interaction and strategies for conducting and attending a meeting. (Chapter 11 surveys group processes in general terms.)

Group Dynamics

Any group is likely to go through three stages in its work: *socialization, conflict,* and *consensus.*

Socialization

First, the group gets to know each other and establishes roles and norms. This socialization process may take several hours—or even several meetings—if the group members are unfamiliar with one another. Leaders emerge. Much communication is nonverbal as participants select their seats, distribute their materials, and include or exclude others when they make casual remarks.

Conflict

In the second stage, meeting participants sort out their conflicts and differences. What conflict is productive? What is wasteful? Power struggles among participants always have the potential for derailing a meeting. Resolving conflicts may require as much work person-to-person outside the meeting environment as inside it. Eventually the range of options and objections narrows as the participants become persuaded of the appropriateness of others' ideas. Some may withdraw their objections—because disagreeing seems futile, because the objection becomes trivial, or because of political pressure from the meeting leader.

Consensus

Success is finally measured in the third stage: consensus. As one solution or issue emerges, it becomes the sense of the group. Unanimity builds enthusiasm for implementation. Holders of minority opinions should be given a positive role in that implementation.

Conducting a Meeting

Before you call a meeting, make sure you understand the dynamics of a group. In addition, clarify the goal and know how you'll measure success. The leaders of meetings often judge them as more successful than the participants do. Why? In part, the leader's control over the meeting gives a vested interest in its outcome. That outcome may remain obscure in the participants' minds. Participants usually feel most productive when the meeting goal is clear, when it is conducted efficiently but without stifling dominance, when its outcome and the next step are well defined—and when they have a role in that next step.

Planning the Logistics

Pay attention to the time and place of the meeting. Some people resent meetings because they feel like hostages to organizers who want to control everyone's calendar. Give adequate notice and accommodate individual schedules as much as possible; an e-mail system aids in negotiating such arrangements. Establish both a starting and an ending time for the meeting. As a device for ensuring promptness and short meetings, some managers avoid scheduling them on the hour. They'll schedule at 9:15 or at 9:30, for example. A meeting scheduled just before lunch also has a built-in control on length: hunger. Forcing all attendees to stand, as one manager does, also tends to keep meetings short.

Arrange the logistics of the meeting site to accommodate the goal. A problem-solving session probably requires a conference table and white boards and flipcharts for recording ideas. An informational meeting might occur in an auditorium with access to more extensive audiovisual equipment. Such facilities are usually in heavy demand in organizations and may require six months or more of lead time. *Check* all equipment in advance. Remember the adage "Don't expect what you don't inspect."

Meetings bringing together employees from all areas of a business provide opportunities for effective communication.

Setting the Agenda

In advance of the meeting, solicit suggestions from the attendees about issues to be placed on the table. You may need a preliminary planning meeting to brainstorm an agenda before setting to work. As you prepare the topics, assess the amount of discussion necessary for each. Keep routine meetings to under two hours. If you have too much to discuss, schedule a series of meetings.

In addition to deciding on the topics for discussion, you'll need to arrange them in order. Depending on the group and your own management style, you may want to begin with easy items to build momentum for approaching the more controversial ones. Or begin with the most taxing items while energies are high and move on to the easier ones later, to end on a note of good feeling. Previewing topics with meeting attendees will provide you with information about what may become controversial. Try to avoid surprises. Remember that an unworkable agenda will undermine your credibility.

To strengthen the discussion you may decide to add special guests for cameo appearances on certain issues; if so, be sure to brief them about the group. Schedule guests only for the time necessary to discuss their particular focus. Holding them for the whole meeting is discourteous and unproductive.

Circulate the agenda well in advance of the meeting so that the participants can prepare and bring with them any appropriate materials. Note any special assignments, as in Figure 21–3.

```
Executive Staff

3 November 1991
10:30–12:00

1. Budget review--2nd quarter results (Maria Luiez)
2. Sales projections (Harry Kwan)
3. Unemployment compensation changes--report on new legislation
   (John Peters)
4. Update
   --cafeteria construction (Tom Levesque)
   --computer backups (Lori Basso)
5. Retreat--schedule and topics (Bill Metzger)
```

FIGURE 21–3.
Agenda for a routine staff meeting.

Leading the Discussion

Leading a meeting well requires both control and flexibility. You need to arrange the agenda and the logistics carefully, as you've seen. In addition,

- Begin on time.
- Open with a statement of the central issue, purpose, or problem to define the bounds of the discussion.
- Keep the participants on target, but allow some slack at the opening and during breaks for small talk.
- Don't let the participants drift—into side conversations, personal squabbles, or passive behavior.
- Perhaps by posing a general question to the whole group, rein in any participants who want to grandstand.
- Use a direct question to gently encourage the contributions of those who seem reluctant—without embarrassing them in public—or to draw in someone who looks angry or bored.
- Periodically summarize the status of the discussion on one topic before moving on to another.
- Close with a summary of all points and a plan for any future action.
- Close at the appointed time.

After a regular meeting, you'll probably circulate minutes, as you read in Chapter 12. In addition, remind individuals personally, as necessary, of any specific tasks for which they are responsible. Talk with dissenters to keep them on the team. Write any documents required by the meeting's purpose, for example, a recommendation report from a task force.

Attending a Meeting

When you are new in a company or organization, attend all meetings to which you are invited. If some meetings overlap, however, then talk with the organizers *in advance* to clarify the issues and to make an informed decision about which meeting to participate in. Don't just *not* attend. If necessary, send a written statement to cover whatever topic or project report you were responsible for.

Before the meeting, *prepare*. Meetings do measure accountability—something that leads people to dislike them. The deadline of the meeting may make you realize that your work is undone. Do it. Review the agenda and clarify your role with the meeting organizer if that role is unclear.

During the meeting, bring your agenda and *participate*. If you are new to the organization, spend time listening and observing to learn the norms for both what you say and what you do—both verbal and nonverbal behavior. Overcome any hesitancy to speak up by good preparation and practice. Temper any tendency to talk too much. *Follow up* afterward with any tasks assigned to you.

Using Meetings to Solve Problems

Although regular meetings may be largely informative, some customized meetings are called to solve extensive problems. Here are guidelines for such meetings.

Guidelines for Solving Problems in Meetings

1. Define the problem.
2. Gather more data.
3. Determine the criteria for evaluating solutions.
4. Generate solutions through brainstorming.
5. Evaluate the solutions against the criteria.
6. Decide on an implementation plan.

1. **Define the problem.**

• Note how urgent, important, or solvable the problem is and who is responsible for its solution.

• Worry about the problem and listen. Avoid hasty negation, for example, "The benefits package doesn't work." Instead, investigate: "What are the components of the package?" "What information do we have about its functioning?" "Who has reported problems?"

• Avoid embedding a solution in the statement of the problem, for example, "We need to increase payments in the dental plan." Increasing payments is one solution, but perhaps not the *best* solution, to problems in the benefits plan. Instead, state the problem in a way that encourages thinking about alternate solutions: "The dental plan seems to cost more than the benefits warrant." Try out the solution in discussion; don't just name it. Avoid a too-narrow or too-broad definition.

• Guard against hidden agendas. A participant who says, ''Let's review inefficiencies in the benefits package,'' may have as her purpose a public attack against the vice president of human resources who instituted the plan.

2. **Gather more data,** as needed, to report at the next meeting. Chapters 8 and 9 provide advice on this step.

3. **Determine the criteria for evaluating solutions.** Some common ones are practicality, economy, acceptability, ease of implementation, simplicity, and safety.

4. **Generate solutions through brainstorming.** As the meeting leader:
   Encourage people to speak.
   Foster diversity.
   Avoid dominance.
   Control conflict.
   Sort issues.
   Encourage synergy.
   Postpone evaluation and criticism.
   Seek an abundance of ideas; nothing is too far-fetched.

5. **Evaluate the solutions against the criteria** and select the best one.

6. **Decide on an implementation plan.** The plan makes the solution concrete. It provides an agenda for action on a set schedule and with (preferably) quantitative measures for success. If the task force decides, for example, that a flexible benefits program is what the organization needs, then the implementation plan addresses such issues as how the old program will be phased out and the new program phased in, how employees will be informed of the change and trained in the use of the new, who will oversee the new program, and how its results will be monitored.

MEETING INTERNATIONALLY

The process for conducting and participating in meetings that you have just read about takes on an added dimension when you meet with business associates abroad or are host to foreign visitors at your organization. The levels of ambiguity, complexity, and inherent confusion often increase. If the meeting is conducted in two languages, it may become twice as long. In ''*FYI:* Deciding to Meet Abroad'' (pages 438–439), Ken Charhut comments on the *purpose* of international meetings. In this section of the text, you'll learn some strategies for achieving that purpose.

Preparing

You can't take as much for granted when you meet internationally as you can when you meet locally. You'll need to learn about meeting customs and logistics in the other culture, and you'll need to prepare documents that ease and reinforce oral messages.

Meeting Customs and Logistics

Read about local customs, currency, taboos, and the like before you venture abroad, and prepare an overview statement for yourself and your team. The CIDA report you saw in Chapter 19 is one such document. Focus particularly on the conduct of meetings in that culture.[5] Learn the rituals for greetings (like bowing in Japan), gift giving, and exchanges of business cards. Know when business discussions are and are not appropriate. Learn the procedures for a first meeting. As you learned in Chapter 20, for example, it's customary to have a go-between arrange an initial meeting in Japan. Learn about who is likely to speak and expected forms of address. Americans are rather spontaneous after an initial presentation, but a foreign team may have only one spokesperson and the team may withdraw for side conversations as a routine behavior—one that may be seen as rude by Americans unless they're prepared.

Consult with your counterpart abroad to arrange logistics. Check holidays there and plan around them. Check customs regulations for bringing into the country whatever documents or equipment you need. Check on the compatibility of local equipment and electrical supply.

Documents

Prepare documents that aid in conducting the meeting and in providing technical information. For example, because it's hard to learn orally and quickly the names and backgrounds of people from other cultures, the Asia Foundation prepared the card shown in Figure 21–4 (page 440) to ease conversations when some high-level visitors attended meetings across the United States. Write such statements in the language of the meeting's setting. If you will be doing extensive business in another country, print your business card (or its back) in that language (see the card at the beginning of the chapter).

Similarly, prepare one or more documents that will reinforce your message in the meeting. Figure 21–5 (pages 442–443) shows such a document used by representatives of Dominion Industrial Fabrics in Europe. Bring annual reports and production statistics in English and provide a short, locally produced summary in the language of your host. Visuals are particularly helpful in crossing language barriers, as you saw in Chapter 6.

Finally, prepare documents that will aid in coordinating your own team. Provide extensive and detailed background on the company you are visiting and your goals for the visit.

Participating

The listening skills—verbal and nonverbal—you learned in Chapter 20 are heavily taxed in international meetings. That's one reason such meetings are tiring. Observe how people refer to themselves and each other, and follow

[5] *The Economist Business Traveller's Guides*, edited by *The Economist*, a leading British business journal, provide excellent introductions to doing business in various cultures and particularly to the etiquette of business meetings. They are published in the United States and Canada by Prentice-Hall.

DECIDING TO MEET ABROAD

Ken Charhut
Director of Marketing,
Automated Distribution,
Baxter Healthcare
Corporation

Business meetings represent an efficient way to share ideas or policies in a group when immediate or personal feedback is required. In the context of international business, meetings become an important method of securing relationships and focusing both sides on the common goal.

We have been working with a Japanese company for product development and manufacturing resources. Our company remains responsible for product research, marketing, and sales. The relationship can be considered a relay race. We present a product concept to the Japanese company; they take the project from there and develop an actual product; then we complete the arrangement by selling the product.

Successful relay teams rely on well trained runners to take and deliver flawless handoffs. We, too, must ensure both successful runs and successful interfacing between runners. That interfacing is the particular communication challenge—both in writing and in oral communication.

The most obvious barrier to communication with the Japanese is language. We settled on English as the language for *written* correspondence. Because our information is highly technical, we also decided to communicate directly with the Japanese engineers and to have information translated by the technical group to enhance precision.

Written correspondence serves well to cover technical specifications and design decisions, but the form breaks down over time as a method of controlling project time lines and commitments. Because each party interprets the documents without consulting the sender, a misinterpretation may occur and may not be corrected immediately.

their lead as you address them. In Japan, for example, your contact in the company will introduce colleagues to you by their family name, in order of seniority. Adding the suffix *-san* to a name implies respect. You may refer to Machi as Mr. Machi, but Machi-san is better. Don't, however, use *-san* in introducing yourself. Wait to be seated in the meeting room until your host designates the proper arrangement. If you are the host, think about that arrangement in advance. In Japan, the most senior host generally sits furthest from the door. The Japanese sit on one side of the table or in a row of chairs that face the visitors on the other side or in another row. The arrangement is "customary rather than confrontational."[6] During the meeting, you may want to designate someone as the detailed notetaker while you talk and listen.

Adjust your expectations *and* your watch to local time. In the United States, meetings tend to begin at the designated time, to end within two hours (except under unusual circumstances), to be free of interruptions, and to move quickly toward an outcome. Elsewhere, a meeting time may be less fixed, and the meeting itself may ramble and be subject to interruptions.

[6] *The Economist Business Traveller's Guides: Japan* (New York: The Economist Publications, Prentice-Hall, 1987).

Major misinterpretations are usually caught quickly, and a phone call or fax corrects them. Minor misunderstandings may go unnoticed and may accumulate over time. These misinterpretations are also coupled with environmental changes such as employee turnover or variations in business conditions. Eventually, we realize that we are no longer in sync. Our clean project handoff is in jeopardy. The triggering event is usually a fax with a new time line or a lack of commitment to a previously agreed-on item. A face-to-face meeting is required to refocus efforts and reevaluate the environment to ensure that the project will remain on track.

The face-to-face meeting serves several purposes. First, it reestablishes the main commitments made in the initial phases of the relationship. Personal contact is critical to reinforce that commitment in human terms between individuals with accountability as opposed to the more abstract terms of companies with no direct accountability. The meeting is conducted in both Japanese and English. Second, within the context of this renewal, changes in the business climate can be evaluated in a positive, supportive environment as opposed to a potentially confrontational one. Finally, more than in documents, the meeting provides an opportunity to deal with misunderstandings through immediate oral give-and-take.

The successful management of an international relationship, then, depends on a balance between oral and written communication. Meetings focus on overall objectives and environmental issues, and documents trace project updates and technical information flow. We believe that the cost of traveling to Japan and holding meetings for these reasons is justified.

MEETING BY PHONE AND ELECTRONICALLY

Thus far you have read about the context and guidelines for face-to-face meetings. In Ken Charhut's *FYI* discussion you saw how he decides that a meeting, rather than more writing, is necessary to advance a project. In this final section, you'll look at some alternative forms and technology for meetings. Some methods include a *merging* of oral and written forms, a trend you saw predicted in Chapters 1 and 10.

Teleconferencing

You can meet with others by phone in a conference call that links several participants who then comment from their desks on an issue or problem posed by the organizer of the call. At a more highly technical level, groups of people at sites remote from one another may gather at speakerphones to

Delegation of

MEMBERS OF JAPANESE NATIONAL DIET

Study-Observation Tour of the United States April 27–May 12, 1990

Sponsored by The Asia Foundation

MOTOHISA IKEDA Kanagawa Prefecture. Japan Socialist Party.

Upon graduation from the School of Political Science and Economics of Waseda University in 1964, Mr. Ikeda joined the Japan Broadcasting Company (NHK). In the course of a twenty-five year career he covered news concerning the Diet, the Prime Minister, political parties, and government ministries. He was also in charge of reporting on elections and other special events. Mr. Ikeda was elected to the Diet in 1990. He is married and has two children.

YOSHIHISA INOUE Tokyo. Komeito or Clean Government Party.

Following graduation from Tohoku University, Mr. Inoue, who was a native of Toyama Prefecture, pursued a career as an official of the Soka Gakkai Buddhist sect and the Komeito. He was elected to the Diet in 1990. He is married and has two children.

KIYOHARU ISHIWATA Kanagawa Prefecture. Liberal Democratic Party.

Mr. Ishiwata was elected to the House of Councillors in July 1989 after serving five terms in the Kanagawa Prefectural Assembly. In 1986 he was elected Speaker of the Assembly. In the House of Councillors, he serves on the Construction and Environmental Affairs Committees. Mr. Ishiwata is a graduate of Keio University and is managing director of a hospital in his native city of Yokohama. He is married and has three children.

HIDEKO ITO Hokkaido Prefecture. Japan Socialist Party.

Ms. Ito is a graduate of the liberal arts faculty of Tokyo University. She served for ten years as an investigator for the Tokyo Family Court before leaving to enter law practice in Sapporo. She was elected to the House of Representatives in February 1990. Ms. Ito is married to a professor at Hokkaido University and has three children.

KIYOKO ONO Tokyo Prefecture. Liberal Democratic Party.

Ms. Ono was elected to the House of Councillors of the Diet in 1986 and serves on the Budget Committee and Committee on Social and Labor Affairs. She is a well-known athlete, who participated in the Tokyo and Rome Olympics. She is a member of the Japan Olympic Committee and Director of her party's Women's Section. Ms. Ono is a graduate of Tokyo Education University, and is the author of books on physical fitness. She is married and has five children.

FIGURE 21–4.
A card introducing members of a U.S. visit sponsored by the Asia Foundation. *(Courtesy of the Asia Foundation.)*

discuss an issue in an *audiographic* teleconference that also allows for the transmission of charts and diagrams. In some systems, these can be developed interactively among participants through an electronic blackboard. Even greater visibility is provided in *full-motion videoconferences* beamed worldwide among specially equipped rooms. Participants see and hear one another, profiting from nonverbal as well as verbal cues. Hard copies of overheads used in presentations can be faxed quickly as well.

Forty percent of the field offices of The Travelers, the insurance company based in Hartford, Connecticut, are now connected to the home office in a teleconferencing network; that number is projected to expand to 80 percent. Fifteen-minute meetings in the early morning connect some 200 employees from both Ireland and the U.S. East Coast to check levels of service (response times of computers, for example, and performances of vendors) and to provide early warning of any problems.[7] Some companies use teleconferencing for major corporate announcements from the home office to branches. The sessions foster group identification and teamwork without requiring travel. But they are expensive. A Travelers spokesperson estimates that equipment costs can run from $10,000 to $15,000 per site; production costs range between $5,000 and $50,000 depending on length and elaborateness; and transmission costs may be $10,000 to $15,000.[8]

Electronic Meetings

The technology of personal computers is leading to another communication form: the electronic meeting. Specialists in management information systems at IBM and Jay F. Nunamaker, a professor at the University of Arizona, for example, are developing software to facilitate "meetings by keyboard."[9] In such a meeting, held in a specially equipped computer room, a leader poses a question or problem. Next, for an hour or so, participants type their responses or solutions; everyone types simultaneously. The computer then searches for common themes and key words and sorts comments into categories that the leader uses to pursue either an oral discussion or further typing. The participants rank the items and vote on priorities.

Companies have used the system to develop the criteria for new projects and to rate senior management on a grid of leadership characteristics. A group from a controller's office developed a billing strategy in one day. "That's a process that would normally require dozens of meetings," said an MIS manager.[10] An electronic meeting "speeds the process, as everyone talks at once; fosters honesty through anonymity; gives participants a sense they played a role in decision-making; creates a printed record of results." But there are also disadvantages: The meeting "requires thinking at a keyboard, gives equal time to bad ideas, does not give credit for brilliance."[11]

[7] Mary Agnes Carey, "Pointless Meetings Are a Waste of Time, Money," *The Hartford Courant,* 26 February 1990, p. 22.

[8] Lawrence B. Rasie, "New Communications Technologies Reducing Company Travel Costs," *The Hartford Courant,* 13 February 1989, p. 3.

[9] Claudia H. Deutsch, "Managing: Business Meetings by Keyboard," *The New York Times,* 21 October 1990, p. 29.

[10] Ibid.

[11] Ibid.

DOMINION
Industrial
Fabrics Co

The **DOMINION** Industrial Fabrics Company manufactures a wide product selection consisting of **spun 100% cotton, polyester/cotton,** and **100% polyester** substrates designed to meet product specification for applications in a variety of sophisticated coating processes.

Our success has resulted from our commitment to develop long term business relationships with our customers.

DOMINIONS' definition of Quality means both Quality of *Service* as well as Quality of *Product*.

We offer the market a broad range of products serving different segments, supported by a program of dedicated customer service and manufacturing flexibility.

Our understanding of customer needs and attention to technical details have contributed to our success.

Experience ***Quality*** with us......

Technical Fabrics
end use

		Scrims	Print Cloth	Sheetings	Flannels	Osnaburgs	Drills	Polyester	Twills	Sateens	Broken Twills	Nomex	Canvas SFD	Plied Ducks	Army Ducks
Abrasives			•	•			•		•	•					
Adhesive Tape Mfg			•	•											
Automotive		•						•							
Buff Trade				•											
Continuous Coaters			•	•	•	•	•			•	•				
Convertors	Apparel			•	•		•		•	•			•		
	Home Furnishing		•	•	•					•					
	Interlining		•	•		•									
Food Packaging		•		•		•									
Footwear Industry			•	•	•	•	•				•		•	•	•
Industrial Cut/Sew	Canvas												•	•	•
	Filtration		•	•	•			•							
	Glove								•				•		
	Promotional		•	•	•					•			•	•	•
	Safety Apparel											•			
Laminators		•	•	•				•							

FIGURE 21–5.
A one-page overview of the Dominion Industrial Fabrics Company—in two languages. *(Courtesy of Sirio DeLuca.)*

La Compagnie des tissus industriels **DOMINION** fabrique une vaste gamme de tissus **tout coton, polyester/ coton** et **tout polyester** conçus selon des spécifications précises pour une variété d'applications du domaine de l'enduction.

Notre succès est dû à notre engagement à développer une longue relation d'affaires avec nos clients.

Chez **DOMINION**, la *qualité* signifie autant la qualité du *service* que la qualité du *produit*.

Nous offrons un large éventail de produits servant différents secteurs du marché, le tout allié à un programme soutenu de service à la clientèle et de souplesse de fabrication.

La compréhension des besoins du client et l'attention aux détails techniques ont contribué à notre succès.

Faites l'expérience de la ***qualité*** avec nous......

Tissus industriels
usages

Usages		Canevas léger	Tissus pour impression	Tissus renfort	Finettes	Osnaburgs	Coutils	Polyester	Sergés	Satin de coton	Sergé interrompu	Nomex	Canevas	Canevas à fils retords	Canevas militaire
Tissus abrasifs			•	•			•		•	•					
Ruban adhésif			•	•											
Tissus pour l'industrie automobile		•						•							
Tissus à polissage				•											
Enduction continue			•	•	•	•	•			•	•				
Finisseurs	Tissus vestimentaires			•	•		•		•	•			•		
	Linge de maison		•	•	•					•					
	Triplures		•	•		•									
Emballage alimentaire		•		•		•									
Industrie de la chaussure			•	•	•	•	•				•		•	•	•
Confection industrielle	Canevas												•	•	•
	Filtration		•	•	•			•							
	Ganterie								•				•		
	Promotion		•	•	•					•			•	•	•
	Vêtements sécuritaires											•			
Contre-Collage		•	•	•				•							

SUMMARY

- **Prepare** before phoning. **Know your goal** and gather any needed material. During the call, run through your questions or information courteously and with dispatch, whether talking with a person or a voice-mail system. **Take notes** on any information or action discussed in the call. **Follow up** as necessary.
- Meetings take time and can dissolve in personal squabbles, trivial issues, or political powwows and ego trips. Those are the risks. But meetings also serve the important organizational goals of **control** and **definition.** Meetings initiate and monitor the work of managers. Task forces develop the long-range plans and problem-solving approaches that define the organization. Meetings further **give visibility** to important ideas and **foster consensus** and goodwill within the organization.
- **Routine meetings** occur at regular intervals, with regular participants, usually members of the same division or department, and often with a regular agenda. **Customized meetings** have a more open structure and are called to meet one-of-a-kind occasions like solving a particular problem or developing policies. **Participants** are specially selected for the task.
- Groups often move through three stages as they meet. The first is a **socialization** process, in which the participants learn or establish their roles and norms. The next stage is **conflict.** Dysfunctional conflicts need to be resolved; positive differences of opinion need to be encouraged to produce abundant ideas for solving the problem. Through conflict, the meeting moves to the third stage, **consensus,** in which participants buy into a group solution or decision on an issue.
- The meeting leader needs to **prepare** for the meeting by setting a clear **goal** and an **agenda** that will achieve that goal and by arranging appropriate **logistics. Leading the discussion** during the meeting requires a balance of control and flexibility. **Periodically summarize discussion** on one topic before moving to another. **End the meeting** on time and with clear guidelines for follow-up activities.
- In arranging a meeting abroad, learn about meeting **customs** and **logistics** in that culture and prepare documents that ease both the conduct of the meeting and the exchange of information. Anticipate differences.
- Through **teleconferencing,** technology has enhanced the ability of businesspeople at remote locations to meet without traveling. An audio-only system connects several phones; more elaborate systems include **electronic blackboards** for interactive graphics; most sophisticated are the **video-enhanced systems** by which people in specially equipped rooms at remote sites can see and hear one another. Other technology includes **meetings by keyboard** as participants jointly use personal computers to come to a consensus on issues.

EXERCISES

For Discussion

1. Observe your telephone behavior over the next several weeks. How do you open and close the discussion? How much time do you tend to allow for small talk before getting to your point? Are you comfortable with

pauses? How do you try to end them? How, in particular, do you close off a conversation when the other person seems to be talking too much? Make notes on your observations. As your instructor directs in class, compile all the responses to each of the questions to generate a profile of telephoning behavior in the class. What are the central tendencies?

2. Here are some statistics:
   - Executives waste at least a month every year on unnecessary or unproductive telephone calls, according to a survey of 200 corporate vice presidents.[12]
   - Business meetings waste more than $37 billion a year in wages and benefits, according to a survey of 1,000 business leaders.[13]

   Read the business press to find other statistics about "waste" in phone calls and meetings. Then discuss the *validity* of these—and your—statistics. On the basis of your reading in this chapter, and elsewhere, develop criteria for measuring waste, and thus productivity, in meetings.

3. Read the following brief case concerning the timing of meetings. Then answer the questions that follow.

> Lisa Dobbins, who supervised 50 wordprocessing operators at a large insurance company, prided herself on being well organized and efficient. She hated to get behind in her work. When her company decided to implement a new flextime plan that would allow the people on her staff to schedule their hours to fit personal needs, she immediately called a staff meeting to describe the plan, even though it was not scheduled to take effect for four months. She wanted all her employees to understand the new system and prepare for it.
>
> During the week after her meeting, eight persons in Dobbins's group started coming in earlier and leaving earlier, and three stopped taking lunch hours so they could go home earlier. She had to remind them that the flextime schedule was not yet officially in place. The week before the schedule was to start, she made some remarks to some workers about getting their schedules in writing to her. They said they didn't realize the new schedules had to be submitted to Dobbins for approval. She curtly reminded them that she had discussed this requirement at the staff meeting nearly four months before. When individuals came to her to ask for more information, she realized that she would have to set up another meeting. She was annoyed because, as she said, she would "have to go over it all again."

   a. Did Lisa Dobbins jump the gun in announcing the flextime plan so far in advance? Why or why not?
   b. Should she have issued a written statement at the beginning? If so, what information should she have included in it?
   c. If she schedules another meeting, how should she begin it? Should she try to explain why she has called another meeting on the same topic?

[12] Albert R. Karr, "Labor Letter," *The Wall Street Journal*, 25 July 1989, p. 1.
[13] Carey, p. 22.

For Writing

4. Keep a log of notes on all phone calls you receive for one week. Record the date and time of the call, the caller's name, the central message, and any action required from you because of the call. If you're a full-time student, most of your calls may be personal ones, but keeping a log is a good habit to cultivate for your days in an office. A phone log there can become a significant document in its own right and as a basis for reports.
5. Write an agenda for a meeting of some organization you belong to at school, in your community, or at your office. Include this information, along with information concerning the logistics of the meeting, in a memo to participants (see Chapter 12).
6. As a participant in a meeting, observe not only *what* is being said, but *how,* that is, the meeting process. Then write up your observations in a brief report. Consider the following questions: How was the meeting announced? How did you know what your role would be? What procedure did the leader establish for running the meeting? Did the meeting get out of control? Did individuals take turns speaking? Did anyone withdraw from the meeting—and did the leader try to bring him or her back in? How? If the meeting included members of both sexes, were there any differences in their group behavior, either verbal or nonverbal?

For Collaboration

7. Divide your class into groups of about five people each. Take one class period for each group to discuss a campus issue and to *propose* a new policy or procedure concerning that issue. All the groups should discuss the same issue. The result of the discussion should be a brief (no more than one-page) statement of the proposal (see Chapter 17). During the next class period, have a spokesperson for each group present the group's statement. Then compare the statements. Discuss in a general session *how* each group arrived at its statement.

   Some General Issues

   Class registration
   Student evaluation of faculty
   The grading system
   College or university policy on alcohol
   The student activities budget

8. Assemble a team to prepare a briefing report on the process of meetings in one culture. Use Canadian or U.S. government publications or privately published guidebooks as references. Each member of the team may develop one topic, for example, greetings, gift giving, ethics, negotiating tactics, or nonverbal behavior.

22 BUSINESS PRESENTATIONS

What's Ahead

THE CONTEXT FOR PRESENTATIONS
DETERMINING THE CONTEXT FOR YOUR TALK
- Analyze the Audience
- Assess the Setting
- Identify the Purpose

ORGANIZING YOUR INFORMATION
- Ho-Hum!
- Why Bring That Up?
- FYI: Corporate Speech Writing: Framing the Facts
- For Instance?
- So What?

PREPARING THE VISUALS
- Overheads and Slides
- Video
- FYI: Seven Cs for Video Success

PRACTICING
PRESENTING
- Keep Control
- Talk with the Audience
- Use Question-and-Answer Sessions Strategically
- Think Multiculturally

SUMMARY
EXERCISES

Do You Know ?

- What are the purposes of business presentations?
- How should you prepare a talk?
- How should you prepare the visuals?
- What can you do to practice the talk?
- What makes for a good performance?

"When they leave one of my presentations, I want them to think about more than where their car is parked."

—A corporate spokesperson

Like the formal written reports you read about in Chapter 19, oral presentations advance company goals and enhance your visibility in the organization. Good presentations also derive from the same principles as good reports: Know your audience, know your information, and structure and express that information to match a clear goal and the needs and interests of the audience. In addition, oral presentations require specialized techniques of delivery. And just thinking about delivering a talk strikes fear in the hearts of many businesspeople. Your organization, and your own career, will benefit, however, if you're an effective presenter.

In this chapter you will learn strategies for delivering effective presentations. After reading about how presentations function in the internal and external communications of organizations in general, you'll read about how to prepare your own talk. "The more you sweat in advance, the less you'll have to sweat once you appear on stage," advises George Plimpton.[1] You'll boost your confidence and effectiveness by preparing well before you perform. In that preparation,

- Determine the context for your talk.
- Organize your information.
- Prepare the visuals.
- Practice.

Then, present the talk—with confidence and effectiveness. Who knows? You may find that you have a knack and enjoy performing.

THE CONTEXT FOR PRESENTATIONS

Many of the meetings you read about in Chapter 21 require participants to prepare and deliver presentations, either informally or formally. You provide

[1] "How to Make a Speech," advertisement of the International Paper Company, © 1981.

an overview of the status of a project to the project team or the division head, or you brief a new member of your organization on the company's benefits package. You propose a new computer system to the vice president of operations as the spokesperson for a company task force charged with the recommendation. As an instructor in the training division, you take a group through the steps in a new quality-control program. As head of marketing, you assemble key salespeople at an Oregon resort and start the two-day event with a presentation aimed at firing their enthusiasm for a new company product. All these presentations are *internal* to your organization.

External presentations serve the company's public relations effort for audiences in the media, the government, or even the public at large. Some aim to keep the press informed of events at the company or in which the company is involved. Such presentations, often called *briefings,* can be tense during a crisis if you represent, for example, an oil company responsible for a major spill, an airline that just lost a plane and several lives in a crash, or a food producer whose contaminated products have caused injury or death. Company representatives may also have to speak at government hearings and at the meetings of review boards.

The CEO and other corporate officers will speak at the annual meeting of stockholders, at sales presentations to customers, and at trade fairs and conventions. Popular business leaders are in demand for speeches at fund raisers, awards ceremonies, and other public service events; at the openings of new franchises, plants, agencies, or stores; and even at national events. The round of dinner talks is often called the *chicken-and-peas circuit,* named for the typical menu at such occasions.

Major presentations, whether internal or external, are often held in large auditoriums and accompanied by elaborate visuals, including films, videos, and multimedia projection on many screens. Speech writers are often enlisted to polish the texts of the talks, as you'll see.

DETERMINING THE CONTEXT FOR YOUR TALK

Why have you decided to give a talk—or why have you been asked to give a presentation? As you begin your preparation, determine the particular context: audience, setting, and purpose.

Analyze the Audience

The critical measure of your presentation's success is whether it works *for your audience.* As in planning a document, match the audience's level of understanding, their purpose in seeking information, and their skills in assimilating that information. But listeners have additional needs. Readers can skim, or read a section slowly, or linger over a figure to extract the details and puzzle out the logic, or pause when they are tired. Listeners, however, are at the mercy of the speaker's ability to impose *one* order and pace that work. Moreover, there's a certain chemistry in a crowd. A speaker has a hard time battling it. As a presenter, then, anticipate the audience's purpose, mood, attention span, and the rate at which they can absorb material.

Characterize

Here are some items to keep in mind as you characterize your audience.

Are you addressing company insiders or people from outside? Your talk will need to set the new information you are presenting within what's familiar ground to them. An internal audience probably shares the same background in your subject, the same expectations about the topics of the talk, and the same vocabulary.

When the audience is *external*—clients, sponsors of research, customers, government officials, the town council, a fifth-grade class—measure their educational level, experience, roles, and knowledge of key terms and visual forms. Can they read a balance sheet? When you must address a mixed audience, aim at the middle. Provide supplemental printed material for those who may not be familiar with the topic. Be sure to review any company constraints on your information. Don't be the one, for example, to divulge an earnings chart with the wrong people.

Be prepared for interruptions if you are addressing your superiors or peers; you have less control than when you address subordinates. Identify the *key people.* Although you will not want to ignore anyone in the audience, find out in advance if there are key people to watch for. Don't let them suddenly pop up and surprise you. Although you may think you'd prefer *not* to know that the CEO is planning to attend your talk, flying blind can be just as scary and much less productive.

Different audiences—different individuals—*listen* in different ways. Fifth-graders may be engaged by stories and pictures and may want you to ask *them* questions before you talk. Accountants may remember best what you present in numbers on standard spreadsheet forms. Assume that everyone's mind will wander.

Assess *why* the participants will be there. Because they were coerced? Because they volunteered? Did managers find them deficient in some way that you are supposed to correct? Being coerced makes many people grumpy or angry—not in a good frame of mind for listening. You'll have to soothe their spirits and entice them to listen in the opening of your talk.

Count

The size of the audience will dictate the relative formality of your approach and the amount of interaction with the audience you can expect. Plan on a somewhat informal structure and lots of give-and-take with a group of 10 to 15. You'll probably have to do most of the talking if the group is larger. For such a presentation, you'll need to assess audience needs even more rigorously because you'll have less opportunity in discussion to respond to specific audience questions that would aid you in saying what the audience needs to hear.

Assess the Setting

Documents must work in a limited number of pages. Your presentation must work in a limited amount of time and in a particular place. Accommodate to that setting, or if the opportunity is available, control it for your purposes.

Timing

Match your timing of the talk to the audience's ability to listen. One aspect of timing is the talk's length; another is the time of day; another, your place in a series of speakers.

You may be given a time slot that indicates the length and time of day of the talk. If so, prepare an appropriate amount of material. Exceeding your time limit is unfair to the audience and may cause them to stop listening before you stop talking and to think less of even the good parts in your talk. It is also unfair to any speakers who follow you. On the other hand, running out of material suggests skimpy preparation or a lack of seriousness.

Making a presentation in front of a group requires preparation, poise, and self-confidence.

If the decision on length is yours, think *short.* No formal presentation should last more than an hour without a break or some other change of pace. Keep presentations within meetings to 10 or 15 minutes.

Be aware of your audience's psychological time at the hour for your presentation. Expect alertness early in the morning and a lull after lunch. Expect fussiness near the end of the day as listeners, particularly in a commuter environment, anticipate making the train or the carpool home. The audience will anticipate some entertainment in an after-dinner talk.

Find out if you are part of a series of speakers. With practice, you'll be able to adjust to most situations, particularly when you hear the speaker before you giving *your* talk. But try to protect yourself from surprises. Learn the approaches of any other speakers, and carve out new territory for your talk. If you're the last speaker, anticipate that others will run over and you'll have less time than promised. During the presentation, plan to *listen* to the other speakers—your audience will be listening—and weave their remarks into at least the opening of your own.

Arrangements

An advertisement for *The New York Times* shows a very small man reading the newspaper in a very large and busy Times Square. The caption: "Every message is at the mercy of its environment."

Your message will be at the mercy of the room in which it is delivered. First, make sure you know where that room is. If possible, visit the site as part of your preparation. Then, assess the situation the room presents and control what you can. Can you move the chairs for a role-playing exercise in groups? Try a U-shaped seating arrangement or a circle if you want the participants to talk with each other as well as listen to you. If you are giving a lecture, chairs in rows are suitable. Are there any distractions? Does a train run by every 15 minutes, obliterating voices? Does sun glare wipe out the image on the screen in the early morning? Will the sound of voices in the next room come through a movable partition? Compensate for what you can't control—by knowing you'll need to pause for the train, close the blinds, or ask the audience to sit on the quieter side of the room. Choose the smallest room that can accommodate the expected audience. A small audience scattered in a large room is hard to address.

Check on any equipment you'll need to support your talk: podium, table, overhead projector, slide projector. Keep spare bulbs handy. Practice with the equipment. Perhaps you've attended a presentation whose opening was postponed while the speaker reversed slides for rear-screen projection. Perhaps, when time was tight, you've even sat through a presentation in which the slides were projected backward, with a nervous speaker translating the labels. Such problems severely reduce the audience's listening comprehension. Logistics are simple matters when they work. But problems in logistics can be devastating.

Identify the Purpose

Your purpose in presenting and your audience's purpose in listening need to mesh, of course. Presentations serve many purposes that fit within the general goals of *informing* or *persuading.*

Assume, for example, that your supervisor has asked you to "review the year-end profit picture" for the finance committee. The goal is *informative*, but the statement leaves the specific scope and approach unclear. By *picture* does he mean that you should look to the future? If so, how far? A five-year plan? Ten years? Or by *picture* does he mean a look backward to trace a graph of profits over the past year? How detailed should you be? Should you consider profitability in light of the patterns of the industry as a whole? Are other speakers addressing any of these issues? Does your invitation represent a new feature for the committee, or is this topic addressed every year at the meeting? If there was such a talk last year, what did it cover?

Many speakers have found themselves thwarted in presentations because they expected to give one kind of talk and the audience expected to hear another. Clarify the assignment in advance. What do you want your audience to remember? To understand? To do? Fill in the blank: "After hearing this presentation, my audience should ___________."

Develop a *control statement* for the talk as you do for a document (see Chapter 4) and deliver it early in the talk and probably again at the end.

ORGANIZING YOUR INFORMATION

Your analysis of the context—audience, setting, and purpose—shapes how you organize your talk. If your talk is based on a document, a common occurrence, reread it to see if new material might be needed—and add it. Then think about how you will begin the talk, how you'll support your control statement in the middle of the talk, and how you'll end it. In "*FYI:* Corporate Speech Writing: Framing the Facts" (pages 454–455), Ellen Roberts provides her advice on organizing a talk.

Another strategy for organizing talks expands on the "framework of image-evoking concepts" that Roberts advocates. In its guide to effective presentations, the General Electric Company identifies four major segments: "Ho-hum!" (the introduction); "Why Bring that Up?" and "For Instance?" (the middle); and "So What?" (the ending).[2]

Ho-Hum!

To overcome the audience's inertia and draw their attention, open with vigor, as Roberts suggests. What are people thinking about that you could put to use? In the first few minutes, show them that they should listen. Use analogies, startling statistics, quotations, jokes, or cartoons. Noting your authorization for the talk as you begin will further draw their attention and will establish your credibility. If you're speaking for the CEO, that authority carries weight that will encourage listening.

Why Bring That Up?

After gaining the audience's attention, provide the control statement. Give the context, the "why" before the "how." Many speakers omit this

[2] General Electric Company, *Effective Presentation of Business Ideas*, rev. ed. (Schenectady, N.Y.: 1967), p. 5.

CORPORATE SPEECH WRITING: FRAMING THE FACTS

Ellen J. Roberts
Manager, Company Communications, ALICO

Scenario: The CEO needs a speech. His deadline? Ten days. The subject? "Emerging Business Opportunities in Latin America." Your level of knowledge on the subject? No match for his 25 years of international experience.

Mission impossible? Not at all. With the right combination of creativity, curiosity, and query, even a novice speech writer can turn an intimidating topic into an interesting talk.

The trick is in framing the facts, in finding ways to tailor the message's technical matter so that it entertains as well as informs.

One technique is to structure the speech inside a framework of image-evoking concepts that captivate the listener. These concepts create points of reference for the audience and can be used to open a speech, close it, and smooth transitions within it.

Commonly used devices include analogies and metaphors, comparisons and contrasts, and famous quotations. Some of the most interesting ones succeed because they surprise. Frequently they have nothing at all to do with the topic itself. Here is an example from a speech on niche-marketing opportunities for newer, smaller companies in competition with larger, more established ones.

In order to survive, the newcomers must be fast and flexible—so the speech writer likened them to elephants and gazelles, creating for the audience an image of limber, fleet-footed animals darting around lumbering pachyderms. The analogy worked well, as the senior executives in the audience hardly expected to hear the president of a large multinational company talk about African animals.

Sometimes the best angles are the simplest and most obvious ones. For example, a speech on "exploring the global market" might begin

step, plunging into the details while the audience strains for an overview. Even more than in a written report, you need to make the organization apparent. As you'll see, visuals are essential for this purpose. Set up the main point *directly* in an informative talk:

```
To prepare you for the meetings next month in Germany, I'll
profile our contacts there and then review our business to
date and target sales for each customer.
```

Under circumstances that demand more *persuasive* strategies, as in delivering bad news or selling an idea or product, you may choose more *indirection* to build common ground before the announcement:

```
Many of you have probably read reports in the media and heard
rumors on the street concerning the impending takeover of our
company. You are understandably uneasy about how such a
change in organizational structure, should it occur, may af-
fect your own positions here. Let me provide you with some
information that's not in the media or on the street to in-
```

with Christopher Columbus, continue with Robert Peary and Sir Edmund Hillary, and include some lesser known trailblazers.

At its most basic, the story of Christopher Columbus is a classic example of how even the best-laid plans can go awry. Anecdotes about Columbus and the other explorers yield numerous business parallels—and give the speaker an easy way to move from point to point.

Sometimes simple audience research elicits angles. Take the example of a 1989 speech on competition with Japan. The audience was comprised of seasoned senior executives, many of whom had fought in World War II. Their reaction to the changes in Japan's economic competitiveness over a relatively short time formulated the foundation for the speech: a series of quarter-century comparisons.

The speech opened with "Let's turn back the clock 25 years" and then described how, in 1964, world attention was focused on Japan not for its business savvy but for the summer Olympics. A humorous reference to the age of the audience sparked an instant connection between speaker and listener. Other "25-years-ago" examples enhanced the speaker's credibility because the time span coincided with his years of experience in the industry.

One word of caution: Make sure the audience understands the analogy. For instance, the writer of the "elephants and gazelles" speech included a brief description of gazelles for listeners who may have been unfamiliar with the mammal.

Speech scenarios can be stockpiled on an ongoing basis, long before the pressure of deadlines sets in. Look for anecdotes, examples, and incidents with universal appeal but less-than-obvious parallels to business situations. Take chances; break some rules; be creative.

```
form you about the company's real position and your options
with us.
```

For Instance?

Once you've set up the main point, prove it. Structure evidence to relate to the audience's needs, and connect new information to what they are already familiar with. Use examples and vivid language to hold attention and foster understanding. The main point is what the audience can remember, not everything you can cram in. Sort minor from major points, and save details for a handout. Periodically summarize one topic before moving on to another.

A *direct* presentation develops each module implied in the control statement. Chapter 4 reviews common patterns for arranging such material. In a *persuasive* presentation, as in a persuasive letter, you may build a buffer of neutral descriptive information in order to encourage listening and entice the audience to agree with your conclusion at the end—in effect, to come up with that conclusion themselves through the inevitable logic of your presentation. Here's how you might organize such a persuasive talk:

1. Criteria for a solution
2. Possible solutions
3. Solution-by-solution discussion, eliminating all but the one *you* support
4. Enlistment of the audience's participation in the solution
5. Description of the new situation with the solution in place
6. A final call to action

So What?

In organizing your talk, keep a cliché in mind: "First, you tell them what you're going to tell them; then, you tell them; then, you tell them what you've told them." Because listeners can't turn back the clock the way readers can turn back the page, you need to build in an obvious framework and repeat main ideas. Outline your talk to establish priorities, and divide the segments into units of time.

Finally, discuss the implications of "what you've told them." Reiterate the main point. Define any actions requested. Even drifting listeners usually snap back when you say "finally" or "in conclusion"; use that attention to build the audience's enthusiasm for implementing the decision you've presented or to reinforce your main point. Try a *call to action:*

```
Now that you are familiar with at least the basic commands
and functions of our e-mail system, try it out in your of-
fices--this afternoon. Don't wait.
```

To ensure compliance, you might add a *test:*

```
I'm eager to welcome you to the system. By Friday, make sure
that each of you has sent me at least one brief e-mail mes-
sage.
```

You might *summarize:*

```
The new e-mail system promises to bring us all closer to-
gether. Other companies have found their communication lines
enhanced, their management more effective, their information
richer and more current. We expect the same benefits.
```

Make the ending *memorable.* A striking image might be just the ticket, as in this ending to a talk at a college athletic banquet:

```
Your education has prepared you for even more challenges in
your careers and your personal lives after the air goes out
of the soccer ball.
```

PREPARING THE VISUALS

In giving a talk, you'll speak in two languages: the words you say and the visuals you show. The audience will probably remember the pictures you present longer than your words, especially if their understanding of the pictures is enhanced by your words. Prepare both simultaneously to reinforce each other. Your goal for the talk, your budget, the audience's expectations, the logistics of the presentation site, the technical capabilities available to you for creating visuals, and your own comfort with them—all will determine the visual forms you select. Figure 22–1 describes the most common forms.

Good visuals can make even a mediocre presenter memorable. Several studies show that presenters who use visuals are seen as better prepared,

Form	Speaker/Audience	Advantages/Disadvantages
Overheads	Faces	Room remains lighted; overheads can be both prepared in advance and written on during the presentation; easy to rearrange at last minute and to recall in a question session; easy to produce. Hard to see at a distance; resolution is often not precise for photographs.
Slides	Faces	High-image resolution; good projection in large rooms for large groups; capable of dramatic artistic and emotional effects. More difficult to produce than overheads and more difficult to arrange at last minute; room must be dark.
Flipcharts	Faces	Easy to move around; may be used for spontaneous jottings during a talk or prepared in advance—in part or completely; room remains lighted. Less polished than overheads or slides; the speaker must have good handwriting.
Blackboards	Turns back	Easy to use for spontaneous notes or may be prepared in advance; often available; room remains lighted. Informal; hard to see at a distance; may become messy; the speaker must have good handwriting; speaker must turn away from audience to write.

FIGURE 22–1.
Common forms of visuals for business communications.

more professional, more interesting—and thus more credible—than those who don't.[3] The visuals also build momentum and encourage compliance, according to Tom Carney of the University of Windsor: "An integrated story-and-picture line-up, especially one containing graphs and charts, is hard to counterthink, off the cuff." Moreover, as the "international language all businesspeople understand," visuals are essential in presentations in multilingual audiences. Before your presentation, distribute translated copies of the visuals for those listeners who are hearing the talk in a language foreign to them. Write any potentially unclear terms—in any language—on a visual. Of course, the context may make the spoken words clear, but listeners may hear something you don't intend. You say *measurability;* they hear *measure ability.* You say *serial attacks;* they hear *cereal attacks.*

Use a wordprocessing or graphics program on a personal computer to prepare polished transparencies (also called "vugraphs" or "flimsies") for overhead projection. Some laser printers can produce them directly, or you can photocopy a printout onto a transparency. Quick-copy centers do this work inexpensively. You may require more professional assistance to produce 35-millimeter slides or videotapes of anything other than routine images.

Overheads and Slides

Few conference rooms (or even classrooms) in the United States lack overhead projectors. Plan to use them. Prepare two types of transparencies or slides: those that will present the *framework* of the talk and those that present *supporting information.*

Framework slides, like Figures 22–2 and 22–3 (pages 459–460), cue listeners visually about where they are in the talk. They preview and remind. Readers of a document can go back to the table of contents and skim through headings to find their place. Listeners need visual cues.

Supporting slides may serve, for example, to gain the listener's attention and to dramatize a point. You might start your presentation with a visual "hook," like a cartoon or a quotation displayed visually. Then use charts, graphs, photographs, and drawings to display the evidence that supports your talk. Chapter 6 provides an overview of such forms. Avoid simply reusing the complete tables and charts you drew to *record* information in a document. Simplify them to show relationships, not details. Use a bar graph to compare statistics or a pie chart to show the relationship of parts to the whole. Use photographs to provide a concrete image of something too large (like an earth-moving machine) or too small (like a microchip) to put on display in the meeting room. Figure 22–4 (page 461) shows a *supporting* transparency.

Keep in mind that visuals *support* your talk. Don't try to put your entire presentation in them. Avoid a string of text-filled slides. After two of these, insert a graph, a photograph, or a table. The checklist offers advice on creating presentation graphics.

[3] "Take Note: Visuals Keep Meetings More Focused," *Meeting Management News,* 1:2 (3M Meeting Management Institute), p. 4.

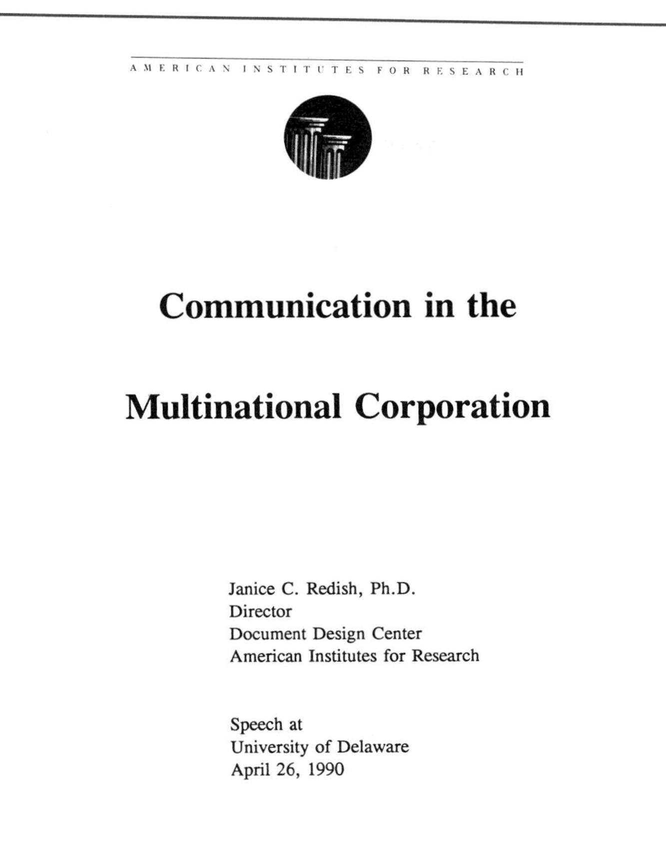

AMERICAN INSTITUTES FOR RESEARCH
Communication in the
Multinational Corporation
Janice C. Redish, Ph.D.
Director
Document Design Center
American Institutes for Research
Speech at
University of Delaware
April 26, 1990
DOCUMENT DESIGN CENTER
3333 K STREET, NW
WASHINGTON, DC 20007
(202) 342-5000

FIGURE 22–2.
A transparency that gives the title of the talk, the name of the presenter, and the setting. *(From the work of Dr. Janice C. Redish. Used with permission.)*

CHECKLIST FOR DEVELOPING PRESENTATION VISUALS[4]

1. Create a master slide that establishes the design of all the other slides that follow—and stick to that consistent design (see Figures 6–15 and 22–4).
2. Present one idea per slide or transparency.
3. Limit textual visuals to five to seven lines, with no more than six or seven words per line.
4. Keep lettering harmonious. Use only one typeface, preferably sans serif, for any text. A good one is Helvetica. Size: 36 points for the title, 24 points for headings, 18 points for subheadings.
5. Use no more than four or five colors for charts and graphs. Inconsistent

(continued on page 462)

[4] For excellent advice on using visuals in presentations—and for presentation skills in general—see the "Meeting Management News" published by the 3M Meeting Management Institute. For copies write to the Institute, Building 225-3N-01, 3M Center, St. Paul MN 55144-1000. Tom Carney of the University of Windsor aided in the creation of this checklist.

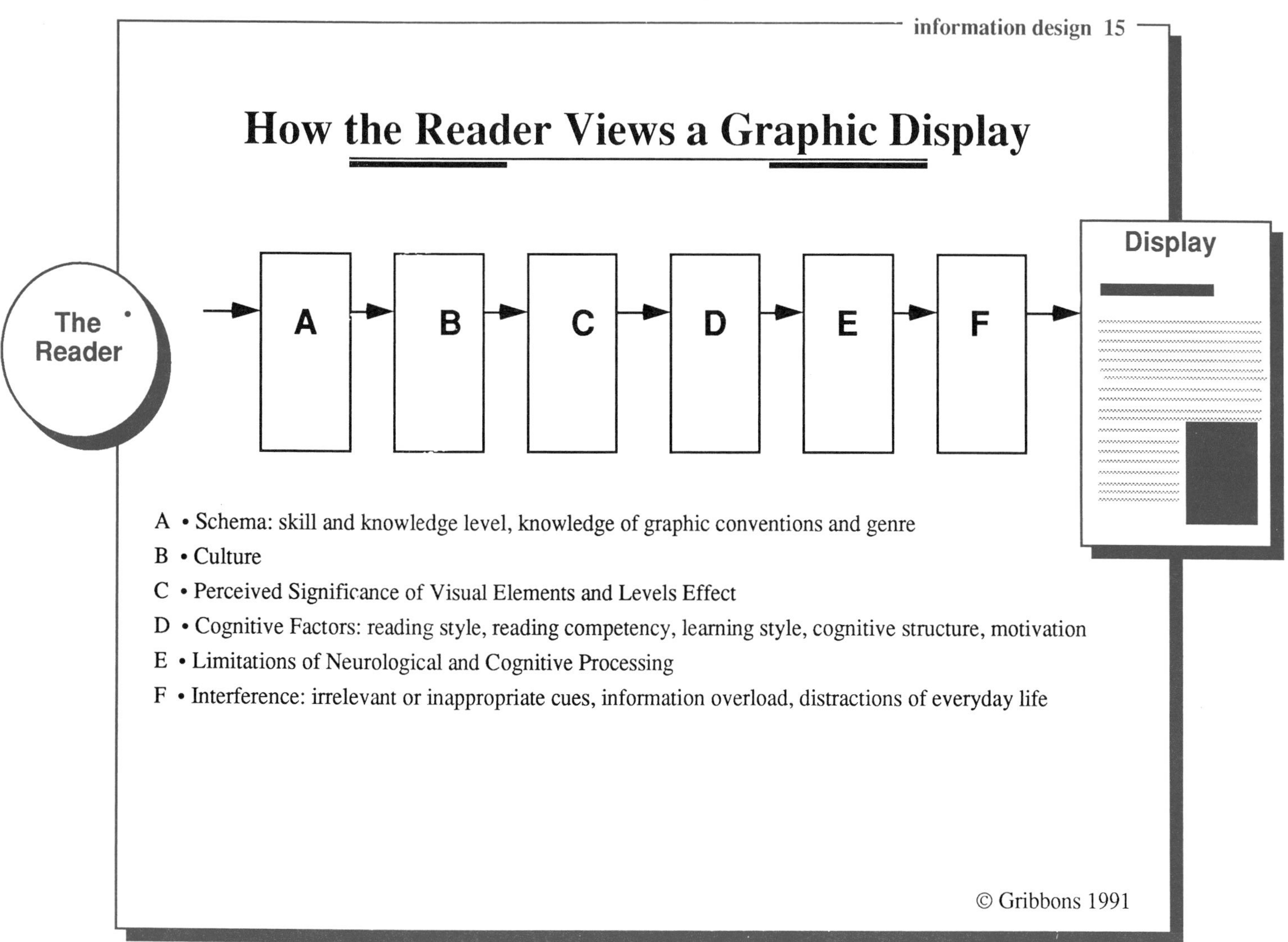

FIGURE 22–3.
An overview of the contents of the talk. *(Courtesy of Dr. William M. Gribbons.)*

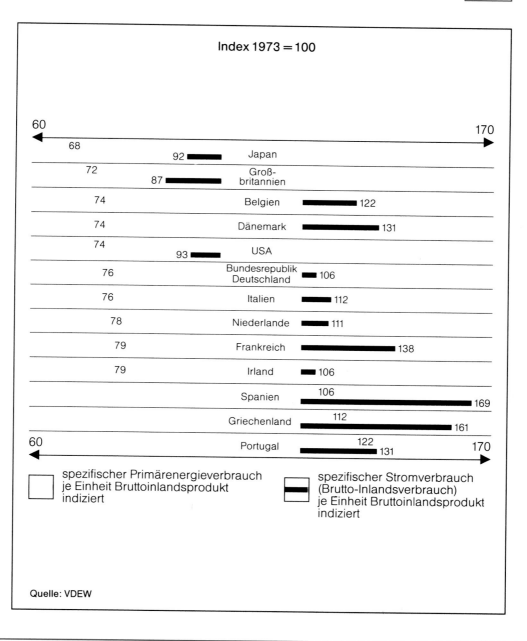

Energieintensitäten im internationalen Vergleich
Entwicklung 1973–1988

Index 1973 = 100

60 — 170

Land	Spezifischer Primärenergieverbrauch	Spezifischer Stromverbrauch
Japan	68	92
Groß-britannien	72	87
Belgien	74	122
Dänemark	74	131
USA	74	93
Bundesrepublik Deutschland	76	106
Italien	76	112
Niederlande	78	111
Frankreich	79	138
Irland	79	106
Spanien	106	169
Griechenland	112	161
Portugal	122	131

60 — 170

spezifischer Primärenergieverbrauch je Einheit Bruttoinlandsprodukt indiziert

spezifischer Stromverbrauch (Brutto-Inlandsverbrauch) je Einheit Bruttoinlandsprodukt indiziert

Quelle: VDEW

FIGURE 22–4.
A supporting transparency. Note the logo in the upper-right corner that indicates the date when the visual was developed and the sequence number of the transparency in the talk (on energy use in Germany). For another visual in this series, see Chapter 6, Figure 6–15. *(Courtesy of IZE, Frankfurt, Germany.)*

use of color, or overuse, confuses more than it clarifies. Watch the *connotations* of the colors you use, especially for multinational audiences.

6. Make sure that the information in the charts is consistent with what you present in your talk.
7. PROOFREAD all visuals. A spelling error can be especially embarrassing when it is several inches tall.
8. To create handouts of your vugraphs, use a photocopy machine to reduce them; paste two or three of these reductions onto an 8½″ × 11″ sheet, leaving room for notes; then photocopy enough of the sheets for the audience. Make sure your name and the source of all data not your own are indicated on the handout.

Video

Recently, the technology for both recording and playing videos has developed significantly. Increases in ease of use have been matched by decreases in cost. Video-enhanced teleconferencing allows "live" meetings among people in remote locations, as you saw in Chapter 21. Videos also provide some of the feeling of a live presentation at greatly reduced costs. Training programs and general corporate announcements can be delivered consistently throughout many dispersed plants and offices of the company. In "*FYI:* Seven Cs for Video Success," Ed Ziegler provides advice on preparing a video presentation.

SEVEN Cs FOR VIDEO SUCCESS

Ed Ziegler
Director of Publications,
Glassboro State College

Business communicators today are asked to use a medium that their predecessors did not have to deal with: *video,* a form companies turn to increasingly to reach a market brought up on television. But many communicators make the mistake of producing nothing more than "animated brochures" that fail to exploit video's strengths.

How can you produce a video that brings your message to the right people? Follow these seven Cs.

Concept. As in any communications campaign, decide what your message is, who your audience is, and why you are using video to bring that message to that audience. Print is the medium of choice for lists and details; the power of video lies in emotion, mood, and motion. Once you've decided, it's time to unleash your

Creativity. As you begin developing ideas, don't stifle yourself with details. Video is theatrical. It depends on moving images to be effective. Print has natural transitions—pages, folds, columns—but you must use different effects to move the audience through a video. Brainstorm with colleagues to explore ways to make your message memorable. A good source of ideas is your

Competition. Gather examples of similar work, both good and bad, and show them to a few representatives of your target audience. Their comments will let you know what works and what doesn't and will help you understand the medium. Once you're committed to an idea, then consider

PRACTICING

You can't sit at your desk, look over your notes, and go through your thoughts in exactly the same amount of time that it will take you to give the presentation. Instead, stand up and say your talk: to an audience of friends, if you can round them up; on video, if the equipment is available to you; in the room reserved for the presentation, if possible; in the shower, if necessary. Time yourself and cut (or add) what's necessary to match the time allotted—or, better, a little under that.

As you practice, too, identify any mannerisms that might distract from your presentation and correct them. Reviewing a videotape of your performance is a great help. Do you push up your eyeglasses? Play with your hair? Shake loose change in your pocket? Cling to the lectern, your white knuckles visible symbols of fear? Such mannerisms will draw the audience's attention away from your talk.

Some acting coaches, who also coach corporate executives, recommend a practice technique called *split-focus concentration.* Try giving your talk while you go through some other activity that you're comfortable with. A basketball player we know dribbles a ball while he practices a speech. Then, when the time comes to talk, so the coaches say, you'll be relaxed with your body and able to use appropriate gestures.

Practice with any equipment you'll be using. Locate on-off switches. Try placing transparencies on an overhead right-side-up. Make sure you can focus them and that the audience can read them from their seats. Practice

Cost. Don't let cost control the creative flow. Knowing what you want to accomplish and how you want it to look, search for a professional who will help you make it work. Consider the producer's service, experience with your type of business, and proximity to your office—and price, last. Remember, the most expensive video is the one that doesn't work. Bob Christenson of RAC Films says one of the biggest mistakes producers make is considering cost before concept: "I prefer to develop a creative idea first, then work backward to see how we can accomplish it with the money the customer has to work with." One way he accomplishes this is by being

Conservative with special effects. Creativity isn't necessarily expensive, and the production should not overshadow the message. Once the project is under way, maintain

Control. Be involved in every step. Don't turn it over to the producer and look the other way. Don't be afraid to ask questions and to learn what you can about video production. Instead of viewing this as one project, think of

Continuity. Think of this video as a first in a series of successful productions. Consider how you can use some of this footage in another project or how someone else can use it. Increase your video literacy.

where you'll stand so that you won't block the screen. Practice loading and starting a video. Note whether the equipment has a counter that will allow you to find a particular frame or starting point on a long tape.

After the practice, ask observers for their comments and evaluate yourself. Figures 22–5 and 22–6 provide evaluation forms that may help you and the observers focus your comments. But don't be too harsh. Correct what's correctable. Let the practice build confidence.

PRESENTING

It's probably scarier to *think* about speaking in public than to do it. The key ingredient is respect for the audience. This means that you prepare well, that you treat them well, and that you work within the agreed-on limits of logistics. Be positive—even if your host mispronounces your name, even if you arrive at the conference room to find a different brand of projector from the one you had specifically requested. Let your preparation build the self-confidence that lets you be flexible when necessary.

The rest of this chapter provides guidelines for performing. If you are part of a team, then review the specific suggestions for group performance in Chapter 11.

Keep Control

When you arrive at the site for your presentation, check the setup of seating, equipment, and acoustics. Greet your host or contact person and others who will be attending. "Remember, as soon as you identify yourself you become the speaker. Project your personality in a positive way."[5] Erase from the blackboard any messages left from the speaker before you.

You *will* be nervous before the talk, especially in the time after someone introduces you and before you begin. Even the pros are. Convert anxiety to energy. After you've been announced, or as you arrive at the podium, pause. Look at the audience. Take a breath. Open with vigor on the note you prepared.

In your performance, ride easy in harness. That is, keep the presentation focused, but keep yourself relaxed. A tense speaker creates tension in the audience; a comfortable speaker makes the audience comfortable. Stand confidently, neither draping yourself over the podium nor bracing stiffly as if waiting to be shot.

Control your voice. Enunciate clearly. Vary your pitch and pace. Adjust your volume to reach the back row. Don't rush. Nervousness often translates into speeded-up delivery. Slow down, especially if your presentation is being translated or is being heard by a multicultural audience. Vary the length of your sentences, keeping them short to allow for easier breathing. Avoid repeating *s* or *p* sounds that grate on the audience. Make particularly sure not to drop words at the ends of sentences.

Control your timing. If you find yourself behind time, skip parts of the middle of your talk but preserve the ending. If necessary, offer to send along supplementary material if you feel valuable information has been sacrificed.

[5] "Giving a Speech," checklist prepared by the Wharton Communication Program.

Speaker:

Date:

Scale 1 Inadequate
3 Adequate
5 Distinguished

CONTENT	
Effectiveness of introduction	1 2 3 4 5
Identification of problem/focus	1 2 3 4 5
Obviousness of organization	1 2 3 4 5
Use of appropriate evidence	1 2 3 4 5
Effectiveness of ending	1 2 3 4 5
Overall content	1 2 3 4 5

DELIVERY	
Posture and presence	1 2 3 4 5
Energy and vigor of delivery	1 2 3 4 5
Timing	1 2 3 4 5
Eye contact	1 2 3 4 5
Voice	1 2 3 4 5
Language	1 2 3 4 5
Use of visuals	1 2 3 4 5
Overall delivery	1 2 3 4 5

Special weaknesses:

Special strengths:

Control statement:

FIGURE 22–5.
A simple evaluation form developed for student oral presentations.

Timing

Started ____ m. Well timed ____
Stopped ____ m. Too long ____
Time ____ min. Too short ____

Organization

Gave suitable introduction:
Yes ____ No ____
Topics discussed in logical order:
Yes ____ No ____

Interrelationships of topics:
Made clear ____ Obscured ____
Fairly clear ____

Closed effectively ____
Or just ran down ____

Manner

Presented paper by:
Talking without notes ____
Talking from manuscript or notes ____
Reading manuscript ____

Looked at audience:
All of the time ____
Part of the time ____
Never ____

Effort to gain audience attention:
Enthusiastic ____
Casual ____
Complacent ____

Mannerisms:
Relaxed and moved easily ____
Stood rigidly ____
Moved excessively ____
Clutched lectern ____
Hands in pockets ____
Nervous effects ____

Gestures:
Impressive ____ Distracting ____
Natural ____ None ____

Speech

Enunciation:
Distinct ____ Heard by all ____
Fairly distinct ____ Partially heard ____
Indistinct ____ Seldom heard ____

Phraseology:
Concise ____ Descriptive ____
Too brief ____ Generalized ____
Verbose ____ Vague ____
Used extraneous transitions ("er," "ah," etc.) Yes ____ No ____

Delivery:
Smooth ____
Jerky ____
Too fast ____
Too slow ____
Appropriate emphasis ____
Periodic inflection ____
Monotone ____

Visual Aids

Quantity: Too many ____ Adequate ____
Too few ____

Quality:
Well composed ____ Lucid ____
Superfluous detail ____ Legible ____
Confusing ____ Illegible ____

Presented: Too fast ____
Too slow ____
Suitably ____
Convincingly ____

Visual aids (would have been) (were)
A hindrance ____
Helpful ____
Exceptionally good ____

Discussion-rebuttal

Attitude toward
Questions: Replies:
Receptive ____ Logical and convincing ____
Indifferent ____ Acceptable ____
Antagonistic ____ Evasive ____
Irrelevant ____

No discussion held ____

General

Have you a clear idea of the speaker's theme?
Yes ____ No ____
Was she or he convincing to you?
Yes ____ No ____
Did she or he hold the attention of the audience?
Yes ____ No ____
Was this an exceptionally good presentation?
Yes ____ No ____

Comment: ________________________________
____

FIGURE 22–6.
A detailed form for evaluating professional presentations. *(Reprinted with permission from The Institute of Electrical and Electronics Engineers, Inc. © IEEE.)*

Talk with the Audience

A presentation to a group around a conference table profits from interaction but may require you to give up some control. A presentation in an auditorium maximizes your control but may make audience interaction difficult. Whatever the setting, however, at least in North America, the audience will expect you to look at *them*—not at the ceiling, not out the window, not at your text. Include the whole room in your gaze. Be particularly careful not to look only at the chief authority in the room.

Use your visuals to connect with the audience. Visuals can become a barrier. Don't be known by your back rather than your face. If you are using an overhead projector, look at it, not the screen. Write on the transparency to point to a topic or feature. Keep talking while you change slides and transparencies, and cover any part of the slide not pertinent to the point you are making at that moment. Don't read the visuals *at* the audience; comment *on* the visuals. And don't get ahead of your visuals. Some presenters keep moving along their outline, forgetting that they have slides to illustrate specific points; they then have to move rapidly through old slides to catch up. Turn off the machine when you have nothing to show.

Don't read the talk. Few people read scripts well, and the reading blocks out the audience. You send a signal that your priority is to protect yourself against the audience. They may react by passivity, daydreaming, and perhaps even sleep, like children read to at bedtime.

The only exception to this guideline is the prepared statement, developed with legal counsel, that has to be read verbatim. In highly sensitive political or legal contexts, you may have to read to avoid repercussions. But most of the time, keep your audience alert by not interposing a printed text between yourself and them.

Use Question-and-Answer Sessions Strategically

Handling questions from the audience can be tricky. When should you take questions? An informal session or a press briefing may develop entirely through questions and answers (Q&A). At routine staff meetings, you may present brief opening remarks and then take questions. You may even find that your audience will interrupt your brief remarks. In a formal presentation, questions may be held until the end—perhaps after a series of presentations of which yours is a part.

Some speakers approach questions as they would a mine field. Crossing the field is easier if the organizer of the talk moderates the questions to keep people on track. Some potential mines in an audience are well known to insiders in the group: the person who always asks about environmental effects, the one who tells stories regardless of the topic of the talk, the one who questions any statistical information presented in a bar chart. The organizer can alert you to these people in advance or gently turn aside their questions if they are inappropriate.

If you don't have such a personal guide, scout the field yourself before the talk. Anticipate likely questions, and bring supporting documents like annual reports to provide background. Stay cool. Here are some guidelines for the strategic use of questions:

Guidelines for Using Questions Strategically

1. In a formal presentation to a large number of people, always repeat the question.
2. If you don't know the answer, don't guess.
3. Gently control unproductive questioners.
4. Guard against highly specialized questions.
5. End on your main point.

1. **In a formal presentation to a large number of people, always repeat the question,** preferably in a short form, before you answer it. In that way you'll be sure that everyone in the audience has heard it. You will also gain time to think about the answer. You may be able to turn the question slightly in a direction that you want to emphasize, even if that direction wasn't exactly implied. Of course, the questioner may not let you get away with this, but the tactic sometimes works.

2. **If you don't know the answer, don't guess.** And don't let a belligerent questioner supply you with an answer to which you agree, only to have the questioner pull the rug out from under you by saying that that is not the right answer. When you don't know, offer to find the answer and to send it to the questioner. And then send it.

3. **Gently control unproductive questioners.** Some questioners are really speech makers themselves. If you are the person's junior, urging an ending to their commentary may be difficult. But some good humor and sensitivity will preserve your control and win you the audience's appreciation, too.

4. **Guard against highly specialized questions** that will take the discussion on a tangent away from the talk and away from the main interests of the audience as a whole. Answer briefly, and then agree to talk with the questioner at greater length after the session.

5. **End on your main point.** Don't let a question period linger too long. When the pace of questions has slowed, avoid prolonging the session artificially. Close. Use the last question as a springboard back to the main theme that your entire presentation was designed to establish.

Knowing how much to leave to a question-and-answer period depends on your own style as a presenter. Some people are much better at answering questions than at giving a formal talk. They should speak briefly and move quickly to the questions. Those better at performing may want to leave only a short part of the allotted time for questions. In answering questions, listen well. Know what's being asked, and answer forthrightly.

Think Multiculturally

Finally, whether you give a talk at home or abroad, be alert to the diversity your audience often presents. Avoid jokes or language that may offend people of a religion, race, gender, or culture different from your own. Anne B. Forrest, Senior Vice President and Asia Regional Director of Hill and Knowlton Asia Ltd. has developed the guidelines shown in Figure 22–7 to aid presenters. "We developed these because we had so many Americans (to

Many of our clients take advantage of visits to Hong Kong by their corporate executives from overseas to set up speaking engagements with business and civic organizations. From our experience, we have developed a few guidelines to make for a successful and effective speech.

1. Citing facts and figures about Hong Kong and Asia is unnecessary and inappropriate. Your audience already knows them. Use local facts only when they illustrate why your company is doing what it's doing or is making a certain decision.

2. Jokes and humour are good icebreakers, but avoid clichés. Jokes about your spouse shopping in Hong Kong, or comments on how astounded you are that Hong Kong is such a vibrant and cosmopolitan city, are particularly tired.

3. Avoid "selling" your company or products, or even appearing to sell, unless you or your company has paid for every guest present. In almost all cases, those attending have paid to hear you. They want to learn, not to hear a sales talk.

4. Do use graphic/descriptive analogies to illustrate or make your key points--analogies are memorable across all cultures. Try to use images familiar to your audience. Not everyone in the audience has been to your hometown.

5. Do keep numbers and percentages to a minimum. Too many become a burden and lessen the likelihood they will be remembered.

6. Do make copies of your speech available after the session. You do not need to read your speech or stick exactly to the text. However, many listeners have trouble with the speaker's accent or language usage, and they like to re-read the speech after the talk and pass it around. The text also will ensure more accurate quotes in the press.

7. Remember to speak clearly and not too quickly. Avoid slang, jargon, and acronyms. Although these are used to achieve a normal, informal-sounding speech, your talk will be more easily understood if you stay with formal English. Many in the audience will not be native English speakers.

8. If you have time, ask your local contact to review your speech to point out any unforeseen pitfalls or sensitivities. Be aware of key taboos which are to be avoided in your speech, references, or actions.

9. Individuals from some countries have sharp humour about their own government and political system, but don't get sucked into agreeing with them, or you might be less than welcome. Try to avoid referring to specific governmental workings--for example, the way the U.S. government runs is difficult for people in other countries to understand. Similarly, few Americans understand the British parliamentary system.

10. During the question and answer period, don't be surprised if questions are not forthcoming. In most countries, audiences are reticent. Keep a few extra comments in reserve to break the ice. People will often come up to talk privately after the presentation.

11. If you use a standard speech, be sure to adapt it to local conditions. Don't speak in Bombay or Mexico City and fail to mention the location of your talk.

FIGURE 22–7.
Guidelines for overseas speakers in Hong Kong. *(Courtesy of Anne B. Forrest, Hill and Knowlton Asia Ltd.)*

be honest) come through and use the latest in-phrases from TV commercials and shows which we had never seen, or use the much-loved acronyms especially when referring to government policies and programs. Even we Americans in Hong Kong couldn't understand them." The guidelines will help you reach your audience—and not set their teeth on edge at the outset—no matter where you talk, no matter to whom.

SUMMARY

- Business presentations serve both to **inform** and to **persuade. Internal** presentations in meetings keep employees up to date, train them in special skills or programs, motivate salespeople, and the like. **External** presentations serve the company's public relations effort for audiences in the government, the media, or even the public at large. In making presentations, you achieve your own goals and enhance your visibility in the organization.
- Good presentations take preparation. Determine the **context. Characterize** your audience: Are they insiders or outsiders? What's their background, their level of understanding, their motivation for attending, their expectations? How many will attend? Then **identify your purpose** in the audience's terms. **Organize** your information to match your determination of the context. Establish a **controlling idea** and support it with evidence arranged in an order that you make obvious to the listeners.
- Audiences at business presentations expect visuals and reward with their attention presenters who use visuals professionally. Use two forms of slides or transparencies: those that establish the **framework** of the talk to preview and reinforce its content and those that present **supporting information.** Establish a **readable and consistent design** for visuals. Use **video** to extend the range of a live presentation via technology and to provide consistent instruction in training programs.
- **Practice** your talk, preferably in front of observers who can evaluate its content and delivery. Lacking a live audience, talk to a video camera and review yourself as you play the video back.
- A good performance works. You keep control of the talk while remaining relaxed and flexible enough to respond to audience queries and interests. You achieve the goal *through the audience,* who remember the main point of what was said and understand and act as required based on that knowledge.

EXERCISES

For Discussion

1. A small-scale industry has developed around people's fears of making presentations. Many consultants offer coaching services for executives. Many authors have produced "how-to" books and even newsletters. From your bookstore or library, collect examples of advice on making speeches. What seems to be the core ingredient? Where do the experts differ? Report on your information in class.

2. In Chapter 16, you read about the "AIDA" approach to sales: attention, interest, desire, and action. In this chapter (pages 453–456) you read about another four-part scheme for organizing a talk. Are the two strategies similar? Is it appropriate for a speaker who is delivering a mainly informative talk still to think in terms of selling the ideas and information to the audience?

For Presenting

3. Use a report in your business communication class as the basis for a six- to eight-minute oral presentation to the class. Don't read the report. *Adapt* it to the new circumstances. If the report addresses a supervisor or client on the job, then address the presentation to the class. Change the emphasis and the content for the new audience. You may be either more general or more particular. For example:

   Report: A Junior Golf Program for the Basking Hills Golf Course
   Presentation: How to Watch a Golf Game and Not Be Bored

   Report: A Safety Program for the Dumont Chemical Company
   Presentation: Tips for Home Safety

   Report: The Color Design for the New Home Offices of FP Industries
   Presentation: The Psychology of Color in the Workplace

4. In arranging your presentation, complete all the tasks indicated in the following list. Under b, for example, *write* your objective. At your teacher's request, hand the list in before the presentation or ask another member of the class to review it with you.
   a. Characterize and count your audience.
   b. Determine your objective.
   c. Plan your strategy.
   d. Organize your talk.
      Ho-Hum!
      Why Bring That Up?
      For Instance?
        1.
        2.
        3.
      So What?
   e. Evaluate the plan before you talk.
   f. Practice, and evaluate your practice.

5. As you learned in this chapter, visuals aid the audience in seeing the structure of a talk and in remembering the main point—and the speaker. Assume that the author of the report at the end of Chapter 19 (on an MIS system for The Whistling Abalone restaurant) has asked you to prepare a set of transparencies to accompany a presentation he will make based on some aspect of the report. Determine the context for the talk—perhaps a briefing for the restaurant's staff, perhaps a talk to a restaurant trade association. Develop at least five transparencies: an opener with the title, the presenter's name, and the occasion of the presentation (how would that differ from the title page in Chapter 19?); an overview of the contents; and three supporting transparencies. Use a "presentation master" software package on a personal computer if one is available to you.

6. Develop a set of overheads or slides for the presentation you prepare in response to Exercises 3 and 4.

For Collaboration

7. If you watch television, you are aware of the impact of visuals on the delivery of information. Divide the class into groups of three persons each and assign each group to watch a different news program every night for a week. Include both local and national news. Record the topics of the news, and observe in particular the *visual* content of the broadcast. Is each story *primarily* visual, or do the visuals enhance a more textual presentation? How does the newscaster handle business news? What forms of visuals are used? Review Chapter 6 for more questions. Then, in class, each group will report on its observations. Based on the reports, compare and contrast the approaches of different newscasters to the use of visuals.

PART VI

EMPLOYMENT COMMUNICATION

23 Resumes and Cover Letters
24 The Interview . . . and Beyond

INTRODUCTION TO PART VI

Many students enroll in a business communication class primarily to learn how to create a good resume and cover letter. You may be one of them. If so, read on. The process is described in detail in Chapter 23. Chapter 24 then guides you through the next phases: the employment interview, follow-up correspondence, and performance reviews once you are on the job.

The job application process is the subject of a good deal of academic and workplace folklore. People tell each other tales of the hunt that sound a lot like fishing stories—the hours spent without yield, the big jobs that got away, the lures and ties lost—like hundreds of letters dropped in the mail without result. The lore of the resume resembles the lore of the fishing spot or the magic reel or the magic bait. Publishers capitalize on the job hunter's vulnerability to folklore and magic by publishing self-help, sure-fire guides that often find their way to the top of the best-seller lists.

Luck—or serendipity—has a part to play in the process, but don't let yourself think it's all luck. Instead, apply the skills you have been learning to your job hunt. Consider your search a test of your ability to listen and talk, to read and write. Review these chapters with the job search in mind:

- Assessing corporate databanks and other sources of business information for job leads and company profiles (Chapters 8 and 9)
- Designing the resume in a visually pleasing form (Chapters 6 and 7)
- Sounding professional and convincing in your cover letter (Chapters 5, 13, and 16)
- Listening and talking effectively (Chapters 20 and 21)

In the following chapters, you'll read about a range of approaches to the documents and conversations that accompany employment. You'll need to learn the conventions. The most important element, however, is simply *excellent* writing and interviewing performance. Gimmicks won't work. Following the procedures for good business communication will.

23 RESUMES AND COVER LETTERS

SELF-INVENTORY
MARKET INVENTORY
- Career-Planning Office or Agency
- State and Federal Employment Offices
- FYI: The Job Search
- Newspapers
- Professional Job Listings
- Sources of Information about Companies
- Word of Mouth

SOLICITING RECOMMENDATIONS
MANAGING THE RESUME—PART I: CONTENT
- Heading
- Objective
- Education
- Experience and Skills
- Personal Information
- References

MANAGING THE RESUME—PART II: DESIGN
WRITING THE COVER LETTER
- Attention
- Interest
- Desire
- Action
- Letters That Work

SUMMARY
EXERCISES

Do You Know 

- What's the first step in looking for a job?
- Where can you find out about the job market?
- Who should write letters of recommendation for you?
- What information belongs in a resume?
- How can you make the cover letter *persuasive?*

''Finding a job is *a job.''*

—A student

For many college students, the hardest step in looking for a job is simply getting started. Even seasoned professionals find that reentering the market demands an initial expenditure of time and energy.

But you can ease your entry or reentry into the market if you think of the job hunt as a process, each step of which is manageable and potentially interesting in itself. It's not all magic. For a while, looking for a job becomes a job—perhaps a second job—that requires certain activities.

This chapter provides guidelines for the process:

- Taking inventory, of yourself and the market
- Soliciting recommendations
- Writing a resume and cover letters

To aid in the process, you may use some of the software now available for both the data-gathering and the writing steps. To find out about *yourself,* try a commercially available program that prompts you to answer questions about your attitudes, values, and skills. The program will then sort your answers against a database to interpret your career interests. To find out about the *market,* ask a librarian to assist you in accessing the vast amounts of corporate data available on CD-ROM. Through such sources as Securities and Exchange Commission filings, financial statements, market studies, and brokerage house reports, you can locate the smaller or more specialized firms that may not recruit on your campus.[1] Personnel directors' names and addresses can be downloaded from the CD files to your wordprocessing program, where you can automatically create personal letters to them. Some e-mail systems will aid you in creating a resume and covering statements and will send what you've created to a prospective employer's terminal or fax machine.

[1] Ronald F. Dow, "Manager's Journal: ROMing Your Corporate Library for Job Leads," *The Wall Street Journal,* 31 December 1990, p. 6.

SELF-INVENTORY

The job search begins with you. Figure out what you want to do on the basis of what you have accomplished, what interests you've shown, and what skills you have developed. Sit down and write the answers to questions like those shown in Figure 23–1. Don't just *think* the answers; write them. In ''*FYI:* The Job Search'' (page 481), Beth Berret underscores the significance of knowing what job you want.

MARKET INVENTORY

In addition to an inventory of your own interests, you need to inventory what jobs are available, and where, in the market. The market search may lead you to recognize a skill or a priority earlier neglected in your thinking. Check these sources:

A career-planning office or agency
State and federal employment offices
Newspapers
Professional job listings
Sources of information about companies
Word of mouth

Career-Planning Office or Agency

The place to begin your market inventory—as well as other steps in the process—may be the career-planning office or officer at your college or university. The office probably maintains a file of potential employers and a collection of books and newsletters about employment, like the *College Placement Annual,* which publishes an updated listing of employment opportunities on a regular basis.

In addition, private career-planning consultants provide such services on a fee-paying basis. Such consultants may be listed in the Yellow Pages or in the classified sections of newspapers. Although recruiting agencies—''headhunters''—have traditionally worked with mid- and upper-level managers, they are expanding their services to place recent college graduates in entry-level jobs. When consulting such agencies, clarify *in advance* the extent of their services, the fee scale, and the method of payment. Sometimes employers pay, and sometimes *you* pay.

State and Federal Employment Offices

Government employment offices keep a file of job openings and opportunities in their region and can also help in a job search. Their listings cover both the private sector and government openings. They also have (as does your college library) government publications concerning job trends, for

1. What decisions have you made in the last year? Can you see any pattern in them? What do they show about your priorities?
2. What would you do (besides sleeping) if you were given an extra day in a week? What do you enjoy doing?
3. Do you work better alone or on a team?
4. Do you like to take charge or to follow directions?
5. Do you like to take risks or to avoid risk?
6. What working conditions do you prefer? Inside or outside? Can you tolerate noise, or do you need quiet conditions?
7. How do you reward yourself when you've done something special?
8. What circumstances make you feel happy? What, on the other hand, frustrates you?
9. Do you meet deadlines easily? Do you work well under pressure?
10. What are your greatest achievements? What skills were needed to achieve them?
    Gathering and analyzing data?
    Getting other people to work?
    Fixing things?
    Seeing patterns where others see chaos?
    Speaking or computing in various languages?
    Operating any special machinery?
11. Think of your courses in high school and college. List the most important ones. Selecting what you consider most important will help you profile your interests. What did you do best in? How have your courses prepared you for the career you are interested in? Given another chance, would you take different courses?
12. How will you know you are successful? What do you note as signs of success in others?
13. Do you weigh job satisfaction or salary more heavily?
14. Do you gravitate toward new ways of doing things, or are you more comfortable with a known routine?
15. Where would you like to be next year? What do you see yourself doing at 10 A.M. one year from today?
16. Where would you like to be in five years? Write a brief statement about what you want to be. You may have a narrow focus:
    - I want to work for a major accounting firm in Denver as an account manager whose responsibilities gradually (but rapidly) increase so that in five years I'm a partner.

    Or you may see yourself in a broad range of positions:
    - I'd like a job offering a lot of contact with the public.
    - I'd like to work in a small, entrepreneurial company aggressively marketing an innovative product.

FIGURE 23–1.
Questions to ask as you inventory your interests and skills.

THE JOB SEARCH

Beth Berret
Instructor, Alvernia College

I warn students not to become discouraged by the job application process. It can be a humbling, frustrating experience, but everyone has gone through it, and you shouldn't take it personally.

Often, new graduates will flood the market with resumes and receive nothing in return, except what has been called the "bozo" letter. You know, that's the one that politely says "don't call us, we'll call you," or "thanks but no thanks." Even more discouraging, sometimes you get no response at all, and you wonder if they even read your letter.

But don't despair. Career planning is the key. Why flood the market with a wish list of jobs just to land one? Often, you're not even sure you're interested in the job or have the qualifications they're looking for. Since you've painstakingly planned the last 4 years of your life getting a bachelor's degree, doesn't it make sense to plan your career search? The steps you've taken in college to prepare for your professional work life will help you land that first job.

Here are a few hints. Know what you want to do. If you're not sure, do your homework. Use all the resources available to you: career services, professors, summer job contacts, internships, and co-op programs. An "I'll do anything if you give me a chance" approach doesn't work in the job application process. Interviewers will interpret your attitude as misguided or uncommitted and will be reluctant to risk training dollars on a candidate who may or may not stick around.

Your knowledge of the job you want will refine your mailing list, and you can spend more time preparing your resume and cover letter. Think of that cover letter as the door to your resume. You want the reader to open the door, or turn the page, to see what your resume offers. Be sure that it's clear, concise, complete, and neat.

A well planned job search, a polished resume and cover letter, and a confident attitude will go a long way toward bringing a job offer rather than a "bozo" letter to your mailbox.

example, the Bureau of Labor Statistics's *Occupational Outlook Handbook* or *Career Index*. *Working for the USA* and the *Federal Career Directory* discuss work with the federal government specifically. The Blue Pages of the telephone book list the government employment agencies in your area.

Newspapers

You're probably familiar with the classified ads in newspapers. When you've decided what *location* you're interested in, check the local newspapers there for job openings. Newspapers like *The New York Times* and *The Wall*

Finding out as much as possible about career opportunities enhances choice and improves one's chances in the competitive marketplace for employment.

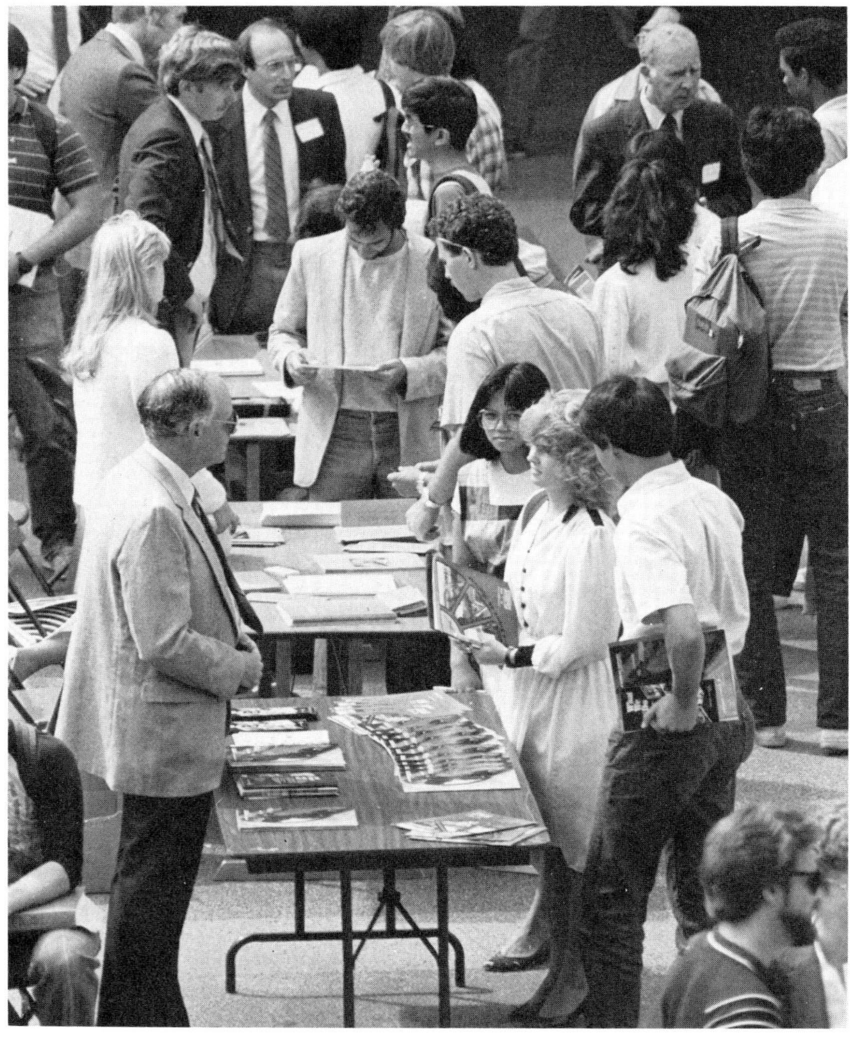

Street Journal list more geographically varied openings. The *Journal* also publishes the *National Business Employment Weekly.*

Professional Job Listings

Some professional societies publish job listings as a regular feature of national and local magazines and newsletters or maintain telephone hotlines listing available positions. English departments are familiar with the Modern Language Association's *Job List.* For information on international careers, read "Communiqué," the newsletter of the International Society for Intercultural Education, Training, and Research (SIETAR) in Washington. Openings in the computer industry are listed online by several professional groups that encourage applicants to respond online to potential employers.

Sources of Information about Companies

Read up on companies that do the kind of work you'd like to be part of (review Chapter 9 on sources of business information). Much information is available on CD. Some primary vendors include Disclosure Inc., Lotus Co., Dun & Bradstreet, and Standard & Poors.[2] The CDs contain essential information on thousands of public and private companies: balance sheets, texts of the president's letter in annual reports, breakdowns of lines of business, the names of officers, and the addresses of offices and plants. A librarian can help you target a search for companies that match your skills and interests.

Word of Mouth

Talk with friends who work for companies that seem appealing to you. Talk with recent graduates from your school in your major to find out what they are doing and what companies they recommend. Ask former supervisors if they know of positions available. Talk with professors. Read jottings on bulletin boards.

You might also engage in "informational interviewing."[3] Ask someone who performs the kind of work you'd like to do if you can talk with him or her about that work and expectations for those who do the work. Talk with your parents, your aunts and uncles, and their friends. In the search, no one is out of bounds. As you shop around, sometimes a lead into one job will send you on a detour to another. Be willing to spend time talking to people ("networking") who may not be able to help you directly, but who may be able to send you to those who can.

SOLICITING RECOMMENDATIONS

As you inventory yourself and talk with people who know the market, select your recommenders. These are people who can write letters of reference for you that comment on what you have done and thus what you can do. You'll probably want to ask your adviser or major professor. You may also ask a supervisor who can describe your work habits. If you have been active in a campus organization, you might ask an adviser to that group for a letter. If you know well someone who works for the company you're interested in, ask her or him. Obviously, it's best if the recommender is known to your potential employer. A familiar source strengthens the force of a good comment.

Chapter 16 provides advice on writing two kinds of letters in this process of recommendations: a letter *requesting* a recommendation and a letter *providing* a recommendation. Here are a few additional suggestions.

- **Never use a recommender's name without asking.** Not to ask is presumptuous, rude, and potentially damaging—to you—if the recommender is called by a potential employer and can't remember you.

[2] Ibid.

[3] Richard N. Bolles, *What Color Is My Parachute? A Practical Manual for Job-Hunters and Career Changers* (Berkeley: Ten Speed Press, yearly updates).

- **Seek an enthusiastic letter.** One student recommends this technique: She asks a potential recommender if he or she could write a positive letter. That question offers the recommender an out. If the response is something like "I could write you a letter, but frankly all I remember is your grade. After all, it was a large lecture course," then the student thanks the professor and leaves. You don't need lukewarm letters.
- **Provide appropriate background and forms for the letter.** Provide the potential recommender with your resume, a brief statement of your goals, and a description of the job you are applying for. Your interest and your willingness to talk with the recommender will probably be reflected in the letter. The more concrete the letter of recommendation, the more convincing. If a form is necessary, complete any parts of the form that require information from you or your signature before giving the form to the recommender.
- **Set up a dossier** with your college placement office. If you do, a recommender will not need to write a letter for each job you are applying for. In special cases, however, you may want to select a particular reference for the job and ask for a tailored letter.

MANAGING THE RESUME—PART 1: CONTENT

"It'll look great on your resume." How often have you heard that as a motivator—for joining a club, assuming a leadership role in an organization, or participating in an exchange program? A resume can become larger than life unless you realize that it is simply a fact sheet like those you read about in Chapter 18. You pull together the most important information from your self-inventory in a format that makes easy reading for potential employers. Your goal is to provide an employer with evidence that supports the appropriateness of your candidacy for the position. The resume also serves as a reference during the interview and reminds the interviewer about you afterward.

The information you present in the resume and its form are not universally dictated. Before you write, however, you should be familiar with certain expectations in content and conventions in form. Moreover, in advance of your reading of guidelines for writing, let us issue a warning: **PROOFREAD.** Recruiters are reading to *eliminate* (their term for this activity is "deselecting"). Spelling errors or errors in grammar give them a watertight excuse. In the heat of your preparation, design, and printing of the resume, don't forget that simple step. Don't "deselect" yourself.

The following guidelines will help you prepare the content of your resume. Design is another matter, which you'll read about shortly. Look at Figures 23–2 to 23–4 as you read about each part of the resume.

Heading

In a heading (which usually appears at the top but may appear at the side), you title the resume. Your name should be prominent. In addition, tell a potential employer how to get in touch with you: mail address; phone

MARTIN ALLENQUIST

College Address (until June 1)	*Permanent Address*
906 Syphert	210 Halsey Ave.
Ithaca, NY 14850	Jericho, NY 11753
607-255-8788	516-432-9655

Objective A position in internal auditing with a large multinational organization in which I can combine my accounting skills with my knowledge of different languages and cultures

Education BS in Accounting, Cornell University, 1993
Courses in managerial accounting, cost accounting, business law, finance, operations management, and marketing
GPA 3.5 out of 4.0
Earned 75% of college expenses

Experience

Summer 1991 — **POM Recoveries,** Syosset, NY.
- Posted financial statements by hand and on computer

Spring 1991 — **Publisher's Clearing House,** Port Washington, NY.
- Sorted checks
- Processed magazine orders
- Validated contest entry forms

Summers 1987–1990 — **Camp Thistle,** Rabbit Lake, NY.
- Organized games
- Taught swimming
- Supervised campers

Activities
- Cornell University Marching Band (3 years)
- Intramural soccer and baseball

Personal
- Born September 17, 1972
- Have traveled widely and attended schools in Switzerland and England
- Fluent in French
- Willing to relocate

References Available upon request.

FIGURE 23–2.
Chronological resume.

SAMANTHA MACDONALD

Campus Address
134 Clark
Laramie, WY 82070
(307)451-8788

Home Address
120 Lake Sundance Crest, S.E.
Calgary, Alberta T2J 2S7
Canada
(403) 522-7811

EDUCATION

University of Wyoming
BS in Business Administration with emphasis in Marketing Management
(expected January 1992)

Dean's List
Attended seminar in the operation and applications of IBM personal computers
Actively participated in marketing research projects

EXPERIENCE

Elaine Powers Figure Salon, Laramie, WY
Service Consultant, 10/90 to present
Instruct aerobic dance and exercise classes. Develop advertising campaigns. Sell membership programs and weight loss products.

University of Wyoming, College of Commerce and Industry
Microcomputer Lab Instructor, 1/90 to present
Instruct faculty and students in use of IBM personal computers. Correct accounting assignments. Work with the following software:

VisiCalc	Visitrend Plot	Peachtree Accounting
WordStar	Lotus 1-2-3	

Bank of Wyoming, Central Marketing Department. Cheyenne, WY
Marketing Research Assistant, 6/91-9/91
Analyzed present and potential markets for new and existing products and services. Interpreted secondary research findings. Input and manipulated research data for statistical analysis. Evaluated current and potential branch sites. Extracted data for market share reports and the analysis of market penetration. Assisted product managers with requests for ongoing research data.

Sid's Pants, Worthington, OH
Sales Clerk, Summers 1985, 1986, 1987
Provided product information and buying recommendations to customers. Arranged merchandise floor plans. Assisted in inventory control. Handled cash transactions.

BACKGROUND

Tutor economics and mathematics. Member of Business Students Association and College of Commerce and Industry Council. Intramural athletics. Interests include jogging, tennis, and travel. Willing to relocate. References available upon request.

FIGURE 23–3.
Chronological resume.

number at home, school, or work; fax number or e-mail address, if appropriate. You might also suggest the best times for calling.

Objective

If you can state your objective clearly, and in at least modestly concrete terms, as in Figures 23–2 and 23–4, then go ahead. Show what you want to *do,* not what you want to *be.* Many resume readers comment that they like to see a clear statement of goals. Here are some concrete statements:

- A supervisory position in production or quality control
- A position in research and development or in technical service, either within the company or in the field

If you are applying for different kinds of positions, write a specific goal statement for each; your wordprocessing system will allow you to pop them in and out.

If you can state your goal only generally—"An entry-level position in the business world"—then omit the statement. The omission will not count against you, but a vague or wide-eyed statement will.

Education

Most recent graduates find that their education is the major selling point. Should you include high school? Perhaps, if you feel the school's identity comments well on your own identity or if you want to note special awards or achievements there. But certainly once you finish college and move on to other degrees or experience, you will drop the high school notation.

List the college (or colleges) you have attended. Start the list with your current college and work backward in time. Indicate any degree or degrees you have received or expect to receive, with your date of graduation and your years of attendance. Avoid obscure abbreviations. You might list relevant courses, with grades if they are good. Again, avoid internal codes: BU 441, E 312. Instead, use course titles: "Business Policy," "Written Communications in Business." Should you include your grade-point average? Recruiters often like to see that, calculated either overall or in major courses. Most students omit their GPA if it is under 2.0 on a 4.0 scale. Be sure to specify the scale.

If you've financed your education largely on your own, note that (see Figures 23–2 and 23–4). Self-financing shows your keen motivation. Indicate scholarship aid if appropriate. You don't need to give the amount.

Note any honors and awards and explain them. If you won the "Golden Shovel Award" for the best sophomore marketing researcher, you'd better tell a reader the meaning, lest he or she interpret the shoveling differently.

Experience and Skills

Two approaches to presenting your experience and skills are common: *chronological* or *functional.* The chronological approach is the most common. You list your education and work experience, job by job, according to time.

Kerri Weidner
16 Papermill Road
Newark, DE 19713
302-731-1111

Objective

To participate in the research and development of efficient methods for using natural resources

Education

Bachelor of Science Degree with Distinction, Agricultural Economics, with a concentration in natural resources, University of Delaware, 1991

Major GPA: 3.54/4.0; Overall GPA: 3.7/4.0

Skills

Research

Individual project: researched and wrote a senior thesis, "Analysis of Resident Concern for Delaware Water Quality." Project scope included designing the initial investigation, including writing a questionnaire; administering the questionnaire to 160 state residents; entering and manipulating the survey data with SAS (Statistical Analysis Software System); writing the thesis and defending it orally.

Team projects: Under the supervision of Dr. John MacKenzie of the University of Delaware, worked with the Delaware Department of Natural Resources and Environmental Control (DNREC) to prepare several reports and papers, including

- The 1990 Statewide Comprehensive Outdoor Recreation Plan for Delaware
- "Participation in Trapping Activities by Delaware Residents"
- "The Demand and Need for Additional Bike Paths in Southern Delaware"

FIGURE 23–4.
Functions (skills) resume *(Courtesy of Kerri Weidner.)*

Kerri Weidner page 2

Skills, continued

Computer

Well versed in several languages and in programs for statistical analysis, database management, and writing, including SAS, Lotus 1-2-3, WordPerfect, Freelance, and Notebook. Experience on both IBM mainframe and personal computers. Instructed students in the use of computers and wrote a manual for using SAS in natural resources research in classes at Delaware.

Communication

Excellent communication skills developed through course work in business communication and as a co-author of papers and reports at DNREC.

Background

Enjoy sailing, downhill skiing, and racquetball

Earned 90% of college expenses through both part-time and full-time work over several years as a waitress and bartender

References

John E. A. MacKenzie
Associate Professor
Department of Food and Resource Economics
University of Delaware
Newark, DE 19716

Wui Chou
Delaware Department of Natural Resources and Environmental Control
Wetlands Branch
P.O. Box 1401
89 Kings Highway
Dover, DE 19903

John Bossacco, Proprietor
The Whistling Abalone Restaurant
12 Ocean Street
Monterey, CA 93940

A functional resume arranges your experience according to the *skills* you can present. Figures 23–2 and 23–3 are chronological resumes. Figure 23–4 is a functional (sometimes called *skills*) resume.

In preparing to write this segment, think about what you did in each job and what you learned. Assess particularly the skills needed simply to be an employee or to supervise others. Such experience is important even if the content of the jobs you have held bears no resemblance to the content of the job you hope to hold. Did you have any specific responsibilities? Did they change? Did you have any part in making them change? Can you quantify the results of your work (the dollar amounts earned in a summer painting job, the number of customers served, the percentage increase in sales, the area covered, the number of tables at a restaurant where you were the sole waiter)? Did you write any reports or other documents on the job? How much time did you work each week? Did you operate any equipment? Were you able to work on your own? Don't forget your experience in internships, cooperative education programs, or campus activities.

Then, decide on an approach. Consider a *functional* approach when you have little experience, or when your experience is scattered both in kinds of jobs and in your amount of time in the work force, or when you are shifting careers after considerable amounts of time in the work force. Incorporate your experience under skill labels like "research," "communication," "management," "supervisory responsibilities," or "proposal preparation" (see Figure 23–4).

Otherwise, use the more common *chronological* approach shown in Figures 23–2 and 23–3. List the title, employer, and dates for your jobs, but don't let your description end there. Describe what you did and what you learned, with particular emphasis on increasing responsibilities and an ability to work without close supervision. Note the skills you developed and your track record as a self-starter. Quantify the description wherever possible, and use active verbs. If you worked with computers on your jobs, be sure to note that, including information about hardware, software, and languages you became proficient with. You might want to group a series of summer jobs.

Personal Information

Use the resume to emphasize your strengths. Affirmative action guidelines caution against revealing such personal information as birth date and marital status, but you may if you'd like. If you speak another language, mention it. Note your computer literacy, an extensive travel record, and your extracurricular activities. Note particularly any offices held that show your leadership ability. Indicate whether you are willing to relocate.

Try to see from an interviewer's perspective the picture of yourself you paint. Noting involvement in group activities like sororities and fraternities and in such "corporate sports" as football, racquetball, and downhill skiing indicates a team player. Listing together such hobbies as long-distance running, mountain biking, cross-country skiing, and vegetarian cooking may suggest more of a loner personality. Look for "red flags" that might raise unwanted questions or might be read to your disadvantage. If, for example, you have always lived in New England, and all your education has been there, a reader at a corporation in Houston may automatically eliminate you as a poor risk in a new geographic environment. Meet that potential misreading head on by including a notation that you are willing to relocate (perhaps even go so far as to indicate your desire to move to the Southwest). As a woman with four children you are proud of, you might note those children and their names and birth dates. But think again. A potential employer may circle that notation and wonder, "When would she have time to work for *us*?" *You* know you can do it; don't raise the issue.

References

In most surveys of what they look for in a resume, recruiters put references in last place. Although the comments from recommenders are vital, noting that such comments are available or where they are available has become an accepted formula:

- `References: Available on request.`

or:

- `References available from the Career Planning Office at the University of the Rockies, Box 352, Laramie, WY 82070.`

MANAGING THE RESUME— PART II: DESIGN

- A Chicago copywriter ends her resume with a coupon offering five dollars from her first paycheck to her next employer.
- A producer seeking a position at a TV network displays his resume on a billboard across from the network president's office.
- A benefits analyst circulates a videotape that provides his credentials in an opening scene and then shows him discussing his abilities and job potential.

Bizarre? Certainly. Such gimmicks may work, especially for positions in advertising and production that demand the creative thinking that these applicants showed. On most occasions, however, too much playing with the conventions of the fact sheet raises resistance rather than enthusiasm in the potential employer. If your resume is *too* slick, the packaging may work against you. Focus on simple and straightforward design—on paper, not billboards, and without coupons.

Figures 23–2, 23–3, and 23–4 show three variations of good design. All were produced by students with a simple desktop publishing program. Keep in mind the checklist below when you design your resume.

CHECKLIST FOR DESIGNING YOUR RESUME

1. **Keep it short.** Experts disagree on whether the resume must be only one page, but few readers are happy with more than two pages. Readers should be able to skim for the gist of the information in under a minute.

2. **Keep it uncluttered.** Leave white space at the left and right margins to direct the reader's attention to the text down the center of the page.
3. **Use type fonts and typefaces strategically, not whimsically.** Figure 23–5 shows an author victimized by a desktop publishing program.
4. **Avoid complete sentences.** Use action verbs to show what you did on the job:

```
Analyzed information from the three national credit bureaus.
Evaluated requests for credit line increases. Assessed in-
formation listed in credit applications. Answered credit-
related questions from customers.
```

5. **Watch parallelism.** Action verbs should be parallel (as above), as should your layout of items in the same category, headings, punctuation, and use of italics, boldface, underlining, and type fonts.

WRITING THE COVER LETTER

The resume provides the facts. To turn the facts into evidence that shows why you're the best candidate for a particular job, you write a cover letter applying for that job. Read the following letter, sent as a photocopy in response to an advertisement for a sales representative to do telemarketing for a bank.

A Poor Approach

```
Dear ____________:

   This communication is relative to inquiry reguarding the
possibility of either immediate or future employment with
your institution or firm.

   The applicant is skilled in communications and in manage-
ment. He has five years' experience in a fast-food chain with
ever increasing responsibilities serving many customers.

   His academic training consists of a BA degree in Politi-
cal Science as well as course work in managment.

   The applicant is 22 years old, in excellent health, and
can furnish superb references and credentials within two days
for your review and consideration.

   Available for immediate employment, interim appointment,
or personal interview. Detailed resume and data on request.
```

Persuasive? In many ways, it's not. The voice is stuffy and impersonal ("this communication," "the applicant," "relative to"). The letter includes misspellings: *reguarding, managment.* It tells the reader something about the applicant but fails to encourage the reader's interest.

OBJECTIVE: To obtain a supervisory position in bank card collection with opportunities for advancement in management.

EXPERIENCE:

120 DAY COLLECTOR

From July 15, 1990 to present was collector in charge of half of the premium Plasticard portfolio of the largest "Silver" card issuer in the world. Maintained the highest standards of quality while exceeding goal three months in a row by collecting 50% of my accounts (figures adjusted for bankruptcy) within 30 days.

PART-TIME COLLECTOR

Started as 30-day part-time collector in January 1989 with Surcharge Plus Bank N.A. and was promoted to 90-day part-time collector a year later. Continued to develop advanced collection techniques and shared responsibility for collection of 45% of $2.5 million in April 1990. Again promoted in May 1990 to the only part-time charge-off collector at Surcharge Plus Bank N.A. Took on added written communication with card holders, gained charge-off experience in the highest rated charge-off unit in the industry. Also executed a bankruptcy prevention program that saved Surcharge Plus Bank N.A. $75,000.

TRAINING:

Directly assisted in the creation, execution, and maintenance of a comprehensive bank-card-collection training program. As a part-time collector was the first employee to be released of collection responsibilities to train new full- and part-time collectors. *Trained twenty collectors within six months in use of SSBBAA computer system and collection method and policy.*

EDUCATION:

McGough University. BA in Political Science, including courses in

Government and Business — Consumer Credit Lending
Public Administration — Macroeconomics
Organizational theory and Administrative Behavior

REFERENCES: Available upon request

FIGURE 23–5.
This resume was prepared on a personal computer with an excellent choice of typefaces, but the author failed to control his choices. The design is crowded; the type size gets smaller in every section, and thus reading is difficult.

When you write, show why the company should be interested in interviewing you—gaining that interview is the goal of the letter. Use both an ethical appeal in your style and attention to detail and a logical appeal in the selection and arrangement of your evidence. Consider incorporating the AIDA approach you learned in Chapter 16.

Attention

Get attention directly in the salutation by using the reader's name. If a name is not included in the job announcement, call the company to find out the name of the personnel director or check a standard source. People pay more attention when they are addressed by their name than when addressed only by their role. Get attention, too, by designing your letter well, with adequate margins, good spacing, and a pleasing typeface. Use good-quality paper. For a marketing or advertising position, you might try a gimmick; one applicant, for example, began his letter at the *last* line on the page and wrote up. He said the letter reflected his willingness to start at the bottom. But think of the reader. Many readers would find upside-down letters upsetting.

Interest

Establish your central selling point *in the reader's terms,* as a way of creating interest. The selling point may be your education, your experience, or both. Choose whether you want to emphasize a single skill or your versatility. For example, note your experience in connection with the reader's product:

```
As a committed user of IBM personal computers and a tutor in
our university IBM microcomputer laboratory, I am writing to
inquire about becoming a participant in your management
training program.
```

Or your knowledge of the reader's company:

```
Because of my experience and education in agricultural eco-
nomics and management, I think I can be an asset to Perdue
Inc. as you maintain your strong position in the poultry in-
dustry.
```

Or your familiarity with the reader's goals:

```
Are you looking for a sales representative with a degree in
marketing and a good technical background in chemistry?
You'll find my academic qualifications and personality are
well suited to a career in pharmaceutical marketing with your
firm.
```

Be positive. The following opener implies that the writer will tell the company how to run its business:

Poor Approach

```
    Last summer, I worked for Pediatrics Associates Inc.,
which uses your office systems. I became very familiar with
all the trouble you have with those systems, their lack of
reliability and difficulty of use. I'd like to apply for a
job with you to straighten these things out.
```

Don't be selfish. Avoid a flat announcement of your availability:

Poor Approach

```
    In June I will receive a B.S. degree in management from
XYZ University.
```

"So what?" a reader may well respond.

If you feel that the reader is conservative and expects a low-keyed, traditional opener, begin by noting where you found out about the job, for example, in an announcement:

```
I am writing in response to your advertisement in the 4 June
issue of The Deseret News.
```

Or through a person:

```
John Maier, my major professor in the Department of Account-
ing at Utah State, suggested that I write to you concerning
your opening for an entry-level accountant.
```

Don't begin with a request for an interview. Save that for later, after you've convinced the reader that you're worth interviewing. Make sure that somewhere in the first paragraph you have applied for a position. Call the position by whatever name you found in the advertisement or heard from your source:

```
I am writing to apply for your position of sales trainee.
```

Desire

With the selling point clear, provide backup evidence to persuade the reader to interview you. Use a *logical* appeal. Match your qualifications to the position. Indeed, let the job description structure your presentation. Here's an advertisement:

```
If you have strong analytical skills, are project-oriented,
have the ability to work on your own, and are looking for a
position where you will participate in and contribute to the
decision-making process in both the operations and strategic
planning areas, this may be the position for you.
```

A response would provide evidence derived from education or experience in each category:

- *Analytical skills:* Courses? Reports written? Problem solving in summer jobs?
- *Project-oriented:* Marketing or other projects in classes? Group assignments? The development of schedules for summer workers where you worked?
- *Work on own:* Employer comments about your independence? Independent-study credits? Entrepreneurial summer activities?
- *Decision making and operations and strategic planning:* Courses in planning? Team work? Case study analyses?

Here's one paragraph from a response to an advertisement for a management trainee in an investment banking company:

```
At college, I have taken courses in financial management that
taught me stock and bond evaluation, dividend analysis, asset
management, and tax policy. Each course required extensive
case analyses and practical problem-solving. High grades in
the courses indicate my strengths in these skills necessary
to do well in your position. In my work with MidLantic Bank
Inc., I gained experience in using several computer programs
for stock analysis and can bring that experience, too, to
your firm.
```

Refer to the resume, but don't just rehash it. Don't editorialize; *show* the reader what you can do, don't just *tell*. Avoid such exaggeration as this:

Poor Approach

```
My extensive course work in marketing and my highly success-
ful summer work experience in a gourmet shop of the utmost
quality have prepared me for an outstanding career in market-
ing. If your opening is commensurate with my own needs, I
might be available for an interview.
```

You want to show that you speak the language of corporate employers, but extensive jargon or stuffiness will probably backfire.

Action

Finally, close the letter with a request for an interview, at which time you can persuade the prospective employer in person. Restate your interest in the job. Anticipate the question of *when* you could attend an interview by providing a time frame:

```
It would be a pleasure to visit you for a personal interview
at your convenience. The best times would be a Monday or a
Wednesday between 1:00 and 5:00, but I could arrange another
time if necessary.
```

You might also retain a bit of control over the situation by noting that you will call the reader in another week or two:

I will call you in two weeks to arrange a convenient time to discuss career opportunities at Syncrude.

Avoid the letterly voice throughout (see Chapters 5 and 13). Especially avoid such cliched endings as "Thank you for your time" or "I hope to hear from you soon." Instead, tailor the ending to the sales approach of the rest of the letter:

I would like to use my background in both marketing and chemistry to represent ICI America and to contribute to your strong growth trend. Please call me for an interview at your convenience. I'm eager to be part of your team.

Letters That Work

You write the letter about yourself, but you need to think in the reader's terms. Resist the temptation simply to describe yourself by repeating information in the resume. As a test, at least make sure that you avoid beginning every paragraph with *I.* Figure 23–6 shows how Kerri Weidner, whose resume you saw in Figure 23–4, interpreted her credentials for a job with the Lamour Corporation.

In the following letter, Jenny Smith uses a hospital's job description to frame her response. Here is the description (*EOE,* by the way, stands for "Equal Opportunity Employer").

Graduate Hospital is seeking highly motivated therapists and certified PT assistants for our 310-bed acute-care teaching hospital with a 20-bed rehabilitation unit. Rehab experience is a plus but not required. Case load will vary. You must be eligible for PA licensure. New graduates are welcome to apply. Excellent salary and benefits. Send resume to Rhonda Pappero, Graduate Hospital, Personnel, 19th and Lombard Sts., Philadelphia PA 19146. EOE.

Here is Smith's letter.

Dear Ms. Pappero:

Because of my academic work and experience in rehabilitation, I can be an asset to your Physical Therapy Department as described in The Forum, 12 May 1992. I am applying for a therapist's position, especially working with young people and with stroke victims of all ages.

The opportunity to work with a varied case load in a teaching hospital, particularly Graduate Hospital, excites me. I hold a B.S. degree in biological sciences from American University and am a recent graduate of Beaver College's graduate program in physical therapy. I am eligible for Pennsylvania licensure. Because I am a recent graduate, my experi-

16 Papermill Road
Newark, DE 19713

January 9, 1991

John Myers, Manager
Research and Development
Lamour Corporation
P.O. Box 52
Milton, VT 05468

Dear Mr. Myers:

My advisor, John MacKenzie, recently told me about openings in your department at Lamour Corporation. I am especially interested in applying for the position of Natural Resource Specialist. I hope you will agree that my qualifications make me well suited for this post.

During my three years as a research assistant at the University of Delaware, I learned proven methods of non-market valuation and cost-benefit analysis from experienced researchers. In addition, I worked closely with the Delaware Department of Natural Resources and Environmental Control in watershed management projects. Through this affiliation and through personal interest, I have become familiar with federal and state conservation policies and programs.

Dr. MacKenzie mentioned that Lamour uses SAS extensively for statistical analysis. I used this program in compiling survey results for my undergraduate thesis on attitudes about Delaware water quality and in developing an outdoor recreational plan for the state. I also received additional training at the SAS institute.

The opportunity to combine my research experience, computer skills, and knowledge of conservation policies in the Natural Resource Specialist position at Lamour is an exciting prospect for me. I also welcome the chance to move to Vermont.

The enclosed resume lists my qualifications. I will be in the Burlington area next month to ski and would be pleased to speak with you about the contribution I might make to your organization. I'll call you in two weeks to arrange an appointment. Thank you.

Sincerely,

Kerri Weidner

Kerri Weidner

Enc.

FIGURE 23–6.
Cover letter based on the resume in Figure 23–4. The letter is in the modified block format. *(Courtesy of Kerri Weidner.)*

ence to date has been clinical rather than job-related, but I have worked directly with both young people and geriatric patients in an internship program at the Moss Rehabilitation Center.

The enclosed resume details my qualifications. At your request, I will be happy to furnish letters of reference that will inform you of my reliability and skill both as a student and as a therapist.

At your convenience, I will be pleased to talk with you. I look forward to learning more about the challenges of rehabilitation medicine and to discussing the role I can play in maintaining the excellent work of Graduate Hospital.

The letter establishes "highly motivated" credentials with words like *excites* and *challenges*. It notes Smith's education, experience, and eligibility for licensure. It mentions the name of the Moss Rehabilitation Center, where Smith interned, because that hospital is also located in Philadelphia and is thus known to—and probably respected by—the reader. The letter emphasizes a broad interest in rehabilitation that reflects the "varied case load" statement in the advertisement.

In the following letter, Susan Hughes describes her personal travel and language skills in the terms of a potential employer at a travel agency. She knows about airline and ground transportation schedules. That knowledge translates into time that Bowman, her potential employer, can save in not having to train Hughes. The details, too, about countries visited and study abroad show enthusiasm for the specific job and are more convincing than a bland statement like "I am an enthusiastic traveler." The agency Hughes is writing to is located in Washington, D.C. Hughes writes from Lawrence, Kansas, so she explains her willingness to travel to Washington for both an interview and eventual relocation.

Dear Mr. Bowman:

Having traveled extensively during the past several years, I was pleased to read in the September issue of Professional Traveler that you are seeking to expand your staff. With my knowledge of much of the United States and several foreign countries, I would like to contribute to maintaining your excellent reputation as you expand your operation.

Currently, I am a student at the University of Kansas and will graduate with a double major in Spanish and business administration. I will be studying in Madrid for five months this spring and would enjoy relocating to Washington after graduation.

Traveling is one of my main interests. I have traveled through a majority of the continental United States and have visited the United Kingdom, South Africa, Brazil, Spain, Mexico, and Guatemala. I have a good knowledge of airlines and ground transportation, gained both as a hobby and during part-time employment with a local agency that serves the university community.

The enclosed resume lists my qualifications. I will be in Washington during my spring break, 6-10 April, and would like to talk with you, at your convenience, during that time, to discuss how I can contribute to your organization. I'll call you in two weeks to see about arranging an appointment.

In the following letter, Rich Hartman writes to an elementary-school principal because of a suggestion from his track coach. The name of the coach is the point of connection with the reader in the first sentence. Note how Hartman uses the ends of Paragraphs 2 and 3 to state his experience in the reader's terms. He shows his knowledge of children by quoting numbers (60) and specific names of programs (HAP). He also establishes his own credentials as a runner. His selling point: He's a runner who has been well coached and who also works well with children.

Dear Mr. Muñoz:

My track coach, Pete Phillips, recently told me about openings in your extracurricular program at Skyline. I am particularly interested in applying for the position of head coach of the boys' track team. I hope you'll agree that my qualifications suit me well for this post.

This past summer, I taught mathematics, in morning sessions, to 60 seventh-graders in the Higher Achievement Program (HAP) at Logan High School. Twice a week, in afternoon sessions, I demonstrated the basic skills of track and other sports to these same students. HAP has provided me with invaluable experience in dealing with boys and girls about the same age as students at Skyline.

I have been running track myself at various levels for 14 years. During this time I have worked closely with five excellent head track coaches (including Pete, of course) and have observed their training techniques. I'm certain I can develop these techniques into a successful program at Skyline.

Highlights of my track career and other pertinent information are outlined on the enclosed resume. I'd like to come to Skyline to talk about working with you and your students to develop a strong track team.

Although it's best to address a specific reader, at times you will need to respond to a blind advertisement in a newspaper. Such advertisements avoid the mention of a company name. Instead, the company is referred to by qualifiers: "a major Fortune 500 firm located in New York City," "a rapidly growing West Coast financial services organization," "an expanding real-estate-syndication firm doing public offerings on real-estate-income programs." The advertisements request responses to a box number at the newspaper. Companies may use these blind ads to keep their own employees from knowing that the company is seeking new workers or to keep job seekers from beating down their doors. In your response, of course, do not write "Dear Box 52." Also avoid "Dear Sir or Madam." Instead, after an inside address of the newspaper, begin your message directly:

```
Now that I have received high marks in my management informa-
tion systems and programming classes and have completed a
summer as a systems analyst for a large organization, I'm
ready to be the "experienced, creative business programmer"
you advertised for on March 17.
```

As you send letters, maintain good records. Keep copies and establish a control sheet with columns for the date you send a letter, the date you receive an acknowledgment, interview dates, dates of follow-up letters, and the like.

Finally, keep in mind that the reader's job is also on the line when he or she decides to interview you. Particularly in large companies, if you survive the initial screening, your letter will be sent along with the blessing of the person you wrote to in the first place. Your letter should make him or her also look good.

SUMMARY

- First, **inventory yourself** as you begin the job search: your own interests, skills, education, and experience. What priorities do you have in location and in the type of job you seek?
- Then, **find out about the market.** Consult with the career-planning office at your college or university. Consult with headhunters and government employment agencies. Read the newspapers and other business information sources. Talk with people familiar with the market.
- Ask people who know you well and, if possible, are known by your potential employer to write **letters of reference** that present your credentials favorably and, if possible, enthusiastically. Consider professors, a supervisor at work, perhaps an adviser to an organization you've been active in. Don't list someone as a reference without asking.
- The **resume** is a simple **fact sheet,** generally on paper, and preferably short: one or two pages. It summarizes what you have done in a way that shows what you can do for a potential employer. It focuses on your education and experience; it may also include personal information and a statement of your career objective. It includes a heading that indicates how someone can reach you by phone or mail.
- Think of the **cover letter** that presents your resume to a potential employer as a **sales letter.** Try the AIDA approach: *a*ttention, *i*nterest, *d*esire, *a*ction. Don't just *tell* things about yourself in a flat description, but *show* how your skills, education, and interests will provide benefits to the potential employer.

EXERCISES

For Discussion

1. Comment on any "red flags" or errors in expression in these descriptions of experience from resumes:

Resident assistant. handled general floor maintenance. presented educational and social programs to residents. Counselled students and provided information about university services.

Waitress, College Hall. Coordinated detailed preparation and service of university and local business banquets.

File Clerk, Johnson Real Estate Agency, Kearny NJ. Maintained the organization of property listing files used by all county realtors, in accordance with the market changes.

Kwan Luggage, Oak Brook Terrace IL. August 1990 to August 1991. Closed and opened store, night deposits, customer service, and inventory.

Sales Assistant, IBM, Stokely FL. Responsible for the follow up and control of IBM's entire line of microcomputers. Duties include: demonstration of hardware and software to groups and individuals, hardware maintenance, keep customer contact to ensure satisfaction (1/90 to present)

Waiter-clown, Smiths FoodHall, Waterville TX. Gain experience working with people and handling cash.

Laborer. Public Works, Ridley Township OH. Worked on the "road crew" fixing and sprucing up Public facilities.

offered position as student tour guide.

2. Comment on any problems in expression in these sections under "Education" in a resume:

   Completed courses in Industrial Psychology, Independent Study dealing with worker evaluation and motivation, Learning and Motivation, Behavioral Statistics, as well as general courses in Computer Science, Business Communications and Economics.

   Have passed BU 614, BU 661, E 451, MU 687, and A111. Expected date of Gratulation: 1993.

3. Comment on these job-objective statements:

   -Acceptance into health care administration with the possibility of advancement.

   -Buyer in the purchasing department with an opportunity for advancement in management.

   -Systems engineer, specializing in computer-related work that will utilize my educational background in the field of finance and personal computers.

```
–Management–level position as liaison between business and
patient care in a moderately sized health–care facility.
```

For Writing

4. As an exercise in making concrete what you are seeking in a job and a career, write a description of your ideal job. The position probably doesn't exist, of course. But use the advertisements in the classified section of a newspaper and the model descriptions in this chapter to prepare your description. Include information about the kind of company you'd like to work in, the responsibilities you'd like to assume, and the skills you'd like to display and continue to develop.
5. Pages 504–505 show a functional resume. Create a revised version with a clearer design and more focus on the candidate's major credentials. Insert current dates where appropriate. Use a desktop publishing program if one is available to you.
6. Pages 506–507 show a chronological resume. Revise as you did in Exercise 5.

For Collaboration

7. "Know thyself" is age-old advice, but following that advice may be difficult. In this chapter you learned about the need for a self-inventory before you tackle the job market. Using the assistance of your career-planning office, of software for career analysis, or of materials from the library, work in a team of three to help each other complete a self-inventory. Jointly derive the appropriate questions and perhaps a form for recording the responses. Help each other to answer the questions. Discuss your questions and forms in class with other teams.
8. Form a team with other students in your major to prepare a market inventory of job prospects in your field. Use CD-ROM sources in your library, if available, as well as others you learned about in this chapter and in Chapter 9. As directed by your instructor, present your results orally in class (see Chapter 22) or in a written report (Chapter 19).

SKILLS

1. Proficiency in planning, writing, and editing business and technical documents, news releases, research reports, and interpretive papers.
2. Ability to communicate orally.
3. Ability to think creatively and to implement new ideas.
4. Abilty to work constructively with a group over a period of time.
5. Ability to direct the activities of others in group projects.
6. Ability to share knowledge and skills.
7. First-aid skills.
8. Ability to learn new ideas and skills rapidly through both oral and written instruction.
9. Ability to travel, to adapt to new cultures, to function on my own without parental or community support.

RELATED TRAINING AND EXPERIENCE

1. • Will graduate June 19xx with a degree in business administration.
   • During a five-week internship with the Cheyenne County Personnel Department, produced annual report for the Personnel Board and report summarizing my statistical research on a special project.
   • News editor for high-school newspaper.

2. • Gave oral presentation on managing personnel resources to my organizational and management behavior class.
   • Gained poise, confidence, and speaking skills while acting in school plays.

3. • Helped found an undergraduate chapter of the International Association of Business Communicators.
   • Started peer advising program for business majors.
   • Started children's acolyte service at church.
   • Choreographed for dance performances.

EXERCISE 5.
A functional resume for revision.

4. • Member of the university dance ensemble, university outing club, intramural sports, Girl Scouts.

5. • Directed short play for a literature class.
   • Advised undergraduate officers of the IABC chapter on leadership.
   • Dormitory government representative.
   • Held several offices in high school.

6. • Tutor for freshman accounting course.
   • Summer counselor and swimming instructor at Girl Scout camp.
   • Spanish teacher for elementary-school program.
   • Sunday school, Bible school teacher.

7. • Worked summers as lifeguard.

8. • Worked part time as library clerk and waitress.

9. • Spent a semester in England, studying and traveling.
   • Familiar with French and Spanish language and culture.

HONORS AND AWARDS

Dean's List, University Honors Program, Rotary Club Service Award, Teacher's Association Scholarship, First-Class Girl Scouting Award, Student of the Month, second runner-up in County Junior Miss Pageant, nominated for People to People Student Ambassador Program, President of National Honor Society.

Peter P. Smith
17 Hyde Dr., Apt A
Mountain View, CA 94043

JOB OBJECTIVE:
Challenging position in business/financial management that will provide an atmosphere conducive to growth and achievement and one where initiative will be welcomed.
EDUCATION:
University of X
B.S. in business administration with concentration in finance. Strong background in accounting and business economics. This program reflected the demand for management capability in every field.
EXPERIENCE:
5/xx–8/xx General Motors Assembly Division, X town CA
Rear-retractable seat-belt operator in the Soft Trim Department. Served as a reliable member of the production team; performed routine testing of components. Emphasis was placed on GM's compliance with the Motor Vehicle Safety Standards Act.

5/xx–8/xx County Country Club, Y town, CA
5/xx–8/xx
Held two positions simultaneously. Waiter in the clubhouse dining room, consisted of such duties as waiting on members for luncheons, dinners, banquets, and poolside occasions. Greenskeeper duties included engineering and maintaining an eighteen-hole private golf course. Tasks carried out were those such as irrigation, planning, landscaping, greens cutting, both pool and tennis-court upkeep.

EXERCISE 6.
A chronological resume for revision.

5/xx–8/xx Pals Cabin Restaurant, Z town CA
Pantry worker, responsible for general food services (cooking and preparation) and managerial assistance in the 75-table restaurant, maintaining beverage and food stocks. Supervised with coordination of brunches, banquets, and private parties (business meetings, personal celebrations, and community club events).

ACTIVITIES:
University of X
Member of the Business and Economics College Council and Business Student Association. Involved in the Residence Hall Government. Member of the Delta Upsilon chapter of Delta Phi Delta national Fraternity. Positions include Corresponding Secretary (responsible for correspondence with national fraternity, community, alumni, and parents, writing necessary documents), Pledge Educator, Rush Chairman, Greek Week Representative, and Outstanding Pledge. Participated in intramural football, waterpolo, basketball and softball. Member of the University of X Marching Band.
INTERESTS:
Participating in football, golf, camping, and music, and tinkering with automobiles.
REFERENCES:
Available on request.

24 THE INTERVIEW . . . AND BEYOND

What's Ahead

GOALS FOR INTERVIEWS
CONDUCTING THE INTERVIEW
- Setting the Stage
- Asking Questions
- Paying Attention
- Taking Notes
- Concluding Gracefully

THE EMPLOYMENT INTERVIEW
- Preparing
- Participating in a Face-to-Face Interview
- FYI: The Employment Interview as Role Play
- Participating in a Telephone Interview

AFTER THE INTERVIEW
- Deciding
- Accepting an Offer
- Declining an Offer
- Responding to a Rejection

PERFORMANCE REVIEWS
SUMMARY
EXERCISES

Do You Know 

- What is the purpose of interviews?
- What strategy should you use when you interview someone?
- What behavior is expected of you as a candidate in an employment interview?
- What follow-up steps are necessary after the interview?
- What should you expect in a performance review?

"Every exit is an entrance someplace else."

—Tom Stoppard, *Rosencrantz and Guildenstern Are Dead*

You'll have many occasions to participate in interviews both during the employment search and on the job. The interview with a recruiter is only one of them, although that interview may weigh heavily on your mind right now. In this chapter, you will first learn about the several goals of interviews. You'll then see how to apply the strategies for listening and talking you learned in Chapter 20 as you interview someone. After that background, you'll read detailed guidelines for performing well in the employment interview and for following up on job offers and rejections after the interview. Finally, you'll read advice about performance reviews that measure your work on the job.

GOALS FOR INTERVIEWS

All interviews have a goal. Most engage just two people, one who initiates the interview and controls its conduct and one who responds, although sometimes a single individual may be interviewed by a team of questioners. You're certainly familiar with journalistic interviews in print or on television or radio. Their goal is to elicit authoritative and perhaps unique information and opinions about such topics as recent or upcoming sporting events, business trends, political events, or wars.

In an organizational setting, many interviews also aim at *gathering information,* as you read in Chapter 9, or at *providing information,* as in instructional interviews. For example, you'll probably learn about your job responsibilities in an interview with your boss; you may learn about the benefits program in an interview with someone from the human resources group. Interviews may also *provide therapy* to help the interviewee deal with work-related personal problems. They serve to *evaluate* an employee's (or a potential employee's) qualifications and job performance. During the course of the evaluation, the interviewer may discipline the interviewee. An employee may also seek an interview to complain about the organization.

Interviews may occur between associates at the same level, but often the two people come from different levels in the organization: a supervisor and a member of the group, a recruiter and a potential employee, a student and a professor.

CONDUCTING THE INTERVIEW

Depending on the goal, routine interviews last from 10 minutes to an hour. More specialized interviews may last for days. Although telephone calls and hallway conversations may be subject to interruption by anything more important that comes along, an interview implies some buffer from any but the most serious interruptions.

As you learned in Chapter 9, schedule the interview well in advance, arrange for the interviewee's permission and for the appropriate equipment if you are going to record the interview on audio- or videotape, and follow up.

The *location* of the interview affects its conduct. Sometimes that location is out of both the interviewer's and the interviewee's control. Many interviews occur in offices, although an office bears signs of authority that may intimidate the visitor. At the least, a good manager steps aside so that the desk doesn't form a barrier against the interviewee. Neutral settings, like a conference room or a quiet corner of a cafeteria at a nonmeal time, are better.

Setting the Stage

Unless you are deliberately trying to intimidate the other person, begin the interview with small talk on neutral topics, like the weather or the interviewee's trip to the interview site, or on topics dear to the interviewee, for example, a sports team or hobby. Then use open-ended questions to establish a level of discussion. These require more than a yes or no answer and may suggest areas the interviewee considers important. Starting too specifically may cause you to ignore an important topic.

Asking Questions

Good questioning takes practice—as you've seen if you watch such news programs as the "McNeil/Lehrer News Hour" on Public Television. You need to weave what you want to say and know with what the interviewee wants to say and know. The kinds of questions you can ask, particularly in employment-related interviews, are also constrained by law and by ethical business practices. Figure 24–1 shows the advice given by Conoco Inc. concerning interviewing practices.

Paying Attention

Listen to the interviewee. A serious flaw in an interviewer is talking too much. Think:

- How does this information compare with information from others?
- How does this information compare with what you already know about the issues or the interviewee?

Conoco Inc., a fully integrated energy company and subsidiary of E. I. du Pont de Nemours and Company, is headquartered in Houston, Texas. In support of its commitment to diversity in hiring, Conoco subscribes to a behavioral approach to interviewing called *Targeted Selection. Targeted Selection* was developed by Development Dimensions International (DDI), headquartered in Pittsburgh, Pennsylvania. Use of *Targeted Selection* allows Conoco Inc. to focus on the information needed to match the candidate to the job while minimizing biases and stereotypes.

The methodology:

1. *Trains interviewers to base hiring decisions on applicant's past behavior.* Behavior is less likely to be misinterpreted because the interviewer follows up to clarify the behavior and the reasoning behind it. Little interpretation is required. Past behavior is extrapolated to predict future behavior.
2. *Uses job-related dimensions.* This system focuses on dimensions determined to be important as a result of a job analysis. Questions are aimed at these dimensions and the discussion of the applicant is structured by them.
3. *Avoids areas of illegal questioning.* Through background reading, examples, and self-tests, interviewers are taught what they can and cannot legally ask. Throughout the system, the emphasis is on questions that produce meaningful, job-related information. If interviewers feel confident that they can legally get all the information needed, they will not be tempted to ask illegal questions.
4. *Uses a selection system to fill positions.* Having an organized selection system that covers all components of the selection process ensures that each applicant is treated in the same way—a key element in equal opportunity.
5. *Minimizes biases and stereotypes.* Decisions made using these procedures are more objective because information on each applicant is obtained, shared, and discussed by several supervisors and managers before final ratings are made. This review exposes biases and stereotypes and provides a check on the legality of interviewer's questions.
6. *Provides skills for managers engaged in the selection process.* Supervisors and managers are trained to interpret and rate the target dimensions fairly and accurately. They're also trained in interviewing techniques, including how to maintain the applicant's self-esteem during the interview—an important requirement when interviewing some applicants.
7. *Trains interviewers in effective note taking.* Note taking is encouraged; interviewers are taught to record behavioral data that can be used to document selection and promotion decisions.
8. *Promotes recordkeeping.* A section of the Administrator's Manual obtained in the Administrator Training program discusses recordkeeping procedures and retention requirements.

Conoco is convinced that a behavioral approach improves its chances of matching candidates to specific job requirements in a fair and equitable manner.

FIGURE 24–1.
Conoco Inc. guidelines for interviewing. *(Courtesy of Russell Jolivet and Judith Raines, Conoco Inc.)*

- Do you really understand, or are you just nodding to be polite?
- Is the interviewee focusing on important matters or wandering into trivial territory?
- Is he or she self-confident? Hesitant?

If your mind wanders, consider *why* it's wandering. Are you bored because you've heard all this before? Or because this information seems far removed from what you need? Take steps early in the interview to correct your boredom:

- Ask the interviewee to repeat what he or she was saying when your mind started to wander—and ask early enough to retrace the line of discussion.
- Cordially suggest another line of response.
- If the comments seem vague, ask for examples.
- Rephrase key issues to confirm your understanding and to encourage the interviewee's elaboration of those points.

Taking Notes

Note taking helps to keep you alert and active as a listener. Moreover, good notes provide an essential and accurate record of the interview:

- Don't note only negative information. Take notes from the beginning. Otherwise, your note taking may intimidate the respondent into silence.
- Reread the salient points from your notes at the closing to ensure agreement on main points.
- After the interview, review the notes to clarify any vague issues and to add any information needed to make the notes a good record for later reference.

Concluding Gracefully

As you opened the interview, finish it on a bit of small talk. Don't be abrupt. Perhaps make reference to the future: another meeting, a date for notification of the results of the interview, documents that you will send or that the interviewee should send to you.

THE EMPLOYMENT INTERVIEW

An interview is a two-way street. Although the person who requests the interview generally controls its direction, as you have seen, a good interviewer is also flexible. She or he lets the other person have a say and changes the interview's direction if those comments warrant. Being interviewed also requires preparation and participation, as you will see in the following discussion of strategies for the employment interview.

Your goal in the interview is to convince the recruiter that you are the best candidate for the job. In addition, you will learn about opportunities that the company can offer you. An employment interview can take many forms. Some are brief, cordial, and highly positive. Some are deliberately stressful. Some require only conversation. Some require tests. They may occur at the potential employer's office, at an interview site maintained by a college or a university, at a hotel during a professional meeting, at a restaurant, or even over dinner at a potential employer's home. Each occasion, of course, requires specific responses.

Preparing

Don't go into any interview cold. Do your homework. Find out about the company interviewing you and, if possible, the person interviewing you—at least that person's name. Talk with company employees and read the company's annual report and other literature. Know enough background to ask specific questions about the position or about projects the company is now undertaking. You might even bring a list of questions with you to the interview.

Anticipate, too, some questions the interviewer may ask. Figure 24–2 lists common questions. Remember, however, that you can't just recite a memorized text in the interview.

Participating in a Face-to-Face Interview

Good preparation will build your confidence, but unless you are unusual, you will be nervous before and during an employment interview. Expect that.

Among the many stories you've probably heard about interviews is the one about first impressions: Some interviewers decide on candidates within

The employment interview, potentially a stressful occasion, offers the chance to promote oneself as well as to learn about career opportunities.

For openers:
Did you have any trouble finding the company?
How's your [fill in the blank] team doing this season?

About your education:
What's your favorite course? Your least favorite course?
Do you think your grades really reflect your understanding of the field?
Why did you decide to go to [fill in the name of your college]?
Why did you major in [fill in your major]?
How did you finance your education?
Do you plan to do graduate work? In what field?
Did you live in a dorm during college? A fraternity or sorority? An apartment? How did you decide on those living arrangements?
Were you active in any extracurricular activities? Sports?
What college project interested you most?

About your work history:
How did you spend your summers during college?
What was the most satisfying job you ever held? Why?
What have you learned from all the jobs you've held?
What makes a good boss? Tell me about the best boss you ever worked for. The worst?
What is your salary history?
What are your salary expectations for this position?

About your career plans:
Tell me about yourself.
What do you see yourself doing in five years?
What are your greatest strengths? Weaknesses?
Do you prefer working on teams or working alone?
How will you measure your own success?
Are you willing to travel? To relocate?

About the interviewer's company:
Why do you think you'd like to work for us?
Do you know people who work here?
What division of the company most interests you?
How did you find out about this position?

For closing off the discussion:
When could you start work?
What else would you like me to know about you?

FIGURE 24–2.
Some questions interviewers often ask.

30 seconds of meeting them, about the time it takes you to enter a room and say hello. You've also probably heard how important body language is in an interview: proper posture, proper dress, no twitching, no drumming of fingers, no awkward movements or cracking of your voice. Your poise, your ability to think on your feet—your *stage presence*—drives an interviewer's response. Some job hunters hire coaches to help them make a memorable entrance and follow up convincingly. You may at least want to practice interviewing; your college or university may provide videotaping services for such practice. You might also think about the interview as an exercise in role playing; for advice on that technique, see "*FYI:* The Employment Interview as Role Play" (pages 516–517).

One word of warning: Don't be afraid that the interview will require you to be somebody you are not. It should not. Neither you nor the potential employer will be served by your masquerade, even if you do manage to carry it off. The employer will expect long-term behavior from you that you might find uncomfortable, and you'll lose the opportunity to find out if your long-term self could really flourish in the role the company would like you to perform. So be honest. That doesn't mean, of course, "Be sloppy," or "Be self-defeating." It means prepare well so that you can display your *best* self.

Start by arriving on time for the interview. Perhaps arrive a bit early. Bring with you items that support your credentials, including a copy of your resume (just in case the interviewer doesn't have one at hand) and perhaps a portfolio of your writings or other work.

As the interviewer introduces himself or herself, remember that name to use later in the interview. Use the formal "Mr." or "Ms." unless the interviewer indicates that a first name is appropriate.

Stay alert. Answer questions directly. *Listen.* Respond not to the question you wished the interviewer had asked, but to the real question. Don't be afraid to use your notes to make sure you've covered essential questions you want to ask. Such preparation shows your commitment and your seriousness about the company.

If, because of inattention or a deliberate attempt to create stress, an interviewer makes malicious comments or asks embarrassing questions, respond to these for what they are: clues to your possible future with that company. They may reflect the company's lack of interest in you. So be it. Or, more significant, they may reflect something about the *interviewer* and his or her sense of self and role in the company. If you are really serious about the company, try to talk with someone else to confirm or correct your impression. The conduct of the interview may point to political or other problems at the company that suggest you would not be happy there.

By law in the United States, interviewers may not ask about your age, marital status or spouse's employment, children, religion, national origin, or political preference. So when you interview in the United States, if such questions are raised, you can simply decline to answer. That refusal may, indeed, *enhance* your image with an interviewer who is looking for someone who will take a stand. You may feel, however, that declining will eliminate you from a position you are seriously interested in, especially if you are talking with a company based in a culture that regards the answers to such questions as important in the hiring process. It's up to you to decide what you'll reveal about yourself.

THE EMPLOYMENT INTERVIEW AS ROLE PLAY

Robert J. Myers
President, The Association for Business Communication and Associate Professor, Baruch College, City University of New York

Thinking of an employment interview as a role play will help you prepare wisely and perform effectively.

You're probably familiar with role playing from a sociology, communication, or management course. You're asked to act out a role along with other students. The context or situation and the various roles are described. The role players act accordingly as, for example, a manager trying to solve a conflict between two subordinates.

You need to prepare before the role play to understand the situation and sympathize with the roles. You also need to improvise during the role play. There's no script; you make up the behavior and dialogue appropriate to your assigned role.

Why approach an employment interview as a role play? Because it forces you to remember what a job interview is all about. It's not about being a bright and attractive college student or graduate (although these qualities rarely hurt). It's not about clever answers to interview questions gleaned from the latest sure-fire, interview-for-success, self-help book. It's about *hiring employees.* When you approach the interview as a role play, you are saying to your prospective employer, "Look at me. Listen to me. What you see and what you hear are what you'll get, *if you hire me.*"

Preparing to Role-Play

Before the interview, think about the role you'll assume if hired: Sales representative? Credit manager? Benefits analyst? Public accountant?

What personal and professional qualities do you associate with someone who successfully assumes that role? Talk to professionals in the field, read about the role, and talk with your professors. You will be generalizing and stereotyping, of course, but that's all right.

For example, here's a profile of a sales representative: outgoing, personable, energetic, ambitious, persistent, and aggressive (in a con-

Be positive. Don't criticize or dwell on excuses. Avoid revealing any negative information early in the interview. Interviewers do tend to form impressions quickly. A negative item that occurs late in an otherwise pleasant interview is not likely to change the interviewer's impression. And don't talk too much. Interviewers like to hear themselves talk, too.

Often an interviewer's last question is "Is there anything you'd like to ask me about the job?" Be prepared with some questions. Then clarify the next step in the hiring process.

Participating in a Telephone Interview

Most employment interviews are conducted in person, precisely because body language and general poise and energy are such important indicators of a candidate's skills and potential. But you may need to respond to a telephone interview if the distance between you and the potential employer is great. Sometimes an initial screening by phone precedes an in-person

trolled manner); a good listener; able to work independently; dynamic in oral presentations, effective on the telephone, persuasive in letters and other written communication.

Then, narrow your thinking to the specific type of position, the specific industry, and the specific company. Assess how that context will affect your performance. For example, is it a large, well-established, and conservative company? A small, informal, and innovative firm?

To match your analysis, choose your costume and props. Costume? Sure. Dress appropriately for the role, as dress contributes to credibility. Most public accountants calling on corporate clients dress conservatively. Creative types in the advertising industry generally don't. Props like portfolios, attaché cases, and pens are important, too. Use them to make the appropriate impression.

Playing the Role

At the moment you decide to seek employment with a specific firm, all future actions should be "in-role."

When you write to the firm, write as you would if you were the professional they are to hire. If you call the firm, sound professional. A company sales rep, for example, is likely to write to a prospective client and then follow up with a phone call. Because you are role-playing, do the same. Write and then call the company. Be assertive, positive, and assured *like a sales rep.*

As you meet the interviewer, slip once more into your sales-rep role play. Be personable, enthusiastic, persistent, and confident. Display good listening skills. Ask pertinent questions. Reinforce the role in your answers to the interviewer's questions. Close the sale. Ask, "Is the job mine?" or "May I call you next Monday to find out your decision?" Aggressive? You bet. But if you're playing the role of sales rep, go for it. That's what you'll do for this firm, *if you are hired.*

interview. If you have a telephone that registers the caller's number, that will give you a few minute's warning in which to prepare yourself. Otherwise, you'll have to respond quickly—something the potential employer may be banking on as a way to test how you think on your feet.

If you *don't* feel comfortable responding at the time you are called, say so, and arrange a time to call back or be called. Such a response is better than a bad performance and shouldn't lower your standing in the interviewer's mind. Moreover, calling the interviewer allows you to check on the validity of his or her identity in the company.

Prepare your questions, in writing, and then be ready when you call or they call. You won't be able to judge the impression you are making as easily as in person. It may be hard to talk simply to a voice. But particularly if the job you are applying for demands telephone skills, show yours. Make sure you don't shout—nervousness tends to cause people to raise their voices on the phone. Move away if possible from any distracting background noises; turn off a radio or dishwasher. Take notes.

AFTER THE INTERVIEW

After the interview, both the interviewer and the applicant still have work to do—more, of course, for the interviewer. The interviewer compiles data from several interviews to continue the selection process. Often, a second round of interviews is in order for a smaller group of the most promising candidates.

As an applicant, you can remind the interviewer about yourself while she or he is making those decisions. Send a brief note to reiterate your interest in the position. Enclose any further documentation of your credentials that may have been requested. Here is the text of such a follow-up letter:[1]

I enjoyed talking with you yesterday at the Career Planning and Placement office here. You only increased my already great interest in working for Premier Systems.

As you requested, I've enclosed a copy of the article on software houses that I mentioned. It appeared in last Tuesday's issue of the *Triangle*, our biweekly campus newspaper. It mentions Premier Systems on the second page.

Again, thank you for taking the time to talk with me yesterday. I look forward to hearing from you.

Deciding

You'll probably participate in several interviews in the course of your job search. Compare information from all the interviews as well as from your background reading. Here are some elements to look for:

The Organization

Salary and benefits package
Size
Reputation for employee support
Financial position
Anticipated growth and mergers
Facilities

Job Description

Typical career paths and opportunities for advancement
Opportunities for training
Criteria for performance evaluation
Amount of travel
Routine versus innovative work

[1] Courtesy of Kitsel Outlaw, who wrote each of the following letters to Premier Systems.

Supervisor(s)

Style of work compared to your own
Opportunities for mentoring
Political position within the organization

Location

Convenience to where you'd like to be
Commuting patterns
Cultural and recreational benefits

Weigh these elements according to your own priorities. Many Europeans, for example, find Americans distressingly job-oriented; Americans will move wherever they are asked in order to find the *job* they want. Europeans are more likely to favor *location;* they look for a job in a place (like Vienna) where they'd like to be. What's more important to you? Your potential relationship with a supervisor may also be the key. You may look for someone who can "mentor" you through the complexities of promotion, particularly in a large organization, and who can show you how best to achieve your professional potential.

Accepting an Offer

The person who interviewed you, or the personnel department of the company, may make you an offer. The offer may come over the phone, with a follow-up letter explaining the details. Or you may receive a letter with the initial offer. Reply promptly to the offer. If you need more time to think about the offer, say when you plan to give an answer. You may need to negotiate that time.

Saying yes to a job offer is easy. Briefly express your pleasure and your acceptance, show the company you're eager to work for them, and confirm the starting date and any other conditions of employment necessary, as in the following letter:

I happily accept your offer of employment as Assistant Product Information Analyst in the Product Integration Department, reporting to John Port.

As you recommended, I talked with Mr. Port. He answered a few questions I had about the position before making my decision. I have informed him that I will be accepting the job, and we agreed on June 17 as the starting date.

Thank you for sending me the description of the benefits package. The completed health survey is enclosed.

If you need other information from me or if you have further information for me, please write or call. I am looking forward to working for Premier Systems.

Declining an Offer

Saying no is more difficult. Wrap the statement declining the offer in an explanation that retains goodwill with the company and confirms your professionalism, as in the following letter:

```
Thank you for your offer of employment with Premier Systems.
As you suggested, I talked with Mr. Jackson about the spe-
cific job description. After reviewing the information he
gave me concerning the work load in conjunction with the fi-
nal salary offer, I'm afraid I won't be able to accept your
offer.

I would be happy to reconsider this position in the future if
you do indeed decide to raise the salary. Premier Systems re-
mains most attractive, and I hope you will keep me in mind.
Again, thank you for your consideration. I regret that I
won't be joining you at this time.
```

Responding to a Rejection

If your interview does *not* result in a job offer—if the company calls or writes to say they've hired someone else—you still have one more communication task if you are seriously interested in the company. Write to acknowledge the refusal. You may be angry or hurt, but don't let those feelings override professional strategy. Close out your file with the company on a positive note of your own by sending a letter that expresses your regret in not getting the job but that reconfirms your interest in the company and in any future openings. The company's representative may then remember you well and write or call again. Here's a brief letter:

```
Thank you for your letter of July 8. I, too, am sorry that
you do not have an opening for me at this time.

I did enjoy talking with you and learning more about Premier
Systems, which remains very attractive to me. I hope you'll
keep me in mind for any future openings.
```

PERFORMANCE REVIEWS

After you've successfully negotiated the hiring process, you show what you can do on the job. In six months to a year, you'll probably engage in an interview with your supervisor to review how well you are performing your responsibilities.

Such performance reviews are standard organizational tools. Although the review may be informal and only oral in a small organization, large organizations use both written and oral forms. In these organizations, your supervisor will also be rated by upper management on an ability to evaluate employees and hence to develop them. Someone who consistently writes positive performance evaluations, for example, and then recommends the person for a low raise or termination is going to have to explain the inconsistency—to a higher manager, to the employee, and perhaps even to a judge.

Periodic written evaluations that consistently point to major weaknesses and report no progress on overcoming them represent helpful support if it becomes necessary to demote or to fire someone, particularly if those evaluations are reinforced by other evidence, like coworker complaints. The evaluations thus aid in justifying corporate actions when they become subject to individual suits or review by outside agencies, which are increasingly intervening in corporate affairs. For both positive and negative (protective) reasons, then, organizations take performance evaluations seriously. As an employee, you should take such evaluations seriously as well.

The evaluation should derive from a set of agreed-on areas of performance, usually stated in the job description (see Chapter 23). Your supervisor may interview you before writing the report and will almost certainly meet with you afterward to confirm the conclusions and to allow for clarification and dissent. Some organizations use forms that call for numerical ratings and/or comments in various categories of behavior (see Figure 24–3). Some forms are more open-ended and discursive.

Even experts disagree on what constitutes an ideal performance evaluation. Some argue for an entirely quantitative rating; others argue for open-ended narratives; others advocate various mixes. In general, however, you should look for an evaluation that is concrete, honest, and objective.

Concreteness. The evaluation should direct your attention to measurable and concrete strengths or weaknesses. Instead of "Inattentive to detail," the evaluation should note, "Fails to complete purchase orders in normal company fashion and neglects to maintain attendance records of subordinates."

Honesty. Honesty doesn't require brutality, but it does require that the report avoid fudging, obscuring, and equivocating. Lies are terribly easy to detect and can lead to deep trouble if a real personnel problem develops. They show someone shirking responsibility for helping you build on strengths and overcome weaknesses.

Objectivity. In *rating* you, your supervisor may be tempted to *judge* you. The line between rating and judgment, after all, is fine. But good evaluations hold the line. For example, instead of noting, "Ms. McCauley fails to behave in a manner consistent with the professional atmosphere in this office," a good evaluation notes, "Ms. McCauley should refrain from chewing gum, playing the radio loudly, and eating at her desk, as these activities detract from her professional image."

SUMMARY

- Interviews are meetings between one person and another person, or one person and a team of interviewers, that serve a **goal.** The purpose may be to **gather (or provide) information,** to **provide therapy,** to **evaluate** an individual, or to **offer an opinion or complaint.**
- Leading an interview requires both control and flexibility. **Set the stage** with small talk or other forms of neutral conversation. In **asking prepared questions** during the interview itself, probe as your goal requires. But be flexible enough to abandon unproductive or unnecessarily antagonistic lines of questioning and to pursue new issues as they arise and seem promising. **Pay attention.** Listening well is more important than talking once you have asked the right questions. **Take notes. Conclude gracefully.**

(continued on page 524)

MANAGEMENT DEVELOPMENT PROGRAM

Participant Evaluation

Employee ____

Date of Hire ____________________ Date Began MDP ________________

Department ____________________

Evaluator ____________________ Date ____________________

I. Rate the MDP participant on his/her work behavior in the following areas, using a scale of 1 to 5 (1=unacceptable, 2=needs improvement, 3=satisfactory, 4=good, 5=outstanding):

Understands assignments ______
Accepts direction ______
Cooperates with others ______
Follows through on work ______
Achieves goals ______
Contributes new ideas ______

II. Identify **both** the strengths and weaknesses of the participant during his/her rotation period in the department. Be specific, and be sure to base your comments on work-related activities.

Strengths:

Weaknesses:

III. Record any suggestions you have to help the MDP participant improve his/her capacity to continue developing as a manager/leader.

FIGURE 24–3.
A performance evaluation form.

IV. In general, what is your assessment of the participant's potential for eventual management assignment?

Signed ____________________________________ Date ____________________

To participants: This regular evaluation of your performance in the Management Development Program is conducted to assist both you and the company. Its contents should be discussed orally with you by your supervisor. You also have the right to comment in the space below on the written evaluation. Even if you do not choose to comment, you should sign on the line provided below to indicate that you have discussed the evaluation with your supervisor. Signing the form indicates only that you have discussed the evaluation and does not signify your agreement with it.

Participant comments:

I have discussed the contents of this evaluation with the supervisor making it and have/have not entered my own comments above.

Signed ____________________________________ Date ____________________

- Employment interviews make job hunters nervous. But if you **prepare** well, that helps. Anticipate questions and learn about the company. Practice. Arrive at the interview on time. Be aware of your body language. Listen and respond carefully and vigorously to the questions you are asked. Ask questions.
- After the interview, **follow up** with whatever steps were outlined for you. Call to check on the review process—but don't badger. Write to thank the interviewer. If you receive an offer, weigh it against any other offers to determine the best job fit for you. Write a letter accepting or rejecting the offer. If you are rejected for the job, write to acknowledge the rejection—and to close your file with the company on a positive note of your own.
- **Performance reviews** are important organizational tools conducted both orally and, especially in large companies, in writing. The review aids you as an employee in knowing how your performance measures up to expectations and in changing course if necessary. Reviews aid upper management in measuring supervisors' ability to encourage and evaluate employee development. They also serve to document any problems in performance and to justify corporate actions on the basis of those problems for audiences inside the company and for oversight agencies and the courts outside. For those reasons, a review should be **concrete, honest,** and **objective.**

EXERCISES

For Discussion

1. Check the career-planning or placement office at your school or college to see what brochures or guidelines they have produced to assist you in your employment interview. Several schools also maintain a library of videotapes, including mock interviews and presentations about companies that recruit frequently there.

For Writing

2. Assume that Premier Systems, a producer of software for data management in small businesses, is interviewing you. The recruiter seems pleased with your credentials, particularly your knowledge of personal computers and your experience as a tutor in a microcomputer laboratory on campus. She'd like to hire you as a sales representative who will travel to various businesses demonstrating the product and then training office personnel in its use.

   In the interview, she asks you to sketch your approach to sales and training in a two- or three-page memo you'll write on the spot. The reader of the memo will be your supervisor in the training department. In writing, describe what you consider the *goal* of a training program and what approach you'll take in structuring information and practice for the office staff you'll train. The sessions will be conducted in-house at the several companies who purchase Premier systems. If you have indeed tutored other students, keep in mind what worked in your tutoring. If not, then remember how you learned about computers and incorporate that learning in your suggestions. Time yourself in your writing; you have half an hour.

3. Assume that the First National Bank of Lincoln (address: One Bank Place, Lincoln, NB 68583) has offered you a position as a junior auditor. Write to accept the position. Then write another letter declining the offer for some reason, for example, the benefits package or your acceptance of another job. Maintain goodwill.

For Collaboration

4. To develop your interviewing skills, *practice* with a friend. Assume the role of interviewer yourself, and then ask the friend to assume that role. Each of you should try to outwit the other. See what happens with uncomfortable questions. You might also want to videotape the session.

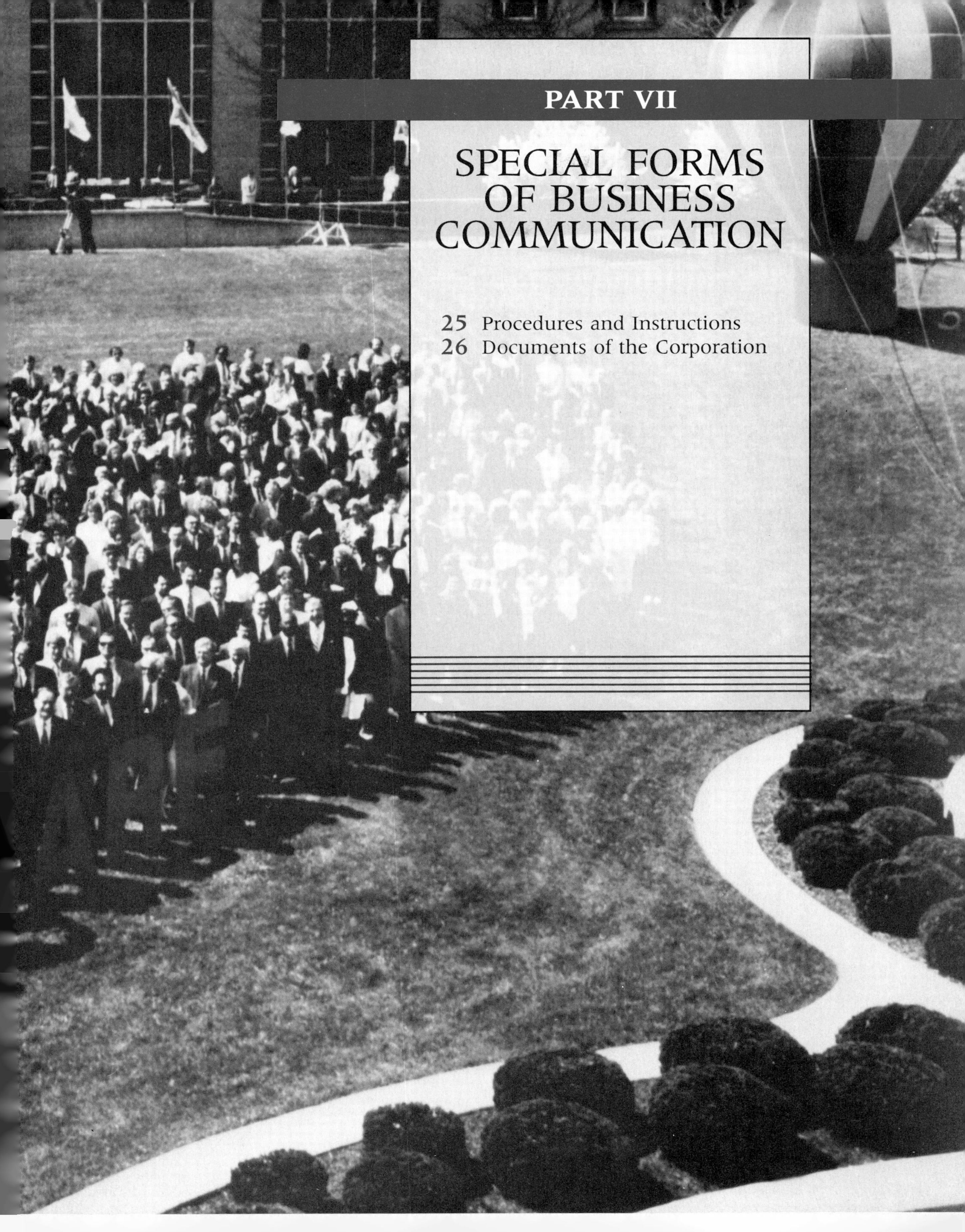

PART VII

SPECIAL FORMS OF BUSINESS COMMUNICATION

25 Procedures and Instructions
26 Documents of the Corporation

INTRODUCTION TO PART VII

''Under the moose and to the right.''

Even to a native speaker of English, the quotation above may seem a bit bizarre—until you know its context. It's a business instruction, what a person at an information desk said in reply to a customer's question: ''Where can I exchange this shirt for a larger one?'' To go from the information desk at the L. L. Bean store in Freeport, Maine, to customer service, you walk under an archway (where the moose head hangs) and turn right. You can't miss it.

This part rounds out the picture of organizational communication you've been seeing in *Business Communication.* In Chapter 25, you'll find advice about composing instructions—those that tell you how to get somewhere (with or without a moose) or how to do something. Instructions, sometimes called *procedures,* range from the simple to the complex, from those given orally to those in writing.

In Chapter 26, you'll find a brief overview of some special forms of organizational communication that you are likely to read on the job, if not to write right away. Some of the forms function in downward *internal* communication to define, control, and maintain the organization and to ensure a climate for good work and goodwill. These include goal statements, strategic plans, operational plans, and in-house newsletters. Other forms are directed at *external* communication with customers, investors, and the public. The most important of these is the corporate annual report for stockholders, but you'll also look at product and policy announcements and press releases.

Often, to an even greater extent than other corporate reports or correspondence, these special forms embody the corporate culture. To return once more to the moose: L. L. Bean's corporate theme is ''The Store That Knows the Outdoors.'' That theme percolates through its documents and presentations. It makes the presence of a moose head (and a trout pond) at its flagship facility not only appropriate, but expected.

25 PROCEDURES AND INSTRUCTIONS

What's Ahead

GETTING READY TO WRITE
- Target the User
- Set the Goals
- Understand the Procedure

WRITING THREE TYPES OF PROCEDURES
- Step-by-Step Instructions
- Manuals
- Codes of Practice and Behavior

DESIGNING THE PROCEDURE

TESTING THE PROCEDURE
- Validating and Verifying
- Revising to Simplify

YOUR VOICE AS AN INSTRUCTOR

SUMMARY

EXERCISES

Do You Know 

- What are procedures and instructions, and what business purposes do they serve?
- What do you need to do as you get ready to write procedures and instructions?
- How do you explain how to do something and how to get somewhere?
- What are manuals, and how do you write them?
- What are codes of conduct and behavior, and how do you write them?
- What process should you follow to design procedures and instructions?
- How do you test the effectiveness of procedures and instructions?
- What voice should you use in giving instructions?

"If all else fails . . . read the instructions."

Instructions tell others how to do something. In business, documents that instruct are typically called *procedures.* Sometimes they are also called *directives, guidelines, codes,* or *performance aids.* In this chapter we use *instructions* and *procedures* as interchangeable terms.

Procedures help people both inside and outside organizations. Procedures for *internal* use are tools of *control* and *maintenance:* for example, instructions for purchasing, safety rules, dress and behavior codes, parking regulations, hiring guidelines, and so forth. Such documents guide the operations of an organization and help keep its day-to-day functions on track and running smoothly. Procedures for *external* use are *customer relations* documents: for example, instructions on how to assemble and use a product, procedures for registering a complaint or making an inquiry, procedures for paying a bill, directions on how to get to the store or hospital from various locations. Aimed at helping the customer use the firm's product or service, these serve the marketing function.

Procedures vary in length. A few lines of instructions often appear at the top of a form. A memo may instruct employees about how to sign up for vacation. A letter to students might instruct them about registering for classes. Full-page or several-page inserts boxed with equipment tell readers how to assemble and install what's in the box. Extensive manuals and guidebooks, some in volumes, describe procedures for operating and maintaining major machines and systems or for performing complex activities.

Early in your business career you may more often be a *user* than a creator of procedures. In that role you need to be familiar with procedures and how they should be prepared. This chapter will help you develop such an understanding. If you are called on to write procedures and instructions, the advice given here will be particularly appropriate.

Although writing procedures and instructions is often a specialized function, assigned to experts, all businesspeople sometimes have to prepare instructions: to instruct subordinates in office procedures, to assist customers in using a product or service, to aid visitors in finding locations within a facility.

Of course, you often describe a procedure orally. But you will need to write when

- You don't have direct access to the person who needs the instructions and thus cannot converse with him or her.
- The procedure is difficult.
- Many people will need to perform the procedure.
- You require a record to check your performance against.

This chapter discusses three types of procedures: step-by-step instructions, manuals, and codes of behavior and practice. Before you look at each of these in detail, you need to understand some basic strategies for preparing to write them.

GETTING READY TO WRITE

How can you tell someone how to do something? Here are three strategies for getting ready:

1. Target the user.
2. Set the goals.
3. Understand the procedure.

Target the User

Always start with the reader, the person who will use your instructions. Procedures must work for particular readers. Failure is immediately obvious: The reader can't follow the instructions. Making assumptions about the user is tricky. An elaborate discourse on running a machine won't work if the reader can't find the on-off switch. A reference manual on a printer hooked up to a computer won't work if the manual assumes incorrectly that the reader knows about the presence of a reset button—one of the first things to push if the printer stops.

As with any marketing project, establish a *baseline* for your target users. Interview a sample of potential clients or customers. If your company has a toll-free telephone number to handle questions on the procedure you need to describe or on similar procedures, record those questions for a period to make sure your description covers those most frequently asked. Moreover, you need to guard against telling the reader *everything*. As an expert, you know far more about the topic than your reader needs to know. Tell only what the reader needs to know to achieve the specific goal you have set.

Different tasks have different degrees of difficulty. For the task you are describing, assess the skill level required and clearly target the description only to those capable of achieving the skill. Make sure that a process you design for beginners does not include any individual steps that can be accomplished only by experts, as a beginner's trail on a ski slope should include no expert pitches (unless, of course, you provide a beginner's bypass).

Envision, too, the reader as he or she reads. Some readers merely skim the instructions at their desk or in the field before plunging into the project. Some consult the procedure only in times of trouble. Even the most conscientious readers usually do not read straight through; to write the instructions assuming that the reader will begin on page 1 and continue uninterrupted page by page is to deny reality. Readers read and perform interactively. You'll need to accommodate their reading habits in the document's design, as we'll see.

Set the Goals

The central goal of any procedure, of course, is "to instruct." But as a goal this is hard to measure. How will you know if your instructions have worked? How will the reader know?

State goals as actions. And state goals in either individual terms or organizational terms. Note, for example, what the reader should know or should have produced at the end of the process:

- `When you have finished filling out this questionnaire, you will know`
  - `Your strengths`
  - `Your weaknesses`
  - `Your most probable career path`

- `This dress code tells you how to dress every day on the job to match the clean, neat, well groomed look our customers expect.`

Understand the Procedure

To write instructions for any reader to meet any goal, you, the writer, obviously have to understand the procedure thoroughly yourself. Sometimes only an expert on the topic is assigned the task. The advantage is obvious, but a potential disadvantage lurks: The expert knows so much that he or she may have trouble ferreting out the essential steps and presenting them simply for users who begin with a blank slate. For this reason, someone who is not an expert often is assigned to write instructions. That person needs to gather all relevant information about the process or item and to understand it thoroughly.

Whether your sources are your own experience, interviews, or books, master certain information:

1. What *materials* and *tools* are necessary to perform the procedure?
2. What are the *time* constraints?
3. What is the *range* of possible steps or actions?
4. What is the *best* sequence of steps or actions?
5. What are the necessary *precautions?*
6. Where can a user find *further information?*

Materials and Tools

First, clarify whatever materials and tools are necessary. The materials are the resources, the ingredients which will be transformed in the process—like the chocolate chips before they become the basis of chocolate chip cookies (see Figure 25–9). The tools aid in the transformation. Remember how you once (perhaps even now) tried to get a toy up and running? Most *materials* probably came in the box—the parts of a helicopter, for example. But another material, batteries, might well have been missing—the object of midnight searches in convenience stores. As a writer, make sure you know all the materials that will be needed and can alert the reader to them early in the procedure. Examine the required tools. If you are writing about a particular piece of software, learn in advance what hardware it is compatible with, along with its requirements for memory, terminal type, and the like.

Time

Assess how long the process should take. Steps in some procedures are pegged to the calendar. For example, readers may have to abide by closing dates for certain financial transactions or filings. Waiting periods may also be necessary. Account for the process time.

Range of Steps or Actions

Sometimes there is only one way to do something. When you ask several individuals about how *they* complete the procedure, they all list the same steps or activities. But often you find as you read about the process and talk with performers that you can reach the same goal by different routes. Collect instances of how the process can be performed. At this stage, develop a list of steps, including alternate routes. Isolate trouble spots and look for short-cuts.

Best Sequence

If appropriate, while you are researching the procedure you may want to try it out yourself. You'll gain confidence for the writing that will translate into credibility in your instructions. You may not be the best performer. Indeed, many people who know how to do something well are unable to show others what they know. But you do need to analyze well what an expert performer does. In testing out a procedure yourself, based upon readings and interviews, establish a critical path to the goal of the procedure—the steps that absolutely must be taken in a specified sequence. Along the way, sort through alternate approaches.

Necessary Precautions

It's important to keep people safe while they work. Although someone faces fewer safety hazards filling out forms in an office than working with explosives in a laboratory, still, flag any possible dangers in the procedure. Less drastically, note where one might go wrong, and suggest alternatives.

Further Information

Particularly for long or complicated processes, compile a bibliography of sources for further information about details of the procedure. For example, if you are writing a guide to using a wordprocessing program in a business writing class, you will gather your information from such references as the operator's guides to the computer hardware, the user's manual for the operating system that the hardware runs, and the manual for the complete wordprocessing package. You'll then list these manuals as references for your readers.

WRITING THREE TYPES OF PROCEDURES

Once you have identifed the user, established the goal, and thoroughly analyzed the process yourself, you should be in good shape to draft a procedure. Let's look at three different types of procedures. First, we'll examine the most common: a *set of steps* in chronological order to achieve some goal. Second, we'll look briefly at guidelines for writing *manuals* that show how to operate a system or some equipment—and how to get out of trouble if the system or equipment does not operate. Third, we'll look at statements concerning employee *practices and behavior* that carry out organizational policy.

Step-by-Step Instructions

Instructions on how to do something or how to get somewhere are very common. They seem to be easy: Just describe each step in sequence. However, if you've ever assembled a lawnmower and found you put the handle on backward or tried to locate a scenic covered bridge based on directions from someone you met at a gas station, you know that step-by-step instructions are not always perfect.

How to Do Something

Figure 25–1 is a procedure to be used by crew persons at McDonald's to carry out the corporate policy of "satisfying the customer." (See Chapter 26 for a statement of this policy.) The procedure presents in sequence the steps that the reader must follow, from greeting the customer to thanking him or her. The directions are specific and detailed. Questions are anticipated and answered. The procedure works: One can follow it step by step to complete the function.

Directions for paying bills are a particularly common form of step-by-step instructions. Consider these instructions from an electric utility:

Dear Customer:

Your bill should be paid by the date indicated above. There are three ways to pay:

1. Pay by mail. Mail your check or money order (do not send cash) along with the top stub or the bill in the addressed envelope provided.
2. Pay in person. Bring the complete bill with your check, money order, or cash to any of our offices or participating banks listed on the back of the bill.

SERVICE: SIX STEPS

1. GREET EVERY CUSTOMER: "Good morning" or "Hi." Just saying, "Can I help you?" is not a greeting. Be enthusiastic and smile. You never get a second chance to make a first impression.

2. TAKE THE ORDER: "May I help you please?"
   a. Listen attentively and do not interrupt the customer.
   b. Note only one item of suggestive selling.
   c. Explain delay (if applicable in case of grill).

3. ASSEMBLE THE ORDER: REMEMBER TENDER LOVING CARE AND ACCURACY.
   a. If tray is needed, assemble and put on counter.
   b. If everything is ready, use the fastest possible assembly.
   c. Handle cups by sides only.
   d. Be sure all drinks are filled, clean and capped.
   e. Select proper bag. Do not pop bag open.
   f. Bag food only if EVERYTHING is ready.
   g. Place sandwiches in bottom, fries on top.
   h. Pick up no more product than you can handle.
   i. Take items from right to left.
   j. Pick up fries from side, not from top.
   k. Double-fold top of bag neatly and place logo (McDonald's emblem) toward the customer.

4. PRESENT THE ORDER: Slide tray or bag toward the customer.

5. RECEIVE PAYMENT: "Sir, your order will be $1.42, please."
   a. Call out sales and amount given you ("out of five").
   b. Place bill on register ledge until sale is completed.
   c. Count change to yourself, then into the customer's hand.
   d. Do not count coins, just bills.

6. THANK CUSTOMER AND ASK FOR REPEAT BUSINESS: "Thank you, sir, and come back again."
   a. Be polite and enthusiastic and remember to SMILE.
   b. Put bill in register and close the drawer.

FIGURE 25–1.
Workable procedure. *(Courtesy of McDonald's, Dukart Management Corporation.)*

3. Pay by phone. If you have a checking account with telephone bill-paying privileges, you can have the amount of your bill deducted directly from your account. Follow all instructions provided by your bank.

Notice how the alternative methods of payment are enumerated following the general statement. Each method is adequately but very simply described. These are effective instructions. By contrast, consider these instructions accompanying a physician's bill:

A Poor Approach

Dear Patient:

The full amount of your bill ("Due to physician" section of the statement, above) is due on receipt. You are responsible for this amount. As a courtesy, we have forwarded your insurance claim, if any, to your carrier. Any amount paid by the carrier will be deducted from the amount you will owe.

Please send your check or money order for the full amount immediately. We cannot accept credit cards, unless you gave us an impression of your card *before* billing. If you are experiencing any trouble paying your bill, please feel free to discuss this with your physician. Any other questions about your bill should be referred to your insurance carrier. Joan in our office cannot answer questions about insurance but will be happy to discuss with you the amount you owe.

Thank you.

Internal Medicine Associates

The lack of logical progression, the internal inconsistency (how can the insurance company's payment later be deducted from the amount you owe now?), and the failure to outline a clear process of inquiry in case of questions make these instructions more confusing than illuminating. Because few persons approach bill paying with delight, the instructions for carrying it out need to be especially clear and to the point.

How to Get Somewhere

Figures 25–2 and 25–3 present parts of the directions for getting from Narita Airport near Tokyo to the International University of Japan (IUJ) in Urasa, a trip that takes about three hours and involves two buses and two trains. The overview (Figure 25–2) is not a map but a visual rendering of the basic steps into which the trip is divided. Symbols of modes of transportation (bus, train, shoe—for walking) tell the user what to expect, and words capture the names of stations and times. Complementing this overview is a set of verbal instructions (Figure 25–3), arranged according to the segments of the trip. These are precise and concrete directions that efficiently guide

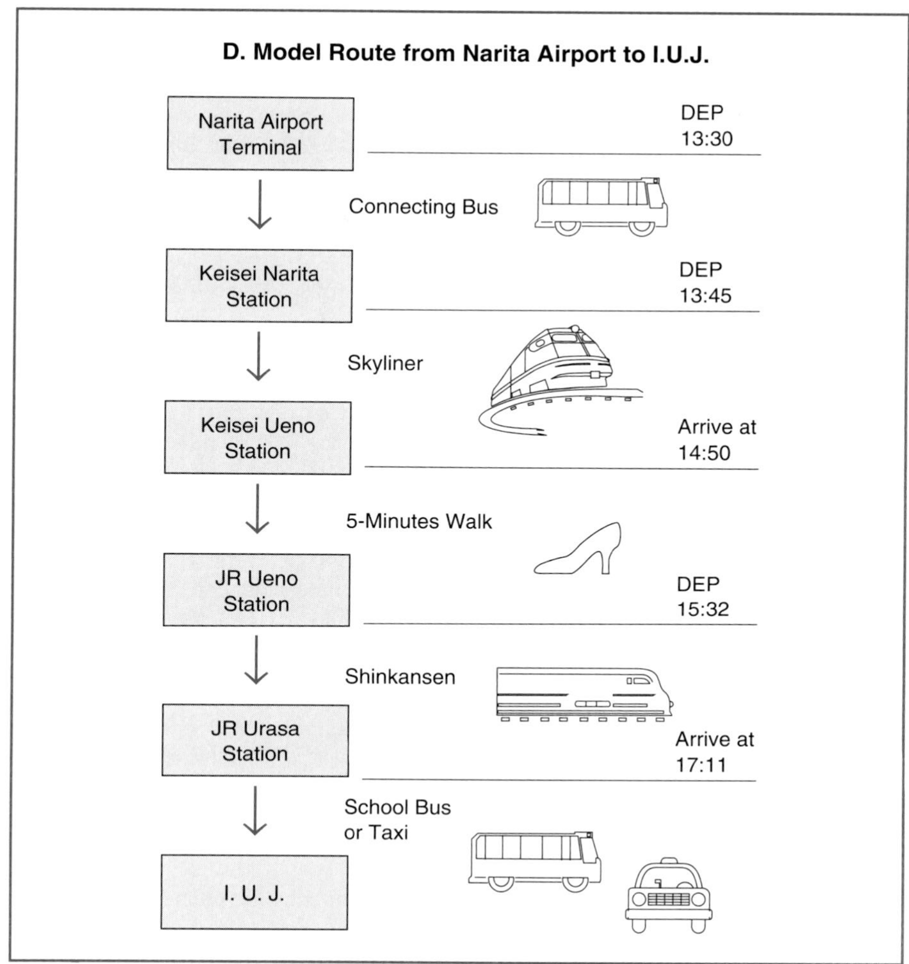

FIGURE 25–2.
Visual overview of directions for getting from Narita Airport to the International University of Japan. *(Used by permission of I. U. J.)*

the (English-speaking) traveler. They succeed because they segment the whole process into logical and manageable steps and provide simple but specific help.

Maps, of course, are often used to give directions. In general, maps—accompanied by text or standing alone—are more appropriate for describing small-scale situations. For example, you don't need to provide a map of Western Europe when you tell someone how to find the Hotel Uhland on Uhlandstrasse in Munich. But a map of Munich, with a detailed map of the section in which the Uhlandstrasse lies, would be appropriate.

In writing instructions on how to get somewhere, you should be particularly careful about *points of connection,* for example, those steps that require transition from one means of transportation to another (bus to train, walking to taking the subway), or one highway or street to another (I-76 to Route 202, Stevens Avenue to Waverly Street). Special caution is also needed to

Skyliner

Narita Airport Station is located down in the basement near the airport control tower. There is an all day shuttle bus service between Airport Station and **Keisei Narita Airport Station**, the starting point for the Skyliner. The required time of the shuttle bus is 6 minutes.

All seats on Skyliner are reserved, and you must purchase your ticket at the ticket counter 10–40 minutes prior to the Skyliner you would like to take. The tickets are only sold for the next immediate Skyliner. As soon as tickets for that Skyliner are sold out, they will start selling tickets for the following Skyliner.

The Skyliner leaves from Keisei Narita Airport Station every 40 minutes. The trip to Ueno takes about an hour.

Keisei Ueno Station to JR Ueno Station

There are two ways to get to Ueno Station of Japan Railways (JR):

- When you come out of the gate for Skyliner, walk up the stairs on the LEFT of the ticket gate to the main road and turn LEFT at the street level. A 5-minute walk in this direction will take you to the **JR Ueno Station**. Walk along the road, under the overpasses and into the main entrance of the JR Ueno station.
- When you come out of the ticket gate for Skyliner, you are in the underground Keisei Ueno Station. As it is connected with JR Ueno Station by an underground walkway, look for a sign for JR Ueno Station and follow the sign.

If you carry a big suitcase with you, the latter route would be easier for you.

If you get lost looking for the station, show someone the following sentence:

Please show me the way to JR Ueno Station.

JR上野駅はどこですか

Purchasing Shinkansen Tickets

Once at JR Ueno Station, look for the Shinkansen (bullet train) Ticket Office with a green sign.

Here is another sentence to get you to the right place:

Where is the ticket office for Shinkansen?

新幹線の切符売場(みどりの窓口)はどこですか

(continued)

FIGURE 25–3.
Excerpts from verbal directions for getting from Narita Airport to the International University of Japan. *(Used by permission of I.U.J.)*

Go to the "Reserved Tickets" counter and buy a ticket for Toki Shinkansen #409—leaving Ueno at 10:40 a.m. and arriving at Urasa at 12:19 p.m. Please use the attached Train Ticket Order Form.

There are two kinds of Shinkansens to Niigata: Asahi (express) and Toki (milk run). Only Toki Shinkansen stops at your destination, Urasa.

Your seat number is written on the ticket. The first number in the middle of your ticket is your car number, the number with a letter indicates the aisle and seat assignment. The non-smoking reserved car number is usually Number 8.

Going Down to the Shinkansen Platform

Go through the Shinkansen ticket gate and take the escalator to go down to the underground floor level 4. Shinkansen Platform 19 or 20 is your platform. Make sure that you are taking the **Joetsu** Shinkansen **Toki** for Niigata. You can check this by looking up at the display board hanging down from the ceiling.

alert users to *guideposts,* for example, "Take the first turning after the red barn"; "Look for a green sign saying 'Gamm II' "; "Three miles after the stoplight, turn left."

Manuals

Manuals pose different challenges. You should know that manuals are big business. They cost from $200 to $1,000 a page to produce. When their production lags behind the production of the items they document (a common occurrence), that lag can cost thousands of dollars a day. Moreover, up-to-date manuals are essential for the safe and effective operation of equipment. By one estimate, the U.S. Navy alone has 200,000 manuals that must be kept up to date, but because of the difficulties in keeping current, 25 percent are out of date.[1]

Broadly speaking, there are two types of manuals: *standard* manuals that arrive with the item and serve all customers, and *custom* manuals written for specific applications or users. Because of the need for updating, manuals of either type are often contained in a three-ring binder so that customers can insert new instructions when items change, or they are provided on disks to be used on your computer.

Software Manuals

The documents accompanying a software package are among the most common manuals used in business. By reviewing them you can learn how manuals work.

First, an operating manual *records* the system. It is written from the

[1] Ron Winslow, "Technical Manual Production Finally Enters Computer Age," *The Wall Street Journal,* 21 June 1985, p. 29.

Effective instructions and user's manuals are important sales tools because they help customers make the best use of often complex products and services.

perspective of system operation and notes, in technical detail, all of the system's specifications and capabilities. It is thorough and extensive.

Several other documents aim to *inform* the reader about how to use the system. Standard documents include, for example, a tutorial that describes the basics of loading and using the program for a first-time user. The tutorial may also include exercises sequenced for ease of use. Some of the instruction may be online as well as on paper. Increasingly, too, videotapes and videodisks are included. Most software houses provide a reference card listing appropriate commands and a template to place on the keyboard as a reminder of the functions and keys.

Because good documentation is key to selling a system, software houses develop manuals that *persuade* the reader as well as inform him or her. They pay attention to design and avoid the colorless, dense, marginless, small-type pages of traditional manuals. Drawings and other visuals are used abundantly to get interest as well as to illustrate functions.

Cross-Cultural Concerns

In considering the content and design of a manual, producers must understand how different cultures learn. For American readers, this means putting an overview of each system or function before the details. For readers from other cultures, the approach must be different—one reason that mere translation of manuals rarely works. Japanese readers, for example, learn better through a more gradual introduction to the parts before the whole. A manual for Japanese users of the Apple IIc begins with a fairy tale, complete with four-color illustrations, and other introductory material that is meant to reduce fear and build confidence.[2] Then sections discuss distinct functions. The authors designed the manual to be like a traditional Japanese dinner:

[2] "Writing User Manuals for Japanese Readers," *Simply Stated* (Washington, D.C.: The Document Design Center, American Institutes for Research), July 1985.

All the food is placed on the table at once, and the diners eat the courses in any order they choose.

Codes of Practice and Behavior

In addition to process descriptions and manuals, you may have to write instructions for general behavior on a job to put corporate policy into practice. Figure 25–4 presents a procedure for dressing and personal appearance ("dress code") that supports the McDonald's policy quoted in part in Chapter 26. In its simple language and details, the statement is well tailored to an anticipated readership of young people, particularly students.

NEATNESS COUNTS AT McDONALD'S

We have learned over a long period of time that our customers like a crew with a clean, neat, well groomed look. This means:

Dress Code for Males and Females

A. Males

1. Dark, clean, hard-soled shoes.
2. Hair must be above collar, back and neat on the sides. Sideburns will not be permitted to grow long and bushy. No beards.
3. McDonald's crew uniform will be worn, including a crew hat and name tag. Aprons will be worn on grill. Hats will be issued once a week. If you feel the uniform must be replaced because of wear, you must see a manager.
4. Hair must be kept under the hat.
5. All buttons on the shirt must be buttoned except for the top button, and proper personal hygiene standards must be followed.

B. Females

1. White, nonskid soles or saddle shoes (brown and white) will be worn and kept clean and polished. Shoes must conform to uniform. We recommend white nurse shoes for looks and for comfort.
2. Hair will be neatly combed and tied back if it is long.
3. No excess or gaudy jewelry will be permitted. Makeup must not be worn to excess.
4. McDonald's crew uniforms will be worn, including a crew hat and a name tag.
5. Fingernail polish is unsanitary for the grill people.
6. Only white sweaters may be worn. All buttons on blouse except for the top one must be buttoned.
7. Proper personal hygiene standards must be followed.

Remember, your name tag is part of your uniform. A lost name tag will cost you 50 cents.

FIGURE 25–4.
McDonald's dress code. *(Courtesy of McDonald's, Dukart Management Corporation.)*

```
We value and respect people:

   • Dealing with each other as individuals, and treating each
other as we would like to be treated
   • Developing people to their fullest potential
   • Working together in a common endeavor; recognizing each other
as important elements in the success of the whole
   • Having a common understanding of each other's role and how we
fit with the corporate objectives
   • Collaborating with each other and having a sense of team
   • Recognizing and accepting differences among people, but
sharing the same values
```

FIGURE 25–5.
Code of practice—ineffective.

Whereas a dress code is quite specific and concrete, a code of corporate practice is necessarily broader, more general. Most large companies, however, have published statements to guide employee behavior, especially with respect to ethical concerns. These resemble corporate policy statements (see Chapter 26) but are meant to implement or make operational the general policies phrased in a mission statement. A large insurance company issues a guide called "Values," which contains four key statements:

```
   We take pride in ourselves and the organization's leader-
ship position.
   We value and respect people.
   We value customers.
   We value communication.
```

Under each of these "value" statements is a list of proper behavior in related activities. Figure 25–5 presents the statements under "We value and respect people." This listing touches on key points of ethical behavior but lacks punch, clarity, and specificity. One reason is fuzzy language: "Collaborating with each other," for example, is redundant. Indeed, the third, fourth, fifth, and sixth statements repeat the same basic point.

Another reason for the lack of clarity is the use of gerunds (words ending in *ing*) instead of finite verbs. Instructions are best presented *as instructions.* Figure 25–6 presents a revised version of the code of practice.

Even rephrased and sharpened as they are in Figure 25–6, instructions to employees for ethical behavior are necessarily more general than, say, instructions for how to dress. Businesses, however, gain much from detailing

```
Because we value and respect people we:

   • Deal with others as individuals; treat each as you would like
to be treated.
   • Help each person develop his or her fullest potential.
   • Recognize and accept differences among people.
   • Work with others as a team, recognizing that each member
brings strengths and weaknesses but that all share a common goal
and common values.
```

FIGURE 25–6.
Code of practice—effective.

their expectations. At a minimum, codes of corporate practice take away employee excuses for bad conduct. Good ones provide direction and even inspiration.

DESIGNING THE PROCEDURE

The *design* of a set of instructions is at least as important as the text itself—perhaps even more important. A crowded page layout and small print both frighten and confuse the reader. The procedure looks unwelcoming, intimidating. To ease the reader's task, design the document for both clarity and attractiveness. Throughout the text, in both words and graphics, build in cues that indicate steps and allow the reader to move back and forth easily between text and action. Make it easy for readers to find their place again. Here are some points to watch, particularly as you revise your draft.

- **Headings.** Use headings that describe *action,* in verb form, rather than mere noun titles. Or use questions as headings. Use first- and second-level headings, but avoid subdivision beyond the second level. Choose a design to highlight the headings and clearly segment the text.
- **Indentation.** Write procedures in short sentences and short paragraphs. The document is a place for isolated units of meaning that a reader can easily check off. There is little room for the more leisurely discussions that occur in long paragraphs.
- **Numbering.** If possible, number the steps for ease of reference. The numbers also provide a way for the reader to keep score; the reader can mark progress by checking off steps as he or she moves through the process.

• **Layout.** Don't crowd the page. Encourage reading and remembering with a pleasing design. Choose a typeface and size that accommodate the readers. For example, a text aimed at the elderly is best composed in a fairly large type size. Avoid using all capital letters (some people read these as a reprimand). If you need to warn the reader about a particularly dangerous step, make that warning stand out visually on the page. Allow adequate margins for the reader's own notes.

Many procedures are first drafted as a drawing or chart. Then the writer adds words to explain. A visual can summarize an entire procedure in one whole picture, as in the flowchart shown in Figure 25–7. The chart both *documents* the procedure for writing reports in the author's organization and *instructs* report writers about the procedure. Words can describe only the segments, not the overall process.

Visuals also motivate a reader. For some audiences, cartoons and other

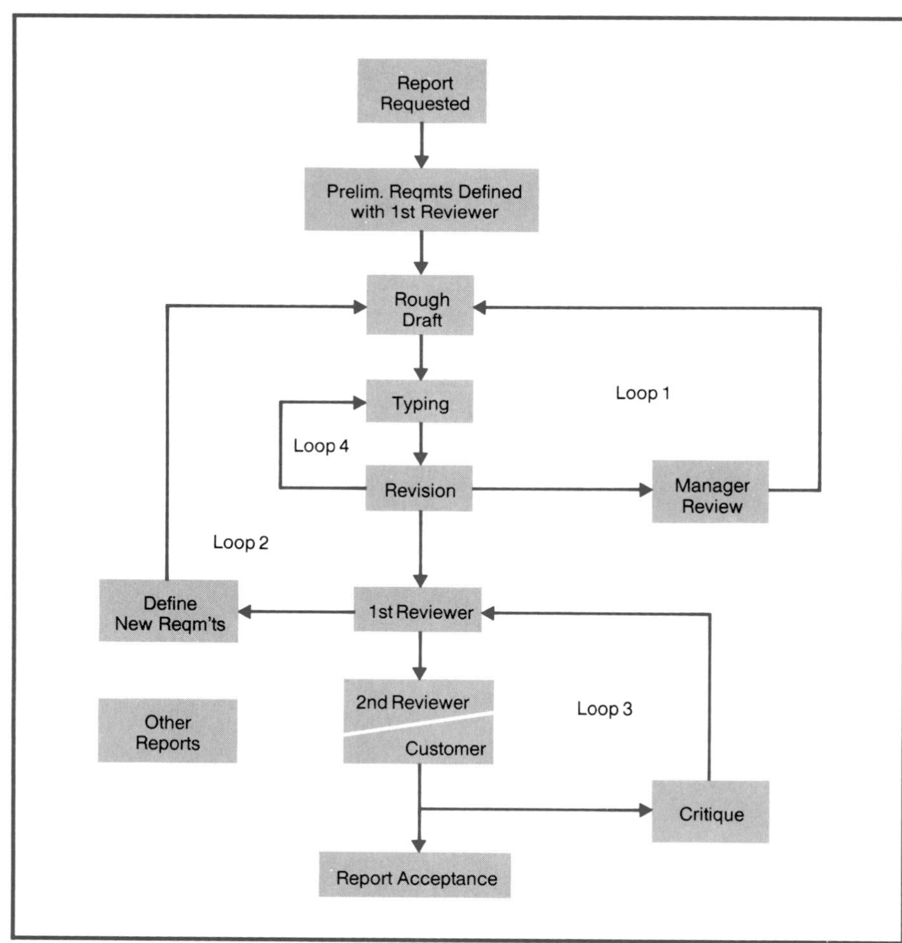

FIGURE 25–7.
Flowchart of report production.

drawings provide welcome relief from the tediousness of the procedure. Novice users may respond particularly well to visual analogies. For example, some wordprocessing programs use icons to instruct. The user is told to consider the entire screen a desk. Icons represent actions, such as a trash can for something the user wants to delete or a folder for a file. The analogies simplify the understanding of the tasks performed electronically by the system.

Some instructions, particularly those that must serve several language communities or those addressed to children, are almost entirely visual (see Figure 25–8). Instead of a document, you may even use a videotape of someone performing the procedure as a method for training new users.

TESTING THE PROCEDURE

Writers revise and rewrite procedures probably more often than they redo other documents. The instructions have to work.

Validating and Verifying

You may not get rid of every bug before you issue a procedure, but try to spot as many as you can. *Validate* and *verify* the procedure. Both reviews are tests of *performance.*

Validation

A procedure may fail because of inaccuracies in the content. For example, a manual may lack information concerning a last-minute enhancement in a new product. Check the procedure for accuracy.

Verification

A procedure may also fail because of ambiguous language, insufficient detail, confusing format, or confusing visuals. To verify the procedure, test it on yourself, although as an informed user you may overlook what others will find troublesome, and particularly the ways in which someone may go wrong.

A better route is to test the procedure on a sample of users before you issue it widely. Watch them and ask them to comment aloud as they work through your written instructions. Or devise a questionnaire to determine their ability to read and follow the instructions or to remember the steps.

Revising to Simplify

In general, revise to *simplify.* Tell the users only what they need to know—no more. If you really feel a wholesale explanation of the system is in order, consider placing such a description in an appendix. Listen when readers ask, "Does that mean . . . ?" Make sure to include any necessary cautions (like reminding someone to unplug a toaster oven before cleaning it). You might also warn readers about any common mistakes in following the procedure and provide ways out of them.

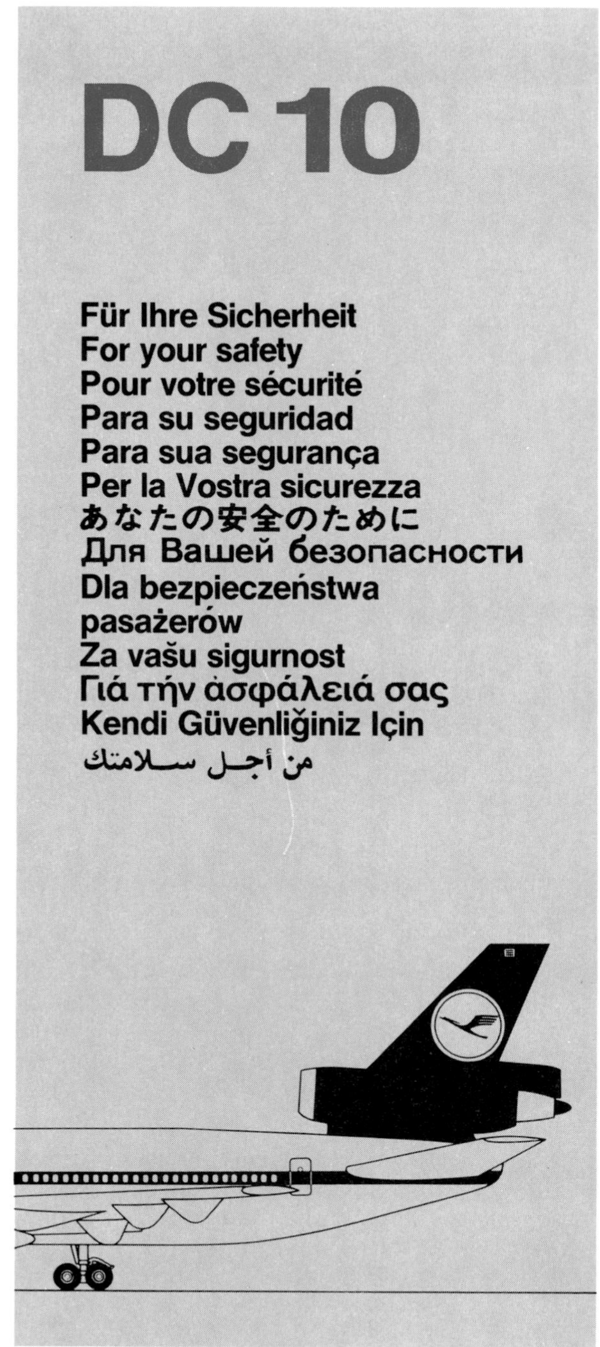

FIGURE 25–8.
Instructions for an international audience. *(Courtesy of Lufthansa German Airlines.)*

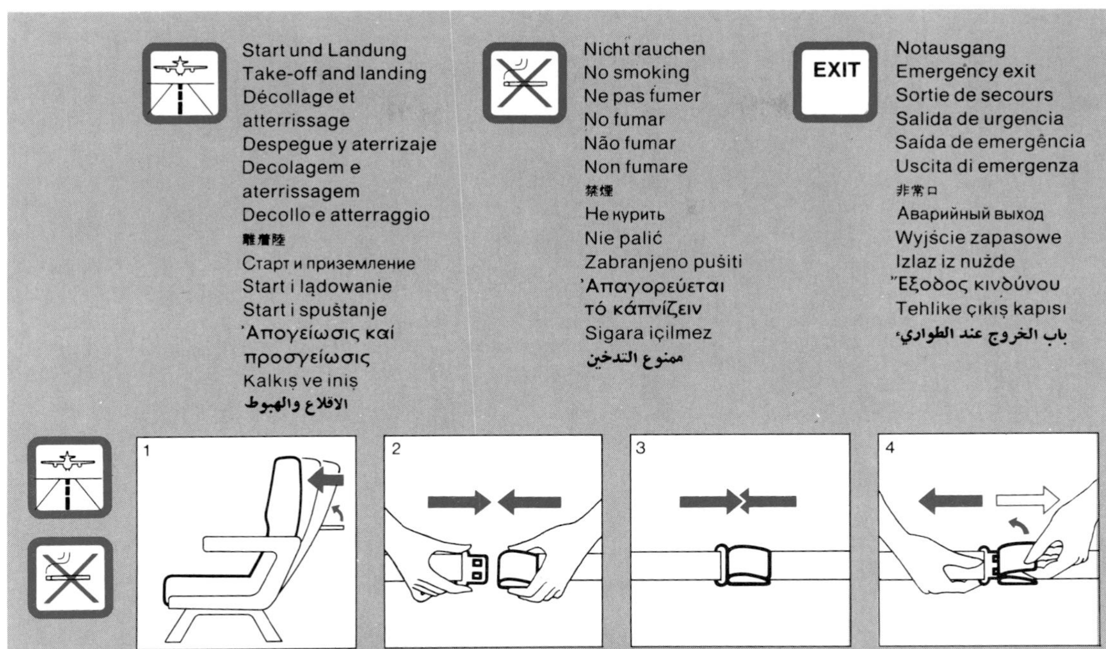

FIGURE 25–8 (continued).

YOUR VOICE AS AN INSTRUCTOR

Read through your procedure to hear how your voice comes off the page. Check your style and tone. It's easy to preach or to chide. Instead, put yourself in the reader's shoes. C. Northcote Parkinson (creator of Parkinson's Law) notes:

> Bad instructions are sometimes deliberate, arising from some muddled motive, the desire to humiliate, the desire to reveal somebody's stupidity, the desire to show that the coming disaster was not our fault. In such instances the will to communicate is absent. More often, however, the will is there, but the imagination is not.[3]

Being imaginative requires, in part, rethinking the process from the reader's perspective and escaping from the "corporate voice." Figure 25–9 pokes fun at that voice; but this parody works because it's not far from what one reads every day in offices.

And watch your biases. Here is a set of instructions from a student newspaper at a university in Philadelphia:

```
   There are undoubtedly some of you out there who want to
go to Salt Lake City, and who are
   a. immune to auto sickness.
```

[3] "Parkinson's Law of the Vacuum (or, Hoover for President)," *Forbes*, 12 May 1980, p. 138.

For those government employees and bureaucrats who have problems with standard recipes, here's one that should make the grade—a classic version of the chocolate chip cookie translated for easy reading.
Total Lead Time: 35 minutes.

Inputs:

1 cup packed brown sugar
½ cup granulated sugar
½ cup softened butter
½ cup shortening
2 eggs
1½ teaspoons vanilla
2½ cups all-purpose flour
1 teaspoon baking soda
½ teaspoon salt
12-ounce package semisweet chocolate pieces
1 cup chopped walnuts or pecans

Guidance:

After procurement actions, decontainerize inputs. Perform measurement tasks on a case-by-case basis. In a mixing type bowl, impact heavily on brown sugar, granulated sugar, softened butter and shortening. Coordinate the interface of eggs and vanilla, avoiding an overrun scenario to the best of your skills and abilities.

At this point in time, leverage flour, baking soda and salt into a bowl and aggregate. Equalize with prior mixture and develop intense and continuous liaison among inputs until well-coordinated. Associate key chocolate and nut subsystems and execute stirring operations.

Within this time frame, take action to prepare the heating environment for throughput by manually setting the oven baking unit by hand to a temperature of 375 degrees Fahrenheit (190 degrees Celsius). Drop mixture in an ongoing fashion from a teaspoon implement onto an ungreased cookie sheet at intervals sufficient enough apart to permit total and permanent separation of throughputs to the maximum extent practicable under operating conditions.

Position cookie sheet in a bake situation and surveil for 8 to 10 minutes or until cooking action terminates. Initiate coordination of outputs within the cooling rack function. Containerize, wrap in red tape and disseminate to authorized staff personnel on a timely and expeditious basis.

Output:

Six dozen official government chocolate chip cookie units.

FIGURE 25–9.
A bureaucrat's guide to chocolate chip cookies. *(Source: Susan E. Russ.)*

b. not independently wealthy.
c. not particularly interested in your classwork.

The solution: Drive. In your own car, or in a Hertz special. It only takes 48 hours, and the directions are simple.

Take Spruce Street over the South Street Bridge and make a left on the Schuylkill Expressway (I-76 West). Stay on this road for an eternity, all the way through Pennsylvania and into Ohio.

When you get to Youngstown, I-76 turns into I-80 (the Ohio Turnpike). Stay on I-80, even when it becomes the Indiana Turnpike.

Stay on 80 when it goes past Chicago.

Past Des Moines, Iowa.
Past Omaha, Nebraska.
Past Lincoln, Nebraska.

```
    Past Cheyenne, Wyoming. Cheyenne, Wyoming!

The next big town is Salt Lake City. You can't miss it.⁴
```

The school's basketball team was playing in a tournament in Salt Lake City, and the editors gave advice on how to get there. The approach is fine: The text defines the intended readers (in the first paragraph) and then gives the routes. Note, however, the change of scale—from minute instructions about leaving Philadelphia to the broad scale of the rest of the country. The distortion is clearly funny, reflecting an Easterner's sense that the rest of the country shrinks beyond the city limits of Philadelphia. But be wary of unintentional—and thus harmful—distortions when you write.

The engaging voice (see Chapter 5) is often hard to find in business writing. But preparing instructions gives you a welcome chance to be yourself because you need to establish a direct relationship with your reader. You need to build confidence, make the reader comfortable, assure her or him that the instructions will work. The voice of instruction should be direct and personal. The test of good procedures and instructions is that they work: The reader achieves the goal you set, masters the information, and performs the task or completes the process. A friendly and engaging voice of instruction goes a long way to make all that happen.

SUMMARY

- **Procedures** and **instructions** are written for **internal** use in an organization to serve **control** and **maintenance** functions: They help the firm monitor its operations and keep it running efficiently. They are also written for external use, as customer relations documents that show how to use a product properly.
- Before you write procedures and instructions, you need to **target the user, set the goals** (what the user will learn or be able to do), and **understand the procedure** thoroughly yourself so you can tell it to the user.
- **Step-by-step instructions** on how to do something or how to get somewhere present separate steps in chronological order, taking the user through the process in a pattern that he or she can check off as each step is accomplished. Visuals are helpful in reinforcing instructions. Charts and diagrams aid in telling how to do something, and maps assist in telling how to get somewhere.
- **Manuals** are comprehensive guides to the functioning of a machine or system. You have to present an overview of what you are describing and then inform the user about each separate step in the use. Manuals are also persuasive documents because they help sell the user on the desirability of the machine or system.
- **Codes of conduct and behavior** provide detailed instructions on how to behave, for example, on ethical and appropriate treatment of customers. You need to make users aware of the underlying goals of the code as well as to instruct them in the specific practices they should follow.

[4] *The Daily Pennsylvanian*, 21 March 1979.

- Design procedures and instructions with special attention to both the text and the visual elements. They need to be well integrated. Because users often need to visualize a process as they work through it, you should consider providing a **visual map** both to give an overview of the process and to elucidate the steps in it.
- The effectiveness of procedures and instructions needs to be **tested for validity** (Are they accurate?) and **verified** (Do they work?). Trying out a draft of the procedure on a sample audience can provide useful information about whether your procedure will meet its users' needs. Revise your drafts to simplify, making the complex simple.
- In writing procedures and instructions, avoid the corporate voice and try to speak directly and personally to the user. He or she needs to have confidence that you understand the process or item yourself and can be trusted to give accurate and easy-to-follow instructions on its use. Through your voice, establish your position as a concerned and friendly instructor, someone who will help and not confuse the user.

EXERCISES

For Discussion

1. Here are two descriptions of the registration procedure at a university. These are general descriptions intended for a brochure about the activities of the records office. Note that these are not instructions intended to guide users through the process but are meant to give an overview of how the procedure works.

A REGISTRATION PROCEDURE

Preregistration:

1. Preregistration forms are mailed to all undergraduate and graduate students, by the Records Office.
2. Students wishing to preregister return the completed form to the Records Office within two weeks.
3. After all forms are received, class request lists are compiled by the computer. A list for each class is made that contains the name of every student who requested the class.
4. The class request lists are then sent to the individual professors. The professors "red-line" or eliminate any students who are not qualified to take the course (i.e., students who do not have the proper prerequisites or who are not in the proper department).
5. After the lists are returned to the Records Office, the remaining students on the lists are assigned a point value as follows:

Freshman	100
Sophomore	200
Junior	300
Senior	400

The student's total number of credits earned is added to the class specification points to determine each student's point value.

6. After the point values are assigned, each class is filled with students in order of point value, until the class limit is reached.

Drop-Add and Late Registration:

1. Students who did not preregister or who didn't get a class through preregistration can add classes at the beginning of the semester through the drop-add system.
2. Drop-add forms are filled out exactly as preregistration forms are except that drop-add forms require a professor's signature for each class.
3. After the drop-add form is signed by the professor, the student is added to the class, and a point value does not have to be determined.

B REGISTRATION PROCEDURE

Each current full-time student is given a two-week advance registration period. The students are given a blue form, which is used only for requesting up to 17 credit hours. Statistics show that only 80 percent of the students advance-register.

After the forms are collected and stamped, they are processed into a computer. The computer stores the information in its memory by social security number, not by first come, first served, as is commonly believed.

Then the process of trial assignment begins. This is when the computer scans through its tapes and assigns the requested courses. Each student is given a number through a point system that is obtained from the number of earned credit hours multiplied by 400 points for a senior, 300 points for a junior, etc. The students with the highest numbers get priority in course selections.

The computer scans the first gridded box and determines if the particular class is open and then enrolls the student. The following boxes are processed the same way, and the computer continues downward in numerical order.

Finally, the student gets his program and receives only three courses when he requested six. The reason for this is a procedure called red-lining. Red-lining occurs when a student requests a course but he is not in that major or doesn't have the prerequisites. For example, it is very difficult to obtain a communication or business course if you are not in that particular college.

The student must now drop-add, which is in the hands of the individual professor. The faculty decide how many students they will offer the class to. If there is room, stu-

```
dents can add the course; this is a first come, first
served process.
```

Discuss these questions:

a. How do the two descriptions differ?
b. Do they give the same details? Can *both* be accurate?
c. Which would be easier to follow, if indeed you needed to register for classes?

2. Comment on the *style* (that is, the *voice*) of the following instructions, from a university faculty member telling readers how to get from the university to his home:

```
Drive east on Route 2 (Kirkwood Hwy.). Turn left on Polly
Drummond Rd. (1st left turn after Red Hill Nursery sign).
Drive up the hill for about a mile, then turn right onto
Linden Hill Rd. at the 2nd pair of flashing yellow lights
(bypassing Polly Drummond Plaza in the process). Turn at
the 2nd right turn, where a small black-and-white English
Village sign marks the way. Follow the winding road until
you see another English Village sign, where you turn left
into a declivity. Keep right until you pass the tree in
the middle of the road; then turn left around a sharp
hairpin curve down another declivity. Look for two brown
dumpsters fronting an elevated walkway leading to Jill
Hall (adjacent to the woods). Walk right in and go up to
the top floor, #17, last door on the right. If lost call
737-8661. (It sounds complicated but I find my way home
nearly every night.)[5]
```

Could you draw a map from the above instructions? Could the map *replace* the written instruction or *complement* them?

3. Obtain a set of instructions, a manual, or a code of behavior or conduct from a business (perhaps one that you work for). Identify the document (instructions, manual, code) and then discuss its effectiveness. Is the intended *user* clear? Does there seem to be a *goal?* Does it seem that the writer mastered the process sufficiently to tell it to someone else?

4. The chapter discussed problems in writing instructions for different cultures. Review several sets of instructions with multilanguage origins. Note word usage, of course. Often, such usage is a source of humor, as in a translation of *hydraulic ram* as "water goat." But beyond this literal level, note any differences in structure or assumptions about the reader that are inherent in your sample of English-language instructions for devices manufactured abroad.

For Writing

5. The two descriptions of registration procedures in Exercise 1 are meant to give an overview of the process. Convert them to a set of step-by-step instructions for students who wish to register for courses.

[5] Courtesy of Ted Billy.

6. Write a set of instructions to tell a reader how to go from some Point A to some Point B. Assume that the reader knows nothing about either location. Use no visuals. Then change the conditions. *Use* a visual. Assume a reader who is generally familiar with the area, and with one location, but not with the other. What differences appear in the instructions?

7. Choose one of the following topics. Then write a procedure on the subject. Use at least one visual. *Before* you write, define these constraints:
   - Audience and assumptions concerning their prior knowledge
   - Purpose of the procedure
   - Your point of view: A set of instructions? A reference description? A narrative of how *you* did this once?

   Topics

   a. What to do when your car won't start
   b. How to get access to a computer on campus
   c. How to make a hoagie (submarine, grinder—whatever you call a long sandwich with various meats)
   d. How to cure a headache
   e. How to sell something (select one thing you know something about)
   f. How to read a corporate annual report

For Collaboration

8. As a class project, collect instructions from different household or office devices, preferably instructions in multiple languages and with pictures. How do these differ: Size? Shape? Devices for courting the reader? Visuals? Forms of address (*you?* generalized?)? What makes them easy or hard to read? As you discuss these issues, note differences among members of the class. How do you account for these differences? What do these differences tell you about the importance of testing (especially *validating*) procedures?

9. Form teams of three or four members each. Each team must prepare a *code of class conduct* to guide how students should conduct themselves during class. Work together to produce a single document in each team. Present the results to the entire class and discuss differences in the documents. Which is most effective? Why? How can the less effective ones be improved?

26 DOCUMENTS OF THE CORPORATION

INTERNAL DOCUMENTS
- Documents That Define
- Documents That Control
- Documents That Maintain
- Employee Publications

EXTERNAL DOCUMENTS
- FYI: Redirecting and Redesigning the Hercules *Horizons*
- Customer-Relations Documents
- Reports for Investors
- FYI: The CEO's Letter to Shareholders
- Press Releases
- FYI: A Glimpse at PR in the 21st Century

SUMMARY

EXERCISES

Do You Know ?

- What three goals do internal corporate documents serve?
- How does a strategic plan differ from an operational plan?
- How can in-house documents maintain good employee relations?
- What external audiences do companies address?
- What is the function of annual reports?

The photograph that opens this part of *Business Communication* originally appeared in *Horizons,* the employee publication of Hercules, Inc., producer of specialty chemicals based in Wilmington, Delaware. The company's employees formed the "We care" pennant to send a message to the community that symbolized Hercules's commitment to the environment. For readers inside Hercules, this issue of the publication provided additional information on corporate environmental policies and procedures.

You will read a variety of specialized documents produced by corporations and government agencies in your role as employee, as client, as customer, as stockholder, or as concerned citizen. This chapter briefly reviews some of the most significant ones. First, you'll read about *internal* documents that meet the three organizational goals discussed in Chapter 2: definition, control, and maintenance. Then you'll see documents, primarily the corporate annual report, aimed at *external* audiences.

INTERNAL DOCUMENTS

The array of documents required to trail every decision or action in an organization may baffle an office newcomer. In general, the larger the organization, the more numerous the forms and handbooks and the more likely that items will be known by acronyms or numbers understandable only to the initiated: a PIN, a 16-J-18, Form 52-X. Although many of these documents may seem designed more to prevent work than to enable it, some are critical. Let's look at the most significant ones.

Documents That Define

Statements from management organize corporate life. At the highest level, *definition* documents codify the very meaning of an organization. They identify goals and strategies, set an agenda for action, and shape an image that governs the organization's culture. Three definition documents are common:

Goal statement
Policy statement
Strategic plan

Goal Statement

A *goal statement* is sometimes called a *strategy* or *mission statement.* It codifies in general terms what the organization is and what it aims to accomplish. Figure 26–1 presents the mission statement of Metropolitan Hospital. The statement describes levels of service and emphasizes the hospital's "people orientation," both toward patients and toward employees. Many mission statements are mere stuffy talk, as you read in Chapter 5. But Figure 26–1 avoids the twin traps of pomposity and vagueness.

The mission statement sets a direction. It establishes a controlling idea and a corporate style that then reverberate through each employee and corporate action. As you read in the part opener, "The Store That Knows the Outdoors" is a brief statement of the mission of L. L. Bean. Figure 26–2 is another goal (or mission) statement—from the manager of several McDonald's restaurants.

Policy Statement

A *policy statement* translates goals into standards. Such statements address personnel issues (hiring, firing, promotion, and compensation), corporate social responsibility, the use of company facilities for nonbusiness purposes, and advertising and promotion standards. Figure 26–3, for example, provides a policy statement on patient relations derived from Metropolitan Hospital's

Metropolitan Hospital is a private, not-for-profit organization established to provide medical care for the residents of the Tri-County area. It offers three levels of service: emergency treatment, basic diagnostic and surgical care, and--through its Metropolitan HomeCare Facility--long-term nursing care for the elderly.

Metropolitan Hospital seeks to provide the best possible care in all categories at the lowest cost consistent with sound medical and fiscal practice. It is committed to personal service, attention to individual patient needs, and courteous professional relationships with its clients.

People make Metropolitan Hospital work. Therefore Metropolitan is people-oriented in its employment practices as in its medical service. It seeks to help its employees at all levels to develop their skills and abilities to the highest level they are capable of and provides support services to help all employees reach their maximum potential as individuals and as providers of health care. Relationships among employees at all levels are governed by professional courtesy and with the ultimate goal of making Metropolitan a truly caring institution.

FIGURE 26–1.
Mission statement for Metropolitan Hospital.

OUR OBJECTIVES

Our philosophy is really very simple, but making it work takes the best effort of everyone on the team. Our prime objective is

TO SATISFY THE CUSTOMER

The customer is the most important factor in our business. We do this by giving the best QUALITY, SERVICE, CLEANLINESS, and VALUE.

Q McDonald's reputation for quality is internationally known. We are unique because the highest quality standards are maintained at very reasonable prices. We use the finest available products and carefully developed formulas. But all of this can be lost without your help. Always check the products you prepare and serve. If they are not right, do not serve them, and tell your manager. One of the keys to quality is Tender Loving Care--"T.L.C." All our efforts can be lost if you crush or drop a sandwich. Handle all products with "T.L.C."

S Quality and cleanliness are wasted without fast, courteous service. A smile does as much to bring a customer back as the best food in the world. And remember--the customer is the most important single factor in our business. Courtesy is always easier if we remember the GOLDEN RULE: "Treat everyone, especially the customer, the way you want to be treated yourself." The customer appreciates courtesy and appreciates speed. Sometimes it is hard to give them both at the same time, but that is what makes McDonald's unique.

C Cleanliness is like a magnet drawing customers to McDonald's. Our stores must be spotless at all times, both inside and out. Only through the best efforts of everyone will that happen.

V Value is a subjective judgment by our customers--how they view the product received in relation to the price they pay for it. Value is the combination of a quality product served quickly and courteously in a clean environment. Only by maintaining the highest standards of QSC will our customers view McDonald's as a true value.

OUR EMPLOYMENT POLICY

It is the policy of McDonald's to offer employment and promotional opportunities to the most qualified individuals and to establish a Wage and Salary Program consistent and equitable for all employees.

Further, it is the policy of the company to prohibit actions or practices which would discriminate in the implementation of the above or general personnel programs for reasons of race, color, age, creed, national origin, or sex. We are an Equal Opportunity Employer.

If you have any questions about this policy, please contact your Store Manager.

FIGURE 26–2.
Goal statement *(Courtesy of McDonald's, Dukart Management Corporation.)*

Metropolitan Hospital is committed to dealing with its patients and their families in a courteous and professional manner that ensures maximum attention to individual needs consistent with the overall goal of providing excellent medical care. To achieve this goal, the staff of the hospital should at all times treat patients and their families with respect and with sensitivity to their emotional needs. Adult patients are always addressed as Mr. or Ms. Children are called by their first names. Staff should avoid becoming too familiar with patients and families or developing personal relationships that interfere with professional standards of treatment. Staff should not allow personal attitudes toward patients to obstruct the professional delivery of health care. Patients or families with special emotional problems or social difficulties should be referred to the counseling staff, which provides specialized psychological help. All patients and families should be treated equally and fairly; favoritism shown to individual patients or families is counterproductive to the effective operation of the hospital.

FIGURE 26–3.
Policy statement on patient relations, Metropolitan Hospital.

mission statement: ". . . committed to personal service, attention to individual patient needs, and courteous professional relationships with its clients."

The policy statement provides guidelines for action: Be sensitive and respectful; address adults as Mr. or Ms.; don't become emotionally attached to patients; refer special problems to counseling; treat everyone equally. A policy statement sets broad directions in behavior; *procedures,* as you read in Chapter 25, then provide specific steps for implementing the policy. The hospital's policy statement might be broken out into a specific *procedure* for checking patients into the emergency room—a procedure that would put these guidelines into practice.

Strategic Plan

Like goal statements and policy statements, a third type of document that defines an organization is a *strategic* or *business plan.* Such plans convert mission statements into agendas for action. Figure 26–4, for example, shows how Metropolitan Hospital's concern for people gave rise to a strategic plan for human resource development. This brief segment of a larger planning document outlines an approach to meeting a goal (a new position of assistant director) and includes a deadline for action.

Documents That Control

Control documents monitor progress toward the organization's goals. To set a standard for that monitoring, companies create an operational plan that

```
Because our people are our major asset, the hospital regards staff
development as a function of the highest priority. To encourage it,
we will create a position of assistant director of personnel for
staff development and will hire the best-qualified person for that
position. He or she will be charged with developing a master plan
for staff development in consultation with divisional and
departmental supervisors. A budget for this function will then be
developed and submitted to the board for approval. The Staff
Development Program should become operational within nine months,
pending Board approval.
```

FIGURE 26–4.
Segment of a plan for human resource development, Metropolitan Hospital.

translates strategies into guidelines for action. Such a plan contains quantitative measures and establishes schedules.

For example, assume that Niblex Inc., which manufactures and sells salty snack foods, has established as one linchpin in its strategic plan the need to maintain a return on investment (ROI) at 18 percent. To achieve this goal, Niblex requires that profit margins for its Niblex brand be 28 percent. To achieve that subgoal, Niblex has determined that unit costs must be maintained at 50 cents per package. Thus the operational plan is as follows:

```
To maintain acceptable profit margins to meet corporate ROI
goals, direct unit costs per package of Niblex must be held
at a maximum of $.50. Unit labor cost should be $.35 and ma-
terials cost $.15.
```

The statement is precise, concrete, and unambiguous, like a good statement in any operational plan. It should leave no doubt in the mind of the reader about how to carry out the plan. The routine reports you read about in Chapter 18 cover most of the monitoring of progress toward the goal. In Figure 18–6, you saw a report responding directly to the Niblex plan.

Documents that Maintain

Maintenance documents keep the corporate house in good order. Memos and reports deal with purchasing, building maintenance, security, property control, parking, and facilities use. Routine notices and employee handbooks include rules and regulations for behavior: hiring, firing, promotion, compensation, schedules, vacations, coffeebreaks, and dress codes. You've certainly seen (and have probably written) memos and short reports aimed at housekeeping. The job descriptions you read about in Chapter 23, the performance evaluations you read about in Chapter 24, and the personnel procedures you read about in Chapter 25 are further examples of maintenance documents.

Employee Publications

All three purposes—definition, control, and maintenance—are reflected in the employee relations documents that reinforce positive aspects of the corporate culture. Keeping employees informed about company goals and news, especially news about people, is an important step in making sure the organization is functioning at its maximum—and that everyone knows that. Publications for employees go beyond bulletin boards and grapevines in disseminating information. Desktop publishing systems have encouraged an increase in such publications; even small companies can produce professional-looking newsletters with the software available on personal computers. In "*FYI:* Redirecting and Redesigning the Hercules *Horizons*," Ida G. Crist comments on how corporate publications keep up to date.

EXTERNAL DOCUMENTS

We've examined *internal documents* in light of the particular organizational purposes they perform. *External documents* are more easily grouped according to the audiences they address. As they provide information (sometimes in response to government regulation, as in annual reports), most external documents also serve the common purpose of making the organization look

REDIRECTING AND REDESIGNING THE HERCULES *HORIZONS*

Ida G. Crist
Publications Manager,
Hercules, Inc.

Business publications help project a company's image as well as serve as a communications vehicle for a specific audience.

As companies and their relationship to employees change, the content and design of employee publications must keep pace with those changes.

Over the past 25 years, employee publications have stressed business news and management decisions. Although they encourage personal achievements, they emphasize accomplishments in the workplace or the community over those in bowling alleys.

The *Horizons*, a weekly newspaper for employees of Hercules, Inc., and its biweekly predecessors have explained and interpreted company decisions and policies since 1942. Like other successful employee publications, *Horizons* fosters such corporate values as safety, quality, and protection of the environment through specific, appealing articles that emphasize policies.

For example, a few years ago, when a drought in the Midwest backed up barges on the Mississippi and delayed the transportation of raw material, *Horizons* told a dramatic story of how Hercules's Transportation Department anticipated the problem and joined several other company departments in creating an alternative route structure. *Horizons* capitalized on a national news story to promote the importance of quality decisions at home.

FIGURE 26–5.
Two designs for the flag of *Hercules Horizons.* The one on top emphasized the company's new building. Seven years later, the redesigned flag emphasizes the company's global business. *(Courtesy of Hercules, Inc.)*

Besides being interesting to read, business publications must be visually appealing. For this reason, *Horizons* was redesigned in 1990. It had been known as the *Hercules Horizons* since 1983, when the company moved its corporate headquarters to a new building. That move marked a new horizon—hence the name, with the new building prominently displayed on the publication's flag (nameplate). (See Figure 26–5.)

Seven years later, however, the graphic of the building seemed outdated, and the company was becoming more global. Hercules had recently undergone a corporate reorganization integrating foreign markets and customers into the individual business groups rather than treating them as separate units. The revamped design of *Horizons* reflects this change. The flag emphasizes a new global horizon with a solid red *O* in Horizons raised slightly above the rest of the letters.

The new publication measures 9¼″ × 12¼″, slightly smaller than the previous version. Its size distinguishes it from hundreds of other 8½″ × 11″ documents. With three columns of text rather than four, the new design also features more white space to encourage reading and a "scholar's margin" at the edge of each page to be used for large quotations, photographs, captions, or news briefs to capture readers' attention.

good. They both inform and persuade. Here's a brief look at documents produced for three audiences: customers, investors, and the public.

Customer-Relations Documents

You've already seen many documents addressed to customers: sales letters, responses to complaints, bids, proposals, and final reports. Correspondence with customers and business proposals may originate in any of several divisions of a company. In a large company, a marketing department may oversee the care and feeding of customers, particularly through advertising, product announcements, and sales brochures. Some consumer-oriented companies maintain special customer-relations departments supported by multimillion-dollar budgets. You've seen toll-free numbers for such departments on cereal boxes, for example.

Service Announcements

In a small organization, a simple typed notice may suffice to announce a product or service, as in Figure 26–6. Woody is concise and direct. Considering its audience, this simple notice, tucked under a windshield wiper, conveys the right message.

Newsletters

Figure 26–7 shows a more sophisticated customer-relations document. *Energy News You Can Use* is an insert in the form of a newsletter that accompanies monthly bills sent by Delmarva Power of Delaware. Julie Williams, editor of the newsletter, cites this insert as a factor in improving the utility's favorability rating—a measure of customer acceptance—from 46 percent in 1982 to 82 percent in 1990. Sixty-two percent of all customers read the insert, and that segment has an even higher rate of favorability.

To Our Valued Customers:

Beginning in August, Woody's Garage will be providing complete service on Hondas, Toyotas, and Datsuns. We have hired John Politz to supervise work on Japanese automobiles. John has had years of experience and will be happy to discuss your automotive needs.

Thanks for your continuing patronage. Please tell your friends about our new service.

FIGURE 26–6.
A simple service announcement.

JANUARY 1991

ENERGY NEWS
YOU CAN USE

Save Energy With Compact Fluorescent Light Bulbs

Saving energy helps protect the environment. Using less energy means a reduction in air pollution and preservation of non-renewable resources. The more energy we save now, the more energy will be available for future generations.

Compact fluorescent light bulbs use one-quarter as much electricity and last about 10 times longer than ordinary light bulbs. An 18-watt compact fluorescent produces about the same amount of light as a regular 75-watt bulb.

These energy-saving bulbs can be used in many light fixtures including table lamps and ceiling fixtures, but may not fit in all lamps because of their size.

Compact fluorescents are expensive. They cost between $10 and $26. But the bulbs have a life of 7,500 to 12,000 hours.

Ten thousand hours is equal to about five years burning the light five hours per day. This example translates to a five year energy savings of about $50.

Good applications for the bulbs include lamps used for general lighting in the family room, work areas, porch or post lamps (outdoor models), and security lights.

For more information on compact fluorescent light bulbs, write to Delmarva Power, Marketing Dept., Rt. 273 & I-95, Newark, DE 19714, or call 302-454-4356. Call collect if you live outside New Castle County, Delaware.

Want To Win An Energy-Saving Light Bulb Worth $20?

Delmarva Power is giving away 1,000 energy-efficient, compact fluorescent light bulbs to people throughout the Delmarva Peninsula to highlight the importance of energy conservation. This project is part of the company's environmental stewardship program, "Serving & Conserving Delmarva."

By taking the short quiz enclosed with your bill (also available at all Delmarva Power district offices) and detaching and mailing in the entry form by February 25, 1991, you will be eligible to win one of these energy-efficient light bulbs.* Each bulb is a $20 value.

One thousand entries will be randomly drawn and winners will receive their compact fluorescent light bulbs in the mail. We will publish the names of winners in early March.

If you would like a chance to win a compact fluorescent bulb, answer the questions on the quiz enclosed with your bill (also available at all Delmarva Power district offices). You don't have to answer correctly, just make sure your entry form reaches us by February 25, 1991 to be eligible for the drawing.

*Delmarva Power employees are not eligible to enter. The drawing is open to everyone else — you need not be a Delmarva Power customer to enter.

SERVING • CONSERVING • DELMARVA

FIGURE 26–7.
Customer service insert. *(Courtesy of Delmarva Power & Light Company.)*

Advances in desktop publishing are enabling even small organizations and professional practices to create newsletters, as you see in Figure 26–8, which shows a newsletter that a veterinary practice distributes to its patients (or to the people who live with them).

Ski areas, hotel chains, museums, zoos, airlines, and baseball teams—a wide variety of organizations keep in touch with their customers or members through newsletters.

Reports for Investors

Government agencies, nonprofit organizations, and profit-seeking organizations that are privately owned need not worry about reporting to shareholders. They may have analogous constituencies (voters, in the case of government agencies, for example) to whom they are accountable and to whom they must therefore provide information and with whom they must cultivate a good image. But in the United States and Canada, publicly owned corporations must, as a legal requirement, report certain basic financial and marketing data to shareholders every quarter. Securities laws stipulate minimum reporting requirements: an income statement, a balance sheet, sources and uses of funds, a statement of accounting principles, notes on valuations, research investment, foreign currency effects, and so on. Although some corporations comply only at the minimum level, firms that have many stockholders almost always dress up these statements.

The Context for Annual Reports

Quarterly reports are usually brief and straightforward. They often fold into a standard business envelope. Annual reports, however, are more elaborate. They represent the company's best occasion for communicating to its owners what it is doing and why. The reports aim to bolster the investor confidence needed to maintain stock prices and to make the company an attractive one for potential owners as well.

Annual reports also function as recruiting devices. Job applicants often look at such reports to assess both the financial standing and the corporate culture of a potential employer. And annual reports serve as marketing tools to explain company goals to potential customers. For all these reasons, companies shower lots of attention on the preparation of annual reports. That attention is reflected in the report's cost: an average of $3.52 a copy in 1988.[1] Visuals contribute a good deal to that cost (see the special feature on photography in corporate annual reports).

Reading Annual Reports

You'll certainly want to read annual reports as you gain information about corporations throughout the world and make decisions concerning your own career goals. Look for the following features in information and presentation:

- **Financial highlights up front.** A lack of numbers near the beginning may signal the covering over of a bad year.

[1] Pamela Sebastian, "Business Bulletin," *The Wall Street Journal,* 17 August 1989, p. 1.

Fall News Bulletin

Fall 1990 Edition

the **Companion**

North Deering Veterinary Hospital

456 Auburn Street
Portland, Maine 04103
207/797-4855

Now's the time to tackle those pesky fleas

As veterinarians we spend hundreds of hours a year in our exam rooms and on the telephone talking about fleas, or, more specifically, how to deal with them.

Generally mid- to late summer is the time of year that we really notice the effect of fleas: the scratching dog, cat or owner.

The problems caused by fleas extend far beyond the simple itch. Fleas have been implicated in severe cases of dermatitis (skin inflammation), ear and anal sac disease, and they can exacerbate cases of allergic skin disease in our pets.

We have many potent products to use against fleas; unfortunately, therapeutic failure is reported fairly frequently. The most common cause for therapeutic failure is not being thorough enough in treating the fleas on and *off* the animal. We have found that it is just as important to thoroughly treat the pet's environment as it is to treat all the animals in the house.

Another complicating factor is that fleas lay their eggs not on the pet itself, but in the pet's (and owner's) environment. These pesky eggs are very resistant to all but the strongest chemicals. A total treatment plan for de-fleaing a pet should take into consideration these points:

Treating the pet

1. ***Bathing.*** Easy to do, but due to rinsing afterwards, has little or no preventative effect to keep fleas off pets later.
2. ***Sprays and powders.*** Also easy to do, and the effects last three to four days, necessitating a twice-weekly application.
3. ***Dipping.*** This is the application, by a thorough wetting, of a dilute solution which is allowed to dry on the animal. Effective dips can keep fleas away for up to two weeks.
4. ***Pro-Spot.*** This is the application of a tiny amount of a concentrated chemical to the area of skin between the shoulder blades of dogs (only). Effective for up to two weeks.

Treating the environment

This is as important as treating the animals, but is probably the area that gets overlooked most often. The environment, including the house, dog house, kennel and possibly the yard, needs to be treated at the same time the pet is treated. Be very thorough — expose closets, underneath cushions and furniture, basement, attic and even the car, truck or recreational vehicle to the treatment, especially if the pet spends any time there.

FIGURE 26–8.
A desktop-published newsletter for a professional practice. *(Courtesy of Thomas A. Judd, DVM: Denise L. McNitt, DVM; designed by Michael Kitchen, Eleventh Hour Graphics, Newton, MA © 1990. All rights reserved.)*

- Information on the company's **competition and market share.**
- **Extensive financial disclosure.** If you don't see numbers near the front, then begin reading at the back, with the auditor's letter that shows if the company's report conforms to "generally accepted accounting principles." If you see the phrase "subject to," in the letter, that may mean trouble: The accountant isn't sure you should take the company's word about some piece of business.
- A **dominant theme** expressed in an attention-getting statement that then shapes the information presented.
- **Comparative statistics on several years' performance**—or an explanation of why such statistics are unavailable or meaningless.
- **Management comments,** as well as those of the auditors, concerning financial information (you'll read more about the important letter from the CEO shortly).
- **Clean layout, text, and graphics** for ease of reading.

Pay particular attention to how companies treat bad news. The problems of corporations often end up in the popular press. Tankers spill oil; airplanes crash or slide off runways; foodstuffs become contaminated; new products fail to sell as projected. Readers expect, then, to see those accounts somehow acknowledged in the company's annual report, along with any other bad news that might affect operations. "The issue is credibility," notes one man-

THE CEO'S LETTER TO SHAREHOLDERS

Crystal C. Bell
Director of Financial Communications,
Enserch Corporation

Writing the letter to shareholders in an annual report is like writing a letter for God. At least it seems that significant. The letter is written under the signature of your public company's chief executive, either the chair or the president, primarily for shareholders.

The letter is usually drafted by a ghostwriter, a copywriting professional on the corporate investor-relations or communications staff. As the letter writer, you sit in the middle of two forces. As an insider, you must satisfy the organization's CEO as you explain the company's financial results, good or bad, for the previous year and describe future operational strategies—all without diminishing the picture of his or her leadership ability.

As a writer, you must also satisfy your external audience: the shareholders. Some are sophisticated institutions that hold thousands, maybe millions of shares. Others are like Aunt Jane, who may only own 10 shares in her IRA. There are also employees (who may not be shareholders), financial analysts, suppliers, customers, potential employees, the media—to name a few readers.

Your message must reach all these people, and thus you must write in broad strokes. What message? The reader, no matter who, should perceive quickly that the company's CEO is a leader who knows where the company is going and what problems must be faced.

First, think. Take some quiet time to puzzle out what the CEO should say. What issues should be discussed? What significant events happened during the year? What challenges has your company faced?

agement consultant. "If you don't address the bad news, people won't believe your good news."[2] In "*FYI:* The CEO's Letter to Shareholders," Crystal Bell of Enserch Corporation provides insight into that important component of the annual report.

Other Reporting Occasions

Between quarterly and annual reporting occasions, publicly held companies may need to communicate special news to shareholders: a takeover bid from an unfriendly source that requires shareholder resistance, a major new product that will improve the company's financial prospects, a change in top management, the results of litigation that may affect the company's stability, a reduction in the dividend. Typically, these messages come as letters from the CEO; you saw such a letter from the CEO of The Travelers in Chapter 15. If the information warrants, the company may produce a brochure, with a covering note from the CEO, to describe the issue, as in Figure 26–9, which shows the CEO's note and the first two pages of the Mobil Corporation's 23-page brochure stating its environmental policy, "Protecting the Environment—1990."

[2] Timothy D. Schellhardt, "Managing: Handling Bad News in Annual Reports," *The Wall Street Journal,* 1 June 1990, p. B1.

How should these topics be discussed? Put yourself behind your CEO's desk.

Next, develop an outline, organizing these topics by priority and looking for transitions between them. Do some research. Interview corporate officers. And read, read—industry stories and financial news. Arm yourself with background.

At this point, some copywriters will start the letter. If you're lucky, you'll be able to take an interim—and important—step: discussing the issues with your CEO. What does he or she think is important? What topics should be covered, and how?

Whether you write the letter with some or no guidance, the letter should sound like the CEO's style of management. Note that I said *management,* not style of *writing.* The CEO's writing may not communicate enough for this letter and the diverse audiences that must be addressed. The language should show a management style that is forthright and direct.

One final point. To write an exceptionally good shareholder letter, *you* should be a shareholder. You should know the company. You should know the pressures and the problems the CEO faces. You should know the industry and the business context in which the company operates. Only if you know your subject and understand your CEO can you write an effective letter—a letter, by the way, that will face a barrage of revisions. Because the shareholder letter is sacred within the company, don't be surprised if it's changed, over and over again.

A message from Allen E. Murray, Chairman, Mobil Corporation

Dear Shareholder:

A year ago we sent you a booklet outlining Mobil's accomplishments and commitment to environmental excellence. We called the booklet "Protecting the environment" and, judging from your reaction, the environment is a subject of great interest and importance to many of you. It is to us, too. And to bring you up-to-date on our continuing environmental initiatives, we offer this new edition, "Protecting the environment—1990."

Our environmental efforts last year cost more than ever before—about $780 million. But striving for excellence requires more than simply throwing dollars at the environment. It takes the commitment of not just the 650 Mobil professionals who work full time on environmental, health and safety activities, but that of *all* Mobil employees.

I'm proud to say that our people understand this, believe it and put it into practice every day. That's because "Protecting the environment" is an integral part of my job and the job of every other Mobil employee, as well.

Allen E. Murray
Chairman, Mobil Corporation

1990: Building on nearly four decades of environmental achievement . . .
In 1990, Mobil strengthened its long-standing formal commitment to environmental protection. Management approved an even more stringent corporate policy which calls for minimizing emissions, discharges and wastes wherever technically and economically feasible. The new policy encourages initiatives in pollution prevention—through source reduction and recycling—to eliminate emissions and waste *before* they become a problem. This builds on our essential practice of proper waste management, including environmentally sound treatment, storage and disposal.

With this mandate, Mobil departments, divisions and affiliates worldwide are establishing even more ambitious goals, encouraging more technology development and transfer, and regularly reviewing their accomplishments.

The policy calls for plants and facilities to handle raw material and products in a manner which protects the environment and to work with suppliers, customers and the public to resolve problems created by the

2

In 1990, Mobil strengthened its long-standing formal commitment to environmental protection.

handling and disposal of hazardous substances wherever possible.

It also calls for employees to be kept informed of this policy and directs them to prevent and minimize emissions, discharges and wastes in planning, setting objectives, and in their day-to-day jobs.

Adoption of an umbrella corporate policy gives new rigor to achieving the goal we've pursued for nearly four decades—a cleaner and healthier environment. On the following pages are highlights of our environmental accomplishments in 1990—examples of how we're meeting that goal.

We made major advances in recycling used motor oil, plastic grocery bags and foam packaging . . .
A Mobil program introduced in 1990 helps motorists dispose of used oil safely and will raise national awareness about recycling. In Florida and the Washington/Baltimore area, participating Mobil service stations began accepting used motor oil and arranging for it to be transported to oil recyclers. Several hundred more dealers are participating in our consumer education campaign.

3

FIGURE 26–9.
Section from a well presented brochure describing the Mobil Corporation's environmental policy. *(Courtesy of Mobil Corporation.)*

Press Releases

In addition to customers and investors—those groups often overlap—companies also communicate with the public at large. One form of communication is advertising. The advertising may be broad-based, like billboards on highways, or targeted, as in direct-mail solicitations. Another form of company-based communication is the press release circulated to newspapers and magazines, radio, and television.

The goal of a press release (or a series of releases) is to promote the goodwill of the media and to maintain name recognition. A release may cover such events as the appointment of a new president, the promotion of a key employee, the acquisition of another company, the sale of a division, the expansion of a plant, the resolution of a legal action, an invitation to an open house, the sponsorship of a softball team, or the sponsorship of research. Figure 26–10 is a press release announcing a promotion. People experienced with press releases, both writers and readers, would recognize the style and

British Classics
Lakewood, Louisiana

For immediate release:

British Classics of Lakewood, Louisiana, announced today the promotion of Henry Blakely to the position of President and Chief Operating Officer.

Mr. Blakely joined the company in 1978 as Sales Manager after fourteen years in the automobile sales field throughout Louisiana. A native of Dallas, Texas, he graduated from Rice University in 1962 with a degree in business administration and served in the U.S. Army in Germany as a Staff Specialist in purchasing. Mr. Blakely is married to the former Julie Watts. He is a member of the Rotary of Lakewood and served as director of its Youth Sports Activities Program. He owns and services several classic British sportscars and is active in the Sports Car Club of America.

Mr. Blakely said, "I am honored by my appointment as President of British Classics and look forward to working with the very dedicated staff of this great company and with our many customers nationwide. I pledge to continue the excellent service that has been the hallmark of British Classics under my predecessor, Ryan Tatum. Our company has a great future."

Mr. Tatum retires from the presidency after eight years and will continue to live in the Lakewood area. He remains a director of British Classics.

British Classics, founded in 1960, imports British Leyland and other fine automobiles from the United Kingdom. It offers sales and service on all makes of British cars, including Jaguars, Rovers, Austins, and the popular Land Rover and Range Rover four-wheel-drive recreational vehicles.

Contact: Henry Lukens, Public Relations, 504-636-3588

FIGURE 26–10.
A typical press release.

content here immediately, even without the "for immediate release" line. It's obviously positive—about Blakely, about Tatum, about British Classics. To gain attention and provide personality, it includes a quotation (perhaps real, probably something invented by the writer). It gives the company's background. It identifies a contact person for follow-up questions and confirmation. Such releases find their way to local newspapers and radio and TV stations; they also go to trade publications and alumni offices.

Writing and circulating press releases is, of course, a specialized function

A GLIMPSE AT PR IN THE 21ST CENTURY*

Wilma K. Mathews
PR and Advertising Director, AT&T Network Systems

Publications editors who would not have accepted a faxed news release a few years ago now insist on them. Faxes have speeded up the sending of releases and increased their numbers. The next step will be individual electronic delivery. You'll send a release from your computer to an editor's computer, and you'll edit together.

You'll also use satellite transmission to hold press tours and news conferences live, simultaneously, in London, New York, California, and Tokyo. International journalists can tour your facility on a live television walk-through.

Beware the wonders of technology, however. Editors and reporters will need the reassurance of personal service to offset the cold impartiality of high-tech equipment. Don't let the technology replace you; let it enhance you.

Audiences, too, have come to expect sensationalism from the media. We've all become technological voyeurs, peering through the camera lens into the courtroom to hear live testimony in murder trials and into patrol cars to participate in drug busts. Audiences look at stories

typically falling to people who have an eye for media events and know the right people in the media. Trained and experienced public relations people cultivate contacts in the press, arrange for special tours, schedule press conferences on major news, and generally develop the publications program that ensures a positive company image—and ensures that the image will be kept in the public eye. In "*FYI:* A Glimpse at PR in the 21st Century," you see a brief picture of some changes that technology produces in both the methods of delivering corporate information and the audiences who will receive that information.

SUMMARY

- **Internal corporate documents** serve to **define** the organization (in goal statements, policy statements, and strategic plans), to **control** activities (in, for example, operational plans), and, finally, to **maintain** the corporate house in good order.
- A **strategic plan** translates goals and standards into a broad agenda for action. It details behavior to meet the plan. That agenda is then converted into an **operational plan** that sets specific tasks. In the plan, those tasks are scheduled, and measures for their accomplishment are established.
- Employee publications aid in disseminating and interpreting management's goals and strategies for the organization as well as in enhancing employees' goodwill and sense of teamwork and pride in the organization's accomplishments.
- Companies address a variety of external audiences, including customers, investors, government agencies, and the public at large.
- By law, publicly held companies in the United States and Canada must

for their shock value rather than their issues; you have to work that much harder to make the issues understood.

Audiences are also increasingly tolerant of disaster. The first earthquake was horrifying to watch; the photos from the second one looked like those from the first one. What's causing this growing acceptance of disasters is a surreal juxtaposition of fact and fantasy. On "Dallas," an oil spill was cleaned up in three weeks; we don't understand why we can't do the same in Alaska. We also no longer have time to anticipate bad news. The bad news arrives in real-time broadcasts from anywhere in the world. A political assassination on the movie of the week is interrupted by news of a real assassination.

You have to address a public that craves sensationalism, avoids complex issues, and gets its information and forms its opinions from 10-second sound bites.

* The comments are adapted from remarks delivered to the International Association of Business Communicators.

produce quarterly and year-end statements disclosing certain financial and market information. The **annual report** is usually given special attention as companies keep investors informed, attract new investors, recruit new hires, and otherwise promote themselves. A good annual report is both honest and clear. It accurately assesses the company's year in financial and managerial terms and presents the assessment in words, pictures, and numbers that are readable and attractive.

EXERCISES

For Discussion

1. What is the *goal* of your college or university? Where would you look for a goal statement? Review the brochures, videotapes, and catalogs produced by your school. In class, jointly develop a one- or two-sentence statement of the goal of your college or university.
2. The vision or culture of your school may find its most direct expression in the brochures and videotapes used to recruit students. If the admissions office of your school has such a tape, view it in class. Then discuss the assumptions the presentation makes about the intended audience, the use of visuals in the tape, and the message the tape sends concerning the goal of your school. Is it the same message you came up with in the documents you reviewed for Exercise 1? If there are inconsistencies, can they be explained?
3. As a student and probably as an employee of some organization, you have read documents that perform housekeeping tasks: parking regulations, dormitory regulations, regulations for the use of such facilities as gyms and classrooms, regulations on smoking and the drinking of alcoholic beverages, dress codes, telephone authorizations, and the like. Collect a sample of such documents to discuss in class. Who is the intended

audience? Do the language and structure of the documents meet that audience's expectations and needs? What vision of the organization as a whole comes through these documents? How do the documents serve the organization's goals? What is the method for distributing the documents—and is that method appropriate?

4. In her *FYI,* Wilma Mathews paints a somewhat stark picture of audience expectations in the 21st century. Do you agree with her description? Find evidence in the media that either supports or contradicts her prediction. How important do you think the electronic media will be in disseminating business news? How will electronic transmission affect that news?

For Writing

5. A major source of business information is the annual reports of publicly held companies in the United States and Canada. Write an analysis of one such report from a company that interests you.[3] Focus on four areas: content, illustrations, format and layout, and readability.

    a. *Content*
    What does the report discuss? New projects? New products? Progress or expansion of existing projects and products? Financial prospects? Environmental issues? Government regulations? Ethical issues? Accomplishments of a single individual or of teams within the company? Company plans and goals? Try to quantify the content. For example, if the report is 24 pages long, how many pages are devoted to descriptions of products? Summarize the "corporate image" the report projects.

    b. *Illustrations*
    How many pages are visuals? (Contrast that number with the number of pages of text.) What do the visuals picture—people, buildings, scenery, technical equipment? What size are the visuals (double-page, full page, half, quarter)? Where are they located? Are they black-and-white or color? What kind of captions do they have? What is the purpose of individual photographs and of photography as a whole in the publication?

    c. *Format and Layout*
    What is the publication's size (dimensions and number of pages)? How wide are the margins? How much of each page is taken up with text and illustrations? What design elements does the report feature?

    d. *Readability*
    Does the publication seem to have a plan? Who is the report's intended audience? Is the company widely held? How readable are the text and visuals? Review Chapters 4, 5, 6, and 7 to answer that last question.

For Collaboration

6. Assemble a team to analyze and summarize the financial, the visual, and the verbal content of one corporate annual report, preferably the report

[3] This assignment is adapted from one created by Rebecca Worley. Used by permission.

of a company that has experienced some difficulties in the year of the report. Other teams will summarize the same report. Deliver the summaries orally in class. Note any discrepancies in the summaries. Is the report deliberately evasive? Does it contradict itself? Do the pictures and the financial data tell different stories? Does the auditor's letter contain any cautions about the company's financial health?

7. Collaborate with two or three other students in your class to create a newsletter for some campus organization or small business you may be associated with. Include information about the organization and its members and about activities, policies, or national news that may have local implications for you. Use a wordprocessing program to develop a good use of type fonts, typefaces, and layout. Use graphics and a more sophisticated desktop publishing system, if they are available.

HANDBOOK

ERROR MESSAGES
- Faulty Agreement
- Fragments
- Lack of Parallelism
- Misplaced Modifiers
- Dangling Modifiers
- Shifts in Point of View
- Shifty or Missing Subjects
- Mixed Metaphors

PUNCTUATION
- The Comma
- The Semicolon
- The Colon
- The Dash
- Parentheses
- Brackets
- The Period
- The Exclamation Point
- Quotation Marks
- The Apostrophe
- The Hyphen
- Underlining and Boldface

ABBREVIATION, CAPITALIZATION, AND NUMBER USE
- Abbreviation
- Capitalization
- Numbers

FREQUENTLY MISUSED WORDS AND PHRASES

Business Communication emphasizes how to set up your writing so that your prose is *right:* efficiently composed and effectively read. Sometimes in the process, however, things do go wrong. Chapter 7 discusses strategies for revising troublesome drafts at the macro- and microlevels to increase readability. This brief handbook notes some quick guidelines for detecting errors—"error messages" like those you receive on a terminal when the computer can't read your instructions—and for correcting them. Be aware of signs that indicate a reader may have trouble deciphering your message.

In addition, the handbook provides generally accepted conventions of punctuation, abbreviation, capitalization, and number use. Such conventions vary from organization to organization; if the group you are part of adheres to different usage, observe its guidelines. Finally, the handbook notes some frequently misused words and phrases and the correct usage.

ERROR MESSAGES

Faulty Agreement

A sentence's subject must agree in number with its verb. A pronoun must agree with its antecedent (the noun it substitutes for). Check in revision to make sure that intervening words have not caused you to pull the sentence elements out of agreement. Some rules often violated:

• Connective phrases like *together with, as well as,* and *in addition to* do not change the number of the subject:

`A list of courses, along with the names of all instructors and the locations of all classes, is attached.` [The subject is *list,* a singular.]

• A collective noun takes a singular verb when the group is thought of as a unit and a plural verb to emphasize the individuals in the group:

```
The number of case studies assigned is large.
A number of case studies were analyzed in class.
```

• When *or* or *nor* connects two or more subjects, the verb agrees with the noun closest to it:

```
Neither the accounting firm nor the internal auditors
were responsible.

Neither the internal auditors nor the accounting firm was
responsible.
```

• Singular verbs are required by such singular pronouns as *another, anybody, anyone, anything, each, either, everyone, everybody, everything, neither, nobody, nothing, one, somebody, someone,* and *something:*

```
Each of the teams has its own style of play.
```

• A pronoun must have a clear antecedent with which it agrees in number:

Error: A manager should not interview a subordinate in his or her office. (*Whose* office?)
One correction: The manager's own office is not the right place in which to interview a subordinate.

Fragments

A fragment is a group of words that looks like a sentence, with a capital letter at the beginning and a period at the end, but that lacks an essential sentence element—a subject or a finite form of a verb. Some fragments are acceptable for emphasis:

> You'd think that after 50 hours at the terminal, you'd have a working program. *Wrong again.*

Most of the time, fragments are errors that mislead the reader and indicate a careless author. Avoid them in formal writing:

Error: The reason being that industrial growth did not outpace the inflation rate. [This statement lacks a finite verb, that is, one that shows person and tense.]
One correction: The reason is that industrial growth did not outpace the inflation rate.

Error: A position that has forced him to be insensitive, cold, and calculating to his staff. [This statement also lacks a finite verb.]
One correction: The position has forced him to be insensitive, cold, and calculating to his staff.

Error: A business system that enables us to manage discrete product flows from the supplier to the store shelf in a way that we will bound off people and systems and manage by standards so that a means is in place to concentrate and focus resources and assets in arenas where significant rates of change are required in 1991 and beyond to establish an enduring competitive position. [This statement, from a management consultant, lacks a verb—and lacks good sense and meaning, too.]

Lack of Parallelism

Items in a series must be equal in logic and in expression. The *logic* of the series is governed by an *enumerator term,* either expressed or understood. The *expression* of the series is governed by the first item, whose form must be followed in all other items:

Error in logic: Medical services that are not available from the college clinic include X rays, cuts and lacerations requiring sutures, broken bones, and any ailment requiring hospitalization and surgery. [The announced enumerator term here is *medical services.* X rays fit, but then the list shifts to *injuries* rather than services—without telling the reader.]

Error in logic: There is to be no smoking, eating, or bever-

ages in the conference room. [The implied enumerator here is *unacceptable behavior.* Logically, the third item should be *drinking,* but the writer felt that this word suggested a ban only on *alcoholic* beverages; soda drinkers might not think it applied to them.]
One correction: Do not smoke, eat, or drink any beverages in the conference room.

Error in logic—faulty comparison: This new power line should improve the overall efficiency of the system and decrease fuel costs because the Whitemarsh district will now be supplied with nuclear power from Peach Bottom nuclear power plant that is connected to Plymouth Meeting instead of fuel oil. [The sentence intends to compare two sources of power for the Whitemarsh district: nuclear power and fuel oil. But the balance is lost with the phrase "instead of fuel oil."]
One correction: This new power line will allow the Whitemarsh district to operate with cheap nuclear power from the Peach Bottom plant rather than with more costly fuel oil; it will thus improve the overall efficiency of the system and decrease cost.

Error in expression: Argentina (Ar) and West Germany (WG) met four times in World Cup competition. They met in the first round of the World Cup at Malmö, Sweden, in 1958: WG 3, AR 1. Then again in 1966, they met in the first round of the World Cup at Birmingham, England, and they tied, 0–0. In 1986, they met in the final of the World Cup in Mexico City, and WG lost to AR 3–2. In 1990, in Italy, WG beat AR 1–0 in the final of the World Cup there.
One correction: [A series of parallel items in sentences often becomes more emphatic and easier to read in either a formal or an informal table, as you saw in Chapter 6.]

Argentina and West Germany met four times in World Cup competition, with these results:

Date	Place	Round	Argentina	W. Germany
1958	Malmö, Sweden	1	1	3
1966	Birmingham, UK	1	0	0
1986	Mexico City	Final	3	2
1990	Rome, Italy	Final	0	1

Misplaced Modifiers

Modifiers that limit, in some way, the meaning of another word should be located in the sentence close to that word. Misplacement may well distort the meaning of the sentence:

Error: Smith questioned just how much security is required to prevent terrorism at the outset of this meeting. [Meeting participants discussed terrorism; they didn't expect an attack at the meeting.]
One correction: At the outset of the meeting, Smith questioned just how much security is required to prevent terrorism.

Error: Many arrests were possible because a suspect was observed stealing from a lookout booth. [Security agents *observed* through a lookout booth; the sentence seems to indicate that the suspect stole something from the booth.]
One correction: Many arrests were possible because agents used a lookout booth to observe suspects in the act of stealing.

Watch particularly how words like *only* change the meaning of a sentence as they move about. Each of the following sentences has a different meaning:

The board has established guidelines regulating <u>only</u> the age of the swimmers competing in the league.
<u>Only</u> the board has established guidelines regulating the age of the swimmers competing in the league.
The board has established guidelines regulating the age of <u>only</u> the swimmers competing in the league.
The board has established guidelines regulating the age of the swimmers competing <u>only</u> in the league.

Some humor—at the author's expense—may result from misplacement:

My client has discussed your proposal to fill the drainage ditch with his partners. [Poor partners!]

Dangling Modifiers

A dangling modifier is usually a verbal, often at the beginning or the end of a sentence, that denotes an action of which the sentence's subject is not capable. Like a misplaced modifier, a dangler can be the source of unintentional humor:

I saw the owl <u>driving down the road</u>. [Presumably the owl wasn't driving.]

The mouse was caught <u>using the trap</u>. [To catch the homeowner?]

<u>After trudging through alder thickets, muskeg, and rain-swollen marshes to reach the railroad</u>, the big diesel came into sight almost immediately. [Comments one reader, "Footsore, but glad to see rails again."]

<u>When making a sundae</u>, the chopped toppings are sprinkled over the ice cream. [The *toppings* don't *make* the sundae—except in the sense of making it delicious.]

Here are some other danglers and corrections:

Error: Made of 100 percent cotton, styled in two of cotton's favorite fabrics, the special stone-washing process has left these shirts feeling wonderfully soft. [The subject of this sentence is *process*. The modifying phrases beginning with *made* and *styled* express actions that a "process" can't achieve. The modifiers dangle. They should be attached to *shirts*.]
One correction: Made of 100 percent cotton, styled in two

of cotton's favorite fabrics, these shirts have further been made wonderfully soft by the stone-washing process.

Error: Driving down the streets of the suburbs, nothing looks out of place.
One correction: A drive down the streets of the suburbs reveals nothing out of place.
Another correction: As I drive down the streets of the suburbs, I see nothing out of place.

Error: After placing the order, the food was promptly delivered.
Corrected: I received my food soon after I placed the order.

Error: In order to organize the cash flow problem, new procedures were needed to keep track of spending.
Corrected: To organize the cash flow, we needed new procedures to keep track of spending.

Shifts in Point of View

Point of view is the author's way of looking at a subject in a sentence, a paragraph, and a whole document. In the whole document, consistency in point of view requires careful control of the logic of the presentation. At the sentence and paragraph level, consistency requires the careful control of pronouns, voice (active and passive), and tense:

Shift in number: An accountant plays many roles. They quantify the value system of the company. They keep records of expenditures. An accountant also makes sure expenditures and receipts are recorded and manipulated according to generally accepted principles. [This paragraph shifts from *an accountant* to *they* and back to *an* again. The subjects should be consistently either singular or plural.]

Shift in person: Warning! Don't park in unmarked spaces. Violators will be tagged and towed at your expense. [This warning, on a parking receipt, shifts from *you* to *violators* and then back to *you*—but with the second *you* covering *all violators,* clearly not what's meant.]

Shift in person: Managers should attend the meetings if you want to.
Corrected: Managers should attend the meetings if they want to.

Shift in tense: No sooner had the meeting ended than the president arrives. [The sentence sets up actions in the past and should continue in the past.]
Corrected: No sooner had the meeting ended than the president arrived.

Shift in tense: First, we sent the form to the computing office. They look it over and approve it. Then, with their approval, we sent it on to purchasing, which sends it out for competitive bidding. [These sentences mix the past tense (what we *did*) with the present (what these offices *do*). Each approach is fine separately, but the writer should choose either the *present* tense consistently, to show the general routing of the form, or the *past* tense consistently, to show what happened with this one form submitted in the past.]

Shift in voice: The president rushed us into writing the report, and we were asked by him to present it Wednesday. [The sentence shifts from the active, *rushed,* to the passive, *were asked.*]
Corrected: The president rushed us into writing the report and asked us to present it Wednesday.

Shift in voice: "Category killer" stores are described in a Journal article, and the article discussed Ikea as one such store.
Corrected: A Journal article describes "category killer" stores and discusses Ikea as one such store.

Shifty or Missing Subjects

When a writer changes subjects in midsentence without telling the reader about the substitution, confusion often results:

Shift in subject: Pizza Headquarters promises to deliver its pizzas within 30 minutes after placing an order; otherwise, it will give the purchaser a discount. [The subject is *Pizza Headquarters,* but the *purchaser* places the order.]

Omission of subject in second clause: On January 6, the ABC Board of Directors declared the regular quarterly dividend of $.12 per common share payable on January 29 to shareholders of record January 18 and is enclosed. [Problem: *What* is enclosed?]

Mixed Metaphors

Figurative language is useful, particularly in documents for popular audiences, but the images must be consistent. Be careful to analyze the roots of clichés:

Mixed metaphor: Planning has blossomed and percolated during the past decade and now occupies an important niche in the public eye. [This sentence derails on inconsistent images: *blossom, percolate, niche,* and *eye.*]

Mixed metaphor: The investor fell victim to a window of opportunity.

PUNCTUATION

Punctuation helps a writer tell a reader how to read the discussion: what belongs with what and what needs to be emphasized or subordinated. It paces the reading. Like words themselves, punctuation is an element of a writer's style. Here are some generally accepted rules for punctuating. But within guidelines for *correctness,* a writer makes personal choices to achieve clarity for the reader.

The Comma

Commas are relatively soft marks of punctuation used under certain circumstances to separate one part of a sentence from another or to enclose a sentence element. In current practice, good writers tend to use commas sparingly.

Use a single comma:

1. To separate two independent clauses in a compound sentence when the second clause begins with a coordinating conjunction (*and, but, or, for, nor, yet*):

> Magee set a still-untouched record of 2,242 career points, and he was a Boston Celtic draft choice in 1963.

Omit the comma if the two clauses are short:

> He is handsome and he is wise.

2. To set off introductory phrases and clauses:

> After reading the proposal, the sponsor fainted.

3. To separate items in a series of more than two:

> The writers' poll routinely came up with these college soccer teams as the best in the country: Hartwick, UCLA, American University, University of Virginia, Indiana, and Clemson. [Note: Practice varies, but in business writing, a comma is generally used before the final *and.*]

4. To separate two or more adjectives, each of which modifies a noun independently:

> durable, cool, breatheable wear [*Test:* Use a comma if you could logically place an *and* between the adjectives.]

5. To separate the year from the month and day, and the state from the city:

> September 17, 1991 [*But:* "17 September 1991" and "September 1991."]
>
> Acton, Maine

6. To indicate the omission of a word or phrase:

> The accounting department brought coleslaw; logistics, ham salad.

Use a pair of commas:

1. To enclose interrupters and parenthetical expressions:

I will, of course, be happy to come to your office for an interview at your convenience.

He always gives 100 percent, that is, when his own best interests demand it.

2. To enclose nonrestrictive modifiers or appositives. A modifier or appositive is *restrictive* when it is essential to the meaning of the sentence. The modifying elements underlined in these sentences are restrictive and are thus not set off:

The woman who is walking toward us is my boss.

The statistical package that runs on our mainframe system still has some bugs in it.

If you are merely adding parenthetical information, however, you do set the modifier off with commas. The modifiers underlined in these sentences are *nonrestrictive:*

My boss, who is walking toward us, is fairly capable.

The PASS statistical package, which runs on our mainframe system, still has some bugs in it.

Do *not* use a comma:

1. To separate the subject of the sentence from the verb:

Error: The development of an organizational focus on areas of strategic business importance, marks a turning point in a corporation's profile.

2. To separate a compound verb:

Error: Ben and Jerry's "Butter pecan brickle fudge ripple" ice cream whets the appetite, and enchants the mind.

The Semicolon

The semicolon indicates a stronger separation of sentence elements than the comma. Use a semicolon:

1. To separate two closely related independent clauses not joined by a coordinating conjunction:

The first half was played in constant rain; the second half was played in constant sunshine.

In the beginning of the summer, she spent her time sailing and swimming; by summer's end, she was devoted to the sailboard, which she rode from dawn to dusk, tacking back and forth across the pond, carving a sleek and silent path across the water.

A *comma fault* or *comma splice* (the terms denote the same error) results if a comma is used between two independent clauses unconnected by a conjunction:

Comma fault: The athletic director thought he was a good writer, he always elected himself spokesperson for the faculty.

2. To separate independent clauses joined by such conjunctive adverbs as *however, nonetheless,* and *consequently* and phrases like *on the other hand:*

She studied hard every day and did all the homework; nonetheless, she failed the final exam and thus failed the course.

3. To separate items in a list when the items themselves are also punctuated:

He arrived at the campsite with an axe (purchased at EMS for $25); an outfit including shorts, hiking boots, shirt, and hat, all of the latest fashion and obviously recently purchased at L.L.Bean; and a fear of the wilderness that no amount of reading and conversation could abate.

The Colon

The colon builds anticipation while it marks (more strongly than a comma or semicolon) a division in sentence elements. Use a colon:

1. To precede examples, equations, explanations, illustrations, lists, quotations, and the like after an expressed enumerator term:

The planning phase is divided into three steps:

1. Worrying
2. Brainstorming options
3. Prioritizing options

She scheduled division meetings for four dates: 10 October, 16 October, 3 November, and 18 November.

Do not separate a verb and its objects with a colon:

Error: The three most common errors are: faulty diction, faulty spelling, and faulty punctuation. [To correct, simply delete the colon.]

2. To separate two clauses when the second expands on or amplifies the first:

All this concern about readability can be summed up in one statement: The document works.

The first letter of the word following the colon is usually capitalized only if the second clause is a complete sentence, but usage varies. Consult the style guide of the organization you work for. Be consistent in any one document.

3. To mark the end of the greeting in a formal letter:

```
Dear Professor Frawley:
```

The colon is a formal mark; an informal greeting usually ends in a comma:

```
Dear Bill,
```

Never use a semicolon after a greeting.

The Dash

The dash is a fairly informal mark that sometimes replaces a semicolon, a colon, or parentheses. A dash can be brisk and effective, just what you need, but use it with caution:

```
There is no more valuable lesson for the student than ob-
serving the research process firsthand and--even more im-
portant--participating in it.
```

Parentheses

Always used as a pair, parentheses subordinate material within a sentence and serve some conventional functions in documentation. Note that the period is placed outside the final parenthesis if the parenthetical expression is part of another sentence; inside, if the parenthetical expression is a sentence in itself. Here are some examples of the use of parentheses:

The Early Avalanche Warning Program (EAWP)

Our profit picture remains bright (Figure 1). [*But* Figure 1 shows a bright profit picture.]

Our profit picture remains bright. (Figure 1 shows a chart of profitability over the last five years.)

The Acton (Maine) Landfill permit . . .
Manual of Professional Practice (New York: Macmillan, 1991).

Never place a comma immediately before either the opening or the closing parenthesis. The parentheses alone properly enclose the sentence element:

Error: Such an approach, (each person trying to usurp control of the meeting) was typically American, or so they thought.

Brackets

Brackets enclose interpolations or comments that a writer inserts within quoted material or parenthetical statements inserted within a text already in parentheses. Some documentation systems also require the use of brackets:

```
"With his dynamic and graceful play, Diego [Maradona]
carried the day for Argentina."

(See the complete explanation of funds accounting [Refer-
ence 5] for a more detailed discussion.)
```

The Period

A period marks the end of a sentence. Many consultants on writing say only half in jest that the period is the most underused mark of punctuation. Beyond ending a sentence, other uses of the period are less fixed, but in general:

1. Use a period with nontechnical abbreviations:

```
Mr., Fig., Dr., Vol.
```

2. Use a period when an abbreviation spells a word:

```
in., no., sect.
```

The Exclamation Point

The exclamation point puts an emotional finish to a sentence. It tells the reader that the writer is (or wants to appear to be) excited or surprised, and that the reader should respond similarly. Exclamation points are common in sales messages:

```
You may already have won!
You'll never see an offer like this again!
Productivity is up to a record level in the third quar-
ter!
```

The exclamation point, however, is generally considered too colloquial and too pushy for reports and other routine and sober business documents.

Quotation Marks

Quotation marks enclose directly quoted material:

```
"The players were tight," noted Loren Kline, the soccer
coach. "They kept trying for the perfect play rather than
relaxing and making the easy play."
```

By American convention, periods and commas belong *inside* the final quotation mark, even though they are not part of the original material; question marks, exclamation points, semicolons, and colons belong *outside* quotation marks, unless they are part of the quoted material:

```
He had what his supervisor termed "an intuitive grasp of
finance"; he could sniff out phony balance sheets without
doing any arithmetic.
```

An exception to this usage occurs when quotation marks surround a command in computer documentation. In that case, *all* other punctuation is put *outside* the quotation marks to prevent a misreading that the comma, for example, is part of the command. Quotation marks may also be used to enclose certain elements in a reference citation (see Appendix: Documenting Sources of Information):

```
D. P. Richardson, "Duel Career Marriages: An Exercise in
the Fine Art of Fencing," The Journal of Personality, 11
(1991) 64–82.
```

The Apostrophe

The apostrophe indicates possession. It can make a real difference in the meaning of a word or phrase. For example, this headline appeared in *The New York Times:*

```
Queens Grandmother Wins Lottery
```

As it stands, the headline means that a grandmother in Queens, a borough of New York City, won. With an apostrophe, however, *(Queen's)*, the lottery would have gone to the grandmother of the queen. Make sure you use the apostrophe where necessary:

1. Use the apostrophe plus *s* to form the possessive of nouns, abbreviations, and acronyms:

```
the college's campus; the book's cover; the company's im-
age; GE's approach; DCA's style
```

Form the possessive of a singular that ends in *s* by adding *'s.*

```
Professor Andrews's textbook
```

[*Note:* The possessive of *it* is *its,* with *no apostrophe. It's* is a contraction for *it is.*]

2. Use the apostrophe *after* the *s* of plural nouns:

```
the nations' joint approach; the companies' joint action
```

3. To show joint possession, use an apostrophe and an *s* added to the last member of the group; indicate separate possession by an *s* added to each member:

```
Frawley and Bowen's article was widely cited.
Frawley's and Bowen's priorities differ markedly.
```

The apostrophe is not used to form normal plurals, nor with plurals of a date or an all-capital abbreviation:

```
books; companies; the 1990s; IRAs; 5s; As
```

The Hyphen

Where such other marks of punctuation as commas, semicolons, and periods *separate* items, the hyphen *connects*. It connects two or more words that form a compound noun and two or more words that form a compound adjective before a noun.

1. Hyphenate compound nouns. Such forms are often transitional ones as two separate words grow together. No general rules apply; just be consistent in any one document and adhere to the conventions of your organization. Here are a few examples:

```
know-how
a merry-go-round of mergers
a Mercedes-Benz
```

2. Hyphenate compound numbers from 21 through 99 when they are spelled out:

```
fifty-five
twenty-nine
```

3. Hyphenate compound adjectives that express a unified idea and precede the noun:

```
a high-tech future
full-page advertisements
135-year-old sewing-machine business
seven-inch-thick file
private-sector financing
deficit-cutting move
small-business owners
Indiana-based program
truth-in-lending laws
```

The hyphen is not used if the compound is easily read without it or is a proper noun:

`government-licensed` [hyphen for clarity] `venture capital`
[no hyphen] `companies`
`New York-based broker` [no hyphen between "New" and "York"]

The hyphen is also not used if the first word is an adverb ending in *ly* or a comparative form:

```
a recently developed plan
a more convincing approach
```

4. Hyphenate words divided at the end of a line and carried to the next line. Divide only between syllables (check a dictionary for correct syllabication).

Underlining and Boldface

Underlining and boldface are both used to highlight certain words and phrases in a text. Computer text processing makes such usage easy. Traditionally, an underlined passage in manuscript has been printed in italics in the published document, but that distinction is fading as computer text processing allows the writer to create *both* underlining and italics for final printing from a terminal. Consult standard sources like the *MLA Handbook,* published by the Modern Language Association, or *The Chicago Manual of Style,* published by the University of Chicago Press, for advice about the use of italics or underlining in footnotes and bibliographies. In addition, use underlining:

1. To set off a word being defined or discussed as a word:

   In this report, we use the word organization to refer to a company of more than 500 employees.

2. To designate words from a foreign language:

   His middle years were punctuated with a Weltschmertz that his den full of trophies could not alleviate.

3. To highlight important information:

   If he had not responded to the request that very minute he would never have joined the firm.

Don't overdo underlining. Too much underlining screams at the readers and may deafen them.

Use boldface:

1. To set off certain headings in a text, usually chapter titles and first-order heads (underlining may also be used for headings at other levels; see Chapter 7):

   CHAPTER ONE: DAWN

2. To highlight material in a text as an alternative to underlining. Again, be cautious, and don't overdo.

ABBREVIATION, CAPITALIZATION, AND NUMBER USE

Abbreviation

One obvious sign of business writing, particularly the writing of bureaucracies, is an abundance of acronyms (as you saw in Chapter 5) and other abbreviations. Such shorthand alone may make a text unintelligible to outsiders. Use abbreviations, of course, but be consistent in their use. And if you have reason to think that *any* of the readers of your report may not understand a particular abbreviation, write out the word or phrase. Here are some general guidelines:

1. Use commonly accepted acronyms for the names of groups or organizations. No periods are used, and the letters are typed with no spaces

between them. In internal communication, the acronym alone is probably enough. For external communication, give the full title and the acronym at the first mention:

For an insider: `RE: PPD update`
For an outsider: `The Packaged Products Division (PPD) rolled up a record year in 1991.`

2. Use an abbreviation for a long word or phrase to be repeated frequently in a report as long as you explain the full phrase at the first mention:

```
Our profitability picture was enhanced this year by our
new Pride in Excellence (PIE) program and our highly vis-
ible PIE charts.
```

3. Use standard abbreviations after numbers denoting a definite quantity. In general, the abbreviation is used in the singular only, and without periods (exceptions: *figs., vols., nos.*):

```
256k RAM; 2000 rpm; a 10-k race
```

4. Form the plural of an uppercase acronym by adding a lowercase *s* (no apostrophe):

```
CRTs, FTEs
```

Capitalization

Be sparing, conventional, and consistent in your use of capital letters. Capitalize:

1. The first word of a sentence.

2. The first word of a direct quotation when the quoted material begins a sentence:

```
The coach said, "Relax, boys. This is a piece of cake."
```

An indirect quotation is not capitalized:

```
The coach told the team to relax because the game would
be a "piece of cake."
```

3. The first letter of certain words in report titles and section headings (be consistent).

4. Most proper nouns, including titles, names of languages, companies, peoples, races, political parties, religions, historical periods, states, cities, countries, and geographic regions. Sometimes *the* is part of a company or university name and is also capitalized:

```
The Ohio State University
```

5. Registered trademarks, whether used as nouns or adjectives:

```
a Xerox® copier
```

6. Common nouns when used in certain specialized senses. For example, some companies refer to themselves throughout a text as *The Company.* In some reports, the terms *Figure* and *Table* are capitalized. Again, consult the style guide for your organization and be consistent.

Numbers

Much business information is expressed in numbers, often in tabular form. Here are some general guidelines for using numbers in the text itself. Again, styles of presentation differ markedly from company to company. Conform to whatever standards are set and be consistent:

1. Don't start a sentence with a number; rephrase the sentence or write the number out.

2. Use arabic numerals unless your organization's style guide recommends, for example, writing out numbers through nine and using numerals above that number:

```
He bought only nine PCs even though his division has more
than 50 employees.
```

3. Write out approximations or indefinite measurements:

```
About one hundred people attended the picnic.
```

4. Use arabic numbers for figures and tables:

```
Figure 10; Table 4
```

5. Present all sums of money in arabic numbers. Repeat the symbol for the currency in a series. For figures over a million, indicate the multiplier in numerals and the zeros in a word (*thousand, million,* and so on):

```
£250
$40
He collected the following amounts: $1200 (from Account-
ing); $1500 (from Logistics); and $4500 (from Mainte-
nance).
$60 million
```

6. Use numerals for the days but not the months in dates:

`May 10, 1991` [*Not* "5/10/91"; the use of numerals is informal and potentially confusing in an international context, as European countries, for example, reverse the order of the day and month common in the U.S.: "May 10, 1991" would be "10/5/91."]

FREQUENTLY MISUSED WORDS AND PHRASES

Words and phrases in the documents of organizational life must be *precise.* The misuse of words may confuse or mislead the reader. Here are some commonly misused terms; add to this list any you know you are apt to use incorrectly.

Adapt/Adopt/Adept

Adapt means to modify:

Adapt these planning methods to fit your own composing style.

Adopt means to take over:

We adopted the PERT planning technique in our department.

Adept, an adjective, means skillful:

He is adept at planning large projects.

Advice/Advise

Advice, a noun, means an opinion given on how to handle some situation:

She profited from her broker's advice.

Advise, a verb, means to give such an opinion, to suggest something:

Her broker advises her on market trends every week.

Affect/Effect

Affect is most frequently used as a verb meaning to influence:

The inflation rate affects unemployment.

Effect is most frequently used as a noun meaning a result or a consequence:

The effect of spiraling inflation was an increase in unemployment.

Affect can also be used as a noun meaning the feeling accompanying an idea; *effect* can be used as a verb meaning to bring about or cause to occur:

She effected a compromise between union and management on the right-to-work issue.

Among/Between

Among is used for more than two items; *between* is used for only two.

Assure/Ensure/Insure

All of these words mean *to make certain,* but with different connotations. *Assure* is used in the sense of making a person sure of something:

Let me assure you that I'll look over your letter today.

Ensure and *insure* suggest a guarantee against harm or failure:

An adequate budget is needed to ensure the success of the project.

Insure is used in the technical sense of guaranteeing property or life:

```
Have you insured your bike against loss or theft?
```

Case

This term is frequently overused in business documents. Save it for specific reference to, for example, a *case study* or a *legal* or *medical case.* The expression in brackets can often be substituted for the phrase on the left; sentences thus gain in brevity and precision:

```
In case [if]
In many cases [often]
In this case [here]
In all cases [always]
```

Continuous/Continual

Continuous means without interruption; *continual* means steady but with brief interruptions.

Criterion/Criteria

Criterion is singular, meaning a rule or test; *criteria* is plural, meaning a number of such rules.

Data

Data refers to observations and facts gathered in an investigation and usually used in a raw state, as opposed to *information,* which refers to interpreted data. The term *data* is technically plural (the singular, in Latin, is *datum*), but it is now begining to be thought of as a collective that takes a singular verb. Abide by the usage set by your organization.

Discreet/Discrete

People can be *discreet,* that is, careful about what they say or do; *things* and *information* can be divided into *discrete*—that is, separate—components:

```
Managers must be discreet in their attentions to employ-
ees.
We performed three discrete tasks.
```

Due to the Fact That

Avoid this phrase in formal reports because it is long and roundabout. Instead, substitute *because.*

Etc.

Avoid. Instead, begin a representative rather than inclusive list with a phrase like "such as" or "for example."

Fewer/Less

Fewer refers to numbers, *less* to degree:

```
This yogurt has fewer calories than Brand Y.
This yogurt is less fattening than Brand Y.
```

Imply/Infer

A writer *implies;* the reader *infers.* An *implication* is thus something given; an *inference* is something taken:

```
By his snickers and giggles, he implied that this train-
ing program was not to be taken seriously.
From the chatter and snickers of the participants, we in-
ferred that they didn't take this training program seri-
ously.
```

It's/Its

It's is a contraction meaning *it is; its* is the possessive form of *it:*

```
It's clear that this accounting system has outlived its
usefulness.
```

-ize Words

One sign of jargon is the creation of verbs with the ending *-ize* (*prioritize, accessorize,* and the like) from nouns. Although such usage is often accepted in conversation, refrain from it in writing.

Oral/Verbal

Oral refers to something spoken; *verbal* refers to something expressed in words, either in writing or in speech. When you say, "She has a *verbal* agreement with the vendor," all you are saying is that she has exchanged words with the vendor, either in writing or in speaking. If you mean that she has only *spoken* with the vendor and has no contract in writing, say, "She has an *oral* agreement with the vendor."

Percent/Percentage

Percent, meaning "hundredths of," should be used only after a figure; *percentage* is used to express a given part or amount of every hundred and not with a figure:

```
His car has an efficiency rating of 80 percent.
Only a small percentage of the fuel's energy is wasted.
```

Personnel/Personal

Personnel are the persons working for a given organization at a given time. *Personal* means private:

> He deals effectively with personnel issues [issues regarding employees].
> His personal life [his *private* life] is a mess.

Precede/Proceed/Procedure

Precede means to go before; *proceed* means to take action. The noun form of the verb *proceed* is *procedure:*

```
Theoretical understanding often precedes practical appli-
cation.
He gave him the green light to proceed with the case
study.
```

Respectfully/Respectively

Respectfully means with respect or deference, as in the complimentary close of a letter, "Respectfully yours." *Respectively* means in the order designated:

```
Hughes Aircraft and Boeing Helicopters contributed $5000
and $7000, respectively.
```

Respectively can become confusing, however, and forces the reader to return to the beginning of the sentence. Prefer this sentence form:

```
Hughes Aircraft contributed $5000; Boeing Helicopters,
$7000.
```

Use/Using/Utilize

These words appear too frequently in business writing when other, more precise words should activate the sentence. Eliminate as many as you can in revision.

Your/You're

Your indicates possession; *you're* is a contraction for *you are:*

```
You're about to read the last word in this handbook.
```

APPENDIX

Documenting Sources of Information

WHEN TO DOCUMENT SOURCES
WHEN TO REQUEST PERMISSION TO REPRINT MATERIAL
DOCUMENTING WRITTEN COMMUNICATIONS
Citing Published Material
Citing Unpublished Material
DOCUMENTING ORAL PRESENTATIONS

In business documents (especially reports) and in oral presentations, you need to cite the source of information used. This process is called *documentation:* You *document* or cite the origin of information. Why?

1. For ethical and legal reasons: to give proper credit to the work of others
2. For persuasive reasons: to add credibility to any claim you are making
3. For practical reasons: to allow the reader to seek additional information

When information is proprietary—that is, when it comes from and belongs to someone else—honesty requires documentation. For example, if *The Economist* hired reporters and paid their expenses to get a story, the information in the story is theirs, and if you use it you must give proper credit. (You may also need permission to reprint material, as discussed below.) Failure to give proper credit puts you in violation of the law and subjects you to legal penalties. Failure to document may also subject you to academic penalties; plagiarism, the use of someone else's material as if it were your own, is a serious offense in colleges.

Documentation is also a tool of persuasion. Quoting *The Economist* or *The Wall Street Journal* or a government report adds credibility to your case by showing people that it is based on more than your own ideas. A report that draws on the work of recognized experts published in known journals will commonly find readier acceptance than one that cites no supporting evidence or quotes unrecognized researchers.

Finally, careful documentation allows your reader to follow up on what you've said, to dig into a topic by referring to the sources you've cited. For example, while you may quote only a few statistics from a report on demographic trends in Latin America, your reader may want to learn more about the topic. Your cited sources can guide the reader to more information on the topic.

WHEN TO DOCUMENT SOURCES

Before you look at specific techniques for documentation, you need to know *when* to document. Students who are unsure of when to cite sources tend to swing to one of two extremes: providing no specific documentation at all or putting footnotes on every sentence. Common sense should help you find the balance between these two extremes. When in doubt, refer to the three reasons for documentation:

- Am I ethically or legally obliged to cite the source?
- Will my case be stronger if I refer to sources?
- Will I help my reader find more information if I document?

Three rules help:

1. Always document direct quotations.
2. Always document proprietary information, that is, specific informa-

tion (for example, statistics) that was discovered or developed by someone else.
3. Generally, document information that is not common knowledge.

The first two rules are quite clear. The third is tricky. What is "common knowledge"? It's common knowledge that the pound sterling is the official currency of the United Kingdom. You don't need to tack a note on that. But it is not common knowledge that the relationship between the pound and the Japanese yen fluctuates in indirect proportion to the fate of British cricket teams. If indeed someone has made that argument, you need to document it because few people would regard such a relationship as "common knowledge."

WHEN TO REQUEST PERMISSION TO REPRINT MATERIAL

Much published material is copyrighted; that is, it is legally protected against use by others. It is considered "intellectual property" and hence, like any other form of property, cannot be taken by others. This is true of almost all newspapers, magazines, scholarly journals, books, and reports.

Copyrighted material may not be reproduced for publication without written permission from the owner of the copyright. Many publishers require you to pay a fee for their permission to reprint material. However, the law allows for what is called "fair use." For example, prose passages of up to 250 words (but not such condensed material as tables) can generally be reprinted without specific permission.

Copyright issues are legally quite complex and may require specific advice from a specialist. However, copyright is generally applicable only if you are *publishing* the quoted material. In a report done for class use, you don't have to seek permission to reprint material even if it exceeds "fair-use" standards. You must, however, *document* the source. And if you intend to publish a report or submit an article to a journal, you need to secure formal permission from the owner of the copyrighted material you quote.

DOCUMENTING WRITTEN COMMUNICATIONS

When you prepare a written report for class or on the job and need to credit a source, you can select from two general systems of documentation: notes and references. Although they appear to be similar, notes and references are quite distinct as systems of citing sources.

(You should be aware that writers sometimes use notes for purposes other than documentation. Notes can define complex or unfamiliar terms or explain concepts or procedures. Because such explanatory notes are not intended to cite information and credit sources, they are not discussed in this appendix.)

Both notes and references are attached in the text to the specific information that comes from another source. They appear in the text as numbers, generally after the quotation reproduced or the fact cited. Notes appear as superscripts—numbers above the line of text. References generally appear on the same line but within parentheses. The number of the text note or reference is then repeated elsewhere along with the full information about the source. The number that appears in the text *refers* the reader to the full information. Notes are called *footnotes* if the information for that number is given at the foot of the page on which the text note appears. They are called *endnotes* or simply *notes* if they are accumulated at the end of the section, the chapter, or the whole document.

Should you use notes or references? The first rule in answering that question is to determine *required* or *recommended* style. Does your company insist on references? Does the journal for which you are writing a report demand notes? If one form of documentation is standard, use it. The second rule is: Be consistent. Once you have adopted the note system, don't slip midway in the report into the reference system. Stick with one form of documentation in each report or other written communication.

Of course if no standard exists—that is, if you are not required by corporate or other policy to use one system—you must select one of the two and use it consistently. Your choice depends on which form you feel most knowledgeable about, which one you can use with greatest ease. If you follow the technique both consistently and well, the reader will be well served by either system.

Now look at how the two systems differ. In Figure A–1, *notes* are used as the documentation system.[1] In Figure A–2, the *reference* system is used.

Notice the differences. In the *note* system, the text notes appear as superscripts. The information to which they refer appears at the foot of the page. The numbers run consecutively through the text, from 1 to 4. Now look at the *reference* system. The text numbers are on the same line but within parentheses. The information to which they refer appears at the end of the text in a section labeled "References." The numbers do *not* run consecutively through the text. Instead, the articles are grouped *alphabetically* by the last names of the authors, and the first is numbered 1, the next 2, and so forth. Within the *text,* the numbers 3 and 4 come before the number 2. That's because the last name of the author of Number 2 comes earlier in the alphabet.

Confused? It's really a simple system once you get the hang of it. But just to make things a bit more confusing, consider that some reference systems group articles by the *year of publication* rather than alphabetically by the author's last name. The numbers then run consecutively (from 1 to whatever) within the reference section, but within the text you may go from 8 to 3 to 9 before coming to 1. The reason is that the text numbers *refer* the reader to the grouped items under "References," and these items are arranged by date of publication.

The difference: Note numbers run consecutively in the text; reference numbers run consecutively not in the text but in the collection of items,

[1] The material in Figures A–1 and A–2 is from Jerry Harr and Sharon Kossack, "Employee Benefit Packages: How Understandable Are They?" *Journal of Business Communication,* 27 (1990), 185. Reprinted by permission of the authors.

While business communication traditionally focused on the composition of personally transmitted messages (e.g., letters, speeches), recent years have witnessed increasing attention to various forms of "mass" business communication. Employee publications, annual reports, and benefits packages have attracted business communication scholars. For example, Clampitt, Crevcoure, and Hartel explored the nature and impact of employee publications within complex organizations.[1] The extent, coverage, costs, and benefits of written corporate communication policy were analyzed by Gilsdorf.[2] Another study assessed the gender representation in corporate annual reports.[3] The effectiveness of contemporary corporate annual report prose communication was studied by another researcher, who found his sample of 65 Canadian annual reports to be beyond the fluent comprehension ease of 92 percent of the adult population and 56 percent of the investor population.[4]

Notes

[1] P. G. Clampitt, J. M. Crevcoure, and R. L. Hartel, "Exploratory Research on Employee Publications," The Journal of Business Communication, 23 (1986), 5–17.

[2] J. W. Gilsdorf, "Written Corporate Communication Policy: Extent, Coverage, Costs, Benefits," The Journal of Business Communication, 24 (1987), 32–52.

[3] S. Kuiper, "Gender Representation in Corporate Annual Reports and Perception of Corporate Climate," The Journal of Business Communication, 25 (1988), 87–93.

[4] J. K. Courtis, "Fry, Smog, Lix, and Rix: Insinuations about Corporate Business Communications," The Journal of Business Communication, 24 (1987), 19–27.

FIGURE A–1.
Citations using notes. *(Kossack, S., and Haar, J., "Employee Benefit Packages: How Understandable Are They?"* Journal of Business Communication 27 *(1990), p. 185.)*

which may be arranged alphabetically by author's last names or by the dates of publication of the items.

You should be aware of one other variation on the *reference* system. Sometimes the name of the author is used rather than a number. That is, the references are not numbered but instead are listed alphabetically by authors' last names, and the author's name, rather than a number, is cited in parentheses in the *text*. For example:

While business communication traditionally focused on the composition of personally transmitted messages (e.g., letters, speeches), recent years have witnessed increasing attention to various forms of "mass" business communication. Employee publications, annual reports, and benefits packages have attracted business communication scholars. For example, Clampitt, Crevcoure, and Hartel (1) explored the nature and impact of employee publications within complex organizations. The extent, coverage, costs, and benefits of written corporate communication policy were analyzed by Gilsdorf (3). Kuiper (4) assessed the gender representation in corporate annual reports. Courtis (2) found his sample of 65 Canadian annual reports to be beyond the fluent comprehension ease of 92 percent of the adult population and 56 percent of the investor population.

References

1. Clampitt, P. G., J. M. Crevcoure, and R. L. Hartel. "Exploratory Research on Employee Publications." The Journal of Business Communication, 23 (1986), 5–17.

2. Courtis, J. K. "Fry, Smog, Lix, and Rix: Insinuations about Corporate Business Communication." The Journal of Business Communication, 24 (1987), 19–27.

3. Gilsdorf, J. W. "Written Corporate Communication Policy: Extent, Coverage, Costs, Benefits." The Journal of Business Communication, 24 (1987), 35–52.

4. Kuiper, S. "Gender Representation in Corporate Annual Reports and Perception of Corporate Climate," The Journal of Business Communication, 25 (1988), 87–93.

FIGURE A–2.
Citations using references. *(Kossack, S., and Haar, J., ''Employee Benefit Packages: How Understandable Are They?''* Journal of Business Communication 27 *(1990), p. 185.)*

Research shows that 34 percent of those living in areas with potential flood problems inquire about flood insurance (Harvey). Still, flood insurance is a bargain (Lopez).

In this instance, Harvey and Lopez are authors of published material, and full citations of their works are given at the end of the section or document, labeled as ''References'' and listed (but without numbers) alphabetically by the authors' last names. The advantage of this variation in the reference system is that it avoids numbers and also shows directly within the text the authors cited. Full details are still saved for the listing at the end.

Notes and references are used in reports and other forms of written business communication to document both published and unpublished information. The details you need to supply in the note or reference depend on whether the source is published or unpublished.

Citing Published Material

When you cite published material, include the following information:

- Name of the author(s), if given
- Title of the work
- Publishing information
- Page(s) on which the information appears

The publishing information given depends on whether the published source you are citing is a book, an article, or a report. For a book, you include the publisher's name and the place and date of publication. For an article, you include the journal in which the article appeared and the date (generally only the year) of publication, but not the publisher's name or the place of publication. For a report, you include the name and location of the publisher (the sponsor or group under whose auspices the report was issued) and the date of publication.

Arranging all this information requires you to master the required or standard form of documentation you are using. There are dozens of versions, variations, and permutations. There is no one right way. The sample notes and sample references in Figure A–3 show one way. There are others. Follow one system, consistently, either the one you select or the one imposed on you.

One hint: When you gather information, be certain to record all the details that you will need to prepare either notes or references when you finally pull everything together in a report. If you know the required form of arranging the details, record them that way as you do your research because that record will make it easy to prepare the documentation. Researchers who take sloppy notes on the sources find that they do extra work, often at the very last minute, having to go back and find, for example, the place and date of a report's publication when they need to document it in their own report.

Citing Unpublished Material

Sometimes the information you need to document in a written report comes from unpublished sources, for example, interviews or surveys. Whereas there are clear standards for what details to include when you cite published material, such standards don't exist for citing unpublished material. You should be guided by the ethical, persuasive, and practical concerns that lead to documentation in the first place: What must I tell to be honest, to lend credibility to my argument, and to help the reader?

Whatever details you present, you can include them in either the note or the reference system, depending on which of these you are using. For

Sample Notes

Book	[1]Thomas J. Peters and Robert H. Waterman, Jr., In Search of Excellence: Lessons from America's Best-Run Companies (New York: Harper & Row, 1982), p. 81.
Article	[2]Bryan Burrough, "Collapse of an Old-Boy Oil Network Places Tesoro in Vulnerable Position for Takeover," The Wall Street Journal, 12 June 1984, p. 37.
Report	[3]U.S. Department of Education, The Nation Responds: Recent Efforts to Improve Education, Washington, D.C., 1984, pp. 8-12.

Sample References (in Alphabetical Arrangement)

1. Burrough, Bryan. "Collapse of an Old-Boy Oil Network Places Tesoro in Vulnerable Position for Takeover," The Wall Street Journal, 12 June 1984, 1.
2. Peters, Thomas, and Robert H. Waterman, Jr. In Search of Excellence: Lessons from America's Best-Run Companies. New York: Harper & Row, 1982.
3. U.S. Department of Education. The Nation Responds: Recent Efforts to Improve Education. Washington, D.C., 1984.

FIGURE A–3.
Sample notes and references.

example, if you are using *notes* and want to cite an interview, the note could read this way:

[1] Interview with James Harley, 23 January 199–.

As a *reference* it would appear this way:

7. Harley, James. Interview on 23 January 199–.

You can avoid a separate reference if you incorporate into the text a statement about the information. For example: "In an interview on 23 January 199-, James Harley made several observations on this subject. First, he noted. . . ."

Information obtained from a survey can be treated similarly: either with a statement in the text itself or with a note that covers the relevant section. For example, after the presentation of some information, you might attach a number referring to this note:

[5] These data were developed in a survey of 35 college students conducted in January 199– at the University of South Florida.

Or you might put a general statement in the text itself conveying the same information: "The information in this report comes from a survey of 35 college students conducted in January 199- at the University of South Florida."

If your report is based largely on a survey, some part of the report should be devoted to discussing the survey itself: how and when it was conducted, the statistical assumptions made, and so forth. From then on in the text you can omit specific documentation as long as the source is clear.

DOCUMENTING ORAL PRESENTATIONS

Once you master a consistent form, notes and references are relatively easy to do in written business communications—in reports, for example. But what do you do if you are giving a talk?

Many business presentations are based on information derived from other sources and thus also need to be documented. In a speech, if you are quoting someone, you should clearly indicate the source (by name if that is appropriate) and show through the use of your hands or voice where the quotation begins and ends. Similarly, when you use information that is not directly quoted but that is the result of someone else's work, indicate in the speech that you are now using data you found in such-and-such a report, article, or book. It's not necessary in such cases to provide all the details (title, place and date of publication, page numbers, and so forth) that you would in a written report. Source information, however, should be included in the appropriate form on any overhead or slide you use in a talk.

Documentation in a talk is oral, but be ready to back it up in writing. You should have available a list of your sources keyed to your text so you can hand it to anyone in the audience who expresses an interest or challenges a point. Some speakers like to hand out a sheet of references before or after their talk. This practice not only ensures conformity with fairness and the law but also strengthens the point you are making and enhances your credibility as a knowledgeable person who has done her or his homework. Such a list can also be helpful to members of the audience who want to pursue the topic in greater detail.

In documenting oral presentations, the same standards apply as to *why* you do it (to be honest, to be persuasive, and to help your audience) and *when* you do it (to cite quotations, proprietary information, and information not considered common knowledge).

PHOTO CREDITS

Page	
xv & xxxvi-1	© Imtek Imagineering/Masterfile
xvii & 50-51	© Tim Bieber/The Image Bank
xxii & 216-17	© Peter Garfield/The Stock Market
xxv & 320-21	© Jon Feingersh/Stock Boston
xxvii & 400-401	© Larry Dale Gordon/The Image Bank
xxix & 474-75	© William Strode/Superstock
xxxi & 526-27	Courtesy of Hercules, Inc.
5	© Akos Szilvasi/Stock Boston
6-7	Courtesy Arthur Andersen & Co., S.C.
10	Courtesy European Communities
11	© Nancy D'Antonio/Photo Researchers, Inc.
21	© William Strode/Woodfin Camp & Associates
23	Courtesy Xerox Corporation
SF-1	© Jeffrey Vordis/The Travelers Corporation
SF-2	Photo © Douglas Johns/AT&T Paradyne
SF-3	Courtesy of the Transamerica Corporation
SF-4	Courtesy Phillips Petroleum Company
SF-5	Courtesy Pfizer Inc.
SF-6	Photo © Eric Meola/Courtesy General Motors Corporation
SF-7	Photo © Steve Niedorf/Courtesy 3M
SF-8	Courtesy of The Williams Companies, Inc.
153	Courtesy of Comstock
175	© Cheryl Klauss/Innervisions
191	© W. Eastep/Stock Market
200	Turner & Devries/The Image Bank
208	© Michael Abramson/The Image Bank
226	© Jeffrey W. Myers/Stock Boston
232	© Stacy Pick, 1989/Stock Boston
346	© Lou Jones/The Image Bank
406	© Robert A. Isaac/Photo Researchers, Inc.
409	© Bobbie Kingsley/Photo Researchers, Inc.
424	© Steven Frame/Stock Boston
433	© John S. Abbott/Manhattan Inc.
451	© Sepp Seitz/Woodfin Camp & Associates
482	© Spencer Grant/Stock Boston
518	© Richard Hackett
540	© Hazel Hankin/Stock Boston

INDEX

A

Abbreviations, 588–89
Abstract, 175, 377
Abstract words, 79–80
Accounts
  letters concerning, 271
Acronyms, 83–84
  FYI, 84
  in letters, 244
  in memos, 235
Active voice, 81–82
Adaptive Process Model of Reading, 143
Adler, Nancy, 38
Address
  in letters, 250
Agenda, 433–34
Agreement
  pronoun and antecedent, 575–76
  subject and verb, 575
Ahmed, Mohammed, 413
AIDA plan (Attention, Interest, Desire, Action)
  in cover letters (letters of application), 494–97
  in sales letters, 301–305
ALICO, 454–55
American Institutes for Research, 144, 459
Analysis
  in reports, 366, 371
  as a structuring tool, 60–61
Andersen Consulting, 5
Andrews, D.C., 204–205
Andrews, W.D., 204–205
Annual reports, 564, 566–67, SF-1–SF-8
  FYI, 566–67
Apostrophe, 586
Appendix, 379
ARASERVE, 106
Arthur D. Little, Inc., 191
Asia Foundation, 437, 440
AT&T, 187, 570–71
Attention line, in letters, 250
Audience
  imagining the reader, 56–57
  for letters, 243–45, 300–301
  multiple, 57
  for presentations, 449–50
  for procedures, 531–32
  for reports, 364, 367
  role in persuasion, 24
Audiovisual equipment, 457, 462–64

B

Back matter, in formal reports, 364, 379
Bad news
  in annual reports, 566–67
  letters about, 276–93
  structuring the message, 54–56
Bailey, Jon, 303–304
Bar charts, 107–108, 113–15
Battelle Memorial Institute, 345
Baxter Healthcare Corporation, 254–57, 423, 438–39

Beamer, Linda, 368–69
Behavior guidelines, 541
Bell, Crystal, 566–67
Berret, Beth, 481
Bibliographies, 379
Bids, 324, 326–28
  guidelines for preparing, 326–28
Bilingual publications, 45, 241–42, 267, 437, 442–43
  FYI, 45
Block style in letters, 48, 253, 291
Body language, 25–26, 407–408
Bohner, Jean, 292–93
Boilerplate, in a proposal, 339–40
Boldface, 587–88
Boolean operators, 176–77
Boucher, Maurice, 45
Brackets, 585
Brainstorming
  FYI, 66–67
  in a meeting, 436
  in organizing writing, 62–64, 66–67
Branching, in sentences, 86–87
Briefing. *See* Presentations
British Telecom, 187
Brown, William R., 88
Budd, Edward H., 283–85
Budget (in a proposal), 340
Buffer (in customized letters), 280–83
Bush, Vannevar, 187
Business (definition), 16
Business, changes in 21st century, 4–7
Business communication, 7–11, 14–28
  FYI, 8–9

C

Canadian International Development Agency (CIDA), 364–66, 382
Capitalization, 589–90
Captions, for visuals, 121, 123
Career planning. *See* Job search
Carney, Thomas F., 66–67, 458–59
Cause and effect
  in interpreting information, 159
  in reports, 371, 383–94
  as a structuring tool, 60
Centre Canadien d'Architecture (CCA), 44–45, 241–42, 266–67
Charhut, Ken, 254–57, 423, 438–39
Chartjunk, 121
Charts
  bar, 107–108, 113–15
  flow, 112–13
  Gantt, 113
  organizational, 19, 112
  pictorial (pictogram), 116–17
  pie, 107, 115–16
Cheney, Donna Lee, 84
Cheney, William, 225
Chronology, in sentences, 111
Citibank (Maine) NA, 302
Claim
  letter refusing, 278–79
  See also Complaint
Classification
  of information, 151–52
  in reports, 366, 371
  as a structuring tool, 60–61
Clustering
  FYI, 66–67
Collaboration, 197–213
  advantages, 199–200
  decision making, 40
  FYI, 204–205, 206–207
  formation of groups, 202
  forms of group writing, 198–99
  group presentations, 209–12
  guidelines for group writing, 203–209
  reviewing someone else's writing, 212–13
  responsibilities in groups, 200–201
  sideways communication, 5, 18–19
Colon, 583–84
Color (as an element of visuals), 97, 100, 103, 105
  FYI, 106
Comma, 581–82
Comma fault (comma splice), 583
Communication
  importance in business, 9–10
  definition, 16
Communication model, 16–18
Comparison and contrast
  in reports, 371–73
  as a structuring tool, 60
Complaint, customer, 287–93
  FYI, 292–93
  letter of, 288–90

letter responding to, 27, 281–82, 289, 291
Compliance
gaining, 78–79, 417–19
reports, 346
Complimentary close, 251
CompuServe, 187
Computers
graphics, 97, 101
literature search services, 174, 175–77
patterns of use, 180–81
personal costs, 191–93
in revising, 133
writing with, 181–82
See also Desktop publishing, Electronic technology
Conclusion, *See* Ending
Concrete words, 79–80
Conflicts, managing, 417–19
Connotation, 80, 244
of colors internationally, 106
Conoco Inc., 510–11
Content words, 80–81
Context
high-context and low-context cultures, 39–41
for reports, 346–48
Control
corporate control documents, 558–59
as a function of organizational communication, 21–22
role of memos in, 220, 222
role of procedures in, 530
role of reports in, 353
Control statement
defined, 58–59
in a mission statement, 556
in presentations, 453
in revision, 134
Conventions. *See* Formats
Corporate culture
reflected in a logo, 103
effect on communication, 405
Corporate voice, 88–90
Correspondence. *See* Letters, Memos
Cover (of a report), 365, 376
Cover letter
defined, 273
letter of application, 492–501
routine, 272
See also Transmittal
Credit
letter denying, 283, 286
requesting, 271
Crist, Ida G., 560–61
Culture
corporate, 103, 405
defined, 37
effect on decision to speak or write, 405
FYI, 44, 45
high-context and low-context, 39–40
language differences, 38
stereotypes, 41–42
Customer relations
in documents, 562–65
in procedures, 530
See also Complaints
Customized communication
definition, 27–28
in letters with negative information, 280–93
in persuasive letters, 299–315
in reports, 347, 364–95

D

Dangling modifier, 578–79
Dash, 584
Data base, computer search, 174–77
Data dump, 62–64
Decentralization of work, 190–91
Definition
corporate documents that define, 555–58
as a goal of organizational communication, 20
Delmarva Power, 562–63
DeLuca, Sirio, 349, 351–52, 442–43
Denotation, 80
Desktop publishing, 139–41, 182–84
for employee relations documents, 560
for newsletters, 562, 565
for reports, 381
Development Dimensions International, 511
Dictation, 71, 246–47
Digital Equipment Company, 308
Direct mail, 301
Direct order
defined, 56, 59
in presentations, 454

Direct order *(Continued)*
in reports, 368–70
Distribution list, in memos, 230, 234
Documentation, 596–605
of visuals, 120
Document design, 139–41
procedures, 543–45
reports, 381
resumes, 491–92
the visual page, 120–21
Document Design Center, 143
Dominion Textile, Inc., 34–35, 347, 349, 351–52, 442–43
Dossier, 484
Doublespeak, NCTE Committee on, 91
Douglis, Philip, 119
Downward communication, 5, 18–19, 40
memos in, 230
Drawings, 118–19
Duffield Associates, 272, 348, 350, 356–59, 372–73, 375, 378
Du Pont Company, 270, 510–11

E

Editing, 141–42
common errors in writing, 575–80
with a computer, 133
in group projects, 212–13
of memos, 235
punctuation, 580–88
Edris, James A., 268–69, 310–15
Education section of a resume, 487
Effect/affect, 591
Electronic mail, 186–88, 249
ethics of, 191–92
FYI, 188–89
Electronic technology, 6, 180–94
bulletin boards and conferences, 188–89
effects on business, 7
effects on document organization, 185
facsimile, 185–86
as a form of communication, 26
FYI, 186–87, 188–89
in the global economy, 34, 36
hypermedia, 185–87
mail, 186
meetings, 441
voice mail, 185, 426–28
workplace, 189–91
Employee relations documents, 560–61
FYI, 560–61
Employment. *See* Job search
Enclosure notation, 251
Ending
of documents, 59
of presentations, 456
of reports, 374
Energy News, 561–62
Enserch Corporation, 566–67
Environmentalism—effect on corporate decision-making, 5
Ethics in business communication, 10–11
of collaboration, 200–201
corporate policy concerning gifts, 270
defined, 10
in documentation, 596
of letter writing, 243–45, 301
of oral communication, 416–17
of voice, 90–91
Euphemisms, 80
in "strategic misrepresentation," 90–91
European Economic Community, 8
Exclamation point, 585
Executive summary, 377–78, 386
Experience section of a resume, 487, 490
Expletives, 81

F

Facsimile (Fax), 185–86, 241, 244, 249
Fact
definition, 151–54
problem of, 328
Fact sheet, 347, 349, 351
Farquharson, John R., 106
Faulty agreement, 575–76
Favors, 270
See also Persuade
Figurative language, 85, 415–16, 580
Figures, 106–108, 110–19
See also Visuals
Final reports. *See* Reports
Flatley, Marie, 176–77
Flat organizations
definition, 5, 18–19
effect of electronic communication, 190
Flip chart, 457
Footnotes, 598–99
Ford Motor Company, 224

Foreword, 379
Formats, 134
  for formal reports, 364–95
  for letters, 249–52
  for memos, 224, 234–35
Form letters, 246
Formal reports. *See* Reports
Forrest, Anne B., 414, 468–70
Fragment, 576
Frameworks of business communication, 15–28
  forms, 24–26
  functions, 20–22
  purposes, 22–24
  modes, 26–28
  See also Control, Customized communication, Definition, Electronic technology, Inform, Letters, Maintenance, Memos, Nonverbal communication, Oral communication, Persuade, Presentations, Reports, Routine communication, Visuals
Front matter
  in formal proposals, 337
  in formal reports, 364, 374–79
Functional (skills) resume, 488–90

G

Galbraith, John Kenneth, 88
Gallert, Petra M., 44
Gates, William, 190
Gathering information, 164–77, 348–51
General Motors, SF-6
Gibson, Walker, 88, 91
Gieselman, Robert D., 8
Gillett, H.W., 345
Global economy
  definition, 6, 33–34
  effects on culture, 38–39
  FYI, 44, 45, 413, 438–39
  listening internationally, 411–14
  meeting internationally, 436–41
  role of electronic technology, 180–81, 192
  speaking internationally, 468–70
  visuals as an international language, 106, 122
  writing letters internationally, 252, 254–57
Goals
  of business presentations, 452–53
  of communication, 16
  corporate statement of, 556–57
  of the cover letter (letter of application), 493–94
  of interviews, 509–10
  of meetings, 429–30
  of memos, 225–30
  of oral communication, 405–407
  organizational, 18, 20
  of procedures, 532
  of telephone calls, 425
  of writing, 56
Graphs, 110–11
Graphics. *See* Visuals
Grateful Dead, 188
Gribbons, William M., 460
Groups
  dynamics, 431–32
  formation and function, 201–203
Group communication. *See* Collaboration
Groupthink, 428

H

Hall, Edward T., 39
Handbooks on international business, 173
Headings, 134–36
  in procedures, 543
Hercules, Inc., 555, 560–61
Hershey Foods Corporation, 268–69, 310–15
High-context culture, 39–40
Hill and Knowlton Asia Ltd., 414, 468
Horizons, 555, 560–61
Hypermedia, 185–87
  FYI, 186–87
Hyphen, 587

I

IBM, 84, 190, 441
Icons, SF-2, 545
Illustrations. *See* Visuals
Index
  for business information—print, 173–75
  electronic, 175–77
  FYI, 176–77
  of a report, 379

Indirect order, 59
with bad news, 54–55, 280–83
in persuasive presentations, 454–55
in persuasive reports, 369
in revising, 135
Inform, communicating to, 23
with letters, 266, 267–73
with manuals, 540
with memos, 220, 222
passive role of information, 151, 157
with presentations, 452
with reports, 346, 348–59
Informal language, 83–84
Information, 6, 150–77
classification, 151–52
digital, 193
FYI, 176–77, 348–49, 368–69
gathering for a report, 348–49
guidelines for interpreting, 158–60
letter requesting, 266, 268
letter responding to a request for, 268–69
objectivity in, 368–69
quality, 154–56
search, 164–66
sources, 166–77
Inquiry. *See* Request
Inside address, 250
Instructions. *See* Procedures
Interim report, 353–356
Internal documents in a corporation, 555–60
See also Memos
International business, careers in, 482
International business communication, 6, 33–45
See also Global economy, Multiculturalism
International University of Japan, 536–37
Interpretation, 152–54, 167, 169
Interviews, 167–69, 509–17
conducting, 510–12
employment, 512–17
questions often asked, 514
FYI, 516–17
for gathering information, 167–69
goals of, 509–10
informational, in job search, 483
telephone, 516–17
Introduction, 59
introductory paragraphs, 136–37
in presentations, 453–55
in reports, 360–72
Introduction-Middle-Ending pattern, 59
displayed in paragraphs, 136–38
in memos, 231–32
in reports, 368–74
in routine letters, 262
Investors
FYI, 566–67
reports for, 564, 566–68
Invitation
FYI, 44
letter declining, 278
persuasive letter of, 305–306
printed, 267
routine letter of, 264, 266
Italics, 588
IZE (Informationszentrale der Elektrizitatswirtschaft EV), 112, 461

J

Jargon, 84–85, 412
Job description, 495–96, 497
Job search, 478–520
cover letter (letter of application), 492–501
deciding on offers, 518–19
FYI, 481
interview, 512–17
market inventory, 479–83
recommendations (references), 307, 309, 483–84, 491
responding to offers, 519–20
resume, 484–92
Johns, Douglas, SF-2
Johns, Kathy, SF-2
Justification section (proposal), 339–40

K

Key word. *See* Search word
Korea, dinner invitation in, 44

L

Labels, for visuals, 121, 123
Legal issues
FYI, 98–99
the legal voice, 90
in letters, 247

Length
  FYI, 225
  of letters, 244
  of memos, 224–25
  of sentences, 85
Letters, 241–316
  with complex information, 310–15
  conventions and format, 249–52
  customized, 245–46, 299–315
  dictation of, 246–47
  elements of writing, 241–56
  ethics of, 243–45
  informative, 247–70
  international, 252, 254–57
  legal considerations in, 247
  letterly voice, 248–49
  negative information in, 277–93
  planning, 245–46
  routine, 245–46, 263–73
  sales, 300–305
  transmittal, 272, 374–76
Levels of usage, 83–85
  See also Figurative language, Jargon
Listening, 409–15
  barriers to, 409–11
  cross cultural, 412–14
  effects of gender differences, 414–15
  FYI, 413
  guidelines for, 410–15
List of figures and tables, 377, 385
Lists. *See* Parallelism
Literature, 172–77
L.L. Bean, 425, 528
Local area networks, 187
Logo, 103, 141, 220
Low-context culture, 39–40

M

McAllister, Glenn, 302–303
McDonald's Corporation, 84, 534–35, 541, 556–57
McKinsey and Company, 15
McNamara, Robert, 224
Macrostructure, in revising, 133–41
Maintenance
  corporate documents that maintain, 559–60
  as a function of organizational communication, 22
  memos, 220–22
  procedures, 530
Major Appliance Consumer Action Panel, 281–82
Management
  style shown in a writer's voice, 79
  success in, 10
  of the writing process, 69–72
Mapping a text, 134, 139
Maps, 118, 536–37
Market inventory in the job search, 479–83
Marks & Spencer, 287–88
Mathes, J.C., 57
Mathews, Wilma K., 570–71
Matrixes, 110
MCI, 187
Meetings, 428–44
  electronic, 441
  FYI, 438–39
  international, 436–39
  minutes, 226–28, 434
  process of, 431–36
  risks and rewards, 428–30
  routine and customized, 430–31
  of writing groups, 209
  See also Collaboration
Meishis, 413
Memos, 220–37
  audience for, 230–31, 234
  conventions, 224, 234–35
  definition, 221–25
  electronic, 236
  FYI, 225
  goals, 225–30
  guidelines for writing, 230–36
  voice, 78–79
Microsoft Corporation, 190
Microstructure, in revising, 141–44
Middle
  of documents, 59
  of presentations, 455–56
  of reports, 371, 373
Minutes, 226–28, 434
Mission statement, 556–57
Misused words and phrases, 590–94
Mixed metaphors, 580
Mobil Corporation, 567–68
Modified block style in letters, 253, 284–85, 290, 304, 312–15

Modifiers
  dangling, 578–79
  misplaced, 577–78
Motorola, 180
Multiculturalism, 37–38
  culture avoiding discriminatory language, 82–83
  in presentations, 468–70
  See also Global economy
Myers, Robert J., 516–17

N

Narrative, 61
Newsletters, 562–65
Nonverbal communication, 25–26, 43, 407–409
North Deering Veterinary Hospital *Companion,* 565
Notes, 597–603
Note-taking, 411, 512
Numbers, 590

O

Objective statement
  in a proposal, 339
  in a resume, 487
Objectivity
  FYI, 368–69
Observation, 152–54, 166–67
Opinion, 152–54, 167, 169
Oral communication, 405–70
  across cultures, 44–45, 412–14
  ethics of, 416–19
  as a form of business communication, 25
  in high- and low-context cultures, 40–43
  listening, 409–15
  meetings, 428–44
  organizing messages in, 58
  talking, 415–16
  telephone calls, 423–28
  See also Listening, Meetings, Nonverbal communication, Presentations, Telephone calls
Oral reports. *See* Presentations
Order
  electronic, 246
  letter concerning a problem, 278
  letter confirming, 266
  letter placing, 264–65
Organization
  conventional patterns, 60–61
  of memos, 231–34
  principles, 55–58
  tools and techniques, 58–68
  of yourself as a writer, 69–72
Organizations
  definition, 16
  forms in the 21st Century, 7
  in the global economy, 38–39
  See also Flat organizations, Tall organizations
Outlining, 67–69
Overhead transparencies (vugraphs), 458–62

P

PACE International, 225
Page design, 120–21, 139–41
Pagination, 381
Pancake organizations. *See* Flat organizations
Paperless office, 24, 182, 236
Paradyne Corporation, SF-2
Paragraphs, 136–39
Parallelism
  in headings, 134–36
  lack of, 576–77
  in lists, 576–77
  in paragraphs, 136
  in sentences, 86
  as a structuring tool, 61
Parentheses, 584–85
Parkinson, C. Northcote, 547
Passive voice, 81–82
Patricia Seybold's Office Computing Group, 84
Performance aids. *See* Procedures
Performance review, 520–23
Period, 585
Periodicals, 172–73
Periodic report, 353–56
Permission to reprint, 597
Personal information section of a resume, 490–91

Persuade
  active role of information in, 151, 157–58
  communicating to, 24
  compliance gaining, 417–18
  using documentation to, 596
  indirect order in, 59
  with letters, 245–46, 299–315
  with manuals, 540
  with memos, 220, 223–24
  with presentations, 452–53
  with reports, 347, 370–71, 383–94
  with visuals, 121–23
Pfizer, SF-5
Phillips Petroleum Company, SF-4
Phone calls. *See* Telephone calls
Photographs, 119–120
  FYI, 119
  Special Feature (SF): Communicating with Photographs in Corporate Annual Reports, SF-1–SF-8
Pictograms, 116–17
Pie Charts, 107, 115–16
Plan
  business (strategic), 558–59
Planning
  group projects, 203–209
  the search for information, 164–65
  writing projects, 69–72
Point of view, 579–80
Policy
  different from a procedure, 534
  letter announcing, 270–71
  statement of corporate, 556–58
Preface, 377
Presentations, 448–70
  context for, 448–52
  dealing with questions in, 467–68
  documenting, 602–603
  FYI, 454–55, 462–63
  guidelines for group, 209–12
  multicultural, 468–70
  organization, 453–56
  practicing, 463–63
  presenting, 464–70
  purpose, 452–53
  visuals in, 456–63
Press release, 568–71
  FYI, 570–71
Problems
  business, 324–25
  classified, 324–25
  of fact, 328
  of means, 328–29
  solving in meetings, 435–36
  solving in proposals, 334, 338
  of value, 329
Procedures, 530–49
  behavior guidelines, 541
  code of practice, 542–43
  composing with visuals, 544–45
  cross-cultural, 540–41
  designing, 543–45
  letter announcing, 271
  manuals, 539–41
  preparing, 531–34
  step-by-step, 534–39
  testing, 545
  voice in, 547–49
Procter and Gamble, 224, 298
Progress reports, 353–56
Proofreading, 142
  by computer, 133
  of letters, 247
  of a resume, 484
Proposals, 324–25, 328–40
  case study, 329–33
  FYI, 336–37
  solicited and unsolicited, 329, 338
  strategies for preparing, 330–31, 334–36
  structure, 336
Proverbs, 42
Public relations documents, 570–71
  See also Customer relations
Puglisi, Thomas, 383–94
Punctuation, 580–88
  See also individual marks
Purpose. *See* Goals

Q

Question-and-answer periods, in presentations, 467–68
Questionnaire, 170–71
  cover letter for, 306–308
Quotation marks, 585–86

R

Ratsep, A. Ingrid, 348, 350, 356–59, 372–73, 375, 378
Readability, 142
  Adaptive Process Model, 143
  differences in readers, 56–57
  formulas, 144
  FYI, 144–45
  pace in paragraphs, 138–39
  of reports, 380–81
  screen vs. print, 182
  See also Audience
Readers. *See* Audience
Reading, 43–45, 143
Recommendation
  letter of, 309–10
  letter requesting, 307, 309
  noting references on a resume, 491
  report, 383–94
  selecting references (recommenders), 483–84
Record
  communicating to, 22–23
  with letters, 241, 243
  with manuals, 539–40
  with memos, 220–22
  with reports, 345–46
  with visuals, 100
Recruiting, international differences in, 40–41
Redish, Janice C., 144–45, 459
References, in documentation, 597–603
References, to recommend. *See* Recommendation
Reliability, of surveys, 169–70
Repetitive Motion Syndrome, 192
Reporting lines, 18
  role in report writing, 345–46
Reports
  annual, 564, 566–67, SF-1–SF-8
  context for, 346–48
  customized/persuasive, 329, 347, 364–95
  ending of, 374
  formal, 364–95
  FYI, 348–49, 368–69
  informative, 328, 346–47
  interpretive, 328–29, 347
  introduction to, 368–71
  measures of accountability, 345–46
  middle of, 371
  model corporate, 356–59
  model student, 383–94
  progress, 353–56
  readability of, 380–81
  readers, 367
  routine, 346–47, 349–60
  trip, 353
Request
  for bid (RFB), 325–27
  letter answering, 283–87
  letter of, 264–66
  for proposal (RFP), 329–30
Resale, 287, 289, 291
Research, *See* Gathering Information, Reports
Restrictive clause or phrase, 582
Resume, 484–93
  chronological, 485–87, 490
  content, 484–91
  design, 491–93
  functional (skills), 488–90
Reviewing someone else's writing, 212–13
Revising, 129–45
  with a computer, 133
  memos, 235
  procedures, 545
  routine for, 132–33
  using a table to reduce text, 105
  See also Editing, Readability
RFB (request for bid), 325–27
RFP (request for proposal), 329–30
Ringi decision making, 40
Roberts, Ellen, 454–55
Rogerian argument, 417–18
Routine communication
  definition, 27
  letters, 263–73, 277–79
  organization of a message, 59–60
  reports, 346–47, 349–60
Rymer, Jone, 206–207

S

Sales letters, 300–305
  AIDA in, 301–303
Salutation (in letters), 250–51
Sampling, 171–72

Schedules
  for airplanes, 101–103
  Gantt charts, 113
  for writing, 70
Search word, 175
Segmented bar chart, 114–15
Self-inventory, 479–80
Semicolon, 582–83
Sentence, 85–87
  branching, 86–87
  connecting in paragraphs, 137
  length, 85
  parallelism in, 86, 136–37
SEPTA, 54–56
Serials. *See* Periodicals
Series
  of visuals, 103
  See also Parallelism
Service announcement, 562
Sexist language, 82–83
Sherman, Wendy, SF-2
Shirk, Henrietta Nickels, 348–49
Sideways communication, 5, 18–19
  effect of culture on, 40
  memos for, 230
Sieff, Marcus, 287
Signature, 251
Simplified style in letters, 253, 265
Slides, 458–62
Sound bites, 193, 571
South Freeport Marine, 15
Speakers. *See* Presentations
Spelling checkers, 133
Status report. *See* Progress reports
Stevenson, Dwight, 57
Strategic misrepresentation, 90
Strategic plan, 558
Structure words, 80–81
Stuffy talk, 88
Style. *See* Voice
Subject line
  in letters, 250
  in memos, 225, 234
Summary, executive, 377–78
Survey, 169–72
Sweet talk, 88
Swissair, 122

T

Table of contents, 366, 377, 385
Tables, 108–10
Talking
  compared to writing, 405–407
  guidelines for, 415–16
  nonverbal elements in, 407–409
  See also Oral communication
Tall organizations, 5, 18–19
Targeted selection, in hiring, 511
Teleconferences, 439–41
Telemarketing, 425
Telephone calls, 423–28
  for customer complaints, 288
  guidelines, 425–28
  for orders, 424–25
  rather than letters, 241, 246
  rather than memos, 231
Thanking
  customized letter, 303, 305
  routine letter, 266
That and *Which*, 582
3M, SF-7
Timberline Lodge, 103
Time
  differences in international communication, 34–36
Title
  for reports, 376, 384
  for visuals, 121, 123
Tokyo Sanyo Electric Co., Ltd., 254–57
Touch, 408
Transamerica Corporation, SF-3
Transmittal
  customized letter with formal report, 374–76
  form letter, 272
Transparencies, 458–62
The Travelers, 283–85, 441, SF-1
Trip report, 353
Typefaces, 140

U

Underlining, 587–88
United Airlines, 279
United Way, 15, 302–303
Upward communication, 5, 18–19, 40

usage, levels of, 83–85
USAir, Inc., 100–103
USSprint, 187

V

Validity
  of procedures, 545
  of surveys, 169
Verbs, 81–82
  active and passive, 81–82
  verbiage, 82
Verification of a procedure, 545
Video, 462–63
  FYI, 462–63
  in hypermedia, 186–87, 348–49
  practice for interview and presentation, 463–64
Visuals, 97–124
  bar charts, 107–108, 113–15
  computer-generated, 97, 101, 107, 108, 111, 114, 118
  designing text as a visual, 139–41
  documenting, 120
  drawings, 118–19
  figures, 106–108, 110–19
  flowcharts, 112
  FYI, 98–99, 106, 119
  graphs, 110–11
  guidelines for, 100–106, 121, 123
  how reader views, 460
  maps, 118, 536–37
  matrixes, 110
  organizational charts, 19, 112
  photographs, 119
  pictograms, 116–17
  pie charts, 107, 115–16
  in presentations, 456–63
  in procedures, 544–45
  in reports, 381–82
  schedules, 70, 101–103
  tables, 108–10
  testing, 119–20
  tool for thinking, 97
  tool for writing, 65–67
Voice, 77–92
  active and passive, 81–82
  corporate, 88–90
  ethics of, 90–91
  legal, 90
  letterly, 248–49
  in letters with negative information, 281–82
  in memos, 78–79
  in procedures, 547–49
  in visuals, 120–21
Voice mail, 185, 241
  guidelines, 426–28
Vugraph, 458–62

W

We attitude, 243
White space, 139
WHYY, 303, 305
Williams, Julie, 562
Williams Companies, SF-8
Wolfson, Bertram, 98–100
Word choice, 79–85
  frequently misused words, 590–94
Wordprocessing, 181–82
Worley, Brent, 336–37
Worley, Rebecca B., 186–87
Writer's block, 70–71
Writing at Work, Inc., 292
Writing process
  composing with visuals, 97–124
  computers and, 181–82
  in groups, 203–209
  macrocomposing, 54–72
  managing yourself, 69–72
  microcomposing, 77–92
WSFS, 89

X

Xerox Corporation, 23, 112

Y

Yates, JoAnne, 188–89
You attitude, 243

Z

Ziegler, Ed, 462–63
Zoological Society of Philadelphia, 110, 262–64